POLAND
in the
BRITISH
PARLIAMENT
1939-1945

POLAND IN THE BRITISH PARLIAMENT

1939-1945

Compiled and edited by
WACŁAW JĘDRZEJEWICZ
Professor of Slavic Studies
Ripon College, Wisconsin

With the Assistance of
PAULINE C. RAMSEY

VOLUME III

Summer 1944 — Summer 1945

JÓZEF PIŁSUDSKI INSTITUTE OF AMERICA
FOR RESEARCH IN THE MODERN HISTORY OF POLAND, INC.
New York, 1962

JÓZEF PIŁSUDSKI INSTITUTE OF AMERICA
FOR RESEARCH IN THE MODERN HISTORY OF POLAND, INC.
289 Park Avenue, South
New York 10, N.Y.

Library of Congress Catalog Card Number 48–702

PRINTED IN THE UNITED STATES OF AMERICA
WALDON PRESS, INC., NEW YORK

DEBATES ON POLAND AND EXPLANATORY NOTES

POLAND
in the
BRITISH
PARLIAMENT
1939-1945

1. MIKOŁAJCZYK'S FIRST VISIT TO MOSCOW*

PREMIER MIKOŁAJCZYK *made a long-planned visit to Washington on June 5–14, 1944.*[1] *During this period he had four talks with Pres. Roosevelt and many conferences with Acting Secretary of State Stettinius. Accompanying Mikołajczyk was Gen. Tabor, recently arrived from Warsaw, who presented in detail to Pres. Roosevelt and U. S. Army authorities the actual situation in Poland.*

In these conversations Pres. Roosevelt explained that for political reasons he did not see his way clear to approach Marshal Stalin at that time with definite suggestions for a final solution of the Polish-Soviet conflict. Moreover, the President indicated that the policy of the U. S. Government was against the settlement of territorial problems before the end of the war. He assured Premier Mikołajczyk that at the appropriate time he would help Poland to retain Lwów, Drohobycz ~~at~~ and Tarnopol, and to obtain East Prussia, including Koenigsberg, as well as Silesia. On the other hand, the President believed that a useful purpose would be served if personal conversations between Marshal Stalin and Premier Mikołajczyk could take place and asked Mr. Mikołajczyk if he would go to Moscow for this purpose. Both the President and Premier Mikołajczyk were of the opinion that at that particular moment a somewhat more promising atmosphere seemed to prevail which might justify the initiation of such a personal and direct contact. Premier Mikołajczyk had reasons which led him to believe that the Soviets were probably more inclined at that moment to favor such a contact which might make an exchange of views possible.[2]

Premier Mikołajczyk asked the President if he would act as a sponsor or "moderator" with a view to bringing about the personal contact—possibly a visit to Moscow of Premier

---

* House of Commons. Vol. 402, Aug. 2, 1944, p. 1481–1482.
[1] Vol. 2, no. 62.
[2] Stosunki polsko-sowieckie, 1943–46, p. 128.

Mikołajczyk, as the President suggested. The President did not reject such a possibility but in further conversations it was realized that an appropriate moment and an appropriate way would have to be found to put this into effect. Premier Mikołajczyk pointed out that if such a meeting were to take place the following points had to be clearly agreed upon: No preliminary condition to be insisted on by either side; the meeting would have to concentrate primarily on the question of collaboration between the Soviet Army and the Polish Underground Army and Administration in the joint effort, which was of real importance not only to the Soviet Armies, but also to the Allied Western invasion and to Poland.[3]

The Washington talks included the subject of credit to the Polish Underground Army, and, on July 13, it was agreed that the U. S. would give a credit in the amount of 10 million dollars to the Underground Army, as well as an additional 2½ million dollars annually for the support of diplomatic posts.[4] *With respect to the credit for the Underground Army the Combined Chiefs of Staff asked whether, in view of Soviet opposition and the lack of an understanding between the Polish and Soviet Governments, the Underground Army would continue battle against the Germans. The Polish Ambassador in Washington, Jan Ciechanowski, assured them that the continuing aim of the Polish Underground was to fight against the Germans until victory was won.*[5]

On June 15 Pres. Roosevelt sent a cable to Stalin suggesting that Mikołajczyk come to Moscow. Stalin's answer was in the negative:

> "You are familiar with the point of view of the Soviet Government and its endeavor to see Poland strong, independent and democratic and the Polish-Soviet relations good-neighborly and based upon durable friendship. The Soviet Government sees the most important promises of this in the reorganization of the émigré Polish Government which would provide the participation in it of Polish statesmen in England, as well as Polish statesmen in the U.S.A. and the USSR, and especially Polish democratic

---

[3] Ibid., p. 129.
[4] Ibid, p. 151.
[5] Ibid, p. 149.

statesmen in Poland itself and also in the recognition by the Polish Government of the Curzon Line as the new border between the USSR and Poland. It is necessary to say, however, that from the statement of Mr. Mikołajczyk in Washington it is not seen that he makes in this matter any step forward. That is why it is difficult for me at the present moment to offer any opinion about Mr. Mikołajczyk's trip to Moscow."[6]

Despite this Premier Mikołajczyk and part of the Polish Government in London believed that because of existing circumstances only a direct conversation between Mikołajczyk and Stalin could break the impasse on the Polish problem.

Just before his visit to Washington, Mikołajczyk, in spite of the non-existence of diplomatic relations between Poland and the USSR, met in London twice and talk with Soviet Ambassador Lebiediev. They had an additional conversation on June 20 after Mikołajczyk's return to London. Prime Minister Churchill, strongly supporting direct conversations between the Polish Government and Stalin, sent another cable to Stalin July 20 again suggesting that Mikołajczyk come to Moscow.[7]

Stalin finally agreed to receive Mikołajczyk the first week of August. Thus, the following flew to Moscow by way of Cairo and Teheran on July 26: Premier Mikołajczyk, Prof. Stanisław Grabski, Speaker of the National Council, and Minister for Foreign Affairs T. Romer. They arrived in Moscow on July 30. When they began the trip they had absolutely no idea that on July 26 the Soviet Government had recognized the Polish Committee of National Liberation, nor did they know of the agreement ratified by this Committee with respect of administrative powers and authority on Polish territory.[8] *This news reached Mikołajczyk and his party only in Cairo and Teheran, but this did not change their plans to go to Moscow.*

Immediately after the creation of the Polish Committee of National Liberation the Catholic Hierarchy in Scotland issued on August 4, 1944 a manifesto. This manifesto was read

---

6 Mikołajczyk, S. The Rape of Poland, p. 64.
7 Stosunki polso-sowieckie, 1943–46, p. 161.
8 See Vol. 2, no. 65.

from the pulpits of all Catholic churches. It emphasized that the Polish Committee of National Liberation had been created without any valid authority or legal mandate. Such an arbitrary setting up of a communist form of government, totally foreign to the religion and ethics of the Polish people, and with a brazen disregard of international law and the laws of nations, undermines the very foundations of Christian ethics.

The Scottish bishops stated that they could not remain silent if the sovereign rights of the Polish nation were forcibly snatched through illegitimate pressure or flagrant violence on the part of a foreign country.

This manifesto was sent on August 14 to all Members of Parliament along with a letter from Archbishop McDonald, O.S.B. (St. Andrew's and Edinburgh) with a question as to whether each Member "is prepared to stand by Britain's pledge to defend against aggression the free and independent State of Poland."

There were 158 replies (1/3 of the total Members); the majority supported the stand taken by the bishops in their manifesto.[9]

THE PRIME MINISTER (MR. CHURCHILL): . . . This in my opinion is a hopeful moment for Poland, for whose rights and independence we entered the war against Germany. We therefore did our best, my right hon. Friend and I and others, late into the night to promote the visit of M. Mikołajczyk and other members of his Cabinet to Moscow, where Marshal Stalin was willing to receive them. The President of the United States was also favorable. How could it be otherwise in these matters, considering his deep interest in the Polish Question? The Russian Armies now stand before the gates of Warsaw. They bring the liberation of Poland in their hands. They offer freedom, sovereignty and independence to the Poles. They ask that there should be a Poland friendly to Russia. This seems to me very reasonable, considering the injuries which Russia

[9] Britain's Pledge to Poland. Replies from Members of Parliament to His Grace Archbishop McDonald (MS in the Library of Prof. Stanisław Kot).

has suffered through the Germans marching across Poland to attack her. The Allies would welcome any general rally or fusion of Polish Forces, both those who are working with the Western Powers and those who are working with the Soviets. We have several gallant Polish divisions fighting the Germans in our Armies now and there are others who have been fighting in Russia. Let them come together. We desire this union and it would be a marvelous thing if it could be proclaimed, or at least its foundations laid, at the moment when the famous capital of Poland, which so valiantly defended itself against the Germans, has been liberated by the bravery of the Russian Armies.

2. WARSAW UPRISING*

IN THE MIDDLE OF JULY 1944 *the German Army on the eastern front was in a catastrophic situation. The Soviet attack, begun on June 23 between the marshes of Polesie and the Dvina River, completely routed Gen. Bush's German Army. Towards the north the 3d German Panzer Army on the Dvina River suffered great losses and retreated to the west. On the south the 4th and 9th German armies were thoroughly beaten. Only the 2d German Army maintained its troops and retreated to the Brest region. The German front on Polish territory practically ceased to exist. Gen. H. Guderian, named on July 21 the Chief of Staff of the German forces on the eastern front, later summarized the situation as follows:*

> "After my appointment the whole front—if it can be called a 'front'—was hardly more than an agglomeration of the remains of our armies which were endeavoring to withdraw to the line of the Vistula; twenty-five divisions were completely annihilated."[1]

The Soviet attacks on the 1st White Russian front (Gen. Rokossovsky) and on the 1st Ukrainian front (Gen. Koniev) resulted in the occupation of Lublin and Łuków (July 24),

---

* House of Commons. Vol. 403, Sept. 26, 27, Oct. 5, 11, 1944, p. 25–27, 217–220, 233–234, 1139–1140, 1724.

1 Komorowski, T. The Secret Army, p. 208.

Białystok, Puławy and Dęblin (July 26). That same day the Soviet Army crossed the Vistula River below Puławy. On July 27 they occupied Lwów—in the battle for this city a Home Army of 3,000 took part. As usual, at first, relations between the Soviet authorities and the Home Army were good—to be followed later by arrests of officers and soldiers, and deportation.

Brest fell on July 28 and the defending German Corps was taken prisoner by the Russians. The Red Army was now only a few miles from Warsaw, practically in the suburb of Praga.[2] *The Germans evacuated their civil offices between July 23 and July 25. But, on July 26 a part of the German administration returned to defend the city.*[3]

Polish underground authorities, both civilian and military, decided to defend Warsaw against the Germans. The code name for the defensive action was "Burza" (Tempest, in English). The Home Army organized similar defensive action in several localities, near the front, at Volhynia,[4] *Wilno,*[5] *and other places, thus helping the Soviet armies.*

The decision for project "Burza" was made at Home Army Headquarters between July 20 and 22. It was agreed to by S. J. Jankowski, Vice-Prime Minister and Delegate of the Polish Government, and by a committee of the Council of National Unity. Polish military and political officials felt that Warsaw, as the capital of Poland, ought to be liberated from the German yoke by Polish soldiers, and that the Soviet Army, approaching Warsaw, should find the city already in Polish hands and should meet and accept the Poles as the legal authorities in the Polish capital. The Home Army felt that it was possible for the underground army to occupy Warsaw, in view of the fact that the rapidly approaching Soviet Army could soon come in to help.[6]

It must be remembered that once before—in September

---

[2] Warsaw is situated on the left, higher side of the Vistula; Praga is on the right, lower side, connected with Warsaw by four bridges.
[3] Polskie Siły Zbrojne, vol. 3, p. 697–699.
[4] Vol. 2, no. 62
[5] Vol. 2, no. 65.
[6] Polskie Siły Zbrojne, vol. 3, p. 653.

1939—Warsaw fought bravely against the Germans,[7] and for five years was the locale for anti-German underground battles. So, now that the German occupation was coming to an end, the Polish capital could not remain passive. From a political point of view, Poland, like her allies, had to make her contribution to the victory, and to fight for her own liberation on Polish soil. Battles beyond Poland's boundaries (such as Monte Cassino) were not on home soil, and while helping the allied cause, did not help directly to liberate Poland.[8] The Home Army wanted to show the world that it was not the Red Army which freed Poland, but that the Poles themselves fought for their country in order to free it from the German occupation. The battle for Warsaw would show the whole civilized world that Soviet plans with respect to Poland recognized her independence and sovereignty.[9]

Polish authorities had to take into account also the psychic factors which were the spontaneous will and desire of the Polish nation to finally settle accounts with the hated German invaders.

On July 25 the Commander of the Home Army, Gen. Bor-Komorowski, sent the following message to the Polish Commander-in-Chief: "We are ready to fight for Warsaw at any moment. I will report the date and hour of the beginning of the fight." In the same message he asked that the Polish Parachute Brigade should be used in the fight for Warsaw, and requested air attack against the German airfields near Warsaw.[10]

This message crossed en route Premier Mikołajczyk's message sent to the Delegate of the Polish Government in Warsaw on July 26, that is, the day of Mikołajczyk's departure for Moscow: "At a session of the Government of the Republic, it was unanimously decided to empower you to proclaim the insurrection at a moment which you will decide as most opportune. If possible, let us know beforehand."[11]

---

[7] Vol. 1, no. 54.
[8] Piłsudski Institute of America, New York. Archives.
[9] Polskie Siły Zbrojne, vol. 3, p. 659.
[10] Komorowski, T. The Secret Army, p. 208.
[11] Ibid, p. 204.

Commander-in-Chief Gen. Sosnkowski was against a general uprising, on account of the patent lack of goodwill on the part of the Russians. He was at that time with the 2d Polish Corps on the Italian front, and on July 28 wired Gen. Bor-Komorowski, via London:[12]

> "In the face of Soviet political pressures and known actions, a heroic uprising would be an act lacking in political value—and it could require unnecessary sacrifices. If the aim of the uprising is the occupation of part of Polish territory, it must be taken into account that in this case it will be necessary to defend Poland's sovereignty on recaptured territory, against whatever power questions this sovereignty. Remember, to put this into its proper perspective, that a heroic uprising and cooperation mean nothing in the face of Soviet lack of goodwill."

This message was not forwarded from London to Warsaw because the Government had already authorized the uprising.

There were also persons in Warsaw, among the members of political groups, who were critical of a Warsaw uprising. One of the more prominent members of the National Democratic Party, Z. Stypułkowski, who was then in Warsaw, made this evaluation of the London Government's decision to allow the uprising:[13]

> "The leadership of the nation had two political foci: the Polish Government in London and the Underground Government in Poland. The former possessed all the information necessary to assess the international situation, and had come to realize what the community in Poland could not believe—that cooperation of the Western Powers with the Soviets had sealed the fate of their country. Every step which might entail further heavy sacrifices had to be very carefully weighed in the balance, particularly where it was a question of throwing thousands of badly armed people against the still powerful German Army. In these circumstances it was a paramount error on the part of the London Government to leave to the Underground the momentous decision as to whether and, if so, when Warsaw should stage a revolt."

In the last days of July propaganda from Moscow showed that they were counting on a swift liberation of Warsaw. On

---

12 Polskie Siły Zbrojne, v. 3, p. 664.
13 Stypułkowski, Z. Invitation to Moscow, p. 122.

July 29 Radio Moscow sent, in Polish, the following appeal to Warsaw:[14]

"No doubt Warsaw already hears guns of the battle which is soon to bring liberation. Those who have never bowed their heads to the Hitlerite power will again, as in 1939, join battle with the Germans, this time for the decisive action. The Polish Army now entering Polish territory, trained in the USSR is now joined to the People's Army to form the corps of the Polish Armed Forces, the armed core of our nation in its struggle for independence. Its ranks will be joined tomorrow by the sons of Warsaw. They will, together with the Allied Army pursue the enemy westward, drive the Hitlerite vermin from the Polish land, and strike a mortal blow at the last of Prussian imperialism. For Warsaw, which did not yield, but fought on, the hour of action has already arrived. The Germans will no doubt try to defend themselves in Warsaw, and add new destruction and more thousands of victims. Our houses and parks, our bridges and railway stations, our factories and our public buildings will be turned into defense positions. They will expose the city to ruin and its inhabitants to death. They will try to take away all the most precious possessions and turn into dust all that they have to leave behind. It is therefore a hundred times more necessary than ever to remember that in the flood of Hitlerite destruction all is lost that is not saved by active effort, that by direct active struggle in the streets of Warsaw, in its houses, factories and stores we not only hasten the moment of final liberation, but also save the nation's property and the lives of our brethren."

The following day (July 30) the Union of Polish Patriots announced from a Moscow radio station the following Polish appeal:[15]

"Warsaw trembles in its foundations from the roaring guns. The Soviet Army is attacking and moving in on Praga. They are approaching to bring you liberty. The Germans, on being driven out of Praga, will strengthen their forces to defend Warsaw. They will try to destroy everything. In Białystok they have destroyed things for 6 days. They murdered thousands of our brothers. Let us do all we can to prevent their doing the same in Warsaw.

"People of Warsaw, to arms! The whole population should gather round the National Council and the Underground Army. Attack the Germans . . . assist the Red Army in crossing the Vistula.

14 Komorowski ,T. The Secret Army, p. 212.
15 Polskie Siły Zbrojne, vol. 3, p. 702.

Give information and show the best fords. The more than a million inhabitants ought to become an army of a million men fighting for liberation and destroying the German invaders."

These appeals from the Soviets for the Home Army to begin battle for Warsaw were repeated several times, and were worded in a very explicit and emphatic way; they seemed to indicate to the commander of the Home Army that the Russians judged the situation ripe for the beginning of the fight and that the fight would be supported by the Red Army.

As far as the military authorities of the U. S. and Great Britain are concerned, the question of carrying out any large-scale operations in Poland by the Home Army had not been anticipated in the plans of the Combined Chiefs of Staff. Rather, they seemed to feel that the role of the Home Army should be limited to diversionary sabotage and to intelligence activities. Col. Leon Z. Mitkiewicz, the Polish representative to the Combined Chiefs of Staff in Washington was notified by a Combined Chiefs of Staff statement of Sept. 23, 1943 that "... the Secret Army could not openly take an active part against the Axis until direct land or sea communication were immediately in prospect; there is also a lack of suitable aircraft for the delivery of large quantities of supplies to Poland ... The supplies requested from U. S. and British sources for sabotage and intelligence activities in Poland have been approved ..."[16]

This position was confirmed by a Combined Chiefs of Staff document of January 20, 1944 pointing out that "with the request to a pronouncement of joint British-American strategic responsibility over Polish territory, the Combined Chiefs of Staff consider that this question is basically political rather than military, and therefore can only be determined by the Chiefs of State." Orally, too, Col. Mitkiewicz was notified that Great Britain and the U. S. took no responsibility for equipping the Home Army with arms, or for any

---

16 Mitkiewicz, Leon. "Powstanie" warszawskie" in "Zeszyty Historyczne" no. 1. Paris, Instytut Literacki, 1962, p. 123 and ff.

activities of the Home Army, inasmuch as they did not consider that Polish territory fell within their strategic scope.

The Polish Government in London informed political and military authorities in the British Government of the planned uprising—this was done in detail when Premier Mikołajczyk talked with Minister Eden on July 25, as well as in conferences with Ambassador Raczyński on July 27 and 28.[17]

Thus, on August 1, at 5:00 P.M. the Warsaw uprising began.

The first few days of battle were highly successful and much of the town was occupied by the insurgents. But, on August 4 a reorganized and re-armed German Army came back to the extent that the Home Army had to limit its fighting to defending the areas seized during the first attack. The more so, because the Soviet offensive which was strong before and just after the start of the uprising ceased completely on August 4. Located on the other side of the Vistula River Gen. Rokossovsky's Soviet Army, including Berling's Polish divisions, stopped its attack on Warsaw and left the Home Army in the tragic position of fighting the Germans alone.

Soviet authorities explained their failure to attack Warsaw on a surprise action of the 2nd German Army concentrated at the Bug River which, reinforced by a couple of panzer divisions, attacked Gen. Rokossovsky's right wing in the early days of August. This, they claimed, resulted in a battle lasting several days—ending on Aug. 12 when the Germans were forced to retreat to the Małkinia-Tłuszcz-Praga line. But, Gen. Rokossovsky's Army waited at Warsaw's gates without doing anything until Sept. 10 when they began an attack on Praga, occupying it on Sept. 14.

The Home Army's active defense of Warsaw lasted until Sept. 1. Other Polish units had to desist from attack and had to limit themselves to passive defense, fighting for each house and building. Battles continued but the situation became progressively more hopeless, the more so that all calls of the Home Army to the Red Army for help remained unanswered. Like-

[17] Stosunki polsko-sowieckie, 1943–46, p. 204.

wise, it became clear that help could not be expected from the west. In this situation, on Oct. 2, 1944, after 63 days of fighting, the Poles capitulated to the Germans.

The Home Army had expected the uprising to last only a few days—just long enough to allow the Soviet Army to enter Warsaw and occupy it. They had a supply of ammunition for only this short time. But the unexpected holding back of the Soviet attack forced the insurgents to continue to fight. It was expected that provisions and ammunition would arrive from the west and would be dropped from airplanes. A voluminous and tragic correspondence began between the Underground authorities in Poland and the Polish Government in London. The difficulty lay in the distances to allied airfields (in England and in Italy) from Warsaw, and the undertaking of such long round-trip flights without landing was very risky. Prime Minister Churchill and Pres. Roosevelt wired Stalin to allow British airplanes to land on Soviet airfields, hardly 100 miles from Warsaw. Vice Minister for Home Affairs, Vyshinsky, told the U. S. Ambassador in Moscow on Aug. 16 that the Soviet Government could not of course object to English or American aircraft dropping arms in the region of Warsaw, since this was an American and British affair; but they decidedly objected to American or British aircraft, after dropping arms in the region of Warsaw, landing on Soviet territory, since the Soviet government did not wish to associate themselves either directly or indirectly with the Warsaw uprising.[18]

Gen. Sosnkowski, Polish Commander-in-Chief, and members of the Government did their best to prevail on English authorities to help Warsaw. They wanted: to send to Warsaw a Polish parachute brigade from Great Britain; to have the Polish Home Army soldiers be recognized as combatant forces, entitled to the rights of the Geneva Convention dated Aug. 27, 1929, concerning the treatment of prisoners of war; to bomb Warsaw airfields; and to arrange for a continuous drop of war supplies and ammunition to designated spots in War-

[18] Churchill, W. Triumph and Tragedy, p. 133.

saw. English authorities rejected the sending of the parachute brigade and the bombing of airfields as being too risky. Rights of the Home Army soldiers as combatant troops were recognized only on Aug. 30, and the dropping of supplies was limited in spite of the fact that there were Polish air crew volunteers to do this. During the 63 days of the Warsaw uprising, Warsaw and surrounding points received from the west 73 deliveries dropped from airplanes, or about 104 tons; of this, 82.3 tons were ammunition and 21.7 tons were provisions and medicine. For this, about 296 airplanes were used of which the Germans shot down 34, or only 12%. During the 2nd half of September there were received some 55 tons by air from the Soviets—of these about 15 tons were provisions.[19] *But the Soviet supplies arrived too late to have any effect on the outcome of the uprising which was then nearing its end. Besides, these supplies were dropped without parachutes and arrived in damaged condition.*

Recognition for the Home Army soldiers as combatant troops took so long because the Allies wanted to release a joint declaration, together with the Soviets. But, the Soviets objected, and finally on August 30 a declaration was issued signed only by Great Britain and the U. S. Following is the text:[20]

"His Majesty's Government have consistently done all in their power to ensure that all members of the armed forces of the Powers at war with Germany should be treated by the German military authorities in accordance with the laws and customs of war. They are, however, receiving numerous reports which show that members of the Polish Home Army, which is engaged in active operations in the struggle against the common enemy, are being treated by the German military authorities in a manner contrary to the laws and customs of war.

His Majesty's Government therefore make this formal declaration:

(1) The Polish Home Army, which is now mobilized, constitutes a combatant force forming an integral part of the Polish Armed Forces.

(2) Members of the Polish Home Army are instructed to

---

19 Polskie Siły Zbrojne, vol. 3, p. 799–800.
20 Stosunki polsko-sowieckie, 1943–46, p. 220.

conduct their military operations in accordance with the rules of war, and in so doing they bear their arms openly against the enemy. They operate in units under responsible commanders. They are provided with a distinctive emblem or with Polish uniforms.

(3) In these circumstances reprisals against members of the Polish Army violate the rules of war, by which Germany is bound. His Majesty's Government therefore solemnly warn all Germans who take any part in or are in any way responsible for such violations that they do so at their peril and will be held answerable for their crimes."

The Soviet Government did not like the idea of a Warsaw uprising. They knew the Polish Home Army was under the authority of the Polish Government in London which they did not recognize. So, for them to occupy Warsaw along with the Home Army would present political complications. In his talks with Mikołajczyk during the first days of August in Moscow, Stalin played down the news of the uprising—the same was true in his talks on Aug. 6 with representatives of the Polish Committee of National Liberation.[21] *Atlhough a Red Army liaison officer was parachuted to Warsaw, the Russian High Command did not want to have a permanent contact with the Polish Home Army, and the numerous dispatches from Gen. Bor-Komorowski to Gen. Rokossowsky were not answered. The Soviets did not want to help the insurrection in Warsaw. They would not permit allied planes to land on Russian airfields, thus forcing them to make non-stop trips from Italy to Warsaw to Italy, a most difficult feat. On Sept. 1 Premier Mikołajczyk discussed this situation with Prime Minister Churchill, who was outraged at the Soviet attitude. Churchill said he had already suggested to Pres. Roosevelt that they present the Soviets with a "fait accompli" and send out daily a large number of American bombers to Warsaw with the idea they would land on Soviet airfields, but Pres. Roosevelt did not agree to this. Churchill regretted this as it was probably the best tactical move and presented the only possible chance of real success. Planes from Italy could not*

---

[21] Mikołajczyk, S. Op. cit., p. 74–75.

guarantee any success and a massive night attack on Warsaw could not be undertaken by the British Air Force. On Sept. 4 the British Government again suggested that the American Government send planes with the intention of landing on Soviet airfields without previous Soviet approval.[22]

The problem of help for Warsaw was discussed at a session of the British War Cabinet on Sept. 4. Prime Minister Churchill wrote in his memoirs:[23]

"When the Cabinet met on the night of Sept. 4 I thought the issue so important that though I had a touch of fever I went from my bed to our underground room. We had met together on many unpleasant affairs. I do not remember any occasion when such deep anger was shown by all our members, Tory, Labor, Liberal, alike. I should have liked to say: 'We are sending our aeroplanes to land in your territory, after delivering supplies to Warsaw. If you do not treat them properly all convoys will be stopped from this moment by us.' But the reader of these pages in after-years must realize that everyone always has to keep in mind the fortunes of millions of men fighting in a world-wide struggle, and that terrible and even humbling submissions must at times be made to the general aim. I did not therefore propose this drastic step. It might have been effective, because we were dealing with men in the Kremlin who were governed by calculations and not by emotion. They did not mean to let the spirit of Poland rise again at Warsaw. Their plans were based on the Lublin Committee. That was the only Poland they cared about. The cutting off of the convoys at this critical moment in their great advance would perhaps have bulked in their minds as much as considerations of honor, humanity, decent commonplace good faith, usually count with ordinary people."

The same day the following telegram was sent to the British Ambassador in Moscow to present to the Soviet Government:[24]

"The War Cabinet at their meeting today considered the latest reports of the situation in Warsaw, which show that the Poles fighting against the Germans there are in desperate straits. The War Cabinet wish the Soviet Government to know that public opinion in this country is deeply moved by the events in Warsaw

22 Sikorski Historical Institute, London. Archives.
23 Churchill, W. Op. cit., p. 141.
24 Ibid, p. 142.

and by the terrible sufferings of the Poles there. Whatever the rights and wrongs about the beginnings of the Warsaw uprising, the people of Warsaw themselves cannot be held responsible for the decision taken. Our people cannot understand why no material help has been sent from outside to the Poles in Warsaw. The fact that such help could not be sent on account of your Government's refusal to allow United States aircraft to land on aerodromes in Russian hands is now becoming publicly known. If on top of all this the Poles in Warsaw should now be overwhelmed by the Germans, as we are told they must be within two or three days, the shock of public opinion here will be incalculable. The War Cabinet themselves find it hard to understand your Government's refusal to take account of the obligations of the British and American governments to help the Poles in Warsaw. Your Government's action in preventing this help being sent seems to us at variance with the spirit of Allied cooperation to which you and we attach so much importance both for the present and the future.

Out of regard for Marshal Stalin and for the Soviet peoples, with whom it is our earnest desire to work in future years, the War Cabinet have asked me to make this further appeal to the Soviet Government to give whatever help may be in their power, and above all to provide facilities for United States aircraft to land on your airfields for this purpose."

Only on Sept. 10 did the Soviet Government agree to allow allied planes to land on Soviet airfields. On Sept. 18, 110 American planes left England and, after dropping supplies over Warsaw, landed on a Soviet air-strip. That was the last air drop over Warsaw.

Sept. 1, 1944 was the 5th anniversary of the outbreak of World War II. On that day Prime Minister Churchill sent this message to the Polish people:[25]

"On September 1st, five years ago, the German armies launched on Poland their unprovoked attack. This attack precipitated the world conflagration which has brought about untold misery to millions of human beings.

In 1939 the Polish armies, despite a gallant resistance, were overwhelmed. But Poland fought on. For five years, despite the most barbarous treatment at the hands of the Nazi thugs and torturers, Polish courage and Polish constancy have never faltered At home and abroad, the Poles, under the leadership first of

25 The Times, London, Sept. 1, 1944.

Gen. Sikorski and then of his distinguished successor Mikołajczyk, have remained at one in their determination to continue with the United Nations to struggle against the German oppressors of their country.

Polish armies have won and are still winning renown, fighting on all the main fronts in the great final battle which will liberate Europe and make possible the restoration of a strong and independent Poland. In Warsaw the heroic struggle continues, watched attentively by the world.

The day of liberation is drawing near and at this time it is fitting that we should pay homage to all those gallant Poles both at home and abroad who have continued the struggle against terrible odds and have earned the lasting admiration of all free peoples. From their sacrifices a new Poland will be born."

President Raczkiewicz and Premier Mikołajczyk spoke to the Polish nation by radio and the Commander-in-Chief, Gen. Sosnkowski issued an Order of the Day, No. 19, to the soldiers of the Home Army, as follows:[26]

Soldiers of the Home Army!

"Five years have passed since the day when Poland, encouraged by the British Government and having received its guarantees, stood up to a lonely struggle against the German might. The September campaign gave the Allies eight months of invaluable time, enabling Great Britain to complete her war preparations to such an extent that the Battle of Britain—a turning point in history—was won. History has still to pass the verdict on the significance of the Polish September campaign in the destinies of the world.

Since then, the deadly struggle of the Polish Armed Forces against German imperialism has never ceased. The darkness of enslavement had barely time to enshroud the ruins of Polish towns and villages, when Polish Forces were already re-forming abroad. For five years they have been fighting without respite on the oceans and continents, in defense of the liberty of the nation—believing that they were thus following the road leading to the restoration of their country, undiminished and truly independent. . . .

For a whole month the soldiers of the Home Army, together with the people of Warsaw, have been shedding their blood alone behind street barricades in a merciless struggle against the enemy's overwhelming superiority. The loneliness in which the

[26] Stosunki polsko-sowieckie, 1943–46, p. 229.

Poles fought the September Campaign and the loneliness in which they are now fighting in Warsaw are entirely different one from the other. The people of Warsaw, left to their own devices and abandoned on the common battlefront against the Germans,—this is a tragic and ghastly riddle which we Poles are unable to solve, considering the background of the great strength of the Allies on the threshold of the sixth year of war.

We are unable to do so, because we have not yet lost faith in the belief that the world is still governed by moral rights. We do not understand as we are unable to believe that a policy devoid of moral principles, could do otherwise than to write on the pages of history, for her own condemnation, the ominous words: "Mane, Tekel, Fares." We cannot believe that reasons of expediency in the face of physical might could lead so far as to cause indifference to the agony of the capital of a country whose soldiers have shielded so many other capitals with their own bodies, besides lending aid in their liberation.

Experts endeavor to explain to us that the lack of help for Warsaw is due to difficulties of a technical nature. Calculation of loss and profit are put forward. The loss of 27 aircraft over Warsaw in the space of one month means little to the Allied Air Forces which possess several score of thousands of planes of all kinds and types at their disposal. If figures have to be mentioned, let us recall that during the battle of London, Polish airmen suffered losses amounting to over 40 per cent. In the effort to aid Warsaw, the losses in aircraft and crews have been 15 per cent. . . .

Warsaw is fighting—not for empty words of praise, not for approval, not for assurances of pity and sympathy. She is waiting for arms and ammuniation. She does not ask, in the manner of a poor relative, for crumbs from the lordly table; she demands the means to fight—in the knowledge of the provisions of the Alliance and the obligations contained therein.

Warsaw is fighting and waiting. The soldiers of the Home Army, the workmen and intellectuals, girls and children—all. The whole Nation is fighting, having—in its passionate yearning for the truth, liberty and victory—achieved the miracle of complete unity.

If the population of Warsaw were to perish for the lack of adequate aid under the ruins of its houses—if it were to be abandoned to mass slaughter through passivity, indifference or cold calculation—then the world's conscience would be burdened with a frightful wrong, a wrong unprecedented in history. There are qualms of conscience which kill. . . .

. . . Reproach is made to the Poles for their alleged lack of coordination, in their fight, with the general operational plans in Eastern Europe. If needed, we will prove how many of our endeavors to achieve such coordination were in vain. For five years the Home Army has been systematically accused of passivity and of feigning combat against the Germans. Today, it is being accused of fighting too much and too well. . . .

I wish to give you an assurance in the name of your brothers who are fighting now on all the fronts in the world, that their deepest concern and their loving thoughts accompany you faithfully in your stern and glorious battle. May this knowledge aid to alleviate, however slightly, the burden you are carrying and to assist you in bearing these days of anguish which resemble a nightmare. But first and foremost know that no sacrifice, conceived from a clear heart, can be vain; and that your strife is rendering the Polish Cause great and indisputable services."

This Order of the Day angered British authorities and part of the Polish Government and was, later, one of the causes for the dismissal of Gen. Sosnkowski.

When Hitler and Himmler learned of the Warsaw Uprising, their immediate reaction was one of raging anger with the Polish soldiers fighting in the Home Army and with the civilian population. According to Gen. Von dem Bach who was in charge of combating the Warsaw Uprising, upon learning of the fighting in the city Hitler immediately ordered the withdrawal of all German troops from Warsaw, in order to level the whole city to the ground with the help of German airplanes, and thus to strangle the fire of rebellion. In Hitler's own words, this was to be "an awesome example for all of Europe."

However, it was not possible to withdraw the German troops immediately because they were already in battle with the insurgents. So, the order was revised: as soon as the German soldiers could be removed, Warsaw was to be razed to the ground, no prisoners were to be taken, but all inhabitants of the city to be killed.[27] *This order was issued on Sept. 1 by Himmler to the Warsaw commander, with the authorization "to kill anyone you please."*[28]

---

27 Borkiewicz, A. Powstanie warszawskie, p. 94.
28 Ibid, p. 96.

Thus began the murder of Polish soldiers and civilians in the besieged city, atrocities unparalleled in the history of war.

Following are several illustrations, chosen from among hundreds.[29]

Already in the first days of the fighting the Germans used Polish women, men, and children as shields for their tanks while attacking the barricades of the insurgents. On Aug. 2 at 2 P.M. in the region of Powązki, the Germans launched a severe attack, headed by a column of tanks and armored panzer cars in front of which the Germans pushed some 50 Poles who had been tied to a ladder. (Borkiewicz, p. 111). On Aug. 3, in reprisal for the uprising, 200 persons were murdered on Olesińska Street; others were driven into cellars and then bombarded with grenades; many were wounded and burned. This attack was led by SS Stormtrooper Stein (p. 136). On Aug. 5 the Germans attacked in the Wola suburbs. From noon on they conducted a mass slaughter of people, with no regard for age or sex. About 38,000 persons were thus murdered (p. 148). On the same day, in another part of the city, Col. Geibel organized a relief for a telephone station under the protection of a live barricade of several hundred Polish women seized in the vicinity of Lithuanian Union Square. These women were pushed along, under penalty of shooting, by a column of four tanks on which women had been placed to deter the insurgents from shooting. Women were also forced to walk in 2 rows alongside the tanks and they were followed by an escort of soldiers dressed in womens' kerchiefs and coats . . . The women were ordered to wave white kerchiefs (p. 312). On Aug. 7 Gen. Reinefarth led the majority of his soldiers into Chłodna Street. At the head, and following two heavy tanks, marched Dirlewanger's 2d battalion pushing ahead of it civilians as cover (p. 154). On Aug. 25 five insurrectionists were taken prisoner along with a badly wounded man and two aides carrying him on a stretcher—all of these had been

---

[29] Ibid, Documentary material on atrocities appears on pages 71, 76, 78, 89, 111, 119, 122, 124, 126, 127, 136, 147, 148, 154, 156, 161, 178, 211, 212, 222,, 255, 258, 270, 302, 308, 309, 312, 314, 319, 323, 357, 376, 413, 443, 470, 483, 492, 528, 550, 569, 571, 585, 593, 594, 602, 616, 639, 660, 677.

Without help from outside, without heavy guns, ammunition, light, water, or food, the Rising engaged an opponent with modern equipment and no scruple in making every brutal use of it. The battle lasted for nine weeks. So it was not an unimportant local military diversion, but a serious political and military demonstration by the entire Polish community, determined to struggle to their last breath.

In this, the final phase of the war, the Warsaw Rising challenges the world again with the problem of Poland. This is no problem for diplomatic chaffering among the cabinets. It is the problem of a great nation, fighting gallantly and uncompromisingly for liberty, integrity and social justice in the life of peoples and nations, for the noble principles of the Atlantic Charter, and all that the finer part of the world is fighting for today.

The blood beyond price which we have shed, the losses we have suffered will not have been in vain. They form an enormous political and moral capital, which will turn the indifference of the world and will weigh in the scales in our favor, when the political results of this war are assessed.

May the Warsaw August Rising cement and bind our nation into a single block. May the fusion of our soldiers, workers, peasants and thinkers, the brotherhood of forest and barricade shared in the struggle against the common enemy, the magnificent maturity and determination of the common people seal the inner solidarity and strength of our Nation, and so ensure the essential consolidation of our political life; may it unite us in the future in such fashion that we shall be able to deal with the difficult tasks which harsh reality sets before us. If that be the result of the August struggles in Warsaw, we shall be able to think hopefully about the future of Poland.

Warsaw—Warsaw, the legendary Capital of Poland—how many times in history has she not stood the terrible test on her own smoking ruins?

The soldiers whose only weapons against tanks, aeroplanes and guns were pistols and bottles of petrol, are heroes. The women, under fire tending the wounded and carrying reports, somehow, in cellars collapsing under bombs and shells, preparing food for children and men, moving among dying people with unshaken cheerfulness and tranquillity, they too are heroes. The children who played calmly on the smoking ruins and in the cellars, are heroes. The common people of Warsaw are heroes.

And the nation which can rise to such heroism is immortal. For those who have died have already conquered, and those who live will go on fighting, will conquer and again bear testimony of the truth that Poland lives wherever Poles live."

Debate on September 26, 1944.

MR. W. J. BROWN (Ind.) asked the Prime Minister if he can make a statement in regard to the rising in Warsaw and the measures taken by the Allies to assist the Polish Forces.

COMMANDER BOWER (C) asked the Prime Minister whether the scale of local assistance to be afforded to the rising of General Bor's forces in Warsaw at the beginning of August was determined beforehand by the Allied staffs; and to what extent it has been found possible to implement such decisions.

THE PRIME MINISTER (MR. CHURCHILL): I welcome this opportunity of paying tribute to the heroism and tenacity of the Polish Home Army and population of Warsaw, who, after five years of oppression, have yet fought for nearly two months to contribute all in their power to the expulsion of the Germans from the capital of Poland.

His Majest's Government have always made it clear to all concerned that they were too far from the scene to undertake responsibility for ordering or supporting a general rising in Poland. At the same time, they have consistently used their good offices to promote cooperation and coordination of plans in regard to such matters between the Polish and Soviet authorities, and, despite the formidable practical difficulties, they have furnished military supplies by air to the Polish Home Army. As soon as His Majesty's Government learned that the rising in Warsaw had begun, they expressed to the Soviet Government their hope that, although such coordination had not yet been achieved, they would nevertheless bring such aid to the Polish insurgents as lay in their power. The Soviet armies were at that time engaged in heavy fighting with strong German forces to the east and northeast of Warsaw, but when their operational plans permitted and direct contact had been established with the Polish Commander-in-Chief in Warsaw, they sent supplies to the Polish Forces and provided them with air cover and anti-aircraft support. This assistance has been gratefully acknowledged by the Polish

Prime Minister and by the Polish Commander-in-Chief in Warsaw.

Meanwhile, the Royal Air Force, despite the very great practical difficulties and in the face of heavy losses, themselves made the long flight from Mediterranean bases to Warsaw with supplies on all occasions when weather conditions permitted. In their statement issued on Sept. 13, the Polish Government published particulars and expressed appreciation of this assistance. On Sept. 18 a large escorted force of United States heavy bombers carried out a successful operation, which was planned in cooperation with the Soviet High Command but which was unavoidably postponed for several days because of bad weather. This force, after dropping a large quantity of supplies in Warsaw, the bulk of which came from British sources, flew on to bases in Soviet territory, escorted by Soviet aircraft.

These successful combined operations have played an important part in sustaining the gallant resistance of the Polish Forces and in enabling them to contribute so effectively to the liberation of their country's capital, which will not, I hope, be much longer delayed.

* * *

Debate on September 27, 1944.

MAJOR-GENERAL SIR ALFRED KNOX (C.) asked the Secretary of State for Foreign Affairs what reason was given by the Government of the USSR for their refusal of permission for R.A.F. planes to land in Soviet territory after dropping munitions and supplies for the patriot forces in Warsaw.

THE SECRETARY OF STATE FOR FOREIGN AFFAIRS (MR. EDEN): There has never been any question of aircraft of the Royal Air Force undertaking such shuttle flights to bases in Soviet territory for these operations. As my right hon. Friend the Prime Minister stated yesterday, in reply to questions, the Soviet Government have now agreed to the use of Soviet bases, and on Sept. 18 a strong force of United States aircraft carried out a supply operation to Warsaw, in collaboration with the Soviet High Command.

SIR A. KNOX: Is it not a fact that on July 30 the Soviet Government, by repeated broadcasts from Moscow, urged the Underground Army to rise, to facilitate the passage of the Vistula by the Red Army, and that by Sept. 14, six weeks later, they had not given permission for Allied aircraft to land supplies in Warsaw and to land in Soviet territory, and that, therefore, they rendered the position of the Polish Forces in Warsaw tragic?

SIR JOHN WARDLAW-MILNE (C.): May I urge my right hon. Friend to consider, in view of the very specific efforts which were made by the British authorities, and especially by the Royal Air Force, to make the statement which the Prime Minister made yesterday very widely public, because there is a very erroneous impression in this country about what has been done by our Forces?

MR. EDEN: I think there is very good cause for my hon. Friend's supplementary. In fact, the Royal Air Force did everything in their power to assist in that way, and I think I can also say that His Majesty's Government did everything in their power to bring about unity and understanding in this matter between our Allies.

SIR A. KNOX: Is it not a fact that the Soviet Government refused to give permission until Sept. 14?

MR. EDEN: My hon. and gallant Friend is asking me why one of our Allies did not give assistance to another of our Allies. That is a question which might well be discussed in this House, but I would rather give consideration to my reply.

SIR A. KNOX asked the Secretary of State for Foreign Affairs if he is aware that members of the Polish Underground Army, who, acting under orders from the Polish Government, have cooperated with the Soviet forces in the liberation of their country, have been arrested and deported by the Soviet authorities in Tarnopol, the province of Lublin, and other districts; and if he will make representations on the subject to the Government of the USSR in the general interest of Allied relations.

MR. EDEN: Yes, Sir. My attention has been drawn to the reports to which my hon. and gallant Friend refers, and I have brought them to the notice of the Soviet Government. The latter have now informed me that they do not consider that these reports give a true picture of events in the areas in question. They state that almost all Polish Army detachments found in Poland when the Soviet armies advanced are now fighting beside the Russians against the Germans.

SIR A. KNOX: Is it not true that several individuals have been arrested and deported because they refused to take the oath of allegiance to the so-called Committee of Liberation?

MR. EDEN: As I have said, as soon as these reports were brought to my notice, I brought them to the notice of the Soviet Government, as I thought it my duty to do. The House will understand that there is no matter which causes more concern to His Majesty's Government at this time than the relations between our Polish and our Russian Allies.

EARL WINTERTON (C.): Is it not a fact that my right hon. Friend cannot be responsible for differences of opinion between our Allies, and that it is not for this House to say how they should be resolved?

MR. MCGOVERN (I.L.P.): Does the right hon. Gentleman think that there is anything to be gained by covering up the fact that an Ally of ours is both deporting and shooting Nationalists and Socialists in Poland?

MR. EDEN: The hon. Gentleman talks about covering up matters, but I must tell the House that not only are these affairs of delicacy between Allies, but also that there is some difficulty in ascertaining the facts. Therefore, we should treat these matters with caution and with reserve at the present time.

EARL WINTERTON: Could my right hon. Friend not make it clear, in reply to my question, that His Majesty's Government can be responsible only for the conduct of His Majesty's Government, and cannot be responsible for the conduct of other nations?

MR. EDEN: My right hon. Friend is absolutely correct. That is why I explained that I was asked a question about affairs which concern two of our Allies, for which my responsibility is not direct.

COMMANDER SIR ARCHIBALD SOUTHBY (C.): While it is true that these are matters of delicacy, are not matters concerning our responsibility to our Ally, Poland, also matters of principle?

MR. EDEN: Yes, Sir, and our responsibility has been fully, and I might add gallantly, discharged.

MR. ASTOR (C.): Are there not liaison officers on the spot, from whom the Government get information?

MR. EDEN: We have been supplied with information from Warsaw; but perhaps my hon. Friend will put that question down.

COMMANDER BOWER (C.) asked the Prime Minister, whether, having regard to the conflicting reports which have reached the public concerning the rising of General Bor's forces in Warsaw, he will make a full statement on the matter.

THE DEPUTY PRIME MINISTER (MR. ATTLEE) (Lab.): I would refer my hon. and gallant Friend to the statement which was made yesterday in reply to Question on this subject.

COMMANDER BOWER: While fully appreciating the statement which was made yesterday, does my right hon. Friend realize that the public so far have heard a great deal of rumor, very few facts and an absolute spate of extremely tendentious Communist propaganda; and is it not necessary and desirable that a very full and frank statement should be made?

MR. ATTLEE: I cannot agree with my hon. and gallant Friend's description of what information has been given to the public and I am quite certain that full opportunity will be taken to give any information that is possible on the very gallant defense of Warsaw.

MR. GALLACHER (Com.): Is it not the case that, instead of a campaign of Communist propaganda, we have had a tendentious campaign of anti-Soviet propaganda?...

COMMANDER BOWER (C.) asked the Minister of Information to what extent restriction on publication of the reports of the Polish rising in Warsaw at the beginning of August was imposed by the Ministry of Information either by prohibition or request.

PARLIAMENTARY SECRETARY TO THE MINISTRY OF INFORMATION (MR. THURTLE): No restriction was imposed nor any request to this effect made by the Ministry of Information.

COMMANDER BOWER: Are we then to assume that by some peculiar feat of telepathy almost the entire Press of this country held up this extremely important information for several days?

MR. THURTLE: I do not know what assumptions my hon. and gallant Friend makes, but it is the fact, as I say, that we have nothing at all to do with it. We did not impose any restrictions on its publication nor did we make any request to that effect.

MR. PETHERICK (C.): Has the Ministry of Information made no such representations to any of the Service Departments?

MR. THURTLE: I am unable to speak for the Service Departments.

* * *

Debate on October 5, 1944.

THE PRIME MINISTER (MR. CHURCHILL): I have a statement to make. I am sure that I am expressing the feelings of the House, as well as those of His Majesty's Government, in paying tribute to the heroic stand of the Polish Home Army and of the Polish civilian population at Warsaw. Their resistance to overwhelming odds, under inconceivable conditions of hardship, came to an end on Oct. 3, after a fight which had lasted 63 days. Despite all the efforts of the Soviet Army, the strong German positions on the Vistula could not be taken, and relief could not come in time. British, American, Polish and Soviet airmen did what they could to succour the Poles at Warsaw, but although this sustained the Polish resistance beyond what would have seemed possible, it could not turn the tide. In the battle for Warsaw, terrible damage has been inflicted upon that noble city, and its heroic population has undergone sufferings and privations unsurpassed even among the miseries of this war.

The final fall of Warsaw, at a time when Allied Armies are everywhere victorious, and when the final defeat of Germany is in sight, must come as a very bitter blow to all Poles. At such a moment, I wish to express our respect to all those Poles who fell, fought or suffered at Warsaw and our sympathy with the Polish nation in this further grievous loss. Our confidence that the days of their tribulation are rapidly drawing to an end is unshakable. When the final Allied victory is achieved, the epic of Warsaw will not be forgotten. It will remain a deathless memory for the Poles, and for the friends of freedom all over the world.

* * *

Debate on October 11, 1944.

CAPTAIN DUNCAN (C.) asked the Secretary of State for Foreign Affairs if he has any official information as to the German claim to have captured General Bor in Warsaw.

THE PARLIAMENTARY UNDER-SECRETARY TO THE FOREIGN OFFICE (MR. LAW): The Polish Government have authorized me to say that on the morning of Oct. 4 they received a message from Warsaw, in which General Bor stated that, as all ways of escape were now closed, he and his staff would have to surrender at midday. There is therefore no reason whatever to doubt that the German claim to have captured General Bor is correct.

CAPTAIN DUNCAN: Does that not vitiate the accuracy of the information put out by the Lublin Committee, which stated, time and again, that General Bor had never been in Warsaw, and will he convey that information to the Ministry of Information so they may decrease the amount of publicity given to the Lublin Committee's report?

MR. LAW: I have no doubt my right hon. Friend the Minister of Information will see the reply to this Question, and my hon. and gallant Friend's supplementary question.

3. POLISH-SOVIET RELATIONS*

A. THE POLISH GOVERNMENT AND RUSSIA

PREMIER MIKOŁAJCZYK'S VISIT *to Moscow lasted 11 days, from July 30 to Aug. 9. His two talks with Stalin were without result; Stalin insisted very strongly that Poland's eastern boundary should be the Curzon Line, and the western boundary should be on the Oder, including therein Breslau, Stettin and part of East Prussia (Koenigsberg to go to Russia). As to the Warsaw uprising, Stalin at first refused to acknowledge that any fighting was going on, and claimed the Home Army simply refused to fight the Germans. On the subject of Poland's internal affairs he suggested that Mikołajczyk come to an understanding with the Polish Committee of National Liberation (the so-called Lublin Committee), whose representatives (E. Osóbka-Morawski, Wanda Wasilewska, Gen. Rola-Zymierski and B. Bierut) had come to Moscow for just that purpose.*

* House of Commons. Vol. 403, Sept. 28-29, 1944, p. 473, 489–491, 501–524, 543–561, 583–589, 615—632, 642–704; House of Lords, Vol. 133. Oct. 3, 1944, p. 273, 281–282, 299–300.

In the talks of Aug. 6 and 7 Mikołajczyk asked the Committee of National Liberation to try to influence the Soviet Government to help Warsaw in her fight against the Germans. Premier Mikołajczyk had not been authorized by the London Government to talk with the Lublin Committee—he had been instructed before his departure on July 26 that he was to deal with the Soviet Government and not with the Lublin Committee.[1] *Evidently, just like Stalin, the Lublin Committee insisted still on Aug. 6 that Warsaw was not in revolt.*[2] *The Lublin Committee demanded the Curzon Line as a boundary and refused to allow the common appeal with the London Delegation to Stalin on the subject of including Wilno and Lwów within Poland. In creating a new government in Poland, the Lublin Committee wanted to discard the 1935 Constitution and adopt instead the 1921 Constitution with Bierut as president, Mikołajczyk as premier and the remaining 18 members of the government to include 3 from London and the rest named by the Warsaw National Council of Poland. Pres. Raczkiewicz and Gen. Sosnkowski were to be removed completely.*

Mikołajczyk did not accept these conditions, and instead presented his proposal: retain the 1935 Constitution as interpreted currently (with limited rights for the President of the Republic). The Government would be composed of members of the 4 parties represented in the London Government as well as members of the Polish Workers Party (or the Communist Party if it really existed in Poland)—a number in proportion to their influence in the country. This Government would conduct talks on Polish-Soviet cooperation and boundaries and would conclude with the Soviet Government an agreement on administration of the country and the Polish Armed Forces.

Mikołajczyk also rejected the recognition of the National Council of Poland as the sovereign authority in Poland. He suggested that the Government be named by the current pres-

---

1 National Committee of Americans of Polish Descent. Biuletyn Organizacyjny, no. 23, p. 15–16.

2 Mikołajczyk, S. Op. cit., p. 75.

ident (Mr. Racczkiewicz), and that democratic elections then be quickly held for members to the Sejm, and the Sejm would elect a new president and would present a new constitution.[3]

The Lublin Committee would not agree to this. Thus Mikołajczyk and his group left Moscow on Aug. 9 and returned to London.

Within the Polish Government in London things were very confused and complicated. The policy conducted by Premier Mikołajczyk of appeasing Soviet demands by accepting the Curzon Line and joining with the Committee of National Liberation was opposed by much of the Polish population and even by members of the Government itself. The Army, and Commander-in-Chief Gen. Sosnkowski especially, strongly opposed this policy. To remove this opposition, Pres. Raczkiewicz, on Aug. 7 under pressure from Premier Mikołajczyk, dismissed Gen. Sosnkowski as successor to the presidency and named to this position T. Arciszewski, newly arrived from Warsaw, a member of the Polish Socialist Party, and unanimously nominated for this position by the Council of National Unity in Warsaw.

Besides these internal difficulties and the problems of the continuing battles in Warsaw, the English and American Governments were putting pressure on the Polish Government to compromise with the Lublin Committee. In answer to a request from Mikołajczyk to Pres. Roosevelt for help for fighting Warsaw, Roosevelt said on Aug. 24 that both he and Prime Minister Churchill had consulted with Stalin on additional ammunition and provisions for Warsaw, and then he added:[4]

> "In regard to the broader question of the solution of Polish-Soviet differences, I fully realize the difficulties which confront you, particularly in the light of the heroic and unequal struggle of the Warsaw garrison. I feel, however, that these unfortunate developments should not deter you from presenting reasonable proposals to the Polish Committee of National Liberation and I am of the firm opinion that if reasonable proposals are not pre-

[3] Stosunki polsko-sowieckie, 1943–46, p. 207.
[4] Mikołajczyk, S. Op. cit . p. 287.

sented to the Committee, and if a crisis should arise in the Polish Government, such developments could only worsen the situation."

So, on Aug. 29 the Polish Government drew up a new plan for agreement with the Soviets, which they sent as a memorandum to England, the United States and the USSR:[5]

"After the liberation of the capital of Poland the Polish Government will be reconstructed on the following lines:

The parties mentioned below will, in equal strength, form the basis of the government: the Peasant Party, the National Party, the Polish Socialist Party, the Christian Labor Party, and the Polish Workers' Communist Party.

The possibility of joining the government by representatives of the Fascist-minded and nondemocratic political groups, also by those responsible for the pre-September 1939 system of government, is ruled out.

Agreement between the Prime Minister and the political parties concerning the choice of candidates for the government from amongst these Parties will take place in Warsaw, and thereafter the President of the Republic will, on the motion of the Prime Minister, appoint a new government.

The program of the government will rest on the following bases:

The government will bring about the resumption of diplomatic relations between Poland and the USSR.

The government will immediately proceed to take over the administration of the liberated Polish lands and prepare the taking over of the new areas to be surrendered by Germany. To this end the government will conclude with the Soviet government an agreement with the view to defining the forms of collaboration with the Red Army in the military sphere. This agreement will be modelled on, and carried out in the spirit of, agreements concluded by the Allied Powers with the governments of the liberated countries of Western Europe. The government will assure order in the rear of the Soviet Army.

All foreign troops will be withdrawn from Polish territories on the cessation of hostilities.

The government will, as soon as possible, arrange for elections to the Constitutional Diet as well as for elections to the local government authorities on the basis of a decree providing for universal, equal, direct, secret, and proportional suffrage. Elections will take place as soon as normal conditions are established in the country.

---

5 Stosunki polsko-sowieckie, 1943–46, p. 218.

The new democratic constitution will be passed immediately after the convocation of the Constitutional Diet. A new President of the Republic will be elected on the basis of the constitution.

The government will undertake the carrying out of social reforms based on the declarations of principles made during the period of occupation by the representatives of the nation in the homeland and by the Polish Government abroad. In particular, the agricultural reforms will be enacted without delay.

Until the convocation of the Constitutional Diet a National Council will be appointed to assist the government as an advisory body. It will be composed of representatives of the aforesaid five political parties, each of which will be represented by equal numbers. Small democratic political groups may also be represented on a correspondingly lesser scale.

The government will bring about an agreement with the Soviet Government with the view to joint prosecution of the war against Germany and the laying of foundations for a durable Polish-Soviet friendship after the war based on a Polish-Soviet alliance aiming at close political and economic collaboration between Poland and the USSR while respecting the principle of the sovereignty of both states and of the mutual obligation on non-interference in the internal affairs of the other states. It will be the object of the alliances to devote constant care to the elimination of all German influence in central Europe and the prevention of the possibility of renewed German aggression.

This object will also be served by the alliance between Poland and Great Britain and France, by the conclusion of a Polish-Czechoslovakian alliance, and by the maintenance of the closest ties of friendship between Poland and the United States of America.

Poland would expect fully to participate in the planning for the safeguarding of peace by a system of general security of peace-loving nations. Also to take part in the occupation of Germany, especially of her eastern territories adjacent to the future western boundaries of Poland.

With regard to the settlement of the frontiers of Poland, the Polish Government will act on the following principles agreed upon with the Soviet Government in the spirit of friendship and the respect of the fundamental interests of the Polish nation.

Poland, which has made so many sacrifices in this war and is the only country under German occupation that produced no Quisling, cannot emerge from this war diminished in territory. In the east the main centers of Polish cultural life and the sources of raw materials indispensable to the economic life of the country shall remain within Polish boundaries. A final settlement of the Polish-Soviet frontier on the basis of these principles will be made by the Constitutional Diet in accordance with democratic principles.

All Germans will be removed from the territories incorporated into Poland in the north and the west by mutual Soviet-Polish cooperation.

Questions of citizenship and repatriation will be duly settled. Polish citizens who have been interned, arrested, or deported both in Poland and on territories of the USSR will immediately be released by the Soviet authorities who will assist in their repatriation.

A voluntary exchange of the Polish, White Russian, and Ukrainian population will be carried out.

The prosecution of the war and the general direction of all matters concerning the Polish armed forces will pass into the hands of the Polish Government, who will form to this end a war cabinet. The latter will, in particular, be combatant in the following matters:

(a) problems connected with the general prosecution of the war;

(b) Polish-Soviet military collaboration;

(c) Polish-British military collaboration;

(d) military cooperation between Poland and other Allied nations;

(e) unification of all armed forces of the Polish Republic.

The discussions of the war cabinet may be attended apart from Ministers appointed by the Council of Ministers, by the Chief of the General Staff, and, if necessary, by the chiefs of the services and the commanders of individual groups of the Polish armed forces.

The Polish armed forces will operate under Polish Command; in the eastern zone of operations under Soviet Supreme Operational Command; in the other theatres of war under the Supreme Operational Allied Command in the respective area."

There was opposition from some political parties to this plan. The Polish Socialist Party presented its own plan[6] and representatives of the National Democratic Party in London sent their opinion to Warsaw in a message on Aug. 24:[7]

---

[6] National Committee of Americans of Polish Descent. Biuletyn Organizacyjny, no. 25, p. 9. Polskie Siły Zbrojne, vol. 3, p. 848.

[7] Piłsudski Institute of America, New York, Archives.

"The bankruptcy of the Polish Government's politics can be seen in its inability to get effective help for Warsaw and in its tendency to capitulate to the Soviets. We regret the lack of an independent government policy, the kind for which we have been fighting since the beginning of the war. We are very sorry that we cannot help you in the struggle which you are waging single-handedly against the enemy. . . . The Premier's trip to Moscow brought nothing but humiliation; it served only to give equal legal status to the Soviet-formed Committee of National Liberation. The British are pressing hard for us to come to an agreement with Russia at any price, so they can be relieved of the Polish problem. Changes in the Constitution, election of a president, and ratification of boundaries are to be left to the Sejm—we fear that elections will be held under Soviet bayonets. The Riga boundaries have been completely discarded. We are apt to lose our cultural centers and our raw materials in eastern Poland. They want to liquidate the Chief Command and put all the armed forces under the War Office of a new government containing Communist elements. To enter into this without Anglo-Saxon guarantees and without concrete obligations from Russia would mean surrendering to the Soviets, the end of our independence, transforming a sovereign Poland into a Soviet protectorate with Mikołajczyk as premier at the beginning, and freeing England from its responsibilities towards us. Government circles are motivated by their attitude that it is necessary to preserve the physical strength of the Polish nation. This is a delusion; such a policy helps neither the people, nor the nation. . . . There is apprehension that Mikołajczyk might, in spite of everything, go to Warsaw and try to present us with a 'fait accompli.' We very badly need the most energetic opposition from the nation, and a demand for a change of government and premier. We don't see any other way out. A new government would have to undo the mistakes of this most difficult situation."

The Polish Government also sent its plan to the underground authorities in Poland for approval. The Council of National Unity, composed of representatives of all parties, came to a decision which they forwarded to London on Aug. 26:[8]

"In the fourth week of the rising, the Council of National Unity has been called upon to make an urgent decision in a matter which constitutes a factual modification of the line of policy hitherto followed by the Government and the authorities at home. The

[8] Polskie Siły Zbrojne, vol. 3, p. 850. Komorowski, T. The Secret Army, p. 325.

plan changes our foreign policy, rendering possible a retirement on our part from the frontiers determined by the Riga Treaty, and an interference by a foreign power into our internal and military affairs—permitting the Polish Workers Party—really a Russian tool—equal rights in Polish affairs. The Council of National Unity has been forced to make its decision in the face of a complete lack of information regarding the basic elements of the international position, in spite of constant demands on the part of the Council and the Government Delegate for exhaustive and continuous notification. Under the pressure of circumstances, we have agreed to adopt your plan.

The Council of National Unity agreed unanimously not to stand in the way of the Government's policy, even though the Council does not understand the motives behind the policy. The Council of National Unity feels however that a solid front of Polish political parties in the Government and in the Council is more important than anything else at this critical time. The Council calls attention to the fact that a normalization of Polish-Soviet relations should not delay the sending of help to the Warsaw insurgents—this call for help should be the most urgent item on the political agenda of the Government. . . ."

This message then proposed several changes to be made in the text of the plan.

The opinion of Gen. Bor-Komorowski, commander-in-chief of the Home Army, sent on Aug. 28, was even more critical:[9]

"To the Commander-in-Chief and to the Prime Minister:

"I have seen the proposal of the Prime Minister, forwarded here to the Government delegate, as to waiting for the solution of our relations with the Soviets until the occupation of Warsaw by the latter. This plan is total capitulation and envisages a series of capital political issues which are based on the postulation of goodwill on the part of the Soviets without any prior guarantees from either the USSR or the Allies. The plan is a complete reversal of the policy followed up till now and is also a blow to our national independence.

"In this crucial moment for Poland's future, in the face of an impending decision of extreme historic importance, I consider it my duty to state, on behalf of the Polish Home Army which I command and in full accordance with the convictions of the entire patriotically disposed Polish people, that Poland has not fought the Germans for five years under the worst conditions and made

9 Komorowski T. The Secret Army, p. 326–327.

the appalling sacrifices she has merely to end up by capitulating to the Soviets.

"Warsaw took up the battle a month ago, with insignificant aid from outside, and is now being crushed to ruin simply to enable the Government to bow to the pressure of circumstance and to impose on the nation an attitude of submission to alien force—an attitude which shall be put to shame by history.

"The undaunted attitude hitherto maintained by the the Government gives us the hope that it will not give way and that it will seek a solution with Russia based on a promise of independence, full sovereignty and as far-reaching an integrity as possible for the Polish Republic."

Gen. Sosnkowski's order of the day on Sept. 1[10] *containing a sharp criticism of England's attitude, brought about a crisis concerning his status as commander-in-chief. The Polish Constitution (article 13) gave the president authority to name the commander-in-chief. Premier Mikołajczyk twice demanded (Sept. 9 and 11) that the President dismiss Gen. Sosnkowski. On Sept. 21 British Ambassador O'Malley, and on Sept. 22 Minister Eden visited Pres. Raczkiewicz and communicated the same request. On Sept. 22 the Polish Government officially resolved to ask the president to relieve Gen. Sosnkowski.*[11] *Under these pressures, Pres. Raczkiewicz dismissed Gen. Sosnkowski on Sept. 30 and named as his successor Gen. Bor-Komorowski who was at that time fighting in Warsaw.*

B. POLISH ARMY BATTLES

During the summer of 1944 Polish Army units were fighting on all fronts.

IN POLAND. For 63 days (from Aug. 1 to Oct. 2) bloody battles were fought by 47,000 soldiers of the Home Army in Warsaw under the command of Gen. Bor-Komorowski.[12]

IN ITALY. Here the Polish 2nd Corps fought under Gen. W. Anders. After the battle for Monte Cassino[13] *this Corps proceeded about the middle of June to the Adriatic front at*

[10] See No. 2.
[11] Anders, W. Op. cit., p. 230.
[12] See No. 2.
[13] See Vol. 2, no. 62.

Pescara. From here they marched north, along the Adriatic. On July 2 they fought at Loreto and on July 18 they occupied Ancona. During the 2nd half of August the 2nd Corps fought a bloody battle at the Metauro River. At this time (Aug. 25–26) Prime Minister Churchill visited the 2nd Corps and discussed for a long time with Gen. Anders the subject of Polish-Soviet relations.[14] *At the end of August Polish units attacked the strongly fortified German Gothic Line and came out victorious on Sept. 2 after heavy fighting.*

IN FRANCE. The 1st Polish Armored Division had been organized in Scotland in Feb. 1942. In the spring of 1944 it consisted of 885 officers and 15,210 soldiers, commanded by Gen. Stanisław Maczek.[15]

Late in July 1944 this division was shipped to France and on Aug. 7 went into battle at Normandy as part of the 2nd Canadian Corps. It distinguished itself in the heavy battles for Falaise during the middle of August. It continued fighting northwards and on Aug. 31 it was east of Rouen fighting to cross the Somme River which it did on Sept. 3. They pursued the Germans to Ypres and Bruges; on Sept. 11 they were in the region of Ghent; on Sept. 20 they reached the mouth of the Scheldt River; and at the end of September they were at the boundary between Belgium and Holland. During all this campaign the Polish Armored Division displayed outstanding valor and bravery which were recognized by high military authorities.

The Polish Parachute Brigade was organized in Great Britain in 1942 under Gen. S. Sosabowski. It was shipped to Holland in October 1944 where it fought under Field-Marshal Montgomery at Arnhem (bridgehead of the Rhine), together with the 1st British Airborne Division and other units (Sept. 17–25). Cut off from allied armies which were not able to cross the Rhine, this unit was commanded by Field-Marshal Montgomery to come back—which it did with very heavy losses, but still displaying untold heroism and bravery.

14 Anders, W. Op. cit., p. 209–213.
15 Pierwsza Dywizja Pancerna w Walce, p. 21.

Debate on September 28, 1944.

THE PRIME MINISTER (MR. CHURCHILL): . . . Very hard and successful fighting on a major scale has also proceeded on the Italian Front. General Alexander, who commands the armies in Italy with complete operational discretion, has under him the Fifth and Eighth Armies. The Fifth Army, half American and half British, with whom are serving the fine Brazilian Division, some of whose troops I had the opportunity of seeing—a magnificent band of men—is commanded by the United States General Clark, an officer of the highest quality and bearing, with a proud record of achievements behind him and his troops. The Eighth Army, under General Oliver Leese, whose qualities are also of the highest order, comprises the Polish Corps which fought so gallantly under General Anders, and a Greek Brigade which in happier surroundings has already distinguished itself in the forefront of the battle...

... It would be affectation to pretend that the attitude of the British and, I believe, the United States Governments towards Poland is identical with that of the Soviet Union. Every allowance must be made for the different conditions of history and geography which governs the relationship of the Western democracies on the one hand and of the Soviet Government on the other with the Polish nation. Marshal Stalin has repeatedly declared himself in favor of a strongly, friendly Poland, sovereign and independent. In this our great Eastern Ally is in the fullest accord with His Majesty's Government and also, judging from American public statements, in the fullest accord with the United States. We in this island and throughout our Empire who drew the sword against mighty Germany, we who are the only great unconquered nation which declared war on Germany on account of her aggression against Poland, have sentiments and duties towards Poland which deeply stir the British race. Everything in our power has been and will be done to achieve, both in the letter and in the spirit, the declared purposes towards Poland of the three great Allies.

Territorial changes on the frontiers of Poland there will have to be. Russia has a right to our support in this matter, because it is the Russian armies which alone can deliver Poland from the German talons; and after all the Russian people have suffered at the hands of Germany they are entitled to safe frontiers and to have friendly neighbor on their Western flank. All the more do I trust that the Soviet Government will make it possible for us to act unitedly with them in the solution of the Polish problem, and that we shall not witness the unhappy spectacle of rival Governments in Poland, one recognized by the Soviet Union and the other firmly adhered to by the Western Powers. I have fervent hopes that M. Mikołajczyk, the worthy successor of General Sikorski, a man firmly desirous of friendly understanding and settlement with Russia, and his colleagues may shortly resume those important conversations at Moscow which were interrupted some months ago.

It is my duty to impress upon the House the embarrassment to our affairs and the possible injury to Polish fortunes which might be caused by intemperate language about Polish and Russian relations in the course of this Debate. It is my firm hope, and also my belief, that a good arrangement will be achieved and that a united Polish Government will be brought into being, which will command the confidence of the three great Powers concerned and will assure for Poland those conditions of strength, sovereignty and independence which we have all three proclaimed as our aim and our resolve. Nothing is easier than to create by violent words a prospect far less hopeful than that which now opens before us. Hon. Members will take upon themselves a very grave responsibility if they embroil themselves precipitately in these controversies and thus mar the hopes we cherish of an honorable and satisfactory solution and settlement. We recognize our special responsibilities towards Poland, and I am confident that I can trust the House not to engage in language which would make our task harder.

We must never lose sight of our prime and overwhelming duty, namely, to bring about the speediest possible destruction of the Nazi power. We owe this to the soldiers, who are shedding their blood and giving their lives in the cause at this moment. They are shedding their blood in the effort to bring this fearful struggle in Europe to a close; and that must be our paramount task. Every problem—and there are many; they are as legion; they crop up in vast array—which now faces the nations of the world will present itself in a far easier and more adaptable form once the cannons have ceased to thunder in Europe and once the victorious Allies gather round the table of armistice or peace. I have every hope that wise and harmonious settlements will be made, in confidence and amity, between the great Powers thus affording the foundations upon which to raise a lasting structure of European and world peace. I say these words on the Polish situation; and I am sure that our friends on both sides will realize how long and anxious has been the study which the Cabinet have given to this matter, how constantly we see representatives of the Poles, how frequent and intimate our correspondence is with Russia on this subject.

I cannot conceive that it is not possible to make a good solution whereby Russia gets the security which she is entitled to have, and which I have resolved that we shall do our utmost to secure for her, on her Western Frontier, and, at the same time, the Polish Nation have restored to them that national sovereignty and independence, for which, across the centuries of oppression and struggle, they have never ceased to strive...

MR. ARTHUR GREENWOOD (Lab.): . . . I would myself unhesitatingly follow the advice of the right hon. Gentleman with regard to Poland. There are differences of opinion, as he has admitted, between the Powers great or small. There may be action taken which some of us may regard as unfortunate. We, my right hon. Friend pointed out, are bound by special ties to Poland. When her territory was invaded there was little delay before Britain declared her willingness to stand by her side. We are forever indebted to the great part played by the Soviet Union in this struggle. We are aware of the part that she must play in the future, and if this country can in any way heal any breaches there may be, any differences of opinion that may have arisen, any misunderstandings that might have occurred, I think it is our duty to do so, and I am quite satisfied myself that in recent weeks Britain has played a great part in working for the salvation of the Polish capital...

CAPTAIN ALAN GRAHAM (C.): . . . In the settlement of Europe that will follow our victory it is essential that we should see that in the future might does not prevail over right, and that the prosperity of a nation should not cause its neighbors jealousy, or fear of aggression. In other words, it is essential that we should develop in Europe a community spirit among the nations of Europe. I fear it will be generations before either in Germany or in Bulgaria it will be possible for any such sense of a European community spirit to arise, but if only we give a firm lead in that direction to the rest of Europe I think we can have far greater confidence that there we may see it flourish.

It is in that spirit that we should approach the Russian-Polish problem. Both these heroic nations are Allies of ours, and both of them are publicly pledged, as we are, to recognition of the rights of small nations to independence and genuine self-government. But it all depends on us British. We cannot abdicate from our position as defenders of European civilization; it depends on us to see that it is in that spirit of the European community that the Russian-Polish problem should be solved, since there can be no possible future peace for Europe if genuine Polish independence were to be crushed, directly or indirectly, by Russia. Russia's best security against any future aggression from Germany or the West is a friendly and independent Poland. Marshal Stalin himself has declared that he wishes for such a Poland, and it is devoutly to be trusted that those who carry out his policy will carry that into effect. Such a friendly Poland Russia can have for the asking if only she will abstain from interfering in internal Polish politics, and if she will not override the national feeling of all true Poles by imposing upon them the authority of, and lending Russian power to, the completely unrepresentative Council of National Liberation sitting in Lublin. Surely the martyred, heroic citizens of Warsaw have earned the gratitude and respect of all their Allies for their epic struggle in the last few months against the Germans. Have not such heroes earned the right, above all men, to be masters of their own destiny? What would the world think of Russia if, after the entry of Russian troops into Warsaw, such heroes as the defenders of that city were placed in concentration camps or deported to Kaluga or Siberia?

Russia now has the greatest chance she has ever had of solving this Polish question and of assuring herself for all time of Polish friendship by helping the Poles to rid themselves of their only real enemies—the Germans—and also by themselves abstaining from interference in Polish internal politics. Ninety-nine per cent of the Poles in this country and in Poland know that Russian friendship is indispensable to their own security, and the Poles are prepared to work for that end. But in return Russia must leave the Poles free to manage their own future. While His Majesty's Government deserve the thanks of the whole world for their unremitting efforts to try and resolve this problem I think we all must be on our guard against offending the Polish nation in Poland by appearing to pick and choose one Polish politician rather than another. If fate says that Poland is to dig her political grave let her by all means dig it herself, but let it never be said that we put our arm behind the spade. Let her also show her own capacity of achieving agreement with Russia. We cannot, however, escape our duty, as a Western Christian nation, of standing up resolutely for the ideals for which we have fought. Among those ideals is the right of a small nation to continue her own existence, just as in a democracy we stand for the rights of every individual, however humble or however small.

MR. MANDER (L.): I cannot help thinking that the Prime Minister gave some very wise advice to the House as to the spirit in which Members should approach some of the difficult questions facing us at the present time. First, I would like to say a word or two about Poland. I am convinced that the Government are doing everything they possible can to resolve this difficult problem and bring the three great Allies into greater unity. The situation has undoubtedly improved, and there seems to be a real prospect, on the lines the Prime Minister suggested, that agreement may be reached. I think the wisest course, so far as Poland is concerned, is to trust in the wise, patient, far-seeing and statesmanlike attitude of the Polish Prime Minister, M. Mikołajczyk, to trust his co-operation with the three great Allies to bring to fruition the efforts that are being made to solve the Polish problem.

LORD DUNGLASS (C.) : . . . In all this fair prospect there is one very black spot, and that is the political relationship between Russia and Poland. The Prime Minister made a particular appeal to back benchers to exercise restraint, and of course I shall try to respond; but I have had considerable experience of the Prime Minister as a back bencher. When he felt strongly upon matters he tried to exercise restraint and responsibility, and that must be my aim this afternoon. This matter between Poland and Russia cannot be left to be settled between the two countries without any intervention from ourselves. Not only from the wide point of view of the organization of world peace has this matter to be looked at, for clearly it will be a test case of the relationship between a great Power and a weaker neighbor. Not only because we are the Allies of each of them, also because, under Treaty, we have accepted not only definite legal, and moral, commitments to Poland. It is our habit to honor our treaties.

I remember very well the day when the guarantee was given to Poland by Mr. Chamberlain's Government.* At that time the British Government and the Polish Government were thinking in terms of the frontiers which held the field in the summer of 1939. At that time they were unchallenged by any

---

* Vol. I, Nos. 1 and 2.

other Power except Germany. I was glad to hear the Prime Minister mention this point because we owe it to ourselves to make it clear that if it had not been for Russia's decision to partake in the partition of Poland this country would have fulfilled that Treaty in the spirit and in the letter; but equally we owe it to the Poles to recognize the situation as it is today. That situation is fundamentally changed. No one in 1939 could have foreseen those changes. No one could have foreseen that Russia, from being a potential enemy would become our Ally, nor the stupendous Russian military effort without which, I think it is admitted—so strong was Germany's strength in the field revealed to be—that Poland might never have been freed. No one could have foreseen that Russia, after her prodigious feat of arms, would determine to annex Polish territory in order to put the best possible strategic frontier between herself and the German people. Those things were not seen at that time. The question for this House, which has a real responsibility in the matter, is: Can we, in these new circumstances, fulfill our guarantee to Poland?

We must be absolutely frank and state the position as we see it today. To the Poles, I take it we should have to say that we cannot hope to restore the old Poland, and that our aim now must be to restore a Poland independent and free, and as nearly equivalent as possible in territory, economic resources and in international status to the Poland of 1939. If that is our intention and aim, the question inevitably follows whether in view of the Russian attitude, we can make that independence and that freedom into a reality. If, after the defeat of Germany, this gallant but unhappy people are still left in bondage, and if this country has failed to do anything that we ought to have done or might have done, then our national conscience will be uneasy for generations.

I believe we can succeed in this matter, but that success will elude us unless we realize two things. The first is that Russia operates under a code of ethics which is by no means the same as our own. For that I am not blaming the Russians. They are at a different point on the historical road. Let me give examples. When the British Government say: "We will promise to restore an independent and free Poland," they mean it in the unqualified sense of the words; but when Marshal Stalin says, "We will restore your independence and freedom," he says, in the name of the Russian Government, to Poland; "Yes, you may have your independence but Russia will dictate your frontiers, and you may have your freedom but Russia will choose your Government and, by implication, will control your policy." Those are two different interpretations and we must face them. Unless we face the fact that, at the present moment, this country and Russia operate under two different sets of standards, there will stretch before us a long vista of political difficulties, misunderstandings and disillusion.

The second thing which I think we have to realize in our political negotiations with Russia is that we must not shirk plain speaking. To that and that alone will the Russians respond. If a criticism lies against His Majesty's Government—and I do not know that it does—I believe it is that they have used a sense of delicacy in negotiation which simply is not understood by a people whose diplomatic methods are, by comparison, crude and direct. May I give an illustration or two? I am afraid that while attempting to use restraint I shall have to pose a dilemma to the Foreign Secretary. I hope we shall get an answer from him tomorrow, although the matter is of some difficulty. Let me take the House back to Teheran. Months before the Prime Minister, President Roosevelt and Stalin met at Teheran, Russo-Polish relations had been in a state of acute tension. An expectant world, after the Conference, received an impression of harmony. "We are friends," said the communique, "in fact, in spirit and in purpose," and the reaction of the world to those words was not that this was an effervescent friendship such as naturally follows after good wine and good dinners, but was something more permanent.

What was Marshal Stalin's reaction? He went home, and within a few weeks there followed an ultimatum to Poland demanding territory, and declaring that this could not be, except for a few details, a matter of negotiation. It seems to me that this action is capable of only two interpretations; either Russia's reading of the Atlantic Charter is fundamentally different from our own, or Russia feels herself strong enough, when it suits her own purpose, to go her own way. [*Interruption.*] I am putting those two possible interpretations and I cannot see any other. Did the Prime Minister or the Foreign Secretary tell Marshal Stalin at Teheran that this question of the method of conduct of relationships between Russia and Poland would be looked upon as a test case in this country, or did they not? If they did not, then the mistake can be rectified. If they did, and in spite of it Marshal Stalin went his own way, it is time that this House knew about it in order that we might assess the implication.

DR. HADEN GUEST (Lab.): Will the Noble Lord deal also with the situation created by the Polish invasion of Soviet Russia in 1920—[HON. MEMBERS: "Oh"]—which has a great deal to do with frontiers, and also with the Nazi reorientation of Poland in 1936?

LORD DUNGLASS: I will deal with those matters. Russia had a Treaty with Poland, which recognized the *status quo* as it was in 1939, but apart from that, I was arguing, not on the grounds of this or that frontier between Russia and Poland, but on the ground of the Atlantic Charter, which postulates the principle that questions of frontier should be settled by negotiation and not by force. One other illustration—and I shall cut these short because it is touchy ground. Many months ago, in the winter of last year, notice was given in the Moscow State-controlled Press, of the formation of a Union of Polish Patriots, a Committee of Poles to look after Polish interests, and it was perfectly clear at that time to anyone who understood the Russian technique that this was the first move towards undermining the authority of the Polish Government in London. Many weeks passed before the Foreign Secretary in this House perfectly rightly reiterated our support of the Polish Government. From that time on the Soviet Government have known that both ourselves and the Americans recognize the Polish Government in London but have refused to listen to our representations. Somewhere the machinery of cooperation has gone wrong.

Let me take this latest case. I am thinking of the support given to the Poles in Warsaw. We do not know the facts, but I think it is worth noting that very little account was taken by the Russian Government of the representations made in private, and it was only when public clamor reached such a stage in this country and America that it could not be stifled, that the Russians began to take notice and send in supplies. This is the dilemma which seems to me, all through this series of events, to face us. Either these incidents are a series of rebuffs from one great Ally to another, or there is genuine misunderstanding. I am willing to believe that, but if that is so it indicates something wrong with the machinery of cooperation which must be put right at once.

So that there will no longer be any doubt, I have a suggestion to make that we should make an immediate and definite approach to the Russian Government on this question of Anglo-Polish-Russian relations, and do it in this way: We should declare to the Russian Government that Great Britain has legal and moral commitments to post-war Poland, to secure for her independence and freedom, and that we expect Russian co-operation to make them a reality. Secondly, that we justify this expectation by invoking the three Agreements to which Great Britain and the Soviet Union have jointly put their signatures. First, the Atlantic Charter, the first three points of which cover exactly just such a case as this, and which upholds the principle of negotiation as against the principle of force. Secondly, there is the Moscow Agreement, by which the Soviet Government and ourselves both agreed to cooperate and consult at every stage in just this sort of political dispute. And, lastly, and more particularly, I would invoke the 20 years' Treaty of Agreement between the Soviet Government and ourselves which was signed in 1942.* In the pre-

---

* Vol. II, No. 16.

amble of that Agreement, the principles of the Atlantic Charter are repeated. But may I read to the House some operative words of Article 5? After the first paragraph, in which the two Powers agree to work closely together, it reads as follows:

> "They (that is, the High Contracting Parties) will take into account the interests of the United Nations in these objects, and they will act in accordance with the two principles of not seeking territorial aggrandizement for themselves and of non-interference in the internal affairs of other States."

That is a definite Clause in a definite Treaty, a Treaty by which we in this country set great store. We hope to make it the foundation of permanently good Anglo-Russian relations, but we shall never make it into a permanent instrument of good relations if either side connives at what it considers to be a breach by another. It is much better for us to call the attention of the Russian Government to this, and say where we think they are going wrong. Only on the basis of that kind of plain speaking can we possibly achieve these good relations.

In this country there is a great store of good will towards Russia, but I think we serve our friendship best by a plain warning now, that in her attitude towards her smaller neighbors she is doing much to forfeit and sacrifice the good will which her heroism has won. For myself, I have never looked upon the Anglo-American-Soviet association as a kind of moral rearmament society. It is a military alliance, and as such it is highly successful, but if these three great Powers wish to go further than that, if they wish to offer themselves to humanity as the founder Powers of a wider world organization for peace, if, in addition to their undoubted ability to dispense power, they also seek to dispense justice, then there is an obligation upon each and upon all to agree, at least, upon a common interpretation of independence and freedom.

MR. MCGOVERN (I.L.P.): I desire to congratulate the Noble Lord on the speech he has made and for having stated sincerely and logically what he thinks should be done in present circumstances. I do not intend to pursue the arguments he has used in relation to this problem. All I would say is that I agree with him that Russia has a tremendous amount of good feeling in this country, which is just in the balance at this moment, and it will depend largely upon her attitude to her small neighboring States whether that good feeling is to be "cashed in on" by the Soviet in an amiable form, or turned to hatred of a great Power's effort against smaller countries. In relation to Poland, we must remember that while it is fair to say, as the Noble Lord did, that Poland might never have been freed if it had not been for the military effort of Russia, it is also true to a large extent, that if it had not been for Russia and her pact with Germany, the whole Continent might never have been placed completely under the heel of Germany, and France might not have collapsed as she did in the military field. Therefore, without any recriminations, I should say that from the lessons to be learned from this war and the benefits to be obtained for humanity, Russia could build up in this world a tremendous amount of good will if she would restrain herself in her attitude towards those Powers on her own frontiers.

While I have appeared from time to time as being very antagonistic to the Soviet Union, I say that I am not antagonistic to the Soviet Union, to the Russian people, but I am antagonistic to the methods that are being thrown up by the bureaucracy of Russia. I wish it were otherwise. I would never attempt to dictate to Russia the line she should take in her own country, but I do say she must allow the rest of the world to determine, according to public feeling, education and reason, the developments they aspire to in their own logical manner. Therefore, I trust that this problem is capable of solution, although I have all the doubts in the world in relation to it, not from a superficial knowledge of Stalin but from a lifetime of experience. I would like to see it possible but just because of the methods in the working-class movement of this country of those who espouse the cause of Russia I find they have a similar type of mind to that shown by the development going on in Russia today. Therefore, it is with regret, because I cannot see unity of purpose in the working-class movement with those forces which have a common objective, that I cannot see those forces pursuing different tactics as between Russia and this country. That was the cause of the estrangement between Lenin and Trotsky in the old days. Trotsky believed that if any change were effected in any country by force, the revolution must come from the bottom, and must be the desire of the people for social change. That, later, under the government of Stalin, was changed for government in accordance with the wishes of the top, and with blood baths. Freedom had to be exterminated with the physical extermination of those who opposed the regime. Seeing that, although I have no desire to dictate what line Russia should pursue in her own country, I thank God that I was born and live in Britain, rather than that I should have to live under conditions of that kind in any other country. . . .

SIR JOHN WARDLAW-MILNE (C.) . . . The Prime Minister made more than one appeal today to Members to be cautious in what they said about the foreign situation. I think we all appreciate that matters are very delicate and that it is desirable to be extremely careful in what one says. I appreciated what my right hon. Friend said in this connection about the Russian-Polish situation. I think it would be wise, although it may be against the feelings of some of us, to refrain from going into details, but I think that one matter which requires to be made public, or at least get more publicity than it has secured in the last few weeks is the tremendous effort which has been made by this country to try and carry out our obligations to Poland and to relieve Warsaw. In particular, I refer to the work of the Royal Air Force; I do not think it known even in this country how desperate were the attempts we made and the losses we unfortunately suffered in trying to do our best for the beleagured people of Warsaw. . . .

MR. TINKER (Lab.): . . . Imagine a difference between Russia and Poland. The United Powers might say to Poland, "You have to have this," though they might feel that Poland was badly treated, and Russia would go her way, as has happened in the past. Every big nation in the past has said, "This is what I intend to do and it is right, because I have might." The aggrieved nation has gathered around her a lot of other nations, who say, "That ought not to happen," and war inevitably follows. I would say to Russia, or to any other nation, "If you have a grievance and satisfaction is not arrived at, submit your case to the international body, which will say who is right." This international force will have full power to act and to determine what should be done. Britain in the past has always regarded herself as above everyone else, but other nations may not have had the same view. We should have to submit our case to the international body and take its decision. If we believe in peace at all, there can be no objection to that.

COMMANDER SIR ARCHIBALD SOUTHBY (C.): . . . This is no time for diplomatic casuistry. This is a time for plain and honest speaking between leaders and between nations and, above all, it is a time for adherence to the fundamental principles of justice and honor, no matter what such adherence may cost.

I intend to confine myself in the main to the consideration of the affairs of Poland and of the three Baltic republics, Latvia, Estonia and Lithuania, so far as they concern us, because I believe our policy in respect of those States must color the whole of our outlook as regards foreign affairs. It cannot be denied that not only Members of this House, but the general public outside, are seriously perturbed regarding the existing relationships between our two Allies, Russia and Poland, and between them and ourselves. It would, I think, be fair to assume three things. Firstly, that the British people consider that we went to war in the first instance to defend the independence of Poland; secondly, that Russia now desires to acquire by negotiation if possible but otherwise by *force majeure*, certain portions of Poland which she wants to add to Soviet territory; and thirdly, that it has been generally thought that we were, in some way, letting Poland down. I believe that both the Prime Minister and the Foreign Secretary are——

EARL WINTERTON (C.): Who are the people in this country who believe that we are letting Poland down?

SIR A. SOUTHBY: The noble Lord's speeches in this House nearly always consist of interruptions of someone else, though he always resents anyone daring to interrupt him.

EARL WINTERTON: That means that the hon. and gallant Gentleman cannot answer the question.

SIR A. SOUTHBY: If the noble Lord will go to his own constituents, he will get a pretty good answer. I believe that both the Prime Minister and the Foreign Secretary are deserving of the utmost praise for their untiring efforts to find a solution of the Soviet-Polish difficulty, more particularly during the past few weeks and I shall try to heed the advice given by the Prime Minister in his speech today but justice demands that although speech should be restrained it should also be plain. Everyone in the House, including the noble Lord, is entitled to have his own views.

EARL WINTERTON: The hon. and gallant Gentleman's graciousness and courtesy are most unusual.

SIR A. SOUTHBY: It is always a marvel to me that after the 44—or is it 54 years—that the noble Lord has sat in the House, his courtesy would remain so little as it is. I pay a heartfelt tribute to our Russian Ally, for her magnificent achievements in the field which have in conjunction with the efforts made by ourselves and the United States ensured the final defeat of Nazi tyranny. It would, however, be both wrong and unwise, for those who guide the destinies of the Soviet Union, to imagine that the fate of Poland and the Baltic republics and the demarcation of their boundaries are no concern of ours nor that the British people did not feel that their honor was involved. May I remind the House that after the Russo-Polish war of 1920 it was we who suggested to the

Poles that they should retire behind what is now called the Curzon Line, but that it was the Soviet Government who refused to accept the mediation of the great Powers and insisted upon negotiating direct with Poland alone? As a result of those negotiations the treaty of Riga was signed in March, 1921. Article 3 of that treaty said:

> "Russia and the Ukraine abandoned all rights and claims to the west of the frontier."

On 15th March, 1923, a representative conference of ambassadors passed a resolution recognizing the eastern boundaries of Poland as set out in the treaty of Riga, and that resolution was assented to by the United States of America on 25th April, 1923.* In May, 1939, the Polish foreign minister received from the Soviet Vice-Commissar for foreign affairs an assurance that in the event of war between Poland and Germany Russia would adopt an attitude of benevolence towards the Poles. That event took place, and on 17th September, 1939, Russian troops invaded Poland. Eleven days later what is called the Ribbentrop-Molotov agreement was published under which each of the signatories took approximately half Poland. Anyone who reads "The Times," as most people do, and observes the way in which the Polish case is played down, must marvel at the change which seems to have come over that paper's point of view. This is what "The Times" said on 30th September, 1939, when writing of the Nazi-Soviet pact announced two days before:

> "The Allied pledge to Poland stood irrefregable, fortified if that be possible by the valor and self-sacrifice of the Poles themselves."

It went on to speak of

> "freedom and independence for the Polish nation within frontiers as unchallengeable as that which Germany violated on 1st September."

It was not long before Germany turned on Russia, as the result of which the Soviet Government on 30th July, 1941, re-

* See Vol. II, No. 54–C.

nounced the Ribbentrop-Molotov agreement.** Nothing could have been more categorical than the admission of the Soviet Government that the terms of the agreement with Germany regarding territorial changes in Poland had lost their force. On the same day our Foreign Secretary declared specifically that we did not recognize any territorial changes made in Poland since 1939. The following day a similar declaration was made by Mr. Sumner Welles on behalf of the United States Government. In January, 1943, it became clear that the Soviet Government intended to insist upon a Russo-Polish frontier, in effect the one laid down in the Ribbentrop-Molotov agreement which the Soviet had themselves renounced on 30th July, 1941. These are historical facts.

Russia's desire for a rectification of her frontier is quite understandable, but that rectification must take place by agreement and not by force. We could agree to the so-called Curzon Line only if the Polish Government and the Polish people agreed to it of their own freewill and not under coercion.

Dare anyone deny that the Poles have scrupulously discharged all their obligations in the war against Germany? By sea, land and air Poles have fought alongside our own men with incomparable valor. Never for one moment has their spirit or their heroism faltered. Until the war is over and it is possible for the Polish people, unfettered and uncoerced, to express their views as to how they shall be governed and by whom, the Polish President in London, the Polish Prime Minister in London, and the Polish Government in London are the rightful rulers and leaders of Poland. Meanwhile, the present situation and, maybe, post-war harmony among the Allies are being imperilled by the activities of the organization called the Polish Committee of National Liberation. Let us face facts. It is, in effect, a government set up in Moscow in opposition to the lawfully constituted Government of Poland whose ministers are here in London. Weeks ago the Polish Prime Minister put forward a memorandum which it was hoped would form the basis for an agreement between the Soviet and Polish

** Vol. I, No. 132.

Governments. In spite of that, the Polish Committee of National Liberation has taken upon itself to sign agreements with the Government of the Ukraine Soviet Republic and the White Russian Republic concerning the transfer of Polish and Soviet populations, which is surely a matter for the proper Polish Government.

Answering questions in the House on 26th January this year, the Foreign Secretary reaffirmed the statement which was made by the Prime Minister on 5th September, 1940, namely, that we should not recognize any territorial changes which had taken place during the war unless they took place with the free consent and good will of the parties concerned.* He also reaffirmed the categorical note which he had addressed to the late General Sikorski after the signature of the Russo-Polish agreement in 1941. The Prime Minister is constantly faced with situations of great complexity which daunt a lesser man than he. I realize how difficult must be many of the decisions which he has to take, but I cannot believe that I was the only person in the House on 22nd February this year who felt some disquiet when I heard him say:

> "I cannot feel that the Russian demand for a reassurance about her western frontiers goes beyond the limits of what is reasonable and just."—[OFFCIAL REPORT, 22nd February, 1944; Vol. 397, c. 698.]

The Russo-Polish frontier which the Soviet Government now seeks to establish is the same frontier established by force in 1939. The British Government in September, 1939, said regarding Poland:

> "This attack made upon an Ally at a moment when she is prostrate in the face of the overwhelming forces brought against her by Germany cannot in the view of His Majesty's Government be justified by the arguments put forward by the Soviet Government."

That was endorsed two days later by the right hon. Gentleman the Member for Wakefield (Mr. Greenwood) speaking for the party opposite who said:

* Vol. I, No. 114.

"There can be no doubt that the justification of it was a justification which reasonable people who had seen, as we have seen, previous acts of aggression, could not accept for one moment."—[OFFICIAL REPORT, 20th September, 1937; Vol. 351, c. 984.]

Recent events in Warsaw have served to stimulate public interest in Polish affairs. On 1st August the heroic Poles rose against their German oppressors. It has been most unfairly suggested in some quarters that the rising was premature and unauthorized, but the fact is that the local commanders acted in accordance with general instructions, which had been submitted both to President Roosevelt and to the Prime Minister, and the Polish Prime Minister has stated that on 31st July this year he also informed M. Molotov, the Russian Commissar for Foreign Affairs. Quite apart from that, for months past both the Soviet-sponsored wireless station, Kosciuszko, and in the broadcasts by the Union of Polish patriots, appeals were being made for an armed revolt against the Germans in Poland, and attacks were being made on General Bor, who commands the Polish Army in Warsaw on the ground of his alleged inactivity. In June the Moscow radio said that it was generally believed that the time to strike had come. On 29th July, a direct appeal was made by wireless to the Patriot Forces to the effect that direct armed action in the streets of Warsaw would hasten the time of final liberation. On 30th July another appeal went out by wireless. It said:

"Warsaw shakes from the roar of guns. The Soviet armies are pushing forward and are nearing Praga. The Germans when pushed out of Praga will attempt to hold Warsaw and will try to destroy everything. People of Warsaw to arms! Attack the Germans! Assist the Red Army in crossing the Vistula."

Two days later General Bor and his men went into action. Nobody could deny that the rising benefitted the advancing Red Army, because it delayed the passage of German reinforcements on their way to the front. Unfortunately, the Russian advance was held up by very heavy German resistance from at least three panzer divisions. Surely one would have imagined that every effort would then have been made to assist the

Poles in Warsaw. What they needed was arms, ammunition and food, and yet in spite of frantic appeals from General Bor and from the Polish Prime Minister and Government in London they were left to their own resources. It was not until 15th or 16th August that bombers, manned by British, Polish and South African crews, who had to fly a round trip of 1,750 miles, and who lost 21 out of 100 bombers, brought some succor to our hard-pressed Allies in Warsaw. Since then, thank God, assistance has gone to Warsaw both from us, the Russians and Americans.

Two questions demand an answer. First, we have been told repeatedly that Russia has virtual command of the air on the Eastern Front. Why, then, should General Bor have had to write on 5th August that German bombers were active and were operating with no interference from the Russian Air Force. Why were Russian machines not dropping the arms and ammunition that Warsaw needed. It may well be that other military considerations were of so urgent a nature that no Soviet machines could be spared, but if that be true then the second question arises. Why did our machines have to fly this immensely long flight instead of being allowed to use Russian airfields which must have been in reasonably close proximity to Warsaw? They were denied the right to land on Russian aerodromes until fairly recently.

THE SECRETARY OF STATE FOR FOREIGN AFFAIRS (MR. EDEN): I am sure that my hon. and gallant Friend does not wish to put the case wrong and add to a difficult situation. There was never a question of our asking for facilities on Russian airfields. Our flights were done from Italy direct.

SIR A. SOUTHBY: I of course accept my right hon. Friend's correction. I should have said United States aircraft were refused the right to land.

MR. WOODBURN: (Lab): I gather that the hon. and gallant Gentleman is anxious to help Poland, as we all are. Is he not aware that one of the main troubles, as far as we can judge, is the Russian fear that Poland is being supported by people who are anti-Russian? Is not the tenor of the hon. and gallant Gentleman's speech such as to suggest that he is a friend of Poland and anti-Russian, and instead of helping the situation between Poland and Russia, he is actually contributing to the misunderstandings that are causing the trouble?

SIR A. SOUTHBY: I pay my tribute, as I always have done to what has been done by the Soviet armies. I believe that the future of the world lies in an understanding between the Soviet Government, ourselves and the United States, but I believe with all my heart and soul that you will never get on with the Soviet Government unless there is plain speaking between them and us, and that no useful purpose is served by denying justice to Poland because you wish to put down the soft pedal with the Soviet Government. I am being scrupulously careful in what I have been saying and am anxious not to be led away by interruptions. On 29th August the R.A.F. did a 2,000-mile flight in bad weather in order to assist the Russian army by bombing the Baltic ports of Stettin and Koenigsberg, and the operation cost us 41 aircraft. If we could do this to help our Russian Ally, surely they could have found some machines to fly the infinitely shorter distance which would have brought help to Warsaw. I have tried to state the Polish case moderately and fairly. It deserves in justice to be stated. What we do as regards Poland will color the opinion of the whole of Europe so far as Britain is concerned when the war is over.

I wish now to say a few words regarding the Baltic Republics. War reports have deliberately used such phrases as "The Latvian Soviet Republic," and similar references have been made in B.B.C. announcements. It is being insidiously suggested that these three independent Republics desire to become part of the Soviet Union. There is no justification for any such assumption, and we owe it to our national honor that the true facts should be clearly stated and the British people, whom we represent in this House, should be made aware of them. These three Republics have at this time proper legally accredited representative Ministers in this country. I want to ask the Secretary of State for Foreign Affairs whether he has or has not received from those Ministers formal declarations to the effect that the Republics desire to maintain their independence and not to become part of the Soviet Union.

It is frequently said of enemy-occupied States that their Governments, or their Ministers resident in London, are not representative of the true feelings of their nationals at home, and that where national Committees of Liberation have been set up their views are the only ones which should be accepted. I wish to be as brief as possible, so I will take the case of only one of these Republics, namely Lithuania.

The Red Army occupied Lithuania on 15th June, 1940. The lawful Government of Lithuania was replaced by a Government which, under the direct control of Soviet officials, held an election at which all existing political parties were proscribed, and only candidates of the newly created Working People's Union, approved by the Soviet Legation in Lithuania, were allowed to stand for election. This so-called Parliament met on 21st July, 1940, and was forced to vote for the incorporation of Lithuania into the Soviet Union. On 3rd August, 1940, the Soviet Government declared Lithuania to be the 14th Soviet Lithuanian Republic of the U.S.S.R. Both the British and United States Ministers in Lithuania were resident in Lithuania at that time and can bear witness to what exactly took place.

Let the British people note that the Government of the United States of America publicly condemned the action of the Soviet. Mr. Sumner Welles, the acting Secretary of State in Washington, made a public statement on 23rd July, 1940, in which he said:

> "During the past few days, the devious processes whereunder the political independence and territorial integrity of the three small Baltic Republics, Estonia, Latvia and Lithuania, were to be deliberately annihilated by one of their more powerful neighbors, have been rapidly drawing to their conclusion. The people of the United States have watched the admirable progress of these Baltic Republics with sympathy and interest and are opposed to predatory acts, no matter whether they are carried out by the use of force or by the threat of force. They are likewise opposed to any

form of intervention on the part of one State, however powerful, in the domestic concerns of any other sovereign State, however weak."

On 15th October, 1940, the President of the United States, in the course of replying to an address which had been submitted to him by a delegation of Americans of Lithuanian origin said this:

"It is stated here that Lithuania has lost her independence. It is a mistake to say so. Lithuania did not lose her independence. Lithuania's independence was only temporarily put aside."

He went on to say:

"Even the smallest nation has the same right to enjoy independence as the largest nation."

After Germany had attacked Russia, and when the Red Army had left Lithuania, the former members of the People's Parliament met, on 30th August, 1942, and passed a Resolution which said that the People's Diet, which was that Parliament, could not and did not express the will of the Lithuanian nation because the structure of the People's Diet had been decided upon in advance by the Communist Party in accordance with orders received from Moscow's representatives in Lithuania, and because the actual voting for incorporation into the Soviet Union was irregular, only 16 to 18 per cent of the voting cards being valid.

I apologize to the House, but it is necessary to give this story in full. On 14th October, 1943, a joint declaration was drawn up by members of various Lithuanian political parties and combat organizations. It was signed by the Lithuanian National Union, the Peasant Populist Union of Lithuania, the Union of Combatants for the Liberty of Lithuania, the Lithuanian Nationalist Party, the Social Democratic Party of Lithuania, the Lithuanian Christian Democratic party and the Lithuanian Front. Could anything be more representative, coming from an occupied country, than that? This declaration begins by saying that the Lithuanian nation desires the true voice of the Lithuanian people to be heard by the outside world, and goes on to point out that, in the Treaty between Russia and Lithuania on the 12th July, 1920,

> "Russia, without any reservation, recognizes Lithuania as a separate and independent State with all the juridical consequences ensuing from such a recognition, and voluntarily renounces for all time the rights of sovereignty which it has exercised over the Lithuanian people and their territory."

It also records that, on 12th October, 1939, speaking of treaties with the Baltic States, the Soviet Commissar for Foreign Affairs said:

> "We stand for the conscientious and exact observation of the treaties concluded, on the principle of entire reciprocity, and declare the idle talk about the Sovietization of the Baltic States to be profitable only to our common enemies, and to all kinds of anti-Soviet provocatuers."

His joint declaration must be accepted as coming from the Lithuanian people who make this definite statement:

> "From the very beginning, the Lithuanian nation has held the Sovietization of Lithuania and her incorporation into the Soviet Union to be null and void."

I ask the House to bear with me, while I quote from one other document. On 16th February this year, the Supreme Committee for Liberation of Lithuania addressed an appeal to the Lithuanian people. It is an appeal to all shades of political opinion in Lithuania, and it declares that the independence of Lithuania is an indispensable condition for the nation's existence and well-being. Let the House note that the three documents from which I have quoted, are not the statements of any one Minister, but of representative organizations of the Lithuanian people, which makes it clear, beyond all shadow of doubt, that the suggestion that Lithuania desired to become part of Soviet Russia is utterly false. I assume that all these documents are in the possession of our Foreign Office. If I am wrong, perhaps my right hon. Friend and Foreign Secretary will correct me. The same overwhelming case could be made out for both Latvia and Estonia. I should like to conclude this part of my speech by quoting what Lord Halifax said in the House of Lords on 24th August, 1939:

> "In failing to uphold the liberty of others, we run the great risk of betraying the principle of liberty itself and with it our own freedom and independence."

MR. VERNON BARTLETT (Ind.): My hon. and gallant Friend who has just spoken will, I hope forgive me if I do not follow him in his historical dissertation. There are three reasons. The first is that there is no part of the globe which so teaches us how little objective a study history can be as Eastern Europe. Another reason is that I do not want to complicate the already heart-breakingly difficult task in front of the Foreign Secretary. The third reason is that I have as great a respect for the Poles as any person in this House and I have as great a sympathy with the citizens of Warsaw as any one. In fact, only a few weeks ago, because I expressed my feelings rather pointedly, I was called "Fascist scum" by one of the principal Soviet papers. Nevertheless, I do not think these discussions can help the Poles at the present time, when we are all waiting to hear what is going to happen to General Sosnkowski and to the proposals put up by this Polish Government to the Soviet Government in Moscow. For those reasons I do not follow my hon. and gallant Friend's line today. . . .

MR. QUINTIN HOGG (C.): . . . I do not believe that Members of the House are the judges of all the moral and political issues which divide the world, but I believe that this country would be well advised to pursue, in accordance with its power and with its conscience, a policy which is honorable in itself without necessarily condemning those with whom we are not always in complete agreement and a policy which we can, in fact, enforce by the resources at our command. That brings me to the question of Poland. I hope I shall not be thought to utter a word of criticism of the Poles. Even if I disagreed with them I should regard it as an impertinence in a Member of this House, a British subject, who has not suffered anything comparable to what the least of these Poles has suffered, to utter a word of criticism of anything that they may have done. On the contrary, we should constantly remember our debt of gratitude to them, how in the hour of calamity they were a constant source of inspiration, their fidelity as Allies, their bravery as soldiers and their loyalty as comrades. We should seek to assert again and again that it is our purpose and our hope to restore a free and independent Poland which may one day, we trust, enjoy the prosperity which we so much desire for them and which we believe they so much deserve.

But if the events of the last five years have meant anything they mean that neither we nor any other Power in the world can enable the Poles to afford to antagonize both Germany and Russia at the same times. Nothing can save them if that is the result, however innocent, of their foreign policy. We should not be able to assist them even if it were consistent with our own independence and freedom to do so. To their eternal honor be it said that never during the whole of these difficult times has there been the slightest evidence that their differences with Russia have driven them to the slightest degree of collusion with our common enemy, Germany. But it must be said, surely, that if we were to let them believe that we were able to do that which our geographical position, the political framework in which we have to live and our military resources alike render impossible, we should, in fact, be committing that very dishonorable action of pretending that we were going to achieve for our friends more, in fact, than we were either disposed or able to do.

It is, I think, well to refer for a moment to the rather partial account which my hon. and gallant Friend the Member for Epsom (Sir A. Southby) gave of the events in Warsaw. I have only followed the reports in the Press. He did not mention what appeared to be at any rate relevant and important facts. The Soviet Armies had advanced for upwards of 300 miles. They must have almost entirely outrun their communications; their forward troops must have been in a state of considerable exhaustion. I do not know and I should not attempt to resolve any issues of fact as to whether the Polish insurrection in Warsaw was opened with or without consultation with Russia. That appears to be immaterial. What is certain is that immediately after the insurrection began the Germans staged a counter-attack which, for the time being, drove the Russians back across the Vistula and undoubtedly gave them a military setback. There were malicious people here and people who were carried away by feelings with which one could only sympathize deeply who believed and allowed it to be said that the Russians did not give the Poles assistance because they desired the insurrection to fail. I do not believe that kind of slander. I can remember that for three years we were in the miserable position of not being able to invade the Continent at the very time that we saw the Russian Armies bleeding. I can remember how very strongly I resented the suggestion, from whatsoever source it came, from Russia or from this country, that we were doing this deliberately in order that our gallant Ally might suffer in the East. I think if we owe the Russians nothing else in this war it is to put the most favorable construction we can on anything they may do, and even if it were not a debt of honor by which we are bound by the terms of our Treaty of Alliance with them, I believe it would be the merest policy based upon the political framework to which I have referred. . . .

MR. COCKS (Lab.) : . . . In considering this Polish question, there is one thing we should first remember, and that is the extreme moderation of Soviet policy. The Prime Minister has told us today how moderate and correct they have been in their armistice terms to Rumania and the neighboring States. In spite of what the Vatican or General Franco seem to think, I do not believe that Marshal Stalin has the least desire to impose the Soviet economic system upon the neighboring States. I do not believe he has the least intention of doing so. I do not believe that Russia desires more than safe frontiers and friendly neighbors. To those she is entitled, as the Prime Minister told us, and in that light the Polish situation must be regarded.

The history of the relations between the Polish Government in London, the Soviet Union and the Polish National Council of Liberation is long and complicated. I have given it some little study, and, as Lord Simon used to say in this House, I thing I have some grasp of it, complex though it is. I do not propose, however, to inflict that information upon this House tonight, but I think it is absurd for the hon. and gallant Member for Wirral to say, as he did, that the National Council of Poland, sitting in Lublin, or the Committee of Polish Liberation which is associated with it, are completely unrepresentative of the Polish people. If it were so, the Polish Prime Minister in London would not have entered into negotiations with it in Moscow, nor would the Polish Government in London have offered or suggested that members of that National Council should be associated with them in the proposed new Government to be set up in Warsaw after its liberation. They would not make any proposal of that kind to a Government or organization which was entirely unrepresentative. It is also absurd for the hon. and gallant Member to suggest that General Zymierski, who is commanding a strong Polish Army in the field at the present time, has no support at all from the Poles who live in the liberated areas of Poland. There is no doubt there is a good deal of support for this organization in the eastern regions of Poland, whatever they may find in the West. If argument is based on these assumptions that the Polish National Council and Committee are not representative, it would make the resumption of friendly relations between the Polish Government and Soviet Russia and the National Council very difficult, even impossible.

I do not deny there have been faults and mistakes on both sides. But what country in the world can say that during the last 20 or 30 years they have been free from error? The fact must be faced that there are certain elements associated with, or surrounding, the Polish Government in London which are violently hostile to the Soviet Government. There may be historical reasons as well as social reasons for this, but the fact remains that these elements do exist, and they are at the present time centering around the personality of the Commander-in-Chief, General Sosnkowski, whose intemperate utterances recently have created great difficulties in the diplomatic field. The general attitude of General Sosnkowski was shown when the late General Sikorski entered into friendly relations with the Soviet Government. General Sonskowski resigned from his position at that time as a protest against the action of General Sikorski. The position of the Commander-in-Chief of the Polish Army is a peculiar one. Under the Constitution of 1935, which was more or less, I would say, of a Fascist nature, the Commander-in-Chief of the Polish Army is appointed personally by the President of Poland.

The Cabinet, the Government, have no control whatever over the appointment, and they have no control over his actions. For example, the Commander-in-Chief can send, as he has done, public messages and secret messages to Warsaw without either consulting the Polish Cabinet in London or even without that Cabinet's knowledge. As a result the Polish Government here have asked General Sosnkowski to resign. He has refused to do so. That being the position they, by unanimous resolution last week, asked the President, who is the only person who has the power, to dismiss the Commander-in-Chief. Up to now no action has been taken by the President, who happens to be anyhow his close personal friend. It seems to me there is no chance of any improved relations between the Polish Government in London and the Polish Committee in Lublin or the Soviet Union as long as he remains in that position. General Sonskowski has got to go. There are many other difficulties which will have to be solved even then, many difficulties and many complexities, but this is the first step which must be taken if better relations are to be established. That is all I intend to say tonight about the Polish situation at the present time.

* * *

Debate on September 29, 1944.

SIR EDWARD GRIGG (C.): . . . The first, most pressing and most difficult problem is, unquestionably, Poland. A great deal turns upon Poland. I was deeply impressed by the speech made yesterday by the noble Lord the Member for Lanark (Lord Dunglass) upon the Polish question. It was a well-argued, well-compacted speech, which did him and the House, too, credit. That is the way in which to deal with foreign problems in this House, and I found myself in much sympathy with him in his arguments. This country can never relinquish its duty to see that, in the future, there is a strong and independent Poland. I think, however, it is also very important to realize, when it comes to frontiers, that you are dealing with one of the most debatable areas in the whole of Europe. The marches from the Baltic in the north to the Black Sea in the south which divide the great nations of Russia and Germany have been fought over, distributed, and redistributed over and over again in the course of centuries of history. You can prove almost anything about their ownership, and therefore I am not very deeply impressed by quotations from this agreement or that declaration. We have to face the realities of the present time and not exercise our historical memories.

From this point of view some speeches which have been made in this House have not been helpful, and I should like to say something about what seems to be the inevitable Russian approach to this issue. Russia has been strongly criticized for her advance into Poland in 1939. I always wonder why, and I wonder very much whether we, ourselves, would not have done the same thing in the same situation—much indeed, as Nelson dealt with the Danish Fleet at Copenhagen. These questions are always debatable, but when the life of a great nation is at stake, decisions have to be taken and debated afterwards. Now what was the position? When Russia advanced into Poland towards the end of 1939, the question was not the frontier between Poland and Russia—Poland had ceased to exist—but solely the frontier between Russia and Germany, and inasmuch as Russia had every reason to suppose that, sooner or later, German military strength would be launched against her, it made all the difference in the world where that frontier was placed, whether the German attack on Russia was launched 200 miles nearer Petrograd, and Moscow and Stalingrad, as it might have been, or 200 miles further to the west. I think we all have reason to be glad, and Poland has reason to be glad, that it was launched 200 miles further west than it might have been. Probably, the fate of Moscow, of Petrograd and of Stalingrad turned upon that action in 1939. Let us remember also that the mere fact that we are now debating the future frontiers of Poland, with all the historical difficulties behind them, is due to the sacrifices and the immense fighting capacity and spirit of the Russian people. This would have been German territory for ever, if it were not for the Russian people. Neither we nor the United States could have done anything comparable to alter that situation in Eastern Europe. We must recognize then that the Russians had some ground for saying that they have a special claim to consideration, and to making their future secure in this matter of frontiers in that area.

I do not think, however, that a readjustment of frontiers need be in any way incompatible with the strength and independence of Poland, which we all wish to see, and I hope, therefore, that there will not be great debate on the past history of frontiers. Russia has some reason still for suspicion. After all, revolutionary countries are suspicious countries; they have usually gone through a long period of ostracism—Russia has—and they have usually suffered unfairly at the hands of other Powers. They have usually had their interests, which may be vital interests, ignored. That has happened to Russia. Let us remember that Russia was not invited to the Munich Conference, although her vital interests were certainly deeply affected. There are other features in pre-war and early war diplomacy which Russia has reason to remember. Russia, therefore, is bound to claim something in the nature of a sphere of influence, which does not menace the independence of other nations but, nevertheless, gives her something in the nature of a special role in that part of Europe.

Let us all recognize that there are good precedents for a claim of that kind. What else is the Monroe Doctrine? We backed that doctrine, which, for nearly 90 years, secured the peace of the whole American continent, North and South. Let us recognize, therefore, that there are good, historical precedents for adoption of action on that line by a great people, and that Russia may have special reasons for adopting it in the East of Europe.

CAPTAIN CUNNINGHAM-REID (Ind.): Before the hon. Gentleman leaves the question of Russia and Poland, I would like to know whether he agrees with the Russian view, frequently expressed, that the newly constituted Poland should go up to the Oder River in Germany, and that it should absorb East Prussia?

SIR E. GRIGG: I have not the knowledge which my hon. and gallant Friend possesses of Russian views in this matter, and I am not going to discuss future frontiers. I have been arguing that it would be a mistake for us, at the present time, to discuss this question of frontiers. The facts cannot be known adequately to any of us here at the moment. I say that our principle in regard to Poland should be to stand up firmly for a strong and independent Poland, but to recognize that Russia has a special sphere of interest in that part of the world, similar to that which we have claimed in other parts of the world. In this respect I would like to congratulate my hon. Friend the Member for Oxford (Mr. Hogg) on the speech which he delivered yesterday. It was a very remarkable contribution to our Debate, and I hope we shall often hear him again on questions of foreign policy. I was sitting in the House all the time, and I think my hon. Friend was heard with great acceptance in all parts of the House and that he certainly got down to the bedrock of the principle upon which British foreign policy at its soundest has been based.

The Prime Minister and the Foreign Secretary have labored, day in and day out, to prevent a break-down in Russian-Polish negotiations. I think there is no doubt whatever that Poland and this country owe a tremendous lot to their united efforts. We know what the strain upon them must be, the tremendous rapidity with which events are happening, and the fact that every day there seems more to be done than can be done in the longest working hours. I think the time and attention, skill and loyalty which they have given and shown in this Russo-Polish question should be acknowledged by all of us, and I would like to throw out the suggestion that, much as we should all miss him in this House, there is something to be said, if it is possible, for the Foreign Secretary going to Moscow in the near future. I believe that my right hon. Friend might help very greatly to produce a solution of what is the paramount and immediate problem in Europe today...

SIR PERCY HARRIS (L.): . . . I shall not say anything about Poland, because I endorse the wise attitude of the Prime Minister. We have a special obligation for the Polish people. They were the first to be overrun and to suffer, but we are not going to be Poland's true friends, if we do not insist that she must come to an understanding with her great and powerful neighbor. If the Foreign Secretary can tear himself away from the Leadership of the House and visit Moscow and help to smooth out the difficulty I hope he will do so, with his charming personality and recognized tact...

MR. A. BEVAN (Lab.): . . . I furthermore believe it would be a nonsensical thing to dismember Germany by taking away from her any part of her territory which she properly regards as Germany. I do not believe we shall settle the world by territorial national mutilations. [An HON. MEMBER: "What about Poland?"] I believe the same thing about Poland, of course I do. I do not believe that Russia's security will be based on this or that frontier. In these days of fly bombs does anybody imagine that the peace of the world can depend on this chain of mountains, or that river line, or that line of fortifications? Those ideas belong to the last century and have nothing to do with the necessities of the modern world...

MAJOR THORNEYCROFT (C.): . . . I do not underestimate the contribution this country must make to a world organization, nor do I underestimate the amount of wishful thinking that goes on about it. There is a form of international Socialism, which believes that all the countries of the world are going to hand over their individual sovereignty to some kind of world government. Let us face the facts. Is there any prospect of Russia or the United States or ourselves handing over our individual sovereignty? What about those countries in Europe: Poland, Czechoslovakia, Belgium, and Holland? They have been fighting for four or five years. Suppose we go to them and say, "Your sole chance of survival is to give up your sovereignty, and hand it over to somebody else." They will say, "What have we been fighting for; we are proud of our history and of our nation." Let us be realists. If we try to build some scheme of world authority, and sell it to the people of this country, on the basis that other countries will surrender their sovereignty, we are going into a very dangerous field. In the end, we will find that other countries will not surrender their sovereignty, and the whole edifice we build up will fall to the ground . . .

COLONEL HAROLD MITCHELL (C.): . . . Perhaps I may be allowed to say something from personal observation of what the Poles, the Belgians and the Dutch have done during this present month. I was glad to hear the Prime Minister recall the reason for our entering the war. For some time there was a danger of that reason being clouded by more recent developments. We cannot overemphasize the fact that we declared war on Germany as the result of her unprovoked aggression on Poland. I know that my right hon. Friend the Foreign Secretary has not spared himself in his efforts to bring about a better feeling between Russia and Poland, and there is, as the Prime Minister said, some improvement. All of us know how assiduous the Foreign Secretary is and we are grateful to him for his part in bringing about that improvement, and we may be sure that he will not relax his efforts before the goal has been reached. I certainly am not going to say anything which will stand in the way of achieving the unity towards which the British Government have been working.

Just before the fall of France in 1940 I made my first contact with the Polish forces in France. They were then being re-formed by General Sikorski, at whose suggestion a little later I was appointed a Liaison Officer with the Polish troops and I have since been associated with them. I was present at the Polish Army's first muster in June, 1940, in Scotland immediately after the fall of France and I have been in close touch since that time with them. I have also had the opportunity of visiting Polish units in various parts of the Middle East. Soon after this House rose for the Summer Recess, at the request of General Kukiel, the Polish Minister of National Defense here in London, I spent some time with the Polish troops in the Low Countries. For obvious reasons I cannot tell the House exactly where they are now, or describe exactly what they are doing, but I can say that they have been in some of the hardest fighting and have acquitted themselves with great courage and remarkable heroism. It has been no easy task, for they have been up against some of the toughest soldiers the enemy has left, men fighting desperately for their lives, and I entirely agree with what the hon. Member of Ebbw Vale (Mr. A. Bevan) said about the strength of the German resistance. Only by supreme skill and valor have these victories over the enemy been secured, and not always without loss.

I joined the Poles at Ypres when they were just beginning the stage in their advance which was to take them right through Belgium into Holland. I accompanied them on this advance and I saw how they surmounted all the obstacles in their path, and they were many in those countries of rivers and canals. I also learned a great deal about what they had done from the Normandy beach-head onwards. One morning after a successful operation I met General Maczek, the Polish Commander. An attack took place outside the village with Polish tanks which had caught a retreating German column and completely destroyed it—an unforgettable scene of destruction. The General, delighted at the outcome of the Polish Forces' engagement of a few hours before, remarked, "This is my revenge for Poland." He commanded the famous Polish Black Brigade which fought so well in 1939 against the Germans until forced over the frontier into Hungary. Many of these troops made their way back to France and he had seen what the enemy had done to his own country. All the troops shared this spirit. They are out to avenge the wrong perpetrated by Hitler and the Nazis against their country and they are glad of the opportunity of fighting side by side with us and with some of the finest units from the British Commonwealth. And I would like to pay a tribute to the excellent cooperation which exists between the Poles and the Canadians, with whom they are serving. These Poles are far too busy fighting to have time for political controversy. They have only one aim, the defeat of Hitler, for by that means they know that they will be able to liberate their country from the tyrant's yoke.

The morale of the Polish troops is very good indeed. I was deeply moved at one point. I saw a soldier sitting on top of his tank, writing. For a moment I hesitated about interrupting him. He looked up and smiled. When I spoke to him he replied in English and his answers were remarkable for their knowledge of news from Britain which he had learned from the Radio. When I asked him where he was writing to he said, "To Scotland." I found that he had maintained a steady correspondence with several families who had befriended him when he had been in that part of the United Kingdom. And here I make an appeal to the Government. All of us know that there are good reasons for withholding information that might be useful to the enemy, but is there any valid reason for not giving something more full than anything so far released about the exploits of the Poles since they first landed in Normandy? This course would bring considerable cheer to their countrymen everywhere. It would encourage not only those fighting in Italy but those of their race in exile and those who are still in their own country resisting the Germans so fiercely. It is a story of amazing heroism comparable with anything in their splendid history. I would ask the Ministers concerned whether they cannot do something in this direction. It would be a fine gesture to a gallant Ally.

I cannot speak of what is happening in any other sector than that in which the Polish troops are operating. But in those areas of Belgium and Holland which I have recently visited I found the Poles and the people of the liberated towns and villages getting on extremely well together. It was an amazing experience to enter places in both countries and see what joy the Poles brought by their victory. I saw people standing in the doorways of their homes, damaged only perhaps an hour before in the fighting, throwing flowers and handing fruit to the troops and cheering themselves hoarse. In one Flanders village I remember going into a shop to make a small purchase. The proprietor behind the counter said to me, "We have had to billet our enemies, the Germans again and again. We are very glad they have been driven out now. Perhaps you will send us a Polish soldier and we will be only too glad to give him a free billet." Just one other incident. There had been a fierce struggle for a small town in Flanders all day with bitter hand-to-hand street fighting. Finally, in the late afternoon, the Poles broke down the German resistance and gained possession of the town. Just after they entered the town I got into conversation with the owner of a small inn on the Market Place. He said to me: "I have waited four years for today. When my windows were smashed this morning by machine gun fire I wept for joy because I knew that liberation was near." Pole and Belgian; and Pole and Dutchman soon became friends. They appreciate that they are comrades in the same struggle...

LIEUT.-COLONEL SIR CUTHBERT HEADLAM (C.): . . . I would like to say a word or two about the present position in Poland with regard to Soviet Russia. I am in the peculiar position of agreeing with the admirable speeches made yesterday both by my Noble Friend the Member for Lanark (Lord Dunglass) who presented the Polish point of view and my hon. Friend the Member for Oxford (Mr. Hogg) who pointed out our position *vis-à-vis* Russia. My noble Friend took the line that the claims of the Poles were of deep concern to us, and that we were more or less pledged to them to see that their independence was maintained, while my hon. Friend the Member for Oxford took the line that the less the Polish situation was discussed in public at present the better. There was much wisdom in the hon. Member's advice. But we cannot forget that we went to war to help the Poles to maintain their independence. It may well be, as the Prime Minister said, that the Soviet Union must be certain that their frontiers are protected amply to their satisfaction against any form of aggression. But I think in this connection the hon. Member for Ebbw Vale rather hit the nail on the head when he pointed out, I think rightly, that the frontiers of the old type no longer count so much as they used to count in the past, and in wars to come are still less likely to be of much avail against new forms of mechanical warfare.

But, putting aside altogether, this aspect of the case and agreeing with the Prime Minister's point of view that Russia must be certain of its frontiers, and admitting, too, that certain parts of Eastern Poland are largely inhabited by Russians, it is difficult for some of us to see why Poland should be deprived of territory. Still less is it easy for us to see why a new government should be brought into existence in Poland by the help of a foreign Power which is opposed to the Polish Government which we recognize here. It is, so it seems to me, an interference by one country in the internal government of another, and I am certain that the Foreign Secretary must be much exercised in his mind by the present situation. All we can do is to point out clearly to our Russian Ally what our point of view is in the matter—Poland is our Ally just as much as Russia—and we should put the views of the Polish Government before the Russian Government as clearly as we possibly can.

When I say the Polish Government, I mean the Polish Government that we recognize here. We cannot, of course, do anything in any way calculated to break down or to make difficult the relationships between us and the Russians; we must do nothing which will in any way weaken the war effort, but I am hopeful that, if we put our case clearly and strongly, and show the Russians that there is a strong public feeling on the matter in this country—and there is strong feeling both here and in the United States of America—that our point of view will have its effect in Moscow. We are always being told that Russia is a democracy and that public opinion counts. Surely we can utilize with Russia the same methods that we adopt with other democracies? One word in conclusion—this is the most crucial moment in the war. It demands unity and energy. We should carry on the fight to the utmost of our vigor, if we are to bring the war to an end as speedily as possible, and then when the fighting is over endeavor to build up a new Europe, in which Germany, no longer in a position to wage another war, will have to play her part in a fellowship of friendly nations.

MR. GALLACHER (Com.) : I do not want to follow the hon. Baronet into his maze of contradictions and tawdry sophistries. It is clear that he does not want interference in Spain which would adversely affect the Fascists but he wants interference against the Soviet Union in regard to Poland.

SIR C. HEADLAM : I do not want interference against the Soviet Union. I only want the point of view of a very large number of people with regard to Poland, made quite clear to the Russian Government.

HON. MEMBERS : Hear, hear.

MR. GALLACHER : Yes, but neither he nor those who "Hear, hear" want the Foreign Secretary to go to Spain and impress on Franco and his gang that the great mass of the people in this country want democracy in Spain. That is what he calls interference with another country.

SIR C. HEADLAM : That is an entirely different point...

MR. GALLACHER (Com.) : . . . Take the question of Poland. Unfortunately, because of certain exigencies I could not hear some of the speeches yesterday, but there were three old Tories who spoke—not old in years, but old in musty, fossilized ideas, the Noble Lord the Member for Lanark (Lord Dunglass), the hon. and gallant Gentleman the Member for Epsom (Sir A. Southby) and another. One young Tory spoke yesterday and one today. I wish we had some lads here always ready to get up after these young Tories. They are very clever lads. They might be dangerous unless they get away from the old Tories. There is a wider gulf between these three old Tories and these two young Tories, than there is between the Benches of this House. No one can suggest for a moment that there is any affinity of spirit between those who speak as young Tories and those old Tories. Thirty-five or 40 years ago, before some of these Members opposite had ever heard of such a place as Poland, I was speaking at mass demonstrations in different parts of the country fighting for freedom and independence for Poland. I have always been a friend of the Polish people. I am certain that the Noble Lord is no more a friend of the Polish people than he is of the people of this country. He is interested in land and landed gentry.

MR. PETHERICK (C.): Will the hon. Member explain what he means by the freedom and independence of Poland? Does he mean freedom and independence from foreign domination, or freedom and independence from certain people with whom he may happen to disagree politically inside?

MR. GALLACHER: The hon. Member does not know anything about Poland. For a long time that country was split into three. No people has such a bitter history of struggle; much of it has been against the Polish gentry. I could tell stories about Poland and the misery, poverty, illiteracy and disease under the Polish gentry, worse than in any other European country. No one can say that the partition of the Ukraine and the partition of White Russia are essential to Polish independence. We have seen what partition means in Ireland. We have a situation there, as a result of partition, in which this Government gives Ireland *de jure* recognition and not *de facto* recognition. We remember the Treaty that was made in connection with the ports; I drew attention to it at the time. That Treaty is between this country and Eire —not the Irish Free State which represented the 26 counties. It was with Eire, which means Ireland, one and indivisible. Although that Treaty is between this country and a United Ireland, *de facto* recognition cannot be given because of the partition. Can we get friendship between Poland and Russia if there is partition of the Ukraine and of White Russia? Does anybody suggest that the partition of these countries is essential for Polish independence? It is not.

But it is essential to Polish independence that the country should not be closed in and that it should have a clear opening to the sea. That is the important thing, and that is the thing that has been taken into account by the Soviet Union. It is the thing in which every Member of this House who is interested in Poland should be concerned. Does any Member who claims to be interested in Poland suggest for a moment that we should reintroduce the Polish Corridor? Is it possible again to have the situation in Europe in which there is that 10-mile strip through Germany? That was an utterly impossible situation, and we cannot have it again. But Poland must have an opening to the sea. How is it to be obtained except on the lines that have been suggested in some circles round about the Soviet Union? This is a question of the deepest interest for Poland. Polish independence depends, not on a bit of territory in the East, but on a real opening-up of the country so that it has a clear passage to the sea, an open connection with all other peoples, and is not hemmed in between a group of neighboring States.

Therefore, the advice of the Prime Minister should be accepted. Do not let us have any of these nasty slanders about the Soviet Union. Let us work for an understanding between the Polish people and the people of the Soviet Union. I am certain that these matters can be ironed in such a way as to bring about a real chance of lasting peace in Europe so that there is a free, independent Poland with its own Government living in the closest harmony and friendship with its mighty neighbor, the Soviet Union, with Great Britain and with its other neighbors.

MR. PRICE (Lab.): The hon. Member for Oxford (Mr. Hogg) made a notable contribution yesterday to this Debate by reminding the House that our forefathers accepted only those foreign obligations which they knew they could effectively carry out. I agree that, as far as Eastern Europe is concerned, we cannot accept obligations without close collaboration with our great Russian Ally. Russia is the only Power in that region that can enable us to implement those obligations. The principles of our foreign policy enunciated by the hon. Member for Oxford were, after all, the policy of Pitt, of Castlereagh and of Canning, and I think it is the policy of the right hon. Gentleman the Foreign Secretary.

It is well in this respect to remember that when the wicked partition of Poland took place, at the end of the eighteenth century, which outraged public opinion in this country, both Whig and Tory, our statesmen nevertheless, without condoning this act of the Holy Alliance, knew that they could not by direct action do anything to help the Poles, and they merely registered their displeasure.

That does not mean that we must renounce all influence in that area. The Moscow Conference did not set up spheres of influence and leave Russia to be the sole controller of Eastern Europe, and we and the United States of Western Europe. It did not set up zones of influence of that kind. On the contrary, as I take it, the whole object of the Conference and its results were to recreate a kind of Concert of the great Powers, out of which a Concert of Europe could later be formed. In that Concert we should have a say in the East, and Russia should have a say in the West. Russia has had a say in the West, in Italian affairs, and we, I think, have also a right to a say in the East. Our duty, therefore, to refuse to bind ourselves to military obligations in the East does not run counter to our rights to use our moral influence in the settlement of disputes, and particularly of Russo-Polish disputes. We can be the honest broker. But we can only play that role if we have the confidence of both sides.

Some speeches I have listened to in this House have not been of the kind to create that confidence—or, if the Government acted on their advice, they would not obtain that confidence. But others have been of the kind that would create that confidence, and I am certain that the right hon. Gentleman the Foreign Secretary is doing his utmost to create it. I was glad that the Noble Lord the Member for East Lanark (Lord Dunglass) sounded a note of realism yesterday. I understood him to warn the Poles that they cannot expect us to champion the idea of their Eastern frontier, on which they have for so long set their hearts. Actually, I think the Poles are becoming more reasonable and realistic on this frontier question now, and I believe also that Russia is prepared to give and take, provided there is one thing, namely, that she is assured of the existence in Poland of a Government friendly to her.

I have the pleasure of the acquaintance of several Poles in prominent positions here, and I am satisfied that many of them are very genuine in their desire for friendly co-operation with Russia. They realize the tragic futility of this age-long quarrel between what are, after all, two sister-Slav-nations, which quarrel, originally, of course, was based upon religion, but has since become largely traditional and quite out of keeping with the modern world. After all, this Russo-Polish frontier dispute, as has been pointed out by the hon. Member for Ebbw Vale (Mr. Bevan), and the frontier question are of far less importance than other questions, in view of the development of military science. It is the creation of a friendly atmosphere between these two countries that is far more important than the actual drawing of the frontier.

For my part, I have confidence that the present Polish Prime Minister, who is himself a peasant and a democrat, is really sincere in his desire for a friendly solution of this question. Unfortunately, and here is the difficult point, there are other prominent Poles who are in high positions here who have made no secret of their strong antipathy to Russia. As long as they hold influential positions here, it is understandable that the attitude of Russia on these matters is bound to be difficult. Russians, of course, have replied by the setting up of this Union of Polish Patriots, and, since then, a new Polish Committee of National Liberation, since Russia has gone beyond the Curzon Line. While those two bodies undoubtedly represent a body of opinion in Poland which is Russophile, I am not satisfied myself that it is fully representative of all shades of public opinion in Poland. I can believe Marshal Stalin when he says he wants to see an independent Poland, because he knows that, otherwise, Poland will be a source of continual trouble and disturbance on Russia's western frontier, but I think it is equally true that no Government based solely upon these two bodies, or whichever is the most important now, in Eastern Europe, will ever be a stable Government unless it contains also the democratic elements of Poland beyond the seas. That, to my mind, is the great task, to try to do all we can to bring about a coalition between these Russophile elements in the occupied part of Poland and the democratic elements of Poland abroad.

Here, of course, we are up against a very delicate situation, because a proud people like the Poles naturally do not want it to appear that their Government is being reconstructed under pressure from any foreign Power. It is a psychological difficulty we are up against. We, in this House, can do no more than wish the Foreign Secretary well in any steps he may take to try to solve this difficult psychological question.

There is the further difficulty that Russian diplomatic methods are indirect, and not always easy to understand. I suppose that is due to the old inheritance from former times. It has gone down in Russian history that their diplomacy is often of that kind, and one of the Tsar's Imperial Chancellors said "Russia does not sulk; she retires and waits." That was said after Russia's defeat in the Crimean war. No doubt, that was a sound method in those days, but I think that Russia today, after her resounding feats of arms and the tremendous prestige she carries now throughout the world, can well afford to be more direct in her diplomatic methods and a little less secretive. As an inveterate Russophile myself, I can say that I hope Russian statesmen will put beyond doubt whatever that they have no intention of imposing upon Poland, either directly or indirectly, a form of government which is not of the Poles own choosing. That is all I have to say on that matter.

MR. HAROLD NICOLSON (N. Lab.): . . . I admire the discretion which has been manifested by the House in discussing this terrible Russo-Polish dispute. I think that among many admirable speeches which have touched upon the subject, the speech made last night by the hon. Member for Oxford (Mr. Quintin Hogg) is among the ten best speeches that I have heard in this Parliament—certainly the ten best Back Bench speeches—and I think he stated great truths.

I hope that two things emerge from this Debate as the expression of the general feeling of this House which, as I said, is the general feeling of the ordinary sensible man in this country, which again means the vast majority of this country because they are ordinary sensible people. This, I think, is perfectly clear. We want to say to the Poles, "Now, do not be insane. You cannot possibly entertain the insane folly of believing that you can ever exist except with friendly relations with Russia. Why be provocative? Why worry about frontiers which you know are quite untenable unless Russia is prepared to uphold them, and why do you not try by every means in your power to place your relations with Russia upon that extremely sensible, permanently realistic basis which the Czechs—I admit in circumstances of far greater ease—established with Moscow?" That is a real model of how a border State is to place itself in a relation of dignity and virtue in regard to its powerful neighbor.

What would I say to the Russians? I admit that the Russians are terribly susceptible and one has to be careful what one says. The merest sigh of perplexity which goes up from here echoes in their ears as a hurricane of abuse. However, I do think we can say, and I think it is important for them to realize, that the perplexity which is felt in this country over this Russo-Polish dispute is not confined to one class or party. It is not a thing which is felt by the enemies of Russia—if there be any such—it is felt profoundly by their deepest friends; we hate the idea that these people, who have behaved with such absolute magnificence in war, and who have, as regards Finland and Rumania, acted with superb generosity, should in this Polish matter, appear to be acting ungenerously. It is a perplexity to us, it is a matter of distress. I should like the Russians to feel that this Debate is not a criticism of their actions but a very definite appeal to them, not merely from the Friends of Poland—or whatever they choose to call themselves—but from the great masses of our people who feel that their admiration and affection for Russia is in some way being chilled. I believe that the tone of this Debate should convey to Russia an appeal from every Bench in this House that Russia should act with that grandeur in this matter which she has shown in the field and elsewhere . . .

THE SECRETARY OF STATE FOR FOREIGN AFFAIRS (MR. EDEN): . . . I want to deal with some of the more difficult questions raised in the Debate and, more particularly, those of the relations between our Soviet and Polish Allies. I think it will be fair to say, and I have listened to almost all the Debate, that each point of view has been put quite fairly in this House. It is all to the good, in my judgment, as Foreign Secretary, that that should happen, and that foreign lands should know what the people of this country think on these problems. There is no subject that causes the Government, or myself as Foreign Secretary, more concern than this, and there is none which, I beg the House to believe, on which we have labored more persistently to try to make our contribution to a solution. In 1941, we reached a happy moment, to which we have never since been able to get back, when we managed to help to secure a Polish-Soviet Agreement, which was signed here in London. Events cut short the life of that Agreement, but I can assure the House that our efforts have been unremitting to try to build again on the foundations which we laid then.

I have been asked certain questions by my Noble Friend the Member for Lanark (Lord Dunglass) in a very admirably phrased speech. He asked me whether, for instance, at Teheran my right hon. Friend and I had made it clear to our Russian Allies how much importance we attached to a settlement of the differences then outstanding between them and the Polish Government. The answer to my Noble Friend is "Yes." We made it plain at Teheran, as we had made it plain earlier at Moscow, at the conference there, and as we have done many times since. There has been a suggestion by one or two of my hon. Friends that perhaps we had failed in the emphasis of our language. I do not accept that. We have spoken as friends to friends and when speaking thus it is, perhaps, wiser and also more effective to speak firmly in private rather than to hector peremptorily in public. Nobody in this House should suppose—and I ask the House to accept the assurance—no member of any party should suppose, that we have failed to make clear our position or our anxiety.

I am going to make only two observations on the present situation, and in particular about developments at Warsaw. I have been asked to give some account of them and I know the House will understand me when I say I do not propose to do so. It would not be very difficult for me to retail events, but I do not think it would be helpful in the light of the outcome of the representations which have been made. Of course we have considered the Warsaw situation. There have been discussions, arguments, representations between the Allies, but I think, on the whole, I will not give a detailed account of these. I will make only two observations. The first is that we ourselves have done everything in our power by military effort to bring help to the garrison at Warsaw since the first day of the rising and every tribute that the House can pay to the Royal Air Force, Polish, British or South African is justified. The second observation is that we have done everything in our power by diplomatic initiative to coordinate the efforts of our Allies in the same sense. For my part, it is a source of thankfulness that, since last week help is being brought to Warsaw by ourselves, the Americans and the Soviet Union also. I believe other problems will equally find themselves capable of solution.

There has been some discussion about the Eastern frontier of Poland and on that I would like to make an observation or two. I have, in one or two of the speeches, found an assumption that these matters were a little clearer than in in fact they are, and that they may be simplified or solved by reference to this treaty or to that. The truth, as the House knows well, is that there has been no more vexed issue in all history than these Eastern frontiers of Poland and His Majesty's Government, bound as they are by treaty to both their Allies—Poland and the Soviet Union—will not swerve in playing their part to try to reach a solution, which will result in in bringing about that to which we are all pledged—all three of us—the creation of a strong, sovereign, independent Poland which can play its full part in the comity of nations.

MR. GALLACHER: Are the Government not making a categorical statement that while Poland should be given an opening to the sea, there will be no question of the renewal of the Polish Corridor?

MR. EDEN: I am not sure I quite got that, unless it means that the hon. Member is against the Polish Corridor and wishes Poland to have an outlet down to the sea. I am in entire agreement with him. If I have spoken with caution about these Polish-Soviet relations—and I ask the attention of the House to this—it is not because of the significance of these matters in themselves, but because of thir inevitable reaction upon our relations with the Soviet Union. When the world emerges from its turmoil, it will yearn for lasting peace and the plain truth is that here can be no guarantee of any such peace unless we, the United States and the Soviet Union, can work together in enduring harmony, and that is to me the overriding importance of this Polish sovereign issue . . .

House of Lords. Debate on October 3, 1944.

LORD ADDISON (Lab.): . . . We all deplore the Polish quarrels. I have nothing to say about them. They emerge as one of the results of the regime which was established in 1935 or round about that date, and they are the inevitable outcome of an autocratic regime. Let us hope that all efforts will be directed to settling them and that soon a sufficient agreement will have been arrived at. I am quite sure that the British Government in the future, as they have done in the past, will do everything they can to help...

LORD VANSITTART: Last week there was in the House of Commons a debate which reached a very high level, and speaker after speaker in the debate referred to Russo-Polish relations in a way which showed the anxiety felt on that subject in all our minds. I do not propose to say anything on Russo-Polish relations, but I think that there is a word which needs saying on Russo-Polish relations.

For a long time past there has been an insistent demand from the Polish Committee in Moscow for the resignation or dismissal of General Sosnkowski. In due course, at the end of last week, that step was taken. I am sure that a great many of us hoped that this would form a fresh starting point for the achievement of the settlement which we so much desire, and that attitude was reflected in almost the entire Press. It was therefore with some disappointment, and indeed almost consternation, that we found that the appointment of his successor was greeted with a veritable outcry by the Polish Committee in Moscow. He was accused of being a criminal for his share in the Warsaw rising, and they even went so far as to intimate that they would try him if he fell into their hands.

In the first place, I do not think that language of that sort comes very well from the Polish Committee in Moscow, who through their radio station Kosciuszko undoubtedly gave some encouragement at least to the rising, but I do not wish to make anything of that point for the moment. Let us pass it over and make every allowance for, and be as generous as possible, to the Committee in Moscow. To the world at large, however, it will seem at least disconcerting that Poles in Russia should be incriminating Poles in Poland, the Poles of the resistance, the Poles of the underground movement, who have borne the heat and burden of the day, because they have fought against Germany, which is, after all, the duty and profession of all the Allies. Nor do I think it a very righteous charge that they should be incriminated because after five years of mortal agony and immortal endurance they failed to synchronize their actions and reactions, their pulses and impulses, with a stop-watch. Again let us make every possible allowance, and assume that these people do feel disposed so to charge each other; I still feel that it was wrong to do so in language so intemperate that only the Germans could have derived any pleasure from it.

I am a straightforward anti-German, and as such I am only one of millions all over the world; but as one of those millions I should like to take this opportunity of saying to the Polish Committee in Moscow that I am sure that the general cause would be greatly enhanced, and that the course of restraint so admirably observed both in another place and always in this House on this topic, would be immensely furthered, if they in their turn would exercise a similar and corresponding restraint . . .

THE SECRETARY OF STATE FOR DOMINION AFFAIRS VISCOUNT CRANBORNE (LORD CECIL): The main difficulty in this sphere still remains, of course, the Polish question, to which Lord Vansittart referred this afternoon. I do not want to go today into the points of detail which were raised by the noble Lord, in the very powerful contribution which he made, but I would say this: to this problem, as the House knows, the Prime Minister and my right honorable friend the Foreign Secretary have devoted an immense amount of work. I am quite certain that the House will agree with them that no trouble can be too great to find a solution of the Polish problem; for, as the Foreign Secretary himself said on Friday last, without a solution of that problem we can have no certain guarantee that Great Britain, the United States and Russia will be able to work together in complete harmony; and on collaboration between these three Powers the hopes of world peace in the future must depend.

In that particular sense the Polish problem is not merely a problem affecting the war with Germany, as was said by Lord Vansittart this afternoon. It is more than that; it is a world problem of the first importance. The Prime Minister, in the speech which he delivered in another place last Thursday, expressed the confident hope that a solution would be found, and that Mr. Mikołajczyk would return to Moscow and continue the conversations which had been interrupted. I am sure that we all share that hope, and share it most warmly; and I am certain, too, that this House will support the Prime Minister and the Foreign Secretary in any contribution which they can make to achieving a successful outcome of the present difficulties.

4. HELP FOR POLISH CIVILIANS*

Debate on October 11, 1944.

MR. R. C. MORRISON (Lab.) asked the Secretary of State for Foreign Affairs whether he is aware that the sending of food parcels from London schoolchildren to individual children in Poland has been stopped; and whether arrangements are being made to resume this service.

THE PARLIAMENTARY UNDER-SECRETARY TO THE FOREIGN OFFICE (MR. LAW): I understand that the dispatch of food parcels to children in Poland had, unfortunately, to be suspended owing to transport difficulties. The resumption of the parcel service to liberated areas is a matter for arrangement in consultation with the Soviet authorities, and, while I am informed that this has not yet been arranged, hon. Members will no doubt have seen Press reports of the distribution of relief in liberated Poland by the Soviet authorities. I cannot

* House of Commons. Vol. 403, Oct. 11, 1944, p. 1724–1725, 1758; Nov. 7, 1944, p. 1257–1258.

say whether the difficulties in the way of the resumption of the dispatch of parcels to those parts of Poland still under enemy occupation can be overcome, but the whole question is at present under consideration.

* * *

MR. R. DUCKWORTH (C.) asked the Parliamentary Secretary to the Ministry of Economic Warfare whether any steps can be taken to assist with food the large numbers of Polish civilians whom the Germans are expelling from Warsaw, especially in view of the coming winter.

PARLIAMENTARY SECRETARY TO THE MINISTRY OF ECONOMIC WARFARE (MR. FOOT): The whole question of relief through the blockade to Poland and other countries still under German occupation is at present under active consideration by His Majesty's Government and the United States Government. I am not yet, however, in a position to make a statement on this subject.

* * *

Debate on November 7, 1944.

SIR A. KNOX (C.) asked the Financial Secretary to the Treasury why the Polish Red Cross in London has been refused permission to send funds to the International Red Cross in Geneva for relief of distress in Poland; and whether it is possible to reverse this decision.

THE FINANCIAL SECRETARY TO THE TREASURY (MR. PEAKE): At the request of the Polish Government, his Majesty's Government have made the sum of 800,000 Swiss francs available to them for the purchase of goods in Switzerland to be sent to Poland through the International Red Cross for the relief of distress there, and I am informed that this amount is not yet exhausted. There seemed, therefore, to be no reason to make further Swiss francs available to the Polish Red Cross.

5. MIKOLAJCZYK'S SECOND VISIT TO MOSCOW*

THERE TOOK PLACE IN THE FALL *of 1944 several events of great importance for the conduct of the war and for future relations between the allies.*

On Sept. 13–16 there was a second conference at Quebec between Pres. Roosevelt and Prime Minister Churchill—for the purpose of discussing problems having to do with the conduct of the war in Europe and the Far East. Since it was evident that the defeat of the Germans was imminent the discussion included the subject of British and American zones of occupation in Germany.

Between August and October representatives of the allied nations, including Russia, met at Dumbarton Oaks in Washington to prepare the statute of the United Nations. This work was not completed during that time and many important topics were left unfinished; voting in the Security Council and the veto were left for future meetings of allied representatives to decide.

At this time Prime Minister Churchill and Minister Eden made a visit to Moscow (Oct. 9–17, 1944). One of the problems Churchill particularly wanted to settle was the question of Poland.

On Oct. 7 Polish Minister for Foreign Affairs, T. Romer described the situation in a note to the U.S. and British Governments, in which he said:[1]

> ". . . Authoritative declarations made by the representatives of the British Government as also the joint declaration made by the United Nations and known as the Atlantic Charter, leave no doubt whatsoever that no unilateral territorial changes will be recognized by the United Nations as legal binding. The Government of the USSR adhered to this principle by signing the Atlantic Charter. They expressly recognized as null and void all agree-

* House of Commons. Vol. 404, Oct. 27, 1944, p. 493–499.
[1] Stosunki polsko-sowieckie, 1943–46, p. 279.

ments previously concluded with the German Reich (Art. 1 Polish-Soviet Agreement of July 30, 1941) concerning the territories of the Polish State. Apart from this the Government of the USSR declared explicitly in a Note presented to the Polish Embassy in Kuibyshev on Dec. 1, 1941, that in their opinion: '. . . the question of frontiers between the USSR and Poland has not been settled and will be subject to a settlement in the future. . . .'

Contrary to the above-mentioned declarations, the Soviet Government are treating the territories incorporated with the Soviet Union in 1939 as their own state territories and are introducing thereon their own administration and their own economic and socal institutions. According to information received by the Polish Government a regular conscription to the Red Army of men between the ages of 18–52 is being carried out on these territories. This is the third call-up to be carried out by the Soviet authorities in these territories. The first took place in the Spring of 1940 and the second in the Spring of 1941, involving a total of about 150,000 men.

Furthermore, the Lithuanian, White-Russian and Ukrainian Soviet Union Republics, acting obviously in accordance with instructions of the Government of the USSR, have concluded agreements with the so-called Polish Committee of National Liberation, on the basis of which an exchange of population on the territories under their administration is being carried out. On the other hand, the relevant agreements do not cover the repatriation of the Polish citizens deported into the interior of Russia in 1939–41, which seems to indicate that in this case the Soviet Government had a purely political effect in view. In this way they are attempting by means of accomplished facts and unilateral decision to change the traditional ethnographic face of these terrisories by arbitrarily moving masses of millions of people. It would be impossible to exaggerate the calamity inflicted on this population by the expulsion from their ancestral homes of a large mass of people who have already endured the afflictions of the last five years and their settlement in new places of domicile while the war is still going on.

The Polish Government are not in a position to ascertain what demarcation line the Soviet Government have laid down between the areas administered by the Soviets and the Committee of National Liberation respectively as no authoritative document, decree or announcement dealing with the matter has been made public. Apart from these obscurities the indisputable fact remains that the Soviet Government have carried out a new partition of Poland and consequent upon it are creating facts, on the strength of their own decisions.

Another part of Polish territory regarded even by the Soviet Government as indisputably Polish State territory has been bequeathed by the Soviet Government with a puppet administration under thinly veiled Soviet leadership. In order to give the impression that this administration represents the Polish nation, the Polish Workers' Party, which used to be a member of the Comintern and is the successor of the Polish Communist Party, founded the so-called National Council of Poland in German-occupied Poland in January 1944. On July 21, 1944, the Council appointed an executive body under the name of the "Committee of National Liberation," most of whose members are members of the Polish Workers' Party or trusted Comintern men who had been active in that capacity in Poland, Russia, Austria and Czechoslovakia before 1939. The Committee also includes Soviet citizens who are members of the highest Soviet authorities.

Immediately on its formation the Committee was given the support of the Soviet Government which concluded an agreement with it on July 26, 1944, authorizing the Committee to take over the administration of the territories of the Polish State liberated from the German occupation. This agreement was not preceded, as happened in all similar cases, by consultations with any Allied Government. In principle it is modelled on the lines of the Russo-Czechoslovak Agreement of May 8, 1944. Furthermore, the Committee and the Soviet Government exchanged representatives, and the Soviet representative, characteristically enough, takes part in the deliberations of the Committee.

The National Council of Poland and the Committee of National Liberation, taking advantage of the support given them by the Soviet Government, are creating further accomplished facts by which they are gradually assuming the attributes of the legal Polish Government. In its resolution of Sept. 11, 1944, the National Council of Poland arrogated to itself the prerogatives of both houses of the Polish Parliament, the Sejm and the Senate. The Council declared in that resolution that the Chairman of the Council would carry out the duties of the President of the Republic. . . .

. . . The formation of the National Council of Poland, the Polish Committee of National Liberation and the Supreme Command of the Polish Army is tantamount to the Soviet Government taking over the attributes of Polish State sovereignty through the medium of Polish Communist elements and of Soviet citizens of Polish descent. . . .

. . . The Committee has declared that 'the emigré Government in London and its agency in Poland are illegal and stated that it does not recognize the Polish Underground Organization and intends to break it up and to use repressive measures against its members—those men, who, with the support of the British and American Governments have for nearly five years risked their lives in the struggle against the German authorities and garrisons of occupation in Poland, thus assisting the war effort of the United Nations to the utmost of their power. In accordance with this announcement the 'Council' issued a decree on Sept. 11, 1944, outlawing the Underground Army in Poland. . . .

. . . In the light of the above there cannot be any doubt that with the approval of the Soviet Government facts have been accomplished on Polish territories designed to impose on the Polish nation an illegal administration which in no way reflects the will of the nation, contrary to repeated assurances of Marshal Stalin that he is striving to rebuild an independent Poland and that he does not intend to interfere in Poland's internal affairs. The enterprises carried out in Poland represent obvious violations of the independence of the Polish State.

In bringing the above facts to the notice of the United States Government I have the honor to state that the Polish Government regard as devoid of all legal validity and in no way binding on them the unilateral facts accomplished by the USSR Government in respect of the territories and the sovereignty of the Polish Republic, either directly or through the so-called Committee of National Liberation, as also the agreements concluded with this Committee and the measures enacted on the strength of these agreements. These facts are a violation of the stipulations of International Law and of the principles proclaimed by the United Nations and in particular a violation of the rights of the Polish Republic and her legal Government. . . ."

During the first Churchill-Stalin talks on Oct. 9 it was decided that it would be necessary to call to Moscow these Polish officials: Premier Mikołajczyk, Prof. S. Grabski and Minister T. Romer. Churchill sent a wire to the Polish Government in London making clear that refusal to come to take part in the conversation would amount to a definite rejection of British advice and would relieve the British from further responsibility towards the London Polish Government.[2]

Churchill wired Harry Hopkins from Moscow on Oct 12:

[2] Churchill, W. Triumph and Tragedy, p. 227.

"Under dire threats from us we persuaded Mikołajczyk and the Poles to accept the invitation we had extracted from the Russians. We hope they will be here tomorrow."[3]

The Poles flew to Moscow on Oct. 12 and on the following day they had their first conference with Stalin and Churchill.[4]

MIKOŁAJCZYK thanked Stalin and Molotov for their hospitality and expressed his gratitude to Churchill for not forgetting Poland.

He began his speech by describing the Polish Memorandum[5] which in his opinion was the best solution of the Polish-Soviet difficulties. He emphasized that he took into account the fact that the Soviet Government had signed an agreement with the Polish Committee of National Liberation on the day before the Polish Delegation had arrived in Moscow for the first time, and the prestige of the Government which had signed it.

The Memorandum dealt with the fundamental problems; the international relations between Poland and the USSR and the Polish international situation. . . . It was his intention—he continued—for the whole Polish Nation thus to take part, as it were, in the understanding with Russia. He ended his long speech by emphasizing that the Memorandum was sent to the Polish Underground authorities and approved unanimously by all political parties .

STALIN asked whether there existed in Poland political parties under German occupation and when Mikolajczyk replied in the affirmative he inquired whether the approval of the parties was obtained on the basis of a published document and whether meetings and public conferences were convened in this connection.

MIKOŁAJCZYK explained that the decision of the parties had to be taken in the course of the heaviest fighting for Warsaw, and that the Memorandum was not published in full but a detailed precis was given by the Premier in a press interview.

STALIN expressed his doubts concerning such methods of approval.

MIKOŁAJCZYK: I know that Marshal Stalin before he became the great leader of his nation knew how to contact his followers in the underground effectively in a similar way.

---

3 Ibid, p. 230.

4 U. S. Congress. House. Select Committee on Communist Aggression. Special report. Polish documents report., p. 116–124.

5 See No. 3.

STALIN: Excuse me, my practice at the time when we were hiding underground from political persecution was entirely different. During that period we held 6 conferences, 6 congresses, 12 meetings and 20 to 25 conferences of the Central Committee of the Party where the program was approved.

MIKOŁAJCZYK: I always looked with great admiration to these methods of underground warfare and today it is with the same admiration that I treat the 5 years of work and combat and methods of liaison of my friends and colleagues of the underground. I want once more to emphasize that in my opinion and in the opinion of other members of the Polish Government our Memorandum is the best way of uniting all forces of the Nation in a program of Polish-Soviet friendship and cooperation. . . .

GRABSKI spoke of the necessity of the new Government in Poland being appointed by the Polish President. So long as the greater part of Poland is occupied by the Germans there is no legal means of changing the Constitution or electing a President.

The Constitution of 1935 is by no means dear to us. Many of us, including myself opposed it vehemently just as we did the Pilsudskiytes.

The person of the President is not of importance in this connection; he has, as a matter of fact, recently changed his successor.

What is however of importance is the legal procedure which is to facilitate a Polish-Soviet agreement. I also spoke of the importance of cooperation between our two nations not only during the war but also, and especially after it when Central Europe will have to be made safe from the danger of a German revenge.

CHURCHILL: I can thus see that these verbal comments were a development of the Memorandum itself which in my understanding, provides a basis for a compromise between the Polish Government and the Committee of National Liberation. For example, the fact that the Polish Workers' Party is to be included among the five parties which are to form the future Government in Poland does not surely imply an intention to diminish the Committee's part in such a Government.

MIKOŁAJCZYK: I am a realist. I realize that the fusion of the Government and the Committee would be impossible. One has therefore to go deeper and to seek support among the political parties.

The Polish Government is based on the four principal parties. The Committee I believe is based on one, although it claims to have a wider basis. It would be useless to quarrel about it. It will suffice to base the Government on the five principal parties each of which would receive a fifth of the ministries, as suggested by the Memorandum.

CHURCHILL: That is not how I understood the matter. I thought that it would be necessary to seek a more equal proportion between the Government and the Committee. We could now fix the numerical ratio.

I imagined that the general agreement for which we are now working would be concluded between the Polish and the Soviet Governments, while its application would be arranged between the Polish Government and the Committee of Liberation.

I also understood that Premier Mikołajczyk and his colleagues would be prepared to discuss the problem of a new constitution with the Soviet Government and with the Committee. I say this, because I think that the Memorandum is only the basis for discussion.

MIKOŁAJCZYK: The actual state of affairs is such: the Soviet Government have concluded an agreement with the Committee. The Polish Government are recognized by the British, American and other governments. These discrepancies should be brought to a common denominator.

The Memorandum envisages the participation in a new government of the representatives of both parties. Thus a new government would be constituted which would be recognized by all of the three principal powers. . . .

STALIN: In my opinion the Polish Memorandum has two important defects which may make an understanding impossible.

The first of them is that it ignores the Committee of National Liberation. How can one ignore such a fact and how can one close one's eyes on reality. Mr. Mikołajczyk should know that the Committee is carrying out an important task in liberated Poland. Recently there took place the conferences of the Socialist and the Peasant parties in the course of which important practical problems were discussed and the opinion of the Liberation Committee was taken into account. Who ignores these facts is against an understanding.

An analysis of the present situation on the Polish sector shows that there is either no Government in Poland or else that there are two, which amounts to the same thing. For this reason a Government must be formed on the basis of a compromise between the two authorities which claim to be the Government.

Another defect of the Memorandum is that it does not settle the problem of the Eastern frontiers of Poland on the basis of the Curzon Line. If you want to have relations with the Soviet

Government you can only do it by recognizing the Curzon Line as the principle.

On the other hand what I find that is good in the Memorandum is the scheme which it contains for future Polish-Soviet relations. That part of the Memorandum merits the approval of everybody who desires good relations between Poland and the USSR. It is a matter, however, which concerns the future but we must also consider the present.

A weak point in the Memorandum is its treatment of the constitution of which Prof. Grabski has spoken. Personally I think that the Polish constitution of 1921 is better than the constitution of 1935. But this should not be an obstacle in the way to improving Polish-Soviet relations. In the long run it is an internal Polish problem.

CHURCHILL: I see a gleam of hope in what Marshal Stalin has just said because I understand that the Polish Government desires a friendly understanding with the Committee and the Memorandum is no obstacle in its way.

As regards the frontier problems, I must declare on behalf of the British Government that the sacrifices made by the Soviet Union in the course of the war against Germany and its effort toward liberating Poland entitle it, in our opinion, to a Western frontier along the Curzon Line. I said so several times to my Polish friends in the course of last year.

I also understand that the Allies will be continuing the struggle against Germany in order to obtain in return for the Polish concessions in the East an equal balance [Mr. Churchill first said "full compensation" and then corrected himself] in the form of territories in the North and in the West, in East Prussia and in Silesia including a good sea coast, an excellent port in Danzig and valuable raw materials in Silesia.

It will be a great country, not quite the same as the one designed at Versailles but constituting a real and solid structure in which the Polish Nation will be able to live and develop in security, prosperity and freedom. Britain attaches the greatest importance to this problem. If I were to take part in the Peace Conference, that is if I should still enjoy the confidence of the Government and of the Parliament, I should use the very same arguments.

MIKOŁAJCZYK: Marshal Stalin stated that our Memorandum ignored the existence of the Committee of National Liberation. To a certain extent this is true, but to a certain extent it is not. Please bear in mind that during five years the Polish Government has struggled to create quite a substantial army, navy and air-force which have fought with distinction on all fronts of the West, the South and on distant seas.

STALIN: That I appreciate.

MIKOŁAJCZYK: For five years the Polish Government has also been organizing an underground army in Poland. But you, Marshal Stalin, ignore this particular Government and recognize the Committee.

STALIN: I do not ignore it as far as a compromise is concerned. And the Memorandum makes no mention of the Committee at all.

MIKOŁAJCZYK: Because it goes down to the very foundations on which both the Government and the Committee are based. . . .

. . . And now as regards the Curzon Line. In this matter I disagree both with Premier Churchill and with Marshal Stalin. I cannot decide this problem for the decision lies with the Polish Nation: you would form a very bad opinion of me were I to agree to ceding 40 per cent of the territory of Poland and 5 million Poles. Were I to concede it would seem that what the Polish soldier and the soldier of the Home Army was shedding his blood for, the politician has sold.

STALIN: It is Ukrainian territory and a non-Polish population is in question.

MIKOŁAJCZYK: The population of the whole territory amounts to 11 million. The soldiers of the Polish Army and of the Polish Home Army are fighting in the hope that they will return to their homes which I am asked to give away.

Were I to do so, I should lose all the confidence I enjoy. It would not serve the Polish-Soviet understanding well, and it is for that understanding that I am working.

STALIN: But you do not seem to notice that a million and a half Ukrainians are fighting for these territories in the ranks of the Red Army. The Ukraine and White Ruthenia have suffered for this reason even more than Poland. Mr. Mikołajczyk does not think of this, he would like to incorporate these territories and by that he proves that he is an imperialist.

MIKOLAJCZYK: I bow my head before the heroism of the Soviet soldiers, but, as a Pole I remember above all else that Poland has lost 5,000,000 men murdered by the Germans in the course of this war.

CHURCHILL: We recognize Poland's sufferings but in order to bring them to an end a new Government will have to be created which would receive the recognition of all principal United powers. If that is not done, further suffering and sacrifices will not be avoided.

STALIN: Quite correct.

MIKOŁAJCZYK: I think that the solution lies in an understanding between the three principal powers and in a generous conciliatory gesture on the part of the Soviet Union. If I am asked to cede 40 percent of our territory and not to demand guarantees of our independence, then . . .

STALIN: [interrupts] Who is it that threatens the independence of Poland? Is it perhaps the Soviet Union?

MIKOŁAJCZYK: I ask for full independence, for the return of all Poles to Poland and for free work for everybody.

CHURCHILL: I thought that we had come to an agreement regarding the return of the population and its exchange.

STALIN: Of course.

MIKOŁAJCZYK: But the facts are different. All the Governments of the liberated countries of Europe were able to return with the one exception of the Polish Government.

CHURCHILL: It is the result of the absence of the understanding for which we are now working. As a matter of fact not all Governments have as yet returned to their countries. Heavy and hard fighting is still in progress, and will still be for some time on all the European fronts.

I had hoped that Mr. Mikołajczyk would have been in a position to state that he recognizes the fact that the British Government support the Soviet Government in their proposals concerning the new Eastern frontiers of Poland. The Poles may deplore this, but it is an important fact. We do not ask Mr. Mikołajczyk to come forward with the initiative for a Polish recognition of the new frontiers but to consider that this is a matter of a new home for the Polish Nation.

As far as I understand Marshal Stalin desires, just as we and our American friends do, a sovereign, strong and independent Poland and of course friendly towards the Soviet Union, though I admit that such feelings cannot be in practice unanimous.

STALIN: [interrupts]. Quite true. The Russians not only say so but are actually helping towards this end.

CHURCHILL: Were we not to reach an understanding in respect of the frontiers I should not be in a position to maintain my efforts any further. I feel it is Russia's attitude that Poland should again arise free, independent and sovereign, and that this is her attitude not because she feels strong but because she considers that she is right.

But no Government could suffer an unfriendly attitude on the part of a neighbor if it had been through what Russia has in this war. [Stalin nods in approval]. I really do not know what would be the best solution to this problem. Perhaps Mr. Mikołajczyk could make a statement concerning the frontiers which would be acceptable to the Soviet Government, but I am afraid that in such a case he would be denounced in the following day by the Polish public opinion which supports him. He could perhaps state that for practical purposes the Polish Government accept the frontier solution but that they reserve the right to appeal in this matter at the peace conference. I do not know whether this would be acceptable to both parties.

MIKOŁAJCZYK: Some time ago I suggested a line of demarcation but I did not imagine that today we were to undertake a new partition of Poland.

STALIN: I am against a partition of Poland but you, on your part want to carry out a partition of the Ukraine and of White Ruthenia.

MIKOŁAJCZYK: I have heard public declarations concerning the partition of Poland but I have so far heard nothing of a partition of Germany.

CHURCHILL: [after having whispered something to Eden]. We have discussed this and the problem of Germany was to be settled here but we avoided any publicity which would only have the result of stiffening resistance.

MOLOTOV: Quite correct.

CHURCHILL: I do not wish to avoid replying to this question. I only appeal to Mr. Mikołajczyk to make a great effort on his part to help the British Government in their endeavor.

Though badly prepared, Britain came into the war to save the Polish Nation from destruction. I think that our duty will have been fulfilled if as a result of this war a great, free, sovereign and independent Poland will arise and will take the whole nation under its wing.

Our attitude is as follows: the Curzon Line, as the Eastern frontier of Poland and in the West and in the North a change of frontiers for Poland's benefit. I do not think in this state of affairs it would be in the interest of the Polish Government to estrange themselves from the British Government.

In the course of this war we were a hair's breadth from defeat: a sword hung over our necks. We have therefore the right to ask the Poles for a great gesture in the interest of European peace. [He turns to Premier Mikołajczyk] I hope that you will not hold against me these unpleasant but frank words which I have spoken with the best of intentions.

MIKOŁAJCZYK: I have already heard so many unpleasant things in the course of this war that one more will not let me lose my balance.

MOLOTOV: I should like to add a few words about what was discussed in Teheran on the subject of Poland. All those who took part are here today with the exception of Pres. Roosevelt. I should like to repeat what he declared and if I am inexact I hope that the other witnesses will correct me.

I can quite well remember that Pres. Roosevelt said that he fully agreed to the Curzon Line and that he considered it to be a just frontier between Poland and the Soviet Union; he thought, however, that for the time being it would be advisable not to give publicity to his view. We can therefore draw the conclusion that the Curzon Line does not only correspond with the attitude of the Soviet Government but it has also the concurrence of all of the three great powers. I wanted to emphasize this as Mr. Mikołajczyk referred to the attitude of three powers.[6]

MIKOŁAJCZYK: And may I learn what was decided in Teheran with regard to the Western frontiers of Poland?

MOLOTOV: The opinion was that the line of the Oder was just. I do not remember anybody objected.

CHURCHILL: I also agreed.

EDEN: The formula in Teheran was that the new frontier of Poland in the West would go as far towards the Oder as the Poles would wish. [All concur].

CHURCHILL: In East Prussia, the territories earmarked for Poland extend to the west and south of Koenigsberg. Would a new united Polish Government accept the Curzon Line, on these conditions, as the de facto Eastern frontier with the reservation that the matter will be settled at the Peace Conference? I must add that I have not yet had the opportunity to discuss this suggestion with the Soviet Government.

MIKOŁAJCZYK: I have no authority to make such a declaration.

CHURCHILL: I have not in mind a solemn declaration but a working formula. I do not want to expose Mr. Mikołajczyk to an immediate denouncement by Polish public opinion, but all the same I think that such a settlement would best help to create a united Polish Government.

---

6 "Shocked, and remembering the earnest assurances I had personally from Roosevelt at the White House, I looked at Churchill and Harriman, silently begging them to call this damnable deal a lie. Harriman looked down at the rug. Churchill looked straight back at me. 'I confirm this'—he said quietly." (Mikołajczyk, op. cit., p. 96.)

"Molotov did not refer to me for confirmation and I decided it would only make matters worse if I being present as an observer had attempted to correct his statement." (Harriman to Roosevelt, Oct. 14, 1944. Yalta Papers, p. 203.)

MIKOŁAJCZYK: Even the Committee of National Liberation has recently announced publicly that they have not lost hope that Lwów may be saved for Poland—and I am asked to be put into a worse condition by being made to agree to the Curzon Line.

STALIN: We do not use Ukrainian soil for barter. The rumor you quoted is without foundation.

CHURCHILL: My attitude should not be given such a ruthless interpretation as the Poles have given it. Danzig is certainly not worth less to Poland than Lwów. Does not Marshall Stalin think that it would be better now to interrupt our discussion and to give the Poles time to think the matter over?

STALIN: I should like to declare that we Russians also speak of including in Poland not only Danzig but also Stettin.

CHURCHILL: Of course.

STALIN: We have all sympathy for this project.

CHURCHILL: So has the British Government. [He turns to Premier Mikołajczyk.] Please consider this in all seriousness. The problems are to us of the greatest importance:

1. acceptance of the Curzon Line as the de facto Eastern frontier of Poland with the right of a final discussion of the matter at the Peace Conference; and
2. a friendly agreement with the Committee of the National Liberation on the subject of forming a united Polish Government which in time could undergo such modifications as circumstances would require.

I think this would be the best solution in this final phase of the war. If before taking a decision Mr. Mikołajczyk would like to talk to me or Mr. Eden, we are of course at his disposal. On my part I consider these two matters as the most important.

ROMER: Are we to understand that Mr. Churchill's suggestion has also the support of the Soviet Government?

STALIN: [who has been standing for some time while all the others were sitting]. In order that the whole matter may be quite clear and that there may be no doubts I want to state categorically that the Soviet Government cannot accept Premier Churchill's formula concerning the Curzon Line. [Churchill makes a gesture of disappointment and helplessness]. I must add the following correction, as far as we are concerned, to this formula:

The Curzon Line must be accepted as the future Polish-Soviet frontier. One cannot keep changing the frontier for the social and economic organizations are different here and different in Poland. We have collective farms which we introduce in all our lands, and Poland has the system of private property of land.

If in these conditions we start questioning to whom certain territories belong it will only increase the suffering of the population.

This is why, just as in the case of Roumania and Finland, we aim at determining a definite frontier with Poland. This is a source of surprise among many of our foreign friends but it is, in our opinion, the only just solution of the problem in view of the difference of our economic systems.

With the rest of Premier Churchill's statement I fully agree.

I repeat once more: The Curzon Line as the basis of the frontier. In its definite delimitation I agree, of course, to certain corrections for local reasons which may move the frontier 3 or 4 [he corrects himself], 6 or 7 miles one way or the other.

MIKOŁAJCZYK: May we be told what is actually considered as the Curzon Line?

CHURCHILL: We shall let you have a map showing it.

MIKOŁAJCZYK: Is the Curzon Line identical to the demarcation line introduced in 1939?

STALIN: No, not by any means. The Curzon Line gives you Białystok, Łomza and Przemysl.

Thus ended the conference.

That same evening, Oct. 13, there was a meeting of Churchill, Stalin and representatives of the Polish Committee of National Liberation. Representatives of the Polish Government in London were not present. The chairman of the Committee, E. Osóbka-Morawski, delivered a speech on the economic and social reforms which the Committee had introduced into Poland, emphasizing results of the new agrarian reforms based on individual ownership of land. In the political field the representatives of the Committee repeated arguments previously put forth by the Soviets. Prime Minister Churchill stated that B. Bierut, president of the Polish National Council, said he was at the meeting to demand on behalf of Poland that Lwów belong to Russia—that such was the will of the Polish people.[7]

The morning of Oct. 14 Churchill and Mikołajczyk had the following heated discussion:[8]

CHURCHILL: It is the crisis of the fortunes of Poland. No such opportunity will ever return and the damage done would

[7] Churchill, W. Op. cit., p. 235.
[8] Stosunki polsko-sowieckie, 1943–46, p. 303 et seq.

be irreparable if we lose today the chance of agreement. Everything hinges on one thing: the eastern frontier of Poland. If this is settled and announced, in one or two sentences, then agreement can be reached easily. How near we got at the beginning of the year. If you had come to an agreement with the Russians at that time, you would not have had today those other people. They are going to be a frightful nuisance to you. They will build up a rival Government and gradually take over authority in Poland. Fighting will begin with the Russians siding with the rival Government. I shall tell Parliament what I have agreed with Stalin and what His Majesty's Government's attitude is. When you have a victorious army behind you, there is quite enough to make a show, especially when the others will be liquidated. They have unlimited means to do this. Therefore you must never leave Russia, but must go to Poland and form a united Government there. Our relations with Russia are much better than they have ever been. I talked to Gen. Anders the other day to whom I took great liking. He entertains the hope that after the defeat of Germany the Russians will be beaten. This is crazy, you cannot defeat the Russians.

I beg you to settle upon the frontier question. You must take responsibilities. If you reach a formula with me I'll go to Stalin at 4 P.M.

What is there else besides the frontier question? It means compensation in the west and the disentanglement of population. If you agree on the frontier then the Russians will withdraw the support from the Committee. When I criticized the Lublin Poles last night Stalin on many occasions supported me. You are really dealing with Russia. The word "basis" is very helpful: we were nearly at it in January. If you do not agree now that means that you are going to use again the "Liberum Veto" which shattered the independence of Poland. What does it matter supposing you lose the support of some of the Poles? Think what you will gain in return! Ambassadors will come. The British Ambassador will be with you. The Americans will have an Ambassador, the greatest military power in the world. You *must* do this. If you miss this moment everything will be lost . . .

MIKOŁAJCZYK: The frontier problem must be settled by the whole Polish nation.

CHURCHILL: If Piłsudski were living, the situation would be quite different. Even though I have never met him, I respect him very much and I am sure that if he had not died, Beck would not have done what he did with Czechs.

MIKOŁAJCZYK, returning to the frontier question, says that

Stalin stated that the Curzon Line must be the frontier between Poland and Russia.

CHURCHILL [irritated]: I wash my hands off; as far as I am concerned we shall give the business up. Because of quarrels between Poles we are not going to wreck the peace of Europe. In your obstinacy you do not see what is at the stake. It is not in friendship that we shall part. We shall tell the world how unreasonable you are. You will start another war in which 25 million lives will be lost. But you don't care.

MIKOŁAJCZYK: I know that our fate was sealed in Teheran.

CHURCHILL: It was *saved* in Teheran.

MIKOŁAJCZYK: I am not a person completely washed out of patriotic feeling to give away half of Poland.

CHURCHILL: What do you mean by saying: "you are not washed out of patriotic feeling"? 25 years ago *we* reconstituted Poland although in the last war more Poles fought against us than for us. Now again we are preserving you from disappearance, but you will not play. You are absolutely crazy.

MIKOŁAJCZYK: But this solution does not change anything.

CHURCHILL: Unless you accept the frontier you are out of the business for ever. The Russians will sweep through your country and your people will be liquidated. You are on the verge of annihilation.

EDEN: Supposing we get an understanding on the Curzon Line, on all the other things we will get agreement from the Russians. You will get a guarantee from us.

CHURCHILL: Poland will be guaranteed by the three Great Powers and certainly by us. The American Constitution makes it difficult for the President to commit the U.S. In any case you are not giving up anything because the Russians are there already.

MIKOŁAJCZYK: We are losing everything.

CHURCHILL: The Pripet marshes and 5 million people. The Ukrainians are not your people. You are saving your own people and enable us to act with vigor.

MIKOŁAJCZYK: If we are going to lose independence, must we sign this?

CHURCHILL: You have only one thing to do. It makes the greatest difference if you agree.

MIKOŁAJCZYK: Couldn't it be announced that the three Powers settled the Polish frontier question without us?

CHURCHILL: We will be sick and tired of you if you go on arguing.

EDEN: Could you say that in view of the declaration made by the British and Soviet Governments you accept a "de facto" formula, under protest if you like, and put the blame on us. I quite see the difficulty of saying it is of your own volition.

The formula suggested by Churchill was not accepted by the Poles. Prof. Grabski gave Churchill his own opinion of the Polish-Soviet dispute, emphasizing that for 30 years he had been working for a Polish-Soviet settlement. Prof. Grabski said that Lwów should belong to Poland, as well as petroleum reserves. He finished by saying that public opinion in Poland would never understand and would never reconcile the paradox that Poland, the first to stand up to German aggression, should come out of the war with a loss of some of her territory.

CHURCHILL (ironically): Rien ne peut empêcher la Pologne de déclarer la guerre à la Russie lorsque celle-ci sera dépourvue du soutien des autres Puissances . . . Qu'est ce que c'est l'opinion publique? Le droit d'être ecrasé . . . Je veux sauver la fleur de la nation polonaise . . .

Before leaving Churchill turned sympathetically to Premier Mikołajczyk and, mentioning the Committee of National Liberation, said: "I don't envy you. I took a considerable dislike to them."

That same afternoon Churchill and Mikołajczyk had further discussions.

In answer to a question from Churchill Mikołajczyk informed him that after renewed consideration he could not give his consent to the acceptance of the Curzon Line as a frontier for the reasons expounded several times. The Polish Government could not agree to the loss of nearly half of the Polish territory in the east without hearing the opinion of the Polish people, which was decisive for the Government.

CHURCHILL: You are no Government if you are incapable of taking any decision. You are callous people who want to wreck Europe. I shall leave you to your own troubles. You have no sense of responsibility when you want to abandon your people at home, to whose sufferings you are indifferent. You do not care about the future of Europe, you have only your own miserable selfish interests in mind. I will have to call on the other Poles and this Lublin Government may function very well. It will be the Government. It is a criminal attempt on your part to wreck, by your "Liberum Veto," agreement between the Allies. It is cowardice on your part.

Mikołajczyk suggested that Churchill could present his proposal to Stalin and that the Polish Government would limit its action to a protest. To this Churchill said: "I am not going to worry Mr. Stalin. If you want to conquer Russia we shall leave you to do it. I feel like being in a lunatic asylum. I don't know whether the British Government will continue to recognize you."

Churchill then stated with passion that Great Britain was powerless towards Russia. To Mikołajczyk's statement that the Polish Government must retain the right to defend Poland's interests at the Peace Conference, Churchill replied: "You are not going to be in a better position at the peace conference. I cannot speak for the American Government. The U.S.A. is not represented here. In the last war more Poles fought against us than for us. In this war what is your contribution to the Allied effort? What did you throw into the common pool? You may withdraw your divisions if you like. You are absolutely incapable of facing facts. Never in my life have I seen such people." Next Churchill recalled Anders' words that "after the German defeat we shall beat the Russians" and said with emphasis: "You hate the Russians, I know you hate them."

After learning of Molotov's statement about the Teheran decision on Poland's boundaries, Mikołajczyk wrote the following letter on Oct. 16 to U.S. Ambassador Harriman:

"Mr. Ambassador: I learned with the shock of surprise from Mr. Molotov's statement at the meeting of Oct. 13 that at the Teheran Conference the representatives of all the three Great Powers had definitely agreed that the so-called Curzon Line should be the frontier between Poland and the Soviet Union.

In this connection I should like to recall that during the conversation which I had the honor to have with the President in Washington in June 1944, I was told that only Marshal Stalin and Prime Minister Churchill had agreed on the Curzon Line. In particular, the President indicated that the policy of the U.S. Government was contrary to the settlement of territorial problems before the end of the War. The President said that at the Teheran Conference he had made it clear that he held the view that the Polish-Soviet conflict should not be settled on the basis of the so-called Curzon Line and he assured me that at the appropriate time he would help Poland to retain Lwów, Drohobycz and Tarnopol and to obtain East Prussia, including Koenigsberg and Silesia. On the other hand, the President expressed the view that Marshal Stalin would not give his consent to the return of Wilno to Poland.

I would be most grateful to you, Mr. Ambassador, if you could help to clear this misunderstanding on a subject of such vital importance to Poland."[9]

This letter was never answered.[10]

On Oct. 16, 1944 the British issued a new (fourth) statement on the Polish question, intended to be the agreement arrived at during the Moscow meeting:[11]

"The British and Soviet Governments, upon the conclusion of the discussions at Moscow in Oct. 1944, between themselves and with the Polish Government, have reached the following agreement:

Upon the unconditional surrender of Germany the territory of Poland in the West will include the Free City of Danzig, the regions of East Prussia west and south of Koenigsberg, the Administrative District of Oppeln Silesia and the lands desired by Poland to the east of the line of the Oder. It is further agreed that the possession of these territories shall be guaranteed to Poland by the Soviet and British Governments. It is understood that the Germans in the said regions shall be repatriated to Germany and that all Poles in Germany shall at their wish be repatriated to Poland.

In consideration of the foregoing agreement, the Polish Government accept the Curzon Line as the line of demarcation[12] between Poland and the USSR.

---

[9] U. S. Congress. House. Select Committee on Communist Aggression. Special report. Part on: Polish documents report, p. 134.

[10] U. S. Congress. House. Select Committee on Communist Aggression. Hearings. 10th interim report, p. 29.

[11] Stosunki polskie-sowieckie, 1943–46, p. 315.

[12] During a conference with Churchill on Oct. 16 Stalin demanded that the words "basis for the frontier" be substituted for "line of demarcation."

Separate Soviet-Polish agreements will regulate reciprocal transfer and the repatriation of the population of both countries and the release of persons detained. It is agreed that the necessary measures will be taken for the transfer of all persons of both countries desiring to change their allegiance in accordance with their freely expressed wishes.

It is agreed that a Polish Government of national unity under Prime Minister Mikołajczyk[13] will be set up at once in the territory already liberated by Russian arms.

The Soviet Government take this occasion of reaffirming their unchanging policy of supporting the establishment, within the territorial limits set forth, of a sovereign, independent Poland, free in every way to manage its own affairs, and their intention to make a treaty of durable friendship and mutual aid with the Polish Government which it is understood will be established on an anti-Fascist and democratic basis.

The treaties and relationships existing between Poland and other countries will be unaffected by this settlement, the parties to which declare again their implacable resolve to wage war against the Nazi tyranny until it has surrendered unconditionally."

The Polish delegation would accept the Curzon Line as a "demarcation line" under the condition that Poland would retain Lwów and the petroleum reserves. Also under the condition that the new government would have Mikołajczyk as the premier. But, since the Soviet Government would not agree to these conditions, the Polish Delegation decided to return to London to prepare Polish public opinion for the change in the Polish situation.

But, before leaving, on Oct. 17 Mikołajczyk had a private conversation with B. Bierut, president of the National Council of Poland.[14] From this conversation he learned that the National Council of Poland had already agreed on the Curzon Line as Poland's eastern boundary; that Bierut would not recognize the 1935 Constitution as the basis for a new Polish president but that he insisted on the 1921 Constitution as the legal basis for a new government; and that 75% of the new

[13] During the same conference Stalin demanded that the words "in accordance with the agreement (or understanding) reached between the Polish Government in London and the Polish Committee of National Liberation in Lublin" be substituted for "under Prime Minister Mikołajczyk."

[14] Stosunki polsko-sowieckie, 1943–46, p. 317, et seq.

government should be composed of representatives from the National Council of Poland. In the face of these demands the conversation was terminated.

On Oct. 18, after his talks with Stalin, Premier Mikołajczyk wrote a letter to the U.S. Ambassador Harriman in which he made the following statement on the Polish question:[15]

"After the meeting held on Oct. 13 I have given much thought to the problem discussed with the view to assess the situation in a most objective way. The results can be summed up as follows:

1. At the Teheran Conference decisions were taken as to the change of Poland's eastern frontier without the knowledge and consultation of the Polish Government.

In view of the fact, however, that there exist public pronouncements of the British and U.S. Governments, which are in force inasmuch as public opinion is concerned namely that the British and U.S. Government do not recognize any territorial changes which take place during the war, except changes arrived at with the consent of the parties concerned, it is now expected that the Polish Government or its Premier should—of their own volition—express consent to the decisions of the Teheran Conference.

2. The Soviet Government have brought into being—without consulting the Allied Governments—the Polish Committee of National Liberation which is a "de facto" rival Polish Government. The prerogatives of the Committee, such as the conclusion of international agreements, the emission of banknotes, conscription to the army, the transfer of the population, the decreeing of laws changing the social and economic structure of the country, etc. etc., require some form of legalization.

It is expected that this would be achieved by the fusion of the legitimate Polish Government with the rival Polish Government created by the Soviets.

The Polish Government or its Premier would now have to:

a/ legalize the Soviet Government's unilateral decision of investing Soviet agents with powers of a Polish Government;

b/ approve before world public opinion the "faits accomplis" created by the Soviet agents with powers of a Polish Government;

c/ ratify all activities of the Committee in Poland, including arrests and deportations.

---

15 Ibid, p. 320.

3. By merging with the Committee of National Liberation the Polish Government would have to renounce its own legal basis of existence. Consequently all possibilities of a return to the legal foundations of the Polish State would be wrecked. All ensuing acts would be imposed on the people of Poland in the presence of the Red Army and the N.K.V.D. Thus the Polish Government is expected voluntarily to destroy—after the ratification of the truncation of Poland and the legislation of the Committee—the legal foundations of the Republic and her supreme authorities.

4. Poland would thus lose her eastern lands and, in the remainder of her territory, Poland's independence would be effaced by the rule of agents of the Comintern in Poland.

No effective guarantees to show that the aforesaid course of events will not take place, have been put forward.

On the other hand it is expected from the Polish Government:

a/ to agree to the loss of Poland's eastern provinces;

b/ to legalize the status of the Polish Committee of National Liberation by its merging with the Polish Government and to approve the Committee's unlawful acts;

c/after the legalization of the Committee to destroy the legal foundations of the Polish Republic;

d/ to express consent to the effacement of independence in the remainder of Poland.

In other words, the Polish Government is expected to commit suicide of its own volition.

The present Polish Government and its premier will not be persuaded to do this and are unwilling to play such a role."

Mikołajczyk's last talk with Stalin took place on Oct. 18. At this time Mikołajczyk once again suggested the possibility of a demarcation line.[16]

MIKOŁAJCZYK: In this historic moment I wish to emphasize once again that your generosity and magnanimity, Mr. Marshal, in the matter of frontiers may win the heart of the entire Polish nation. Then Mikołajczyk discussed at length the necessity of not deciding at present the question of Polish frontiers but suggested the concession of fixing the line of demarcation.

STALIN: A demarcation line is not a frontier. I firmly insist on immediate settlement of frontiers which as I said before shall follow the Curzon Line. And this Curzon Line was not invented by us but by the allies at that time. It was approved by the Amer-

---

[16] U. S. Congress. House. Select Committee on Communist Aggression. Special report. Polish documents report, p. 143–145.

icans, French and English who were our enemies at that time. We cannot depart from the Curzon Line. If we would make concessions from that line we would be ashamed of it. Therefore, we cannot do it. These territories were always the object of conflicts and struggles between Poles, White Russians and Ukrainians and this must end once and for all. Whoever wants peace must accept this. In addition, the Polish nation will not object to it. Messrs. Bierut and Osóbka, representatives of the Lublin Committee, declared that this new frontier was just. Finally, the new frontier line will put an end to mistrust between Poles and Ukrainians. Emigres in London oppose this frontier, but I do not consider them as the nation. In addition, these emigres expect the conflict between Russia and England. We need a final frontier.

MIKOŁAJCZYK again defended the integrity of the Polish frontier and discussed at length the question of Eastern Galicia, stressing that this part of the Polish Republic was not included in the Curzon Line, mentioning also that it was not a part of Russia before the 1914 War.

STALIN: [interrupts] But Warsaw was within the boundaries of Czarist Russia.

MIKOŁAJCZYK mentions the statement of Lenin that Poland should rise free and independent.

STALIN: We also share this view.

MIKOŁAJCZYK once again defends Polish frontiers —

STALIN: I repeat once more that I cannot agree. And what would the Ukrainians say to it, who fought so valiantly against the Germans and suffered so many losses. In addition, as you know English and Americans support us in the matter of these frontiers.

MIKOŁAJCZYK: As you know, Mr. Marshal, Polish soldiers from eastern territories of Poland fought valiantly against the Germans and what would be my position should I come to them and tell that they have no home and place to return to.

STALIN: We have already mobilized our citizens in Eastern Galicia and all of them very willingly fought the Germans. Those, however, from among the Ukrainians who cooperated with the Germans were executed as enemies of the United Nations.

MIKOŁAJCZYK: How do you, Mr. Marshal, imagine the future foreign policy of Poland? Poland besides friendly relations with Russia is in alliance agreements with Great Britain and France.

STALIN: Of course, besides friendly relations with Soviet Russia, Poland has to maintain friendly relations not only with Great Britain and France but also with the United States, the Czechs and the Hungarians. The states bordering upon Poland have to live in friendship together, so that if the Germans would provoke an aggression these states would strike at them.

MIKOŁAJCZYK: Will Poland take part in the occupation of Germany together with the Soviet army?

STALIN: If Poland wishes, we will give part of the German territories for occupation.

I wish to emphasize once again that the Polish policy should be independent.

MIKOŁAJCZYK: As you know, Mr. Marshal, Communists are small in numbers in Poland. Then do you think, Mr. Marshal, that the form of government of Poland will not be Communist?

STALIN: Of course not. The form of government of Poland should be democratic. Private ownership system and free private economic enterprise should be preserved. Under the control of the State over capitalism, of course. There are no conditions for the Communist system in Poland.

MIKOŁAJCZYK: If it comes to an understanding in Poland, would it then be possible to count on the friendliness of Russia for the future Polish Government?

STALIN: I do not doubt it.

MIKOŁAJCZYK: After liberation from the Germans the people in Poland will want to live a free life, there will be various political parties, of course, and the views will conflict. There will be a free interchange of thought at last.

STALIN: It will be permitted only up to some limits: for the work over the reconstruction of the state and not for a revolt.

MIKOŁAJCZYK: Do you think, Mr. Marshal, that the members of the National Democratic Party of western Poland whose representatives always wished friendly collaboration with Russia, will be able to work in Poland?

STALIN: We shall admit all who wish to work in the democratic spirit, both those from the left and those from the right. But we shall not admit those who want under these or those pretenses to come for the purpose of making revolution. It would be best to discuss the matter of returning people from London with the Committee. As you know, in the course of this war the composition of political parties has been completely changed; there are new people everywhere, people bound with the struggle against the Germans. It should be taken into account. To avoid misunderstanding, not even one man shall we admit who in this or another way is connected with reactionary elements of Sosnkowski. You should go to Poland, discuss with the Committee and then you will orientate yourself. One thing is sure. Political parties created now in Poland wish sincere and friendly collaboration with Russia and they must have their voice.

MIKOŁAJCZYK underlines the share of Poland in the war against the Germans, great political significance in Poland of four political parties forming the Government in London, and assures Marshal Stalin that as soon as he returns to London he will endeavor to convince his colleagues in the Cabinet about the necessity of arriving at an understanding with Russia; however, he firmly insists upon postponement of the controversial matters relating to the frontiers to a future time.

On Oct. 22 Churchill wired Pres. Roosevelt that Stalin had seen Mikołajczyk and had had an hour and a half's friendly talk with him, during which Stalin promised to help Mikołajczyk form a government friendly to the Russians, making it clear however that the Lublin Poles would have to have a majority in the government.[17]

On Oct. 20 the Polish delegation left Moscow. On Oct. 21 a communique was issued in Moscow[18] *on the results of the meetings, containing the following statement:*

"Important progress was made towards a solution of the Polish question, which was closely discussed between the Soviet and British Governments. They held consultations both with the Prime Minister and Minister for Foreign Affairs of the Polish Government, and with the president of the National Council and Chairman of the Committee of National Liberation at Lublin. These discussions have notably narrowed and dispelled misconceptions. Conversations are continuing on outstanding points."

Among the Polish nationals in Poland, England, U.S. and other countries the news of Mikołajczyk's 2nd visit to Moscow brought forth violent reactions. Mikołajczyk's agreement to a "demarcation line" and to cooperation with the Lublin Committee were looked on as a betrayal of Poland. Especially bitter were the Polish Army fighting in Poland, Italy and France, the Polish Air Force and the Polish Navy. Miko-

---

17 Churchill, W. Op. cit., p. 240.
18 Stosunki polsko-sowieckie, 1943–46, p. 330.

łajczyk himself admitted during a conversation with Churchill on Oct. 26 after his return from Moscow that among Polish political circles in London he had met with even greater opposition than anticipated, particularly on the question of boundaries.[19] *During this conversation, one day before Churchill's talk in the House of Commons*[20] *the British Prime Minister strongly urged Mikołajczyk and his delegation to return to Moscow as soon as possible for further negotiations. He advised to let it be known in Moscow that although the eastern boundary did not meet with Polish approval, nevertheless, since it was proposed by the British and Russian Governments, the Poles would agree to it on the condition that Mikołajczyk could have a majority in the new government, chosen from a list of candidates chosen by Mikołajczyk himself. In case the Russians would not agree to this, Churchill told Mikołajczyk that he could reject the negotiations with the full support of the British Government.*[21]

THE PRIME MINISTER (MR. CHURCHILL): . . . The most urgent and burning question was of course that of Poland, and, here again, I speak words of hope, of hope reinforced by confidence. To abandon hope in this matter would, indeed, be to surrender to despair. In this sphere there are two crucial issues. The first is the question of the eastern frontier of Poland with Russia and the Curzon Line, as it is called, and the new territories to be added to Poland in the North and in the West. That is the first issue. The second is the relation of the Polish Government with the Lublin National Liberation Committee. On these two points, apart from many subsidiary and ancillary points, we held a series of conferences with both parties. We saw them together and we saw them separately, and, of course, we were in constant discussion with the heads of the Soviet Government. I had several very long talks with Marshal Stalin, and the Foreign Secretary was every day working on these and cognate matters with Mon-

19 Ibid, p. 334.
20 See Churchill's statement in House of Commons on Oct. 27, 1944.
21 Stosunki polsko-sowieckie, 1943–46, p. 335.

sieur Molotov. Two or three times we all four met together without anyone else but the interpreters being present.

I wish I could tell the House that we had reached a solution of these problems. It is certainly not for want of trying. I am quite sure however, that we have got a great deal nearer to the solution of both. I hope Monsieur Mikołajczyk will soon return to Moscow, and it will be a great disappointment to all the sincere friends of Poland, if a good arrangement cannot be made which will enable him to form a Polish Government on Polish soil—a Government recognized by all the great Powers concerned, and indeed by all those Governments of the United Nations which now recognize only the Polish Government in London. Although I do not underrate the difficulties which remain, it is a comfort to feel that Britain and Soviet Russia, and I do not doubt the United States, are all firmly agreed in the re-creation of a strong, free, independent, sovereign Poland loyal to the Allies and friendly to her great neighbor and liberator, Russia. Speaking more particularly for His Majesty's Government it is our persevering and constant aim that the Polish people, after their suffering and vicissitudes, shall find in Europe an abiding home and resting place, which, though it may not entirely coincide or correspond with the pre-war frontiers of Poland, will, nevertheless, be adequate for the needs of the Polish nation and not inferior in character and quality, taking the picture as a whole, to what they previously possessed.

These are critical days and it would be a great pity if time were wasted in indecision or in protracted negotiation. If the Polish Government had taken the advice we tended them at the beginning of this year, the additional complication produced by the formation of the Polish National Committee at Lublin would not have arisen, and anything like a prolonged delay in the settlement can only have the effect of increasing the division between Poles in Poland and also of hampering the common action which the Poles, the Russians and the rest of the Allies are taking against Germany. Therefore, as I say, I hope that no time will be lost in continuing these discussions and pressing them to an effective conclusion . . .

MAJOR LLOYD (C.): I have no desire to take up the time of the House, but I would be grateful to the Prime Minister if he could see his way to answer two or three questions, which, in my judgment, very many people in this country would be grateful to have answered. I realize—none better—the extremely delicate nature of the subject of Russo-Polish relations, and I do not want, and I do not think anybody in the House wants, to say one word that could possibly do anything but smooth those relations. Might I ask the Prime Minister if it is still the Government's policy and wish, as previously expressed on several occasions, to defer the decisions on all territorial and boundary questions between Russia and Poland until after the cessation of hostilities? Could he also say whether the British Government are in general sympathy with the desire of the Polish Government for specific and joint guarantees from Great Britain and the other great Powers—Russia and the United States of America—in support of Poland's continued independence and completely sovereign State after the war? I would much appreciate an answer from the Prime Minister, and I assure him that the questions are not asked in any sense of causing awkwardness or controversy.

THE PRIME MINISTER (MR. CHURCHILL): With regard to the first question, we should welcome a solution between the parties themselves, an agreement that would bring the whole matter to the Peace Conference in a form most helpful and favorable to all concerned, and also tide us over the difficult and potentially tragic period through which we are passing. With regard to the guarantee of the three Great Powers, it is certainly to be hoped that the three Great Powers will guarantee the independent sovereign free Poland which will emerge from any arrangment which is made now, and ratified at the Peace Conference. As far as the Soviet Government are concerned, I understand that that will be their fixed intention, and I have not hesitated to say that His Majesty's Government will certainly conform to and themselves join in such a guarantee. It is not for me to speak of the affairs of the United States of America.

6. POLISH ARMY IN ENGLAND. REQUISITIONED BUILDINGS*

SIR R. GOWER (C.) asked the Secretary of State for War how many buildings in London are used or occupied by the Polish Forces; and whether any supervision is exercised over the requisitioning by Allied Governments or troops of premises used and occupied by British organizations for the direct or indirect purposes of the war.

THE SECRETARY OF THE STATE FOR WAR (SIR J. GRIGG): The number of buildings requisitioned by the War Department and now occupied or used by the Polish Forces in London is 26, including seven garages. No Allied Governments or troops are empowered to carry out any requisitioning of buildings, and any such requisitioning required is effected by the British Department or Ministry concerned.

7. LUBLIN COMMITTEE NEWSPAPER IN LONDON**

MR. ASTOR (C.) asked the Minister of Information whether he will investigate the circumstances in which a newspaper has been started in London in support of the Lublin Committee in spite of the assurances given that no paper would be made available for such a purpose.

THE MINISTER OF INFORMATION (MR. BRACKEN): No license has been granted for the publication of such a newspaper and no paper has been made available. The attention of the authorities administering the Control of Paper Orders

* House of Commons. Vol. 404, Nov. 9, 1944, p. 1553–1554.
** House of Commons. Vol. 404, Nov. 15, 1944, p. 1968–1969.

has been called to the publication of one issue of a paper entitled "Democratic Poland."

MR. ASTOR: Does that mean that no further copies of this paper will be published?

MR. BRACKEN: I hope so, because, if a second copy is published, the editor lays himself open to proceedings.

8. POLISH ARMY IN ENGLAND—CITIZENSHIP PROBLEMS*

MR. HAMMERSLEY (C.) asked the Secretary of State for the Home Department whether favorable consideration will be given to Polish officers anxious to acquire British nationality, who have served with the R.A.F. for over three years; and if necessary will legislation be introduced.

THE SECRETARY OF STATE FOR THE HOME DEPARTMENT (MR. H. MORRISON): While I share my hon. Friend's appreciation of the services rendered to the Allied cause by these officers, there are numerous other aliens who are giving notable assistance to the war effort of the United Nations both in the Armed Forces and in civilian occupations, and I know of no ground on which I would be justified in selecting for differential treatment the particular group of foreigners to whom the Question refers. The second part of the Question does not therefore arise.

9. POLAND AND THE SOVIETS**

VISCOUNT SAMUEL (L.): . . . With regard to conditions in the Allied countries, I would only make reference to one of our Allies, to Poland. We are all distressed to see the great difficulty in establishing a political union there. As I said on

* House of Commons. Vol. 404, Nov. 15, 1944, p. 1973.

** House of Lords. Vo. 134, Nov. 29, 1944, p. 28 (Address in reply to His Majesty's speech).

a previous occasion in this House, the history of the last 200 years has shown that a strong and independent Poland cannot live unless Poland makes friends either with Germany or with Russia. It cannot survive with hostile peoples to the east and to the west, and as in present circumstances it is out of the question that it can be reconciled and establish an abiding friendship with Germany, it is essential for their own security and safety that, even at the cost of great sacrifices, Poland should reconcile herself with her great neighbor on the east. That is, I believe, the conviction of people in this country, and it is to be hoped that that course may be found practicable.

10. ENGLAND AND POLAND*

Debate on November 30, 1944.

CAPTAIN DUNCAN (C.): As one who has served in two wars, and is therefore most anxious to avoid any further wars in my lifetime or the lifetime of our children, I regard the second sentence in the Gracious Speech from the Throne as the most important. Without peace we can do nothing, and unless we can get a satisfactory solution all measures of national insurance or anything else will fall by the way. The sentence is:

> "They now look forward with greater confidence than ever before to those final victories which will give to the peoples of the world the just peace which is our chief desire."

The words "just peace" are absolutely the correct words in this connection. I do not want today, because there will be many opportunities later, to deal with the future set-up of Europe, and the war is not over yet. I do not want, as the hon. Member for North-East Bethnal Green (Mr. Chater) did, to refer to Dumbarton Oaks, but as he has done so, I would

---

* House of Commons. Vol. 406, Nov. 30, Dec. 1, 1944, p. 159–160, 278–279 (Debate on King's Speech).

just say that no form of international peace, international arrangement or international organization can be successful unless it is based on the good will and good faith of the nations concerned. The Dumbarton Oaks proposal suggests a Security Council of the Great Powers, but the Great Powers themselves have to have the will, and to continue to have the will, and, above all, the ability to enforce their will, and nothing set up in the form of an organization can succeed unless the Big Powers in the world have the will to peace and the will to enforce it.

I want to deal with this matter in a slightly different way. Foreign Affairs—and this is a trite remark—are British interests abroad. What are the British interests? I believe, broadly speaking, British interests abroad, at any rate as far as Europe is concerned, are the interests of Europe itself. There is no conflict, because we want nothing from Europe except peace, between British interests in Europe and the interests of Europe. The first want is obviously a just peace, an unassailable peace, as is also mentioned in the Gracious Speech. But that must mean that the people who agree to this peace must really agree to it and that it must be, more or less at any rate, by consent, and the people for whom the peace is made must be, more or less, content with the settlements that are made.

Let us take one or two countries in Europe today and see if contentment and consent are really covered. I know that there is to be a further Debate on Poland and I will not labor the question now, but let me mention Poland in passing. Whatever settlement is come to in Poland it must be obvious from hon. Members' conversations with Poles in this country, from letters in the Press and the general knowledge of what the Poles are feeling in the Fighting Forces and elsewhere, that unless the Poles are given a reasonably decent peace they will never be content with a peace imposed either by the Lublin Committee or by Russia. It would not, in the long run, be in the interests of Russia herself to have a peace which is imposed and which creates such discontent among the Polish people abroad and Polish people in Poland that it may well be a festering sore in that part of Europe for the future...

* * *

Debate on December 1, 1944.

MR. HYND (Lab.): ... I would refer to the peculiar change in the attitude of the Government and political circles generally to our own Ally Poland during the last two or three months. We find the Poles, who after all played such a tremendous part in the Battle of Britain, and formed such a considerable portion of those few to whom so many owed so much, those Poles for whom we understood we went to war in the first instance, who were defending a mighty tradition of independence and democracy and national integrity, are now being toned down, and in our Press and political circles those great emotions which inspired them to put up a tremendous stand against the Nazi menace are now becoming a romantic conception, which they really should be prepared to lay aside and see the realities of politics and the realities of dependence on neighboring Governments. These modifications of policy are a historic development in war circumstances and post-war circumstances, and must obviously give rise to considerable disquiet.

11. RESIGNATION OF THE MIKOŁAJCZYK GOVERNMENT*

AFTER STUDYING THE RESULTS *of the Moscow Conference*[1] *the Polish Government decided to ask Great Britain and the U.S.A. some questions—with the idea that the answers received would form the basis for definitive decisions on Soviet demands for a revision of Poland's eastern boundaries, and on the calling up of a new government in Poland.*

* House of Commons. Vol. 406, Dec. 15, 1944, p. 1478-1578.
[1] See No. 5.

On Oct. 26 Premier Mikołajczyk sent the following communication to Pres. Roosevelt[2]*:*

"Mr. President: From Ambassador Harriman you undoubtedly know the pressure being exercised on the Polish Government definitely to accept at present and without reservations the so-called Curzon Line as the basis of the future frontier between Poland and Soviet Russia. In all my political activities I have proved how fully I realize the necessity of Polish-Soviet understanding and how sincerely I desire to achieve it, not only in the interest of my own country, but also in that of the common cause of the United Nations and of future peace.

I am no less convinced, however, that the Polish nation would feel itself terribly deceived and wronged if, as the response to all its sacrifices, to its indomitable attitude, and its uninterrupted part in the fight in the course of this war it were faced as a result with the loss of nearly one-half of its territory on which are situated great centres of its national and cultural life and considerable economic values. The Polish Government cannot give its agreement to such a solution, as it realizes that it would thereby lose the confidence and following of its nation to such an extent that this would close its way to the exploration of possibilities of reaching understanding with the Government of the USSR in other fields. It would in fact deprive the activities of the Polish Government of practical value.

In the course of the Moscow conversations I have applied all my best efforts to convince Marshal Stalin and Premier Churchill of the importance of the above considerations. In particular I stressed that it would constitute a great conciliatory and amicable gesture on the part of Russia towards Poland—a gesture which would be regarded as such by the Polish people and make it easier for the Polish nation to reconcile itself with the other already so great territorial sacrifices demanded of it, if the City of Lwów and the East Galicia oilfields were left with Poland in accordance with the so-called Line "B". This line would not infringe on the principle of the Curzon Line, as the latter did not formally extend through East Galicia.

However, my endeavors in this direction have hitherto remained unsuccessful. I cannot, in the face of my great responsibility, regard these endeavors as exhausted as long as you, Mr. President, have not expressed your stand in this matter. I retain in vivid and grateful memory your assurances given me

---

2 Yalta Papers, p. 207.

in the course of our conversations in June, last, in Washington, pertaining particularly to Lwów and the adjacent territories. The memory of these assurances has not been dispelled even by Mr Molotov's onesided version about your attitude in Teheran, which he gave me during the last conversations in Moscow. I have no doubt that in your attitude, Mr. President, purely objective arguments have played the most important part. It is known that for the last six hundred years Lwów has been a Polish city no less than Cracow and Warsaw, and one of the sources of Polish civilization. On the other hand, the production of the East Galicia oil fields, so important to the economic system of Poland, constitutes barely one per cent of the oil production of the USSR.

I fully realize how deeply absorbed you are in your duties at this time and in the course of the next days. I believe, however, that in the face of the great importance of the decisions facing the Polish Government, which will bear on the entire future of the Polish Nation, and in a great measure on world relations as a whole, you will not refuse, Mr. President, my fervent prayer once more to throw the weight of your decisive influence and authority on the scales of events.

I am firmly convinced that if you, Mr. President, will consider it possible immediately to address a personal message to Marshal Stalin, pointing out that it is of consequence to you that the Polish question should be settled in such a way that the City of Lwów and the oil field basin of East Galicia should be left in Poland—such a demarche, as forseen by you, would have chances to being effective.

By removing from the way the chief and basic difference of opinions in the present negotiations between the Polish and the Soviet Governments,—such a demarche would render possible the achievment of an over-all Polish-Soviet understanding and would bring to you, Mr. President, not only a new title to the warm gratitude of the Polish people, but likewise an age long merit of having solved one of the capital difficulties on the way of collaboration of the United Nations and the future peace of Europe and the world.

I place in your hands, Mr. President, this matter with the greatest confidence and I shall await your decision."

On Oct. 31 Minister of Foreign Affairs Romer, while talking with British Permanent Under-Secretary to the Foreign Office, Sir Alexander Cadogan, asked the British Government for replies to three questions pertaining to Poland's future.

On Nov. 2 Sir Alexander Cadogan delivered to the Polish Government this reply:[3]

"I duly reported to the Prime Minister the conversation which I had with Your Excellency and the Polish Ambassador on Oct. 31, in the course of which you put me three questions for the consideration of His Majesty's Government.

The Prime Minister, after consultation with the Cabinet, has now directed me to give you the following replies.

You asked in the first place whether, even in the event of the United States Government finding themselves unable to agree to the changes in the Western frontier of Poland foreshadowed in the recent conversations in Moscow, His Majesty's Government would still advocate these changes at the Peace Settlement. The answer of His Majesty's Government to this question is the affirmative.

Secondly, you enquired whether His Majesty's Government were definitely in favor of advancing the Polish frontier up to the line of the Oder, to include the port of Stettin. The answer is that His Majesty's Government do consider that Poland should have the right to extend her territory to this extent.

Finally, you enquired whether His Majesty's Government would guarantee the independence and integrity of the new Poland. To this the answer is that His Majesty's Government are prepared to give such a guarantee jointly with the Soviet Government. If the United States Government could see their way to join also, that would plainly be of the greatest advantage, though His Majesty's Government would not make this a condition of their own guarantee in conjunction with that of the Soviet Government. This Anglo-Soviet guarantee would, in the view of His Majesty's Government, remain valid until effectively merged in the general guarantee which it is hoped may be afforded by the projected world organization.

With regard to what you said in regard to anticipated difficulties in the way of negotations in Moscow for a reformation of the Polish Government, the Prime Minister observes that the success of these negotiations must depend on a solution of the frontier question. It is impossible to ignore the possibility that agreement might be reached on the frontier question and that it might nevertheless prove impossible to reach agreement on the other matter. That would of course be most unfortunate, but the Polish Government would be in a much better position if negotiations broke down on this point, on which they would have the

---

3 Stosunki polsko-sowieckie, 1943–46, p. 355.

support of His Majesty's Government and probably of the United States Government, than on the frontier question."

In the meantime, on Oct. 30 and Nov. 2, there were two meetings of the Polish Council of Ministers at which two courses of action were discussed: 1) to give in to Russia as urged by the British Government—this course was supported by Premier Mikołajczyk; and, 2) to stand fast on the integrality of Polish lands, professing that Poland cannot capitulate to Soviet demands, even though these demands are supported by the British Government. In spite of the fact that the British Government pressed for Mikołajczyk to go quickly to Moscow to negotiate a settlement of the Polish problem, several of the ministers felt that they should wait for an answer from the American Government—an answer delayed in coming because of presidential elections in the U.S.A. They did not want to rush so quickly into a decision which was so fraught with the possibility of Poland's losing her independence.

On Nov. 2 this dramatic and tragic conversation took place between Mikołajczyk and Churchill:[4]

CHURCHILL: How long it is since you gentlemen returned from Moscow? About two weeks ago?

ROMER specifies October 22nd.

MIKOŁAJCZYK: That is correct. Time is pressing and the problem before us is enormous.

CHURCHILL: Delay in deciding threatens that the friendly atmosphere created in Moscow will vanish.

MIKOŁAJCZYK: My Cabinet has demanded, that in a matter so important to us, we consult the American Government. He reads the preliminary reply received today from Pres. Roosevelt, who indicates that he will soon send a more factual reply.

CHURCHILL: What practical value has it at present? Will the Polish-Americans vote against Pres. Roosevelt?

MIKOŁAJCZYK: There is no fear of that.

CHURCHILL: That is good.

MIKOŁAJCZYK: We are concerned, however, with the main-

[4] U. S. Congress. House. Select Committee on Communist Aggression. Special report, pt. 4: Polish documents report, p. 149–155.

taining of Poland's independence, and unfortunately our concern is not without grounds.

CHURCHILL: It would be better if the negotiations broke down on this very point, in which you may count on our standing by you. In the matter of the eastern frontier we cannot support you.

MIKOŁAJCZYK; If we were to agree to the territorial demands made, our Polish people would blame us that we had sold out our independence.

CHURCHILL: If you had followed our counsel in January and accepted the Curzon Line, today you would not have had in Lublin those horrible Lublin Poles!

MIKOŁAJCZYK: The most recent examples of Soviet behavior in Iran and Rumania are not encouraging.

CHURCHILL: You had better attend to your own affairs. In the case of Rumania, it is another matter, since it concerns recent satellites of Germany, who had provoked Russia. In Greece we have a good chance to take control of the situation. But what is our attitude to be towards the Polish Government, who cannot decide to say yes or no? It would be better therefore if you state clearly that you will never agree to a solution which will not give Lwów to Poland. I will then wash my hands of you! You have really reached the limit!

MIKOŁAJCZYK: This is a misunderstanding. Together with the Minister of Foreign Affairs, we endeavour to influence the Government in this spirit to devote due attention to all arguments. I admit that we are meeting with very strong reservations when it comes to the solution proposed in Moscow. One can hardly be surprised. Why is Poland, alone among the United Nations, to bear territorial sacrifices, and so soon?

CHURCHILL: [restraining his impatience]: All right, then. Let the Lublin Poles continue to hold leadership of Polish affairs in their hands, since you do not want to take it away from them. Dirty, filthy brutes, Quisling Poles will be at the head of your country! You may continue to sit here, but Russia will not want to talk with you any more. After all, it concerns the third world power! On my part, I did what I could, I explained to Stalin and convinced him of the need of an understanding with Poland. Today you could again be in Moscow close to success; instead, you sit here perplexed. I am very sorry.

MIKOŁAJCZYK: The difficulty is that even despite our consent, the independence of Poland is not secured.

CHURCHILL: Surely you can say that you recognize the

Curzon Line on condition that the independence of Poland shall be respected and guaranteed in the agreement. If this condition should not be possible of realization and the negotiations break down on that, you will not be bound in the matter of frontiers and us, as also, surely, the Americans, you will have behind you.

MIKOŁAJCZYK: In the circles of Ambassador Lebiedew, unfounded rumors are being spread among Poles that the Soviets await the arrival in Moscow this time, not members of the Polish Government, but a delegation sent by it for the purpose of further negotiation on basis of Soviet territorial concessions, which reach to the east of the Curzon Line. This is a maneuver calculated to obstruct an agreement being reached in Polish circles. In order to frustrate it, I instructed the reply that we are ready at any moment to dispatch such a delegation, should we receive the assurance that the subject of conversations with it in Moscow will be Polish territories to the east of the Curzon Line.

CHURCHILL: That is absurd, pure Utopia! Don't you remember my laborious attempt with Stalin to make it possible for the visit to Moscow for you gentlemen? At present your endeavours will evaporate into thin air; you will lose control over the further development of events. I shall have to tell Stalin that the Polish Government cannot make up its mind. You are returning to the old tradition of Liberum Veto. As far as I am concerned, I shall stop at that and will not follow you. What will be, under those conditions, Poland's prospects for the future? Think only of the terrible massacre which awaits your underground movement!

MIKOŁAJCZYK: I have quoted to you in confidence the manoeuver attributed to the Russians and my reaction to it, which goes to prove that I am not falling for rumours and which has as its purpose only the unmasking of a diversion.

CHURCHILL: You yourself know best what Stalin wants and thinks. Unless you give me an answer by to-day or to-morrow, I shall consider everything finished. Take into consideration what awaits you? I have done everything I could. I shall explain before Parliament. There is indeed no Polish Government, if it is unable to decide anything. I know the view of Mr. Mikołajczyk and Mr. Romer, but what of that, when they are unable to put them into effect. Meantime, the Lublin Poles are active and despite all, gain in their significance.

MIKOŁAJCZYK: I cannot persuade my colleagues of the necessity to accept the heavy conditions made, without proper guarantees. The reply of the British Government to our inquiries which was transmitted to us in the letter from Cadogan, constitute in that respect not so much assistance as obstacle, because it constitutes a step backward in comparison with the stand formulated in Moscow.

CHURCHILL: You say that our letter is an obstacle? Please consider it, therefore, as cancelled of this moment. I withdraw our propositions.

RACZYNSKI attempts to explain the misunderstanding, but CHURCHILL does not let him finish and himself continues further: I have enough of it! On leaving Moscow, you had mentioned the possibility that your stay in London may not be for more than 48 hours before the negotiations are renewed. To-day, after two weeks have passed, you have made no progress whatsoever. You are all able to bargain only about one thing: the Curzon Line. Already in January you had rejected it and here now are the consequences of this step. Do you think perhaps that the Russian armies have once and for all stopped where they are now, and are unable to move on any further?

MIKOŁAJCZYK: Not at all! On the contrary, we anticipate the further advance of the Soviet armies and this is taken into account in our instructions sent by us to Poland.

CHURCHILL: The result of your attitude, Gentlemen, shall be the unavoidable creation in Poland of a rival Government. I don't condemn you, but you are a confused man, who is incapable of saying either yes or no. To us, it will be a relief not to feel bound by anything. I have told Stalin in Moscow, that in the new Polish Government I don't allow the ratio of strength 75 percent to 25 percent in favor of the Committee and I demand at least 50 percent to 50 percent.

MIKOŁAJCZYK: Enormous and extremely difficult things are demanded from us. After all, it concerns the transfer into the sphere of the new regions of Poland of five to six millions of Poles and to remove from them seven million Germans.

CHURCHILL: The main thing is that you find yourself in Lublin as soon as possible. Otherwise regrettable events will take place there, which are not to be mended.

CADOGAN: Was our reply of any use to you, Gentlemen?

MIKOŁAJCZYK explains the difference which occurred in the formulation in Cadogan's letter to Romer of the Polish first question and the effect thereof on the reply. He points out also the small value for Poles of a joint British-Soviet guarantee for the safeguard of the independence and territorial integrity of Poland.

CADOGAN: Perhaps I had not precisely formulated the question which Minister Romer has put to me verbally. This is my fault. As to the joint guarantee, I admit that in the event of aggression by Russia on Poland, the British guarantee does not come into play. But in that case a Soviet aggression would be however a clear violation of international obligations by Russia That alone is already some security.

CHURCHILL: How can you wait helplesly, as if you were paralyzed? You are playing delaying tactics, by posing to us still other new questions, we give ourselves a lot of trouble to reply to them—and I don't hide from you that it has not come to me easy to convince my colleagues on the necessity of giving you satisfaction—and as a result, you pose to us still further questions, because it is all the same to you. I have enough of that and I withdraw my promises.

Here follow a discussion and mutual explanation concerning the particular points of questions and answers; it is conducted in a somewhat chaotic manner by all present, and does not lead to any goal. It only becomes clear from it, that Churchill does not have much of an idea of the legal intricacies of Cadogan's letter and apparently is not familiar with its exact formulation. He stresses only that all Polish questions were submitted for consideration by the British Cabinet, as a result of which to each of these questions he personally made a pencilled reply in the affirmative.

CHURCHILL: If you don't leave tomorrow evening for Moscow, I shall consider everything as finished and shall telegraph Stalin about it. I withdraw our letters containing guarantees. You have brought it about that the Committee of National Liberation exists.

MIKOŁAJCZYK: I cannot agree with that. When Sikorski was at the Kremlin, the very same day the Union of Polish Patriots was constituted, out of which afterwards emerged the Committee of National Liberation. And during my trip to Moscow the Soviet Government hastened to sign an agreement with that Committee. Where is the good will here?

CHURCHILL: Only for you, only in the interest of Poland, I went personally to Moscow. But you care only about your "Liberum Veto," and your extraordinary habits, thanks to which one of the most valiant nations in Europe has in the past fallen into slavery. If you had really wanted to co-operate with Stalin, you could have by now been in Poland in the company of the British and American Ambassadors.

MIKOŁAJCZYK: Only because I have not ceased to contemplate it, have we not yet said: No, although everything induces us to do so.

CHURCHILL repeats once again, the comparison so often used by him, of the losses which Poland would have to accept in the east with the much greater benefits, which the change of frontiers in the west would bring her.

MIKOŁAJCZYK: Among all the countries, not excluding Germany, Poland after this war is to suffer the greatest territorial sacrifices. How is that to be explained?

CHURCHILL: What did you Gentlemen accomplish in these two weeks? What did you return to London for? The Soviet Government intimates to us now that it will not sit at a joint table with the Polish Government at any international conferences and that it shall demand at them a place for the representatives of the Lublin Committee. Step after step you will be liquidated, this you will rightly not escape. Have the courage to say: No! I shall repeat it to Stalin.

MIKOŁAJCZYK: You know well, that I did everything to bring about an understanding with Russia and have done so with no little risk.

CADOGAN: I am only an humble official and would not wish to exceed my competence by interfering in the discussion. Yet I am concerned to establish what we may communicate to Stalin, because since the Moscow Conference we did not make any remarks to him, even one word on Polish matters, despite their importance and urgency. If we are therefore to avoid a fundamental change of atmosphere, which would necessarily reflect also on the British-Soviet relations, then we must inform him without further delay of the situation. Are we to tell the Russians that the Polish Government cannot agree to the Curzon Line?

MIKOŁAJCZYK: At that moment, no.

CHURCHILL: Are you prepared to leave tomorrow evening for Moscow?

MIKOŁAJCZYK: No, I could not do it.

CHURCHILL: And the day after tomorrow?

MIKOŁAJCZYK: I am not certain of receiving within that set time the Polish Government's decision. You will understand that we are concerned with the independence of Poland and this is no small matter in the present state of affairs.

CHURCHILL: This is a matter of your understanding with Bierut. I give you 48 hours' time. In the absence of your reply within that time, I shall telegraph to Stalin and let come what may.

MIKOŁAJCZYK: The attitude of the British Government does not help to a make a decision easier.

CHURCHILL: I shall be glad to withdraw our guarantees given to you.

CADOGAN: We gave in their connection more than we usually give. I shall not betray a secret by pointing out that Prime Minister Churchill had yesterday serious difficulties to force through the resolution in that matter at a meeting of the War Cabinet.

CHURCHILL: If your attitude is negative, then have the courage to say so. I shall not hesitate to stand up against you. Two whole weeks you fruitlessly wasted in continuous debates without any results! Where does it lead? Today I am telling you for the last time. After tonight I shall not speak to you any more!

MIKOŁAJCZYK: Perhaps the same fate awaits me as Maniu,[5] but never mind that!

CADOGAN: Can you give Stalin any indication, suggest anything, because in the event of your silence the last chance of agreement will vanish.

CHURCHILL: You have not moved one inch!

MIKOŁAJCZYK refers to the position of Pres. Roosevelt in the Polish question and to the basic divergence between his definition during his own conversations with the President which he had with him in June in Washington and the interpretation given by Molotov at the Moscow Conference. It is a matter of primary importance to us, which requires clearing up before we undertake a final decision.

CHURCHILL: I had already said I shall still wait 48 hours. A further delay would threaten with incalculable consequences. Again a new campaign of hate shall be set loose by Lublin.

MIKOŁAJCZYK reads the last reports from Poland, which inform of the terrible conditions in which disarmed soldiers of the Home Army are held imprisoned near Siedlce.

CHURCHILL: Only your presence in Poland may bring an end to these horrors.

MIKOŁAJCZYK: If you leave to me only 48 hours and if I am not to have opportunity to await the American reply to our questions, then I warn you that the answer which you will receive

---

[5] Maniu, Juliu, Rumanian politician, head of Rumanian Peasant Party. He as liberal opposed King Carol and dictatorship of gen. Antonescu. After the communists came into power in Rumania he was denounced as reactionary, afterwards arrested and sentenced for life (Nov. 1947), reported dead in prison (1951).

shall be negative. I am quite certain that if you yourself were a Pole you would not act otherwise.

CHURCHILL: I never shirk before a decision nor before responsibility.

MIKOŁAJCZYK: The attitude of America is the more important to us, for, in accordance with your own remarks which I heard in Moscow, on America will depend the material aid with which we are unable to dispense, having to deal with resettlements on such vast scale and the subsequent rebuilding of economies. For after the sacrifices suffered by Poland she will have to pay also for that herself? out of what?

CHURCHILL again reminds of the last demand of the Soviet Government, that at international Conferences in which it is to participate, not the Polish Government will be seated, but the Lublin Committee, on behalf of Poland. This is most embarrassing in connection with the London Conference on inland communications.

ROMER reminds that Poles find ourselves in that respect in company with Swiss and Portuguese "Fascists", as is evident from the absence of Russia at the International Conference of Civilian Airlines in the United States.

CADOGAN explains that with regard to the London Conference mentioned by Churchill, the Foreign Office had made reservations against the attitude taken by the Soviet Government, so that probably this matter shall not for the time being have any unpleasant repercussions.

CHURCHILL: Notwithstanding, the Poles continue to have a hostile attitude towards the Soviet. Was it not madness to appoint after Sosnkowski, Bor, if one was concerned to improve the Polish-Soviet relations?

MIKOŁAJCZYK: After Sosnkowski was removed, the Soviets attacked Bor; when he was taken prisoner by the Germans, Pres. Raczkiewicz is being attacked. Tomorrow the attacks shall be directed against me or whoever replaces me.

CHURCHILL: I like Anders as a valiant soldier, but I remember what he told me: Today we fight the Germans, tomorrow we shall fight the Russians. But this is an aberration! Don't count on us to help you in that. Do you realize how very much your standing has deteriorated in the world since the beginning of this year?

MIKOŁAJCZYK: In the moral sense, not!

CHURCHILL: I am withdrawing my guarantees contained in Cadogan's letter, since you are unable to give me a reply.

CADOGAN: Perhaps Prime Minister Churchill shall agree not to do it yet, because we have learned from Premier Mikołajczyk that he unfortunately received my letter too late to be able to submit it to the Council of Ministers today, consequently the Polish Government had no opportunity whatsoever to become acquainted with the matter. Will it take place tomorrow?

MIKOŁAJCZYK: Yes, I shall call for that purpose a special meeting.

In conclusion of the discussion it was mentioned also on the Polish side, as proof of the existing enormous difficulties the fact that Stalin deleted from the text of the British proposal the name of Premier Mikołajczyk as the chief of the future Polish Government in Poland; also the ratio of strength in this Government, which under the present conditions even with a 50-50 proportion, to which the Lublin Committee does not agree, gives no possibility of governing. The British side explains in the first matter that Stalin gave to Churchill verbal assurance, that he accepts and will honor Mikołajczyk as candidate, and in the second matter that it shall remain a problem for negotiations in Moscow and Lublin, to guarantee a sufficient and permanent majority in the future Government, following Premier Mikołajczyk's idea. If this will not be possible to carry out, an understanding, and together with it, a Polish consent to the Curzon Line, shall not come about, and the whole thing will fall apart on a point on which the Polish Government will be able to count for a continuous support of the British Government, as opposed to the matter of the Polish frontiers in the east.

Under pressure of the Churchill ultimatum, the Polish Council of Ministers on Nov. 3 prepared this resolution:[6]

"The preliminary condition for a Polish-Soviet understanding placed before the Polish Government at the Moscow Conference was the demand for an immediate recognition of the so-called Curzon Line as the basis of the Polish-Soviet frontier.

Seeing that—apart from considerations of a fundamental and formally legal nature—the Polish Government would have to accept immediately and definitely a new Polish frontier without waiting for the end of the war and for the peace conference,

that on the other hand the final delimitation and ratification of the new frontier of Poland in the West and in the North is to take place in the Peace Settlement,

that the independence, sovereignty and territorial integrity

---

[6] Stosunki polsko-sowieckie, 1943–46, p. 369.

of Poland within her new frontiers cannot be under present conditions fully and lastingly guaranteed by the Principal United Nations,

that the Government of the United States has not yet been able to define its attitude towards these questions,

the Polish Government, though fully appreciating the urgent necessity of a Polish-Soviet understanding which they warmly desire and for the attainment of which they will spare no effort, do not find it possible to agree to the conditions placed before them at the conference in Moscow and venture to request that in the near future these matters be reconsidered anew by the three Principal United Nations together with the Polish Government."

During the course of these discussions, Churchill once again assured Stalin of his intention to uphold the decisions reached with regard to Poland's western boundaries. On Nov. 5, 1944 he telegraphed Stalin:[7]

". . . I take this opportunity of assuring you that I stand exactly where we parted and that His Majesty's Government will support at any armistice or peace conference the Soviet claims to the line we have agreed upon. . . ."

On Nov. 7 Pres. Roosevelt was re-elected for a fourth term. On Nov. 17 he wrote a letter to Premier Mikołajczyk—this letter was handed to Mikołajczyk in London by U.S. Ambassador to Moscow Averell Harrimann on Nov. 22, and contained this text:[8]

"I have constantly in mind the problems you are facing in your endeavors to bring about an equitable and permanent solution of the Polish-Soviet difficulties and particularly the questions which you raised in your message of Oct. 26.

While I would have preferred to postpone the entire question of this Government's attitude until the general postwar settlement in Europe, I fully realize your urgent desire to receive some indication of the position of the United States Government with the least possible delay. Therefore I am giving below in broad outline the general position of this Government in the hope that it may be of some assistance to you in your difficult task.

---

7 Correspondence . . . vol. I, no. 344, p. 267.
8 Stosunki polsko-sowieckie, 1943–46, p. 382.

The United States Government stand unequivocal'y for a strong, free and independent Polish State with the untrammeled right of the Polish people to order their internal existence as they see fit.

In regard to the future frontiers of Poland, if a mutual agreement on this subject, including the proposed compensation for Poland from Germany, is reached between the Polish, Soviet and British Governments, this Government would offer no objection. In so far as the United States guarantee of any specific frontiers is concerned I am sure you will understand that this Government, in accordance with its traditional policy, cannot give a guarantee for any specific frontiers.

If the Polish Government and people desire in connection with the new frontiers of the Polish State to bring about the transfer to and from the territory of Poland of national minorities, the United States Government will raise no objection and as far as practicable will facilitate such transfer.

The United States Government is prepared, subject to legislative authority, to assist in so far as practicable in the postwar economic reconstruction of the Polish State."

The text of this letter was immediately studied by the Polish Council of Ministers. There was a conflict of opinion within the Council. Members of the Polish Socialist Party, National Democratic Party, and the Christian Democratic Party were against any concessions which would extend beyond the principles set forth in the Polish memorandum of Aug. 29, 1944.[9] *Mikołajczyk, for his part, felt that it was necessary to agree to the terms of the British Government since rejection of these terms might be followed by difficulties for Poland, difficulties which in the end might mean the authority of the Polish Government in London might be reduced to a minimum.*

Finding himself in a minority Mikołajczyk handed in his resignation to Pres. Raczkiewicz on Nov. 24. Jan Kwapiński, a member of the Polish Socialist Party was asked to form a cabinet. He was not successful, and Tomasz Arciszewski, newly arrived from Poland and a highly esteemed member of the Polish Socialist Party, formed Nov. 29 a government.

Though the Polish Peasant Party (of which Mikołajczyk

[9] See No. 3.

was a member) was not in the cabinet, the party nevertheless promised to support the new government and issued this declaration:[10]

"The Peasant Party declares its support of the legal Polish Government in its arduous struggle in defense of the interests of Poland and of the Polish people. The Peasant Party is temporarily unable to take part in the Government but will make every effort and continue to work toward the rebuilding of a strong, free, independent, and truly democratic Poland, which is the highest aim, desire and hope of all Poles."

The British Government did not like the idea of a new Polish Government. During a talk with Mikołajczyk on Nov. 27 Eden said that this change of government must be looked on as a change in Polish policy towards Russia and under these conditions it was necessary to anticipate that the new Polish Government would not enjoy the same confidence and cooperation of the British Government enjoyed by the Mikołajczyk Government. Eden further stated that there would have to be a change in the special diplomatic privileges accorded to the preceding Polish Government—privileges which were the result of personal confidence in Gen. Sikorski and Premier Mikołajczyk; one of these diplomatic privileges was the use of their own code in contacting the Polish underground fighting the German invaders. Eden did not want to interfere in the internal affairs of the Polish Government and agreed that the new government would have British recognition; but he also felt that this new turn of events played into the hands of the Lublin Committee and would undoubtedly be exploited by the Soviet Government and its Polish accomplices. According to Eden the British Government could not be expected to have personal confidence in the new government and transfer to it the friendship and faith it had in the Mikołajczyk Government. He said that he would send instructions to the British Ambassador in Moscow to make every effort there to maintain things on a peaceful plane and not allow the situation to become inflamed by new events and polemics.[11]

---

10 Polish Facts & Figures, no. 14, p. 2.
11 Stosunki polsko-sowieckie, 1943–46, p. 388.

On the following day Prime Minister Churchill, in saying goodby to Mikołajczyk reaffirmed Eden's opinions.[12] *He said that on the British side Polish statehood would naturally not be questioned and the new government would receive the normal diplomatic privileges which were enjoyed by foreign governments in London; but this relationship would not enjoy the personal confidence and special privileges which were formerly bestowed on Gen. Sikorski and later on Mr. Mikołajczyk; this would be clearly expressed to the representatives of the new Polish Government if they called, though they might not call at all, realizing that they did not stand on the same political ground as the British.*

Churchill informed Stalin of the above in a dispatch dated Dec. 3,[13] *stating that*

> "... The desire of His Majesty's Government for the reconstitution of a strong and independent Poland, friendly to Russia, remains unalterable. We have practical matters to handle with the Polish Government, and more especially the control of the considerable Polish armed forces, over 80,000 excellent fighting men, under our operational command. These are now making an appreciable contribution to the United Nations' war effort in Italy, Holland and elsewhere. Our attitude towards any new Polish Government must therefore be correct, though it will certainly be cold. We cannot of course have the same close relations of confidence with such a government as we have had with Mr. Mikołajczyk or with his predecessor, the late General Sikorski, and we shall do all in our power to ensure that its activities do not endanger the unity between the Allies."

Churchill then predicted that a newly created Polish government would not last long and that for that reason Mikołajczyk would return to power, with even greater prestige. In ending, Churchill begged Stalin to use his influence on the "Poles in Lublin" with respect to this matter.

Stalin's dispatch of Dec. 8[14] *took quite an opposite stand, indicating that Mikołajczyk could not be of any help in solving any Polish problems.*

---

12 Ibid, p. 391.
13 Correspondence . . . vol. 1, no. 362, p. 279.
14 Ibid. no. 367, p. 282.

"It has become obvious since my last meeting with Mr. Mikołajczyk in Moscow that he is incapable of helping a Polish settlement. Indeed, his negative role has been revealed. It is now evident that his negotiations with the Polish National Committee are designed to cover up those who, behind his back, engaged in criminal terror acts against Soviet officers and Soviet people generally on Polish territory. We cannot tolerate this state of affairs. We cannot tolerate terrorists, instigated by the Polish émigrés, assassinating our people in Poland and waging a criminal struggle against the Soviet forces liberating Poland. We look on these people as allies of our common enemy, and as to their radio correspondence with Mr. Mikołajczyk, which we found on émigré agents arrested on Polish territory, it not only exposes their treacherous designs, it also casts a shadow on Mr. Mikołajczyk and his men.

Ministerial changes in the émigré Government no longer deserve serious attention. For these elements, who have lost touch with the national soil and have no contact with their people, are merely marking time. Meanwhile the Polish Committee of National Liberation has made substantial progress in consolidating its national, democratic organizations on Polish soil, in implementing a land reform in favor of the peasants and in expanding its armed forces, and enjoys great prestige among the population.

I think that our task now is to support the National Committee in Lublin and all who want to cooperate and are capable of cooperating with it. This is particularly important to the Allies in view of the need for accelerating the defeat of the Germans."

In Poland and among Poles in exile the Arciszewski Government met with general approval. Poles, the same as Churchill, understood that a new policy had come into being as a result of Soviet demands for Polish submission. They felt that the Soviet demands constituted a new partition of Poland—a partition requiring the approval of a legal Polish Government, the same as the Polish partitions of the 18th century. Mikołajczyk had been ready to give this approval. Arciszewski was against it. Thus, Arciszewski represented the opinion of the majority of the Poles in Poland and in exile all over the world, as well as the Polish Armed Forces. The esteemed Polish journalist, Ignacy Matuszewski, expressed the attitude of the Polish people towards the Arciszewski Government thus:

"The Arciszewski Government is taking on a terrible burden:

the bequest of ignominious obligations, inherited from lawless pronouncements. It will have to follow a long and steep path to return to earlier days when Poland, discussed with England, as an equal, the future of Europe. Poles can praise and blame this government—that is their right. But, praising or blaming, criticizing or approving, they will bestow on it their most valuable gift: they will believe in it. They will believe and trust that the government is fighting for the same aims as they—that it wants what they want: a free and whole Poland, independent and strong. They will have faith that this government will not surrender."[15]

THE PRIME MINISTER (MR. CHURCHILL): In opening this Debate I find myself in a position to read to the House again some extracts from the carefully considered statements that I made to them in February, after I had returned from Teheran, and also in October, of the present year. I rely upon those statements, and when I read them over again last night in preparation for this Debate I found it very difficult to improve upon them or alter them in any way. This may accuse me of infertility of mind, but it also gives me some confidence that I have not misled the House or felt myself stultified, in all respects at any rate, by the harsh and unforeseeable movement of events. It is not often that one wishes to repeat what one said two months ago, and still less 10 months ago, but I propose to do so, because in no other way and in no other words that I can remind the House of and bring home to them the grim, bare bones of the Polish problem.

On 22nd February, I said:*

"At Teheran I took occasion to raise personally with Marshal Stalin the question of the future of Poland and I pointed out that it was in fulfilment of our guarantee to Poland that Great Britain declared war upon Nazi Germany and that we had never weakened in our resolve, even in the period when we were all alone, and that the fate of the Polish nation holds a prime place in the thoughts and policies of His Majesty's Government and of the British Parliament. It was with great pleasure that I heard from Marshal Stalin that he, too, was resolved upon the creation and maintenance of a strong, integral, independent Poland as one of

[15] Matuszewski, I. Wybór Pism, p. 256. (also printed in "Nowy Świat", New York, Dec. 2, 1944).

* Vol. II, No. 54.

the leading Powers in Europe. He has several times repeated these declarations in public and I am convinced that they represent the settled policy of the Soviet Union. Here I may remind the House that we ourselves have never in the past guaranteed, on behalf of His Majesty's Government, any particular frontier line to Poland. We did not approve of the Polish occupation of Vilna in 1920. The British view in 1919 stands expressed in the so-called Curzon Line which attempted to deal, at any rate partially, with the problem. I have always held the opinion that all questions of territorial settlement and re-adjustment should stand over until the end of the war and that the victorious Powers should then arrive at formal and final agreements governing the articulation of Europe as a whole. That is still the wish of His Majesty's Government. However, the advance of the Russian Armies into Polish regions in which the Polish underground army is active makes it indispensable that some kind of friendly working agreement should be arrived at to govern the war-time conditions and to enable all anti-Hitlerite forces to work together with the greatest advantage against the common foe.

"During the last few weeks"—

I may remind the House that I was speaking on 22nd February—

"the Foreign Secretary and I together have labored with the Polish Government in London with the object of establishing a working arrangement upon which the Fighting Forces can act, and upon which, I trust, an increasing structure of good will and comradeship may be built between Russians and Poles. I have an intense sympathy with the Poles, that heroic race whose national spirit centuries of misfortune cannot quench, but I also have sympathy with the Russian standpoint. Twice in our lifetime Russia has been violently assaulted by Germany. Many millions of Russians have been slain and vast tracts of Russian soil devastated as a result of repeated German aggression. Russia has the right of reassurance against future attacks from the West, and we are going all the way with her to see that she gets it, not only by the might of her arms but by the approval and assent of the United Nations. The liberation of Poland may presently be achieved by the Russian Armies after these Armies have suffered millions of casualties in breaking the German military machine. I cannot feel that the Russian demand for a reassurance about her Western frontiers goes beyond limits of what is reasonable or just. Marshal Stalin and I also spoke and agreed upon the need for Poland to obtain compensation at the expense of

Germany both in the north and in the west."—[*Official Report*, 22nd February, 1944; Vol. 397, c. 698].

I said that nearly a year ago. I have nothing to alter in it from the point of view of His Majesty's Government. On 27th October, more recently, I reported upon my last visit to Moscow and I said:*

"The most urgent and burning question was of course that of Poland, and here again, I speak words of hope, of hope reinforced by confidence."

I am afraid this does not hold in the same degree at the present time.

"To abandon hope in this matter would indeed be to surrender to despair. In this sphere there are two crucial issues. The first is the question of the Eastern frontier of Poland with Russia and the Curzon Line, as it is called, and the new territories to be added to Poland in the north and in the west. That is the first issue. The second is the relation of the Polish Government with the Lublin National Liberation Committee. On these two points, apart from many subsidiary and ancillary points, we held a series of conferences with both parties. . . .

I wish I could tell the House that we had reached a solution of these problems. It is certainly not for want of trying. I am quite sure, however, that we have got a great deal nearer to the solution of both."

—I say that this part is subject to some review in the light of events—

"I hope Mr. Mikołajczyk will soon return to Moscow, and it will be a great disappointment to all the sincere friends of Poland, if a good arrangement cannot be made which will enable him to form a Polish Government on Polish soil—a Government recognized by all the great Powers concerned, and indeed by all those Governments of the United Nations which now recognize only the Polish Government in London. Although I do not underrate the difficulties which remain, it is a comfort to feel that Britain and Soviet Russia, and I do not doubt the United States, are all firmly agreed in the re-creation of a strong, free, independent, sovereign Poland loyal to the Allies and friendly to her great neighbor and liberator, Russia. Speaking more particularly

* See No. 5.

for His Majesty's Government it is our persevering and constant aim that the Polish people, after their suffering and vicissitudes, shall find in Europe an abiding home and resting place, which, though it may not entirely coincide or correspond with the pre-war frontiers of Poland, will nevertheless be adequate for the needs of the Polish nation and not inferior in character and quality, taking the picture as a whole, to what they previously possessed.

These are critical days and it would be a great pity if time were wasted in indecision or in protracted negotiation. If the Polish Government had taken the advice we tended them at the beginning of this year, the additional complication produced by the formation of the Polish National Committee of Liberation at Lublin would not have arisen, and anything like a prolonged delay in the settlement can only have the effect of increasing the division between Poles in Poland and also of hampering the common action which the Poles, the Russians and the rest of the Allies are taking against Germany. Therefore, as I say, I hope that no time will be lost in continuing these discussions and pressing them to an effective conclusion."—[*Official Report*, 27th October, 1944; Vol. 404, c. 494-5.].

The hopes which I thought it proper, and indeed necessary, to express in October, have faded. When Mr. Mikołajczyk left Moscow my hope was that he would return within a week or so with the authority of the Polish Government in London to agree about the Polish frontiers on the basis of the Curzon Line and its prolongation to the Southward called "the Curzon Line A," which comprises, on the Russian side, the city of Lvov. I have several times drawn Mr. Mikołajczyk's attention to the dangers of delay. Had he been able to return after the very friendly conversations which passed between him and Marshal Stalin, and also the conversations which he had with the Lublin National Liberation Committee; had he been able to return, with the assent of his colleagues, I believe that the difficulties inherent in the forming of a Polish Government in harmony with the Lublin Committee, might well have been overcome. In that case he would be at this moment at the head of a Polish Government, on Polish soil, recognized by all the United Nations, and awaiting the advance of the Russian Armies moving farther into Poland as the country was delivered from the Germans. He would also be assured in his task of the friendship and help of Marshal Stalin. Thus he could at every stage have established a good relationship between the Polish underground movement and the advancing Russians, and a Polish Administration would have been set up by him in the newly delivered regions as they expanded.

I have the greatest respect for M. Mikołajczyk, and for his able colleagues who joined us at Moscow, Mr. Romer and Mr. Grabski. I am sure they are more qualified to fill the place of the late General Sikorski than any other of the Polish leaders. After endless discussions, into some of which we were drawn, on Mr. Mikołajczyk's return from Moscow the Poles utterly failed to obtain agreement. In consequence, on 24th November, Mr. Mikołajczyk, Mr. Romer and a number of other Polish Ministers resigned from the Polish Government, which has been almost entirely reconstituted in a form which in some respects I certainly am not able to applaud. Mr. Mikołajczyk and his friends remain, in the view of His Majesty's Government, the only light which burns for Poland in the immediate future.

Just as I said that if the Polish Government had agreed, in the early part of this year, upon the frontier there never would have been any Lublin Committee to which Soviet Russia had committed herself, so I now say that if Mr. Mikołajczyk could swiftly have returned to Moscow early in November, as he hoped and expected to do, with the power to conclude an agreement on the frontier line, Poland might now have taken her full place in the ranks of the nations contending against Germany, and would have had the full support and friendship of Marshal Stalin and the Soviet Government. That opportunity, too, has been, for the time being, suspended. This prospect has vanished like the last. One is reminded of the story of the Sybilline books, in which on every occasion the price remained the same and the number of volumes decreased, until at last they had to be bought on the most unfavorable terms. Mr. Mikołajczyk's ordeal has been a most severe and painful one. Torn between the love of his country and the intense desire to reach a settlement with her mighty neighbor, which was most abhorrent to many of his fellow-countrymen, confronted with the obstinate and inflexible resistance of his London colleages, whose veto was like the former Liberum Veto, which played so great a part in the ruin of Poland, with these circumstances around him, Mr. Mikołajczyk decided to resign. Almost a month has passed since then, and now I imagine that the prospects of a reconciliation between the Polish Government and the Lublin Committee, with the Soviet Government behind them, have definitely receded; although they might perhaps advance again were Mr. Mikołajczyk able to speak with authority for the fortunes of the Polish nation.

The consequences of this rescission of hopes of a working agreement between Russia and the Poles have been masked to British eyes by the fact that the Russian Armies on the long Vistula front have been motionless, but when they move forward, as move forward they surely will, and the Germans are expelled from large new tracts of Poland, the area administered by the Lublin Committee will grow, and its contacts with the Soviet Government will become more intimate and strong. I do not know what misfortunes will attend such a development. The absence of an agreement may well be grievous for Poland, and the relationship and misunderstandings between the advancing Russian Armies and the Polish underground movement may take forms which will be most painful to all who have the permanent well-being of Poland and her relationship with Russia at heart. The fact that a Prime Minister resigns and that a new Government is formed does not, of course, affect the formal diplomatic relationship between States. We still recognize the Polish Government in London as the Government of Poland, as we have done since they reached our shores in the early part of this war. This course has been continued up to the present by all the rest of the United Nations, excepting only Russia which is the Power most concerned and the Power whose Armies will first enter the heart of Poland. It is a source of grief to me that all these forces could not have been joined together more speedily against the common foe.

I cannot accept the view that the arrangements which have to be proposed about the frontiers of the new Poland are not solid and satisfactory, or that they would not give to Poland that "abiding home" of which I spoke to the House in February. If Poland concedes Lvov and the surrounding regions in the South, on the line known as Curzon Line A, which my right hon. Friend the Foreign Secretary will deal with in more detail later on in the Debate—if Poland makes this concession and these lands are joined to the Ukraine, she will gain in the North the whole of East Prussia West and South of the fortress of Koenigsberg, including the great city and port of Danzig, one of the most magnificent cities and harbors in the whole of the world, famous for centuries as a great gathering place of the trade of the Baltic, and, indeed, of the world. This will be hers instead of the threatened and artificial Corridor, which was built so laboriously after the last war, and Poland will stretch broadly along the Baltic on a front of over 200 miles. The Poles are free, so far as Russia and Great Britain are concerned, to extend their territory, at the expense of Germany, to the West. I do not propose to go into exact details, but the extensions which will be supported by Britain and Russia, bound together as they are by the 20 years' Alliance, are of high importance. Thus, they gain in the West and the North territories more important and more highly developed than they lose in the East. We hear that a third of Poland is to be conceded, but I must mention that that third includes the vast track of the Pripet Marshes, a most desolate region, which, though it swells the acreage, does not add to the wealth of those who own it.

Thus I have set before the House what is, in outline, the offer which the Russians, on whom the main burden of liberation still falls, make to the Polish people. I cannot believe that such an offer should be rejected by Poland. It would, of course, have to be accompanied by the disentanglement of populations in the East and in the North. The transference of several millions of people would have to be effected from the East to the West or North, as well as the expulsion of the Germans—because that is what is proposed: the total expulsion of the Germans—from the area to be acquired by Poland in the West and the North. For expulsion is the method which, so far as we have been able to see, will be the most satisfactory and lasting. There will be no mixture of populations to cause endless trouble, as has been the case in Alsace-Lorraine. A clean sweep will be made. I am not alarmed by the prospect of the disentanglement of populations, nor even by these large transferences, which are more possible in modern conditions than they ever were before.

The disentanglement of populations which took place between Greece and Turkey after the last war—my noble Friend opposite may remember—was in many ways a success, and has produced friendly relations between Greece and Turkey ever since. That disentanglement, which at first seemed impossible of achievement, and about which it was said that it would strip Turkish life in Anatolia of so many necessary services, and that the extra population could never be assimilated or sustained by Greece having regard to its own area and population—I say that disentanglement solved problems which had before been the causes of immense friction, of wars and of rumours of wars. Nor do I see why there should not be room in Germany for the German populations of East Prussia and of the other territories I have mentioned. After all, 6,000,000 or 7,000,000 Germans have been killed already in this frightful war, into which they did not hesitate, for a second time in a generation, to plunge all Europe. At the present time, we are told that they have 10,000,000 or 12,000,000 prisoners or foreigners used as slaves in Germany, who will, we hope, be restored to their own homes and lands when victory is gained. Moreover, we must expect that many more Germans will be killed in the fighting which will occupy the spring and summer and which we must expect will involve the largest and fiercest battles yet fought in this war.

When these ideas, which arose at the Teheran Conference,

were first foreshadowed by me to the House, the British and American Armies had not landed on the Continent. France was not liberated. She was powerless, not like now when she is rising with great rapidity to a strong and fine position among the nations of the world. The Armies of General Eisenhower did not stand along the Rhine when these matters were discussed. They were still gathering in this island, not along the Rhine, where they are now growing in strength as the waves of American manhood cross the Atlantic and take their places in the crusade and in the line of battle. Nor had the Russians advanced to the Vistula; vast distances separated them even from the frontiers of Poland. Nor was one large German army cut off in Courland, the peninsula which has Memel and Libau at its base. Nor was there that great position which the Russian Armies held in the extreme North, with their right hand, nor was their left hand reaching out beyond Budapest in the South, threatening an advance into the very heart of Austria. Nor had Rome been occupied, nor the Apennines pierced.

In those days, the Poles might well have had some show of reason in asking whether the great Allies would have the power, even if they were so minded, to deliver the new territories to Poland which were to compensate her for what she was giving up in the East, but the situation has changed vastly in favor of the Allies, and it seems to me extremely unlikely that, after the spring and summer campaigns have been fought, if it be necessary to go so far in the business—and we shall go whatever distance is necessary to complete our object—it seems extremely unlikely that the evil and hateful forces in Germany, who plotted, planned and began this war, will have the power to resist the decisions of a peace or armistice conference, at which the principal victorious Powers will be assembled. The prospects of final victory have, in the time that has passed since these matters were first discussed at Teheran, become for the Allies solid and spacious. Therefore, as I say, it has always been said by the Poles, when I have been discussing the matter with them here, "We know what we have to give up; what certainty have we of receiving compensation in other quarters?" They have much more certainty of it now than at this time last year. In fact, I cannot see any doubt whatever that the Great Powers, if they agree, can effect the transference of population.

I find great difficulty in discussing these matters, because the attitude of the United States has not been defined with the precision which His Majesty's Government have thought it wise to use. The friendship of the United States Government for Poland, no less than our own, the large mass of Poles who have made their homes in the United States, and are, or are becoming, American citizens, the constitutional difficulties of the United States in making treaties and foreign agreements of every kind—all these have not enabled the Government of that great nation to speak in the terms which I have thought it my duty, with the assent of my colleagues, to use in this House. We know, however, that the Government and people of the United States have set their hearts upon a world organization to prevent the outbreak of future wars, and that this world organization will be fatally ruptured by a quarrel between any of the three most powerful Empires which compose the Grand Alliance of the United Nations. The President is aware of everything that has passed and of all that is in the minds both of the Russians and of the British. He had, at Moscow, in Mr. Averell Harriman, the U.S. Ambassador, a most accomplished representative, who in the capacity of observer was present at all, or nearly all, of our Polish talks on the occasion of our last visit. The President has, therefore, been kept fully informed, not only by His Majesty's Government, but also by his own highly competent and distinguished representatives, and by all the many sources and channels that are open to the unceasing vigilance of the State Department.

I am particularly careful not ever to pretend to speak in the name of any other Power unless so directed beforehand, and I hope the House will make allowances for the care with which I pick my words upon this point. All I can say is that

I have received no formal disagreement in all these long months upon the way in which the future of Poland seems to be shaping itself—or is being shaped—but no doubt when the time comes the United States will make their own pronouncement on these matters, bearing in mind, as they will, the practical aspect which they assume and also that failure on the part of the three greatest Powers to work together would damage all our hopes for a future structure, a world government which, whatever else it may fail to do, will at any rate be equipped with all the powers necessary to prevent the outbreak of further war.

It is asked, Why cannot all questions of territorial changes be left over till the end of the war? I think that is a most pertinent question and it is, in fact, the answer which I and the Foreign Secretary gave in almost every case that has been presented to us. Well, Sir, I understand the argument. The armies, it is said, may move here and there, their front may advance or recede, this country or that may be in occupation of this space of ground or the other, but it is at the peace table alone that permanent destiny of any land or people will be decided. Why cannot that be said in this case? It can be said in every case, or almost every case, except in that of Poland. So why should Poland be excepted from this general rule? It is only for Polish advantage and to avoid great evils which might occur. The Russian Armies—I know nothing of their intentions, I am speaking only of what is obvious to anyone who studies the war map—will probably, during the early part of next year, traverse large areas of Poland, driving the Germans before them. If, during those marches, fierce quarrels and fighting break out between large sections of the Polish population and the Russian troops, very great suffering—which can still be avoided—will infallibly occur, and new poisoned wounds will be inflicted upon those who must dwell side by side in peace, confidence and good neighborliness if the tranquility of Europe is to be assured or the smooth working of the world organization for the maintenance of peace is to be created and maintained.

All these matters are among the most serious which could possibly be examined as far as our present lights allow. Our British principle has been enunciated that, as I have said, all territorial changes must await the conference at the peace table after the victory has been won, but to that principle there is one exception, and that exception is, changes mutually agreed. It must not be forgotten that in the Atlantic Charter is I think inserted the exception that there should be no changes before the peace table except those mutually agreed. I am absolutly convinced that it is in the profound future interest of the Polish nation that they should reach agreement with the Soviet Government about their disputed frontiers in the East before the march of the Russian Armies through the main part of Poland takes place. That is the great gift they have to make to Russia, a settlement now at this time which gives the firm title of mutual agreement to what might otherwise be disputed at the Peace Conference. I must, however, say, because I am most anxious the House should understand the whole position, speaking on behalf of His Majesty's Government in a way which I believe would probably be held binding by our successors, that at the Conference we shall adhere to the lines which I am now unfolding to the House, and shall not hesitate to proclaim that the Russians are justly treated, and rightly treated, in being granted the claim they make to the Eastern frontiers along the Curzon Line as described.

The Foreign Secretary and I have labored for many months, we have spared no labor of travel, no risk of political rebuff and consequent censure, in our effort to bring about that good understanding between the Poland whom we still recognize and the mighty Ally which has so heavily smitten the German military power. We have never weakened in any way in our resolve that Poland shall be restored and stand erect as a sovereign, independent nation, free to model her social institutions or any other institutions in any way her people choose, provided, I must say, that these are not on Fascist lines, and provided that Poland stands loyally as a barrier and friend of Russia against German aggression from the West. And in this task, of course, Poland will be aided to the full by a Russian and British guarantee and assistance and will also, I cannot doubt, though I cannot declare, be aided by the United States acting at least through the world organization which we are determined to erect—that she and the whole of the United Nations are determined to erect—for the salvation of mankind toiling here below from the horrors of repeated war.

Another great war, especially an ideological war, fought as it would be not only on frontiers but in the heart of every land with weapons far more destructive than men have yet wielded, would spell the doom, perhaps for many centuries, of such civilization as we have been able to erect since history began to be written. It is that peril which, according to the best judgment of this National Government of all parties, which has so lately renewed its troth to stand together for the duration of the war against Germany—it is that peril that we have labored and are striving sincerely and faithfully to ward off. Other powerful States are with us on each side, more powerful States perhaps even than the British Empire and Commonwealth of Nations. We can only try our best, and if we cannot solve the problem we can at least make sure that it is faced in all its sombre magnitude while time remains.

I have spoken of fading hopes and of disappointment at the failure to reach a Russo-Polish Agreement, but there has been another disappointment. It has been impossible to arrange any meeting of the three Great Powers. We had good grounds for believing that we might have met before Christmas. Indeed, I confidently expected that we should, but so far, however, although the prospect is earnestly looked forward to, nothing definite has been settled. Therefore, the strong, authoritative, if provisional decisions which are now required, not only on the Russo-Polish question, but on a host of vital matters, political, international, military and economic, apart from such progress as can be made by correspondence and individual visits, stand at the bar and wait. There ought to be a meeting at least of the three great Powers at the earliest possible moment. So far as I and my right hon. Friend the Foreign Secretary are concerned, we can only repeat what has been said so often, that we will proceed to any place at any time, under any conditions, where we can meet the heads of our two chief Allies, and we should welcome, above all, a meeting in this island, a meeting in Great Britain, which has waged war from the very outset and has risked, without flinching, national annihilation in the cause of freedom.

MR. PRICE (Lab.): The Prime Minister has spoken with a frankness for which I am sure the House will be grateful, and for which all those who, in a much humbler way, have been trying to bring about a reconciliation between Russia and Poland will be especially grateful. His vast knowledge of the issues involved in the maintenance of international peace after this war, his knowledge of those conditions which are dependent upon the maintenance of an alliance between the three great Powers and, subsidiary to that, good Russo-Polish relations, are matters which we know he holds very dearly, as does everyone in the House who thinks about them. I feel very deeply the tragedy of the situation that has arisen between Russia and Poland, and I do not want to say anything which will make that situation worse. I also hope that hon. Members below the Gangway, on the opposite side of the House, who, I know, have many friends in Poland, and who espouse the Polish cause, will also say nothing which will make the situation worse.

But it is as well occasionally to speak a little frankly, as the Prime Minister has rightly done today. In regard to the meeting of the three great Powers, to which he referred in his closing remarks, I hope that the Prime Minister will not risk his health in going abroad again, as he did last year. I hope that it will be possible to induce Marshal Stalin, or some nominee of his, to come out of Russia and meet, if possible, in this country. When we last discussed the Russo-Polish situation in September we hoped that the elements in Poland friendly to Russia would be able to bring about a reconciliation on these important matters. But, alas, I fear that the spirit of Piłsudski still broods over the Council Chamber of the Polish Government in London. There are two great national characteristics which the Poles have; the first is unexampled bravery, and the second is complete inability to get out of the world of make-believe in which they love to live. It was their undoing in the 18th century, and it led to the partition which bedevilled European politics for over a century. This is the world of make-believe in which some Poles, I do not say all, are living today. They think they can perpetuate that highly artificial and quite temporary predominance, both military and diplomatic, which they enjoyed in Eastern Europe between the two wars. At that time Russia was passing through her "troublous time," as she has done before in her past history, and was weak, but now, of course, that period has passed and Russia has become once more, as she has been in the past, a great military power in Europe. A whole system of French Alliances after the last war was built up on the assumption that Russia did not count, and that Poland and Czechoslovakia were the lynch pin of the system which was then built up. That system collapsed with Munich, but I fear that some Poles still do not realize that fact. They still think that Russia can be kept back in the East and remain a weak Power, and that the Polish Eastern frontier can stretch far towards the Eastern Baltic and the Black Sea.

Moreover, I am very much afraid that there are those in the Polish Government in London who think they can utilize two possible factors to attain their ends. They hope to mobilize Roman Catholic opinion throughout the world, and to obtain the diplomatic support of the Vatican, but, more serious than that, they are stipulating on a possible development of friction between ourselves and Russia, and between the United States and Russia. I think it is time to speak a little bluntly. Our patience in this country is not altogether inexhaustible. We have been treated for years to cataracts of propaganda from Polish sources, printed on paper the like of which we have not seen since the beginning of the war for our own use, much of which has tried to create the impression that, although Germany may be the enemy now, Russia will be the enemy in the future. It is argued that these frontier questions ought to be put off until after the war. I think the Prime Minister has answered that very well today. If it is possible to bring about agreement by consent there is nothing to prevent it. Moreover, what reason is there why there should not be agreement on the Eastern frontier question? The Curzon Line, if looked at from the point of view of the racial and religious aggregations of population in that area, is obviously the soundest and most commonsense line. I know it is argued that people in those disputed territories do not speak Russian. I knew those territories well during the last war, and I know that the population there do not speak Great Russian but speak White Russian and Ukrainian. They certainly do not speak Polish, or only a minority do; and as for their religious persuasion, they are Greek Orthodox, with a minority in the Uniate church, which accepts the Eastern liturgy and the authority of the Pope, but these are only a minority and are mainly Eastern Galicians. I happen to be one of the few, I think perhaps the only Englishman, except Sir Bernard Pares, who is now in America, who was with the Russian Army during the last war when they occupied Eastern Galicia, when General Brusiloff defeated the Austrians at the battle of Rawa Ruska and very soon after came into Lvov. There is no question that Lvov is mainly a Polish town—I am quite prepared to grant that—and on this particular matter I should like to see the Russians give way and compromise, provided the Poles recognize themselves that the people in the rural area round there are Ukrainian to a man and that Russia is entitled to a frontier across the Carpathians adjacent with Czechoslovakia.*

---

* In Lwów among 312,000 inhabitants there are 200,000 Poles, 75,000 Jews and 24,000 Ukrainians. In the district of Lwów, excluding the town itself, the Polish population is 56.9 per cent. Also in 8 other districts of South-Eastern Poland east of the river San the Polish population is 50–60 per cent.: Przemyśl 53.2, Mościska 46, Sanok 59.8, Prze-

There, I think, is a basis of compromise. I have reason to think the Russians might be reasonable on this provided they knew that they had a Polish Government friendly to Russia to deal with, but unfortunately they still do not think they have. I know that there are elements in Poland who have been trying, sincerely I think, to bring about an understanding. Such is the Polish Socialist Party and the party to which I belong are in close contact with it, but unfortunately they are so hag-ridden by fears of Communism, seeing a Communist round every corner, that their judgment is, I am afraid, far too often deflected by those fears. Then, of course, there is the Peasant Party of Mr. Mikołajczyk, for whom everyone has the greatest respect, and I think that is the party which is more inclined to and ready to make a settlement than any other. Moreover, they have hitherto shown great interest in and desire for agrarian reforms in Poland, which have gone on in a desultory manner for the last 20 years but are still far from complete. Indeed, it is a tragedy that the internal conditions in Poland have helped to make the international situation more and more difficult. There is no question that Poland was ripe for big agrarian reforms, as Russia was ripe for them and got those reforms in her revolution. Russia went very far, but in Poland they hardly went any distance at all. Under the so-called Nieśwież Agreement Piłsudski came to an understanding with the big landlords which partially suspended agrarian reforms, but meanwhile the big landlords got increased subsidies and tariffs. But the Polish peasants remained in the most povery-stricken conditions. I understand that 64 per cent of the Polish peasants have no more than 12

---

myślany 58.3, Kamionka Strumiłowa 51.1, Tarnopol 66.4, Trembowla 60.9, Zbaraż 50 per cent. In 12 other districts, the Polish population is somewhere near 50 per cent.: Lubaczów 49.8, Rudki 48.4, Sambor 44.5, Drohobycz 47.2, Brzeżany 47.1, Podhajce 48.8, Zborów 47.8, Złoczów 47.9, Buczacz 43.7, Czortków 43.7, Kopyczynce 43.7, Borszczów 45.8 per cent. In the remaining districts the Polish peasant population is between 20 and 30 per cent. Generally speaking in this part of the country between San and Zbrucz apart from Lwów there are over 2 million Poles and less than 3 million Ukrainians. (St. Stronski, "Two Examples" in Glasgow Courier, No. 1/331, 14th January 1945, p. 3, 7.)

acres.[1] Between the wars only a little more than 2,000,000 hectares were distributed to those peasants, which is a mere faction of what the Lublin Commitee are now proposing to give them.[2]

The Lublin Committee have set themselves up in the occupied part of Poland and are apparently preparing to be the Polish Government. I want to be frank and say that I do not consider them to be fully representative. They represent a very important element, certainly, but not everybody, and it would be the wise thing, if it were possible, to get other elements to join them. If the Lublin Government is not fully representative in its personalities, by its actions, at least, it shows itself very representative of the age-long desires of the Polish peasants and that is the thing to remember. The agrarian reforms which the Lublin Committee are proposing and are going some way to carry into effect meet this demand of the Polish peasants. Moreover, according to all the information which comes to me, it is a falsehood to say that they are indiscriminately collectivizing the land there. Of that there is no evidence at all; the peasants are having their existing holdings increased. It seems to be a perennial tragedy that the Poles throughout their history have had their great reforms carried out by foreigners. That is not generally known. For instance, chattel slavery in Poland was abolished by Napoleon and by the Emperor of Austria and the King of Prussia, and it was the Russian Tsar Alexander II who emancipated the serfs, who in 1864 were a very large part of the population of what is now Poland.[3] The Poles themselves fought heroically in the great rebellion of 1863 for a freedom which they could not give themselves. That is the tragedy with Po-

---

[1] In 1921. In Sweden, 55.4% (1932). In Germany, 53.5% (1933).

[2] 2,640,000 hectares were parcelled among 734,000 small farmers. In 1939, 81.5% of all arable land was in small holdings (up to 125 acres), and only 15% was in large holdings. (Polish Facts &Figures, No. 9, p. 6).

[3] This is not correct. The Polish Constitution of May 3, 1791 guaranteed peasants legal protection, though it did not abolish serfdom. The manifesto of Tadeusz Kosciuszko (May 7, 1794) gave peasants their freedom.

land, and the same thing applies today. It is the Lublin Committee which, under Russian influence, I fear, is doing what the Poles ought to be doing themselves.

What is to be done? The Polish Government in London is, I believe, fast losing its hold on the situation in Poland. It may still have a romantic appeal for those Poles who are in exile, but it cannot live on that. I do not know what Mr. Mikołajczyk and his Peasant Party intend to do, but I feel that unless he comes to some terms with the Lublin Committee he will very soon "miss the bus." In that case what will be the use of our continuing to recognize the Polish Government in London? The withdrawal of our recognition of the Polish Government in London is not a step which we could contemplate with any pleasure, having regard to the gallant units of the Polish Army and other Forces that are fighting over here; but the sands are running out. It looks as if we are witnessing once more a Polish tragedy, because the Poles are a people, it seems, who are capable only of grasping a shadow and losing a substance.

MR. RAIKES (C.): It is not a pleasant task to be obliged on this occasion to take an entirely divergent line from that taken by the Prime Minister. I feel bound to say openly that I believe—and that is why I am speaking—that the whole future peace of the world depends beyond all else upon a freely negotiated agreement between Poland and Russia. I use the words "freely negotiated" and I underline them. I have listened to the speech of my right hon. Friend the Prime Minister. What is the picture before us today? We are faced with a Poland which has been devastated by years of war, a Poland which we guaranteed—though not its exact frontiers—in 1939, a Poland that is asked today to hand away practically half her territory, territory which was agreed to by Russia herself under the Treaty of Riga, first in 1920 and then again in the 1930s. I could not help wondering while the Prime Minister was speaking what would have been said if, during the great deays of 1940, when Britain stood alone with her honor untarnished, the one hope of civilization in the world, any hon. or right hon. Member had got up and said, "Of course the guarantee of Poland does not mean more than that when Poland regains her liberty she will have at least half of her former area." I wonder what the people of this country would have said at that time, when Polish airmen, almost alone among those of the nations of the world, were dying by the side of our men in the Battle of Britain, when Polish troops, alone of any troops in the world at that time, were fighting beside us on every battle front.

MR. WOODBURN (Lab.): I agree that it would be desirable to have an agreement, but if people will not agree to give up anything there cannot be agreements. If two parties want to get agreement each must give up something—[HON. MEMBERS: "Each"]—but the hon. Member has gone further and said that in 1939 we guaranteed Poland, and that no hon. Members in this House doubted whether we had the ability to enforce that guarantee.

MR. RAIKES: I was referring to the fact that it was obvious in 1939 that Poland, although guaranteed, would be overrun, but I challenge the hon. Member or anybody else to say that it was not the view of practically everybody in this country that by challenging the might of the aggressor Poland, though at first defeated, would be restored to her former greatness after an Allied victory. What was the position of Moscow? The Prime Minister dealt very sketchily with the Moscow conversations, and I propose, therefore, to go into them in a little more detail, because it is just as well to know how these romantic Poles feel who are accused of demanding the impossible. Mr. Mikołajczyk, for whom I have the highest admiration, went to Moscow under great difficulties. There was the background of Eastern Poland, already occupied by Russian troops, the background of Eastern Poland already being treated as Russian territory without any agreement, mutual or otherwise.

It was with that background that Mr. Mikołajczyk went to Moscow. What are the terms—the Foreign Secretary will correct me if I make any mis-statement of facts, which is the las thing I should desire or intend to do. First, we understand that the Polish Government were told categorically that they had to give up all territories East of the Curzon Line, and that at once—at once. There was no question of a demarcation line until hostilities were over, but those territories were to be given up at once. Those territories included 33 per cent of the Polish population and 47 per cent of the pre-war territory of Poland. It was rather a big bite. Secondly, the Polish Government in London were to amalgamate with the Lublin Government. I think we might sweep away at any rate one subterfuge. Neither the British Government, nor the Russian Government, nor the Polish Government regard Lublin as anything else but a fake. Mr. Mikołajczyk was told I understand at Moscow, first, that in this amalgamation Lublin must have 75 per cent of the representation of the Polish Government and the rest of the parties 25 per cent. I believe it was indicated that if a proper arrangement could be made, if Mr. Mikołajczyk was sufficiently accommodating it might be worked out on a 50–50 basis—a good old British compromise. I wonder what the Prime Minister and his Government would say if it was suggested by a foreign Power that the hon. Member for West Fife (Mr. Gallacher) should have a 50–50 representation.

MR. MESSER (Lab.): What an absurd comparison.

MR. RAIKES: Judging by the representation of the Communist Party in the Polish Parliament in the years between 1920 and 1929 I think, on the whole, the comparison is an apt one, but I am not going to be drawn away by a red herring.

MR. MESSER: The hon. Member floated the red herring.

MR. RAIKES: There is nothing very red about it except the Lublin Committee. Regarding these two reciprocal offers to which the Prime Minister referred as compensation for the Poles, all I say is that the offer of East Prussia means

East Prussia without Koenigsberg, without Pilau, the fortress of Koenigsberg which would dominate the Gulf of Gdynia and also control the port of Dantzig. As regards the offer of German lands to the Oder, it is easy enough to consider on the map depopulating millions of people. But does the House appreciate what that means—4,000,000 Poles East of the Curzon Line dragged from the homes in which they have lived for generations, 4,000,000 Ukrainians left to be Russian citizens, whether they wish it or not, and 5,000,000 Germans again forced from their homes and transferred to Western Germany? What a sum of human misery. I do not know that the basis of the settlement of a new world after the war would be improved by removing 5,000,000 Germans from one side of the Oder to the other, not the sort of settlement the Atlantic Charter proposed to stand for in the days before the Atlantic Charter had become merely a ghost and that ghost was laid today finally by the Prime Minister.

I believe that the error that has been made throughout the negotiations with the Soviet has been the assumption that Soviet will get angry and annoyed if you talk to them in tough language. There is not the least question of any Polish Government being intransigent if there is one real gesture of friendship from Marshal Stalin. It is more important for Poland to be friendly to Russia than it is to Russia to have a a friendly Poland but we can, I think, ask that it should not all be given by the small State and all taken by the big State. Supposing this Government, even at the present stage—and Governments do listen to one of the few free Parliaments left in the world—speaks out boldly with the strength of the British Parliament behind it and talks to Moscow in terms of free negotiation and a fair and reasonable deal in which concessions are to be made by both sides and not only by one, we might achieve much. Certainly we would play a very much more satisfactory part for Poland than we are playing at present.

There is one thing that I deeply regret. Many people may feel that Mr. Mikołajczyk is the ablest Prime Minister Poland has had, but the differentiation between the degree of help likely to be given by our Government to the present Polish Government as compared to the last was an unfortunate phrase on the part of the Prime Minister of England. If we could shoulder the present Polish Government and merely back Mr. Mikołajczyk and the Government of which he is a member we should allow the Prime Minister to turn into a "king-maker" like the Early of Warwick in the 15th century. I do not think it will pay in the long run for the Government of this country to be strongly partisan in regard to the personalities in Cabinets formed by friendly Allied Powers who have a right to select their own Ministers as they will. We have still before us an unsettled Russian-Polish problem. I think it can still be settled but it will only be dealt with effectively if Great Britain is prepared to raise her voice as she has done in the past as a great supporter of international morality and honorable dealing. May I remind the Foreign Secretary of words spoken 100 years ago by a Foreign Secretary, perhaps even greater than he is, Lord Palmerston?

> "I hold that the real policy of England is to be the champion of justice and right. As long as England keeps herself in the right, as long as she wishes to permit no injustice, as long as she sympathizes with right and justice, she will never find herself altogether alone."

That principle has been the foundation of our greatness as a nation, that principle has given us the moral leadership of Europe. When we became weak, when Ministers have found themselves in the past obliged to stand up feebly without a policy, with the hands of irresolution fumbling up and down the sleeves of uncertainty, then the power of Britain for good in the world has diminished and faded. I hope the Foreign Secretary today and in the time that lies ahead will take a little of the vigor, the fire and the buoyancy of the great Lord Palmerston, and play his part in talking strongly and firmly to the great nations of Europe and by doing justice to the weak lay the foundations of a new world in which there will be peace and freedom and honor.

MR. MANDER (L.): I think the hon. Member is refusing to face the facts. He is not looking at the world at all as it is at present. I think the Prime Minister and the Foreign Secretary in their negotiations with the leaders of the other great Powers have done the very thing that he asks. They have struggled and used their influence to secure just what he himself wants to achieve. I do not think the best way is to have Debates in this House. It is much better to have confidence in the known views of the Prime Minister and Foreign Secretary so that they may do all they possibly can to secure the results the hon. Member wants. He has made, as is so easy in these circumstances, an emotional and sentimental speech. There is an immense amount of emotion and sentiment about the Poles. We all have the most profound admiration for the unforgettable deeds that they have performed in the war. They are, as a race, brave, attractive, talented and romantic. They have a keen historic sense and they have long memories—and they have something to remember, their grievances in the long past and in recent days too. But sometimes we have to teach ourselves to forget certain things and not bear them in mind too long.

One thing that the Poles have not had is the opportunity in recent years of practicing democracy. We, in this island, have been more fortunate. We have been able to bring it very near to perfection, but they have not had that opportunity. I believe they desire to attain true democracy after the war. I was in a Parliamentary delegation which visited the Polish Army in France in May, 1940, just before the great storm began. I attended a great open air service on Sunday near Nancy. The whole Polish Army was there with the President and the Commander-in-Chief, and the Chaplain General preached, from a pulpit made up of boughs, what appeared to me to be a most eloquent sermon in Polish. I could not understand it, but I ascertained afterwards that it was a plea not only for Polish victory but for a victory for Polish democracy. I thought that was a true and impressive account of what we were fighting for.

If one is a friend of Poland I do not think that necessarily means that one must encourage them to pursue a path which one thinks will lead them to disaster. Surely a friend can speak frankly and give advice even if it is not altogether palatable. We have to face the facts as they are. First of all, there is no hope for a strong and independent Poland without a real and cordial friendship with Russia. One can understand Russian suspicion and their doubt as to the good will of certain sections of the Poles. We know that there is a great deal of anti-Soviet feeling, and the Russians have to be reassured that any Polish Government after the war will be genuinely friendly with them. But I go further, and say that not only does the whole fate of Poland depend on Russian good will but the whole fate of Europe and the world depends on the cordial and genuine co-operation of the three great Powers. If that fails, all fails and the war will come to an end only as a preparation for another struggle later on. That was the foundation at Dumbarton Oaks on which the new world organization was, rightly to my mind, to be built up. There has been some comment on the undecided question of the veto of the great Powers. Theoretically I should have thought there was everything to be said against it, but in practice I should have thought there was a great deal to be said for it because, if you once get to a stage where these three great Powers cannot settle their difference by agreement and are contemplating action of some kind, the whole thing comes to an end.

I should prefer to see the old Polish boundaries restored after the war. It is natural for Poles to desire that, and for the friends of Poland too, but time has marched on, events have changed and it is a wholly impracticable solution at present. If any attempt is made to insist on that, they may lose all. The hon. Member wants to restore Poland to her former greatness, but his policy would very likely destroy Poland altogether. That is the danger that we have to face. I know that some of my hon. Friends are inclined to say that Poland is going to be Sovietized in any case. I do not take that view.

I believe that the Russian Government are not particularly interested in Communists outside Russia and have no desire to set up their own system in Poland if it is a friendly country. It may be a capitalist or a Social system, but I do not believe they have any intention of insisting that it should be a Soviet system. They have given no indication in Rumania and other places that that is their policy. It is a great mistake to assume that Marshal Stalin's enthusiasm for Communism is unbounded, and I do not think we ought to assume that he has any designs on the Sovietization of Poland.

I cannot help regretting that the policy of this distinguished statesman Mr. Mikołajczyk is not to be pursued. It was extremely wise. I do not want to be in the position of suggesting to a foreign country what Ministers they should have, but his policy of collaboration with Russia should be pursued to the end under whatever Minister is placed in charge by the Polish authorities. I understand that a great part is played in Polish affairs by that distinguished man, the Polish President, of whom I desire to speak in terms of the deepest respect. At the same time, I cannot help wondering whether all his actions are in the real interest of his country. I think that that is a note which ought to be sounded, if I may do it respectfully in that manner. Reference has been made to the settlement of all boundaries. It would be desirable, no doubt, and it is an attractive proposal, but the Prime Minister has given reasons why it does not seem practicable at the present time. Then there is the question of the guarantee of the frontiers. I should have thought that we got that guarantee in the Dumbarton Oaks proposals in another way. The three great Powers have made it clear that they intend to act together in the maintenance of the order that is set up. It cannot think of any other method by which we can obtain that guarantee. I think that to ask the United States for a direct guarantee is most impolitic. We shall get it indirectly through the world organization.

The Prime Minister referred to the word "compensation" in connection with the sacrifices which Poland has made in the East. I have never felt very happy about that word. It seems to me that it is not compensation that is contemplated, but a change of strategic grounds. East Prussia, for instance, has always been a great danger to her neighbors. Germany was able to strike from there, and on those grounds alone there is a good case for taking it away from Germany. I think it is quite right to give it to Poland and to transfer the populations. It is tragic that we should have come to things of this kind. Transfers of population are taking place in Europe under conditions of the most incredible brutality, but an orderly migration such as is contemplated is a wholly different matter. As a matter of fact, I imagine that at the end of this war there will not be many Germans left in East Prussia. There may not be many in the Eastern parts of Germany, because I fancy that, as the Russians approach, they will make rapid strides towards the interior of their country.

There are voices, one knows, in this country—I do not say necessarily in this House—which are giving to the Poles what, to my mind, is very bad advice. There are military persons as well as political persons who are saying to them "Play for time, delay as much as possible." [HON. MEMBERS: "Oh."] It is not necessary for me to specify the persons. It is known to all of us that there are people who sincerely hold that view. I am not accusing hon. Members. The people who hold that view advise Poland, "Play for time and hope that the Allies will quarrel after the war, and then you will have an opportunity of getting back East Prussia." Nothing could be more foolish or disastrous than to give our Polish friends advice of that kind. The new Polish Government that has been set up does not seem to me, from the point of view of succeeding in the negotiations, one that is too impressive. After all, the National Peasant Party is not represented in it. It is true that they are still represented in the underground organization in Poland, but that is quite a different matter and does not involve representation in the Polish Government. When one looks at the other Polish Government, the Lublin Government, one sees that that is even less impressive. The desirable thing is one Polish Government to which all Poles can give their allegiance, one that is really impressive and will rally the nation and we want to see that Government situated in Warsaw at the earliest possible moment. I say to my Polish friends, with deep sadness, what, I think, ought to be said in kindness to them, "Act as quickly as you can in collaboration with the Russians along the lines of the wise policy of Mr. Mikołajczyk. Do it for your own sakes and for the sakes of Europe and the whole world, and so make possible a Polish nation which, in peace as in war, will make a noble contribution, a contribution worthy of her historic past."

MR. PICKTHORN (C.): This has been so far a very sad Debate and, if I may say it without in any way intending to assume superiority, I think rather a disappointing Debate. I do not attribute any blame to anyone—I think it is due, perhaps, to a series of accidents—that this House has, in fact, discussed His Majesty's Government's foreign policy, in the course of the last three weeks, in a way, in my humble judgment, most of all calculated, if it had been a calculation, to make it difficult. We had a two-day Debate leaving out all those parts of foreign policy which really excite most Members of the House; then we had a one-day Debate on one exciting bit of foreign policy; and now we are having another day's Debate on another bit. It seems to me absolutely inevitable that before many more weeks are out we shall have to have a Debate on Yugoslavia. I am anxious to be as short as I can; therefore, I do not wish, although it would be in Order strictly speaking, to draw parallels, but I think this way of debating does mean that hon. Members are rather precluded from comparing what is happening in one part of Europe with what is happening in another, and is not the manner most likely to enlighten us, or our constituents, upon foreign policy.

EARL WINTERTON (C.): There is nothing whatever on this Motion to stop Members discussing any subject of foreign policy.

MR. PICKTHORN: I not only know that, but if the Noble Lord had been willing to pay attention to me, he would have known that I said it. And, incidentally, one of my minor disappointments was when the Noble Lord said that the worst Foreign Secretary he could remember was Palmerston. I thought I knew of better candidates for that position.

We have been warned by one former speaker not to say anything that might make things more difficult for Poland. I will certainly do my best to heed that warning. On every previous occasion on which this matter has been discussed, we have been warned by His Majesty's Government, by "The Times," and by other superior persons and institutions to be very careful not to say anything that would do harm. I think we have been very careful. I think it is at least arguable that we have been so careful not to say things that might do harm, that we have slipped into the opposite error, which is the last error a Parliamentarian ought to slip into, that is, the error of keeping quiet, the error of keeping quiet about things about which public ignorance does harm. It was to avoid that error that Parliaments were invented and developed to the point where they now are.

I make no apology for quoting the Prime Minister. I was going to say I wish he were here, but that might sound like a complaint, and I have no complaint at all.

THE SECRETARY OF STATE FOR FOREIGN AFFAIRS (MR. EDEN): I have had a conversation with the Prime Minister, and it is only fair to tell the House that there are some particularly important problems at the moment which are claiming his attention.

MR. PICKTHORN: I was not meaning to complain in any way, but when one quotes a speech of another hon. Member, even of the Prime Minister himself, one likes as a rule to tell him one is going to quote him, or to have him here. I am the less reluctant to quote the Prime Minister this time because the Prime Minister himself quoted from his earlier speeches at considerable length, and with a great deal of the spirit of

Tom Moore, I think, who was moved to tears by admiration for his genius when younger, on an occasion when somebody sang to him a song he had composed some years before. The Prime Minister quoted for us today the speech which he made on 22nd February, and I agree that it is the best point from which to begin. In this speech he said:

> "It was with great pleasure that I heard from Marshal Stalin that he, too, was resolved upon the creation and maintenance of a strong integral independent Poland as one of the leading Powers in Europe."

I have never known very clearly what "integral" means, but "strong" and "independent" are words which most of us can understand. The Prime Minister went on to say that His Majesty's Government adhered to the principle that territorial changes should be reserved for the permanent peace settlement. But he made it very difficult for anybody to believe that the principle would be very effective when he said:

> "We did not approve of the Polish occupation of Vilna in 1920. The British view in 1919 stands expressed in the so-called Curzon Line."—[*Official Report*, 22nd February, 1944; Vol. 397, c. 697-8.].*

I think that the Prime Minister's history is mistaken on that point. I do not think the Curzon Line does express what had been the British view as to the permanent frontier. But that I would not urge; all I am saying is that the Prime Minister on 22nd February, when stating this principle in regard to territorial changes, indicated that it was to be expected that when those changes did happen, they would be the changes desired by one side rather than any change that might be suggested by the other. It did rather whittle away that principle. With great respect to my right hon. Friend, I would like to refer to what he said about the Atlantic Charter. I have never been an excessive admirer of the Atlantic Charter. It has always seemed to me that making large promises to everybody, in the manner recommended to us by the hon. Member

---

* See Vol. II, No. 54, p. 336.

for East Wolverhampton (Mr. Mander) when he suggested that we need, none of us, desire locks on our front doors or guarantees from our next door neighbors, because we should all get a *holus bolus,* panacea guarantee from Dumbarton Oaks, or Hot Springs, or somewhere else—

MR. MANDER: The hon. Member is making a frivolous reference to my speech, but I can assure him that I referred to the decision at Dumbarton Oaks in all seriousness.

MR. PICKTHORN: The hon. Member should not think that nobody has ever been serious who is not being solemn. He rebuked my hon. Friend who spoke before me from this side of the House for being emotional or sentimental. I hope that I do not sound emotional or sentimental, but one of the best ways of avoiding that indictment when one feels deeply is, not the Liberal method of speaking with a solemnity even greater than that of the subject, but the opposite method of speaking with a certain irony, and even ocassionally with what may appear to opponents to be a disagreeable facetiousness.

The Atlantic Charter always seemed to me likely to do more harm than good, by promising everything to everybody, and making it easier not to keep those comparatively small promises for which there was a genuine obligation. My fears about the Atlantic Charter were very much strengthened by my right hon. Friend today, who did not appear to have read it, which was rather surprising. I do not know who composed it.

MR. STOKES (Lab.): Washington.

MR. PICKTHORN: I had supposed that the Prime Minister had read it. He told us—naturally I have not got HANSARD before me, but I am sure that I am right in my recollection —that there was a special proviso in the Atlantic Charter about mutual agreements for territorial changes. I think I am right in saying that there is nothing of the sort in the Atlantic Charter.

MR. IVOR THOMAS (Lab.): Perhaps there is a secret clause.

MR. PICKTHORN: It may be a secret clause. I had not thought of that. The Atlantic Charter announced that the United Nations desired to see no territorial changes that did not accord with the freely expressed wishes of the people concerned. That is the proviso,

> "the freely expressed wishes of the people concerned,"

and not any proviso about mutual agreement.

I do not wish to argue where the frontiers ought to be of Poland. For all I have to say to the contrary the Eastern frontier of Poland should be the Chilterns and the Western frontier the Alleghenies; but I beg hon. Members, and especially Members on the Government Front Bench, not to use the argument against us that this country has never guaranteed any specific frontier. If anybody ever guaranteed the British Isles or the British State, it would be taken to guarantee its boundaries at the time of the guarantee. If, at the time of the guarantee to Poland, there was any secret proviso either that the guarantee was to work or that it was not to work in circumstances not then immediately contemplated, I think the time has come when the Foreign Secretary ought to tell us about it. If there was not any such secret proviso, I hope we shall never again hear any argument about our not guaranteeing any specific frontier.

On the specific-frontier point and on the guarantee point I should like to ask the Foreign Secretary another question. The Prime Minister, speaking in this House, said to us the other day that it was to be hoped that there would be a guarantee from the three great Powers. "It was certainly to be hoped that the three great Powers will guarantee an intedependent, sovereign, free Poland."* That is what the Prime Minister said to us not so many days ago, on 27th October. Within the month, Mr. Stettinius said:

> "The specific question of a guarantee of the Polish frontier by this Government was not, and could not have been, at issue

* See No. 5.

> since this Government's traditional policy of not guaranteeing frontiers in Europe is well known."

I suppose it was well known to the Foreign Office. I suppose it was well known to those who advised my right hon. Friend the Prime Minister when he spoke in this House on 27th October. If that was well known to them, when did it become well known to the Polish Government, who are not perhaps so familiar as we are with the constitution of the United States? We have had a good many reasons for familiarizing ourselves with that matter in the last 150 years. Perhaps not everybody else has. I would like my right hon. Friend to tell us when certainty was reached that the Poles were aware of that traditional U.S. policy of not guaranteeing frontiers.

But I would not put the main question upon definings or sharings of frontier or of guarantee. Some hon. Member from the other side begged friends of Poland to be careful. I am not a friend of Poland. I am a friend of England, and if I am a friend of any other country in the world, perhaps Scotland and France might compete for that friendship. I speak in this House not in the least as a friend of Poland. I think it is not the business of this House to consider the interests of Poland as such, and that the specific business of this House is to consider the interests of the British Empire and the British people. I am forced to say that it did ring like a knell in my heart —with apologies to the hon. Member for East Wolverhampton* for being emotional—when the Prime Minister said today, for the third time in the last three or four weeks, that this country has two great Allies, "perhaps greater than us." Not greater than us, and if we think them greater than us, greater than us they will be. In my judgment, if they are greater than us, or either or both of them think themselves greater than us, there is no chance of peace in Europe in any time while anyone now present in this Chamber lives.

There is only once chance of peace in Europe and that is that this continent, which has suffered, which has had its morals and its habits and its whole equipment disturbed in

* Mr. Mander.

a way we can hardly imagine, and only one chance of peace when the war is over, and that is that the new growth of mutual confidence should be quick. There is only one chance, in my judgment, for such growth of mutual confidence, and that is that there should be one State through which the confidence can spread from State A to B and from X to Y, and I cannot see how that can be any State but us. If we are to be the State in Europe most trusted by the other States of Europe, then, in that position, the country which is the Ally of the United States and of the USSR, and which is the metropolis of the British Empire, will be, at the very least, as powerful as any other State upon earth. But only if we have that confidence—and that is why I am concerned with the matter before us today. I am not concerned about where Polish frontiers should be. I think it is a very interesting question that we might discuss on another day. What I am concerned about is, wherever the Polish frontier is and however small or great Poland is, will the countries of Europe, at the moment when Germany is defeated, think that those lines of frontier were drawn wherever they have been drawn as a result of complete fidelity on the part of the British Government, or will Europe not think so? I believe that on the answer to that question depends the chance of any peace at all before all of our sons are dead.

Therefore, in a sense I attach much more importance to the Lublin Committee than I do to the actual frontier. In one sense I agree, respectfully, with the hon. Member who said that we need not waste time with the Lublin Committee, because everybody knows it is bogus. Is there anybody who will dare to say that it is less bogus than the Vlasov Committee? The thing is completely and absolutely bogus, and it is not therefore worth while going through the biographies of the members who compose it and guessing which of them have been lifelong paid employees of the O.G.P.U. or who have not, and who have been imprisoned for what and who had not. I do not think that is worth doing. There are two things which I hope the House will forgive me for thinking worth mention, two things which do prove the bogus nature of this Committee.

One is what happened in Warsaw in August and September. That rising, whatever else anybody may think about it, was perhaps the most heroic episode of the war. The whole population rose. Nobody ever denied that the whole population rose. Even broadcasts which were most against Warsaw, both the German controlled and the Russian controlled broadcasts in the early days, when both sides were trying to play the thing down, agreed that it was a 100 per cent affair, and that the whole city rose. That is more convincing than any plebiscite. You could have a plebiscite that gave you 99.99999 "Yesses" and you would not have so convincing a proof as that was, where the allegiance of the Poles went. The allegiance of the Poles went to the so-called "émigré" Government. In that respect, I think we might be a little careful about describing our Allies as émigré Governments, which has become almost a term of abuse, and threatens to be a terrible term of reproach against us. One day, a country which stands up on the same side as ourselves has "found its soul" and two days or two months, no, but at any rate less than two years later it is an "émigré Government." Anyway, that was one proof that the Polish Government was certainly a legitimate Government and also have the highest ground for legitimacy, that it is a Government which are taken for granted and taken as a matter of course by those for whom they are speaking.

The second reason for saying that the Polish Government is the legitimate Government of Poland and the Lublin Government is not, is in the words of the Prime Minister, which he quoted again today. I do not think I can find the exact words, but I think I can quote them fairly exactly. He said: "If only the Poles had taken the advice we tended them at the beginning of this year, the additional complication produced by the formation of the Lublin Committee would not have arisen." I think those words are near enough. He said those in October or February, and he repeated them today. It seems that the Prime Minister has no doubt that the whole thing is bogus, artificial, factitious. There is not the least doubt about it.

What, in those circumstances, becomes the duty of His Majesty's Government? I will tell the House as plainly as I can, I hope without offense to any State or any individual. The duty of His Majesty's Government is to make quite certain, at very nearly whatever risk, that the world knows that whatever regime is set up in Poland, if it is not obviously on the face of it a wholly independent regime, and whatever frontiers are drawn for Poland, if those frontiers are in any respect unfavorable to Poland, that those unfavorable decisions have not been facilitated by us; and, above all, that we have not been parties to any plan for using the Lublin Committee as a lever for squeezing, putting a squeeze on, the Polish Government, to whom we are bound by every tie of honor, or on the Polish people, for whom our hearts must, even in Wolverhampton, continue to bleed.

There is very much more that might be said on this matter, but I do not wish to say any more, except one thing, one thing only. In peace time it is fun to attack the Government, especially if you are in opposition, or to make speeches which appear critical of the Government. In war time I do not think it is fun at all; indeed, in matters of foreign policy and strategy I never thought it legitimate, even in peace time. I always thought that every private Member ought to make a rule for himself equivalent to the Standing Order about money, the Standing Order of Queen Anne, which forbids any back bencher from moving the expenditure of money. I have always thought each one of us should, in the proper sense of the words, be "a law unto himself" in the matter too of spending blood, and should practically never argue for something which might possibly cost the blood of one more British soldier. In time of crisis, most of all in time of war, it is extremely difficult to make any criticism, even any suggestion, to His Majesty's Government about high policy, without running the risk that one might have that guilt upon one's head. But there are times when it is necessary to make clear what some back benchers feel to be the proper action of this country, and the reason why they so regard it. I think those of us who have spoken in this Debate have been justified in trying to do that. I hope we, all of us, will be acquitted of having said anything that could be embarrassing.

MISS RATHBONE (Ind.): I shall not speak long, and I shall not speak at all on the vexed question of Polish frontiers. My opinions on that subject are forming themselves only slowly, and I shoul not be justified in inflicting them on the House. I want to raise two issues which I approach purely from a humanitarian point of view. The first is the issue of the deportations from Poland and the Russian parts of Poland to the USSR, and I shall give the facts as presented to me by those who have studied the question very closely, both British and Polish people. But, mark you, I do not take responsibility for the accuracy of all these facts. The figures may have been, and I think, probably have been, exaggerated; certainly they are only approximate, and the descriptions of hardship which have been brought before me are possibly also exaggerated, seeing that they must be mostly based on hearsay or through very slow-moving underground channels. But I do submit that making allowance for maximum exaggeration possible, the whole position is decidedlv disquieting, and we should be very careful lest we take any responsibility for acquiescing in it.

As to deportations, there are two periods to which I wish to refer, the earlier date being from February, 1940, to June, 1941, at the time when Russia was forced into the war by German aggression. I believe it is not disputed by anyone that during that period vast numbers of Poles and other people besides—the latter I do not intend to discuss—were deported to distant parts of the USSR. The alleged figures given to me are that some 880,000 civilians plus a great number of prisoners of war—and also great numbers who were forcibly mobilized—in all well over 1,000,000 persons, were affected. The civilians included several hundred thousands of women and children. They were sent to various distant parts of European Russia, to Siberia and to Central Asiatic Republics and elsewhere, and owing to the haste with which they were sent off they were sent with exceedingly inadequate provision of food and clothing and in overcrowded conditions so far as transport was concerned. They are said—all those that were fit—to have been put to forced labor, many in an Arctic climate, in such conditions of underfeeding and underclothing that thousands are said to have succumbed. It is reported that in April, 1943, over 270,000 Polish citizens were benefiting from the relief organizations of the Polish Embassy set up in Kuibishev, including 95,000 men, 98,000 women and 78,000 children, when the work of the Polish relief organizations was brought to an end by the rupture of diplomatic relations between the two countries. After that relief stopped and since then, except during a brief period when the Australian representative had some access, there has been no access allowed to those persons by any impartial persons, and neither the International Red Cross, Quakers, nor any other international body, were allowed access.

The second series of deportations is much later—during and since August of the present year. It is alleged to affect large numbers, including many officers and men who had fought actively with the Red Army in the common fight against Germany, and who were afterwards seized upon, and for one reason or other, deported. The facts about that are rather more doubtful. Obviously they come from underground sources which may or may not be reliable. The position is unsatisfactory but the extent of it is less fully established than in the case of the earlier deportations. I merely want to say that all this is very disquieting, and the question is whether the Russian authorities have anything to be ashamed of, anything they would not like impartial people from other countries to see. If not why cannot they allow access, not to any busybodies, but to recognized organizations?

My second point raises the same kind of issue. I will deal with it very shortly. It is a less important issue, but it was confirmed on Wednesday at Question Time that the USSR has so far made no reply to the request received from UNRRA to be allowed to send a delegation and supplies through Russian territory into Poland and to Russian-occupied parts of Poland.* Permission has not been refused, but it is delayed. Bearing in mind that Russia was one of the bodies that helped to set up UNRRA and to designate its functions, could not this permission be more quickly expedited? My right hon. Friend the Foreign Secretary said it was clearly a matter for the USSR themselves, but considering the United States and ourselves were the other Powers mainly concerned in setting up UNRRA, we have a right to be interested in it officially.

I am going to speak rather bluntly. What is the use of university representation if university representatives cannot speak the truth as they see it, and without thinking of anything else but what is the truth? All these delays and these difficulties about the deportees must inevitably strengthen the fear, just or unjust, that the Soviet have reason to dislike impartial witnesses. I see in many quarters, including friends who might be described as more to the Left than to the Right, but also some in quarters in which I would not have expected it, a disposition to treat Russia as a doctor treats a highly hysterical patient, to say, "She is very sensitive, she may have made mistakes, but do not say anything that might displease her." That is an insult for leading Russians, who surely have too much sense of humor and commonsense to want to be treated like that, If we are looking forward to 20 years' post-war close cooperation with Russia, to which we are bound by a Treaty already in existence, let us put it plainly. The Russians have to get accustomed, whether they like or not, to our habit of speaking our mind, not only to our own Government—no one can doubt our free exercise of that right—but about other Governments with which we are in alliance. In

---

* MISS RATHBONE: Is it not the case that the Government of the USSR have not yet given any permission for delegations or supplies to UNRRA to pass through Soviet territory? Cannot a decision on that point be expedited?

MR. EDEN: I cannot answer for the Soviet Government, as the hon. Lady will realize. She asks whether a decision cannot be expedited. It is for them to do that, but the hon. Lady is quite correct in saying that they have not made known their views.

(Debates of Dec. 13, 1944, Hansard, Vol. 406, p. 1208).

the long run there cannot be much hope for the future of the world, or this great international organization foreshadowed at Dumbarton Oaks, about which I shall say nothing, though the Russian views about that are also disquieting, unless there is that kind of speaking.

I do not often agree with the Senior Burgess for Cambridge University (Mr. Pickthorn) but I never agreed with him more than when he said that where we have, through force of circumstances, to give assent to something to which our conscience or reason demurs, do not let us pretend that our conscience or reason does not demur; do not let us say that these things have our full assent. I am justified in asking my right hon. Friend, who will reply, whether he can give us some assurance about these matters, and above all, did he, when he was in Moscow, or will he, in his representations to Moscow, raise this question, "What about the deportees, and why do you not want people to visit them?" And "Why should it not be possible to send supplies to them?" Do not we owe at least that to our hard tried Polish Allies?

CAPTAIN ALAN GRAHAM (C.): May I say first of all how extremely refreshing it has been to listen to the manly forthrightness of the hon. Lady the Member for the Combined English Universities (Miss Rathbone). This debate of course centers round the Russian-Polish situation, and our British attitude towards it, but it seems to me that far bigger issues are involved, namely, the whole future of European civilization. What is the key-note of our civilization in contrast with Asiatic concepts? It is surely the infinite value of the individual human soul. In the East, where nature is so colossal in its features, and so terrifying in its operations, the river Yangtze in China overflows its banks, and a million Chinese are swept away to destruction. If the water level has not reached a certain height another million or so also die of starvation, because the rice crop has failed. To them the individual is next to nothing, but in Europe he is all important.

This is the basic concept on which all our hopes of man's progress are founded: the social services, to assist his bodily infirmities; freedom of religion, so that his soul may prosper; our democratic institutions, so that the State may derive the greatest possible voluntary service from every free, individual citizen. This is an idea of which Nazi Germany is the mortal foe; and for this idea Poland, France and ourselves drew the sword in September, 1939. For this idea, in 1940, when Europe lay prostrate under the Nazi heel, we alone continued to fight; for which Europe and the whole civilized world still pay us their tribute of admiration. Consequently, we were, and we are still, considered the champions of European civilization. From this rôle we cannot withdraw without shame, dishonor, and material danger. The Polish nation has always been a member of our European family, and a worthy contributor to European civilization—indeed, for centuries one of its doughtiest champions. At this moment, the Polish nation is in grave danger of extinction at the hands of our enemy, Germany, and, I am sorry to say, at the hands of our other Ally, Russia. We cannot afford, nor can Europe afford, to allow this to happen.

What does Russia demand of Poland? She demands half her territory, and that she should be governed by the Lublin Committee, which, the world knows, is an utterly unrepresentative body of Poles, provided by Russia, and whose authority and power rest solely on the Russian NKVD, or political police, the child of the OGPU, and Russian bayonets. In other words, the Polish Government are to surrender half their country to Russia, and to accept Russian government in all but name over what remains. Is it any wonder that both Mr. Mikołajczyk and the present Polish Government refused to set their hands to what would have been nothing else but the suicide-warrant of their country and their nation? Further, it was expected of them to agree to this without any positive guarantees of the independence of Poland. We know for a fact that the United States Government have definitely refused any guarantee for Poland. There were some verbal assurances given by the Prime Minister when last he spoke on this subject, and there have been statements by Mr. Stalin; but, unfortunately, there have been other statements by Mr. Stalin which have not subsequently been implemented. Naturally, Mr. Mikołajczyk's Government were unable to agree to these terms and signified their unanimous refusal to the British Government on 3rd November. Therefore, it seems unfair that any persons should charge the present Polish Government with being necessarily less willing to meet the Russian demands than the former Polish Government. It may be asked, What is the moral justification for such demands being put to Poland, our martyred Ally, who gave us such indispensable aid at the time of the Battle of Britain, and who was the first Power to fight against Nazi Germany? The answer is, Absolutely none. In fact, we are morally and textually bound, by Article 3 of our guarantee of 1939 to Poland, to support Poland not only against armed aggression, but against any attempt "to undermine Polish independence, by processes of economic penetration or in any other way." When Hitler, in August, 1939, sought to persuade us to disinterest ourselves in the fate of Poland, the British Government of those days replied:

> "The German Government will be aware that His Majesty's Government have obligations to Poland, by which they are bound, and which they intend to honor. They could not, for any advantage offered to Great Britain, acquiesce in a settlement which put in jeopardy the independence of a State to whom they have given their guarantee."*

That was the voice of Britain in August, 1939, when we were materially a very weak Power; but our moral courage then was indeed great. Has anything happened since then to make us weaker in material force or in any degree less courageous? Has Poland since then done anything to lessen our esteem for her? Perhaps the behavior of Polish troops at Monte Cassino and at Falaise may be mentioned. Has Poland done anything to justify us in ignoring those solemn obligations in which she, then and now, has placed her trust? If any nation has spilled her blood more readily in the common cause than Po-

---

* Vol. I, p. 185.

land, I have yet to hear of it. Five million Poles have so far died in the struggle against Germany—one in every seven of the population—and they are still dying, in Poland and on every battle front. And why? Are 5,000,000 Poles dying for half their territories to pass at once under an alien yoke, and the rest of their territory to be governed by a stranger? If the Briton of 1944 or 1945 were to consent to such an outrage, the Briton of 1939 would be the first to testify against him, and to disown such dishonorable behavior. Why should we now shamelessly cast away our reputation as the defenders of honor and European civilization? Our armed might was never stronger than it is today; our moral standing, in spite of some things that have happened, is still high. But we are honest neither with ourselves nor with Russia if we pretend that we can disinterest ourselves in the fate of Poland.

It is actually said that for the last month—whether or not because of the change in Government I do not know—we have sent no further supplies to the Underground Army in Poland. Can we afford to ignore this organized army of 160,-000 combatants against Germany, recognized by ourselves three months ago as combatants? I should like to know from the right hon. Gentleman whether that statement is true, that we have taken the occasion of the change in the Polish Government to refuse to go on supplying these forces of the Polish Underground Army, who, against heavy odds, are still fighting our battle. They will get arms from somewhere, if not from us. Is not such action calculated to drive them into the arms of Germany? If His Majesty's Government do not now stand up for full Polish independence, they will force all Central Europeans to rally around Germany, even in defeat, and to make Germany, as she claims to be, Europe's defender against the Eastern invader. Poland is the test-case for European civilization. If we desert Poland, Europe will desert us; and that will be our ruin. France, a Power by no means at the maximum of her strength today, has hastened already to declare her concern in what goes on in Eastern Europe, and she considers it of vital importance to her, Western power though she is. The days are past when the Channel served us—

"as a moat . . . Against the envy of less happier lands."

V.1 and V.2 and the progress of aviation have made those sentiments completely obsolete long ago. Even Lord Baldwin admitted, in 1936, that the Rhine was our frontier, although, of course, he did nothing about it. Today our frontier is the Vistula; tomorrow it may be the Dnieper. In the underground war in Germany, which will follow the defeat of her regular armies in the field, the support of these 100 million people living between Russia and Germany may well prove decisive. In any event, all Europe is now so near that, whether we like it or not, we are both in and of it; and that intimately. For our own material safety, therefore, as well as for every moral reason, such as honor between man and man and regard for treaties and for the whole fabric of our European civilization, I say to the Government that the moment has come to say to our great Ally Russia, of whose many services we are abundantly conscious, that she must treat Poland as what she is, a civilized, Christian, European nation, and not as if she was a paltry Asiatic tribe of Uzbegs or Tajiks. Firm and definite language now will save a deal of mounting troubles later on. From my own experience of the Russian nation, I know that there is nothing they despise more than concessions, and there is nothing to which they respond with greater readiness than to firmness.

Lastly, I will make a personal appeal to the Prime Minister. In many Polish towns today the principal street is called Churchill Street, because he is looked up to by the Poles as the savior of Poland and of Europe. In martyred Warsaw, during the last rising against the Germans, 20 barricades in Churchill Street alone were soaked in Polish blood. That happened because they believed that, whatever might happen to them, he at least would see that in the end Poland was free. I cannot believe that, when history comes to award his due to the greatest Englishman since Chatham, it will say, "But he deserted Poland!"

MR. IVOR THOMAS (Lab.): Anyone thinking about the Polish problem must start from two premises, and I shall mention them at the outset, lest I forget, and in order that I may avoid being misrepresented, as otherwise will be the case. Friendship with the Soviet Union is the first essential for the existence of an independent Polish State; and the friendship of the Soviet Union, the United States, and ourselves is essential for the maintenance of world peace. To say that is not to solve the problem, but merely to state it. This Polish problem is the most intractable in the whole field of our foreign relations at present. I have never risen to speak with such a heavy heart as I do today. It is melancholy to think that after more than five years of fighting, in a war which we entered to defend the independence of Poland, we should be debating whether Poland is to be a State at all. For, make no mistake, that is the issue before us. The frontier question is entirely subordinate. I shall develop that in a few moments; but let me say now that if the proposals made by the Prime Minister this morning are in fact carried out—and I am not criticizing the Prime Minister, because I think he may have been caught in what the hon. Member for West Leicester (Mr. H. Nicolson) recently called a chain of circumstances—if these proposals are carried out, the real victors will not be the Lublin Committee. They will be my hon. Friend the Member for Westhoughton (Mr. Rhys Davies) and my hon. Friends who, on most other days except Fridays, sit on the benches below the gangway; if their case is not indeed proved, it will be greatly strengthened, for their case is that war settles nothing. If, at the end of six years of fighting, we see the causes for which we entered the war trampled underfoot, then, indeed, that case will be very much strengthened, and it will lead to a sense of cynicism and shame which will make it very difficult to get the people of this country to go to war again, however sacred the cause. And the Prime Minister's speech has left me with a feeling that the future is very uncertain. that speech was composed of the dragon's teeth which are said to be the seeds of future wars.

I have said that the frontier question is not the most important one, and it is not, but, even so, there are certain considerations which I think ought to be born in mind. The hon. Gentleman the Senior Burgess for Cambridge University (Mr. Pickthorn), with whom I so often disagree but whose eloquence is always worth listening to, was perfectly right when he said that the Prime Minister was not reproducing correctly the British attitude after the last war. The facts can be stated quite briefly. On 8th December, 1919, when the Supreme Council first proposed what later became known as the Curzon Line, it was simply proposed as a line behind which the Polish Government could get on with its administration, leaving the sovereignty of territories East of that line to be settled later. It is true that on 11th July, 1920, the right hon. Gentleman the Member for Carnarvon Boroughs (Mr. David Lloyd-George), in conversation with Mr. Grabski, indicated that line as the legitimate frontier of Poland, but, on the next day, 12th July, when Lord Curzon communicated this line officially to the Polish Government, it was not as a frontier, but as a temporary line of demarcation along which hostilities might cease; it was not the case that this Line was proposed as a permanent frontier between the two countries.

There are many more important considerations to be born in mind. What is proposed by the Prime Minister is that Poland should be shifted bodily Westwards. The right hon. Gentleman did not seem to realize all the problems which that would involve for Poland. She is already involved in considerable hostility with the Soviet Union, and, if anything is calculated to make a permanent enemy of Germany, it is such a proposal. I do not say that it should not be carried out; it looks to me as though it will have to be, but it is certainly going to create immense problems for Poland, and, if the Allies urge the Polish Government to adopt such a solution, they must do one thing more—they must give a joint and several guarantee to Poland. That raises formidable problems for us, because we are traditionally averse to giving such guarantees. But we have no right to urge on Poland a solution bristling with such difficulties unless we are prepared to make our own contribution to it.

The Prime Minister has said that, if the Poles had agreed to the Curzon Line as a frontier—and, really, I wish we could drop the name "Curzon Line"; why not call it the Supreme Council Line, because "Curzon" is a misleading name and has done much harm—if the Poles had adopted the Supreme Council Line, the Lublin Committee would not have been set up. We have no assurance of that, and I am extremely doubtful myself whether that would have been the case. We are not without experience in this matter. Let us consider the case of General Sosnkowski. It may well be that he ought to have been dropped. For what it is worth, I am of that opinion myself. But when the Poles acceded to British pressure and dropped General Sosnkowski and appointed General Bor in his place, what happened? Within a few hours, General Bor, to whom no one in this Assembly is fit to hold a candle, was denounced by the Lublin Committee as a traitor, and the head of this Committee had the impudence to suggest that he should be brought to trial for his life. I am speaking strongly, but as hon. Members have already said, we ought not to be afraid to speak strongly, and I believe the Soviet Union is influenced by opinions expressed in this country and in this Chamber. I think nothing is gained by not speaking according to the light within us.

So much, then, for the question of the frontiers, except that I ought to make one more comment on the Prime Minister's reference to the subject. The right hon. Gentleman admitted that Poland, under these proposals, would lose a great deal of territory. I think the right hon. Gentleman underestimated the amount, because I think it is as large as 46.5 per cent of the area and one-third of her population. The Prime Minister said it contained the large areas of the Pripet Marshes, which are of no value to anybody. I would point out that it also includes the only oilfield in Poland and valuable deposits of phosphates, which are immaterial to Russia but of great value to Poland.

MR. PRICE: Would by hon. Friend bear in mind that the Polish population of this territory is quite a minority?

MR. THOMAS: When my hon. Friend says a minority, he is speaking of a figure just short of 50 per cent. The question which I would like to put to him is: Why does he assume that the Soviet Union alone has the right to be a multi-national State? There are many nationalities in the Soviet Union—about 200—and why should there not be two or three nationalities in Poland? I cannot see the force of the argument that the Soviet Union has the right to include all Ruthenians and all Ukrainians—

MR. PRICE: Is my hon. Friend aware that, not many years ago, there was a rebellion against Poland in these Eastern Polish territories?

PROFESSOR SAVORY (C.): Excited by the Germans and by Hitler's money.

MR. THOMAS: My hon. Friend the Member for Queen's University, Belfast, has given the answer. [*Interruption.*] My hon. Friend says I am in bad company. Well, there are occasions when we must speak our minds, and I am prepared to do it today even if I am in strange company. It was painful to me earlier on to hear the hon. Member for East Wolverhampton (Mr. Mander), who claims to carry the banner of Russell, Palmerston, Gladstone and Asquith, making the speech that he did; his party was once the champion of the rights of small nations. He is not alone; I note that many hon. Members last week were saying very different things in the Greek Debate from what they are saying today about the rights of small nations. Be that as it may, the point I wanted to make, when I was led into a digression, was this. The Soviet Union is asking for Westward extension on strategic' grounds. Surely, we have learned by now that no security can be guaranteed by strategic frontiers?

VISCOUNT HINCHINGBROOKE (C.): Moscow was saved.

MR. THOMAS: Moscow will not be saved by the westward

extension now proposed if unhappily any future war should break out.

MR. QUINTIN HOGG (C.): Are you seriously contending that you know, from a military point of view, what is better for the Soviets than the Soviets themselves? What military experience have you?

MR. THOMAS: I will only reply to that observation by saying that I have had much the same experience as the hon. Member himself.

MR. HOGG: May I say that you—

MR. DEPUTY-SPEAKER (MR. CHARLES WILLIAMS): The hon. Member for Oxford (Mr. Hogg) has been saying "you" once or twice and that refers to me. He must not use "you" in that way. Perhaps we may adjourn this conversation.

MR. THOMAS: Regretfully, I obey your ruling, Mr. Deputy-Speaker, but I think you ought to allow me to say that I have served in the Army.

MR. HOGG: I did not mean to say that my hon. Friend had not, but that, like myself, he served in a relatively humble capacity.

MR. THOMAS: That is true. It is claimed, on strategic grounds, that the Russian frontier should be extended to the West. That may be right and inevitable, but it makes nonsense of the Atlantic Charter. I thought that the Atlantic Charter still stood for something in this country. I do not believe that the proposal will produce security, which must be based on a general organization for peace and, still more, on confidence and mutual trust between the nations. I think we ought to have urged upon the Soviet Union that she should attempt to secure the peace in a different way. In any case, if the Soviet Union is afraid of further aggression from Germany, it is very hard that Poland should be the sufferer.

So much for the frontier question. I have said that, although Poland is being very hardly treated in this matter, it is not the most important matter and, no doubt, could be adjusted. There have been many changes in the Polish frontiers in the past, and, no doubt, there could be changes again. What is important is the question of independence, and that word is apparently understood differently in different quarters. We cannot do much in this Debate today. In fact, I think it is rather ominous that we are having a debate at all; if the Government had much hope that the Polish problem would be solved we should have been asked not to speak at all. There is, however, one thing we can do, and that is to get a firm pledge from the Government that they will not recognize the Lublin Committee. We are entitled to get a firm assurance from them that they will continue to recognize the Polish Government of which Mr. Arciszewski is the head in London. I very much agree with my hon. Friend that we should not refer to it as an *émigré* Government. We are entitled to a firm assurance that the British Government will continue to recognize the Polish Government as the only Government of Poland.

MR. GALLACHER (Com.): Should the Government lay it down that, under no circumstances, will they recognize the Lublin Committee, even though the circumstances may be that the Polish people themselves desire to recognize the Lublin Committee?

MISS RATHBONE: Is it not very dangerous to ask the Government to make an announcement that they will only recognize a certain Government in a foreign country? Are we not criticizing the Russian Government for doing that very thing? Should we not rather say that we will recognize whatever Government it is, even a compromise Government, if it really represents Polish opinion as far as it can be ascertained?

MR. THOMAS: No British Government will enter into the hypothetical future. All I am dealing with is the immediately foreseeable future, and I think we are entitled to the assurance for which I asked. With regard to the hon. Lady's suggestion about a compromise Government, I will deal with that later. What is the general character of these two bodies? I agree with an earlier speaker that it would be idle to go into the personal lives of the members of the Lublin Committee, but I think I may say that, if ever it became a Government, it would be the most curious medley since the administration of Uncle Tom Cobleigh.

It is a Government composed of one party and one party only; nine out of the 14 members of it are avowed members of the Communist Party. It is true that the Union of Polish Patriots, out of which it has arisen, is said to be composed of a very large number of different parties, but we in the Labor Party at least are sufficiently familiar with that technique. We have learned to recognize the Communist Party under many different names, and at any rate nine out of the 14 members of the Lublin Committee are open members of the Communist Party. The Polish Government is solidly based on four parties which, in pre-war times, could count on the support of 80 per cent of the electorate against the two per cent of the Polish Communist Party. The Polish Communist Party was so infected with Trotskyism that in 1937 it had to be disbanded and it does not dare, even now, to call itself the Communist Party, but calls itself instead the Polish Workers' Party.

It is perhaps appropriate here to say something—because the Prime Minister referred to it—about the composition of the present Polish Government. Like the Prime Minister, I have the highest admiration, in common with most hon. Members, for Mr. Mikołajczyk, but it ought to be made perfectly clear that there is no breach between him and the present Polish Government. The reasons why he and his Foreign Secretary, Mr. de Romer—who has also won the admiration of so many of us who have come into contact with him—resigned, are perfectly plain. When one method has been tried and has brought no results, it is necessary to try different methods and different men. That is all that need be said. The Polish Peasant Party have issued a strong public statement—I claim no esoteric knowledge in this matter—in support of the Government now headed by Mr. Arciszewski, which can therefore claim to be fully representative of opinion in Poland as it existed before the war and so far as it can be ascertained now.

Here I would like to address something to my Socialist comrades—I mean, colleagues—in this House. [HON. MEMBERS: "Comrades or colleagues?"] I am sorry, I thought that I was still across the way. I cannot lightly abandon a Government which has a Socialist at its head with such a distinguished record as Mr. Arciszewski, and includes such men as Dr. Pragier and Mr. Kwapinski, supported by such men as Mr. Stańczyk and Mr. Ciołkosz. At our Labor Party Conference across the road they have no doubt been singing today about "dungeons dark," but these men have lived in "dungeons dark." Mr. Kwapinski was sentenced to death on one occasion for his Socialist beliefs and only his tender years secured commutation to imprisonment. Mr. Arciszewski was leading strikes at the age of 13, and taking part in the revolution of 1905 before I was born.

MR. MACK (Lab.): Is it not anti-Socialistic to be participating in revolutions?

MR. GALLACHER: Nonsense; Mussolini was leading strikes at that age.

MR. THOMAS: I was saying, and I do not think it can be refuted, that not one of us Socialist Members of Parliament in this Chamber—not even my right hon. Friend the Member for East Edinburgh (Mr. Pethick-Lawrence), who has had some experience of prison, which most of us have not—is fit to hold a candle to such men as Mr. Arciszewski, Mr. Kwapinski, Dr. Pragier and the others. It is alleged that they are undemocratic, and they are said to be committed to the undemocratic Constitution of 1935. I would point out to my hon. Friends on these benches that two of the Socialist Ministers were put in prison for their stand against the Piłsudski régime and General Kukiel was dismissed from his post for his opposition to it. There is not the slightest reason, therefore, to doubt that this Polish Government is a really democratic Government in the sense in which we understand the word, and that it has given the most practical proofs of its democratic faith.

I said that I would deal with the suggestion of the hon. Lady the Member for the Combined English Universities (Miss Rathbone) that there might be some compromise between this Government and the Lublin Committee. I understand that certain proposals of that nature have been made, but they remind me very much of the rabbit pie which was 50 per cent rabbit and 50 per cent horse, that is to say, one rabbit, one horse. The proposal, as I understand it, would give such a preponderance to the Lublin Committee that it would, in fact, simply be the Lublin Committee. Here again, I say, we have much experience on these benches of working with Communists and it is a very difficult thing to do; it is something we have done our best, hitherto, to avoid.

MR. GALLACHER: I would like to ask the hon. Member what experience he has had in dealing with the Communists in view of the fact that I, a Communist, was in the Labor Movement almost before he was born, and have done more than most members of it to build up the Labor Movement on which he is trading now for personal ambition?

HON. MEMBERS: Oh!

MR. DEPUTY-SPEAKER: The hon. Gentleman must not accuse other hon. Members of personal ambition; I am sure he will modify that.

MR. GALLACHER: On a point of Order, Mr. Deputy-Speaker. If the hon. Member makes innuendoes against me by jeering at Communists in general, surely I have a right to retort to him?

MR. DEPUTY-SPEAKER: The hon. Gentleman must be more careful. The hon. Member for Keighley (Mr. Thomas) was referring to the Communist Party, not an individual.

MR. GALLACHER: That is me.

MR. DEPUTY-SPEAKER: What I was objecting to was the hon. Gentleman accusing the hon. Member for Keighley of personal ambition. I would ask him if he would not modify that statement.

MR. GALLACHER: Further to that point of Order, Mr. Deputy-Speaker. The hon. Member was talking about his experience of the intrigues of the Communist Party. That reflected on the honesty of the Communist Party, and I represent the Communisty Party in this House. If he casts reflections on my honesty, surely I am entitled to make reflections on his? I have a bigger opinion of my own honesty than I have of his.

MR. DEPUTY-SPEAKER: I admit it is rather a difficult position, as the hon. Member is the only representative of a party, so perhaps, under the circumstances, it would be best if the hon. Member for Keighley continued his speech.

MR. THOMAS: It it will help to ease matters, Mr. Deputy-Speaker, I would point out that this is not the kind of speech which is likely to further any personal ambitions I might have; in fact, for all I know, I might be signing a political death warrant for myself. Be that as it may, the point I was trying to make was that in the Labor Party we have had perpetually this problem of working with the Communist Party—not in this House, but outside—and have always been very careful to avoid it. I cannot bring myself now to recommend to another country what I am not prepared to do myself.

The most important thing I wish to say is this. The Polish problem is almost insuperably difficult, and my right hon. Friends on the Front Bench have my deepest sympathy in their responsibility for dealing with it. It may very well be that no satisfactory solution can be achieved, but may I ask one thing? It is, that they should not urge upon the Polish Government a solution which does not command itself to their consciences on its merits. If it cannot commend itself to them as a good solution in itself, let us ask that they shall not urge it upon the Polish Government. Let us cast our minds back to the days of Munich. As I understand the Munich agreement, the real evil was not that it was entered into; in the long chain of circumstances that was probably inevitable.

The wicked thing to my mind was that we tried to compel the Czech Government to accept a solution which we knew was immoral, and that is the danger I see in this present situation, that His Majesty's Government should try to urge upon the Polish Government something which they know to be wrong. I would like to see His Majesty's Government urging a just and generous solution of this question.

I would like them to take up the matter with the Soviet Union and say, "You have every reason to be generous. You have one-sixth of the earth's surface. By 1970 you will have a population of 250,000,000. You have every raw material you can possibly desire in abundant quantities for yourself and for export. You have nothing to fear from any country in the world. What can it possibly matter to you whether you have a few hundred square miles of Polish territory or not? This will guarantee your security; your security will come, above all, from the strength of your own resources, from the fighting qualities of your population, and from the faith that you have given to them since your revolution. These are the things that guarantee your security and, alongside that, will be the general international agreements into which we shall enter." In this spirit His Majesty's Government ought to urge upon the Soviet Union that they can afford to be generous with Poland, and that they ought to be generous, and if His Majesty's Government cannot secure such a settlement, then let us not urge anything else upon the Poles. Let us, as the United States appears to be doing, refrain from making any recommendations which we cannot commend to our own consciences.

We are bound deeply in this matter by our interests and by our honor. I say "our interests" not in any narrow sense, for I do not suppose that British citizens have any considerable material interests in Poland. Our interests are of a different order. The greatest of all British interests is to maintain peace and order throughout the world, and the Polish problem is the most serious threat to that order we have yet faced. If we cannot solve it justly and generously, the outlook for the future is indeed dark. We are bound also in honor by engagements we have signed. I cannot think lightly of that Treaty of Guarantee into which we entered in 1939, or of the Atlantic Charter, or of the other engagements that bind us. Those Treaties are not simply written in ink; they have since been sealed in blood. If it had not been for the Polish airmen who fought in the Battle of Britain we might have gone under in 1940, for the margin was very narrow. Ever since those days, wherever the fighting has been thickest, the Polish soldiers have been there—at Monte Cassino, at Breda, at Arnhem, and a dozen other places where valor is to be seen and distinction to be gained. On the high seas the Polish sailors have fought with a gallantry equal to our own. We have, therefore, a very special interest in trying to see a just settlement of this question, and I urge His Majesty's Government that they shall not lightly abandon the Polish cause, or give up hope too easily, but will urge the Soviet Union to be generous.

MR. TREE (C.): Whether we agree with the hon. Member for Keighley (Mr. Ivor Thomas) or not, I think everybody in the House will agree that he made an extremely courageous speech. Anyone who wishes to take part in this Debate today will do so with a very deep sense of responsibility that a chance word or phrase he might make may exacerbate a situation which all of us in this House deplore, and which we all hope may yet be capable of solution in spite of the Prime Minister's somewhat gloomy prognostications this morning. Before starting to express my own views, I would like to say a word or two of praise to the way in which the Prime Minister and the Foreign Secretary have attempted, over many months and with infinite patience, to solve this extraordinary difficult and complex problem. A journey to Moscow by air is at any time a difficult undertaking, but when it is undertaken in the autumn far advanced by a man of the age of the Prime Minister it does, indeed, show how deeply he has the matter at heart. The reason why the British Government are striving so hard to solve this well-nigh age-long problem is not only because we are bound by a treaty of Alliance, and guarantees with Poland, but because we owe to the Polish people a debt of gratitude which it is extremely difficult to express in mere words.

We welcomed their Government when they were driven out of their second capital four years ago and they have been our welcome guests ever since. As the last speaker said, wherever we have fought the Poles have fought by our side, whether it was on the sea with their ships, fighting beside our own, or doing convoy duty together, or whether it was fighting with our Armies in Norway and France before the fall of France, and afterwards through Egypt and Libya right up to the rugged mountains of Italy, and now in North-West Europe. I was told only recently of what a great honor was felt by a famous British regiment when, having fought side by side with their Polish Allies in Italy, they were asked to wear on their sleeves the insignia of the "Mermaid of Warsaw." We cannot forget either that it was in the Battle of Britain that we were so nobly assisted by a very large number of Polish airmen and that in Poland alone, of all the occupied countries, no quisling has yet been found. These are things we must not, and cannot, forget. Nor should it be forgotten either that we are bound by a treaty of 20 years' alliance with our Russian Allies and that we have a profound admiration for their war effort, which comes closest to our own in a total war effort, and of the way in which they have fought in order that the war may be brought to a speedy conclusion and of the casualties they have suffered. During the period in which we have fought with Russia, and they have been our Allies, there has been on both sides a gradual breaking down of the suspicion and distrust that existed between the two nations in the 20 years between wars. I think everywhere in this country there is a profound realization, as the Prime Minister said so truly today, that unless we and the United States and the USSR can get together on some definite understanding the outlook for the world, for Europe especially, and for Poland, separated from us by many hundreds of miles, will indeed be dark.

It is with this general background in mind that we have to approach the complex and difficult problem that we are facing today—relations between Russia and Poland. It seems to be essential that we should do so not by taking sides or by attempting to aggravate what is already a raw and open wound—

MR. PICKTHORN: When my hon. Friend recommends that we should not takes sides does he mean that we should not take sides with our Allies?

MR. TREE: They are both our Allies. We must try to take the medium course, and mediate between them. Unless this understanding is arrived at, the outlook for the peace of the world is, as I have said, very dark. The dispute between Russia and Poland covers many issues, and on each of them much could be said. They go back into the dark recesses of history. Boundaries and cities, minorities, economics, religions and ideologies all play their part. But it surely all boils down to this: that the majority of Poles today are deeply suspicious of Russia's intentions in regard to them at the end of the war. They believe that Russia intends gradually to whittle away their powers until once more Poland occupies the status of a Grand Duchy, except that instead of having a grand duke there will be a commissar, and that instead of there being a grand duchy they will become a Sovietized member of the USSR. Therefore, because of that suspicion they believe it best to delay coming to any decisions on frontier or other matters, as they were strongly urged to do by the Prime Minister and Premier Stalin at Moscow, because they feel that if they are able to defer and delay, the Soviet Government and the Lublin Committee will get into great difficulties, owing to lack of support when they get into the liberated countries of Poland, and that rather than face a hostile Poland lying athwart their communications between Germany and Russia they will have to come to the Polish Government and ask for help in order to restore law and order.

I think the Prime Minister had the support of the whole House today when he said he would prefer that all discussions in regard to frontiers should be deferred until they could be discussed in the quieter conditions of a Peace Conference, but surely the main thesis of the Poles, in wishing to defer and delay, is the wrong one. Premier Stalin has constantly said—and I think the Prime Minister reiterated it in his speech—that he wishes to see a strong and independent Poland and, moreover, that he has not the slightest interest in the internal affairs of a future Polish State. But he does insist, and I think rightly, that there should be a Polish Government that is friendly in outlook to its neighbor in the East. Further—and this is an important point—as more and more of Poland is liberated there is an obvious danger that if the Lublin Committee is the only Committee on the spot then to it will be assigned the job of administering the liberated countries. Somebody will have to administer them, and it will be to it that this job will be given. I have no more desire than any previous speaker to see more power being given to the Lublin Committee. I believe, from everything I have heard about them, that they are a seedy and obviously unrepresentative group of men. The suggestion, as I understand it, was made in Moscow, that as soon as Mr. Mikołajczyk could get back to this country, and obtain the consent of his Government, he should then return to Lublin and take part in a Coalition Government. While we may all agree that the Lublin Committee should not have, say, 50 per cent representation in that Government surely, if they are not representative and have not got the support of the Polish people, they will ultimately disappear as personalities from the scene. I think it is a tragedy that this did not happen, and that instead a policy of wait and see should have been adopted by the present Polish Government. I quite realize that it is easy to suggest from London what should be done, and I do not think we have any right to interfere in the internal affairs of the Polish Government. Nevertheless, I would urge very strongly that they should make another effort to get into touch, once again, with the Russian Government towards a solution of this problem and that this effort should have the full support of the British Government.

In conclusion, I have one other concrete suggestion I should like to make to the Foreign Secretary. At the end of this war there will be a large number of Poles who have served in the Forces alongside us who, if there is a frontier rectification, will find themselves living outside their country and moreover in a country towards which they have no religious or political leanings. Many will be transferred to the new territories that will be handed over to Poland under the peace treaties, but it may be that a certain number will not wish to make their homes there. The suggestion I should like to make is that any of those people should be given the right, if they so desire, of becoming citizens of this country, and that arrangements should be entered into with the Dominions so that if they wish to settle in one of them they will be able to do so. We all know the intense love of the Poles for their own country. I daresay that only a few would choose to become British citizens, but I think it would be a gesture towards those who may have to be moved from the homes they love, and will do something to repay a debt of gratitude that we owe to Poland and the Polish people.

LIEUT.-COLONEL SIR WALTER SMILES (C.) : I can only speak on this matter as an average Britisher, but at the same time I should like later to speak as I think the average Pole is thinking. I have no particular knowledge of Poland, having been there only two or three times, and all my sympathies are on the side of Russia, because of the many kindnesses which I have received from Russian people. At the end of the last war, when I was asked to volunteer to fight in some of those sideshows at Archangel and down in Odessa I refused, because I did not want to be killing Russians, although I did not mind killing Germans. Certainly I have no prejudice against them, but at the present moment what has happened in Poland? What is the average British person thinking? He thinks that Poland has been murdered, thinks it has been murdered largely by the Germans, and also that many Poles have been murdered by the Russians. He thinks, rightly or wrongly, that a million Poles have been deported to Siberia and elsewhere; and those who have been sent to Siberia will be very fortunate if half of them ever see their homes or their relatives again. The hon. Lady the Member for the Combined English Universities (Miss Rathbone) mentioned all that, and there is no need for me to go into that matter again, but when Czechoslovakia was invaded by Germany in March, 1939, some of us remember a little peccadillo on the part of Poland, who seized Teschen. A lot of people are always inclined to blame their own country for anything in the nature of Imperialism, but occasionally some foreign countries make mistakes along those lines.

I want us to keep our feet upon the ground; not to think of the world as we would like it to be, but as it really is in 1944. Who is going to settle the Western frontiers of Russia? Who is going to decide how much of Finland Russia will take; how much of Estonia, Latvia and Lithuania; how much of Poland; how much of Hungary, Czechoslovakia and Rumania? At any rate let us distinguish between those countries; let us remember those which fought with us and those which fought against us. I have every sympathy with those Polish statesmen who would not sign that agreement. It might have been very much better for this country if many of our statesmen had not signed these various agreements. It might have been better for the right hon. Member for Ross and Cromarty (Mr. Malcolm MacDonald) if he had never signed that agreement giving away the Irish ports, so that 10,000 of our seamen are at the bottom of the sea through him. If I were one of those Polish statemen I would refuse to sign that agreement unless the United States of America, this country and the British Dominions signed at the same time.

We signed a pact to protect Czechoslovakia—that was when the late Mr. Neville Chamberlain went to Munich—and Hitler broke it in March, 1939, when he marched into Prague. It is no use our signing anything which we cannot guarantee.

We signed a pact to defend Poland. Have we done so? Goodness knows how many millions of Poles have died since we signed that pact, and we should be well advised not to sign any more pacts unless we are sure we can carry them out. But if the United States of America sign also it is a very different matter. The hon. Member for South-East Essex (Mr. Raikes) spoke about ghosts. I think the ghost of Woodrow Wilson may be abroad just now. He signed a pact in the Treaty of Versailles, and when he went home to America the Americans rolled him in the gutter. It seems that we need more than the Prime Minister or the President of the United States to sign a pact, and I would say to the Poles, "Be very careful if there is to be a pact that the pact will be kept."

What about our Dominions? I never heard that there was any great enthusiasm on their part to come in with us at the time of Munich, but they did come in with us most wholeheartedly and gallantly when the Germans marched into Poland. Are we certain, with things as they are in Canada today, that Canada will put her name to a pact to guarantee the future frontiers of Poland? Are we sure about Australia? New Zealand we can perhaps rely upon. It took Field-Marshal Smuts all his time to bring South Africa into the war. We may as well face the facts as they really are. But if these various countries do come in and sign on the dotted line to guarantee the frontiers of Poland they would be very well advised to agree to this: I would not mind seeing those people transferred if we were sure that once they had been transferred they would be protected from the hatred of Germany and others who may perhaps be jealous of them.

Let us not forget that all these agreements and disagreements in Europe just now are meat for Hitler. They encourage him to hold out a bit longer, in the hope that the Allies may quarrel among themselves. I would advise the Poles that, if we get these various nations to agree, it would be very wise for them to reconsider the proposals put up by our Prime Minister today, remembering that the world is not what they would wish it to be but is as it is today.

MR. MARTIN (Lab.) : I agree very cordially with the sentence with which my hon. Friend the Member for Harborough (Mr. Tree) opened his remarks, reminding us how tragic this question was, because this is the saddest and most intractable story in the whole history of civilization. I think it is rather melancholy that this House is tending today to divide itself into Right and Left in its sympathies in this matter, to make an ideological problem out of what is really a fundamental political question of the gravest importance to the future of Europe and the world. I came here this afternoon hoping to make a few remarks on the Russian and Polish aspect of this question, but after listening to the speech of the Prime Minister I should like to devote my time to directing attention to what I think is by far the gravest aspect of this situation, the problem of world peace and international relations, which it implies.

I do not think this is an occasion for considering what capital the Germans, Japanese or anyone else are going to make out of divisions amongst the Allies. I think the unity of the Allies towards accomplishing the defeat of the Germans and Japanese and dealing with them at the end of the war is something which cannot and will not be shattered by any differences about the future. I think it is patent that there is a profound distinction between the two great Powers at this moment on these questions. I felt my hon. Friend the Senior Burgess for Cambridge University (Mr. Pickthorn) put his finger on the fundamental point of the Debate when he said the American State Department has declared that it will not be responsible at present for guaranteeing frontiers in Europe. We have based our case largely upon the agreement between this country, the United States and the Soviet Union and that the Soviet Union is determined to alter frontiers in a certain respect in a final sense before the war is concluded and the Peace Conference assembles. That is a matter of great substance and importance. I have always hoped and humbly worked, as far as it was within my power, for the agreement with Russia and for the Treaty. I believe the Poles must face realities and will be obliged, in the nature of things, to understand that the Treaty of Riga and the non-aggression Pact of 1934 and all the other historical and political matters on which she has based so much of her case—[AN HON. MEMBER: "Are mere scraps of paper."] I will not say that, but she must accept the fact that they are not altogether relevant to the situation as it is today. I think the Russians are justified in maintaining that position and I think the Poles must alter their approach to the question. None the less, we have to face the question of drastic and decisive alteration of the frontiers of Europe. If it is true that it is necessary for the peace of Europe for us to agree to these alterations, involving the transposition of large numbers of people of three or four different races—perhaps millions—in circumstances which will involve deep and growing economic problems, what case have we for denying the same claim, or a similar claim, which may be made in a short time by other countries for similar alterations in the map of Europe? What case have we for denying to France the Rhine countries? What case have we for denying adjustments to Czechoslovakia, Denmark and half a dozen other countries? If these adjustments one after the other are conceded to political agitation before peace is signed, we shall find ourselves at the peace table with a situation which it will be almost impossible to unravel. I well understand the position of the American people and the State Department in refusing to commit themselves at this stage.

I turn to the problem of the relations of the three great Powers. The Foreign Secretary is constantly reminding us—in the early days when he did it I had a great deal of sympathy with him—that the future of mankind is based upon the maintenance of good relations between the USA, the USSR and ourselves. I think that was profoundly true, and it is profoundly true today, but reiteration is perhaps giving it a false perspective. Although we shall never build a permanent peace system without unity between those three great Powers, I do not believe that any serious student of these matters believes that the future of the world can be indefinitely maintained on any dictatorship of a triumvirate, however admirable and powerful that triumvirate may be. I think the time must come when other nations will feel that the situation is intolerable. The time must come when, as a result of the psychological and political pressure of other nations, there must be moral and political strains between the three members of that group, and there must be moral and political concessions in which they do not really believe, made by one or other of these three members towards maintaining the harmony of that triumvirate, and when you come to that point you are back again at Munich and the policy of appeasement. What was wrong with the policy of appeasement was not that a concession made to another Power in the interest of peace was in itself necessarily wrong, but that a concession made against the political interests of the world or against the moral integrity of nations must fundamentally carry with it a gradual but increasingly rapid progress towards internecine conflicts between the peoples involved.

I gather from the set-up at present that the position is that we hope to try to tide over the immediate necessities of the moment hoping that after the war things may possibly improve. Unless this arrangement of the triumvirate is maintained from now on with the deliberate purpose of erecting a peace system which shall have functional value for maintaining harmony between the nations of the civilized world, I do not think we shall get anywhere at all. Gradually there is growing up in the world something comparable to the growth of great joint stock companies in the economic and industrial sphere during the last 50 years. We are gradually seeing the emergence of power in the sense of great aggregations of population in various parts of the world. We have Russia with nearly 200,000,000 people, the United States with over 130,000,000, Japan with 100,000,000, and China with 400,000,000. Then we have India, which will probably at no distant date join the comity of nations and may conceivably become a great Power and a great industrial nation with three or four hundred million people. All these great Powers are emerging on the civilized scene. It seems to me that the dangers of some sort of centripetal conflict between them all will gradually emerge after the war unless we can find some satisfactory solution to the problem of these complicated international relations.

I do not see, as I said just now, the tripartite arrangement lasting for ever, but I do see something appearing on the world scene which is not so very different from the conception of federal union advocated so strongly in the years immediately preceding the war. I think that the policy of the United States in the last few years shows that they are very carefully watching the political scene to see whether some kind of world State, some kind of world arrangement, some kind of world organization can be evolved that is likely to function. If such an organization does not seem likely to function, the United States have an alternative. That alternative has always been implicit in United States policy since President Monroe, with the approval of the most eminent of the surviving "Founding Fathers," propounded his famous doctrine, which may grow into a rather novel form of Imperialism.

The nucleus of that Imperial community must necessarily be the American Continent. Of the States of the American Continent, the most important to its success from the United States point of view must obviously be the Dominion of Canada. Canada is related to the United States, not only by ties of a common political outlook and sympathy, by many important racial ties and by the most important economic ties of any other American State, but by the fact that she is obviously in the key position for the development of American strategy in a world that is going to be preparing for conflict rather than for peace. I do think that that is an aspect of the matter we have to consider very seriously. Canada cannot, however, be loyal to—and I think she is very loyal to—and however much she appreciates the Imperial ideal, disregard the fact that her strategic, economic and political interests are bound up with those of the American Continent to a degree which must primarily dictate her political actions in every world problem that may arise. In that respect she is the most important and vital link between ourselves and the United States and can play a great part in that regard. But in the last resort the interests of Canada must follow the situation in which Providence and geography have placed her.

Beyond this we see emerging out of this nucleus of an American commonwealth two important buttresses. One is the Western buttress in the Pacific, consisting of Australia and New Zealand. They, too, must have their place in this new commonwealth. They, too, must play an important part in its development. We should remember that when the Australian Continent was threatened, as it was not long ago, with the most terrible disaster, what the Australians found happening was this. It was not the people of Fremantle and Perth who, looking out over the Western waters, saw the British Fleet coming to their aid; it was the people of Sydney who, from Eastern windows, saw the American Pacific Fleet coming to defend them from the Japanese. It was not to the Prime Minister that they were obliged to turn, but rather to President Roosevelt. It was not Lord Wavell but General MacArthur who became their supreme commander-in-chief. In these changes in the map of Europe we have to take into account that that kind of preponderance in the political set-up will gradually develop. If Australia and New Zealand constitute the Western buttress of this new commonwealth, it is certain where the Eastern buttress is going to be. It is going to be in this island.

The only reason I have dwelt on this aspect of the matter is that we are no longer, after the war is over, if the world is to be a war preparing world again, going to be the deciding factor in the future of the British Empire; that we have to face the fact that major decisions will be taken in Washington; that we, as well as Canada, Australia and New Zealand, must accept the facts of geography; and that the gradual development of the political scene will be in favor of the loss of gravity and of the political importance of this island and of the shifting of the center of importance to Washington and the United States. I commend these considerations, not so much to this House and this country, as to the Union of Soviet Republics. If the three great Powers are allowed to drift apart before they have built up an adequate peace organization, if we begin the peace in a conflict of disagreements and hostility, if we have to accept always solutions to which we cannot give wholehearted moral and political subscription, I suggest that the future trend of events is not necessarily in favor of a happy and progressive growth of the Union of Soviet Republics. I suggest that we may enter a fresh conflict in Europe, which will only be solved by a third world war far more tragic and terrible than anything that has been seen in this war.

I would urge that we turn from this maneuvering to set up a new balance of power in Europe, and try really to solve the problems which the European conflict of a thousand years presents to us; to try, not in a hurry, to commit ourselves to frontiers or agreements or transpositions of population; and to try to accomplish just four things. They are, to defer the final settlements of the peace for a period of from five to ten years after the war with Germany ends and to set up, in that period, four commissions. One of them should be concerned with minorities and might study the problem which frontiers and minorities present; one to be entrusted with the control of certain exemplary raw materials and to see how far it is possible for the world to exercise a common control over important raw materials for an experimental period; one to study the question of international finance; and the last to superintend the problem of controlling national armaments and building up by degrees an international peace system.

None of those things is practicable in the present state of the world or ultimately in a world which consists of nothing but sovereign States, but all are matters upon which we can begin, slowly and carefully over a period of years, to work out, and on which, if we can get, after studied investigation, some reports, it might be possible, at a peace conference five or ten years after the war is over, to have the beginnings of an enduring peace system.

MR. PETHERICK (C.) :I will refrain from following my hon. Friend on the Cook's tour all the way around the Empire with which he has just favored the House and, if he will permit me to do so, I will bring the focus of the Debate back to the question of the Polish-Russian relations. When I listened to the Prime Minister today, I could not help noticing the feeling of the House, as one so often can. Instead of, as we have so often seen recently, cheers and counter cheers for or against the Prime Minister's policy, we heard, all the way through his speech, hardly a cheer and a sort of awful, ugly, apprehensive, cold silence. That was significant, and the speeches that have followed have justified the idea which one had of the way in which this House and the country are feeling in this matter. I am sure that the speeches of my hon. and gallant Friend the Member for South-East Essex (Mr. Raikes), the Senior Burgess for Cambridge University (Mr. Pickthorn) and the hon. Member for Keighley (Mr. Ivor Thomas), who made a first-rate and most courageous speech, and, last, but not least, of the hon. Lady the Member for the Combined English Universities (Miss Rathbone), with whom I have often disagreed in the past, today spoke and I believe represented the real voice of Britain.

Let us consider the situation. My hon. Friend the Member for South-East Essex asked what would have been thought in 1940, supposing we had been told in this House what was going to happen. I will take it back another year. Suppose the late Prime Minister, Mr. Neville Chamberlain, announcing the British declaration of war on behalf of His Majesty's Government on 3rd September, 1939, had said, finishing his speech: "In five years' time, this Poland, which we have come into the war to defend, will be severed, and half will be offered to another Power." It is a horrifying thought, that one dare hardly even contemplate.

I should have liked to refer to the question of the Baltic States, because I believe that their future and the future of Poland are bound up closely together. I do not do so only because I do not wish to take too long, but I would say that the situation in the Baltic States now controlled by Russia is a very serious and a very ugly one. If hon. Members will get the most recent bulletin of the Institute of International Affairs and will read the part which deals with the four countries, I think they will have en eye opener. I believe that Poland should engage our attention even more, because Poland is a test case, not only of what is going to happen between now and the end of the war but of the peace treaties, when we come to that period.

Poland is entitled to full respect from the people of this country. It is not only because, as many hon. Members have said, she has fought so gallantly in the war and not only because we came into the war to defend Poland against German aggression but also because she is a very ancient State which, in spite of four partitions, has still maintained within its borders a strong people, speaking a distinct language and with a strong and powerful racial sense. In spite of all those vicissitudes, she is determined to remain an independent nation. After all those terrible times that they have had, in the last 200 years—and indeed before, when they were standing up to the Asiatic hordes—when Poland was attacked by Germany she was the first country in Europe which stood up and fought, because she was determined not to be overrun by German aggressors. She fought with very little hope, but she fought for six weeks in circumstances of great gallantry.

Now we are asked, and our attention is focused upon this possibility—I do not think it has gone any farther than that for the moment—of handing over half Poland, that is to say, up to the Curzon Line, to Russia. I am not going to ask whether the peoples on the East of the Curzon Line are Russian or mainly Pole and I do not agree with the hon. Member who spoke earlier as to racial alignment. It is not necessary, for the reason that, on four successive occasions, treaties have been made, freely entered into, by the Russian Government and by the Polish Government on the matter. It was first laid down in the Treaty of Riga in 1921, and then confirmed in the treaties of 1932, 1934 and 1941, what those boundaries were. After 1921, at the time of the Treaty of Riga, the boundaries were never in dispute on any occasion. Why then are they in dispute now? There can be only one answer. I beg His Majesty's Government to look at the crude realities. I do not wish to overstate my case in any way. There can be only one answer why they are in dispute now, and that is because Russia says she wants that particular territory. It is the only, the inescapable, conclusion, that we can draw from that.

Since 1921, Russo-Polish relations have been, on the whole, fairly good until of course in 1939 when that unfortunate affair happened, when Russia entered Poland behind the back of the Polish Armies, and seized a certain portion of Polish territory. Then, after that, relations again happily improved when, as a result of the German attack on Russia, Russian views on these matters underwent a very great change. In General Sikorski's Premiership, as we all know—and this is important—a Treaty, the fourth Treaty, was freely entered into between Poland and Russia which read as follows:

> "The Government of the USSR recognize the Soviet-German Treaty of 1939 as to territorial changes in Poland as having lost their validity.
>
> The two Governments agree to render each other material support at all times in the present war against Hitlerite Germany."

The result of that Treaty was clearly to undo the effects of the Russian action in 1939 and to revert to Poland's pre-war frontiers. At that time the present Secretary of State welcomed that agreement, as it was quite natural he should; so I think did the whole of the British people. He handed a note to General Sikorski the operative part of which was as follows:

> "His Majesty's Government in the United Kingdom has not undertaken any obligations to the USSR which would affect the

relations between that State and Poland. I also desire to state that His Majesty's Government does not recognize any territorial change made in Poland since August, 1939."*

I would like to ask, for what reason have they departed from that perfectly explicit statement of their views? There was, further, the Anglo-Polish Treaty made on 25th August, 1939, as a result of which we came into the war. I would like to ask my right hon. Friend a further question on this Treaty. Some of us know that there was an unpublished protocol to that Treaty, a protocol I have seen with my own eyes. It did not come into my hands from any Polish source; there was no breach of faith on the part of anyone. That protocol if I read it correctly, and I believe I did, further reinforces the obligation of His Majesty's Government to the Polish nation.

MR. EDEN: To what was my hon. Friend referring?

MR. PETHERICK: I was referring to the Anglo-Polish Treaty of 1939, to which there was an unpublished protocol.**

In addition, we have the Atlantic Charter. I agree with the Senior Burgess for Cambridge University in having neither particular affection for nor placing enormous reliance on the Atlantic Charter because I thought we should get into very serious trouble as a result of it. But the Prime Minister in his interpretation of the Atlantic Charter today got the wording all wrong. It was not at all what the Atlantic Charter says. It says that they, that is, the high contracting parties,

> "desire to see no territorial changes that do not accord with the freely expressed wishes of the people concerned."

How can the peoples freely express their wishes on the questions of frontiers or Governments? They can only do so by means of free elections, not free elections under a regime which would only allow one party to offer themselves for election, but free elections as we understand them in this country —that is the only way, to my mind, in which we are to fulfil not the spirit but the actual terms of the Atlantic Charter,

---

* Vol. I, p. 471–473.
** Vol. I, p. 191.

and can allow any part of Europe to be changed except, of course, enemy countries.

I come to the Curzon Line because I believe that relations have unfortunately steadily deteriorated in the last few months since the mention of the Curzon Line. We only heard of that immediately after the Conference at Teheran, when the Prime Minister, for the first time, in my opinion highly unfortunately, made mention of the Curzon Line in the House of Commons. What is the Curzon Line? If you go about talking to people outside this House who ought to be quite well informed they have the idea from this name that it must be something respectable, an honest Conservative view given by an honest Conservative statesmen, as to where a line of demarcation between Poland and Russia should be drawn. What was the Curzon Line? It was on 8th December, 1919, that the Supreme Allied Council in Paris made this declaration, in view of the chaos in Eastern Europe and the fighting on the Polish frontiers as the result of all kinds of terrible results coming from the war. They thought it best to make a declaration that the Polish Government then in being should have the right to form a Government and administer territory up to a certain suggested line.

I would draw the attention of the House to this: There was a very distinct proviso, which I can quote in the original French, if anybody would like me to do so, which said that that line up to which the Polish Government was entitled to take over and administer the territory was without prejudice to the ultimate stipulations which will fix the definitive Eastern frontiers of Poland. The Russian-Polish war went on for some time until Mr. Grabski in 1920 agreed to sign an immediate armistice on the basis that

> "the Polish Army retires to and stands on the line fixed by the Peace Conference"—

that was the declaration of 8th December, 1919, as the administrative boundary up to which the then Polish Government was allowed to operate—

"as the provisional boundary of Polish administration; and that the Soviet Armies halt 50 kilometres to the east of that line."

As a result of that the next day His Majesty's Government made a proposal to Russia the terms of which are now being considered by the House.

It seems to make it perfectly plain that at every stage the Curzon Line was nothing more or less than an armistice line, and the statement of the Allied Powers in 1919 made it clear that this boundary which was roughly the Curzon Line up to which the Polish Government were allowed to take over was only a provision line and not in the least definitive. I need not add anything more except to point once again to the fact that that provisional line became a definitive line by free agreement between the Poles and Russia by the Treaty of Riga, 1921, which was re-affirmed three times later.

Mention has been made of the Lublin Committee. I leave that, because, in my opinion, the question of the Lublin Committee is much less important than the question of frontiers, for this reason: A country cannot have independence, it cannot have an independent Government, unless its frontiers are assured, and in my opinion the Lublin Committee was never regarded seriously by the Russians and was merely put up as a stalking horse to give what they thought they wanted so far as boundaries were concerned. I think my right hon. Friend the Secretary of State and, indeed, the Prime Minister in Moscow were perhaps not very wise in paying too much attention to and in treating the Lublin Committee too seriously as they appear to have done. The Lublin Committee is utterly fictitious and the Russians, who are very sensible and wise people in these matters, know perfectly well, just the same as everybody else does, that the Lublin Committee is bogus and was utterly unnecessary except in order to achieve a certain ulterior purpose.

What is the final suggestion? It is that Poland is to lose half her territory, and that she will lose one-third of her population. Apparently the plea is that that is necessary in order to give defense in depth to Moscow. We, whose Armies, with the American armies, are engaged in operations for the defense of the Low Countries might just as well say that we, who have experienced war at the gates of our country, will remain in occupation there after this war, because we require defense in depth for London. What a cry would arise, not only from the Belgians but from the French, our own people, and indeed the Russians, if we made such a monstrous suggestion.

MR. AUSTIN HOPKINSON (Ind.): My hon. Friend has forgotten another point, which would make his analogy complete. Not only should we take part of the country which we have occupied, but, also, we should say to the Government of the remainder of the country, that they should meet only with our approval.

MR. PETHERICK: I am very grateful to my hon. Friend for his interruption, because I know he wished to make an imperfect speech rather better than it was likely to be. I would remind him of another point on the question of so-called compensation. It is suggested that East Prussia should be given to Poland as compensation. But the Poles do not want East Prussia as compensation. It is the same as if you took away East Anglia from Britain, and gave it to Germany, and offered us Normandy instead. It is a monstrous suggestion.

I am coming to the end of my speech, which I fear has been rather controversial. I believe that it is most important, not only in our interests and in Polish interests, but, oddly enough, in Russia's interests too, that we should speak perfectly frankly. Little has been mentioned today of Russian interests and rights; but certainly Russian interests and Russian rights should also be considered in discussing these matters. I believe that the greatest of all Russian interests is the same as the greatest of British interests—that is, peace, and being able to live within her own borders a peaceful life, and so to order her own people as she likes: not as any other country in the world likes, but as she likes. One very important Russian interest is that she must be allowed to carry on her immense work of reconstruction after the ravages of this war, so that she may, after a period of time, try, as we shall have to, to get a better standard of life for her population. Lastly, does it really pay Russia in the long run to have a whole lot of Irelands around her frontiers, all struggling to be free, and troubling not only Europe, but Russia herself?

Four Powers—Great Britain, France, the United States, and Russia—have all suffered terribly together in this war. They are all agreed that Germany must be completely destroyed as a military Power. Each of them, including Russia, is fully entitled to security within its frontiers. When Germany is defeated, and defeated completely, there must no longer be any danger to Russia or anyone else in Europe from Germany, and consequently Russia, so far as Europe is concerned, can feel completely safe. Those great Powers, having won their right to independence and to live their own lives, should also be generous—and I believe that this is a Russian interest too—to those smaller Powers, who cannot always stand up militarily for their own rights and their own independence.

Is it impossible to bring Russia to see this? Some Members believe that it is not possible, but I believe that it is possible. I do not believe that Russia intends to pursue the purely Imperialistic policy which so many hon. Members, and some members of the public, in this country and in the United States, believe is likely. Some effort should be made; because if Great Britain, America, Russia, and France can stand together, the peace of Europe is assured for 100 years to come, but if all that happens is that one aggressor is completely ground in the dust and there is another aggressor arising in Europe, we cannot look forward to peace, not only for a 100 years, but for a single day. The greatest British interest is British honor, and we were deeply committed to Poland when we came into this war. There will be no peace in Europe, or in the world, unless as a result of the Russian policy in respect to Poland, it is clear to the whole world that power is only the man-at-arms of justice.

MR. MACK (Lab.): The hon. Member for Penryn and Falmouth (Mr. Petherick) apologized for the fact that he might be controversial. I can assure him that I did not object, having in mind the controversy that my remarks might arouse; because, unlike practically all the preceding speakers, I am an unrepentant friend of Russia, and have been such not only in the roseate times of today, but in years back, when Russia was not *persona grata* with the powers that be. I have rarely heard in this House so reactionary a speech as that which was delivered by my hon, and gallant Friend the Member for Wirral (Captain Graham), who, if he will not mind my saying so, has established himself as a pitiable stooge of the Polish reactionaries, and does not represent in any sense the Polish people—neither he nor the droning chorus which has gathered around him, and which has been particularly evident in this Debate. I am sorry to say that there are in other parts of the House apologetical hirelings of Poland, who have voiced a feeling——

CAPTAIN GRAHAM: May I ask the hon. Gentleman for a definition of the word "hireling," in case he has to withdraw it?

MR. MACK: I am not here to educate the hon. and gallant Member in the use of language, which no doubt he understands perfectly. Furthermore, I have not referred specifically to any particular Member. Generally speaking, the attitude of Russia can be epitomized in the lines of Shakespeare:

> "it is excellent—
> To have a giant's strength; but it is tyrannous
> To use it like a giant."

I think that all fair-minded people will agree that Russia, in her relations with all the small nations around her, has shown an understanding, and in some cases a solicitude, which has not always been deserved. In the case of Poland, which is being represented as a democratic, Christian country, with all the virtues that one associates with those terms, suffering under the lash of Russia, and liable to be submerged and completely obliterated from the comity of nations, I think that that can only be described as a completely distorted picture. The Poland that we know is not the Poland of Chopin, of Paderewski or even of John Sobieski. Rather it is the Poland of peasants, mostly impoverished, and of a landed feudal aristocracy which has ruled tyrannously for hundreds of years. [*Interruption.*] I am not speaking of the Government that is here at present, but of the Government which had power and control over the Poles in Poland, and which helped reduce that peasantry to the parlous condition in which it remained. [An HON MEMBER: "Which Government?"] We have the assurance of Marshal Stalin—[*Interruption*]—I do not mind interruptions, because the verbosity of hon. Members opposite indicates their paucity of intelligence. The fact remains that, on 28th April, 1943, the Russian Government broke off negotiations with the Polish Government in London for certain reasons, among which may be mentioned the type of propaganda in which the Polish Government indulged in regard to Katyn, in which they supported the propaganda of Goebbels, which claimed that tens of thousands of Polish officers had been cruelly murdered by the Russians.*

More than that, every Member of Parliament in this House is familiar with a type of propaganda received by post casting aspersions on the Russians and their actions by certain sections of the Poles in London. Again, we had the case not long ago, when this House expressed itself very strongly against the attitude of certain Polish military chiefs, who differentiated between minorities of nationals in their own Army in this country. Indeed, they had a very sorry record. Finally, I know, from personal association, that there are internecine quarrels amongst the Poles themselves, and it is quite evident, both from the Press and from utterances from their own lips, that they are unable to manage their own affairs in any coherent manner.

The fact remains that, on 1st December, "The Times" said:

> "The best that can be said of the announcement of the formation of a new Polish Government in London under M. Arci-

---

* Vol. II, No. 30.

> szewski and without the participation of M. Mikołajczyk and the Peasant Party is that a step so clearly out of touch with present realities and future needs cannot be regarded as more than a momentary stop-gap."

And went on to say:

> "Unfortunately, the majority of Polish politicians in London, blindly faithful to a fatal and discredited tradition, have forced the resignation of the only leader of eminence among them whose sense of realities made him capable of recognizing this simple truth and of building on it a workable policy for the Poland of the future."

I want to say, lest there be any misapprehension, that everybody in this House, so far as I am able to ascertain, has a great respect for the many thousands of heroic Poles who have waged war so finely against Germany, and I would be churlish and less than honest if I did not say that I also as much as my hon. Friend wish to pay a great tribute to these people. I would go further and say that the rank and file of the Polish workers and peasants are honest, decent, humble people, who have no desire, fundamentally, to quarrel with their neighbors, but who have been led into this awful position, not of their own volition, but because they have been used by their politicians.

I would remind hon. Members that these sores go back a quarter of a century. It was in the Spring of 1920 that Polish troops invaded the Ukraine and captured Kiev. Months later in the same year, the Russians recaptured that town and, finally, were able to restore some order. As a result of the Treaty of Riga, Russia was forced to concede the Western Ukraine to Poland, a Poland which became temporarily strong, with the advent of General Piłsudski and other military chiefs, all of whom endeavored to weaken the Russian revolution in its tender stages, before the Russians could defend themselves adequately. Then we had the siege of Vilna in 1920. I was very glad that the hon. Gentleman, the Senior Burgess for Cambridge University (Mr. Pickthorn) said, "I am no friend of Poland," although his intentions are probably well disposed towards the Poles. But, if one faces realities, one sees that the actions of some of my hon. Friends are rendering a great disservice to the Polish people at the present moment. I congratulate the Prime Minister for once in a while on having the awareness to understand that, when one is dealing with a big Power like Russia it will not be promptings or urgings on our part, or the speech of my hon. and gallant Friend, that will decide the future of Poland, but that Russia, in the final analysis, will decide it, in any case.

SIR HERBERT WILLIAMS (C.): Is my hon Friend aware that he is talking power politics?

MR. MACK: My hon. Friend knows better than that. I should be the last to urge that an unwarrantable usurpation of power against a weak neighbor would vindicate truth and honor. Far from it, but I do say this, and I make this prophecy to the House, although prophecy is a very dangerous thing in which to indulge, that, after the war, Russia will treat not only Poland, but all these small countries, with great understanding, sympathy, and help and will set an example of bigheartedness that some of us are too purblind to appreciate at the present time.

CAPTAIN GRAHAM rose——

MR. SPEAKER: The hon. and gallant Gentleman cannot make another speech.

MR. MACK: The Prime Minister and Foreign Secretary, who have both visited Russia recently and have had an opportunity of making close contact, know the position rather better than most hon. Members of this House. I am confident that, as far as their actions are concerned, the continuance of friendship with Russia and the futherance of the highest ideals will be accomplished if we do not vitiate their efforts as the result of a reactionary state of mind and by creating pictures which have no historical relationship to the facts. If this object is accomplished I think it will augur an era of understanding between this country and Russia, do much to heal the hurts and misunderstandings of the past, and thus build a better future for millions of poor people who have suffered greatly in this war as a result of Germany's aggression.

MR. BOOTHBY (C.) : This Debate, after all, is only the continuation of a long Debate on foreign policy, but against another background, and in another context. As the hon. Member for South-East Essex (Mr. Raikes) pointed out, in what I venture to say was a very brilliant speech, it raises certain fundamental issues; and I have been asking myself during the last few days what have been the guiding principles underlying the conduct of our foreign policy during this war. I have been able to discover only one, and I do not think it is a bad one. It has been the defeat of Germany. In 1940 and 1941, that sufficed. We attained during those years a prestige which has never been equalled by any nation in the history of the world; but by 1942 I do not think that that single principle, the defeat of Germany, sufficed any longer.

MR. LOFTUS (C.) : May I interrupt the hon. Member? Surely that was a purpose, not a principle?

MR. BOOTHBY: No, I think it was the principle which underlay our foreign policy. We had been joined in 1942 by powerful Allies; and the problems which began to press on us with increasing severity were no longer of a purely military character—they were becoming political. But we had no compass and no ruler to apply to them other than grounds of military necessity, no star to steer by except Mars; and one star, for a lot of mariners, is not enough. There was, of course, the Atlantic Charter, to which frequent reference has been made today. I have never been able to take that document too seriously. It was a pious aspiration. The quotation about the changing of frontiers has been given more than once in this Debate: "We desire that no frontiers shall be changed until the end of the war," or whatever it may be. Yes, but we do not always get in this rough life what we desire. It was, I repeat, a pious aspiration. Some people are inclined to treat the Atlantic Charter as if it were the tablets of Moses, the final commandments. It was a document drafted under great pressure in a battleship, and in a comparatively short time.

MR. KENNETH LINDSAY (Lab.) : Under pressure of what?

MR. BOOTHBY: Under pressure of time, and of events. I am not going to say that the Atlantic Charter should be regarded as sacrosanct for all time in every respect.

In the summer of 1942 I ventured to suggest, in a letter to "The Times," that we should try to set up a Supreme Council of the United Nations. I was taken to task at the time, and told it was a physical impossibility, and that the existing arrangements for co-operation were satisfactory and adequate. Looking back, however, I feel sure that it would have been a right thing to do, if it could have been done; and that a great many of the troubles which have come upon us since would have been averted if we had had a Supreme Council of the United Nations. If the need for it was urgent then, I submit to the House that it is ten times more urgent today. For where are we now heading?

We are heading in the direction of spheres of influence; and that, in my belief, is a dangerous course, which may easily culminate in the final disaster of a third world war, unless it is checked. What in fact happens? We say to the Russians, "Greece is strategically important to us in the Eastern Mediterranean. We shall, therefore, be very much obliged if you would be good enough to clear out of Greece and disinterest yourselves in the future of Greece"; and we are delighted when the Russians meet our wishes. What is the obvious implication when that policy is carried out? Poland, Rumania, Bulgaria are all of admitted strategic importance to Russia. The implication is that the Soviet Union should bring them within their ambit and sphere of influence; and that we should lose interest in those three countries, getting Greece as a *quid pro quo*, or Greece and Yugoslavia, or whatever else you like, as a Mediterranean Power. So the bargaining goes on between the great Powers for spheres of influence. That, I think, is dangerous; and I want to protest against it.

I share M. Litvinov's view that peace is indivisible. Just as I do not think we should ever have been requested or encouraged to accept the sole responsibility for the administration of liberated Greece, so I do not think we can disinterest ourselves in the future of Poland. To that extent I go all the way with my hon. Friends opposite. We have moral obligations to Poland from which escape is quite impossible. That being so, I should like to make it clear that I personally agree with the Prime Minister that the Russian claim for a frontier—subject to modifications—based on the Curzon Line, is valid on strategic and ethnographic grounds. The fact that that Line, whatever anybody may say, was originally drawn by us, certainly lends force and point to that argument. What were the circumstances in which that Line was drawn? We had a Government in this country which was strongly hostile to Russia. Lord Curzon certainly did not take a favorable view of Russia; and my right hon. Friend the Prime Minister, who was an important member of that Administration at that time, took an even less favorable view of Russia than Lord Curzon. On top of that, Russia was actually in a very weak position, having received a severe military defeat. Those were the conditions under which the Curzon Line was drawn; and presumably we must have thought that it was reasonable.

I also think—and here I find myself again in substantial agreement with the Prime Minister—that East Prussia, which remains today what it has been for the last two centuries, the focal point of the infection of Prussian militarism, should be excised from the German body politic by a surgical operation; and that the German population of East Prussia should be, as the Prime Minister said, expelled. It is rough, but, by God, they deserve it.

I would like to say, before I sit down, a word or two about the past, because I do not think we can ignore it completely. If I have any criticism to make of the series of most formidable speeches made by my hon. Friends opposite who are opposed to the Government and to me on this issue the past is what they have rather carefully skated round. There has been a lot of talk about frontiers, guaranted and sacrosanct. I seem to remember something about a guarantee of the frontiers of the new Czechoslovakia after Munich; but when that unfortunate country was finally raped by Germany we did not find my hon. Friends coming down in a white heat of passion to demand that we implement our guarantee of the frontiers of newly constituted Czechoslovakia. Yet only a few weeks before, that had been their main plank in backing the Munich agreement; the claim that by that agreement, we had guaranteed the safety and security of a newer, better and happier Czechoslovakia with all its boundaries set out in beautiful blue print. Anyhow the Germans collared it. And I cannot help asking myself whether it is because Russia is now the alleged offender—it was Germany in those days, at the height of appeasement, when the golden age was alleged to be round the corner—that makes such a marked difference. But the principle is the same. If frontiers are guaranteed, and if so much importance is attached to them, there is no difference between the two.

So far as the last 10 years are concerned, I suggest to hon. Members that the record of the Russians is, in some respects at any rate, better than the record of the Poles. I well remember crossing the Atlantic Ocean in the "Berengaria" with M. Litvinov in the autumn of 1933, and having a long conversation with him on a stormy day while walking around the deck. He foretold the course of coming events with startling accuracy. He named the two aggressor Powers which were about to challenge the existing order; and described in precise terms the methods they would employ. In every detail his prophecy was fulfilled.

SIR H. WILLIAS: As M. Litvinov fixed up the treaty of appeasement between Russia and Germany, did he not fix up what he predicted?

MR. BOOTHBY: M. Litvinov did not fix up that treaty. I am coming to that point, if my hon. Friend will allow me to develop my argument. I asked M. Litvinov what he proposed to do, and what he thought should be done. He said that nothing could stop it except an effective system of collective security based upon the League of Nations; and to the creation of such a system he was going to devote all his energies. Even at that time, however, he was not very sanguine about the result. I was reading last night Mr. Sumner Welles's very interesting book "The Time for Decision," and I came across this short paragraph about Litvinov which I believe to be a true and fair summary:

> "Litvinov is a blunt man. He is often brutal. He has never seemed to me to be devious. So long as he represented his Government in the League, he strove with all his great ability to make the League work. It should never be forgotten that the Soviet Union did not desert the League. It was the great Powers which dominated the League in its later years that deserted the Soviet Union."

There is more than an element of truth in that. We shall have to accept our full share of responsibility for what happened before history; for the fact remains that we turned down the proposal of Litvinov for a conference at Geneva after the rape of Austria, and again for a conference at Bucharest after the rape of Czechoslovakia; and at Munich we served a public notice on the USSR to quit.

But, in the final analysis, the main obstacle to the alliance between Russia and the Western democracies, which we were all desperately striving to achieve in the early months of 1939, was Poland. Poland prejudiced almost everybody in the world against her by seizing the Teschen coal field when Czechoslovakia was on her back which, whatever may be said about it, was not a pretty thing to do. And up to the outbreak of the present war Poland refused any kind of military cooperation with the Soviet Union; and that is the answer to my hon. Friend the Member for South Croydon (Sir. H. Williams), who, I am sorry to see, is no longer in his place. For that is what finally drove the Soviet Union to sign a pact with Nazi Germany. These things cannot and should not be forgotten.

Without a friendly Russia, as many Members on both sides pointed out, Poland can never hope to exist in security and independence. I believe that she could have made an agreement with Russia a year ago, and that had she been well led she would have done so. I believe that General Sikorski, had he lived, would have done it. His death was a European tragedy of the first order. Nevertheless, despite all their failures in the political field, the military record of the Poles everywhere in this war is glorious; and I agree that we cannot disinterest ourselves in the future of Poland. Whatever we may feel about her frontiers—and I am against them on the Curzon Line—we have an obligation to do our best to see that no political regime is forcibly imposed on Poland from without; and we must do our level best to fulfill that obligation, even though we may sometimes think that the Poles themselves are doing their level best to prevent us.

What of the future? The Prime Minister said not long ago that he thought this war was becoming less ideological. He must have been sharply disillusioned in recent weeks. We have first of all to face the fact that all Europe is in the throes of revolution, of which this war is not the cause but merely a symptom. There is nothing that can stop it; we cannot put back Governments of the old regimes; and personally I do not mind that. It is not a Communist revolution. We are inclined to judge these things by our own political standards, forgetting that in the political field we are far ahead of any other country in the world, with the exception of the United States. My hon. Friend the Member for South Croydon* is miles to the Left of many Continental politicians who call themselves Socialists. We are much more advanced in these poltical matters than other European countries. This revolution is the revolt of the common man against tyranny and oppression. It is the clamant assertion on the part of the individual of the right to live. We are familiar with it in this country. Colonel Rainbow in the seventeenth century, who said:

> "The poorest man hath a life to live as the richest he,"

and Robert Burns who, in the eighteenth century, said:

> "A man's a man for a' that,"

* Sir Herbert Williams.

were expressing what the ordinary people in Europe are striving to express today. That is the core of this revolution. In considering the problem that is before us today we have to bear in mind that there was a good deal of tyranny and oppression in Poland before the outbreak of this war. The hon. Member who has just sat down talked of the feudalism and wretchedness of the Polish nation; and he was talking a good deal of sense and truth. The condition of the peasants in Eastern Poland was pretty desperate before this war.

The second fact we have to face up to—some of my hon. Friends may disagree with me on this—is that *emigre* Governments—I do not use the word sarcastically or abusively—which have existed in London during the last four years are unlikely to be acceptable to countries which have been under the German heel during that time. Among them I include the Lublin Committee. General de Gaulle is an exception; he was always the symbol of French resistance, and the acknowledged head of the resistance movement. We should, I think, be better advised to impose law and order ourselves in the liberated countries than impose unpopular Governments; but we cannot do this alone.

This brings me to my final point. We may succeed or we may fail; but unless we can work in closer co-operation with our principal Allies in this war than we have been able to do in recent months, then I think it is possible that this war may have been fought in vain. Some hon. Members said that the Prime Minister's announcement of the terms with regard to Poland, to which he had agreed, were a death knell. I thought that that part of the Prime Minister's speech was courageous and realistic; and I agreed with it. What struck a slight chill in my heart was his statement that it has not yet been found possible to arrange for an early meeting between himself, President Roosevelt and Marshal Stalin. This is a really serious situation. It is no use for Mr. Stettinius to fire sighting salvoes against us across the Atlantic. Some Americans may disapprove of our actions in Italy, Greece, or Poland; but they cannot disapprove more than some of us have disapproved in the past of their policy towards France, particularly at the time of the squalid Darlan affair. If a small group of Members of this House, belonging to no party, had not championed the cause of de Gaulle in his darkest and most difficult hour, God knows what follies might not have been committed.

The remedy for this problem and for many other problems, must be sought, for it can only be found, in closer co-operation between the four major Powers which now form the basis of the United Nations—France, Russia, ourselves and America. If we cannot do that it will be a serious outlook indeed. I know the Prime Minister and the Government are striving to this end; and I hope the Foreign Secretary will be able to give us some reassurance, because of what the Prime Minister said, on the question of the failure up to the present to arrange a four-Power Conference. What the Prime Minister said on this matter deeply perturbed many Members on both sides of the House. It seemed to me by far the most serious aspect of his speech. I beg of His Majesty's Government, before it is too late, to get this meeting; and to set up a Supreme Council of the United Nations, so that in co-operation rather than in competition with our Allies, we may lay the foundations of the new world.

MR. PETHICK-LAWRENCE (Lab.): I once spent a very unhappy week-end. I went to stay with a married couple, both of whom were my intimate and very dear friends, and with whom I had had a close association for a considerable part of my life. To my grievous distress I had been there hardly five minutes when I found that they were wrangling and describing one another in terms of abuse. When I pleaded with them for their sake, for my sake, and for the sake of their children, to get into closer friendly relations they yielded to my entreaties for a time, but shortly afterwards slid back into their altercations. That is how I regard this situation between Poland and Russia.

Perhaps my earliest insight into foreign affairs, when I was a very small child, was derived from the pitiable story of the rape of Poland, which had taken place more than once in history. My pity for the Poles was aroused from that day. I appreciated their desire to recover their country—an appreciation which has lasted for many years, and has been increased by my sympathy for some of the great Polish figures of history, including one whose name has not yet been mentioned. Madame Curie, the great scientist. My knowledge of the splendid fight which the Poles have put up in the present war, and the fact that the Polish Prime Minister is a member of the Socialist Party in Poland, has also inclined me to desire that Poland should be treated with justice and consideration. I think I speak for my party when I say that they share that feeling. They most strongly backed up the demand that the Germans should not be allowed with impunity to attack Poland, and we strongly supported the intimation given, even in the days of the Chamberlain Government, to Germany that if she attacked the Poles we should come in to fight on their behalf.

It is equally true that both I and my party have a feeling of very deep affection for the Soviet Government. We have watched the struggle they have made against many who wanted to see the downfall of the Socialist experiment. We have watched the strength of their success, we have watched the marvelous fight that they have put up in the present war and we have watched the magnanimity with which they have treated the Finns and some of the countries in the Balkan States when at last peace has been declared between them. Therefore, it is not only the hon. Member for South-East Essex (Mr. Raikes) but it is surely all Members of the House who would infinitely prefer a free negotiated settlement if that is in any way possible. In fact, I will go almost further than he does. I do not believe that any settlement of the Polish-Russian problem which does not command the full support of both parties will make for peace. That is not merely the attitude of those who have been, so to speak, pro-Polish. I think it is true of every party and every person in the House. But the question which was addressed to the hon. Member himself, and which he did not answer, was, "Supposing you cannot get a free negotiated settlement?" It reminds me of a passage in "Much Ado About Nothing." This is what Dogberry said to the watch:

> "This is your charge: You shall comprehend all vagrom men; you are to bid any man stand, in the prince's name."

The watch said:

> "How if a will not stand?"

Dogberry said:

> "Take no note of him, but let him go; and presently call the rest of the watch together, and thank God you are rid of a knave."

Then Verges added:

> "If he will not stand when he is bidden, he is none of the prince's subjects."

That is the problem to which we have to address ourselves. What if he will not stand? What if we can get not negotiated settlement? Why is it that a negotiated settlement is not forthcoming? I think I can supply the answer. It is because the history of the relationship of these two countries is blotted with the blood and tears of countless people all down the centuries.

I do not know if the House has heard the story of a Negro preacher rationalizing the passage by the Israelites of the Red Sea. He said, "A cold North wind arose and the Red Sea was frozen solid, and the Israelites walked across the ice as though they were on dry land." One of the congregation said he had been looking at his geography, and the Red Sea was somewhere in the tropics where they did not get frosts. The preacher was not in the least upset by the suggestion. He said that all this happened several thousand years ago, and there was no geography in those days. I sometimes wish there was no history in these days or, if there has to be history, that it had not entered into the bones, the heart, the blood and the emotions of the peoples who live today. I am sure the Foreign Secretary would have a much easier task if the blotted pages of history were not uppermost in the minds of those people with whom he has to deal.

I agree very largely with my hon. Friend with regard to the seriousness of what the Prime Minister said about the relationships of the Allied Powers. The most serious thing with regard to the actual Russian situation is that he appeared to have abandoned all hope of a negotiated settlement and, knowing how hard he and the Foreign Secretary have worked in order to reach a settlement, this was a matter which must be of very grave anxiety and regret to Members of the House, not untouched with very serious misgivings. It is with this background that he asks for the acceptance of the territorial changes which he sketched out to us. These changes are undoubtedly cataclysmic and, though they have been hinted at before, I do not thing that up to now they have been expressed in such a concrete shape. I am speaking on behalf of my party, and I do not think I should be entitled to put forward any precise and specific view in detail, with regard to this quite definite proposal of the terms of the settlement, if settlement it can be called. But I think I can say that it certainly is not a settlement which leaves us very happy. I feel that it raises a very large number of issues which are not easy to see through to the end.

We all see the difficulties of the situation. It may well be that the British Government cannot prevent a settlement somewhat on these lines, but I am not sure that it necessarily follows that they must underwrite the settlement. Are we in any worse position with regard to our great Ally, whom we all wish to support, if we say to them, "We wish we could make a different settlement but, if that is your settlement, we will do anything we can to get it carried," or if we say, "We do not altogether like it. If you must make it, you must make it, but you must not expect us actively to support it." There seems to me to be a distinct shade of difference. I know from what the Prime Minister said in a previous Debate that he has done his best to present to Russia our feeling with regard to this important question, and Mr. Stalin is now fully aware of our position. Shall we worsen our position *vis-a-vis* Mr. Stalin if we do not actively go out to support this proposal? That is the direct suggestion that I make to the Foreign Secretary. I support a great deal of what was said in a very thoughtful speech from my hon. Friend the Member for Central Southwark (Mr. Martin), who gave us a close and interesting analysis, from his point of view, of what we are all feeling so much about today.

I do not propose to say anything further about the specific frontier proposed for Poland on the East. The disadvantages of it are quite apparent. It may be thought that that is what it will be in the end, but I do not propose to go into that any further, but to say a few words about the frontier suggested on the West. I think that the famous Danzig Corridor worked so badly that we are perfectly right to get rid of it, and that on general grounds, quite apart from the present situation, Poland should have proper access to the sea. I do not think that the Germans, considering what they did, have the slightest right to complain of our taking that course. I would go further, and say that, after the transferences of population which the Germans have effected in all parts of the world, the ruthless way in which they have torn people up from their homes and even removed their own people about, they have no right to complain if we on our part forcibly remove some of their people. I would even go further. The Prime Minister quoted certain reasons for thinking that there would be room in Germany, even a smaller Germany, for some of the people who lay outside the inner Reich. The German Government have murdered or driven out of their country a large number of Jews, and the place that these people occupied will also be available for others from outside. So that, although the Germans will complain, I do not think they will have any right to complain about any forcible changes of populations that we may desire to make.

That is not to say that we can play about with territories which have been German and that we can move about not hundreds of thousands but millions of people. I think that there are in the territory about which the Prime Minister is speaking something like 5,000,000 Germans, which is a very large number. That may be an exaggeration, but the number, at any rate, runs into millions. I do not think we can play about with territories and masses of populations of those dimensions except at very grave peril. Whether we incorporate in Poland a great piece of German territory with the Germans in it, or incorporate the territory and turn the Germans out of it, we are creating a situation for the future that will not make for the peace either of Poland or of the world. I do not say that we cannot get over the difficulty of the Danzig Corridor. It may be that we have to take away from Germany that part which rendered the Corridor necessary, but I do not think we should encourage the Poles, still less force the Poles, to have German territory which is not absolutely necessary for the purposes we have in mind. If we encourage too wide an extension of Poland on the west at the expense of Germany, we are sowing the seed of grave danger for the future of the world.

Having expressed what is my view and what I think I can reasonably say is the view of my party, I want to come back to what I said at the beginning. There is no solution—not the Prime Minister's solution, not the Poles' solution, not the Soviet solution—of this problem which will really be lasting unless it is a solution by consent. Unless we have that it will be a continuing sore in the body politic of the world. I beg the Government, and I beg the Prime Minister and the Foreign Secretary, who have done tremendous work in the months that have gone by, to try to bring about a settlement and not even now to despair of efforts for success. Those of us outside who have not, like my right hon. Friend, had all the difficulties and troubles of the negotiation, and to whom the problem may have seemed easier may say, as sometimes those who are outside can say to those who are fighting a battle which appears to be lost: "Go back once more into the struggle and make another effort, because, though it may seem difficult today, perhaps the way is still open." If they do so, it may be that they will achieve a success which will be of lasting value to Europe and mankind.

THE SECRETARY OF STATE FOR FOREIGN AFFAIRS (Mr. Eden) : The right hon. Gentleman the Member for East Edinburgh (Mr. Pethick-Lawrence) has just made a speech of characteristic and constructive thoughtfulness, and I would like to say at once that with a large part—I think I can almost say with by far the greater part—of what he has said I find myself in complete agreement. In speaking about this matter today I want to try as hard as I possibly can to put the position as I see it, not from the angle of Poland or of Russia, but from the angle of those of us in this country who have had to deal with this vexatious problem for all this long period. I shall try very hard, and I hope I shall succeed, in saying nothing that will be regarded as partisan. At any rate, I beg the House to believe this, that having dealt with this subject for so long, I am incapable of being partisan for either one side or the other. All I heartily wish is for a solution, if it can be found, which will be acceptable to both sides.

Let me first answer one or two speeches which were made. I have no complaint whatever as Foreign Secretary about the speeches in this Debate by any hon. Member. As I conceive it, it is the duty of Members of Parliament to express their views on these matters with frankness. It is the principal method by which we make plain to the world the views of British opinion. The fact that those opinions are sometimes contrary to His Majesty's Government, does not necessarily mean that the opinions are always wrong. I therefore assure my hon. Friends who referred to it, that, so far as I am concerned, no complaint lies anywhere that a certain amount of frankness has been used and, as I think, rightly used in the course of this Debate.

I begin with the point raised by my hon. Friend the Senior Burgess for Cambridge University (Mr. Pickthorn) about the reference to my right hon. Friend the Prime Minister to the Atlantic Charter. I start with that, because I would like to clear it out of the way before I get down to the main subject of the Debate. What my right hon. Friend intended to convey was that, in view of His Majesty's Government, there is an exception to the general principle that there should be no territorial changes before the peace table. My hon. Friend is correct in pointing out that that exception is not in the Atlantic Charter. The exception is in cases where the changes are mutually agreed, and that is not part of the Atlantic Charter. It is part of a statement of our own policy which we made in September, 1940, when the Prime Minister said:

> "We have not at any time adopted since this war broke out the line that nothing can be changed in the territorial structures of the various countries. On the other hand, we do not propose to recognize any territorial changes which take place during the war, unless they take place with the free consent and good will of the parties concerned."—[OFFICIAL REPORT, 5th September, 1940; Vol. 365, c. 40.]*

It is to that that my right hon. Friend was referring, and not to the Atlantic Charter, and my hon. Friend was perfectly correct in his observations.

Now I come to the main issue of the Debate, the Polish-Soviet relations and the problem that underlies them. I do not hesitate to say, from the point of view of His Majesty's Government, that this has been for the last three years, or a little more, the most vexatious and anxious problem with which we have to deal. It is not only that it is of the greatest importance that Alied unity should be maintained, and that it cannot be effectively maintained unless our Allies are in general agreement; it is not only because it is important to us who are allied to both those countries that there should be some understanding between them, but it is because, unless there is some understanding we find it difficult to see how there can be confidence, settlement and peace in Eastern Europe, when this war is over; and if there be not this confidence, then the repercussions will be felt by us all.

Both these countries, I have said, are our Allies. We entered this war of our own free will, by our own deed, in fulfillment of our guarantees to Poland. Ours is the only country which has continued with its own territory—our island ter-

* Vol. I, No. 114.

ritory—intact throughout the war, and which did as I say enter the war voluntarily and of its own free will. From time to time it is right that we should remind ourselves and others of that. We have, as the war has progressed, felt a growing, not only esteem, but affection for our Polish Allies: for those we have known, and for those we have seen in this country, and for their armed forces, and for the gallantry of the part that they have played. There is something more than that; we have seen also that, of all the countries that have been under the harrow of this war, Poland has, perhaps, suffered most of all. All those considerations have entered into it, and I do not regard myself, and I do not think any hon. Member should regard himself, as sentimental, if these considerations weigh heavily on us when we approach this problem.

On the other side, we have our 20 years' treaty with Russia. We understand, and we believe that they understand and other nations understand, how much the future peace of Europe is going to depend upon our ability to work together and to understand each other. We remember that in three great wars we have fought together on the same side in the end, although we may not have begun as Allies, and that after each of them, we have fallen apart. We know that if that happens again, the prospects for the peace of Europe are very frail indeed. Those considerations have to be in our minds when we face this problem, as we have to face it now.

So it is that, ever since the German attack on Russia in the summer of 1941, we have labored unceasingly to try to solve these Polish-Soviet differences. We have not been successful always, but we have been successful sometimes. It was here in London, actually in my room at the Foreign Office, that the Soviet-Polish Treaty was signed, in the summer of 1941. Despite a chequered history, many differences, arguments, criticisms and charges and counter-charges, that Treaty did stand until February of last year, when it was denounced—I do not know whether "denounced" is the right word—or when, rather, it was regarded as in abeyance by the Soviet Government. Ever since then, we have tried to bring about a resumption of relations. Sometimes we seemed to be almost in sight of the goal and at others, the prospects became gloomy again. Since I have been much concerned in these long negotiations, I ought today to pay my tribute, which is a heartfelt one, to the courage and patience with which, first, General Sikorski and later M. Mikołajczyk and M. Romer, made their contribution to our work. Now I have to report that the prospects are not as good as they have been, but we shall continue to do all we can to secure a strong and independent Poland as our Ally, and, as we trust, the Ally of Soviet Russia.

Now I come to one of the criticisms—perhaps not criticisms but observations—made in the Debate on a remark which my right hon. Friend the Prime Minister let fall. I have not his exact words here, but I think they were to the effect that we were dealing with two very great Powers, as great, if not perhaps greater than us. I do not think that those words were quite correctly understood. I am absolutely certain that my right hon. Friend had not the least intention of suggesting that in meetings with any of those other great Powers we had any sense of inferiority at all. Certainly we have not. I would ask my hon. Friends who know the Prime Minister to imagine, if they can, my right hon. Friend feeling himself any sense of inferiority over this. So far, that is a spectacle that I have never seen either at home or abroad.

I would like to put the position a little differently. I would say that our position in the world and our sense that we feel the equal, and fully the equal, of even the greatest Powers on the earth's surface, is not in any sense based on geography, on size or on population. I do not think these are the basis of our strength and our authority; I think it is due to something different. I think it comes from the fact that, owing to our island position, our traditions and our long history, we have shown ourselves able, over and over again, in titanic struggles, to be the leader in marshalling a coalition against any Power which has sought to impose its will on Europe. And that is why I say that there is no need for anybody to think for one moment that, in discussions, we feel inferior to any

Ally, however great, to whom we have to speak and to whom we have to express our position. I am bound to say in addition, that if our position is so authoritative in Europe today there is no man who has played a greater part in that than the Prime Minister himself.

I want to say something about some of the criticisms, not uttered today, but which I have seen, particularly in Polish quarters, of the efforts which M. Mikołajczyk, M. Romer and M. Grabski have made to reach agreement with out Russian Allies. Any criticism on that score is misplaced. The truth is that, as I understand it, these Polish leaders understood how essential it was to Poland and to Europe that they should make some effort, and a great effort, to settle these age-long disputes, even though it might involve painful sacrifices.

MR. PETHERICK: Were they not settled five years ago?

MR. EDEN: Forgive me if I say that I do not think that that is a complete answer to this problem. These frontiers have been a matter of vexatious dispute for centuries, and we oversimplify our problems if we treat it in that way. I am going to put all I know about it, as fairly as I can. I do not believe that we can say: "It was settled five years ago and that there is nothing more to be done." I do not think that would be possible, or reasonable, or that many wise Polish leaders would regard it as the way finally to settle this problem.

I want to deal with another point that has been made. There has never been, I must emphasize, in this discussion in London, from the Soviet side, any suggestion that, as a result of any arrangement which might be made between Russia and ourselves, Poland's links with the West should in any way be modified or affected. On the contrary, Marshal Stalin emphasized to M. Mikołajczyk his desire that the Treaty with ourselves and the Polish treaty with France and any relations that were possible between Poland and the United States subject to the constitutional position of the United States, should be continued and if need be reinforced. I think he has said that publicly and I think that it should be stressed because it is not in my judgment true to suggest that the Soviet Government desires that the Polish State and Government should be, as it were, in her orb and have no territorial or political links with other Governments.

I come to slightly more controversial ground. I shall try to give a brief account and I hope an accurate account of the story of the Curzon Line, to which reference has been made by several Members in the course of the Debate.* What was the origin of this Line? It was originally drawn up by the Commission of Polish Affairs of the Paris Supreme Council. They drew it up to mark the eastern limit of what was indisputably Polish territory so that the Polish Government could immediately take over the administration in that area without question, even while the position in relation to Russia was obscure. That was in 1919, and the proposal became associated with Lord Curzon's name only a year later, when this proposal was pulled out, as it were, again, and put before the two parties as an attempt to bring hostilities to an and. Then it came to be called the Curzon Line; but the work upon it was done a year before. It is fair to say that it was from the outset only intended to show the minimum amount of territory which should be assigned to Poland in the east. It is also true to say that the British delegation at the Peace Conference consistently maintained that any further eastward extension of Polish territory beyond the Curzon Line would be highly dangerous to Poland, and before the Treaty of Riga was signed in 1921 we several times warned the Polish Government against such extensions. Thus in the view which my right hon. Friend was expressing earlier today he was not departing so violently as some Members of the House seem to think from what has been our position before in relation to this vexed question.

MR. IVOR THOMAS: Is the Secretary of State able to confirm that the Soviet Foreign Minister, Tchicherin, replied to Lord Curzon that the Curzon Line was unacceptable because it was too unfavorable to the Poles?

* See Vol. II, Appendix 1.

MR. EDEN: I am familiar with that one. It is absolutely correct, and the reason for that was that in the belief of the Soviet Government at that time a district which I think is called Chelm was thought by the Soviet Government to be on the Russian side of the Curzon Line; and they said, and rightly said, that that was Polish territory, and they did not agree with the Curzon Line in regard to that particular area. These are technical matters, but I tried to answer the hon. Member because there is no bias in this. We want to try to see how this position arose.

I go to the next stage which is significant—August, 1920. At that time, the opposite happened to what had happened before. While at the earlier date the Curzon Line was proposed to the Soviet Government by us with the approval of the Polish Government, at the later stage to which I am referring the Soviet Government, in their turn, approached the Polish Government with a proposal—which was approximately in fact the Curzon Line—and the Polish Government asked our opinion. We then told the Polish Government in 1920—the Soviet Government having communicated to us the text of the terms—that we considered such terms would leave her ethnographical frontier unimpaired, and we urged them, the Polish Government, not to refuse these terms. I only mention these facts because it is fair to try to give the House a picture of past events, though I do not myself overemphasize their importance.

I would like to refer to another matter which I think we must try to get into the right perspective—the problem of Galicia. In the extension of the Curzon Line to the south two alternatives were recommended to the Supreme Council's Commission on Polish affairs. At this stage I should perhaps mention that our representative on the Commission was Sir Eyre Crowe, certainly a distinguished holder of that position. There were two proposals. One was line A, which is the line that the Soviet Government now claim as the basis of the frontier itself. Line A was proposed as the boundary between Poland proper and an autonomous Eastern Galicia, which it was hoped to set up under the suzerainty of Poland. Line B further to the East, which left Lvov to Poland, was recommended if the bulk of Eastern Galicia was excluded from Poland and the autonomous State under her suzerainty was not created. I hope that I make this rather complicated business clear.

Our delegation favored Line A—the line which the Soviet Government are now asking for—and it was eventually adopted by the Supreme Council, and embodied in the draft Treaty. Of the reasons which actuated us at that time, one was the economic position in that part of Europe and the necessity, as those who reported thought, of keeping this economic area of Eastern Galicia as a whole. The second reason was the possibility that there might be a larger independent State, perhaps as part of a greater Ukraine. I think the final reason was the population problem. At that time the population of this area between Line A and Line B, which is, as far as territorial matters go, the crux of the dispute—if our Polish friends could get Line B their attitude would probably be modified a good deal, and personally I can well understand their attitude—the populations at that time, out of a total of about 1,500,000, were over 500,000 Ukrainians, little more than 250,000 Poles, and the rest Jews. I think that was the reason why those concerned at that time had in mind to try and arrange some autonomous regime.

I would like to ask the House for a moment to look at the population problem generally in the area between the Riga frontier and the Curzon Line taking Line A. The figures I shall give are those of the 1931 Polish census. They are the latest figures available to us though likely enough there have been very considerable changes since then. They showed that the population in that area, in what might be called the disputed area, was 10,700,000. Of that total, 3,900,000 are Polish-speaking population; 3,200,000 are Roman Catholic population. I think those who are authorities on these matters say, usually, the religious figures are rather nearer to the mark than the language-speaking figures, because, for instance, Jews might be Polish-speaking Jews who would be included in one and not the other. That is about the figure—at the most 3,900,000, at the least 3,200,000. It would be fair to say therefore that while there are no later figures than those of 1931 the Poles have never constituted much more than a third of the total population of this area.

COMMANDER AGNEW (C.): Has my right hon. Friend any figures for Lvov itself?

MR. EDEN: I have not, but I would gladly give them if my hon. and gallant Friend would like to put down a Question. My view is that there is certainly a Polish majority in Lvov itself. I have always taken this view though in the surrounding country there is a Ukrainian majority.

Let me turn to the present situation, and its difficulties. First, I would like to answer a question on supplies, by my hon. and gallant Friend the Member of The Wirral (Captain Graham). This matter is now being examined by the Prime Minister and myself, with our technical advisers. I am unable to say exactly what we shall do in the winter months, but it is under examination, and it is on the basis of what we can do that we shall decide our action.

MR. PETHERICK: Before my right hon. Friend leaves the history of events in the earlier part of the two years immediately after the last war, may I say that he has given a perfectly fair account of the events leading up to the Treaty of Riga, but he has not mentioned the Treaty of Riga, which was the final arrangement between Poland and Russia, and which always operated until 1939?

MR. EDEN: I had not mentioned the Treaty of Riga, but I do not know which point my hon. Friend wishes me to make about it. My point is that the story of this area is a long-disputed one. Before the Treaty was signed, we ourselves advised the Poles—I am not saying whether we were right or wrong—not to go so far East as the frontiers given by the Treaty of Riga. It is true that the Russians accepted the Treaty—nobody disputes that. But you cannot say, "This is where I take my stand, and I refuse to go back any farther"—for if you do, it will be impossible to reach a settlement. It is quite true that it was our initiative—the Prime Minister's and mine—at Moscow which raised this Polish question once again. We went to Moscow with the fullest intention of talking about it, and of putting our point of view to our Russian Ally. I would like some of my hon. Friends to believe that we are capable of putting our case quite strongly, even to an Ally, though we do not necessarily put it in quite the same way on the Floor of the House of Commons—and I hope we shall not put it in quite the same way on the Floor of the House of Commons. The first thing we asked was whether M. Grabski and M. Mikołajczyk, who had been parties to the conversations before, could come to Moscow again. That proposition was at once accepted, on the first night of our arrival, by M. Stalin and M. Molotov; and they came to Moscow. I had hoped—I do not deny that—that, as a result of this discussion, a measure of agreement would arise large enough to enable the conversations to continue, and a final settlement to be reached. But after M. Mikołajczyk got back the Polish Government was reconstituted, and those hopes have been disappointed.

My hon. Friend the Member for South-East Essex (Mr. Raikes), in his very eloquent speech, asked whether I could say a little more about the Moscow conversations. I will say a little, but not much more, because I have not abandoned all hope of working out some solution to this problem. I think it is fair to ask that the House should have some answer. First, my hon. Friend said that the Polish Government were asked to give up at once, and go into the nebulous future, with uncertainty as to what Poland will get. If that were the position, I would agree that it would be quite an unacceptable one from the Polish point of view. But that was not the position. The position was that concessions—I do not like that word, let us say frontier changes, would be made. There was absolute agreement between us and the Russians, as well as the Poles, on the changes there would be in the West. The Poles would not be committed to the Curzon Line unless, as a result of these discussions, agreement was finally reached, and the Polish Government, headed by M. Mikołajczyk, went into Poland and took up their position there. There was no question of our asking the Poles to give up something without agreement being reached. There was also the question of the composition of the Committee, on which my hon. Friend asked whether they were going to be 75 per cent, or not.

MR. RAIKES: Surely the position was not quite that the Poles were at once to receive compensation in the West, and that the whole thing hung together with the Curzon Line; because the Russians had already got into possession of Eastern Poland, and, whatever might be said at Moscow, the Poles could not get the suggested compensation anyhow until the Germans had been defeated?

MR. EDEN: But the very fact that the Russians were in possession was one of the reasons why we wanted to get agreement. I will explain why. I do not know what the Lublin Committee may have wanted, but I think it had never entered our heads to think that such an arrangement would be possible for a moment. In fact, the only thing that was agreed about the future composition of the Polish Government was that M. Mikołajczyk himself should be Prime Minister. That was one thing about which everybody seemed to be agreed—ourselves, the Russians, the Lublin Committee, and the Polish Government in London.

MR. PICKTHORN: May I ask my right hon. Friend to answer a question which I put to him, and which, I think, is relevant to this point? On what date did His Majesty's Government assure themselves that the Polish Government understood the constitutional impossibility of a Washington guarantee?

MR. EDEN: I was coming to that. There was no misunderstanding about that. We do tell our Allies frankly about these matters. We do not try to deceive people. We put it quite plainly to our Polish friends. I do not believe that my hon.

Friend fully understood—I will not say understood, but fully balanced, what the Prime Minister said on this subject. He said:

> "It is certainly to be hoped that the three Great Powers will guarantee the independent, sovereign, free Poland which will emerge from any arrangement which is made now and ratified at the Peace Conference."

That is what my hon. Friend quoted. But my right hon. Friend went on to say, in that very speech, that the question was whether the United States Government would be in a position to give such a guarantee now. He also said:

> "It is not for me to speak of the affairs of the United States of America."—[*Official Report,* 27th October, 1944; Vol. 404, c. 499.]

He said the same thing today. I really think we can say that at no time have we allowed our Polish friends—and I do not think that they would say we had—to think that they would have a guarantee that we could not give. We can speak only for ourselves. I do not doubt that the Poles are as well aware as we are of the constitutional difficulties of the United States. Considering the number of Poles in the United States, there must be plenty of people there to send telegrams to tell them about it.

I come to a question which I do not think has played a great part—and which should have played a greater part—except in the speech of the hon. Gentleman who spoke just now. That is the Corridor. There has been a great deal of discussion about Eastern Poland, but hardly a word about the Corridor. I have taken the view for many years, as an individual, that it is impossible for the Polish State to have an independent national life with the Corridor system perpetuated. I have told the House that once or twice before. I sat at Geneva as rapporteur on this wretched Danzig business. Actually it was quite unworkable. Some people seem to think, quite wrongly, that the Corridor was German. It was not; the population of the Coridor was Polish. But, even so, the cross-traffic and the endless problems of the Free City of Danzig, and the growing *Herrenvolk* attitude of the German officials towards Poles, made it absolutely impossible for there to be any arrangement on those lines. I say to the House that, quite independently of this Polish-Russian problem at all, long ago I think I am on record as having said this. The only way to solve this problem was that East Prussia should go to the Poles and that the population of East Prussia should be shifted out. That is the only way to get a permanent settlement.

MR. GALLACHER: Even if you shut the Poles in?

MR. EDEN: In conclusion, I want to say a word about the movement of population. Of course, my hon. Friend is right —it is an immensely difficult question. I do not think it is impossible, and, if it is the only way to solve this problem of the Corridor, as I am convinced it is, then we have got to face it. The House should remember that there were certain populations of Polish descent when East Prussia was under Polish suzerainty. I repeat my own conviction that it is the only way in which we can hope to obtain a lasting settlement there.

Now I come to the question of what we are going to do now. If I may say so, of the comments and the criticisms I have heard, there has only been one alternative policy suggested, which was to wait until the Peace Conference to settle these matters and to hold our hands meanwhile and make no commitment. I think I was urged by one of my hon Friends: "Do not say something or do something which may be dishonorable, and do not commit yourselves to lines in Eastern Europe for which you will afterwards be blamed." The last consideration does not weigh so heavily as it should, because, in my experience, whatever you do, you are quite certain to be blamed by somebody, so that consideration is not going to weigh very much. At the same time, that is the only alternative—to take no further action and let the matter wait until the Peace Conference. One of my hon. Friends asked why we did not do that originally? My reply is that we foresaw this position arising, with Russian Armies advancing through Poland, with no understanding whatever with the Polish Government, which we were convinced represented majority opinion in Poland, and with no arrangement of any kind, no civil affairs agreement other than some administration being set up to carry on the Government somehow, or else it being done direct by the Russians. We saw all the friction which would inevitably result. We knew, because the Russians told us this, that they were prepared to make, with M. Mikołajczyk's government, if the frontier could be settled, an arrangement similar to the one they had with the Czechs and similar to the one we have with the Belgian, the Dutch and the French.

MR. PETHERICK: May I point out that that is not an absolutely fair analogy? We are advancing through Holland and Belgium now, but not claiming the right to annex Holland and Belgium.

MR. EDEN: My hon. Friend has not understood my observation. What I said was that if we could have got an understanding between the Soviet and M. Mikołajczyk's Government we knew the Soviet Government would make a civil affairs agreement with the Polish Government on the same lines as we have made one with the Belgians and the French. Such an agreement should have provided for the setting up of a Polish administration which would have the confidence of the Polish people, and we should have avoided those incidents and troubles, perhaps serious troubles, which we are likely to see when there is no agreement. That is the reason why we took this risk, and, if you like, burnt our fingers, but it was a case in which, if we had not made this attempt, there would inevitably have been these difficulties.

What is the position now? An hon. Gentleman asked me just now whether we would go on trying. I must honestly say that, at present, the prospects of agreement are pretty bleak. They are, honestly, not as good between this Polish Government and the Soviet as they were between the previous Polish Government and the Soviet Government, but if there was any opportunity, despite the risks, and I know what they are, I think it would still be our duty to try. I think that, among the very many perils that may arise, the worst that I see is the failure to reach a settlement of this question, because I see repercussions that may arise which may affect the relations of ourselves and our Soviet Allies, and the relations of America and ourselves, and of all of us, and which will affect that widespread co-operation which is so indispensable.

I can say this to my hon. Friends. It is quite likely that we shall fail and not get another opportunity. If that happens what is our position? We recognize this Government here in London as we recognized its predecessor. The subject will then have to wait for the Peace Conference, when all the Powers meet, and I can only say that I pray that those who have to handle it then will be more successful than we have been. I am not so optimistic as to see exactly why they should be more successful than we have been, but I am prepared to believe my hon. Friends when they say that they hope they will have that success. There is a danger that developments will occur which I think will not be good for the unity of the United Nations, and that is why we are trying to avoid this position coming about.

My last words are about unity also, because it was raised in questions put by the hon. Member for Aberdeen, East (Mr. Boothby) and the right hon. Gentleman the member for Edinburgh, East.* The Prime Minister referred to this in his speech and both speakers have said that it was an uneasy and gloomy forecast that the three Powers were not going to meet. We ardently wish that they should meet, and I would go further and say that it is immensely desirable that the three men upon whom the chief responsibility falls should meet. I think it is also desirable that, at regular intervals, a second eleven, in the shape of the Foreign Secretaries, should also meet. I believe that, if that could be done regularly, we might be able to iron out some of the problems and avoid some of the difficulties which arise. We might perhaps help to prepare the way for the heads of the Governments to meet themselves.

So far as we are concerned we are perfectly ready to co-

* Mr. Pethick-Lawrence.

operate in any scheme of that kind, to travel anywhere and meet them anywhere and to work with them. It is not in our power to do more than that and it is for others also to make a gesture. The Prime Minister is the oldest of all these men and has had the heaviest burden of them all. For the last four years it has been on his shoulders. I think others ought to move too, and I hope they will, and move soon, so that some of these problems can be dealt with.

Let me finish by saying that I am grateful to the House and to hon. Members in all parts for the way they have spoker in this Debate. I thing hon. Members were right to be frank. and right to say what their feelings were. I cannot hold out hopes of success in agreement between these countries, as matters are, but I think it is sometimes the case, in diplomacy, that, if you stand back and let the problem lie, success may come. Our affection and esteem for our Polish friends are deep and real, and our desire to work with our Soviet Allies is unshaken. We are in the unhappy position of trying to reconcile a problem which does not date from our time but from centuries ago. So far, we have not succeeded, and it is small comfort to know that others have failed before us, but we shall go on trying, confident that in so doing we shall not dishonor our country, but fairly and truly trying to bring together nations who must be friends if their people are to live in happiness and peace in the years to come.

12. EAST PRUSSIA*

VISCOUNT CECIL OF CHELWOOD: . . . When I come to Poland, it seems to me to be another case. The policy that is proposed to be pursued in Poland, as I understand it, is, broadly, this: that a certain portion from the south-east of what was Poland before the war is to be transferred to Russia, and that compensation is to be provided for Poland in the north by the transfer to her of what was certainly before the war, and in

* House of Lords. Vol. 134, Dec. 20, 1944, p. 435–438.

deed for many centuries, the German province of East Prussia. I have nothing to say at all as to any German grievance in the matter; I fully admit that the Germans cannot be heard on that point at all. I must say, however, that this seems to be a disagreeable reminiscence of the worst type of pre-war diplomacy in its very nature. I do not want to go back to the Atlantic Charter unduly, particularly after the very interesting exposition which the President of the United States has given as to the way in which the Atlantic Charter was constructed, but in point of fact the broad principle that territory should not be transferred from one Government to another except with the consent of its inhabitants is a very sound one. It is not because there is a promise to this person or to that person, but because the consent of the people is the very essence and foundation of democracy. I therefore look with great anxiety on this proposal, and my anxiety is scarcely removed at all by the complementary suggestion that in order to enable this to be done the whole German population of East Prussia is to be conveyed to some part of Germany, wherever room can be found for them.

I gather that that is to be done extensively, so that something like five million Germans are to be transferred from the places where they now live, and lived before the war, to some unknown position in Germany, and their places are to be taken by Poles or Russians. I am not concerned with any question of justice or injustice to Germany, because I agree that she has no right to complain, considering what she has done, of any action which may be of use to the peace of the world; but what I am afraid of is that when an attempt is made to carry this proposal out the practical difficulties will turn out to be very great. I have had a little indirect experience of transfers of population, and I know that the difficulties are very great. They produce the greatest possible discomfort; they involve very complicated questions of government and so on. What I am frankly terrified will in fact be the result is that after transferring a certain number of these Germans back to Germany it will be found almost impracticable to go on with the experiment. We cannot adopt the methods which the Germans themselves have tried to adopt—quite unsuccessfully—which consist, roughly, of the murder of anybody who objects to what they do. I hope and trust and believe that we shall not be able to do that; people in this country would not be a party to action of that kind. It will have to be done by persuasion and by moderate means.

The result will be that it will break down, and in this new province to be transferred to Poland the mass of the population will still be hostile to the Government to which they have been transferred. This would seem to me to be the most reckless kind of policy, if that turns out to be the result. It means keeping alive in an important part of Europe a perpetual sore which, sooner or later, is bound to produce disturbance and probably a war similar to that which we are now enduring. I very earnestly beg the Goxernment to consider again whether there is not some way of avoiding this very serious result. I cannot help thinking that in some way or other it ought to be possible to avoid settling anything finally during the progress of the war with regard to transfers of territory. It seems to me a reckless thing to attempt to do. I gather from something which fell from the Prime Minister that he agrees that it would be better to delay action until after the war, when at any rate there will be some prospect of a general cooling of spirits and lessening of irritation. In the meantime, is it not possible to arrive at some kind of *modus vivendi* which will enable Russians and Poles alike to concentrate on the defeat of Germany, which is the first essential to anything being done, leaving the final settlement and the real settlement to be disposed of after the most careful inquiry and impartial consideration, which can be provided only at the end of the war, and indeed, as I think, only after there has been recreated some kind of international organization which will command at any rate a measure of assent from all the countries of the world? . . .

THE EARL OF PERTH: My Lords, I have the greatest sympathy with the ideas put forward by the Noble Viscount who moved this Resolution in his eloquent and thought-provoking speech. I should like to add my tribute of praise to those which have already been paid. I shall not pretend to follow the noble Viscount, Lord Cecil of Chelwood, into the questions of detail which he has raised regarding Germany, regarding Greece and regarding Poland; but I must say that I most strongly dissent from his views as regards East Prussia. I will explain to your Lordships the reason why I hold so strongly that East Prussia should go to Poland when this war is finished. The noble Viscount quoted in support of what he said the Atlantic Charter. Yes, I can quote the Atlantic Charter too in support of my views, and that is in the statement that security is the most important factor in the post-war world. I would add that as far as East Prussia goes it must be remembered that there is a very large population of Polish origin, mostly peasants, which is still resident in that province. I would like to make another point. There will have to be a very large transfer of population in any case. The Germans have moved some eight or ten million people and those people must be resettled in their homes, and I cannot believe that the additional problem of placing a considerable number, say two millions or even more, of Germans back in Germany would present a difficulty which cannot be overcome.

13. POLISH GOVERNMENT IN LONDON—RECOGNITION*

ON JAN. *2, 1945 the following appeared in the New York Times:*

"Secretary of State Edward R. Stettinius, Jr. announced today that despite the formation of the Russian-sponsored Polish Provisional Government in Lublin, the United States wou'd continue to recognize the Polish Government in exile in London. In response to questions from reporters at the State Dept., Mr. Stettinius merely reiterated the Administration's policy of recognizing

* House of Commons. Vol. 407, Jan. 16, 1945, p. 33.

the government of Premier Tomasz Arciszewski in London, and he followed this by inviting that Government's Ambassador in Washington, Jan Ciechanowski, to attend this afternoon's celebration of the third anniversary of the signing of the Declaration of the United Nations. . ."

MR. STOURTON (C.) asked the Prime Minister if he will give an assurance that it still remains the policy of His Majesty's Government to adhere to recognition of the legitimately constituted Polish Government, at present resident in London.

THE PRIME MINISTER (MR. CHURCHILL): Yes, Sir.

MR. STOURTON: Is my right hon. Friend aware that this decision of H. M. Government will hearten all those who believe in constitutional government, not only in this country but throughout the world?

14. POLISH CITIZENS—ADMISSION TO BRITAIN*

LIEUT.-COLONEL THORNTON-KEMSLEY (C) asked the Secretary of State for Foreign Affairs what arrangements are being made for the reception and accommodation in this country of Polish citizens from liberated countries; whether he is satisfied that the accommodation is adequate and suitable; and whether arrangements will be made to find beneficial employment for men whose services are not required in the Polish Armed Forces.

THE SECRETARY OF STATE FOR HOME AFFAIRS (MR. H. MORRISON): I have been asked to reply. His Majesty's Government are unable in present circumstances to grant facilities for the admission of Polish citizens or, indeed, of any other foreigners from liberated countries unless their presence here is required for some purpose advantageous to the war effort of the United Nations.

---

* House of Commons. Vol. 407, Jan. 16, 1945, p. 61.

15. POLAND AND THE SOVIETS*

MR. STOKES (Lab.) asked the Secretary of State for Foreign Affairs whether he will publish as a White Paper the discussions carried on by the Strang Mission to Moscow in 1939.[1]

THE SECRETARY OF STATE FOR FOREIGN AFFAIRS (MR. EDEN): No, Sir.

MR. STOKES: Will not the Foreign Secretary reconsider his decision? Does he not think that the publication of this matter will enable people in this country to understand much more fully the position in Poland today?

MR. EDEN: I can hardly imagine a less helpful contribution than to raise again all the arguments about why agreement was not reached in 1939, at this moment when our Armies are jointly fighting the common enemy.

MAJOR-GENERAL SIR ALFRED KNOX (C.) asked the Secretary of State for Foreign Affairs whether any reply has yet been received from the Soviet Government to the application of UNRRA for permission to send relief to Poland.

MR. EDEN: I understand that negotiations about the transit of UNRRA supplies to liberated Poland through Soviet territories are now proceeding between UNRRA and the Soviet authorities.

SIR A. KNOX: Can the right hon. Gentleman give any idea of when these supplies will reach Poland? Poland has been more devastated that any other country in Europe.

MR. EDEN: I agree as regards the desirability, and negotiations have now begun, as I say. I regret that I cannot say how long they will take.

---

* House of Commons. Vol. 407, Jan. 17, 1945, p. 135–136.

1 Vol. I, No. 94, 99, 116.

SIR A. KNOX: Will the right hon. Gentleman help the case by making representations to the Soviet Government?

MR. EDEN: I think this is a matter between UNRRA and the Soviet Government, rather than a matter for myself, but I will consider what my hon. and gallant Friend says.

MISS RATHBONE (Ind.): Can the right hon. Gentleman say whether permission has yet been given by the USSR for a delegation from UNRRA apart from the provision of supplies?

MR. EDEN: I think that is exactly the point now being discussed.

SIR A. KNOX asked the Secretary of State for Foreign Affairs if his attention has been drawn to an article in the "Soviet War News" of Jan. 8 issued by the Soviet Embassy in London, referring to the Polish Government in London as a flunkey of Hitlerite Germany; and whether he will represent to the Government of Soviet Russia that the publication of libellous statements regarding a Government which is recognized as the lawful Government of Poland by Britain and the U.S.A. does not contribute to good feeling among Allies.

MR. EDEN: The answer to the first part of the Question is, "Yes, Sir." His Majesty's Government must express their regret at the publication of such insinuations against an Allied Government which they recognize.

SIR A. KNOX: Does not my right hon. Friend think it time that this sort of statement should be stopped, as the Polish Government have a cleaner record than the Government of any other country in Europe?

MR. EDEN: I rather thought that the House would feel that what I said was about right.

MR. DRIBERG (Ind.): Could the right hon. Gentleman say whether any of the numerous Polish newspapers published in London has ever contained a word in mild rebuke of the Soviet Union?

16. BALTIC REPUBLICS (STATUS)*

COMMANDER SIR ARCHIBALD SOUTHBY (C.) asked the Secretary of State for Foreign Affairs upon what date His Majesty's Government received from the Ministers representing Latvia, Lithuania and Esthonia formal declarations that the republics which they represented desired to maintain their independence and not become part of the Soviet Union.

THE SECRETARY OF STATE FOR FOREIGN AFFAIRS (MR. EDEN): The three Ministers referred to in the question made to His Majesty's Government communications expressing their views on the events which had just taken place in the Baltic States and expressing the hope that His Majesty's Government would not recognize the incorporation of those States in the Soviet Union. These communications were received upon July 23, 1940.[1]

SIR A. SOUTHBY: Has my right hon. Friend read the statement made by the President of the United States to the effect that even the smallest nations have a right to their own independence;[2] and is not this a case where we might apply the principles of the Atlantic Charter?

MR. EDEN: My hon. and gallant Friend asked when we received these representations and I have told him.

---

* House of Commons. Vol. 407, Jan. 17, 1945, p. 136–137.

1 See Vol. I, p. 443.

2 On Oct. 15, 1940, Pres. Roosevelt, on receiving a delegation of Americans of Lithuanian Descent, said: "Even the smallest nation has the same right to enjoy independence as the largest one." (Bilmanis, Alfred: "Baltic Essay," p. 188).

17. THE ARCISZEWSKI GOVERNMENT*

IN DECEMBER *1944 and January 1945 several things happened on the international front which affected the conduct of the war in its final month.*

Gen. De Gaulle made a visit to Moscow early in December and on Dec. 10 the Franco-Soviet Pact of Mutual Assistance was signed. This decidedly strengthened Russia's role in international politics.

In Athens on Dec. 3 Greek communists tried to take over control of the country. England sent armed forces to fight against the Greek communists. The situation in Athens was so complicated that Prime Minister Churchill and Minister Eden made a sudden trip there. They talked with anti-communist groups; this led to a statement made by Greek King George II in London that he would not return to Greece unless specifically re-called by his people and that he would give up his right to the throne; as a result, an armistice was signed in Greece on Jan. 11. According to the Churchill-Stalin understanding reached during Churchill's visit to Moscow in October of 1944, Great Britain was given 90% predominance in Greece.[1] *The USSR did not intervene directly in the Greek fighting.*

The last big German offensive of the war was begun on Dec. 16 at Ardennes under the command of Marshal Rundstedt. The attack was unexpected; it caught the Allies by surprise and the Germans pushed deep into France and Belgium. But, towards the end of December Marshal Montgomery regained control of the situation and gradually canceled out the German gains.

On the eastern front the December attack of the Russians towards the south brought the Soviets to Budapest. On the

---

* House of Commons. Vol. 407, Jan. 18–19, 30, 1945; p. 397–398, 441–483, 525–526, 565, 1372–1415; House of Lords. Vol. 134, Jan. 25, 1945, p. 711, 738–739, 754–755.

[1] Churchill, W. Op. Cit, p. 227.

Polish front Warsaw fell on Jan. 17 and at the end of January the Soviets reached the German border. East Prussia was occupied, and only Koenigsberg continued to fight.

In London the new Polish Government under T. Arciszewski was striving to make some contact with the British and the USA Governments. With respect to England the efforts were without success. Although recognizing the new Polish Government, the British Government actually had no direct contact with it.[2] *Neither Prime Minister Churchill nor Minister Eden received the members of the new Polish Government; and the Foreign Offiice limited itself to contacts with only Polish Ambassador Raczyński or with lesser Polish officials. This was in conformance with the warning voiced by both Churchill and Eden in their last talks with Mikołajczyk on Nov. 27 and 28.*[3]

The American Government, on the other hand, showed an active interest in the Polish problem. On Dec. 18 Secretary of State Stettinius made the following statement at a press conference:[4]

> The United States Government's position as regards Poland has been steadfastly guided by full understanding and sympathy for the interests of the Polish people. This position has been communicated on previous occasions to the interested Governments, including the Government of Poland. It may be summarized as follows:
>
> 1. The United States Government stands unequivocally for a strong, free and independent Polish state with the untrammled right of the Polish people to order their internal existence as they see fit.
>
> 2. It has been the consistently held policy of the United States Government that questions relating to boundaries should be left in abeyance until the termination of hostilities. As Secretary Hull stated in his address of Apr. 9, 1944. "This does not mean that certain questions may not and should not in the meantime be settled by friendly conference and agreement". In the case of the United Nations directly concerned, this Government would have no objection to such an agreement which could

---

[2] See No. 13.
[3] See No. 11.
[4] U. S. Dept. of State Bulletin, vol. 11, no. 287.

make an essential contribution to the prosecution of the war against the common enemy. If, as a result of such agreement, the Government and people of Poland decide that it would be in the interest of the Polish state to transfer national groups, the United States Government in cooperation with other governments will assist Poland, in so far as practicable, in such transfer. The United States Government continues to adhere to its traditional policy of declining to give guarantees for any specific frontiers. The United States Government is working for the establishment of a world security organization through which the United States together with other member states would assume responsibility for the preservation of general security.

3. It is the announced aim of the United States Government, subject to legislative authority, to assist the countries liberated from the enemy in repairing the devastation of war and thus to bring to their peoples the opportunity to join as full partners in the task of building a more prosperous and secure life for all men and women. This applies to Poland as well as the other United Nations.

The policy of the United States Government regarding Poland outlined above has as its objective the attainment of the announced basic principles of the United States foreign policy.

An exchange of friendly dispatches between Premier Arciszewski (Dec. 14) and Pres. Roosevelt (Dec. 23), the latter referring to the Stettinius statement, showed that cordial relations existed between the two governments.

In Dec. 1944 a group of former Polish senators and representatives, living in Great Britain, sent an appeal to the members of the British Parliament asking for humanitarian support for Poland. Describing the actual state of affairs in Poland which was gradually being taken over by the Soviets, the appeal ended with these words:[5]

"We have no wish to interfere in any way with complicated political arrangementts, but, in view of our loyalty throughout this war to the anti-German alliance, a loyalty proved by the deeds of the entire Polish Nation as well as by those of our fighting men, and on the grounds of human justice, we appeal to the Members of the British Parliament to lend their voice to an opinion which would contribute to:

[5] National Committee of Americans of Polish Descent. Biuletyn Organizacyjny, No. 27–28, p. 15.

1. Dissuading the Soviet authorities from continuing the deportations of the citizens of Poland to Russia;
2. Extending to these territories the beneficial activities of the Red Cross or other institutions aiming at the relief of distress;
3. The recognition, also by the Soviets, of the combatant status of the Polish Home Army;
4. The granting to our country of treatment similar to that afforded to France, Belgium, Holland and Italy."

Lord Dervent made reference to this appeal in his House of Lords speech on Jan. 25, 1945.

While this was going on in London and Washington, Lublin and Moscow were busy creating a temporary Polish Government. Stalin informed Pres. Roosevelt of this in this dispatch of Dec. 27:[6]

". . . A number of facts which took place during the time after the last visit of Mikołajczyk to Moscow, and in particular the radio communications with Mikołajczyk's Government intercepted by us from terrorists arrested in Poland—underground agents of the Polish émigré Government—with all palpability prove that the negotiations of M. Mikołajczyk with the Polish National Committee served as a screen for those elements who conducted from behind Mikołajczyk's back criminal terrorist work against Soviet officers and soldiers on the territory of Poland. We cannot reconcile with such a situation when terrorists instigated by Polish emigrants kill in Poland soldiers and officers of the Red Army, lead a criminal fight against Soviet troops who are liberating Poland, and directly aid our enemies, whose allies they in fact are. The substitution of Mikołajczyk by Arciszewski, and in general transpositions of Ministers in the Polish émigré Government, have made the situation even worse and have created a precipice between Poland and the émigré Government.

Meanwhile the Polish National Committee has made serious achivements in the strengthening of the Polish State and the apparatus of Governmental power on the territory of Poland, in the expansion and strengthening of the Polish Army, in carrying into practice a number of important Governmental measures, and, in the first place, the agrarian reform in favor of the peasants. All this has led to consolidation of democratic powers of Poland and to powerful strengthening of authority of National

6 Yalta Papers, p. 221.

Committee among wide masses in Poland and among wide social Polish circles abroad.

It seems to me that now we should be interested in the support of the Polish National Committee and all those who want and are capable to work together with it, and that is especially important for the Allies and for the solution of our common task —the speeding of the defeat of Hitlerite Germany. For the Soviet Union, which is bearing the whole burden for the liberation of Poland from German occupationists, the question of relations with Poland under present conditions is the task of daily close and friendly relations with a Power which has been established by the Polish people on its own soil and which has already grown strong and has its own army, which, together with the Red Army, is fighting against the Germans.

I have to say frankly that if the Polish Committee of National Liberation will transform itself into a Provisional Polish Government, then, in view of the above-said, the Soviet Government will not have any serious ground for postponement of the question of its recognition. It is necessary to bear in mind that in the strengthening of a pro-Allied and democratic Poland the Soviet Union is interested more than any other Power, not only because the Soviet Union is bearing the main brunt of the battle for liberation of Poland, but also because Poland is a border State with the Soviet Union and the problem of Poland is inseparable from the problem of security of the Soviet Union. To this I have to add that the successes of the Red Army in Poland in the fight against the Germans are to great degree dependent on the presence of a peaceful and trustworthy rear in Poland. And the Polish National Committee fully takes into account these circumstances, while the émigré Government and its underground agents by their terroristic actions are creating a threat of civil war in the rear of the Red Army and counteract the successes of the latter.

On the other hand, under the conditions which exist in Poland at the present time there are no reasons for the continuation of the policy of support of the émigré Government, which has lost all confidence of the Polish population in the country, and besides creates a threat of civil war in the rear of the Red Army, violating thus our common interests of a successful fight against the Germans. I think that it would be natural, just, and profitable for our common cause if the Governments of the Allied countries as the first step have agreed on an immediate exchange of representatives with the Polish National Committee, so that after a certain time it would be recognized as the lawful

Government of Poland after the transformation of the National Committee into a Provisional Government of Poland. Otherwise I am afraid that the confidence of the Polish people in the Allied Powers may weaken. I think that we cannot allow the Polish people to say that we are sacrificing the interests of Poland in favor of the interests of a handful of Polish emigrants in London."

Pres. Roosevelt answered Stalin on Dec. 30 saying he was "disturbed and deeply disappointed" at the news that Stalin wanted to recognize the Lublin Committee as the Polish Government and did not want to wait for a joint conference to discuss the problem. At the same time Pres. Roosevelt said that the USA would continue to accept the London Polish Government and would not recognize the Lublin Committee. He continued that "if at some future date following the liberation of Poland a Provisional Government of Poland with popular support is established the attitude of this Government would of course be governed by the decision of the Polish people."[7] *Pres. Roosevelt then expressed the hope that Stalin would refrain from recognizing the Lublin Committee until such a time as the three heads of governments could have a joint conference.*

Stalin's answer on Jan. 1 was in the negative.[8] *He stated that he naturally comprehended the suggestion that the Soviet Government's recognition of the Provisional Government of Poland be postponed for a month; there was, however, a circumstance which made this impossible: as early as Dec. 27 the Presidium of the Supreme Soviet of the USSR had informed the Poles, in reply to an inquiry on the subject, that it proposed to recognize the Provisional Government of Poland as soon as the latter was formed. For this reason it was impossible for the Soviets to comply with Roosevelt's request.*

As Stalin indicated, the National Council of Poland in Lublin, on Dec. 31, 1944, named the Polish Committee of National Liberation as the "Provisional Government of Poland." That same day the National Council of Poland formed a cab-

---

7 Yalta Papers, p. 224.
8 Churchill, W. Op. Cit, p. 336.

inet with E. Osóbka-Morawski as premier and minister of foreign affairs.[9]

The Polish Government in London reacted to this with a Polish Telegraph Agency communique which included the following:[10]

"All leaders and administrators have remained in Poland, continuing the fight against the Germans, and acting as the Council of Ministers and the Council of National Unity, representing the main Polish political parties. They have not quit their posts after the superhuman efforts of the past 2-month uprising of the Warsaw population, and they are carrying out their obligations in strict accordance with instructions from the Polish Government.

"The Polish government is registering a protest against attempts to rob the Polish nation of its sovereignty, attempts by the Lublin Committee which is calling itself a provisional government, but which is actually an imposter. The Polish Nation will never accept an authority imposed on it by force, or any form of totalitarianism, and it will fight to the end for a truly independent Poland."

The Polish National Council in London (the Parliament in exile) issued this resolution on Jan. 5:[11]

"On Dec. 31, 1944 the so-called "Committee of National Liberation" decided to call itself the "Provisional Government of Poland." This is an example of the new violation and usurpation of Poland's sovereignty which aims to liquidate Poland's existence as an independent state. This imposter group is composed of persons totally unknown to the Polish people and having nothing in common with them; it is forcing itself on the Polish nation with the support of a foreign power. Poland is not a newly-found state which would need a new administrative organization starting from scratch. Reborn after World War I it has existed since 1918, and the fact that the government has been in exile during the present war does not alter its legality. It has been active in exile and is the legal authority of the Polish nation. It is recognizd by all allied and neutral powers, and since July 31, 1944! it has also been recognized by the USSR . . . The Polish National Council, as the only representative of the Polish people, states categorically that the imposter Lublin Committee calling itself the

[9] Stosunki polsko-sowieckie, 1943–46, p. 432–433.
[10] Ibid., p. 436.
[11] Stosunki polsko-sowieckie, 1943–46, p. 437–438.

"Provisional Government of Poland" has neither factual nor legal meaning and all acts of this "government" are absolutely illegal. At the same time the Polish National Council reaffirms that a free and independent Poland is, always has been, and always will be the aim of the Polish people and that they never will recognize a government imposed on it by force."

Early in January Stalin and Churchill exchanged dispatches. On Jan. 4 Stalin informed Churchill:[12]

". . . The transformation of the Polish National Committee into a Provisional Government seems to us entirely opportune, especially since Mikołajczyk has ceased to be a member of the émigré Polish Government and the latter has thus ceased to possess any semblance of a Government. I consider it impossible to leave Poland without a Government. Accordingly, the Soviet Government has consented to recognize the Polish Provisional Government. I much regret that I was unable completely to convince you of the correctness of the Soviet Government's attitude towards the Polish question. I nevertheless hope that future events will show that our recognition of the Polish Government in Lublin is in the interests of the general Allied cause and will contribute to hasten the defeat of Germany . . ."

Prime Minister Churchill felt that further correspondence on this subject was pointless. Only personal contact could give any hope of solution. So, he telegraphed Stalin on Jan. 5:[13]

"I thank you for sending me your two messages to the President on the Polish question. Naturally I and my War Cabinet colleagues are distressed at the course events are taking. I am quite clear that much the best thing is for us three to meet together and talk all these matters over, not only as isolated problems but in relation to the whole world situation both of the war and the transition to peace. Meanwhile our attitude as you know it remains unchanged."

The Soviet Government recognized the Provisional Government of Poland in Lublin on Jan. 5 and simultaneously assigned to it as Envoy Extraordinary and Plenipotentiary Victor Lebediev. This evoked another protest from the Polish Government in London (Jan. 8).

---

12 Churchill, W. Op. Cit., p. 336.

13 Ibid, p. 337.

In this steadily deepening crisis the Polish Government in London turned to the U.S. Government to use its good offices in negotiating for a solution to the Polish-Soviet problem. The U.S. Government accepted the request and accordingly sent instructions to its ambassador in Moscow. On ~~July~~ Jan. 17 the State Dept. in Washington issued this statement:[14]

"Having received officially the request of the Polish Government contained in its public statement of Jan. 14, this Government through its Ambassador in Moscow informed the Soviet Government of its willingness, if agreeable to the Soviet Government, to extend its good offices with a view to arranging for the initiation of discussions between the two Governments looking to a resumption of official relations between them. Without going into the merits of the case, it is our hope that some satisfactory means may be found for the resumption of friendly relations between these two fellow members of the United Nations. No reply has been received from the Soviet Government."

In spite of the difficult situation created by events in Poland and the Soviet support of the impostor government, the Polish Government in London continued to try to reach an understanding with the Soviets which would not entail the loss of Poland's independence and integrality. Thus, Premier Arciszewski made a talk over the radio to Poland (Jan. 19) which ended with these words:[15]

"We hold out our hand to Russia and we do not believe that it will be rejected. The right to true independence of our nation, that is our whole program and all we claim. Right—that means that no bayonet, even though it may be covered with glory, will dictate who shall govern the country. Freedom—that is not only liberation from the German yoke, it is personal freedom, freedom of speech and thought, freedom of the press, of organizations and societies, freedom of religion, it is a Government imposed not by force but established on the basis of democratic elections without outside pressure. If these principles are recognized and the demands contained therein are fulfilled, then not one Russian-Polish problem exists which could not easily and amicably be settled. Humanity, which has begun to lose faith, will eventually see above the ruins and battlefields, the vision of a 'better world' as a tangible aim of this war."

---

14 Stosunki polsko-sowieckie, 1943–46, p. 443.
15 Polish Review, N. Y., No. 4, Feb. 1, 1945.

A meeting of Roosevelt, Churchill, and Stalin was to take place shortly. Counting on the fact that the Polish problem would be on the agenda, the Polish Government in London sent this memorandum to the British and U. S. Governments on Jan. 22:[16]

"Foreseeing that matters concerning Poland will be discussed at the forthcoming meeting of the Heads of the Governments of the three great Powers, and having full confidence in the intentions of the President of the United States of ensuring the Polish State real independence and the guarantee of its rights,—the Polish Government would like to take this opportunity to express the following views:

I.—The Polish Government shares the attitude taken by the Governments of the United States and Great Britain that terriorial questions should be settled only after the termination of hostilities. The Polish Government is ready to reach an amicable settlement of the Polish-Soviet controversy which has arisen as a result of the claims of the USSR to the eastern territories of the Polish Republic and will accept any one of the methods foreseen by international law for the just and fair solution of the controversy with the participation of both parties concerned. Moreover, the Polish Government is decided to conclude with the USSR an alliance guaranteeing the security of both states and closely to collaborate with the USSR in the framework of a general international organization of security and of the economic organization of the States of Central-Eastern Europe.

Under no circumstances will the Polish Government recognize unilateral solutions, mindful of the fact that Poland, belonging as she does to the family of United Nations in the common struggle for freedom of the world, has made enormous sacrifices of her most precious values and has lost practically one-fifth of her population fallen in battle, murdered in penal camps, in Ghettos or deceased in prisons, in exile or in labor camps.

The Polish Government is convinced that the simultaneous establishment and guaranteeing of the over-all territorial status of the Polish State, the solution of the controversy with the USSR, the grant to Poland of territories to which she has rightful claim situated to the North and the West of her frontiers, the insurance of her real independence and full right to organize her internal life in accordance with the will of the Polish Nation untrammeled by any foreign intervention,—is a vital matter not only for Poland, but for the whole of Europe.

---

16 Yalta Papers, p. 228.

II.—Should the Soviet Government, notwithstanding the insistent efforts of the Polish Government, refuse to enter into a voluntary understanding, the Polish Government, desirous of insuring internal peace and freedom to its country, suggests that a Military Inter-Allied Commission should be created under whose control the local administration of Poland could perform its functions until it will be possible for the legal Polish Government to take over authority.

Such a Commission should have at its disposal military contingents of the States represented on it. The statutes of the Commission and the principles upon which the local administration would be based should be established in detail in agreement with the Polish Government. The Polish Government additionally stresses that the authorities of the Polish Republic, abolished by the German occupying authorities in violation of the stipulations of the IV-th Hague Convention of 1907, in effect continued to function underground and should constitute the foundation of the administration of the country.

After the return to Poland her Supreme State Authorities as well as of her citizens who are at present outside her frontiers due to war events, elections will be held on the basis of a universal, secret, equal, direct and proportional electoral law, giving to all political parties full freedom of electoral action, and to all citizens equal and free right of expressing their will.

The Polish Government will retain its authority until the convocation of the Parliament [Sejm] on the above mentioned principles and the creation in Poland of a new legal government.

III.—The Polish Government trusts that the United States Government will not take part in any decisions concerning the Allied Polish State taken without the participation and consent of the Polish Government.

The Polish Government is convinced that at the meeting of the three great Powers the United States Government will express its decision of not recognizing in Poland accomplished facts and particularly of not recognizing a 'puppet government'. The recognition of such a 'government' in Poland would be equivalent to the cancellation of the recognition of an independent Poland, for the maintenance of which the present war started."

In Washington Acting Secretary of State Joseph C. Grew forwarded this memorandum to Press. Roosevelt with his own observation that "the proposals do not appear to offer any real basis for an approach to the Soviet Government."[17]

---

[17] Yalta Papers, p. 227.

In London Under-Secretary Cadogan in a talk with Ambassador Raczyński on Jan. 23 gave the opinion that British authorities looked pessimistically on a possible realization of the postulates listed in the Polish memorandum.

On Feb. 3, one day before the Yalta Conference, Premier Arciszewski sent Pres. Roosevelt this message:[18]

Mr. President:

At this time the fate of many nations rests in your hands and in the hands of Prime Minister Churchill. The whole world expects that these important discussions in which you and the Prime Minister of Great Britain are taking part will result in the creation of foundations for a future peace, a peace which should bring to nations the freedom of conscience and speech and secure for them freedom from fear and want. I trust that these essential freedoms will also be granted to our nation which has been fighting unflinchingly for their realization at the side of the great American and British democraticies.

In particular I trust you will not permit any decisions to be taken which might jeopardize the legitimate rights of Poland or her independence and that you will not recognize any faits accomplis with regard to Poland. If peace in Europe is to be durable it must be based on principles of justice, on respect of law, on good neighborly relations as well as honesty in international life.

While I am writing these words, the lives of many thousands of Poland's best sons are in danger. The so-called Provisional Government of Lublin has openly declared its intention to try as traitors all soldiers of the Polish Home Army and members of the Polish Underground Movement. Mass arrests and deportations have already taken place. You are well aware that they have fought the Germans gallantly and regardless of sacrifice throughout the years of occupation. You assisted them yourself with your aid and in the memorable days of the Warsaw rising the British and American Governments recognized the Home Army as part of the regular Polish Forces fighting alongside the United Nations. To-day the lives of these soldiers are in danger because they recognize the independent, legal Polish Government and because they firmly insist on their rights as men and citizens. I therefore beg of you to urge upon the Soviet Government whose armies are at present in occupation of the territory of Poland to give

18 Ibid, p. 950.

proof that they genuinely desire understanding with Poland and to prevent the execution of the criminal plans of the Lublin men.

This message was forwarded from Washington to Yalta with this annotation by Lt. R. W. Bogue, Watch Officer, Map Room:

"6 February. Shown to Mr. Hiss who took it to show to Doc Matthews. Returned and said that no action was necessary that they were working on Polish problem then, and that perhaps later acknowledgment might be in order."

Pres. Roosevelt acknowledged Arciszewski's message by a telegram dated Feb. 15, 1945 in which he stated: "You may be assured that Poland's problem received most careful and sympathetic consideration at our recent Conference. I hope we may all work together harmoniously to find the correct solution in due time."

Debate on January 18, 1945.

THE PRIME MINISTER (MR. CHURCHILL): We have one principle about the liberated countries or the repentant satellite countries which we strive for according to the best of our ability and resources. Here is the principle. I will state it in the broadest and most familiar terms: Government of the people, by the people, for the people, set up on a basis of free and universal suffrage election, with secrecy of the ballot and no intimidation. That is and has always been the policy of this Government in all countries. That is our only aim, our only interest, and our only care. It is to that goal that we try to make our way across all the difficulties, obstacles and perils of the long road. Trust the people, make sure they have a fair chance to decide their destiny without being terrorized from either quarter or regimented. There is our policy for Italy, for Yugoslavia and for Greece. What other interests have we than that? For that we shall strive and for that alone . . .

MR. LIPSON (Ind. C.): . . . There can be no doubt that what has happened in Greece has been a very great encouragement to the enemy. We know that Hitler and his associates are relying upon a difference of policy between the Allied nations to secure a stalemate peace. They argue to their own people that if they will only hold out long enough the Allies will quarrel among themselves. There can be no doubt that our policy in Greece has caused very great concern, not only in this country but in the United States.

It is not only in this matter that there is a difference of policy between the Allied nations, which is strengthening German morale, and to that extent tending to prolong the war. There is the difference of opinion with regard to Poland. The United States and ourselves recognize the Polish Government in London: the USSR have recognized the Lublin Government.

We want not only to make a clean job of the war, we want to make a clean job of the peace. We want to try and establish a peace that is likely to last. If we are to succeed in that, we must make the kind of peace that will not only appear just and right when it is made immediately after the war, but be a peace which, 10 or 20 years afterwards, the people of this country, if need be, will be prepared to enforce. We do not want to see happen this time what happened after the last war, when the Treaty of Versailles was violated and the people of this country were not united in their determination to resist its violation, because they were not satisfied that there was not some moral justification for the violation.

That is why I am concerned with the Government's announcement with regard to compensating Poland for the loss of territory from Germany in the other direction, to the extent of the whole of East Prussia. Not only will it be extremely difficult to carry out, but the transport, at a time when transport will be very difficult after the war of millions of people will take a long time and cause tremendous suffering. Further, I believe the loss of East Prussia is something that the German people will never accept, and I think we should be on sounder lines—and what I have in mind is a durable peace after the war—if we were to adopt the Curzon Line on the one hand, and allow the Poles to retain the Corridor, because I believe that, until Hitler came into power, the Germans had become reconciled to the Corridor position. If need be, give them Danzig, but certainly do not transport millions of people from East Prussia, which would create bitter feelings and might easily make it very difficult to ensure peace after the war . . .

MR. STOKES (Lab.): . . . I have often thought that some of the peace plans which are turning over in the minds of our great leaders must be too disgraceful for the nation to know. I have now come to the conclusion that that is so. I want to speak with great emphasis on this subject. I believe the principles for which I stand were largely betrayed at Teheran. I believe the scheme of allowing zones of influence, of deciding that America shall deal there, and Great Britain there and Russia there, is the most deplorable and impossible policy to follow if you really want an effective and just and lasting peace. I think the scheme is leaking out, despite the Foreign Secretary's assurance that there were no secrets—he stood up in this House six months or more ago when some of these things were debated, and assured us that there was nothing secret.

We have never had any clear indication of what happened at Teheran, and the birds are now beginning to come home. We are told that Poland is to lose part of what was before the war known as her Eastern territory. I have never disputed the right of Russia to insist that there should be some adjustment of her Western frontier, but equally I have always insisted that it should be done by agreement and not arbitrarily, by force. And so it ought to be. I cannot understand why our Government did not stand out and insist that we should follow that course. At the same time we are told that Poland is to be compensated in the West by giving her East Prussia and, if you believe the refugee Germans here, the cumulative effect of all the changes that are to be made in the West will be the uprooting of 10,000,000 people from their homes and planting them elsewhere. I protest, first of all, against the inhumanity of the thing, which should never be done at all, and, secondly, against the complete and utter idiocy of it, because you will never get peace if you treat millions of people in that way, a way which is indescribably inhuman and absolutely bestial.

So far as East Prussia is concerned, I cannot even follow the Prime Minister's mind. In his own book he writes that East Prussia, though once a Prussian colonial conquest, is more German than Germany herself. How can you expect to get peace if you cut great chunks off Germany and hand them over to people who will have to fight at some time in the future to maintain them? As the hon. Member for Cheltenham (Mr. Lipson) said, peace will not depend on whether you and I think it just at this moment; it will depend on whether our children and the next generation after them really think that what has been done has been fair, and will fight to uphold it. I am quite certain that what has now taken place will bring about a state of things which in the minds of future generations will be considered much worse than the Treaty of Versailles. Where does peace lie under those conditions? We are being led into an impossible position because the Government will not give us a positive and constructive lead. They are funking it. I cannot understand their attitude in this matter at all.

Finally, I come to the question of unconditional surrender. I would like to say something about Poland and the Baltic Provinces but perhaps I have been too long. However, in that connection it seems to me to be quite senseless to deplore the terrible things that have been done by both sides in Greece and to ignore the horrible things that have been going on in Poland and in the Baltic Provinces. What absolutely astonishes me is the cowardice of our own authorities in not allowing the truth to be told in the Press here. My information comes from the American Press, where they are much more outspoken, and it is better they should be. I think that the truth of what is going on should be made available to the public in this country for, while I am second to none in recognizing the marvelous military feats of the Russian Armies, the terrific endeavor of their soldiers, the capability of their command, I loathe and despise and vomit at the beastliness of the political Gestapo that follows in their wake . . .

PROFESSOR SAVORY (C.): The capture of Warsaw and of Cracow have made consideration of the Polish question extremely urgent at the present time. I would appeal to His Majesty's Ministers to do everything in their power to render help to this unfortunate city of Warsaw. We all know of the heroic campaign, lasting 63 days, which that great city carried on in its defense. Now it has been relieved, but I understand there is scarcely a house left intact in that once beautiful and very important city. I feel sure that it would be possible for the Government to take steps to see that medical supplies, food and clothing are sent to those most unfortunate people, who have deserved a very much better fate. The Prime Minister laid stress on the fact that it was in order to carry out our guarantee to Poland that we have gone into this war. There was a Debate on Poland on December 15.*

I will not repeat anything that was said on that occasion, but I should like to call attention to a few points which escaped notice. I feel that this question of the Eastern Provinces of Poland is one of the most vital importance. Great stress was laid on the fact that Poland was being asked to sacrifice 47 per cent of her territory and a third of her population. This proposed border is really almost exactly equivalent to the partition line of 1795, when the whole of Poland was annexed to the three neighboring States. What you are proposing under the arrangement that has been suggested is that you should hand over to Russia everything that she obtained by the final partition of Poland in 1795. One of our greatest historians, a distinguished Member of the House and President of the Board of Education, Mr. H. A. L. Fisher, said of the partitions of Poland that the story was one of the most shameful in the annals of Europe. No one pointed out in the Debate that the proposal to hand over Eastern Galicia is to give Russia something which in the whole course of her history

* See No. 11.

she has never possessed. At the time of the first partition in 1772, part of Galicia was handed over to Austria and the remainder at the third partition of 1795. It remained Austrian down to the outbreak of the last war and, of course, from the time of the Treaty of Peace it was Polish. With regard to the other territories—the Northern territories and the White Russian territories—even those were Polish for more than 400 years before the first partition of 1772. We have heard a very great deal with regard to the question of race and we all know that Eastern Poland is inhabited by a mixed Polo-Ukrainian race but it is certain that the Poles are in a relative majority. In any case—this argument was never brought forward—there are practically no Russians in the whole of that territory. I doubt very much whether the whole Russian population exceeds 100,000—that is one per cent of the whole population.

Further, I would ask the House never to give its consent to handing over those two great centers of Polish culture, Vilno and Lvov, to Russia, because they are essentially Polish. I, as a University Member, entreat you to remember that those great Universities were European centers of culture. If there were time I could tell you what they have done. I could give you a list of the men of science and literature that they have produced. I would, therefore, implore the Government not to force Poland to give up two absolutely essential Polish cities. May I make a comparison? If you were to ask Poland to hand over Lvov it would be just as much as asking Ulster to hand over the sacred and historic city of Derry, commemorated in the graphic and striking pages of Macaulay. You could not do that without provoking a civil war throughout Ireland. The Poles attach exactly the same importance to the ancient and historic city of Lvov that we in Ulster attach to the maiden city, as we call it, the heroine of the great siege —Londonderry. I would make this appeal to our Russian friends. Do not insist on a frontier which will always throughout the ages be a bone of contention. No Pole who is faithful to his country will ever consent to give up that noble heritage of his race, Galicia and the North-Eastern provinces. Do not make the mistake that was made by the Germans in 1870. Bismarck was very much against the proposal to seize Alsace and Lorraine, but he was overborne by the King and by the military party. Germany annexed Alsace and Lorraine and that was a bone of contention for over 40 years. That was a sore which prevented any reconciliation between Germany and France during all that period and was one of the causes which led to the outbreak of the war in 1914. After all, the line of the Treaty of Riga was a very fair compromise. Poland was asked by the Treaty of Riga to give up 120,000 square miles which had belonged to her in 1772 and which that great Ulster statesman Lord Castlereagh was anxious to give her at the time of the Treaty of Vienna, but when the Emperor Alexander got up from his seat, stood against the map and put his hand on it and said, "Poland is mine," he was the master of great legions and it was impossible for justice to be carried out. What have the Russians themselves said with regard to that line of Riga? I have a statement signed by Lenin and Chicherin in July, 1920:

> "The real frontiers which Soviet Russia will establish with the representatives of the Polish people will be to the east of the frontiers marked out by the Imperialists in London and in Paris."

That is to say that the real line would be very different from that suggested in the telegram from Lord Curzon. It would be a line very much more East and corresponding much more to the compromise line adopted in the Treaty of Riga. I would like my hon. Friends to remember this. When war broke out, it broke out 500 miles to the West of the country where it would have broken out if the Poles had accepted the offers made to them by Field-Marshal Goering. We have heard of the hunting expeditions and of the visits of Goering to Marshal Piłsudski. The documents in the Polish White Book give the tempting proposals which were made by the Germans: "Join with us, attack Russia, help us, and then we will guarantee the integrity of Poland." Poland to her honor rejected those proposals, and the consequence was that Russia owes her an immense debt, because when the war broke out it broke out, as I have said, 500 miles further to the West than it would have broken out had Poland accepted them. I would appeal to four brief texts which, I think, are of vital importance. I will give them as briefly as possible. The Prime Minister, on September 5, 1940, said:

> "We do not propose to recognize any territorial changes which take place during the war unless they take place with the free consent and good will of the parties concerned."*

The right hon. Gentleman the Secretary of State for Foreign Affairs on July 31, 1941, wrote to the Polish Prime Minister, General Sikorski:

> "His Majesty's Government in the United Kingdom have entered into no undertaking towards the USSR which affects the relations between that country and Poland. I also desire to assure you that His Majesty's Government do not recognize any territorial changes which have been effected in Poland since August, 1939."**

Then we have that magnificent clause in the Atlantic Charter, Clause 2, signed by the Prime Minister and President Roosevelt on Aug. 14, 1941:

> "They desire to see no territorial changes that do not accord with the freely expressed wishes of the peoples concerned."***

Finally, may I quote Article 5 of the Anglo-Soviet Agreement of May 26, 1942:

> "The high contracting parties will . . . act in accordance with the two principles of not seeking territorial aggrandizement for themselves and of non-interference in the internal affairs of other States."****

We have been told that we were obliged to accept the Munich Agreement and that as it was a question of force, we could not resist it. That may or may not be. All I can say is that it left a nasty taste in the mouth because it handed over 800,000

---

* Vol. I, No. 114.
** Vol. I, No. 132.
*** Vol. I, No. 135.
**** Vol. II, No. 15.

Czechs to Hitler and thousands of Sudeten Germans who had no wish to be Nazified. On this question, let me implore the Government not to hand over these provinces which are sacred to Poland against the will of Poland, or we shall be doing an action which we shall afterwards regret. We may have to submit to force majeure; I do not deny it, but do not let us be a party to it. Do not let us play the Bismarckian role of the honest broker. Do not let us even give our consent to it. Let us remember those glorious words of the "Chanson de Roland," that great monument of the earliest French literature. Let no charge be brought against us in history, as it was brought against the traitor Ganelon: "Il a forfait à l'honneur." . . .

* * *

Debate on January 19, 1495:.

SIR C. HEADLAM (C.): . . . As regards the situation in Poland, I should like to associate myself with the speech made by my hon. Friend the Member for the Queen's University of Belfast (Professor Savory), who spoke so ably yesterday. It is difficult for many of us to see what is going on in Poland without a feeling of depression and disappointment. We are conscious that we are in some degree responsible for modern Poland. I do not think that any of us wants to be associated with another partition of Poland. Although it may be impossible for us to take any effective action to stop it, I am certain that there will never be peace in Eastern Europe unless a satisfactory settlement of Poland can be brought about. I do not look upon the suggestion about East Prussia with much satisfaction. I do not think that you are going to give peace to Europe for any length of time if these drastic alterations of the map are made. But that is another matter. We must do nothing that is in any way calculated to make relations between ourselves and Russia worse. But we have to maintain our honor, and we should make clear to the Russian Government our views regarding the right of the Poles to manage their own affairs in accordance with the wishes of the majority of the Polish people. . . .

COMMANDER SIR ARCHIBALD SOUTHBY (C.): . . . I believe it to be true that the vast majority of the people in this country will have heaved a sigh of relief when they read the Prime Minister's speech. Having followed the events in Greece with great care and attention, and having been much exercised in their minds and subjected to propaganda of all kinds, at last, they have seen the picture drawn clearly by the Prime Minister. At the same time it would be idle to deny that there is a certain amount of public uneasiness regarding Poland and Yugoslavia. I have given at some length in this House my views on the question of Poland. I have no desire to reiterate them, but I will just say this. We are all watching Russia's wonderful military advance at the present time. There is not a soul amongst the Allied Nations who is not grateful to Russia for what she has done. All through this war, while she has been fighting on our side against Germany, she has earned the gratitude of mankind. Is it too much for some of us to dare to hope that, when the meeting takes place, as it soon will, between the President of the United States, the Prime Minister, and that great leader of Russia, Marshal Stalin, realizing the gratitude the world feels to Russia, those who guide the destinies of that great country may perhaps come to the conference table and consent to consider and discuss the whole question of Poland de novo—to make a new start in a spirit of generosity to the Polish people, who have been beyond praise in their courage and tenacity during this war, in spite of all the sacrifices which they have been called upon to make?

* * *

House of Lords. Debate on January 25, 1945.

LORD ADDISON (Lab.): . . . I hope that as part of the deliberations we shall see some machinery set up which will deal with urgent matters of international dispute. First amongst these, of course, is the Polish question, and I sincerely hope that one of the results of this meeting will be some proposals for producing an effective settlement of that long-standing controversy. Unfortunately, for two hundred years or more, we know that history has presented us with disputatious factions—to put it no higher—in Poland, and I suppose that national characteristic will still remain. Well, we have our share of it ourselves. The settlement of the major Polish questions is clearly an essential ingredient in the security of peace in Europe. I think also that we might look for some prompter action and more effective machinery for dealing with the problems of liberated nations as they become liberated. It is true that the conditions that arose, say in Belgium, or France, or Greece, or Yugoslavia, are in themselves different, and I do not see on the horizon, at present anyhow, any inter-Allied agency that can function with authority, with sufficient promptitude, as these territories are liberated. We cannot expect the standing European Council, which is mainly advisory, to exercise functions of that kind, but I think that some more effective machinery and a more authoritative agency is required than we have at present for dealing with the problems of liberated countries as they arise, and particularly for the distribution of food supplies and other necessities . . .

LORD DERWENT: My Lords, in what is inevitably a protracted debate I desire to raise only three points, and to do so with what I consider to be the maximum of brevity; I hope that the noble Viscount, the Leader of the House, and your Lordships will agree with me at any rate on that score. The first concerns an unhappy and tragic country, Poland, a name which has been mentioned in the debate only once, I fancy by Lord Addison. Your Lordships will doubtless, like myself, have received a circular sent out by a number of former members of the Polish Senate and Chamber of Deputies in which, while, as they say, having "no wish to interfere in any way with complicated political arrangements," they adduce their loyalty throughout this war to the "Anti-German alliance" in order to make certain suggestions, amongst which is that the Members of the British Parliament should help to "dissuade the Soviet authorities from continuing the deportation of Polish citizens to Russia." These deportations, they claim, are rife at this time on lines similar to those of 1939 and 1940, when approximately a million Polish citizens "were penally deported to the depths of Russia and Asia."

If these statements are true—and I cannot believe that that circular would have been sent out irresponsibly, or would have been sent out if the statements in it did not contain at any rate a fairly large grain of truth—it is just because I firmly believe that the Poles must, for the future happiness of their country, end by forgetting the past and arriving at some working arrangement with their powerful neighbor, that I do not hesitate to ask His Majesty's Government whether it cannot (if that has not already been done) be arranged that this matter should come under discussion at the next meeting of the Big Three, which has been referred to so often in this debate, which is in everybody's mind and on which we build such high hopes. Autocracy is an old tradition in Russia, a thing which we have a slight tendency to forget, and Marshal Stalin moves in just as mysterious a way as his predecessors; but even if, after all that has passed between Russia and ourselves on the Polish question, it is unlikely that the Marshal is going to modify his intentions in regard to Poland in deference to any representations which we may make, I should personally prefer—and I feel that many of your Lordships would agree with me—the verdict of history to be that we tried to play our part in smoothing the way to an eventually satisfactory relationship between Russia and Poland rather than that we refrained from putting in a timely word when we could. And we still can, and, if we care for what we call democratic institutions, as we say we do, and for the privileges which are supposed to accompany them, I sincerely think that we should . . .

THE LORD PRIVY SEAL (VISCOUNT CRANBORNE) (LORD CECIL): . . . Then there is the problem of Poland, about which Lord Derwent spoke today. That problem may appear to be widely different from that of Yugoslavia, but I would suggest that, in some of its main features, it is exactly the same. There, too, you have a country which has been occupied by the enemy. There, too, the policy of His Majesty's Government is to see the country emerge strong and independent, with a form of government which has been chosen by the whole Polish people. It is the same policy. There, too, there has always been a danger that there might come about the establishment of two authorities, a Government outside the country, and another administration set up inside the country, in those parts liberated from the enemy. That is precisely the situation which His Majesty's Government, which the Prime Minister and the Foreign Secretary, have labored so arduously to avoid. It would have been perfectly easy for us to have stood aside and allowed matters to take their course. Nothing would have been easier. But I believe that it would have been contrary to all our traditions and that we should be bitterly blamed by the people of this country had we done so.

Poland is our Ally. She has fought heroically at the side of the Allies. We were bound to do what we could to assist her, in what were very real and grievous difficulties. The only way in which we could, in practice, help was to try to find a basis of agreement between the Polish Government in London and the Russian Government in Moscow, to enable those two Governments together to reach some solution of the Polish problem which would be acceptable to both. The matter could not be left until the end of the war. Events were moving far too fast for that. It is on this extremely thorny and ungrateful problem that, as your Lordships know, the Prime Minister and the Foreign Secretary have been working for many months now. In Moscow and in London they have sought to find some middle line which would enable agreement to be reached.

A compromise which they supported, and which the Prime Minister announced, was clearly by no means perfect. It involved far-reaching sacrifices on the part of the Poles. It involved sacrifices with regard to Lvov, and with regard to that eastern portion of Poland east of the Curzon Line. Quite clearly, that must have been a very bitter pill for any Polish Government to have to swallow. But it would have given a possibility that the new Poland which was envisaged, and which would have comprised Polish territory west of the Curzon Line, with the addition of East Prussia, could be a free, independent, and powerful nation. At any rate, it offered, I think, the best chance of getting agreement. However, the Polish Government, as the House knows, could not bring themselves to agree to the sacrifices involved, and the negotiations broke down. His Majesty's Government here have been criticized in various quarters for supporting the proposal they did, but I must confess that I have never heard any one put forward any alternative plan which was more likely to be acceptable to the two parties concerned.

Now, just what might have been feared has happened. Two administrations have come into existence, one which is recognized by Russia, and the other which is recognized by ourselves and the United States. What is going to follow upon this I cannot tell your Lordships. No doubt this must be a matter for discussion, sooner or later, between the leaders of the Great Powers. At any rate we can say this: we have done everything which was conceivable to try to find a solution, and I believe that we should have been extremely blameworthy if we had not tried. Lord Derwent raised one or two detailed points, but he will forgive me if I do not go into them today. I assure him that I will bring what he said to the notice of the Foreign Secretary.

House of Commons. Debate on January 30, 1945.

MR. STOKES (Lab.): . . . I want to raise what is to me and, indeed, to every person in this country, a matter of vital importance, that is the conduct of political affairs in relation to our foreign policy today. I know it is a broad issue but, in my view, the principles upon which our foreign policy should be founded are principles which should be enunciated again and again, and as often as possible, and on every opportunity that occurs, and it is for that reason that I have seized this opportunity today.

We meet today under the shadow—I call it a shadow in view of what has happened on preceding occasions—of an impending conference abroad. When or where that is to take place I have not the slightest idea, but I would like, if I could, to make my views reach those celebrated personages who are to represent the cause of this great country and great Empire at that meeting. My mind carries me back to the first Teheran Conference in November, 1943. I have said on other occasions, and I have no hesitation at all in saying it again today, that in my view—I speak only for myself and not for my party—the principles for which I stand were betrayed at that Conference, and conclusions were arrived at and agreements were made at that Conference, of which this House was not sufficiently informed at the time. I know the Prime Minister came back in February, a few months after the Conference, and made a statement to this House couched in strong language, but sufficiently veiled not to rouse the hostility of many people. I am bound to say I felt a bit angry myself. The Foreign Secretary stood up shortly afterwards and assured us in terms that admit of no equivocation, that there had been no secret understanding. I think it is worth while quoting to the House the words he used. In reply, I think, to my hon. Friend the Member for Ebbw Vale (Mr. Bevan), he said on 15th December, 1943:

> "I can also tell the House, lest there is any uneasiness about it, that we have not entered into any kind of secret engagement or treaty or anything which can cause anyone a sleepless night or a sleepless hour, and the hon. Member need not have any fear that the movement of power has been from him to the Treasury Bench. I can give this undertaking, that as long as I have anything to do with the conduct of the Foreign Office, if I make an engagement I shall come and tell the House at once, which is the constitutional practice, and, if they do not like it, they can turn me out."—[*Official Report*, 15th December, 1943, Vol. 395, c. 1651.]*

---

* Vol. II, No. 50.

With the sentiments expressed in the last two sentences, I profoundly agree, but my feeling is that the Foreign Secretary—I am not speaking of my personal regard for him—in the execution of his duty, did not tell the House the true and honest facts.

I want the House to reflect on what happened at the Teheran Conference so far as we have been told. I have been challenged again and again in my constituency by people of the extreme Left, who would kneel down at the feet of Marshal Stalin "for ever and ever, amen," and by people of the extreme Right, who would do the same to the Prime Minister —there is very little difference between them when dictatorship comes into it. I would like to know what are the facts. I have said, and I challenge my right hon. Friend to dispute this, that, in effect, the Atlantic Charter was betrayed at the first Teheran Conference. He cannot deny that. It is true. It may be disagreeable, it might even be unavoidable, I do not know, but surely we should be allowed to know the facts as soon as possible after any step has been taken contrary to what the people of this country believe?

Secondly, what were we told? I know perfectly well that in our first Alliance with Poland all we did was to assure the Western frontier against aggression by Germany. We gave no guarantee as to the Eastern frontier. That is a point which is not sufficiently known but that, I think, can be proven from the records. The general sentiment in this country was, however, that we went to war to stop aggression, to protect the rights of Poland among other things. I can remember saying in the early days, with great unpopularity, that the longer this war went on, the less of Poland would be left, and that is precisely what has happened. The Prime Minister told us on 22nd February last year** that he had agreed with Marshal Stalin for what is tantamount to the forcible adjustment of Russia's Western front. I have never disputed the advisability of adjusting Russia's Western front, I have always recognized that, indeed, would have to be done, the moment Rus-

** Vol. II, No. 54.

sia had gathered herself together from the last war and was able to assert what she considered to be her rights. But surely the essence of the thing should have been that it was to be done by agreement and not by force. That is my quarrel with the Government.

My mind goes to the Strang Mission. I remember that in June, 1939, we sent a mission to Russia to try to arrive at a treaty with Russia against Germany. I asked the Foreign Secretary the other day whether he would publish, as a White Paper, the discussions which took place in Moscow on that very vital point, and he said that it was not in the public interest. My belief is this—and I shall be very glad to have my argument completely destroyed—that, in effect, what the Russians said to us was, "Let us have Poland to the Curzon Line and the Baltic Provinces, and we will have an alliance with you." We said, "No," and I personally, think we were quite right. I do not disagree with that. There was no alliance and what happens next? Off go the Germans to Moscow and Ribbentrop is asked the same question. He says, "Yes, not only may you have the Baltic Provinces, but as much as you want of Poland on the East, and we will take out of those Provinces all the German nationals who might be a nuisance to you." So they had an alliance. Now where do we find ourselves? We find ourselves fighting to give to Russia—I agree that Russia is doing a great deal of the fighting, but the philosophical background is that we are fighting to give to Russia precisely those territories which, had we allowed her to have them in 1939, would have prevented an outbreak of war at all. Is there an answer to that? I should like to know. I do not think there is. It seems to me perfectly terible that, as a result of what is going on, as I said on another occasion, the seeds of the next war have been sown. You are proposing not only to destroy Poland in effect; you are giving away the Baltic Provinces and doing so in no uncertain terms, which I will quote to my hon. Friend in a moment.

MR. SILVERMAN (Lab.): I am trying to follow this, because we agree on so many things that I do not want to differ unnecessarily from my hon. Friend. Would he explain what he meant by the statement that the rectification of Russia's Western frontier in 1939 would have prevented the war?

MR. STOKES: I am stating what is my belief, and I should have thought it was the belief of my hon. Friend. I do not say that war would never have broken out, but surely the belief of a large number of people wo have studied this question is that if there really had been an alliance on the East, which involved, naturally, an adjustment of wrongs which Russia considered needed to be set right, then the Germans would at that moment have been afraid to enter into any war at all.

MR. SILVERMAN: What is wrong with doing it now?

MR. STOKES: I am not arguing that question, I am arguing whether it should be done by force or not. After all if you ask what is wrong with doing it now, I should reply, "Why waste all those lives, why not have done it in the first place?" If you are going to do it at all, then for goodness' sake save all the human lives you can in doing it. To let the war go on for six years, and then agree that this is the right thing to do seems to me entirely crazy. As I have said, I do not dispute the necessity for adjustment but it must be done by agreement and not by force.

I would ask my hon. Friend to think of the Atlantic Charter which he and I, at least, think was a step in the right direction. It said that there shall be no territorial changes except by the wish of the people concerned. You can argue whether that would apply to some parts of Eastern Poland, but you cannot argue whether it does or does not apply to the Baltic Provinces. At the Teheran Conference, largely owing to its secrecy, zones of influence were agreed upon and independent action was allowed. Thus you get all the horrible villainies which are being carried on now. I am not in the least afraid of offending my hon. Friends. I know we did not guarantee the Eastern Frontier of Poland, but Russia did. If she did not, then I do not know what is the meaning of the Soviet-Polish Agreement of 30th July, 1941. It stated:

> "The USSR recognizes the Soviet-German Treaties of 1939 with regard to territorial changes in Poland as having lost their validity. The two Governments mutually undertake to render each other assistance and support of all kinds in the present war against Hitlerite Germany."

I do not know what that means unless it means that you are going to do your best to maintain the *status quo* until a different status is mutually agreed.

I return to the question of East Prussia, and I would remind the House of what the Prime Minister said on this point. I am not talking of the humanity of what the right hon. Gentleman said—which makes one feel so hot with passion—but it seems crazy to contemplate the removal from territory of persons who have lived there for many generations. I do not see how you can get peace like that. We were told that at the Teheran Conference, in consideration of the cession of Eastern Poland up to the Curzon Line, or something like it, Poland was to be compensated by the cession of German territory in the North and West. I understand that specifically to refer to East Prussia. It may be that there are greater authorities on this point than the present Prime Minister, but at least he made a considerable contribution to international affairs in his writings after the last war. In "World Crisis Aftermath," he said:

> "The Province of East Prussia, although originally in the nature of a German colonial conquest, had become a purely German land, whose population was animated, above all other parts of Germany, by the spirit of intense nationalism."

How is it proposed to lift 3,500,000 people from East Prussia, put them down in another place and expect peace, a peace which we hope will be for all time? If you mean only a patched-up peace, which will later mean another war, then I understand the policy. In that case we shall be dead and forgotten, and it will not matter to us. But it is the future we are all thinking of, at least those who fought in the last war and who fought, and are fighting, in this war. If I may take an analogy from part of the country of which I represent, does my right hon. Friend the Under-Secretary really imagine that if the boot had been on the other foot and the unspeakable thing had happened, and we had been "licked" in 1940 and Norfolk and Suffolk had been taken away from us and had been given to the Dutch or Belgians and the population removed to South Wales, this would have meant peace? The moment those people arrived at their new destinations, they would have started to try to recapture their territory. I have been in Suffolk for 20 years, and I am not accepted yet. You cannot change people like that, and every student of international affairs knows perfectly well that you cannot get peace by uprooting people from territory which they consider is theirs, and in which they were born and bred?

I want to say a few words about the Baltic Provinces. I do not pretend to be well informed on the history of those Provinces, but I protest—and I would be a coward if I did not—against the terrible treatment which is being meted out to the people there, if the reports we receive are correct. If the reports are not correct, let us have them contradicted and proved futile. What are we told by the Lithuanian representatives in this country? They say that designated families are selected, are visited suddenly and, without notice, are given an hour to collect a few possessions; that they are carried in lorries to the point of entrainment and that the heads of the families separated from the others, this being kept secret so as not to provoke scenes; that these ruthless separations are enforced upon tens of thousands of private families for no other reason than that they are judged to be unlikely docilely to accept the Bolshevist formation. If that is so, it ought to be condemned outright; if not, it ought to be forcibly denied by the Minister. For the sake of humanity alone, the information which comes to Lithuanians in this country ought to be stated to be entirely without foundation, if that is the case. . . .

MR. E. P. SMITH (C.): The hon. Member has spoken very feelingly of Poland. I assume that he would wish Poland to have access to the sea. Does he wish to perpetuate the Danzig corridor?

MR. STOKES: I am opposed to the corridor and have never considered it essential to give Poland access to the sea. Lots of countries in Europe have not got it and live economically secure.

COLONEL SIR ARTHUR EVANS (C.): The hon. Member for Ipswich (Mr. Stokes) has gone on a long world tour. He has taken us to Russia, to the Far East and to the Middle East, which I gather he knows well, and back again to France all in the space of fifteen minutes. He said he proposed to indulge in a little loud thinking. I think it was Mark Twain who said on one occasion that people sometimes sit and think, but sometimes just sit. The only difference in my view is that sometimes the hon. Member stands instead of sitting, because he seems to take a delight in mischief making at critical times in our fortunes. First of all he attacked the policy of the Foreign Secretary and the Prime Minister in relation to the Teheran Conference, and criticized its findings, though he did not know what those findings were. Of course he does not know. The House knows well that the parleys between Stalin, Roosevelt and Churchill on the prosecution of the war and the state of the world immediately after the war must be secret. It is impracticable to suggest that it is possible for any Government to disclose with complete frankness the decisions arrived at and the discussions which led up to those decisions.

MR. STOKES: I did not say we knew nothing. I said we only knew as much as the Prime Minister chose to tell us. My whole point was with regard to secret treaties on policy.

SIR A. EVANS: Is the hon. Member suggesting that it is possible, when a treaty or understanding is arrived at during the prosecution of the greatest war in history, for those agreements to be published to the world—at the time?

MR. STOKES: Certainly.

MR. SILVERMAN (Lab.): Would the hon. Gentleman draw a distinction between agreements as to the conduct of the war, agreements as to what is to be done during the war and what after the war? Is there any reason why, if the heads of the great United Nations reach an agreement as to the disposal of territories or the organization of human affairs after victory has been achieved, that should not be communicated and the sanction of the House of Commons sought to agreements of that kind?

SIR A. EVANS: I see no reason at all at the opportune moment, when that state of affairs has come about, but is the hon. Member suggesting that those treaties are already in being and that the Government have secretly put their signature to treaties which have not been disclosed to the House of Commons?

MR. SILVERMAN: None of us know what agreements have been arrived at. It may be that we ought or it may be that we ought not. I thought the hon. Gentleman was suggesting that, if an agreement is reached as to what is to be done after victory is achieved, it is impossible to communicate it, and it was that point that I was challenging.

SIR A. EVANS: I am afraid the hon. Member did not follow me. The hon Member for Ipswich charged the Foreign Secretary with making a statement about the Teheran meeting not in accordance with the true and honest fact.

MR. STOKES: Certainly I do.

SIR A. EVANS: Officially we have no knowledge as to what agreements were arrived at Teheran. The hon. Member admitted that, because he asked the Government to tell us what the facts were. The question of Poland is a very difficult and delicate one to discuss at this particular time. Owing to the military efficiency of Russia, Poland is—at this moment—being freed of the enemy. That is fact No. 1. The next fact is that the Prime Minister has disclosed to the country that one of the subjects to be discussed at the coming international conference is that of Poland. It has also been disclosed in the

American Press that President Roosevelt shares the same point of view, that that subject must be reviewed at the forthcoming conference. The hon. Member, in his anxiety to use any weapon with which to hit the Prime Minister over the head and embarrass the Government, chooses this time, on a Debate on the Adjournment of the House, to raise the question of Poland. I do not think he is serving any useful purpose at this time in saying anything which would either embarrass our representatives at the forthcoming conference, or in any way withhold from the glory of Russian arms what they are in fact doing, clearing the Germans out of Poland. To say the least, it is unfortunate and shows little sense of responsibility to seize on opportunities and occasions such as this to add embarrassment to a task which must of itself be difficult.

The hon. Member referred to the treatment likely to be accorded to East Prussia at the conclusion of the war and suggested that, if we ventured to hand over East Prussia and its territory to Poland in compensation for any other territory that might be ceded to another nation, we were doing something which would sow seeds for further trouble. I believe, rightly or wrongly, that it is not only Hitler but the German people themselves who must be called upon to pay the price of their errors. If we are to befriend the people of Poland, on whose behalf we entered this war, and the British people have made such enormous sacrifices; if we are to aid them in compensating them for some of their losses by taking away territory from a part of the German Reich, I should be the last to say them nay. I feel that we must review the situation in the realm of reality, realize on the one hand the just claims of Russia, and on the other that what we might wish to do, will not always accord with the views of our Allies, with whom we have to work not only now but in the future. I regret profoundly that, in his anxiety, the hon. Member decides on anything to attack and embarrass the Government, instead of addressing himself to the larger problem of a lasting peace and using his undoubted ability to make a practical contribution to that end.

MR. SILVERMAN (Lab.): I should like to say to my hon. Friend the Member for Ipswich (Mr. Stokes) that in this matter of Poland I think he is batting on an extremely sticky wicket. I do not know what the complaint is. It is apparently conceded that the Curzon Line was not a line that was unfair to Poland. After all, it was agreed upon at the Versailles Conference. It was agreed upon at the Peace Conference at which Russia had no representatives. It secured the approval of a Commission presided over by Lord Curzon, and there is nobody, as far as I know, who has ever accused him of being too friendly to Bolshevik Russia. It was accepted by the Poles themselves. The Treaty of Versailles and the Treaties accompanying it which created the republic of Poland had the acquiescence of the Polish representatives at that time. The very Treaty which created the modern republic of Poland created it on the basis of the Eastern frontier between Poland and Russia, which has since come to be known as the Curzon Line.

MR. STOKES: I do not want to get at loggerheads with my hon. Friend, but is he correct in saying that the Curzon Line was agreed on in the Versailles Treaty? I do not think so.

MR. SILVERMAN: This is a Debate, which, as my hon. Friend has said, has been staged without any notice to anybody, so that none of us have had much opportunity of looking up the facts. My impression is, however, that the Curzon Line, the border between Poland and Russia, was agreed upon by a Commission appointed under the authority of the Versailles Conference, and was incorporated into the Treaties which created the modern republic of Poland and which, at that time, had the consent of the Polish representatives.

MR. HAROLD NICOLSON (Lab.): My hon. Friend is almost right, but not quite. What happened was that the western frontier was decided in the Treaty of Versailles, but the eastern frontier was left vague and was decided two years after.

MR. SILVERMAN: I said it was decided under the authority of negotiations commenced at the Versailles Conference and that ultimately, when the final boundaries on both sides were decided, it had the concurrence of the Polish representatives.

MR. NICOLSON: The Treaty of Versailles had nothing to do with it. It was after the Russians had invaded Poland.

MR. SILVERMAN: I speak with all respect to my hon. Friend's much greater knowledge and experience, but surely it is no good saying that the Treaty of Versailles had nothing to do with it. But for Versailles there would have been no Poland at all.

MR. PICKTHORN (C.): The same might be said about the apple and the Garden of Eden.

MR. SILVERMAN: I have yet to learn that the Versailles Treaty had anything to do with the Garden of Eden or the apple.

MR. PICKTHORN: I really believe that this is wholly irrelevant to the arguments of the hon. Member for Ipswich (Mr. Stokes), but since the hon. Gentleman has introduced all this learning, which has been corrected and replenished by the hon. Member for West Leicester (Mr. H. Nicolson), and has brought in the argument that it has something to do with and is, indeed, part of and dependent on the Treaty of Versailles, because if there had not been that Treaty Poland would not have happened, let me say that this is an argument which you can apply as between any two events in history, from the first chapter of Genesis to this moment. As the hon. Gentleman has called me to my feet, perhaps I may contribute my learning. I do so with great diffidence because I like to look these things up, but when the so-called Curzon Line was drawn it was drawn, not as a political line, but as an armistice line, as a line to keep the two armies apart.

MR. SILVERMAN: This goes far beyond anything started by my hon. Friend the Member for Ipswich, and I doubt very much whether he would endorse many of the things that are being said in his support. The main point is—and I withdraw it completely if it is challenged—that, so far as I understand the argument, nobody really contends that there is anything ethically wrong with the Curzon Line as the border between Poland and Russia. My hon. Friend the Member for Ipswich conceded that. If I am wrong as to the details of what happened at the Versailles Conference or afterwards, or on what the historical moralities may be, let it be so, but the argument I put—and I do not understand that anybody challenges it— is that nobody now disputes that the border that has come to be known as the Curzon Line between Poland and Russia is in itself a just and fair border, and that everybody would concede it.

MR. PICKTHORN: No Pole would.

MR. STOKES: Concede the principle, yes, but I say that the adjustment must be made by agreement.

MR. SILVERMAN: That is another point. If we are agreed that the Line iself is conceded and that it is conceded that it is a fair Line, we can go on and deal with the other point, whether it has now been established by force or by agreement. I deny that it has been done unilaterally or by force. As I understand the situation, a provisional agreement was reached between Stalin, the Prime Minister of this country and the Prime Minister at that time of Poland. As I understand it M. Mikołajczyk was party to the agreement so far as this Line was concerned. It is true that the Polish Provisional Government in London did not endorse it and that M. Mikołajczyk resigned the premiership of Poland because they did not.

MR. STOKES: May I ask my hon. Friend on what authority he said that the Polish Prime Minister agreed to this? I have not seen it.

MR. SILVERMAN: My hon. Friend and I are equally in a difficulty, and I sympathize with him and join with him in his protest that none of us have been given enough of the facts. I am only trying to do what he did and reach a fair inference from such facts as are known. It is known that there was a conference, that these three gentlemen were present, that it was announced that a provisional agreement had been reached between them, that M. Mikołajczyk came back to London, that he reported on the conference to his Government, that they did not agree with him, and that he resigned. It is not an unfair inference from those facts that if he had had his way he would still have been Premier of Poland and there would have been no question of anybody imposing by force. It is a great pity that he did not do it.

If there was anything wrong ethically with the Curzon Line, it might be a different story. I am dealing with my hon. Friend the Member for Ipswich, who concedes that there is nothing much wrong with it as a frontier. If there is any-tihng much wrong with it as a frontier, whatever happened in 1939, I still say it is a pity from Poland's point of view that the Polish Government in London could not agree with its then Premier. If they had done so, there would have been a settlement of this question by agreement. There would have been no dispute, and the Polish Government in London would have been recognized today by all the great nations as the lawful Government of Poland, and very soon it would have been back on its own territory and governing it with the consent of everybody. I cannot help feeling it was a very great pity that those concerned in London could not be persuaded to take that view. It would have removed a great many of their difficulties and a great many of the difficulties of the world.

My hon. Friend says, and says very rightly, some things about East Prussia and the population of East Prussia. I take it that his reference to the Atlantic Charter does not affect the Eastern side at all. He is surely not suggesting there ought to be a plebiscite there, that the population on the East of the Curzon Line ought to be consulted? If so, he is on very dangerous ground. There is a place called Teschen, which was taken by Poland from Czechoslovakia after Munich in September, 1938, and the guarantee to Poland, even of the Western frontier, could not be taken to have included that.

MR. RAIKES (C.): May I ask the hon. Member one question on Teschen? This question has been raised often. Is it not a fact that Teschen was taken by the Poles when Hitler, after Munich, had marched into Czechoslovakia, and so far from Teschen having been taken from Czechoslovakia, Poland only marched in to prevent it being taken by Hitler?

MR. SILVERMAN: I daresay they marched in with the most altruistic motives in the world, but if they did, and did not desire anything for themselves, I have no doubt they would be perfectly ready to agree, and I think they have already agreed, that it should go back to Czechoslovakia when the time comes. No one would suggest that the Atlantic Charter provision that the population should be consulted by some kind of plebiscite, should apply to circumstances of that kind. Therefore, it cannot apply to the population East of the Curzon Line either. [AN HON. MEMBER: "Why?"] For the obvious reason it should be on that side. [AN HON. MEMBER: "That is not agreed."] My argument has been based on the supposition that that frontier is a fair frontier. I have not heard it challenged. If it is, I will address my argument to the challenge.

East Prussia, I concede, is a totally different case, but after all, the concession of East Prussia to the new Poland was not a Russian or British interest. It was done in order to compensate Poland for the loss of territory on the other side. It may be very wrong, but I have yet to hear that the Polish Government in London have ever repudiated the idea. If Poland does not want it, the Polish Government have only to say so. They have never said no. I am afraid that some members, at any rate, of the Polish Government in London are actuated by ideas of territorial megalomania that go far beyond East Prussia on one side, and far beyond the Curzon Line on the other. I think this case of Poland is a very bad one from my hon. Friend's point of view.

MR. STOKES: It is only part of the issue. The main issue

is whether there shall or shall not be secret treaties of which this House would not approve.

MR. SILVERMAN: On the main issue I am with my hon. Friend, as he knows. I only detain the House for a moment longer to say as I entirely agree with what was said by the hon. and gallant Gentleman below the Gangway. Even if it involve temporary territorial aggression, no one in his senses would embarrass any Government charged with the successful prosecution of the war by bringing all these issues to the House, or to any assembly, as matters of debate, argument and vote. But I think that when you are dealing with the reconstruction of the world after victory has been achieved, you are in very different country.

I am one of a small group of people in this House who, right from the beginning of this war, have taken the view that so far from doing any harm to our war effort, it would have been of the greatest possible benefit to our war effort if we had defined and put down in clear terms our aims and objects in the war. I do not mean that we should seek to draw or redraw an exact new political map of Europe. That is not necessary. But at any rate we ought to have been able to make up our minds what our main objects were. We ought to have been able to set them down in clear terms and invited our Allies and others to join with us. There ought not to have been any kind of doubt, ambiguity or hesitation, or doubtful controversial debate about our objects in the war. These ought to have been clearly stated from the start. Enemy peoples ought to have known from the start what we proposed to do after the victory had been achieved.

I have never quarrelled very much with the idea of unconditional surrender. I do not quarrel with it now. On the contrary, I agree with it, but I urge that it should be understood that unconditional surrender is not a policy. Unconditional surrender means that you undertake yourself the sole responsibility for what happens after victory has been achieved. Unconditional surrender means that you do not negotiate with anybody about it, you do not bargain with anybody about it. It surely means also that you know what you want it for. Unconditional surrender, without saying what ultimate purposes you have, is a mere slogan and nothing else. If you get your unconditional surrender—and I hope we shall get it soon—you are then at the beginning of your problems. You have still to evolve your policy of reconstruction. Why wait until then? Why not do it now? Why not take the House and our Allies into consultation? Why not take the world into consultation, as far as that can be done, in framing a clear picture of the kind of world we want to see, in place of the ugly, murderous world out of which we are emerging?

I think the Government have been rather inclined, because of difficulties and possible disagreements in doing that, to burke the issue, and to cloak the difficulties under this curtain of the reiterated slogan of unconditional surrender. Those of us who object to it, are not objecting because we want to make terms with Hitler—far from it. I do not want to make terms with Hitler, or the Nazis and Fascists, in Germany, or anywhere else. I want unconditional surrender so far as they are concerned. But I do want to see a clean, decent, sane world afterwards. I want the responsibility which we assume when we insist on unconditional surrender to be adequately discharged. I want it to be clear on what lines and on what basis we propose to rebuild shattered Europe and the shattered world. I think the Government are very much to blame in not having formulated long before this a plan, which would be known and understood, which would be clear and sincere, and accepted by the world, so that wherever there may be people prepared to support us in rebuilding the world along those lines they would know that we were with them, and that we would support them.

MR. BEVERLEY BAXTER (C.) : I find myself in the odd position of disagreeing with my colleague the hon. and gallant Member for Cardiff South (Colonel Sir A. Evans) and, for once, agreeing largely with the hon. Member for Ipswich (Mr. Stokes). I think the hon. Member has done a good service in raising this matter today. My hon. and gallant Friend says that the hon. Member has always tried to cause trouble, and that this is not the time to embarrass the Government by expressing convictions upon matters of foreign policy. With great respect, I think that is an entirely wrong attitude to take.

SIR A. EVANS: I said that this was not the time. After all, if we are to discuss matters of such importance as this, it is essential that hon. Members should have an opportunity of informing themselves of the facts and of hearing from the Government their views on the situation. They should not have to deal with the matter on what I might call an irresponsible occasion, on the Adjournment Motion.

MR. BAXTER: I do not think it is an irresponsible occasion. The House of Commons is a very adjustable place where Debates of great value can quite suddenly and unexpectedly arise, such as the Debate today, which none of us expected. Nor do I think it right that on matters of eternal values, we should have Government construction. I feel that there is altogether too much legalism and expediency in our foreign policy today. The Prime Minister and the Foreign Secretary are tried to the utmost of their patience; they have had a hard task and carry enormous burdens, but there is always a danger that Ministers who are too close to things, will lose track of the philosophy which must be behind Government and foreign policy, as it must be behind human life. There is an old joke to the effect that we never like to have a Foreign Secretary who speaks French, because he becomes too much involved with French influence and French policy. There is a danger of the Foreign Secretary of this country becoming too intimate with the personalities and problems on the European chess board.

It seems to me that we have to fall back upon the eternal governing principles which have made this country so honored through the centuries. None of us would try to minimize the dreadful problem of Poland, quite outside the justification of Russia's case and the necessities of Russia's strategical position, but is there any one of us who does not wish with all his heart that Stalin would approach the matter in an entirely different spirit?

MR. SILVERMAN: What other line could he possibly have taken?

MR. BAXTER: There is a beautiful word in our language, "magnanimity." There has not been to my knowledge, in the last two years, a speech by this great and mighty leader of the Russian people, expressing any warmth or pity or feeling for the Polish people.

MR. SILVERMAN: Surely the hon. Member, who I know speaks with a great sense of responsibility, is speaking too hastily now. There have been a number of speeches quite recenty in which the Russian Premier has said how much he wants a strong and independent Poland. This difficulty about the frontier, which has been handled with great magnanimity and great patience over a long period of time, was only settled as it was when it became necessary in order to advance towards the West. So many people who talk about this Polish issue seem to wish that the Russians had been able to advance from Russia to Berlin without touching Polish territory at all. Unfortunately, geographically that was not possible.

MR. BAXTER: I am sorry to interrupt the hon. Gentleman's interruption, but it does seem to me that there are times when the legal mind does not speak for this country as well as the more simple and uninstructed mind that I am going to use today. Is it true or is it not true that there have been cruel deportations from Poland? I am not speaking with the least idea of embarrassing the Prime Minister or the Foreign Secretary, but I am not happy about the dexterity of our dealing with foreign Powers in Europe. It seems to me that we might get back to very simple things, one of which is our desire that the weak shall be free, and to give every country the right to choose its own form of government. We ought to be true to those who have been our honorable friends, and no considerations of policy, or strategy, or expediency should take away from a nation or from a man the right to be true to those whom they regard as their friends in this cause for which we are all fighting.

MR. COVE (Lab.): Including India.

MR. BAXTER: We went into this war for Poland, because Poland represented a point in the history of humanity, and it has not been made easier for us by the Russian Government, who want us to stand aside and see the Polish nation treated almost as if it were an enemy State. Look at the attack this morning on General Bor, the man who led the tragic but wonderfully brave rising of patriots in Warsaw. Today, he is accused by Moscow of being a Quisling. It is in "The Daily Worker" and I presume that it has come from reliable sources. Is there any man in this country who believes for one moment, that General Bor was a traitor to Poland. I doubt it. From the same source, we are told that the Polish Government here are in league with the Germans. We must realize that Poland and Russia have to live together, but if this is the approach to it, God help them.

If ever this troubled world was in need of magnanimity, consideration and compassion, that moment is now. Poland has seldom or never, in the history of mankind, had such a chance of starting well. I sometimes wonder whether the Kremlin, in their lack of knowledge of the Western world, realizes the immense reservoir of good-will in this country from which they could draw from all classes. There is no longer the prejudice against Russia that there was formerly. We realize that Russia has emerged into the world as one of the greatest, and perhaps the greatest, dominating factor in the future. We want to do business with Russia, and march side by side with her, but we do not want to make concessions to Russia of everything in which we believe. That matter should be taken into account. If we are to be true to our friends and to our alliances and ideals, I wonder whether the Party opposite would consider their attitude towards such men as King George of Greece and this young boy, King Peter of Yugoslavia. . . .

MR. G. STRAUSS (Lab.): . . . I want to speak about the wider issue referred to by the hon. Member for Ipswich (Mr. Stokes) and my hon. Friend the Member for Nelson and Colne (Mr. Silverman), particularly in regard to Poland. A great deal has been said this afternoon about dexterity and manipulation, and so on. I submit that we should still consider these problems not so much as questions of power politics, in the sense of what one nation can do or cannot do, but in relation to certain basic principles on which Members of the Labor Party should at least be agreed. The principles are two. One is embodied in the Atlantic Charter, which was supported, I think, not only by everybody in this House, but by everybody in every democratic country throughout the world. That is, that there should be no transfers of territory without the consent of the people concerned.

The other principle—perhaps "principle" is not quite the word—arises from the first. It is to consider all these problems from the angle of what is most likely to bring about peace and contentment in Europe, and to make a future war less likely. It is from that angle that I feel that this problem should be regarded, and from that angle primarily. In the past I have heard my hon. Friend the Member for Nelson and Colne speak very eloquently, and indeed vehemently, on behalf of that first principle in the Atlantic Charter, because it is the right principle. It is certainly a Socialist principle, that there should be no transfer of territory or populations on any large scale unless it is going to lead to the greater contentment of the people concerned. It may very well be and, in fact, I have said so in this House—that probably it would lead to the greater contentment of the peoples concerned if those who live on the East of the Curzon Line were incorporated in the Soviet Union. That is my view. But the people who live there may take a different view. There has so far been no agreement whatever about the transfer of that territory. No Polish Government has agreed to it. I would point out, particularly to my hon. Friends, that the Polish Socialists have not agreed to it. People living there have not agreed to it, because they have not been asked. There has been no referendum nor has an election been held. The only people who have agreed are the Lublin Committee.

It may be perfectly right that this territory should be transferred, but there is a question of principle involved that is going to arise throughout Europe, and I, as a Socialist, would be very much happier if my belief that this suggestion is justified could be confirmed by some sort of plebiscite among the people concerned, as soon as the war is over. There is no reason, as I see it, why it should be finally concluded now. There could be a provisional government meanwhile. I would like to see, not only here, but in regard to all the major territorial adjustments proposed by various nations for the post-war period, that the people concerned should be asked their views. That is the principle which has been agreed and accepted by the whole democratic world in the Atlantic Charter, and I think it is tragic that it has now been abandoned. It is tragic, not only for the people concerned, who are going to be pushed about here and there as on a draughts-board but because I believe the violation of that principle is going to make another war highly probable.

MR. SILVERMAN: The hon. Member is not being quite fair about this. This is not a transfer of territory in the ordinary sense. This is territory which the Russians have always said, and most of us agree with them, had been wrongfully taken by the Poles from the Russians when the Russians were weak. The Russians had to advance over that territory if they had to make any advance, and, if they did not make any advance, we were all sunk together. Was it very unreasonable for the Russians to say, with regard to this territory, which should never have been Polish and was never rightfully Polish, "We want this settled, and we are prepared to make compensation and do everything we can to make a strong, free and independent Poland, but this bit of territory——"

MR. DEPUTY-SPEAKER (MR. CHARLES WILLIAMS): Is not the

hon. Member's intervention getting near to being a second speech?

MR. STRAUSS: I think they are perfectly entitled to put forward the demand for the return of that territory, and, if their case is strong, as I believe it is, I think it would be acceptable in any international conference afterwards, particularly if the same view were taken by the majority of the people concerned. Certainly, some areas which Russia is claiming today are almost wholly Polish. All that could be a matter of compromise.

SIR GEOFFREY MANDER (C.): I am not quite clear how far my hon. Friend goes. Would he apply the principle he lays down to enemy territory, and insist that the Germans in East Prussia or other places must give their consent and be consenting parties, before there can be any transfer of territory?

MR. STRAUSS: The Government of this country signed the Atlantic Charter, which said that the Allies required no aggrandizement of territory, and that there should be no transfers of territory without the consent of the people concerned. This was accepted by everybody at the time, and not challenged in any quarter, to apply to all territories, including enemy territories. It was only subsequently that various nations have put forward demands for cutting off a bit of Germany, saying that the Charter was never meant to apply to the enemy. If it was never meant to apply to Germany, to whom was it meant to apply? Nobody has ever answered that question. Of course, it was meant to apply to Germany. I say that, for the future peace of Europe, it is the height of folly to make any considerable transfers of population without the consent of the people involved. A minor frontier adjustment here and there may be highly desirable from every point of view but, when you are proposing to move, as these proposals suggest, 7,500,000—that is the population of East and West Prussia, North and South Silesia, involved in the Polish issue —without taking into account the feelings of the present population, I say that, to move all those people against their will, people who have lived there for generations, is not likely to lead to a permanent settlement of European affairs.

SIR G. MANDER: Have they not gone already? Are they not going as fast as they can? The transfer is taking place.

MR. STRAUSS: Maybe they are. I do not know what the situation is, but the point I am trying to make is really a simple one. In this Polish issue, there are certain matters of important principle involved which affect the whole European scene. I would like to see these principles, which I believe are correct principles, carried out and accepted in the Russo-Polish dispute and elsewhere.

If the Russian demand in this case is a perfectly sound and good one, as I believe it is, I do not understand their suggestion that Poland should be compensated by taking over part of another country. If the people on the East of the Curzon Line will be happier if they were part of the Soviet Union, I cannot understand why the question of compensation arises at all. I think that, if compensation is to be forthcoming, it should be on the lines of making the Polish worker and peasant a more prosperous and contented person than before by giving him, from Germany and elsewhere, machinery, fertilizers, and capital of all sorts. I am convinced that if Poland is to take over the territory which is suggested, she would be creating, on her West, a permanently hostile people, more hostile than before. We should be doing our best to plant the seeds of hatred and discontent in the hearts of people now children who will grow up and want, inevitably, to go back to the land in which they lived as children and their parents and grandparents.

I should have thought that, if we wanted a settlement of Europe, not only should we disarm Germany so that she may never have the power of going to war again, but we should see that the German people lose the will to go to war again. But here you are presenting the young people of Germany today with such grievances, that the time will inevitably arise when they will want to readjust their frontiers, peaceably, if possible, and if not, by other means.

I suggest that we should look upon all these matters from the point of view of these basic principles, because they apply everywhere through Europe. If we once say "good-bye" to these principles, and everybody tries to get bits of territory here, there and everywhere, putting forward claims which may or may not be good, that process of bargaining will end in chaos, and we shall make almost certain that there will be another war. I feel that my hon. Friends and I and those who think along these lines, should press, today and constantly, for an adherence to these principles set out very admirably in the Atlantic Charter, which, not only hon. Members on this side of the House but the whole Parliament and country agreed are the only principles upon which permanent peace can be secured.

MR. RAIKES (C.) : I find myself largely in agreement with what the hon. Member for North Lambeth (Mr. G. Strauss) has just said. There is one thing that is quite certain. If at the end of this war there is a sphere of influence, say, a Russian sphere of influence over half of Europe or a British sphere of influence over the other half, we shall be inevitably drifting towards another great conflagration at an early date. The only hope for the future lies in the nations of Europe deciding by free consent their own forms of government, whatever that government may be, and providing that position is reached, I would sooner see States in Europe adopting forms of government of which I disapprove rather than seeing them compelled to accept forms of government which are contrary to their desires.

I feel bound to say a word or two with regard to Poland. The hon Member for Nelson and Colne (Mr. Silverman) was nearly right, but not quite. He said that the Curzon Line had been really agreed upon by both sides at the end of the last war. As a demarcation line, yes, but the hon. Member will bear in mind that it was also stated that that was to be a demarcation line subject to any rights that Poland might have East of that line. The hon. Member also left out a further point that the Russians themselves stated directly that, with that demarcation line, they were prepared to offer Poland something rather more than the Curzon Line. The Curzon Line at that time did not include Eastern Silesia* as part of Russia. The Curzon Line pressed for by Russia today includes Eastern Silesia* as well as territories which are East of that line. I do not regard the pre-war boundaries of Poland as being sacrosanct, but it is a tall order that Russia, who not only recognized the Curzon Line but re-ratified it in 1932 and 1934 and re-ratified it again in 1941, should suddenly say, "We have come to the conclusion that we are going to have half the territory of prewar Poland." I would be willing, like the hon. Member opposite, to see these Eastern territories, if it could be done, going into other areas if they wished to do so. Russia because she is powerful—and she is powerful—because she has fought well—and she has fought well—is saying, "I am going to take so and so not because of the right of it but because I want it."

MR. SILVERMAN: When did Russia say that? Surely the Russian claim has been that they were having it because, on the merits, they were entitled to it and because the Polish authority had agreed to it.

MR. RAIKES: It is easy to talk about the merits, but it was on the merits that the Russian Government four times ratified the Treaty of Riga. Why has the Treaty of Riga suddenly become out of date? The hon. Member cannot find an answer to that. M. Stalin has not attempted to find it. I want to go a little beyond that. I think that a Debate like this is a good thing, as we are able to clear up matters which it is not possible to clear up at any other time. If Mikołajczyk had remained Prime Minister all would have been well and there would not have been any of this trouble. The Curzon Line was not the only thing considered at Moscow. At Moscow the Russian terms were clearly laid down—first of all the Curzon

* Must be Galicia.

Line; secondly, the majority of the new Government were to be members of the Lublin Committee; and thirdly, Poland was to be compensated by certain territories in the West subject to conditions which would mean that Russia would have control of Poland's outlet to the sea. Whatever Mikołajczyk agreed to, he did not agree to those terms in Moscow. He came back and said he must discuss those matters with the Cabinet, and that as far as he was concerned, the terms, as they stood, could not be accepted. The Polish Cabinet met, and at their first meeting they unanimously decided that they were not prepared to agree to the Russian terms, which covered all those other things to which I have referred. Later there was disagreement between Mikołajczyk and the majority of his Cabinet as to whether it would be worth while to go back to Moscow and negotiate on the basis of those terms and try to get something better. It is not for me to express an opinion one way or the other, but Mikołajczyk took the view that it might be well to negotiate, and the majority of his Government took the view that further negotiations would not be worth while on those terms because they were already so bad. That, I understand, was the position of Poland, and it is rather a different picture from that which the hon. Member for Nelson and Colne painted.

MR. SILVERMAN: Surely the picture which the hon. Member is giving is much more unfavorable to the London Government than the picture I gave.

MR. RAIKES: I have some difficulty in following that intervention. There was this difference of view in the London Government. The terms meant the end of Polish independence and they may well be right. Mikołajczyk felt that it might still be worth while to try and negotiate something better than that which the Russians had offered. But the question of Poland is really only a small part of the picture. It is an important part. If the future of Poland is to be decided not by the will of the Poles themselves, or indeed by the will of many Germans on the Oder, but by the decision of Russia and by what they want in contradiction of their own treaty signed and re-ratified time after time, the whole future for peace is not very great. I agree with the hon. Member opposite that it would not be a satisfactory agreement by which Poland was given completely non-Polish territories as part of the west. I would accept the corridor, because I think the corridor is a different matter, but to say that Poland is to have a large proportion of territory to the west in exchange will not be of any use.

I sometimes think that His Majesty's Government do not always sufficiently realize the degree of misery and despair caused by the moving of millions of people of different races from their homes in order to make a geographical settlement. The hon. Member for Ipswich (Mr. Stokes) is interjecting mildly to himself and I know that he will not agree with what I say, but that will not prevent me from saying it. I recall to the attention of the House, and particularly to the Under-Secretary of State for Foreign Affairs, a decree which has recently been issued by the Lublin Committee—it was signed by President Bierut and reported in the "Daily Telegraph" of 20th January—which called for a round-up of "irreconcilable members of the Polish Home Army and followers of the London Government." It urged all armed forces in the liberated areas to co-operate with the Soviet and Polish military authorities to outlaw "the Home Army murderers who are provoking civil strife." Whatever our views of the future of Poland may be, the Government which the right hon. Member the Under-Secretary is representing on that Bench at the moment is a Government which still recognizes the London Government of Poland.

It is a government which has power to speak to Marshal Stalin and inform him of our own views, and I think that whenever the meeting of the great three takes place it must be urged that if there is to be any hope for future friendly relationships between East and West, you cannot have decree after decree issued by the present Lublin Committe, recognized by Russia, calling for the death penalty on all persons not connected with Lublin, for hundreds of thousands of these people have fought against Germany in the underground movement for a considerable number of years. . . .

. . . Other countries will also be involved, but if only this House can come clearly down to the real principle in the years after the war—I do not believe there is a great difference over this—that we want to see a free Europe, a Europe not carved up in spheres of influence, a Europe in which the ordinary man and ordinary woman can live in his own home, in his own place, without being forcibly transferred, a Europe in which Governments can operate by free consent of the peoples themselves, a Europe in which the small state will have the rule of law enforced in its favor against the great—if we build such a Europe we shall have peace; but if we have to consent to a dictatorship Europe where Russian influence may be building spheres of influence in one part so that she forces us to set up something to offset them, perhaps, in the West, we shall not have peace but an uneasy armistice and, in that uneasy armistice we shall sow the seeds of a greater and worse war than the present one.

PROFESSOR GRUFFYDD (L.): I think it is necessary that someone from my Party should make quite clear what our views are on this question. For my own part, I am in very general agreement with what was said by the hon. Member for Ipswich (Mr. Stokes) and with the very grave words which have come with great significance from the other side of the House. I speak with all the more confidence because I know that any words from an obscure back-bencher cannot possibly embarrass the Prime Minister or the Government in any negotiations they may be conducting at present or in the future. It may be well, however, to assure the Prime Minister that the country as a whole is not quite as acquiescent in everything he does as is the present House of Commons, that there is a feeling in the country that at this very moment we may be hanging a tragedy around the necks of our children and our grandchildren.

The hon. and gallant Member for South Cardiff (Sir A.

Evans) protested violently against any discussion of peace negotiations before peace had actually been signed or before the enemy had been conquered. I can only say this, I am convinced that unless we discuss now, in general, the principles which we would see applied at once, and in the future, we shall never have an opportunity of doing so. That was the great trouble after the last war—when the time came for the country as a whole to make its voice heard in the councils of Europe, it simply was not heard, because it had not prepared itself, it had not informed itself of the problems, and the people in the Government, the people responsible at the time, had not educated the country to the problems that were to arise and which they knew perfectly well were to be the issues of the future.

Mussolini once used a phrase which has been condemned at large—*sacro egoisimo*—the holy or the sacred egoism. I appeal to this House to use a little of that *sacro egoisimo* in its proper sense. One would think that we are the most altruistic people in the world. We discuss the fate of Poland, we discuss the future of Germany, we discuss what Greece is going to do, what America feels, but we never think of the one thing of which the House ought to think before anything else —what will happen to our own children and grandchildren after this War. I appeal to the House to think of that and to keep that in their minds when we are discussing the fate of other countries, because the fate of our children and our grandchildren will depend directly on whether we take the right line and whether we judge rightly in the matter of the external politics of Europe. That will depend very much on the amount of discipline which this House exercises over the Foreign Office.

At the end of the last war I was interested in a society called the Union of Democratic Control. At that time, we found it was very necessary to protest in season and out of season against the secret commitments which were made then by the Government. There has been no difference, as far as I can see, in the last 30 years in the method which the Foreign

Office has followed from that time to this. In one respect they have not learned a single lesson from the last war. They have not learned that they ought, first of all, to have learned some indication of the feeling of the country in general, not merely the feeling of Parliament but of the country before they enter into undertakings of which we know nothing. With those words, I will sit down. I am glad to have had the opportunity of stating a view with which I am confident most of my party will agree.

COMMANDER PRIOR (C.) : If I may say so with all courtesy, the hon. Member for Ipswich (Mr. Stokes) made a most pro-Nazi speech, a speech which will give immense satisfaction to the German High Command. What we are all searching for is the peace of the world, not only in our own time but in the future. I have had dealings with many young Nazis. I picked one out of the sea not long ago, and the first thing he said to me was, "When we invade England." I asked him how he proposed to do it. These young men now living in Germany love war. They are filled with vengeance and the lust for blood. What we are all searching for now is the peace of the world. How is that to be gained? Hon. Members have taken exception to the transfer of East Prussia, I am unaware that any great musicians, authors or artists ever came out of that country.

PROFESSOR GRUFFYDD: The greatest classical scholar in the world, Mollendorf-Williamowitz, came out of East Prussia.

COMMANDER PRIOR: I am unware of him, but let me correct myself. Many more soldiers and generals have come out of East Prussia than men of peace. We are told that we have to get the consent of the East Prussians before their will to war is stifled for good. Exception is taken to the French advancing to their natural boundary, the Rhine. In my humble opinion unless the means to make war are removed from Germany we will always have war. The Germans want war; they are thirsting for vengeance. How is that to be stopped unless by the dismemberment of Germany, and the break-up of their war potential?

MR. KENNETH LINDSAY (Lab.) : . . . As I read "Soviet War News," which comes in a little packet to my breakfast table, and the Lublin Pol-Press communiques, I see, in Russia, a clear-cut policy. They know what they want, and so far as I am concerned they appeal to my interests when they talk about Lublin, because they say they are starting the schools again. I do not know whether they are or not; I do not know whether to believe a word of it. I am told by hon. Members that it is all puppetry and nonsense. But at any rate it is power politics, and how can power politics sit down side by side with the Atlantic Charter? My hon. Friend the Member for North Lambeth (Mr. G. Strauss) talked in eloquent terms about the Atlantic Charter. I have heard it ridiculed and laughed at by many of my Conservative friends, who say that it is just a sheet of paper. It may well represent deep feeling in the country, and so far as I am concerned it does represent something. But it has not become the touchstone of our foreign policy. What is that touchstone? What is it we stand for, as distinct from the Communist clear-cut creed which has cells in France, Greece, and Poland and, for all I know, in this country? The cells may not necessarily be connected, but they talk about a common thing. It is a common conception of society.

I am not so sure that we have not, in this Debate, arrived a little nearer to the kind of unity which must be forged if we are to succeed. You cannot force unity on the people. There is a great deal of nonsense in the talk about unity of the people of this country, which has been forced on us by Hitler. If, out of the sufferings and experiences of this war, we are to build a unity which represents the voice of Britain we must agree on the main principles of our policy. The only point which seems to have been agreed upon by every hon. Member is that we should let each country choose its own form of government. But is that a sufficiently clear and heroic policy? Can we say that, in accents which only the Prime Minister himself could use, to the people of Europe? How is this country going to talk about the glory of Europe—which is a phrase the Prime Minister used the other day—and about being good Europeans, if there is a suspicion, at any rate on this side of the House, that arrangements have already been made about spheres of influence? I do not know.

Unlike the Debates in which we tend, inevitably, to have long speeches from the Government benches, when the Prime Minister comes back from a conference, there has emerged today a further principle, and that is that hon. Members who usually take opposite sides, Royalist and Republicans alike, have agreed that there is something very unsatisfactory about the condition of Poland at the present time. My hon. Friend the Member for North Lambeth, my hon. Friend the Member for Ipswich, and certainly, hon. Members on the other side, seemed to be in very strong agreement on this one point. I wish there could be more Debates of this kind, of an unofficial sort, where we get not merely reports from conferences, and where the House of Commons—it is better to do it here than upstairs in a foreign affairs committee—can work out what it thinks and can, possibly, influence the Prime Minister and Foreign Secretary before they go to future Conferences.

THE UNDER-SECRETARY OF STATE FOR FOREIGN AFFAIRS (MR. GEORGE HALL): I commence the few remarks which I desire to make on the basis of the speech of my hon. Friend the Member for Kilmarnock (Mr. Lindsay). I have no complaint —and I am sure the House has no complaint—at my hon. Friend the Member for Ipswich (Mr. Stokes) initiating this Debate. I would have liked, of course, a little more time in which to deal with some of the points which have been raised today, although my hon. Friend pointed out very clearly that the Debate was not initiated for the purpose of a reply but to create much more interest in foreign affairs than he thought existed. For that reason I can say, not only of his speech but of those subsequently delivered, that we have had some interesting speeches, covering much of the same ground as previous speeches but in some ways laying greater emphasis on the points that have been put, and the Debate has been most interesting in the sense that we have seen a rather strange line-up, the hon. Member for South-East Essex (Mr. Raikes) agreeing with my hon. Friend the Member for Ipswich (Mr. Stokes), whereas my hon. Friend the Member for Nelson and Colne (Mr. Silverman) violently disagreed with him.

In almost all the speeches points of very high policy have been raised, points which have previously been made and fully dealt with. I know of no time during my stay in the House when so much time has been given to foreign affairs as during the last month or five weeks. Six whole days have been devoted to these very important questions, three very long and important speeches have been made by the Prime Minister and three by the Foreign Secretary. Poland has been very fully dealt with—I am sure a number of my hon. Friends will say not satisfactorily, but the Prime Minister has taken the House into his complete confidence and pointed out the difficulties that have arisen, and there can be no ambiguity at all in our minds as to the position of the Government. The same can be said of Greece—no subject has been debated more fully during the last fortnight or three weeks—the Baltic States, Yugoslavia and many other matters, and I feel that there is nothing I can usefully add to the statements of the Prime Minister and the Foreign Secretary. The hon. Member for Ipswich questioned the statement of the Foreign Secretary that no secret engagement had been entered into at the conferences which he and the Prime Minister had attended. As far as I know, that still stands, and there is nothing further that I can say on that matter. The hon. Member for South-East Essex raised the question of certain decrees which have been issued by the Lublin Committee. I will certainly see that this matter is brought to the notice of the Secretary of State. The hon. Member wanted it made clear that whichever leader controls or whatever Government governs Yugoslavia should be appointed by popular vote. I think it has been made absolutely clear by the Prime Minister that in each of the liberated countries opportunities must be given for a popular vote of the people to decide their Government. That still stands.

I wish there was a little more confidence reposed in the Government in dealing with these deeply important matters. One would imagine that it was the British Government that was entirely responsible for framing the new world policy. The British Government is working in the closest possible co-operation with its Allies, America, Russia and France and the smaller nations are being taken into consultation in connection with matters of very high policy. I have no doubt that at the forthcoming conference—where and when it is to be held one cannot say—many of the matters that have been discussed today will be subjects for consideration, and that after their report is given to the House by the Prime Minister and the Foreign Secretary the House will have the satisfaction that it usually has as the result of conferences of this kind attended by representatives of the great Allied nations.

MR. RHYS DAVIES (Lab.): The speech of my right hon. Friend the Under-Secretary for Foreign Affairs was quite proper but it did not enlighten us very much. It was typical of a Minister in this Government saying as little as possible. In that respect my right hon. Friend has, of course, succeeded very well indeed. The hon. and gallant Member for South Cardiff (Sir A. Evans) was very critical of my hon. Friend the Member for Ipswich (Mr. Stokes) for raising this issue of foreign affairs at all; he added that his speech was mischievous and embarrassing. I can tell him from my experience in this House that no one ever reaches the Front Government bench at any time unless he is mischievous and embarrassing to the Government. I fear indeed that if my hon. Friend persists in what he has done today he may arrive there himself ultimately.

MR. MUFF (Lab.): Will my hon. Friend tell us how he got on the Front Bench in 1924?

MR. DAVIES: By not saying too many nice things of the Tory Government of the day. I do not know as much about foreign affairs as some hon. Members, and I envy them their wider knowledge. I have, however, been in Poland and East

Prussia and without very intimate knowledge of those parts I have a fair idea of what the people of those territories think. I have come to the conclusion that it is as necessary to find out what the foreigner thinks of us, as to say what we think of him. The Polish question does, of course, provide a puzzle; and my right hon. Friend who represents the Foreign Office will forgive me if I tell him bluntly that the average individual in this country is completely unable to understand how it comes about that there is a Polish Government in London which our Government recognizes to the full, and which is apparently living at our expense, and that our Ally, Russia, recognizes another Government in Lublin, inside Poland. It does not require a university education to make a person bewildered at that state of affairs; and my right hon. Friend has said nothing which would help us to clear away that difficulty. It is an impossible situation; and when the "great Three," as they are called, meet, one of the first things they will have to do is to clear away that difficulty of two Allies supporting separate governments who claim to represent the very same nation. Then somebody has repeated today that the whole of the German people must be held responsible for what has been done in this war. How simple! I wish that they would read the history of the Napoleonic wars—

SIR HENRY MORRIS-JONES (L. Nat.): Is it not a fact that Himmler, in his message yesterday, stated that the whole German people must be held responsible?

MR. DAVIES: I do not descend so low as to read or believe what Himmler says; and I am surprised that the hon. Gentleman should do so. The main point that emerges from this Debate is whether Great Britain will lend its power to see to it at the end of the war, whoever are our Allies or our enemies, it shall be laid down as a fundamental principle of British policy that any people living in any territory anywhere, shall have the right to decide for themselves what form of government they want.

MR. BAXTER: Does the hon. Gentleman seriously suggest

that when the war is over, the Germans should be allowed to elect a Nazi Government?

MR. DAVIES: I feel like Voltaire about that interruption. He said:

> "I disagree with what you say, but would defend to the death your right to say it."

That is my philosophy. If the German people were foolish enough to elect a Nazi regime, it would be, in my view, as stupid as if the British working class elected a Tory Government.

MR. LINDSAY: We have the Russian communiques taking a completely opposite view, so that there is a war about ideas as well, is there not?

MR. DAVIES: That may be so. This is a war of ideas but those ideas are a little bit mixed up with capitalism and rackets of that kind. Let me come to a point which has occurred to me about the Ukrainian problem. It is not commonly known that there are, fighting with the Canadian Forces in Europe, about 6,000 Canadian soldiers of Ukrainian origin; and it may astonish hon. Members to know that I was invited to address them some time ago in spite of the unpopular beliefs I hold. It is as well to understand that these men hold strong views as to whether any portion of the Ukraine should be incorporated in Russia or in Poland. They hold the view that the Ukrainian people should have the right even to determine whether there shall be an independent Ukraine or whether it should be part of the Russian or Polish republics. They are beginning to issue publications in this country giving voice to their views on that. There are more people living in the Ukraine than there are in these islands—about 48,000,000 I believe. That is another problem which may crop up in due course. . . .

MR. LOFTUS (C.): Today, to take one case, the hon. Lady the Member for the Combined English Universities (Miss Rathbone) in a recent Debate, referred to the deportees from

Poland. As she pointed out it was not a question of politics, it was a question of common humanity, about which, in the Victorian age, every man and woman in the country would have rallied and tried to do something to ameliorate the position. These people, a million to a million and a half, were deported in 1939, many of them to the wastes of Siberia and some to the arctic forests. I have heard stories—whether true or not I do not know—that women teachers, women professors from universities and people like that, in summer clothes, were sent to the Arctic and that there they died in great numbers. Today, hardly a voice is raised——

It being Six o'Clock, the Motion for the Adjournment of the House lapsed, without Question put.

Question proposed, "That this House do now adjourn."—[*Mr. Mathers.*]

MR. LOFTUS: —with few honorable exceptions, in Press or in Parliament on behalf of doing something to ameliorate the conditions of the people and to find out what has happened to them in order to try to bring families together again. Now we have entered Europe we shall be met by all the specters that haunted the entrance to Hades as described by Virgil in Book 6 of the Aenied. Have we any guideposts to help us, when we thread our way through the labyrinth of Europe which is blazing with hates, with fires ready to burst out, and full of appalling unhappiness? Have we any indications to help us, any principles? I suggest—and here I agree with the hon. Member for Kilmarnock (Mr. Lindsay)—that the Atlantic Charter does provide us with such principles. I know it is the fashion in some quarters to deride it, but when it was promulgated to the world in 1941 it embodied the hopes and commanded the enthusiastic support of millions of people in this country and throughout the world. That Charter has been flagrantly broken in some instances, and certainly with regard to Poland.

We talk at Dumbarton Oaks and elsewhere of building the peace structure after the war, but treaties broken with the ink scarcely dry upon them will be an ill foundation for any enduring peace structure. The Atlantic Charter was not signed in 1941, but it was signed by all the Allied nations on 1st January, 1942, and that ratification had the signatures of the President of the United States, our Prime Minister and of Mr. Litvinov on behalf of the USSR. Have we any other guidance? I suggest that we have. The Prime Minister gave an admirable farewell message to the Italian people. He put forward there certain tests of freedom. Hon. Members will probably remember that they included freedom of the Press, of criticism of the Government, freedom to form opposition parties, Constitutional means of changing the Government. Fair play for all citizens and not only for Government officials. He went on to point out that courts of justice should administer known laws, not under pressure from any one party or from the Executive.

. . . I would add this word about Poland. I think we have to do our utmost, within the frontiers which will be decided for Poland, though not by us or by Poland, to see that Poland gets the government which her people really desire, and, with it, absolute independence. Poland has suffered as no nation in the world has suffered in this war. I would also add a word about Germany. We have heard discussions as to the future of Germany, and the suggestion of moving masses of people from Prussia. We have heard of the Morgenthau plan for reducing Germany to a purely agricultural country, and have read the vague plans set forth in "The Times" yesterday and today. What are the essential things that we must do about Germany? They are two. We must make absolutely sure that she cannot rearm; the second thing we ought to endeavor to do is to see that Germany, to the utmost capacity, makes reparation for the material injuries she has done to other countries. . . .

18. JEWISH SURVIVORS IN POLAND*

MR. SILVERMAN (Lab.) asked the Minister of Information whether his attention has been called to broadcasts from Lublin of the names and addresses of Jewish survivors in Poland who desire to contact relatives in other parts of the world; whether any record is made of these broadcasts; and whether such records can be made available to persons and organizations who may be interested.

PARLIAMENTARY SECRETARY TO THE MINISTRY OF INFORMATION (MR. THURTLE): These broadcasts are not recorded by the B. B. C. Monitoring Service. Their resources are already heavily taxed, but consideration will certainly be given to my hon. Friend's suggestion.

19. ELECTIONS IN LIBERATED COUNTRIES**

MRS. CAZALET KEIR (C.) asked the Secretary of State for Foreign Affairs whether it is the agreed policy of the United Nations that no Government in liberated countries will be formally recognized before a properly constituted general election with a secret ballot takes place.

PARLIAMENTARY UNDER-SECRETARY TO THE FOREIGN OFFICE (MR. LAW): The policy of His Majesty's Government as regards the recognition of governments in liberated territory must depend on the circumstances of each case. It would not be possible to lay down rigid criteria in advance as suggested by my hon. Friend.

MRS. KEIR: Does not my right hon. Friend think we ought to stand for, and insist on, free elections and secret ballots in all the liberated countries?

---

* House of Commons. Vol. 407, Feb. 1, 1945, p. 1644.
** House of Commons. Vol. 407, Feb. 7, 1945, p. 2049–2051.

MR. LAW: I think the attitude of His Majesty's Government was made perfectly clear by the Prime Minister, in his speech on the war situation the other day. We do stand for certain principles, and we will do all we can to see that they are carried out. That is one thing, but it is quite another thing to constitute ourselves as a kind of honorary nursery governess in the countries of our Allies.

MISS RATHBONE (Ind.): Will my right hon. Friend bear in mind that the results of the elections will not be indicative of the real feeling of the people, if, for example, the women's votes are excluded, and only half the community exercise franchise?

MR. LOFTUS (C.): Does my right hon. Friend propose to apply the tests of freedom as given by the Prime Minister in his farewell message to the Italian people, as tests by which the Government will be judged?

MRS. KEIR asked the Secretary of State for Foreign Affairs whether, in view of the Government's policy of ensuring that a General Election takes place in all liberated countries at the earliest possible date, it is the Government's intention to stipulate that universal adult suffrage should be a condition of such elections.

MISS WARD (C.) asked the Secretary for Foreign Affairs whether it is the intention of the Allied Governments to ensure that a free election and secret ballot is carried out in each liberated country by the supervision of the election in each country being undertaken by the Allied Powers with the least national interest.

MR. LAW: It has recently been made clear by my right hon. Friends the Prime Minister and the Foreign Secretary[1] that His Majesty's Government will exert their influence to ensure that elections on the broadest possible democratic basis shall be held at an early date in all liberated countries. We

---

[1] See No. 17.

clearly cannot, however, prescribe to the Governments concerned the exact conditions in which such elections should be held.

As regards the suggestion that the Allies might supervise such elections, I would recall the reply which my right hon. Friend the Deputy Prime Minister gave on December 21 to the hon. Member for Bridgewater.[2] His Majesty's Government would be prepared to assist in supervising elections if invited to do so by the Governments and peoples concerned, but they sincerely hope that such exceptional measures of intervention in the affairs of other States will not be called for.

MRS KEIR: In view of the important part taken by women in the resistance movements, does not my right hon. Friend think that they should have some say in the future government of their countries; and could not our Government make a statement on this question?

MR. LAW: I think that that must be a matter for the Governments and peoples concerned.

MISS WARD: Has Russia the same ideas as the British Government with regard to free elections for the liberated countries?

MR. LAW: I can only speak for His Majesty's Government.

---

[2] House of Commons, December 21, 1944.

Mr. Vernon Bartlett (Ind.) asked the Prime Minister whether, in view of the political difficulties involved in holding elections in liberated countries and of the importance of holding elections with the least possible delay, he will propose the establishment of a United Nations commission to arrange and to supervise elections in those liberated countries which would welcome the commission's co-operation?

The Deputy Prime Minister (Mr. Attlee): I can see no advantage in a general commission of the sort suggested by the hon. Member. My right hon. Friend the Foreign Secretary informed the House yesterday that His Majesty's Government would be prepared to help in supervising elections in Greece and would welcome the co-operation of their Allies. We should no doubt do our best to give similar assistance elsewhere if conditions demanded it and if it were clearly desired and requested by the Government and people concerned. But I believe and sincerely hope that such exceptional measures, involving close intervention in the affairs of another State, will not prove to be necessary in other liberated countries.

MR. SILVERMAN (Lab).: Does not the right hon. Gentleman think that questions of this kind will come with a better grace in this House, after we have had an election of our own?

20. ATLANTIC CHARTER*

Debate on February 15, 1945.

MR. RHYS DAVIES (Lab.) asked the Prime Minister whether, in view of his declarations as to which countries the provisions of the Atlantic Charter do not apply, he will now state to which countries those provisions do apply.

THE DEPUTY PR ME MINISTER (MR. ATTLEE): I think my hon. Friend is under a misapprehension. My right hon. Friend the Prime Minister has been at pains to make it clear in past statements in the House that the Charter cannot be regarded as applying as a matter of right to our enemies, or as constituting any sort of pact or bargain with them.

MR. RHYS DAVIES: Does not the right hon. Gentleman understand that people are being deceived by statements made by the Prime Minister on this subject? The Prime Minister told us some time ago that the Charter does not apply to certain countries. Why cannot the Government, therefore, tell us what countries the provisions of the Charter do actually apply?

MR. SORENSON (Lab.): Why was the particular interpretation now given by the Deputy Prime Minister not made perfectly clear at the time of the signing of the Charter?

MR. ATTLEE: I think it was perfectly obvious at the time the Charter was made that it was a statement giving the general principles on which the United Nations were acting. There

* House of Commons. Vol. 408, Feb. 15, 1945, p. 396–397; Feb. 21, 1945, p. 794. See also Vol. II, No. 56.

was never any suggestion that it was a bargain with our enemies.

SIR H. WILLIAMS (C.) : Does it apply to the Baltic Republics of Latvia, Lithuania and Estonia?

HON. MEMBERS: Answer.

MR. DE LA BERE (C.) : And answer came there none.

* * *

Debate on February 21, 1945.

MR. PETHERICK (C.) asked the Prime Minister whether Article 2 of the Atlantic Charter which declares that the Powers desire to see no territorial changes that do not accord with the freely expressed wishes of the people concerned applies to Latvia, Lithuania, Estonia, and Poland.

THE PRIME MINISTER (MR. CHURCHILL): The Atlantic Charter is a guide, not a rule.

21. BRITISH NATIONALITY FOR POLISH SOLDIERS*

CAPTAIN MCEVEN (C.) asked the Secretary of State for the Home Department whether he is aware of the number of Polish soldiers, who are anxious to obtain British nationality after the war; and whether he has in consideration any measure which will render this object more easy of achievement for them.

THE SECRETARY OF STATE FOR THE HOME DEPARTMENT (MR. H. MORRISON): Among the many foreigners who are assisting the war effort of the United Nations, both in the Armed Forces and in civilian occupations, there are numerous people who are anxious to obtain British nationality, and I know of no

* House of Commons. Vol. 408, Feb. 15, 1945, p. 378–379.

ground on which I should be justified in selecting for preferential treatment the particular group to which my hon. and gallant Friend refers. . . .

MR. MCGOVERN (I. L. P.) : Is the Minister aware that this country is under a special obligation to these men, many of whom will not want to return to Stalinized Poland? In view of the gross betrayal of Poland at the present moment, should not these people get special treatment?

MR. MORRISON: The views of my hon. Friend on foreign affairs generally, and on this matter, will be given due consideration.

22. POLISH UNDERGROUND ARMY*

CAPTAIN A. GRAHAM (C.) asked the Secretary of State for War if he will instruct the British representative at Soviet military headquarters to ascertain the fate of Allied officers and non-commissioned officers of the Polish Underground Army liberated by the Soviet troops from German concentration camps and, if necessary, to take steps to secure their complete freedom.

THE UNDER-SECRETARY OF STATE FOR FOREIGN AFFAIRS (MR. GEORGE HALL) : I have been asked to reply. The freeing of all members of the former Underground Army in Poland who fought against the Germans is a matter to which His Majesty's Government attach great importance, and it is hoped that the matter will be fully explored with the Soviet Government in the near future when such cases, if any, as those referred to by my hon. Friend will be kept in mind.

---

* House of Commons. Vol. 408, Feb. 20, 1945, p. 643–644.

23. CURZON LINE. LWOW PROBLEM*

PROFESSOR SAVORY (C.) asked the Secretary of State for Foreign Affairs in view of the fact that Eastern Galicia has never been in the possession of Russia, what evidence he has that the inhabitants to the east of the so-called Curzon Line have any desire to be incorporated in Russia.

THE SECRETARY OF STATE FOR FOREIGN AFFAIRS (MR. EDEN): My hon. Friend and the House are no doubt aware of the strength of the Ukrainian national movement which has existed for many years in this territory but this is clearly not a matter on which His Majesty's Government can be expected to have detailed, factual and up-to-date evidence.

PROFESSOR SAVORY: Is not the right hon. Gentleman bound by the Atlantic Charter to consult these populations before transferring them?

MR. EDEN: My hon. Friend is well aware that this is not purely a Polish-Russian question, but also very much a Ukrainian question. I have no factual up-to-date information on that, though I know there is a large Ukrainian population in this territory.

MR. STOKES (Lab.): How did the Government arrive at their decision, if they had not sufficient factual information?

MR. EDEN: As regards the Ukrainian majority, there is, as far as I know, no dispute. If the hon. Member wishes to debate the matter further, I will gladly do so next week.

MAJOR-GENERAL SIR ALFRED KNOX (C.): Is not this purely a surrender to power politics?

PROFESSOR SAVORY asked the Secretary of State for Foreign Affairs the number of Polish inhabitants of Lwów; what proportion they bear to the population of the city as a whole;

* House of Commons. Vol. 408, Feb. 21, 1945, p. 766–768, 794.

and if it is proposed to modify the Curzon Line in respect of this city.

MR. EDEN: As regards the first part of the Question, the latest available figures are those of the Polish census of 1931. This gave the number of Polish-speaking inhabitants of the city of Lwów as 198,200 or 64 per cent of the total population at that time. It is impossible to make any estimate of the present-day figures but it would be unwise to assume that they bear any close relationship to those of 1931. It is also necessary to recall that the city of Lwów has always been a predominantly Polish island in the midst of a predominantly non-Polish countryside. This is clear from the fact that in 1920, at the time when the Peace Conference was studying the question of Eastern Galicia, it was estimated that the population of the area lying between so-called Lines A and B which include the city of Lwów,[1] contained a population of rather less than 1,500,000 inhabitants, of whom more than half were Ukrainians, a little over a quarter Poles and the rest Jews.

As regards the last part of the Question, the views of the three major Allies on this matter have been expressed in the declaration issued by the Crimea Conference to which I have nothing at present to add.

PROFESSOR SAVORY: Is my right hon. Friend not aware that the genuine Russian population of Lwów is less than a half per cent?

MR. EDEN: As I explained before, and as my hon. Friend knows very well, this is not a Russian-Polish problem but largely a Ukrainian problem and the question is whether or not the new arrangement will create more Ukrainian unity than there was before. My hon. Friend knows the difficulties that there were between the Poles and the Ukrainians in this area between the two wars.

MR. PETHERICK (C.): Is my right hon. Friend not under

[1] See No. 11.

the misapprehension of assuming that the Ukrainians are Russians?

MR. EDEN: I did not say they were Russians. I merely said they were Ukrainians.

24. RELIEF FOR POLAND*

CAPTAIN ALAN GRAHAM (C.) asked the Secretary of State for Foreign Affairs what arrangements have been made either by the Soviet Government, the International Red Cross or by the UNRRA for the provision of at least as much food, clothing and medical supplies as was possible under the German occupation to the remaining 700,000 of the former population of Warsaw.

THE SECRETARY OF STATE FOR FOREIGN AFFAIRS (MR. EDEN): I understand that relief is being supplied to Poland by the Soviet Government, but I am not in a position to make a statement on the quantities involved. I have had inquiries made and find that relief taken to Poland by the International Red Cross Committee during the later stages of the German occupation was increasingly hampered by the interruption of communications, and has now been brought to a stop by the development of an active battle front between Switzerland and Poland. UNRRA has for some time been preparing food, clothing and medical supplies for dispatch to Poland, and I am informed that the first ship of supplies from UNRRA is in process of loading now. It is expected that shipments will be made on an increased scale as additional port facilities and means of overland transport in Eastern Europe become available.

MISS RATHBONE (Ind.): Have the Soviet Government at last consented to the sending of these supplies by UNRRA; and have they also consented to the sending of a personal dele-

* House of Commons. Vol. 408, Feb. 21, 1945, p. 766–768, 794. See also No. 4.

gation from UNRRA, as there is considerable anxiety on this matter among circles which are much further to the Left than those represented by the hon. and gallant Gentleman who asked the question?

MR. EDEN: I am glad of that little instruction. As I understand it, the matter in fact has been settled, but I should like the hon. Lady to put her question down.

25. POLISH SEAMEN*

MR. MACK (Lab.) asked the Parliamentary Secretary to the Ministry of War Transport whether steps will be taken to prevent the victimization of 14 Polish seamen, stationed at Birkenhead, and supporters of the Provisional Government in Poland, by the Polish Ministry of Industry, Commerce and Shipping, which has withheld from the men payment of reserve pay and will no longer direct them to work on Polish ships.

THE PARLIAMENTARY SECRETARY TO THE MINISTRY OF WAR TRANSPORT (MR. NOEL-BAKER): I am making inquiries and I will communicate with my hon. Friend.

26. YALTA CONFERENCE**

ON Feb. 1, 1945, during a stop-over at Malta on the way to the Crimea Eden and Stettinius had a conference. They discussed the Polish question among other things. They agreed on several points which they were supposed to present to their chiefs (Roosevelt and Churchill) in the form of a memorandum. Minister Eden's memorandum was as follows:[1]

* House of Commons. Vol. 408, Feb. 28, 1945, p. 1380.

** House of Commons. Vol. 408, Feb. 27–28, Mar. 1, 1945, p. 1275–1284, 1298–1345, 1421–1520, 1591–1672. House of Lords, Vol. 135, Mar. 1, 1945, p. 223–237, 247–254, 260–294.

1 Yalta Papers, p. 508.

Conversation with Mr. Stettinius.
Poland.

1. We found that we were in broad agreement on the necessity for finding a solution and that it was impossible for our Governments to recognize the Lublin Government. Mr. Stettinius stressed that failure to find a solution would greatly disturb American public opinion, and might prejudice the whole question of American participation in the World Organization.

2. I agreed that a "Russian" solution of the question would be very likely to produce the latter result.

3. We found that we had very similar ideas on the lines of a possible solution. We should have to stress to Marshal Stalin the unsatisfactory nature of the present state of affairs, with the Soviets recognizing one Government in Lublin and ourselves another Government in London. (We, of course, ourselves have the added problem of the Polish forces, acting with ours, who owe allegiance to the London Government). There would be apparent to the world a definite divergence of view on a point of first rate importance. This would give rise to uneasiness amongst our peoples and would afford valuable material to enemy propaganda.

4. The time has probably gone by for a "fusion" of London and Lublin, and the only remedy that we can see is the creation of a *new* interim Government in Poland, pledged to hold free elections as soon as conditions permit. This would be representative of all Polish political parties and would no doubt include elements from the Lublin Government, from Poles in Poland, and from Poles abroad. There are no good candidates from the Government in London, but if M. Mikołajczyk and, perhaps, M. Romer and others such as M. Grabski could be included, that would make it much easier for us to recognize the new Government, which should be far more representative of Poland as a whole than is the Lublin Government.

5. If it would facilitate the realization of this plan, we should be ready to see the adoption of M. Mikołajczyk's idea of a "Presidential Council"[2] consisting of such men as the former Prime

[2] Summary of Mikołajczyk's Memorandum presented to the British and U.S. Governments at the end of Jan. 1945:

The Polish people in the homeland desire to regulate Polish-Soviet relations; they fear Poland will be forced into Communism; they pin their hopes of independence on Great Britain and the United States and advocate a guarantee by all the three great powers; frontier changes should embrace all frontiers simultaneously; delineation of the eastern frontiers should be effected by compromise, not unilateral dictation; the eastern frontier should be more favorable to Poland than the Curzon Line and should be arrived at only in conjunction with the guaranteeing

Minister, V. Witos, Archbishop of Sapieha, M. Żuławski and M. Bierut. Such a Council could appoint the new Government.

6. If the Russians persist in their present policy, that would only neutralize the efforts of all those in our two countries most anxious to work with Russia.

7. There remains the territorial problem. As regards Poland's eastern frontier, H.M.G. have already agreed with the Russians and announced publicly that this should be the Curzon Line, giving Lwów to the USSR. The Americans may however still wish to press the Russians to leave Lwów to Poland. As regards Poland's western frontier, we and the Americans agreed that Poland should certainly have East Prussia south and west of Koenigsberg, Danzig, the eastern tip of Pomerania and the whole of Upper Silesia. The Lublin Poles, no doubt with Soviet approval, are however also claiming not only the Oder line frontier, including Stettin and Breslau, but also the western Neisse frontier.

8. The cession upon which we and the Americans are agreed would involve the transfer of some 2½ million Germans. The Oder frontier, without Breslau and Stettin would involve a fur-

---

of restitution to Poland of Danzig, East Prussia and western lands taken from Poland by Germany.

Mikołajczyk states that questions of frontiers and independence closely interwine. If Poland loses territory, it must not lose the Polish population living in it. Plan for the eviction of Germans as well as transfer of Poles in Russia must be prepared in advance and coupled with plan of credits. Mikołajczyk supports plans for modification of Curzon Line in Poland's favor and states that in the west the new frontier should include East Prussia, Danzig, the region of Oppeln, the region of Gruenberg on the left bank of the Oder and, northward, the whole right bank of the Oder including Stettin.

He presents the following alternative solutions of problems of government and administration during transition period:

1. Return of Polish President to Poland where he would appoint new government.

2. President to resign in favor of a person in Poland who would appoint new government.

3. Representatives of Council of National Unity and the Lublin Committee to choose a new government in presence of representatives of the three great powers.

4. Creation in Poland of Presidential Council composed of widely-known leaders which would summon conference of the political parties only or, alternatively, of the political parties and the Lublin National Council and Provisional Government, the Council of National Unity in Poland and Polish Ministers who lived in Poland throughout the war.

Memorandum concludes that the prompt establishment of government based on all democratic political movements is decisive for independence of Poland. Schoenfeld (American Embassy near the Government of Poland, in London) adds list of persons whom Mikołajczyk considers as possible candidates for the Presidential Council. (Yalta Papers, p. 953).

ther $2\frac{1}{4}$ millions. The western Neisse frontier with Breslau and Stettin would involve an additional $3\frac{1}{4}$ millions making 8 millions in all.

9. We were prepared last October in Moscow to let M. Mikołajczyk's Government have any territories they chose to claim up to the Oder, but this was conditional upon agreement then being reached between him and the Russians and there was no question of our agreeing to the western Neisse frontier. It was agreed before we left London that we should oppose the western Neisse frontier. I also think that we should keep the position fluid as regards the Oder line frontier, and take the line that H.M.G. cannot be considered as having accepted any definite line for the western frontier of Poland, since we need not make the same concessions to the Lublin Poles which we were prepared to make to M. Mikołajczyk in order to obtain a solution of the Polish problem. Even the Oder line frontier would severely tax the Polish capacity for absorption and would increase the formidable difficulties involved in the transfer of millions of Germans. We agreed with the Americans that in any event these transfers should be gradual and not precipitate.

10. If the Russians refuse to accept any solution such as that outlined above, the present deadlock must continue. That would be bad, but a simple recognition of the Lublin Government would be even worse.

(Malta) 1st February, 1945.

The State Dept. memorandum was given to Pres. Roosevelt at Yalta on Feb. 4. Point 4 referred to Poland and consisted of the following:[3]

"(a) Boundaries: We favor the Curzon Line in the north and center and, in the south, the eastern line of Lwów province, which would correspond generally with one of the frontiers proposed in 1919 to the Supreme Allied Council. Transfer of German territory to be limited to East Prussia (except Koenigsberg to Russia), and a small coastal salient of Pomerania, and Upper Silesia.

(b) We should be prepared to assist in the formation of a new representative interim government pledged to free elections when conditions permit. We should urge inclusion in a provisional government of Mikołajczyk (Peasant Party is most important in Poland) and other moderate Poles abroad. We should not agree to recognize the Lublin government in its present form."

---

[3] Stettinius, E. Roosevelt and the Russians, p. 88.

Roosevelt felt that if Russia did not agree to leave Lwow in Poland, it might at least agree to let them retain the oil fields, he also felt that the territory Poland would gain on the west would amount to one-third less than that which she would lose on the east; and, he did not feel he could recognize the Lublin Government.

On Feb. 6 a discussion of the Polish problem was taken up at a plenary meeting of the Big Three at Yalta.[4]

> ROOSEVELT: I should like to bring up Poland. I come from a great distance and therefore have advantage of a more distant point of view of this problem. There are six or seven million Poles in the United States, mostly of the second generation and most of them were generally in favor of the Curzon Line as the eastern frontier of Poland.[5] As I said in Teheran I am in favor of the Curzon Line. Most Poles, like Chinese, want to save face.
>
> STALIN: (interrupting) Who will save face, the Poles in Poland or the émigré Poles?
>
> ROOSEVELT: The Poles would like East Prussia and part of Germany. It would make it easier for me at home if the Soviet Government would give something to Poland. I raised in Teheran the question of giving them Lwów. It has now been suggested that the oil lands in the southwest of Lwów might be given them. That would have a very salutary effect. I am not making a definite statement but I am merely putting forth the suggestion for consideration and I would not insist on it. I hope that Marshal Stalin can make a gesture in this direction.
>
> But the most important matter is that of a permanent government for Poland. Opinion in the United States is against recognition of the Lublin Government on the ground that it represents

---

4 All these discussions that follow here, unless otherwise indicated, were taken from: "Foreign Relations of the U.S. Diplomatic Papers. The Conferences at Malta and Yalta", otherwise called the "Yalta Papers." Particularly, these are notes made by H. Matthews, Charles Bohlen, complemented with statements from Churchill's "Triumph and Tragedy" James Byrnes' "Speaking Frankly," and Edward R. Stettinius'. Jr. "Roosevelt and the Russians, The Yalta Conference."

5 Wandycz, D.S. "Polish Americans and the Curzon Line. President Roosevelt's statement at Yalta." In this publication the author presents documents showing that during 1942–44 representatives of Polish Americans kept Pres. Roosevelt and the State Dept. informed of their political postulates with respect to Poland, and particularly with respect to the eastern boundaries. Polish Americans continuously and unanimously came out against recognition of the Curzon Line as Poland's eastern boundary.

a small portion of the Polish people. I wish to see the creation of a representative government of national unity which could have the support of all the great powers and which would be composed of representatives of the principal five parties of Poland: Polish Workers Party, Polish Peasant Party, Polish Socialist Party, National Democratic Party and Christian Labor Party. It may interest Marshal Stalin that I do not know any of the London or of the Lublin Government. Mikołajczyk came to Washington and I was greatly impressed by him. I felt that he was an honest man.

The main suggestion I want to make is that there be created an ad interim government which will have the support of the majority of the Polish people. There are many ways of creating such a government. One of the many suggestions is the possibility of creating a Presidential Council made up of a small number of men who would be the controlling force ad interim and set up a more permanent government. I make this suggestion as from the distance of 3,000 miles. Sometimes distance is an advantage. We want a Poland that will be throughly friendly to the Soviet for years to come. This is essential.

STALIN: (interrupting) Friendly not only to the Soviets but all three Allies.

ROOSEVELT: This is my only suggestion. If we can work out some solution of this problem it will make peace much easier.

CHURCHILL: I have made repeated declarations in Parliament in support of the Soviet claims to the Curzon Line, that is to say, leaving Lwów with Soviet Russia. I have been much criticized and so has Mr. Eden especially by the party which I represent. But I have always considered that after all Russia has suffered in fighting Germany and after all her efforts in liberating Poland, her claim is one not founded on force but upon right. In that position I abide. But of course if the mighly power, the Soviet Union, made a gesture of magnanimity to a much weaker Power and some territorial concession, suggested by the President, we would heartily admire and acclaim the Soviet action.

However, I am more interested in the question of Poland's sovereign independence and freedom than in particular frontier lines. I want the Poles to have a home in Europe and to be free to live their own lives there. That is an objective which I have always heard Marshal Stalin proclaim with the most firmness. It is because I put my trust in his declaration about the sovereign independence and freedom of Poland that the frontier question I consider not of supreme importance. This is what is dear to the hearts of the nation of Britain. This is what we went to war against Germany for—that Poland should be free and sovereign. Everyone here knows what a terrible risk we took unprepared as we were and that it nearly cost us our life in the world, not only as an Empire but as a nation. Great Britain had no material interest in Poland. Her interest is only one of honor because we drew the sword for Poland against Hitler's brutal attack. Never could I be content with any solution that would not leave Poland as a free, independent, and sovereign state. Poland must be mistrees in her own house and captain in her own soul. However, I have one qualification: I do not think that the freedom of Poland could be made to cover hostile designs by any Polish government, perhaps by intrigue with Germany, against the Soviets. I cannot conceive that the world organization would ever tolerate such action or leave it only to Soviet Russia to take proper measures. I earnestly hope that we shall not separate without taking a practical step with this objective. At the present time there are two governments about which we differ. I have never seen any of the present London Government. We recognize them but have not sought their company. But Mikołajczyk, Romer and Grabski are men of good sense and we have confidence in them. We remain in informal but friendly contact with them. There will be great criticism against us all if we let them divide us when we have such great tasks and common hopes. Can we not make a government here for Poland—provisional or interim government, as the President said, pending free elections so that all three of us can extend recognition as well as the other United Nations. Can we not pave the way for a free future constitution and administration of Poland? If we could do that we should leave the table with one great step accomplished toward future peace and the prosperity of central Europe. I am sure that effective guarantees can be laid down to secure the line of communications of the victorious Red Army in its battle to defeat Germany. His Majesty's Government cordially support the President's suggestion and present the question to our Russian allies.

STALIN: (after a ten-minute intermission) The Prime Minister has said that for Great Britain the question of Poland is a question of honor. For Russia it is not only a question of honor but also of security. It is a question of honor for Russia for we shall have to eliminate many things from the books. But it is also a question of security of the state not only because we are on Poland's frontier but also because throughout history Poland has always been a corridor for attack on Russia. It is sufficient that during the last thirty years our German enemy has passed through this corridor twice. This is because Poland was weak. It is in the Russian interest as well as that of Poland that Poland be strong and powerful and in a position in her own and in our interests to shut the corridor by her own forces. The corridor cannot be mechanically shut from outside by Russia. It could be shut from inside only by Poland. It is necessary that Poland be free, independent and powerful. It is not only a question of honor but of life and death for the Soviet state. That is why Russia today is against the Czarist policy of abolition of Poland. We have completely changed this inhuman policy and started a policy of friendship and independence for Poland. This is the basis to our policy and we favor a free, strong and independent Poland.

I refer now to our allies' appeal with regard to the Curzon Line. The President has suggested modification, giving Poland Lwów and the Lwów Province. The Prime Minister thinks that we should make a gesture of magnanimity. But I must remind you that the Curzon Line was invented not by Russians but by foreigners. The Curzon Line was made by Curzon, Clemenceau and the Americans in 1918-1919 in the conference which then took place. Russia was not invited and did not participate. The line was accepted against the will of the Russians on the basis of ethnographical data. Lenin opposed it. He did not want to give Białystok and Białystok Province to Poland but the Curzon Line gives them to Poland. We have retreated from Lenin's position. Some want us to be less Russian than Curzon and Clemenceau. You would drive us into shame. What will the Russians say at Moscow, the White Russians and the Ukrainians? They will say that Stalin and Molotov are far less defenders of Russia than Curzon and Clemenceau. I cannot take such a position and return to Moscow with an open face. I prefer that the war continue a little longer although it costs us blood and to give Poland compensation in the west at the expense of Germany. I asked Mikołajczyk what frontier he wanted. Mikołajczyk was delighted to hear of a western frontier to the River Neisse. I must say that I will maintain this line and ask this conference to support it. There are two Neisse Rivers: one near Breslau, and another farther west. I favor the west.

Now about the government. The Prime Minister has said that he wants to create a Polish government here. I am afraid that was a slip of the tongue. Without the participation of Poles we can create no Polish government. They all say I am a dictator but I have enough democratic feeling not to set up a Polish government without Poles. It must be with participation of Poles. We had the opportunity in Moscow to create a Polish government with Poles. Both London and Lublin groups met in Moscow and certain points of agreement were reached. Mikołajczyk returned to London and was kicked out of the government. The present London Government of Arciszewski, is in reality under President Raczkiewicz. All this people were against the agreement and hostile to the idea. They called the Lublin Government "bandits" and "traitors". Naturally the Lublin Government paid the same coin to the London Government. It is difficult to bring them together. The principal personalities, Bierut, Osóbka-Morawski, won't hear of the London Government. I ask what kind of concessions can be made. They can tolerate Grabski and General Zeligowski, but they won't hear of Mikołajczyk becoming Prime Minister. Under these circumstances I am prepared to support any attempt to create unity if there is some chance of success. I am prepared to call the Warsaw Poles here or better to see them in Moscow. But frankly, the Warsaw Government has as great a democratic basis in Poland as de Gaulle has in France.

Now as a military man I must say what I demand of a country liberated by the Red Army. First, there should be peace and quiet in the wake of the army. The men of the Red Army are indifferent as to what kind of government there is in Poland but they do want one that will maintain order behind the lines. The Lublin-Warsaw Government fulfills this role not badly. There are agents of the London Government connected with the so-called underground. They are called resistance forces. We have had nothing good from them but much evil. So far their agents have killed 212 Russian military men. They have attacked supply bases for arms. It was announced that all wireless stations must be registered but these forces continued to break all the laws of war and complained of being arrested. If they attack the Red Army any more they will be shot. When I compare the agents of both governments I find that the Lublin ones are useful and the others the contrary. The military must have peace and quiet. The military will support such a government and I cannot do otherwise. Such is the situation.

CHURCHILL: I must put on record that both the British and Soviet Governments have different sources of information in Poland and get different facts. Perhaps we are mistaken but I do not feel that the Lublin Government represents even one third of Polish people. This is my honest opinion and I may be wrong. Still, I have felt that the underground might have collisions with the Lublin Government. I have feared bloodshed, arrests, deportation, and I fear the effect on the whole Polish question. Anyone who attacks the Red Army should be punished but I cannot feel that the Lublin Government has any right to represent the Polish nation.

That same evening (Feb. 6) Pres. Roosevelt sent a letter[6] *to Stalin complaining*

"that the three great powers do not have a meeting of minds about the political setup in Poland . . . I was very much impressed with some of the things you said today, particularly your determination that your rear must be safeguarded as your army moves into Berlin . . . I have had to make it clear to you that we cannot recognize the Lublin Government as now composed, and the world would regard it as a lamentable outcome of our work here if we parted with an open and obvious divergence between us on this issue . . .

. . . I would like to develop your proposal a little and suggest that we invite here to Yalta at once Mr. Bierut and Mr. Osóbka-Morawski from the Lublin government and also two or three from the following list of Poles, which according to our information would be desirable as representatives of the other elements of the Polish people in the development of a new temporary government which all three of us could recognize and support: Bishop Sapieha of Cracow, Vincente Witos, Mr. Zuławski, Prof. Bujak, and Prof. Kutrzeba. If, as result of the presence of these Polish leaders here, we could jointly agree with them on a provisional government in Poland which should no doubt include some Polish leaders from abroad such as Mr. Mikołajczyk, Mr. Grabski and Mr. Romer, the U.S. Government, and I feel sure the British Government as well, would then be prepared to examine with you conditions in which they would dissociate themselves from the London government and transfer their recognition to the new provisional government.

I hope I do not have to assure you that the U.S. will never lend its support in any way to any provisional government in Poland that would be inimical to your interests . . ."

At the next meeting of the Big Three, on Feb. 7, the discussion on the Polish questioned was continued.

ROOSEVELT: I think we should take up the Polish question. When we concluded our meeting yesterday Marshal Stalin had explained his views. I have nothing special to add to what I said yesterday. I think it is particularly important to find a solution of the governmental question. I am not so concerned with frontiers, I am likewise not so concerned on the question of the con-

[6] Yalta Papers, p. 727.

tinuity of the government. There hasn't really been any Polish government since 1939. It is entirely in the province of the three of us to help set up a government—something to last until the Polish people can choose. I discard the idea of continuity. I think we want something new and drastic—like a breath of fresh air. But before we go on with Poland I think Mr. Molotov should report to us on the meeting of three foreign ministers.

(Molotov reads his report about the dismemberment of Germany).

ROOSEVELT: Shall we go on with the discussion of Poland?

STALIN: I have received the President's message. It contains a proposal to call from Poland two representatives of the Lublin government and two from the opposite camp, so that in our presence these four would settle the question of the new Polish government. If this is successful, the new provisional government should in the shortest possible time organize elections in Poland. This message of the President's also proposes that some more Poles from London—Mikołajczyk, Romer and Grabski, should also take part in the new government. I received this letter an hour and a half ago. I immediately gave instructions to find Bierut and Osóbka-Morawski so that I could talk with them on the phone. The result was that at the moment they are outside Warsaw at Lodz or Cracow but they will be found and I must ask them how to find the representatives on the other side and what they think of the possibility of their coming. I can then tell how soon they will arrive. If Vincente Witos or Sapieha could come here it would facilitate a solution but I do not know their addresses. I am afraid we have not sufficient time. Meanwhile, Molotov has prepared a draft to meet in a certain extent the President's proposal. Let us hear it when it arrives as the translation is not yet finished. Meanwhile, we might talk of Dumbarton Oaks.

Molotov presented the Soviet attitude in the following note:

"1. It was agreed that the line of Curzon should be the Eastern frontier of Poland with a digression from it in some regions of 5-8 kilometers in favor of Poland.

2. It was decided that the Western frontier of Poland should be traced from the town of Stettin (Polish) and farther to the south along the River Oder and still farther along the River Neisse (western).

3. It was deemed desirable to add to the provisional Polish Government some democratic leaders from Polish émigré circles.[7]

4. It was regarded desirable that the enlarged Provisional Polish Government should be recognized by the Allied Governments.

5. It was deemed desirable that the Provisional Polish Government, enlarged as was mentioned above in Paragraph 3, should as soon as possible call the population of Poland to the polls for organization by general voting of permanent organs of the Polish Government.

6. V. M. Molotov, Mr. Harriman and Sir Archibald Clark Kerr were entrusted with the discussion of the question of enlarging the Provisional Polish Government and submitting their proposals to the consideration of three governments."

MOLOTOV: We are still trying to telephone the Polish leaders but without success and I am afraid there will not be time for them to come to this conference. That makes it impossible to try the President's proposal. On the other hand I think these proposals meet the President's wishes.

ROOSEVELT: I think we are making definite progress in the light of Mr. Molotov's suggestions. I should like to wait until tomorrow to study these proposals and to talk them over with the Secretary of State and officials of the State Dept. There is one word in them I do not like. This is 'émigré'. It is not necessary to take émigrés. I know none of the people concerned except Mikołajczyk but I do not think we need only contact émigrés. We should also find some people in Poland itself. May we postpone discussion?

STALIN: Yes, certainly.

CHURCHILL: I share the President's dislike of the word 'émigré'. It was applied during the French Revolution to the French aristocracy driven out by their own countrymen, but the Poles were driven out by brutal German attacks and I suggest that the words 'Poles temporarily abroad' should be submitted for 'émigrés'.

With regard to the frontier on the River Neisse I should like to say a word. I have always qualified a movement west by the Poles, but say that the Poles should be free to take territory but not more than they wish or can manage. I do not wish to stuff the Polish goose until it dies of German indigestion. I also feel conscious of the large school of thought in England which is shocked at the idea of transferring millions of people by force.

---

[7] The words "and from inside Poland" were added at the end of this paragraph in the subsequent discussion.

Personally I am not shocked but much of the opinion in England is. However, the exchange of Greeks and Turks was a great success, and the two countries had enjoyed good relations ever since; but that only involved two million. If the Poles take East Prussia and Silesia as far as the Oder, that alone would mean moving six million Germans back to Germany. It might be managed, subject to the moral question, which I would have to settle with my own people.

STALIN: There will be no more Germans there for when our troops come in the Germans run away and no Germans are left.

CHURCHILL: Then there is the problem of how to handle them in Germany. We have killed six or seven million and probably will kill another million before the end of the war.

STALIN: One or two?

CHURCHILL: Oh, I am not proposing any limitation on them. So there should be room in Germany for some who will need to fill the vacancy. I am not afraid of the problem of the transfer of populations as long as it is in proportion to what the Poles can manage and what can be put in the place of the dead in Germany.

I have only one other comment. It is a reference in Mr. Molotov's plan to the utilization of some democratic leaders from 'émigré' circles. Would Marshal Stalin be willing to add 'and some within Poland itself'. This was also suggested in the President's message.

STALIN: Yes, that is acceptable.

CHURCHILL: Well. I am in agreement with the President's suggestion that we should sleep on this till morning.

STALIN: I likewise find this acceptable.

On Feb. 8 Pres. Roosevelt presented his opinions on the Polish question, and in general agreed with Molotov, in the following:[8]

"The proposals submitted by Mr. Molotov in regard to the Polish question in reply to the President's letter to Marshal Stalin dated Feb. 6, 1945, have been given careful study.

In regard to the frontier question, no objection is perceived to point One of the Soviet proposal, namely, that the Eastern boundary of Poland should be the Curzon line with modifications in favor of Poland in some areas of from five to eight kilometers.

In regard to point Two, while agreeing that compensation should be given to Poland at the expense of Germany, including

---

8 Yalta Papers, p. 792.

that portion of East Prussia south of the Koenigsberg line, Upper Silesia, and up to the line of the Oder, there would appear to be little justification to the extension of the western boundary of Poland up to the Western Neisse River.

In regard to the proposals of the Soviet Government concerning the future Government of Poland, it is proposed that Mr. Molotov, Mr. Harriman and Sir Archibald Clark Kerr be authorized on behalf of the three Governments to invite to Moscow Mr. Bierut, Mr. Osóbka-Morawski, Archbishop Sapieha, Mr. Vincente Witos, Mr. Mikołajczyk and Mr. Grabski to form a Polish Government of National Unity along the following lines:

1. There will be formed a Presidential Committee of three, possibly consisting of Mr. Bierut, Mr. Grabski and Archbishop Sapieha, to represent the Presidential office of the Polish Republic.
2. This Presidential Committee will undertake the formation of a government consisting of representative leaders from the present Polish provisional government in Warsaw, from other democratic elements inside Poland, and from Polish democratic leaders abroad.
3. This interim government, when formed, will pledge itself to the holding of free elections in Poland as soon as conditions permit for a constituent assembly to establish a new Polish constitution under which a permanent Government would be elected.
4. When a Polish Government of National Unity is formed, the three Governments will then proceed to accord it recognition as the Provisional Government of Poland."

At a plenary session on Feb. 8 Churchill presented the following proposal:[9]

"1. It was agreed that the Curzon Line should be the eastern frontier of Poland, with adjustments in some regions of 5 to 8 kilometers in favor of Poland.

2. It was decided that the territory of Poland in the west should include the free city of Danzig, the region of East Prussia west and south of Koenigsberg, the administrative district of Oppeln in Silesia, and the lands desired by Poland to the east of the Oder. It was understood that the Germans in said region should be repatriated to Germany and that all Poles in Germany should at their wish be repatriated to Poland.

3. Having regard to the recent liberation of western Poland

[9] Yalta Papers, p. 869.

by the Soviet Army, it was deemed desirable to facilitate the establishment of a fully representative Provisional Polish Government, based upon all the democratic and anti-fascist forces in Poland, and including democratic leaders from Poles abroad. That Government should be so constituted as to command recognition by the three Allied Governments.

4. It was agreed that establishment of such a Provisional Government was primarily the responsibility of the Polish people, and that pending the possibility of free elections representative Polish leaders should consult together on the composition of this Provisional Government. Mr. Molotov, Mr. Harriman, and Sir Archibald Clark Kerr were entrusted with the task of approaching such leaders and submitting their proposals to the consideration of the Allied Governments.

5. It was deemed desirable that the Provisional Polish Government thus established should as soon as possible hold free and unfettered elections on the basis of universal suffrage and secret ballot, in which all democratic parties would have the right to participate and to promote candidatures in order to ensure the establishment of a Government truly representative of the will of the Polish people."

ROOSEVELT: Has Mr. Molotov had time to read the proposal I have made with regard to Poland?

STALIN: I have received it.

ROOSEVELT: Just to make it clear let me read it. (President reads the proposal).

STALIN: Does this mean that you would withdraw recognition from the London Government?

ROOSEVELT: Yes.

CHURCHILL explains that with the recognition of a new interim government recognition would be transferred from the London Government to that regime.

STALIN: What about the property of the London Government? Would they remain in the possession of Arciszewski?

ROOSEVELT: That automatically would go to the new government.

CHURCHILL: I had prepared an alternative suggestion, but since discussion has already begun on the President's proposal I would rather continue on that.

MOLOTOV: I should like to make a few remarks on the proposal of the President and the Prime Minister. Our proposal of yesterday had been based on certain realities existing in Poland.

We think it would be useful to have discussions on the Polish question on the basis of the present government being extended. We cannot ignore the fact that the present government exists at Warsaw. It is now at the head of the Polish people and has great authority. It has been enthusiastically acclaimed by the Polish people and enjoys great authority and prestige. If we put forward a proposal to ignore this fact we might be placed in a position where the Poles themselves would never agree to any solution which would greatly change the Provisional Government. If we start on the basis that the present government could be enlarged, the basis of probable success is more secure. Those now in the Provisional Government are closely connected with great national events taking place in Poland. Messrs Mikołajczyk, Grabski, Romer and Witos have not been directly connected with these events. If we wish to reach a practical end we must take as the basis that the present government be enlarged. How many and who should be taken in is the question to be discussed by us. There may be differences but in any event it depends upon the Poles now working in liberated Poland. The President proposes a new thought, namely agreement not only on the government but on a Presidential Committee. I have some doubts on that. I am afraid instead of one we will then have two difficult problems, since there already exists a National Council of Poland (Rada Krayova)—that of the Government and that of the Presidential Committee. This will increase our difficulties, not decrease them. There is a National Council, a representative body of Poland which could also be enlarged. We could discuss how this could be done. It would be better to talk on the basis of the existing situation and then how to improve it. Therefore, my conclusions are how to enlarge and by what basis the National Council. The National Council and Government are temporary and provisional. All three proposals have one point of view, namely, the holding of free elections in Poland. That is the best way to build up stable rule in Poland which we all consider of fundamental importance.

On the frontier question with regard to the east, we are in complete agreement. On the west there is no unanimous feeling. But I know that the Poles and the Polish Government are definitely in favor of a frontier on the Neisse River. Of course we can ask them, but I have not the slightest doubt of their desire. Also about holding negotations in Moscow between myself, Harriman and Clark Kerr, I think there is full agreement.

The Poles usually select three people, Bierut, Osóbka-Morawski and Gen. Rola Zymierski. Usually all three take part.

Then there are those to be invited from the other side whom the President proposed yesterday. With some people the Provisional Government would not like to talk at all, for instance Mikołajczyk. Since his visit to Moscow relations have greatly deteriorated. Yesterday the President had proposed five names. Two of the five should be invited. If three of the provisional government, whom I have mentioned and two of those mentioned in the President's letter be invited, negotiations could be started. That is my proposal.

ROOSEVELT: I should like to keep the Presidential Committee and then there is the question of election.

MOLOTOV: It would be better to avoid the Presidential Committee and to enlarge the National Council. I think the two ambassadors and I could discuss how to enlarge the Council. Any proposals to be finally adopted by the committee of three would, of course, be submitted to the three governments. My remarks have been addressed to the American proposal since the Prime Minister agreed to this.

CHURCHILL: Of course we are at the crucial point of this great conference. This is the question for which the world is waiting. If we accept that each recognize separate governments this will be Soviet Government on the one hand and the U.S. and British Governments on the other. The consequences would be most lamentable in the world and would stamp the conference as a failure. On the other hand, I take a different view about the basic facts in Poland, or at any rate some of them. According to our information, the present Lublin, now Warsaw government does not commend itself to the vast majority of the Polish people, and we cannot feel that it would be accepted abroad as representing them. If we were to brush away the London government and lend all our weight to the Lublin government there would be a world outcry. As far as we can see, the Poles outside Poland would make a virtually united protest. We have an army of 150,000 Poles who have been gathered from all who have been able to come together from outside Poland. This army has fought, and is still fighting, very bravely. That army would not be reconciled to the Lublin government. It would regard our action in transferring recognition as a betrayal.

As Molotov and the Marshal know, I do not agree with the London government's action, which has been foolish at every stage. But the formal act of transfer of recognition to a new government would cause the very gravest criticism. It would be said that we have broken altogether with the lawful government of Poland which we have recognized during the five years of war. It would be said that we have no knowledge of conditions in Poland. We cannot enter the country and must accept in toto the view of Lublin government. Therefore, it would be charged in London that we are forsaking the cause of Poland. Debates would follow in Parliament which would be most painful and embarrasing to units of the allies if we were to agree. The proposals of Mr. Molotov do not go up nearly far enough. If we give up the Poles in London it should be for a new start on both sides, more or less on equal terms. Before His Majesty's Government could leave its present position on continuing recognition of the London government we would have to be satisfied that the new government was fairly representative of the Polish nation, I agree that this can be only a view because we do not know the facts. Our doubts would be removed by elections with full secret ballot and free candidacies to be held in Poland. When such elections were held, His Majesty's Government will salute the government that emerges without regard to the Polish Government in London. It is the interval before the elections that is causing us so much anxiety.

MOLOTOV: Perhaps the discussions in Moscow will have a useful result. It is difficult to consider the Polish question without the presence of Poles.

CHURCHILL: It is frigthfully important that this conference separate on a note of agreement. We must struggle precisely for that.

ROOSEVELT: From another hemisphere I should like to say that we are agreed on free elections. The only problem is how to govern in the meantime for a relatively few months.

STALIN: The Prime Minister complains that he had no information and no way of getting it.

CHURCHILL: I have a certain amount.

STALIN: It does not coincide with ours. I think Great Britain and the United States can have their own sources of information there whenever they like. I do not see why Great Britain and the United States could not send their own people into Poland.

What is the basis of the popularity of the provisional government? I can assure you that these people are really very popular. Bierut and Osóbka-Morawski and Gen. Rola-Zymierski —they are the people who did not leave Poland. They have come from the underground. We should bear in mind the peculiar mentality of those who live under occupation. The Poland people consider these three as those who stayed. It may be that Arciszewski has in his government clever people but they are not liked in Poland because during the time of stress they did not seek the underground.[10] Perhaps this attitude is a little primitive but it must be taken into consideration. What troubles the Polish people? It is a great consolation that their country has been liberated by the Red Army. This has completely changed their psychology. The Poles for many years have not liked Russia because Russia took part in three partitions of Poland. But the advance of the Soviet Army and the liberation of Poland from Hitler has completely changed that, the old resentment has completely disappeared. Now there is good will toward Russia.

It is natural that the Polish people are delighted to see the Germans flee their country and to feel themselves liberated. My impression is that the Polish people consider this a great historical holiday. The population is surprised, even astounded that the people of the London government do not take any part in this liberation. Members of the provisional government they see there, but where are the London Poles? These two circumstances produce the fact that the members of the Warsaw Government, though they may not be great men, enjoy great popularity. Cannot we take account of this fact? We cannot ignore it—the feelings of the Polish people. You are afraid also that we may separate before agreement. We have different information and have reached different conclusions. Perhaps to begin with we should call the Poles of the two different camps to hear them and learn from them. We are agreed to the fact that the Polish government must be democratically elected. It is much better to have a government based on free elections. But until now the war has prevented elections. The day for them is near but until then we must deal with the provisional government.

---

10 Thomas Arciszewski, prime minister of Polish Government in Exile and leader of the Polish Socialist Party was a prominent member of the underground movement in Poland for five years from the very beginning of autumn 1939 until his arrival in London in August 1944. Many other active members of Polish underground movement and Home Army arrived in London to report the situation in Poland, like Jan Karski (author of the book "Story of the Secret State") and Gen. Tabor. The frequent messages sent by radio from Poland gave a lot of detailed information and the British and U.S. Governments were very well informed about the situation in Poland during the entire war.

Churchill and Roosevelt were both very well acquainted with the fact that part of the Polish Government, headed by a vice-premier, was in Warsaw all through the war (vol. 2, p. xiv, 314 and following). Furthermore, they knew that the Polish Representation of the Home Country (Council of National Unity) and the Home Army (Armia Krajowa) numbering about 350,000 were active in Poland throughout the whole war. Part of this Home Army engaged in bloody warfare in Warsaw with the Germans during August and September of 1944.

It is like that of de Gaulle who is also not elected. Who is more popular, de Gaulle or Bierut? We have considered it possible to deal with de Gaulle and make treaties with him. Why not deal with an enlarged Polish provisional government? We cannot demand more of Poland then of France. So far the French Government has not carried out any reforms to create enthusiasm. The Polish Government has carried out a great land reform which gives it great popularity. If we approve this government without prejudice we can find a solution. We will not attach too much importance to secondary matters and concentrate on the primary ones. It is better to reconstruct than to create a new government. Molotov is right. We could not talk about a Presidential Committee without Poles. Perhaps they would agree, but as a result of their amour propre and feelings, the prestige of the provisional government is greatly increased. If we do not talk to them they would accuse us of being occupiers and not liberators.

ROOSEVELT: How long before elections could be held?

STALIN: In about one month unless there is a catastrophe on the front and the Germans defeat us. (Smiling). I do not think this will happen.[11]

CHURCHILL: Free elections would of course settle the worries of the British Government at least. That would supersede at a stroke all questions of legality. Of course, we must not ask anything that would impair military operations. But if it is possible to learn the opinion of the population in Poland in one or even two months no one could object.

ROOSEVELT: That is why it is worth pursuing the subject. I move that we adjourn our talks until tomorrow. I suggest that meanwhile the matter be referred to the three Foreign Secretaries. They are very effective.

MOLOTOV: The other two will outvote me. (Laughing).

During the afternoon of Feb. 9 there was a conference of the three foreign ministers at which they discussed the Polish problem:

STETTINIUS stated that he would like briefly to comment upon one important point which had not been previously raised. There had been quite a struggle in the United States on American participation in the World Organization. From the standpoint of psychology and public opinion the Polish situation was of great importance at this time to the U. S. He hoped with all his heart

[11] The elections took place 23 months later, on Jan. 19, 1947.

that the Polish question could be settled before the Crimean Conference broke up.

Then he read the following statement:

"After further consideration I agree with Mr. Molotov's statement that the question of the creation of a Presidential Committee should be dropped and am therefore prepared to withdraw our suggestion on that point.

I believe that, with this change, our three positions are not far apart on the substance of the governmental question. Mr. Molotov spoke of the reorganization of the Polish Government. The British formula suggests the establishment of a fully representative 'Provisional Polish Government' and we speak of the formation of a 'Government of National Unity.' All three agree that this government should be composed of members of the present Polish Provisional Government and in addition representatives of other democratic elements inside Poland and some Polish democratic leaders from abroad.

The following formula might therefore be considered:

That the present Polish Provisional Government be reorganized into a fully representative government based on all democratic forces in Poland and including democratic leaders from Poland abroad, to be termed "The Provisional Government of National Unity'; Mr. Molotov, Mr. Harriman and Sir Archibald Kerr to be authorized to consult in the first instance in Moscow with members of the present Provisional Government and other democratic leaders from within Poland and from abroad with a view to the reorganization of the present government along the above lines. This 'Government of National Unity' would be pledged to the holding of free and unfettered elections as soon as practicable on the basis of universal suffrage and secret ballot in which all democratic parties would have the right to participate and to put forward candidates.

When a 'Provisional Government of National Unity' is satisfactorily formed, the three Governments will then proceed to accord it recognition. The Ambassadors of the three powers in Warsaw following such recognition would be charged with the responsibility of observing and reporting to their respective Governments on carrying out the pledge in regard to free and unfettered elections.'

MOLOTOV stated that he would like to obtain a copy of the text of the statement in the Russian language as he did not feel prepared to reply to the oral statement.

EDEN said that he had some preliminary remarks on Mr. Stettinius' proposal. He must tell his colleagues frankly of his difficulties in this matter. Many people thought that the Poles had been harshly treated by the British readiness to acquiesce on frontier on the Curzon Line. He himself had been troubled for some time because, quite apart from the merits of the case, it might become a cause of difficulty between the Soviet Government and the British.

As regards the Lublin Government, it was possible that he might be quite wrong but he thought it was a fact that hardly anyone in Great Britain believed that the Lublin Government was representative of Poland. He should have thought that that view was widely held in the rest of Europe and in the United States of America. It was for that reason that the document which he had put forward the previous day[12] had avoided all mention of adding to the Lublin Government and had stressed that a new start was necessary.

If agreement were reached here, this would involve a transfer of recognition from the London Government to the new Government. The British Government should have to abandon recognition of the London Government and such abandonment would be much easier for it if were not made in favor of the existing Lublin Government but in favor of a new Government.

The British Government had considerable Polish forces fighting with it—about 150,000 at present—and these forces would increase as more Poles were liberated or escaped from Switzerland. It naturally desired very much to carry them along in any settlement. The task would be easier if a fresh start were made.

He had one other comment which concerned a personality. It had been said that there was considerable opposition to Mr. Mikołajczyk in the Lublin Government. He was not convinced of that. But in any case the presence of Mikołajczyk in a Polish Government would do more than anything else to add to the authority of that Government, and to convince the British people of its representative character.

MOLOTOV stated that while the American document was being translated he wished to make some comments. Although he could not, of course, go farther than what Marshal Stalin had said yesterday, he recalled that the President had stated that the Polish situation was temporary and could not last for a long time. In the Russian opinion the most important question was the holding as soon as practical of general elections in Poland. These elections would give a basis for a permanent Government

[12] See above Churchill's proposal on the plenary meeting Feb. 8th.

and do away with all difficulties that were facing the Allies at the present time. Marshal Stalin had referred to the provisional period as lasting perhaps one month, whereas the Prime Minister had mentioned two. In any event, It would be a short interval. However, at the present time it was not only a question of Poland but also the rear of the Red Army. Even for a short period, it was essential to the Soviet Union, the United States and the United Kingdom to take this military situation into consideration. If there were any obstacles in the rear of the Red Army an impossible situation would arise. That was why Mr. Molotov had suggested yesterday that the reorganization of the Polish Government should be on the basis of the present Lublin Government with democratic elements from within and without the country added to it.

With respect to Mikołajczyk, Mr. Molotov stated that it might be a mistake to say that he was unacceptable. The Poles themselves must decide this. Conversations must be held with the Poles in and out of Poland. Perhaps the Mikołajczyk question was not as acute as it appeared. However, it could not be cleared up in the Crimea without consulting the Poles. Furthermore, reorganization of the Polish Government could not be undertaken without speaking to the Poles. The Moscow Commission made up of the British and American Ambassadors and Mr. Molotov would have serious tasks to perform. They should discuss the entire question with the Poles and make clear to them the basis reached in the Crimea on the Polish question.

EDEN said he entirely agreed with Mr. Molotov in respect to his remarks on the importance of the Polish elections. However, he felt sure that British opinion would agree that if the elections were controlled by the Lublin Government they would not be free elections or represent the will of the Polish people.

STETTINIUS stated that he supported Mr. Eden's views in full in this respect.

After a brief interruption, Mr. MOLOTOV, on reading a translation of the American proposal, stated that he would be unable to give a final answer to the new American considerations until he had consulted Marshal Stalin. He hoped to be able to do this by four o'clock. However, at the present time, he would like to make a few preliminary comments.

Firstly, it would be inadvisable to place too much emphasis on the formula of the question of the Polish Government before consulting the Poles themselves. He still believed that the new Polish Government should be created on the basis of the Lublin

Government. If the three Foreign Ministers agreed to this in principle, it would not be difficult to find a formula.

Secondly, it might be better to leave out reference to the Allied Ambassadors in Warsaw since this reference would undoubtedly be offensive to the Poles as it would indicate that they, the Poles, were under the control of foreign diplomatic representatives. The Ambassadors would, of course, see and report as they desired. In the last analysis the question of a formula was not important—the question of an agreement on the fundamental issues was more so.

EDEN stated that the three Allied Governments considered that a new situation would be created by the complete liberation of Poland by the Red Army. This would call for the establishment of a fully representative provisional Polish Government which could be more broadly representative than was possible before the liberation of Poland. This Government should be comprised of members of the Lublin Government and other democratic leaders in Poland and abroad.

He felt that this Government should be called the Provisional Government of National Unity.

MOLOTOV continued to stress the advisability of forming the new Government on the basis of the Lublin Government. Otherwise an unstable situation would be established in the rear of the Red Army. This Government would include other representatives from Poland and from without the country.

STETTINIUS maintained that it would be preferable to start with an entirely new Government and stated that unless the Foreign Ministers could get away from the words "Existing Polish Government," no agreement could be reached on this question. He suggested that Mr. Molotov give consideration to a formula which would state that the Polish Government should be based upon the old *and also* on the democratic leaders which will be brought in.

MOLOTOV maintained that it was very difficult to deal with the Poles and that a serious situation would arise if a period should be created in which there were no Government in Poland. The authority of the present Lublin Government would be undermined. He maintained that if the American or British proposals were adopted everything would be standing in air and a period of instability would be created in Poland.

STETTINIUS pointed out that the present Polish Government would continue until the new Government was formed.

MOLOTOV maintained that the Poles would know that negotiations were proceeding on a change in government and that the present government would not endure. This would create a situation which might well cause difficulties for the Red Army.

STETTINIUS stated that Mr. Eden's formula avoided this situation.

MOLOTOV, however adhered to his former position of insisting that the new Polish Government be formed on the basis of the Lublin Government. He maintained that the matter would have to be discussed with the Poles themselves before any decision could be reached.

STETTINIUS inquired as to Mr. Molotov's reactions with respect to the name of the new Polish Government.

MOLOTOV replied that this could be taken up at later date.

STETTINIUS stated that under present circumstances it would probably be best to report to the plenary session that the Foreign Ministers had discussed at length the Polish Government question on the basis of the memorandum submitted by the American Delegation and that although they had not yet reached an agreement on the matter they had decided to continue discussions at later date.

HARRIMAN asked Mr. Molotov to consider a redraft of the American formula which would contain the words "based on the old *and also* on other democratic elements from outside and inside Poland".

MOLOTOV's reaction to this suggestion was negative. He appeared to prefer the wording "based on the old government and with the calling in of representatives . . ."

In the plenary session of Feb. 9 Roosevelt opened the meeting by calling on Mr. Stettinius to report on the 12 o'clock meeting of the foreign ministers. Mr. Stettinius read his report (see above).

MOLOTOV: We accept as a basis the proposal put forward this morning by Mr. Stettinius. We would like to come to an agreement, adding only some amendments. The first sentence we would modify to read that the provisional government should be "reorganized on a wider democratic basis with the inclusion of democratic statesmen in Poland and Poles abroad." I have a second amendment to suggest. In the sentence on the holding of elections, I would revise to read: "In these elections all non-Fascist and anti-Fascist democratic parties would have the right to take part and to put forward candidates." My third amendment is the omission of the last sentence of Mr. Stettinius' draft which we feel would seriously offend the sensibilities of the Poles.

(After an intermission).

ROOSEVELT: I find that it is now largely a question of etymology—of finding the right words. We are nearer than we have been before. I believe there is a chance of real agreement to settle this question of the period before the Poles can hold their election. I have two examples of what I mean by the use of words. Mr. Molotov says that the present Polish government should be reorganized on a wider basis. This is difficult for those recognizing the Polish Government in London. I suggest that the words be changed to "The Polish provisional government now functioning in Poland". I have another example. Mr. Molotov proposes the elimination of the last sentence. I suggest that some gesture be made to show that there will be an honest election. Therefore, I think that a little more work by the foreign ministers tonight—we are sufficiently close—might settle the question. They can report the results of tonight's meeting to us tomorrow.

CHURCHILL: I agree with the President that there has been continuous progress towards a united declaration by three principal powers. I agree with the President that the matter should be tidied up by the three foreign secretaries and reported to us tomorrow. But there are two points which I should like to emphasize now. The first is a small one. It arises out of what Marshal Stalin said yesterday. He said that Poland has been liberated and the enemy driven away—that is a great new fact. It is a good point to make before the world that the Red Army has liberated Poland. Therefore, a new situation has been created. This calls for the establishment of a new provisional Polish government, that this now be more broad-based than before liberation. That gives a good chance for what we say to be received favorably by the world. It is ornamental but it is important to us.

The other point is much more important. That is the last sentence of the United States draft. I want to make an appeal to Marshal Stalin. We are at great disadvantage in discussing Polish affairs for we knew very little but must take great responsibilities. We know there are very bitter feelings among the Poles. Very fierce language has been used by Mr. Morawski. I am informed that the Lublin government has openly declared its intentions to try as traitors all members of the Polish Home Army and underground movement.[13] This causes us great anxiety and distress. We are perplexed in forming our view. Of course, I put first the

[13] See No. 17, Arciszewski's message to Roosevelt of Feb. 3, 1945.

nonhampering of the operations of the Red Army against Germany. But I would ask the Marshal with patience and kindness to consider our position. We really do not know what is going on except through a few people we parachuted in and a few we brought out through the underground. I don't like to obtain information that way. How can this be remedied without hampering the movements of the Red Army, which movements are, of course, before everything else in importance? Could any facilities be granted to the British—and the United States would no doubt like to participate—in order to see how the Polish quarrels are being settled? That is why the last sentence is so important for us. Might I say if elections take place in Yugoslavia, Tito will have no objection to Russian, British and American observers to assure the world that they are impartial. So far as Greece is concerned, when elections are held, which we hope will be soon, we would greatly welcome U.S., Russian and British observers to show the world and make sure the elections were conducted as the people wished. The same question would arise in Italy. When Northern Italy was delivered there would be a vast change in the Italian political situation, and there would have to be an election before it was possible to form a Constituent Assembly or Parliament. The British formula there was the same—Russian, American, and British observers should be present to assure the world that everything had been done in a fair way. These are no idle requests. In Egypt whatever government conducts the elections wins. Nahas wanted elections when he quarreled with the King. The King said, "No, not while you are in office." When he turned Nahas out the King's people won.

STALIN: I do not believe much in Egyptian elections. It is all rotten corruption there. They buy each other.

CHURCHILL: Anyway, we seek this formula.

STALIN: What percentage of the people read and write in Egypt? In Poland 70% can read and write.

CHURCHILL: I do not know the Egyptian percentage, but I meant no comparison with Poland. I only wanted fair elections. This should be considered with the Poles. I do not want to go on any longer. We have agreed to think this over. But I must be able to tell Parliament that elections will be free and fair. For instance, would Mikołajczyk be able to go back to Poland and organize his party for the elections?

STALIN: Mikołajczyk is a representative of the Peasant Party. The Peasant Party is not Fascist and will take part in the elections. Those candidates will be allowed to stand.

CHURCHILL: Yes, specifically as a government is formed.

STALIN: Yes, the Peasant Party will be represented. This can be done in the presence of the Poles with various people present.

CHURCHILL: I must be able to tell the House of Commons that the elections will be free and that there will be effective guarantees that they are freely and fairly carried out. I do not care much about Poles myself.

STALIN: There are some very good people among the Poles. They are good fighters and they have some good scientists and musicians. Of course, they fight among themselves too. I think on both sides there are non-Fascist and anti-Fascist elements.

CHURCHILL: I do not like this division. Anybody can call anybody anything. We prefer the terminology democratic parties. All I want is for all sides to get a fair hearing.

STALIN: I refer to the declaration on liberated areas (see below). On the whole I approve it. I find in a certain paragraph the same expression, anti-Nazism and anti-Fascism.

ROOSEVELT: This is the first example for the use of the declaration. It has the phrase to create democratic institutions of their own choice. The next paragraph contains the following: (c) to form interim governmental authorities broadly representative of all democratic elements in the population and pledged to the earliest possible establishment through free elections of governments responsive to the will of the people.

STALIN: We accept that paragraph three.

ROOSEVELT: I want this election in Poland to be the first one beyond question. It should be like Ceasar's wife. I did not know her but they said she was pure. I want some kind of assurance to give to the world, and I don't want anybody to be able to question their purity. It is matter of good politics rather than principle.

STALIN: It was said so about Ceasar's wife, but, in fact, she had certain sins.

MOLOTOV: We are afraid to leave this phrase in without consulting with the Poles. They will feel that it shows a lack of confidence in them. It is better to leave it to the Poles.

ROOSEVELT: Why not leave this for the foreign ministers and talk about it tomorrow?

STALIN: I think in the first place in the words "present provisional Polish government" we can delete the word "present." We can say, "the Polish government which acts in Poland."

That same evening (Feb. 9, 10:30 P. M.) Stettinius, Eden and Molotov continued their discussion of Poland. Eden said that he had just received a strong cable from the War Cabinet in London to the effect that if something very close to the English proposal of Feb. 8 were not accepted, there was very little chance that the British Government would agree to any statement whatsoever on the Polish question. After a prolonged discussion the following was decided on:

"A new situation has been created by the complete liberation of Poland by the Red Army. This calls for the establishment of a provisional Polish government more broadly based than was possible before the recent liberation of western Poland. The provisional government now functioning in Poland should be reorganized on a broader democratic basis with the inclusion of democratic leaders from Poland itself and from those living abroad. This new government will then be called the "Polish Provisional Government of National Unity." Mr. Molotov, Mr. Harriman, and Sir Archibald Clark Kerr, are authorized to consult in the first instance in Moscow with members of the present provisional government and with other democratic leaders from within Poland and from abroad with a view to the reorganization of the present government along the above lines. This "Polish Provisional Government of National Unty" would be pledged to the holding of free and unfettered elections as soon as practicable on the basis of universal suffrage and secret ballot. In these elections all democratic and anti-Nazi parties would have the right to take part and to put forth candidates.

When a "Polish Provisional Government of National Unity" has been properly formed in conformity with the above, the three governments will then accord it recognition."

The three Foreign Secretaries were unable, however, to agree on the addition of a further sentence:

"The ambassadors of the three powers in Warsaw, following such recognition, would be charged with the responsibility of observing and reporting to their respective governments on the carrying out of the pledge in regard to free and unfettered elections."

Mr. Stettinius then proposed a variation of that sentence, reading as following:

"The three governments recognizing their responsibility as a result of the present agreement for the future right of the Polish people freely to choose the government and institutions under which they are to live, will receive reports on this subject from their ambassadors in Warsaw."

Mr. Mooltov had the same objections to this sentence. It was felt that the question would be put up to the Big Three Meeting.

On Feb. 10, during a conference held in the morning between Stettinius and Roosevelt on the subject of the above sentence, President Roosevelt said:[14]

"If we agree to withdraw this sentence it must clearly be understood that we fully expect our ambassadors to observe and report on the elections. If the statement of this fact in the agreement irritates the Russians, we can drop the statement, but they must understand our firm determination that the ambassadors will observe and report on the elections in any case."

At a conference of the ministers of foreign affairs held at noon on the same day, Stettinius, on instructions from Roosevelt, withdrew his proposed variation of the sentence, despite objections from Eden. Eventually the three foreign ministers decided on a text of the resolution which they planned to present for approval at an afternoon meeting of the Big Three.

This text was subsequently published on Feb. 12 (see below), lacking only the last paragraph relating to Poland's boundaries.

That same day, during a private conversation with Stalin, Churchill brought up the point that the British Government had no representative in Poland and that this presented difficulties, since a British ambassador or British correspondent ought to be stationed there. Stalin promised that, after recognizing the new Polish Government, Great Britain could send an ambassador to Warsaw, who, if it was a question of the Red Army, would be able to travel anywhere in Poland without any difficulty or limitation.

On the plenary session of Feb. 10, the problem of Poland was discussed farther.

EDEN: I should like to report that with the exception of two points outstanding we have reached a decision on the Polish

[14] Stettinius. Op. Cit., p. 252.

question. I believe that we have since worked out an agreement with regard to these two points. (He reads the declaration about Poland—see below—without the last paragraph about frontiers.)

CHURCHILL: There is no reference in this formula to the frontier question. The world at large will ask about that. We are all agreed I believe about the eastern frontier. We are all agreed in principle about the western frontier. The only question is where the line is to be drawn and how much to say about it in our communiqué. We are doubtful about going further in mentioning frontiers at this stage. I have received a telegram from the War Cabinet deprecating any frontier going as far as the Neisse. They feel that the population problem is too large to handle.

ROOSEVELT: My position is that I would rather hear from the new government of national unity what they think about it. Therefore, I think we had better leave out all references to frontiers.

CHURCHILL: On the west?

STALIN: It is important to say something.

CHURCHILL: I agree. People will immediately ask what is the settlement on the question of the frontiers. We think that the eastern frontier is settled. On the west the wishes of the Polish Provisional Government of National Unity must be consulted.

ROOSEVELT: I do not believe we should say anything in the communiqué. I have no right to make an agreement on boundaries at this time. That must be done by the Senate later. Let the Prime Minister make some public statement when he returns if that is necessary.

MOLOTOV: I think it would be very good if something could be said about full agreement of the three heads of government on the eastern frontier. We could say that the Curzon line is generally representative of the opinion of all present. It is possible that there might be criticism of this for some time but that would be better in the long run. We should either agree or leave to the three foreign ministers to find a formula. I agree that we need say nothing about the western frontier.

CHURCHILL: I agree we must say something.

MOLOTOV: Yes, but less specific if you wish.

CHURCHILL: We must say that Poland is to get compensation in the west; also that this is to be left for discussion with the Polish government before the line is drawn.

MOLOTOV: Very good.

(Matter is referred to the three foreign ministers.)

ROOSEVELT: The only thing left now is the amended text on the frontiers of Poland.

ROOSEVELT then said he wished to propose some small amendments in the paragraph regarding frontiers in the Polish statement. He said these amendments were necessary for American Constitutional reasons. He suggested that instead of the first words "The three powers" he would like to substitute "The three heads of government" and that in the second sentence the words "three powers" be eliminated, and in the last sentence the word "feel" instead of "agree" should be used.

STALIN: I should like to suggest an amendment in the phraseology to indicate that Poland should receive the return of her ancient frontier of East Prussia and the Oder.

ROOSEVELT: (Laughing to Prime Minister) Perhaps you would want us back?

CHURCHILL: Well you might be as indigestible for us as it might be for the Poles if they took too much German territory.

MOLOTOV: This change would give great encouragement to the Poles.

CHURCHILL: I prefer to leave it as it is.

MOLOTOV: But there is no mention of frontiers in the west. What about Oder? No exchange was mentioned.

CHURCHILL: Well, between what we propose and the question of specifying ancient territories up to the Oder there seems to be no stopping place.

STALIN: I withdraw my suggestion and agree to leave it as drawn. The President suggested changes (change "agreed" to "consider" in the first sentence and change "the three powers" to "the three heads of government" in the third sentence) are accepted. This, I believe is our last point of decision.

The amendments were accepted by the conference, and the following text approved:

> "The three Heads of Government consider that the Eastern frontier of Poland should follow the Curzon Line with digressions from it in some regions of five to eight kilometres in favor of Poland. It is recognized that Poland must receive substantial accessions of territory in the North and West. They feel that the opinion of the new Polish Provisional Government of National Unity should be sought in due course on the extent of these accessions and that the final delineation of the Western frontier of Poland should thereafter await the Peace Conference."

A communique published at the end of the Yalta Conference (on Feb. 12, 1945) contained the following text on the "Declaration of Poland" (chapter VI) and "Declaration on Liberated Europe" (chapter V):

VI. POLAND

"We came to the Crimea Conference resolved to settle our differences about Poland. We discussed fully all aspects of the question. We reaffirm our common desire to see established a strong, free, independent, and democratic Poland. As a result of our discussions we have agreed on the conditions in which a new Polish Provisional Government of National Unity may be formed in such a manner as to command recognition by the three major Powers.

The agreement reached is as follows:

A new situation has been created in Poland as a result of her complete liberation by the Red Army. This calls for the establishment of a Polish Provisional Government which can be more broadly based than was possible before the recent liberation of Western Poland. The Provisional Government which is now functioning in Poland should therefore be reorganized on a broader democratic basis, with the inclusion of democratic leaders from Poland itself and from Poles abroad. This new Government should then be called the Polish Provisional Government of National Unity.

Mr. Molotov, Mr. Harriman, and Sir A. Clark Kerr are authorized as a commission to consult in the first instance in Moscow with members of the present Provisional Government and with other Polish democratic leaders from within Poland and from abroad with a view to the reorganization of the present Government along the above lines. This Polish Provisional Government of National Unity shall be pledged to the holding of free and unfettered elections as soon as possible on the basis of universal suffrage and secret ballot. In these elections all democratic and anti-Nazi parties shall have the right to take part and to put forward candidates.

When a Polish Provisional Government of National Unity has been properly formed in conformity with the above, the Government of the Union of Soviet Socialist Republics, which now maintains diplomatic relations with the present Provisional Government of Poland, and the Government of the United Kingdom and the Government of the United States will establish diplomatic relations with the new Polish Government of National

Unity, and will exchange Ambassadors, by whose reports the respective Governments will be kept informed about the situation in Poland.

The three heads of Governments consider that the eastern frontier of Poland should follow the Curzon Line, with digressions from it in some regions of five to eight kilometres in favor of Poland. They recognize that Poland must receive substantial accessions of territory in the north and west. They feel that the opinion of the new Polish Provisional Government of National Unity should be sought in due course on the extent of these accessions, and that the final delineation of the western frontier of Poland should thereafter await the Peace Conference."

V. DECLARATION ON LIBERATED EUROPE

"We have drawn up and subscribed to a Declaration on liberated Europe. This Declaration provides for concerting the policies of the three Powers and for joint action by them in meeting the political and economic problems of liberated Europe in accordance with democratic principles. The text of the Declaration is as follows:

The Premier of the Union of Soviet Socialist Republics, the Prime Minister of the United Kingdom, and the President of the United States of America have consulted with each other in the common interests of the peoples of their countries and those of liberated Europe. They jointly declare their mutual agreement to concert during the temporary period of instability in liberated Europe the policies of their three governments in assisting the peoples liberated from the domination of Nazi Germany and the peoples of the former Axis satellite states of Europe to solve by democratic means their pressing political and economic problems.

The establishment of order in Europe and the rebuilding of national economic life must be achieved by processes which will enable the liberated peoples to destroy the last vestiges of Nazism and Fascism and to create democratic institutions of their own choice. This is a principle of the Atlantic Charter—the right of all peoples to choose the form of government under which they will live—the restoration of sovereign rights and self-government to those peoples who have been forcibly deprived of them by the aggressor nations.

To foster the conditions in which the liberated peoples may exercise these rights, the three governments will jointly assist the people in any European liberated state or former Axis satellite state in Europe where in their judgment conditions require (a) to establish conditions of internal peace; (b) to carry out emergency measures for the relief of distressed people; (c) to form interim governmental authorities broadly representative of all democratic elements in the population and pledged to the earliest possible establishment through free elections of governments responsive to the will of the people; and (d) to facilitate where necessary the holding of such elections.

The three governments will consult the other United Nations and provisional authorities or other governments in Europe when matters of direct interest to them are under consideration.

When, in the opinion of the three governments, conditions in any European liberated state or any former Axis satellite state in Europe make such action necessary, they will immediately consult together on the measures necessary to discharge the joint responsibilities set forth in this declaration.

By this declaration we reaffirm our faith in the principles of the Atlantic Charter, our pledge in the Declaration by the United Nations, and our determination to build in cooperation with other peace-loving nations a world order under law, dedicated to peace, security, freedom and the general well-being of all mankind.

In issuing this declaration, the Three Powers express the hope that the Provisional Government of the French Republic may be associated with them in the procedure suggested."

Upon receipt of the text of this resolution at Yalta, the Polish Government in London on Feb. 13 issued the following declaration:[15]

"On February 12th, at 7.30 p.m. the British Foreign Office handed to the Polish Ambassador in London the text of the resolution concerning Poland adopted by President Roosevelt, Prime Minister Churchill and Marshal Stalin at the Yalta Conference between February 4th-11th.

Before the Conference began the Polish Government handed to the Governments of Great Britain and the United States a Memorandum in which the hope was expressed that these Governments would not be a party to any decisions regarding the Allied Polish State without previous consultation and without the consent of the Polish Government. At the same time, the Polish Government declared themselves willing to seek the solution of the dispute initiated by Soviet Russia through normal international procedure and with due respect for the rights of the parties concerned.

---

15 Stosunki polsko-sowieckie, p. 461.

In spite of this the decisions of the Three Powers Conference were prepared and taken not only without the participation and authorisation of the Polish Government but also without their knowledge.

The method adopted in the case of Poland is a contradiction of the elementary principles binding the Allies and constitutes a violation of the letter and spirit of the Atlantic Charter and the right of every nation to defend its own interests.

The Polish Government declare that the decision of the Three Powers Conference concerning Poland cannot be recognized by the Polish Government and cannot bind the Polish Nation.

The Polish Government will consider the severance of the eastern half of the territory of Poland through the imposition of a Polish-Soviet frontier following along the so-called Curzon Line as a fifth partition of Poland, now accomplished by her Allies.

The intention of the Three Powers to create a "Provisional Polish Government of National Unity" by enlarging the foreign appointed Lublin Committee with persons vaguely described as "democratic leaders from Poland itself and Poles abroad" can only legalize Soviet interference in Polish internal affairs. As long as the territory of Poland will remain under the sole occupation of Soviet troops, a Government of that kind will not safeguard to the Polish Nation even in the presence of the British and American diplomats the unfettered right of free expression.

The Polish Government who are the sole legal and generally recognized Government of Poland and who for five and half years have directed the struggle of the Polish State and Nation against the Axis countries both through the underground movement in the Homeland and through the Polish Armed Forces in all the theatres of war have expressed their readiness—in a Memorandum presented to the Governments of Great Britain and United States—to cooperate in the creation of a Government in Poland truly representative of the will of the Polish Nation. The Polish Government maintain this offer."

At the same time the Polish Government issued the following proclamation to the Polish army:

"In view of the heavy blow which the Polish cause has suffered—the Polish Government realizing the worries and disquiet pervading the Polish Forces—appeals to its commanders and soldiers for further carrying out of duty, retaining peace, dignity and solidarity as well as maintaining brotherhood in arms with soldiers of Forces of Great Britain, Canada, United States and

France, with whom they have been tied by bloodshed in common battles.

The esteem and friendship for Poland, grown during service full of sacrifice by the Polish Armed Forces among free peoples of the West, are still in possession of the Polish Republic, which her soldiers must retain and multiply."

In addition, the Polish Minister for Foreign Affairs Adam Tarnowski presented a long note, complete with documents, to the British Ambassador in which he stated that the decisions reached at Yalta with respect to Poland's eastern boundaries constitute an infringement of both the Polish-British Alliance and the Atlantic Charter.[16] *As to other decisions reached at Yalta, he stated that the Polish Government could not recognize them as legally valid and was thus entering a solemn protest against them. The note ended with this statement:*

"The Polish Government cannot believe, therefore, that the Resolutions of the Crimea Conference could be regarded as the final expression of the attitude of the British Government with regard to Poland and consequently, they express their readiness to discuss with His Majesty's Government all questions contained in the Crimea Resolutions with regard to Poland."

On March 1 Pres. Roosevelt informed the U. S. Congress as follows:[17]

"... One outstanding sample of joint action by the three major Allied powers in the liberated areas was the solution reached on Poland. The whole Polish question was a potential source of trouble in postwar Europe—as it has been sometimes before—and we came to the Conference determined to find a common ground for its solution. And we did—even though everybody does not agree with us, obviously.

Our objective was to create a strong, independent, and prosperous Nation. That is the thing we must always remember, those words, agreed to by Russia, by Britain, and by the United States: the objective of making Poland a strong, independent, and prosperous Nation, with a government ultimately to be selected by the Polish people themselves.

To achieve that objective, it was necessary to provide for

---

16 Stosunki polsko-sowieckie, p. 465–468.

17 The Public Papers and Addresses of Franklin D. Roosevelt, 1944–45 Volume, p. 581.

the formation of a new government much more representative than had been possible while Poland was enslaved. There were, as you know, two governments—one in London, one in Lublin—practically in Russia. Accordingly, steps were taken at Yalta to reorganize the existing Provisional Government in Poland on a broader democratic basis, so as to include democratic leaders now in Poland and those abroad. This new, reorganized government will be recognized by all of us as the temporary government of Poland. Poland needs a temporary government in the worst way—an ad interim government, I think is another way of putting it.

However, the new Polish Provisional Government of National Unity will be pledged to holding a free election as soon as possible on the basis of universal suffrage and a secret ballot.

Throughout history, Poland has been the corridor through which attacks on Russia have been made. Twice in this generation, Germany has struck at Russia through this corridor. To insure European security and world peace, a strong and independent Poland is necessary to prevent that from happening again.

The decision with respect to the boundaries of Poland was, frankly, a compromise. I did not agree with all of it, by any means, but we did not go as far as Britain wanted, in certain areas; we did not go so far as Russia wanted, in certain areas; and we did not go so far as I wanted, in certain areas. It was a compromise. The decision is one, however, under which the Poles will receive compensation in territory in the North and West in exchange for what they lose by the Curzon Line in the East. The limits of the western border will be permanently fixed in the final Peace Conference. We know, roughly, that it will include—in the new, strong Poland—quite a large slice of what now is called Germany. And it was agreed, also, that the new Poland will have a large and long coast line, and many new harbors. Also, that most of East Prussia will go to Poland. A corner of it will go to Russia. Also, that the anomaly of the Free State of Danzig will come to an end; I think Danzig would be a lot better if it were Polish.

It is well known that the people east of the Curzon Line—just for example, here is why I compromised—are predominantly white Russian and Ukrainian—they are not Polish; and a very great majority of the people west of the Line are predominantly Polish, except in that part of East Prussia and eastern Germany, which will go to the new Poland. As far back as 1919, representatives of the Allies agreed that the Curzon Line represented a fair boundary between the two peoples. And you must remember, also, that there had not been any Polish government before 1919 for a great many generations."[18]

I am convinced that the agreement on Poland, under the circumstances, is the most hopeful agreement possible for a free, independent, and prosperous Polish state. . ."

When the results of the Yalta Conference became known Poles, both in Poland and in exile, were very much shocked and reacted quite forcefully. The Polish Government expressed the opinion of the majority of the Poles when it called this the 5th partition of Poland,[19] *this one perpetrated by allies. Protests came forth from Polish political parties, groups, and societies all over the world. In the U. S., where just a couple of months earlier a majority of the Americans of Polish Descent had voted to re-elect Pres. Roosevelt feeling that he was a protector of Polish interests, the reaction was particularly strong. The Polish American Congress and the National Committee of Americans of Polish Descent issued protests couched in very strong language.*

An especially dramatic event took place in units of the Polish Armed Forces fighting in Italy, Germany, in the air and on the seas. Expressing the feeling of the soldiers in the Polish 2nd Corps in Italy, its commander, Gen. Anders, wrote the following letter on Feb. 13 to the Army Commander, Gen. McCreery, requesting the withdrawal of Polish troops from the front:[20]

"We left along our path, which we regarded as our battle route to Poland, thousands of graves of our comrades in arms. The soldier of the 2nd Polish Corps, therefore, feels this last decision of the Three Power Conference to be the gravest injustice and in complete contradiction to his sense of what is honorable. . . . This soldier now asks me what is the object of his struggle? Today I am unable to answer this question. What has come about is more than grave; we find ourselves in a situation from which,

---

[18] For facts about the Curzon Line see Vol. 2, No. 50, p. 293 (footnote 2) and Appendix 1.

[19] 1st partition, 1772 (Russia, Germany, Austria); 2nd partition, 1793 (Russia, Germany); 3d partition, 1795 (Russia, Germany, Austria); 4th partition, 1939 (Ribbentrop-Molotov Pact).

[20] Anders, W. Op. Cit, p. 251.

so far, I can see no way out. . . . I can see little but necessity of relieving those of my troops now in the line, owing to (a) the feelings of my men as I have described them above, and (b) the fact that neither I nor my subordinate commanders feel, in our consciences, the right to demand new sacrifices from our men."

But, owing to the general situation at the Italian front, the Polish soldiers remained in line of battle and fought on. Gen. Anders was called to London and on Feb. 21 he had this conversation with Churchill:[21]

CHURCHILL: You are not satisfied with the Yalta Conference.

ANDERS: It is not enough to say that I am dissatisfied. I consider that a great calamity has occurred. The Polish nation did not deserve to see matters settled the way they have been, and we who have fought on the Allied side had no reason to expect it. Poland was the first to shed blood in this war, and sustained terrible losses. She was an ally of Great Britain from the very beginning and throughout the most crucial times. Abroad we made the greatest effort possible in the air, on land and sea, while at home we had a most important resistance movement against the Germans. Our soldiers fought for Poland, fought for the freedom of their country. What can we, their commanders, tell them now? Soviet Russia, until 1941 in close alliance with Germany, now takes half our territory, and in the rest of it she wants to establish her power. We know by experience what her intentions are.

CHURCHILL (*irascibly*): It is your own fault. For a long time I advised you to settle frontier matters with Soviet Russia and to surrender the territories east of the Curzon Line. Had you listened to me the whole matter would now have been different. We have never guaranteed your eastern frontiers. We have enough troops today, and we do not need your help. You can take your divisions. We shall do without them.

ANDERS: That is not what you said during the last few years. We still want to fight for Poland, free and independent. Russia has no right to our territory, and she never questioned our possession of it. She broke all treaties and grabbed these territories on the strength of an agreement and an alliance with Hitler. There are no Russians in these territories. Apart from Poles, there are only Ukrainians and White Ruthenians. No one asked them to which country they would like to belong. You under-

---

[21] Anders, W. Op. Cit, p. 256.

stand that the elections held in 1939 under the pressure of Russian bayonets were a sheer mockery.

Gen. Anders said that he was very much against a government being based on the Lublin Committee, which was composed exclusively of Soviet citizens and of traitors directed from Moscow.

Sir Alexander Cadogan interrupted to say: "Then you would prefer that the Polish Government should be organized by Russia alone, from members of the Lublin Committee."

ANDERS: Certainly, that would not change things a lot. And at least the whole world would know that it was not a Polish Government. Public opinion in Poland and abroad would thus not be deceived.

Churchill ended the conversation by saying that Great Britain would only recognize a government composed of representatives of all political trends. The Provisional Government would only have the task of organizing elections. He said that he would soon be making a speech on Polish matters in the House of Commons.

Debate on February 27, 1945.

THE PRIME MINISTER (MR. CHURCHILL): I beg to move, "That this House approves the declaration of joint policy agreed to by the three Great Powers at the Crimea Conference and, in particular, welcomes their determination to maintain unity of action not only in achieving the final defeat of the common enemy but, thereafter, in peace as in war."

THE PRIME MINISTER (MR. CHURCHILL): . . . I now come to the most difficult and agitating part of the statement which I have to make to the House—the question of Poland. For more than a year past, and since the tide of war has turned so strongly against Germany, the Polish problem has been divided into two main issues—the frontiers of Poland and the freedom of Poland.

The House is well aware from the speeches I have made to them that the freedom, independence, integrity and sovereignty of Poland have always seemed to His Majesty's Government more important than the actual frontiers. To establish a free Polish nation, with a good home to live in, has always far outweighed, in my mind, the actual tracing of the frontier line, or whether these boundaries should be shifted on both sides of Poland further to the West. The Russian claim, first advanced at Teheran in November, 1943, has always been unchanged for the Curzon Line in the East, and the Russian offer has always been that ample compensation should be gained for Poland at the expense of Germany in the North and in the West. All these matters are tolerably well-known now. My right hon. Friend the Foreign Secretary explained in detail last December the story of the Curzon Line.* I have never concealed from the House, that personally, I think the Russian claim is just and right. If I champion this frontier for Russia, it is not because I bow to force. It is because I believe it is the fairest division of territory that can in all the circumstances be made between the two countries whose history has been so checkered and intermingled.

The Curzon Line was drawn in 1919 by an expert Commission, of which one of our most distinguished foreign representatives of those days, Sir Eyre Crowe, was a member. It was drawn at a time when Russia had few friends among the Allies. In fact, I may say that she was extremely unpopular. One cannot feel that either the circumstances or the personalities concerned would have given undue favor to Soviet Russia. They just tried to find out what was the right and proper line to draw. The British Government in those days approved this Line including, of course, the exclusion of Lwow from Poland. Apart from all that has happened since, I cannot conceive that we should not regard it as a well-informed and fair proposal.

There are two things to be remembered in justice to our great Ally. I can look back to August, 1914, when Germany first declared war against Russia under the Tsar. In those days the Russian frontiers on the West were far more spacious than those for which Russia is now asking after all her sufferings and victories. The Tsarist frontiers included all Finland and the whole of the vast Warsaw salient stretching to

* No. 11.

within 60 miles of Breslau. Russia is, in fact, accepting a frontier which over immense distances is 200 or 300 miles further to the East than what was Russian territory and had been Russian territory for many generations under the Tsarist regime. Marshal Stalin told me one day that Lenin objected to the Curzon Line because Bialystok and the region round it were taken from Russia. Marshal Stalin and the modern Soviet Government make no such claim and freely agree with the view taken by the Allied Commission of 1919 that the Bialystok region should go to Poland because of the Polish population predominating there.

We speak of the Curzon Line. A line is not a frontier. A frontier has to be surveyed and traced on the ground and not merely cut in on a map by a pencil and ruler. When my right hon. Friend and I were at Moscow in October Marshal Stalin made this point to me, and at that time he said that there might be deviations of 8 to 10 kilometers in either direction in order to follow the courses of streams and hills or the actual sites of particular villages. It seems to me that this was an eminently sensible way of looking at the problem. However, when we met at Yalta the Russian proposal was changed. It was made clear that all such minor alterations would be at the expense of Russia and not at the expense of Poland in order that the Poles might have their minds set at rest once and for all and there would be no further discussion about that part of the business. We welcomed this Soviet proposal.

One must regard these 30 years or more of strife, turmoil and suffering in Europe as part of one story. I have lived through the whole story since 1911 when I was sent to the Admiralty to prepare the Fleet for an impending German war. In its main essentials it seems to me to be one story of a 30 years' war, in which British, Russians, Americans and French have struggled to their utmost to resist German aggression at a cost most grievous to all of them, but to none more frightful than to the Russian people, whose country has twice been ravaged over vast areas and whose blood has been poured out in tens of millions of lives in a common cause now reaching final accomplishment.

There is a second reason which appeals to me apart from this sense of continuity which I personally feel. But for the prodigious exertions and sacrifices of Russia, Poland was doomed to utter destruction at the hands of the Germans. Not only Poland as a State and as a nation, but the Poles as a race were doomed by Hitler to be destroyed or reduced to a servile station. Three and a half million Polish Jews are said to have been actually slaughtered. It is certain that enormous numbers have perished in one of the most horrifying acts of cruelty, probably the most horrifying act of cruelty, which has ever darkened the passage of man on the earth. When the Germans had clearly avowed their intention of making the Poles a subject and lower-grade race under the Herrenvolk, suddenly, by a superb effort of military force and skill, the Russian Armies, in little more than three weeks, since in fact we spoke on these matters here, have advanced from the Vistula to the Oder, driving the Germans in ruin before them and freeing the whole of Poland from the awful cruelty and oppression under which the Poles were writhing.

In supporting the Russian claim to the Curzon Line, I repudiate and repulse any suggestion that we are making a questionable compromise or yielding to force or fear, and I assert with the utmost conviction the broad justice of the policy upon which, for the first time, all the three great Allies have now taken their stand. Moreover, the three Powers have now agreed that Poland shall receive substantial accessions of territory both in the North and in the West. In the North she will certainly receive, in the place of a precarious Corridor, the great city of Danzig, the greater part of East Prussia West and South of Koenigsberg and a long, wide sea front on the Baltic. In the West she will receive the important industrial province of Upper Silesia and, in addition, such other territories to the East of the Oder as it may be decided at the peace settlement to detach from Germany after the views of a broadly based Polish Government have been ascertained.

Thus, it seems to me that this talk of cutting half of Poland off is very misleading. In fact, the part which is to be East of the Curzon Line cannot in any case be measured by its size. It includes the enormous, dismal region of the Pripet Marshes, which Poland held between two wars, and it exchanges for that the far more fruitful and developed land in the West, from which a very large portion of the German population has already departed. We need not fear that the task of holding these new lines will be too heavy for Poland, or that it will bring about another German revenge or that it will, to use a conventional phrase, sow the seeds of future wars. We intend to take steps far more drastic and effective that those which followed the last war, because we know much more about this business, so as to render all offensive action by Germany utterly impossible for generations to come.

Finally, under the world organization all nations great and small, victors and vanquished will be secured against aggression by indisputable law and by overwhelming international force. The published Crimea Agreement is not a ready-made plan, imposed by the great Powers on the Polish people. It sets out the agreed views of the three major Allies on the means whereby their common desire to see established a strong, free, independent Poland may be fulfilled in co-operation with the Poles themselves, and whereby a Polish Government which all the United Nations can recognize may be set up in Poland. This has become for the first time a possibility now that practically the whole country has been liberated by the Soviet Army. The fulfillment of the plan will depend upon the willingness of all sections of democratic Polish opinion in Poland or abroad to work together in giving it effect. The plan should be studied as a whole, and with the main common objective always in view. The three Powers are agreed that acceptance by the Poles of the provisions on the Eastern frontiers and, so far as can now be ascertained, on the Western frontiers, is an essential condition of the establishment and future welfare and security of a strong, independent, homogeneous Polish State.

The proposals of frontiers are in complete accordance, as the House will remember, with the views expressed by me in Parliament on behalf of His Majesty's Government many times during the past year. I ventured to make pronouncements upon this subject at a time when a great measure of agreement was not expressed by the other important parties to the affair. The Eastern frontier must be settled now, if the new Polish administration is to be able to carry on its work in its own territory, and to do this in amity with the Russians and behind their fighting fronts. The Western frontiers, which will involve a substantial accession of German territory to Poland, cannot be fixed except as part of the whole German settlement until after the Allies have occupied German territory and after a fully representative Polish Government has been able to make its wishes known. It would be a great mistake to press Poland to take a larger portion of these lands than is considered by her and by her friends and Allies to be within her compass to man, to develop, and, with the aid of the Allies and the world organization, to maintain.

I have now dealt with the frontiers of Poland. I must say I think it is a case which I can outline with great confidence to the House. An impartial line traced long ago by a British commission in which Britain took a leading part; the moderation with which the Russians have strictly confined themselves to that line; the enormous sacrifices they have made and the sufferings they have undergone; the contributions they have made to our present victory; the great interest, the vital interest, which Poland has in having complete agreement with her powerful neighbor to the East—when you consider all those matters and the way they have been put forward, the temperate, patient manner in which they have been put forward and discussed, I say that I have rarely seen a case in this House which I could commend with more confidence to the good sense of Members of all sides.

But even more important than the frontiers of Poland, within the limits now disclosed, is the freedom of Poland. The home of the Poles is settled. Are they to be masters in their own house? Are they to be free, as we in Britain and the United States or France are free? Are their sovereignty and their independence to be untrammeled, or are they to become a mere projection of the Soviet State, forced against their will by an armed minority, to adopt a Communist or totalitarian system? Well, I am putting the case in all its bluntness. It is a touchstone far more sensitive and vital than the drawing of frontier lines. Where does Poland stand? Where do we all stand on this?

Most solemn declarations have been made by Marshal Stalin and the Soviet Union that the sovereign independence of Poland is to be maintained, and this decision is now joined in both by Great Britain and the United States. Here also, the world organization will in due course assume a measure of responsibility. The Poles will have their future in their own hands, with the single limitation that they must honestly follow, in harmony with their Allies, a policy friendly to Russia. That is surely reasonable—[*Interruption*].

The procedure which the three Great Powers have unitedly adopted to achieve this vital aim is set forth in unmistakable terms in the Crimea declaration. The agreement provides for consultation with a view to the establishment in Poland of a new Polish Provisional Government of National Unity, with which the three major Powers can all enter into diplomatic relations, instead of some recognizing one Polish Government and the rest another, a situation which, if it had survived the Yalta Conference, would have proclaimed to the world disunity and confusion. We had to settle it, and we settled it there. No binding restrictions have been imposed upon the scope and method of these consultations. His Majesty's Government intend to do all in their power to ensure that they shall be as wide as possible and that representative Poles of all democratic parties are given full freedom to come and make their views known. Arrangements for this are now being made in Moscow by the Commission of three, comprising M. Molotov, and Mr. Harriman and Sir Archibald Clark Kerr, representing the United States and Great Britain respectively.

It will be for the Poles themselves, with such assistance as the Allies are able to give them, to agree upon the composition and constitution of the New Polish Government of National Unity. Thereafter, His Majesty's Government, through their representative in Poland, will use all their influence to ensure that the free elections to which the new Polish Government will be pledged shall be fairly carried out under all proper democratic safeguards.

Our two guiding principles in dealing with all these problems of the Continent and of liberated countries have been clear: While the war is on, we give help to anyone who can kill a Hun; when the war is over we look to the solution of a free, unfettered, democratic election. Those are the two principles which this Coalition Government have applied, to the best of their ability, to the circumstances and situations in this entangled and infinitely varied development.

LORD DUNGLASS (C.): I am sorry to interrupt the Prime Minister, but this point is highly important. So much depends upon the interpretation of the words which the Prime Minister is now using. My only reason for interrupting him is to ask whether he can possibly develop this point a little more. For instance, is there going to be some kind of international supervision? His interpretation will make a great difference to many of us.

THE PRIME MINISTER: I should certainly like that, but we have to wait until the new Polish Government is set up and to see what are the proposals they make for the carrying out of these free, unfettered elections, to which they will be pledged and to which we are pledged by the responsibility we have assumed.* But I have not finished. Perhaps some further words of comfort may come for my Noble Friend. I should be very sorry if I could not reassure him that the course we have adopted is simple, direct and trustworthy. The agreement does not affect the continued recognition by His Majesty's Government of the Polish Government in London. This will be maintained until such time as His Majesty's Government

* About elections in Poland see No. 53.

consider that a new Provisional Government has been properly formed in Poland, in accordance with the agreed provisions; nor does it involve the previous or immediate recognition by His Majesty's Government of the present Provisional Government which is now functioning in Poland. We are awaiting—[*Interruption.*] Let me remind the House and those who have undertaken what I regard as an honorable task, of being very careful that our affairs in Poland are regulated in accordance with the dignity and honor of this country—I have no quarrel with them at all, only a difference of opinion on the facts, which I hope to clear away. That is all that is between us.

Let me remind them that there would have been no Lublin Committee or Lublin Provisional Government in Poland if the Polish Government in London had accepted our faithful council given to them a year ago. They would have entered into Poland as its active Government, with the liberating Armies of Russia. Even in October, when the Foreign Secretary and I toiled night and day in Moscow, M. Mikołajczyk could have gone from Moscow to Lublin, with every assurance of Marshal Stalin's friendship, and become the Prime Minister of a more broadly constructed Government, which would now be seated at Warsaw, or wherever, in view of the ruin of Warsaw, the center of government is placed.

But these opportunities were cast aside. Meanwhile, the expulsion of the Germans from Poland has taken place, and of course the new Government, the Lublin Government, advanced with the victorious Russian Armies, who were received with great joy in very great areas in Poland, many great cities changing hands without a shot fired, and with none of the terrible business of underground armies being shot by both sides, and so forth, which we feared so much, having actually taken place during the great forward advance. These opportunities were cast aside. The Russians, who are executing and preparing military operations on the largest scale against the heart of Germany, have the right to have the communications of their Armies protected by an orderly countryside, under a government acting in accordance with their needs.

It was not therefore possible, so far as recognition was concerned, to procure the dissolution of the Lublin Government as well as of the London Government simultaneously, and start from a swept table. To do that would be to endanger the success of the Russian offensive, and consequently to prolong the war, with increased loss of Russian, British and American blood. The house should read carefully again and again, those Members who have doubts, the words and terms of the Declaration, every word of which was the subject of the most profound and searching attention by the Heads of the three Governments, and by the Foreign Secretaries and all their experts.

How will this Declaration be carried out? How will phrases like

> "Free and unfettered elections on the basis of universal suffrage and secret ballot."

be interpreted? Will the "new" Government be "properly" constituted, with a fair representation of the Polish people, as far as can be made practicable at the moment, and as soon as possible? Will the elections be free and unfettered? Will the candidates of all democratic parties be able to present themselves to the electors, and to conduct their compaigns? What are democratic parties? People always take different views. Even in our own country there has been from time to time an effort by one party or the other to claim that they are the true democratic party, and the rest are either Bolsheviks or Tory landlords. What are democratic parties? Obviously this is capable of being settled. Will the election be what we should say was fair and free in this country, making some allowance for the great confusion and disorder which prevail?

MR. GALLACHER (Com.) : Will there be any caucuses?

THE PRIME MINISTER: One cannot entirely avoid some nucleus of party inspiration being formed, even in this country, and no doubt sometimes very able Members find themselves a little out of joint with the party arrangements. But there are a great number of parties in Poland. We have agreed that all those that are democratic parties—not Nazi or Fascist parties or parties of collaborators with the enemy—all these will be able to take their part.

There are questions upon which we have the clearest views, in accordance with the principles of the Declaration on liberated Europe, to which all three Governments have duly subscribed. It is on that basis that the Moscow Commission of three was intended to work, and it is on that basis it has already begun to work.

The impression I brought back from the Crimea, and from all my other contacts, is that Marshal Stalin and the Soviet leaders wish to live in honorable friendship and equality with the Western democracies. I feel also that their word is their bond. I know of no Government which stands to its obligations, even in its own despite, more solidly than the Russian Soviet Government. I decline absolutely to embark here on a discussion about Russian good faith. It is quite evident that these matters touch the whole future of the world. Somber indeed would be the fortunes of mankind if some awful schism arose between the Western democracies and the Russian Soviet Union, if all the future world organization were rent asunder, and if new cataclysms of inconceivable violence destroyed all that is left of the treasures and liberties of mankind.

Finally on this subject, His Majesty's Government recognizes that the large forces of Polish troops, soldiers, sailors and airmen, now fighting gallantly, as they have fought during the whole war, under British command, owe allegiance to the Polish Government in London. We have every confidence that once the new Government, more fully representative of the will of the Polish people than either the present Government in London or the Provisional Administration in Poland, has been established, and recognized by the Great Powers, means will be found of overcoming these formal difficulties in the wider interest of Poland. Above all, His Majesty's government are resolved that as many as possible of the Polish troops shall be enabled to return in due course to Poland, of their own free will, and under every safeguard, to play their part in the future life of their country.

In any event, His Majesty's Government will never forget the debt they owe to the Polish troops who have served them so valiantly, and to all those who have fought under our command I earnestly hope it may be possible to offer the citizenship and freedom of the British Empire, if they so desire. I am not able to make a declaration on that subject today, because all matters affecting citizenship require to be discussed between this country and the Dominions, and that takes time. But so far as we are concerned we should think it an honor to have such faithful and valiant warriors dwelling among us as if they were men of our own blood.

MR. ARTHUR GREENWOOD (Lab.): . . . I leave aside the United Nations' Conference to come to the section of the White Paper dealing with the declaration on liberated Europe. The Big Three must not in any event regard themselves as the overlords of Europe, and I was glad of some words used by the Prime Minister this afternoon which indicated that that was not in his mind. I do not think that the Big Three ought to determine the fate of the smaller—the dozen or whatever number it may be—nations which do not possess either our economic resources or our military power. The value of a nation to human life, culture and civilization is not measured by its size, it is measured by its quality, and I hope that in dealing with liberated Europe that will be borne in mind.

This section links with the following section on Poland, to which my right hon. Friend paid a good deal of attention this morning. In the previous section dealing with liberated Europe as a whole there is this sentence:

> "The three Governments will consult the other United Nations and provisional authorities or other Governments in Europe when matters of direct interest to them are under consideration."

I follow the arguments of my right hon. Friend with regard to territorial readjustment.

I agree that what is far more important is the preservation of a free, independent, sovereign Poland in the fullest sense of the term. As I have said, it is not the size of the body, it is the quality of the body that matters, and that is so in the case of Poland. I do not wish to exacerbate a situation which has already become somewhat acute, but I would point out to the House, that it is foreign to the principles of British justice that the fate of a nation should be decided in its absence and behind its back. I do not regard the territorial problem as vital, but the other problem is vital—that there should be in the East of Europe the living beacon of Poland free and independent, as a warning note to any future aggressive Germany. I do not hold any brief for the Polish Government. I do not think it has been too well treated by His Majesty's Government. I think it has made mistakes. I have told my Polish friends that it has made mistakes. I admit all that, but I say it really is a cardinal sin for the three Great Powers—one of whom has an interest which we have not got—in the absence of the people whose lives are being bartered away, to determine the future of any country.

THE PRIME MINISTER: The whole object is to create a Polish Government which can, unitedly, decide upon the future.

MR. GREENWOOD: I think we all want a united Polish Government which can decide upon the future but, as regards the territorial issue, the Poles have been allowed to say very little about how their coat is to be cut. The fact is that before a decision of this kind is taken, I really do feel that the Poles—all the Poles—might have been consulted in the matter. If I were to enter into the realms of controversy on this issue, I would say that an authority has been given to the Polish end of the Polish Government, rather than to the Government which has hitherto been recognized by this country and is still recognized. However, it is perfectly clear—and I have expressed this view to what Polish friends I have, during past months—that there must be a provisional Government, national in character, representative of all organized political movements, to prepare for the future of the Polish people. [HON. MEMBERS: "All?"] Yes, all recognized political movements, and I include the Communists in that, if that is what my hon. Friends are thinking about. My Socialist friends in Belgium are not enamored of the Communist Party, but they realize that in their country there is a strong Communist movement, and they are prepared to co-operate with it during these interim days. Then, when we get free and unfettered elections, the people can decide for themselves. It is a pity that in these initial arrangements, both the Lublin Government and the Government here were not properly consulted.

THE PRIME MINISTER: They are being consulted now. It was not possible to invite a Polish Government to Yalta, because one of the Great Powers recognized one Government and the others recognized another, and it was absolutely necessary for us to adjust our views upon that great division before any invitation could be sent and before we knew to which Government it should be sent. What is happening now is that a Government recognized by all the Powers is being brought into being representative of the broad elements of Polish national life. That Government will settle, subject to what I have said about the election being free and unfettered, the future course of affairs in Poland and will have the recognition of all the United Governments, I trust, until such time as its situation can be placed on unchallengeable footing by free, unfettered, universal suffrage exercised at the elections.

VISCOUNTESS ASTOR (C.) : May I ask a question?

HON. MEMBERS: Order.

MR. DEPUTY-SPEAKER (MR. CHARLES WILLIAMS) : We must keep to one speech at a time.

MR. GREENWOOD: I will stick to the point I made before. I realize the right. Hon. Gentleman's difficulties, with one Government recognized by one State, and another Government recognized by two other States. But I still feel that a decision on those lines and of that character, scope, magnitude and importance to the Polish people of the future ought not to have been taken, so to speak, behind their backs. I hope I am not hurting my right hon. Friend's feelings. . . .

LORD DUNGLASS (C.): . . . One reason why there is world concern over the differences between Russia and Poland, is because it is the first test case, a test case, in the relationship between a Great Power wielding great military might, and her smaller and weaker neighbor. That is the reason why there is world concern over this matter. As far as Poland is concerned there is no country which by reason of its opposition to tyranny has earned a greater right to independence. There is no country to which independence has been more specifically pledged in treaty and declaration, and there is no country which in its weakness has a greater claim upon the magnanimity of its friends. The British approach to this problem cannot rest upon sentiment, but our hearts would need to be of stone if we were not moved by these considerations. But our relations are generally specific undertakings given in treaty, both to Poland and to Russia.

This House is familiar with our obligations to Poland. What are the instruments which govern our relationships to Russia? First, there is the Atlantic Charter, which is not as ethereal as some people would have us believe. It is in the Preamble to the Anglo-Russian Treaty of 1942.* It is deliberately brought into this Agreement as a guide to the conduct of Great Powers towards other Powers in the world. Certain questions, therefore, ought to be posed and have to be answered to see whether this agreement can, in fact, come within the framework of the Atlantic Charter. What about territorial questions, and what about territorial settlements, the question of the Curzon Line, and the strict limitation of modifications in Poland's favor? Does the treaty conform to that section of the Atlantic Charter which reads:

> "The High Contracting Parties desire to see no territorial changes that do not conform with the freely expressed wishes of the people concerned"?

---

* Vol. II, No. 15.

What about the free elections about which I asked the Prime Minister, and to which I shall return? Do they give a real hope that that section will be fulfilled which reads

> "that they wish to respect the rights of all people to those forms of Government under which they wish to live"?

Are there arrangements to end the shootings and deportations and the outlawing of the Polish Home Army? Do they give real promises that the conditions will be fulfilled in which

> "all the men in all the lands may live out their lives in freedom from fear"?

The questions which arise at the moment are under the last two headings, but the Prime Minister is right about the territorial settlement. The Russians have never receded for one moment, from the view that in this matter they alone are the judges and what they have taken, they will keep. That is their attitude, and I feel rather different from some other Members about this territorial matter. I believe that if you try to force what is an act of power, within the framework of the Atlantic Charter, you will not whitewash the Act but you will break the Charter. When the Prime Minister says that he accepts this as an act of justice, I must take a fundamentally opposite view. We have, dozens of times in our history, accepted this kind of arrangement as a fact of power. I accept it as a fact of power, but I cannot be asked to underwrite it as an act of justice. This is not a quibble in words. It is not a quibbling legalistic interpretation. I believe, most profoundly, that it is an essential British interest that we should be seen to preserve our moral standards in international behavior. When our plenipotentiaries go abroad and sign agreements for us, they go, it is true, in command of great Imperial power, but they also go as representatives of a great Christian people.

I am going to leave that territorial settlement to one side with that reservation, which, although I do not like it, would not prevent me from voting for the Government on this occasion, because I would never encourage the Poles to believe that they could get this territory back. I would not encourage them to believe that we can help them to do it. All we can do is to aid them to achieve a Poland as nearly as possible equal in status to what it was before the war. I turn, therefore, to the second instrument which regulates our relations with Russia, the Anglo-Russian Treaty of 1942. If I might interpret the word "treaty" to the Prime Minister it would be that a treaty "is a rule and not a guide." Perhaps the House will allow me to read Article 5:

> "The High Contracting Parties agree to act according to the principles of not seeking territorial aggrandizement for themselves, and of non-interference in the internal affairs of other States."

On that basis it was our hope—it is our hope—to build up good relations with Russia. In 1944, the Russians signed a Treaty with the French which, otherwise closely parallel with our own, had no such Clause. It was an ostentatious omission and it is natural that we should ask ourselves, which is the genuine edition of Russian foreign policy, the 1942 or the 1944, because the Foreign Secretary did not put this clause into the Anglo-Russian Treaty without reason. To us, it represents a fundamental conception, namely, that of a Europe of small, free, sovereign, independent States, in which we wish to be one of the family. That is the conception of Europe which we want to see, and it is not entirely selfish—not entirely governed by reasons of security. We do not measure a country's contribution to civilization merely by the numbers within its borders. Therefore a Europe of small, free, independent States is a fundamental British interest, and we interpret this Clause as covering the right of Poland and other sovereign States to real independence. We could never be a party to a process under which a whole range of the smaller countries of Europe was drawn, by a mixture of military pressure from without and political disruption from within, into the orbit of another and a greater Power.

Therefore, for me, two vital questions arise in this Debate. First of all, does Russia recognize this Clause as valid and binding, and will she make her actions correspond to her pledged word? Secondly, does Russia hold approximately the same ideas and conceptions of the structure of Europe as we do? On the answer to those two questions, very much depends. Unless you have sanctity of treaties, unless nations are going to keep their pledged word, there is not even the minimum condition present for the coherence of international society, and unless all the great nations start with at least some common principles and common agreement on fundamentals, all the machinery that we create at San Francisco, or wherever it may be, will contribute nothing to the security of these islands, or to the peace of the world. Machinery is nothing, if good will and agreement are not there.

I want to put before the Foreign Secretary some of the questions which were left unanswered by the Prime Minister. As long as they are unanswered, I am unable to decide how I am going to vote, reluctant as I am even to abstain on an issue of this kind. I want to vote for the Government, if I can, and to give them authority to go forth to more world Conferences and to wider agreement. What answers will the Foreign Secretary give to these difficulties in which I find myself? As the White Paper is framed, and as Press reports have come to us, it looks as though the Lublin Committee is going to be the foundation of the new Government. Is that intended or is it not? It would have been cleaner to scrap both Governments, and start afresh. If you want a new Government, it would have been a fairer thing to do. Is it intended that this Government should really be new and that Lublin should not be its foundation? I come to the question of free election. It is imperative that these elections should be really and truly free, and a good deal depends on what is our Government's intention with regard to the machinery to achieve it. I should have liked to see joint machinery set up between ourselves and the Russians and the Americans, with the possible addition of other nations, which would cover the case of elections not only in Poland but in Yugoslavia, Greece, or wherever it might be—in other words, that this should be real international supervision and that there should be no doubt about it.

SIR WILLIAM BEVERIDGE (L.): It was Mazzini who said once that the morrow of victory was more dangerous than its eve. We all realize that, and all of us in this House will respond to that appeal with which, at the end of his speech, the Prime Minister crowned his work at the Crimea Conference, that we should approach the problem which now lies before us with restraint and deep responsibility. I will confine myself to touch on four points only—the boundaries of Poland, the Government of Poland, the future of Germany and the future world organization. With regard to the boundaries of Poland, I am thinking of the Eastern boundaries. There we have the choice, broadly, between the Curzon Line, which was accepted by the Supreme Council in 1919, and the 1939 boundary which was secured by the Poles under the Treaty of Riga in 1920. For three years the Powers in Paris tried to get the Poles to give this up, offering one amendment alternatively after another, including a 25-year mandate. Finally, in March, 1923, the Powers capitulated to the Poles and accepted the 1920 boundary which lasted to 1939. When this capitulation was announced in this House by the Prime Minister, Mr. Bonar Law, many questions were asked.* Among them he was asked under what conditions the supreme Powers had accepted the Treaty of 1920, and he said they had done it on the condition that Poland, which had been in occupation of Eastern Galicia for three or four years, must recognize that ethnographical conditions made autonomy necessary in that region. I am not sure whether there has been any autonomy in that region since then or not.

As between these two lines, the Curzon Line has the moral basis of an impartial investigation, while the line of 1939, going back to 1772, rests on history and on force. We must all realize that to rest an international arrangement on history and force rather than on impartial decision, is the

---

* Vol. II, No. 54.

way to return to war. I have no hesitation in supporting the Curzon Line as a starting point in defining the Eastern boundary of Poland. I would only ask those who are dealing with the drawing of the frontier in detail to remember that the Curzon Line was laid down as the minimum for Poland on the East; according to Professor Temperley's history of the Peace Conference, the American and French delegates thought that the boundary should be more to the East. I hope that we shall be able to obtain whatever modifications to the East are justified by fair ethnographical considerations.

If we accept the Curzon Line now on the ground that it is really justice, it leaves no real ground for compensation for the Poles on the West or elsewhere. In spite of that difficulty, I personally, would also support the proposal to make East Prussia and Danzig Polish and to remove the German population from those regions. I support that not on the ground of compensation for Poland for taking away from her something she should never have had, but on the practical ground of giving to Poland a compact territory inhabited by Poles only, of giving her an adequate seaboard, and of making room for those Poles who find themselves beyond the Eastern boundary under Soviet rule and wish to move into Poland. They ought to be able to do so on terms of ample compensation. The giving of Danzig and East Prussia to the Poles and taking them away from Germany is also an act of poetic justice. Is it not the origin and occasion of war? After all, what was the German objection to the Polish Corridor? It was the ridiculous objection that Germans could not go to another part of Germany by sea and that therefore Poland must be cut off from the sea. For a country which was claiming Colonies to object that they were required to travel by sea to East Prussia, was ridiculous. I suggest that they should in future be saved from that necessity. By the cutting off of East Prussia we could make the source of this quarrel into a monument and symbol of their defeat.

It may be said that these territorial adjustments conflict with the Atlantic Charter. I do not think that they really do.

The Atlantic Charter implies that no peoples should be required to live in a State, in which they do not wish to live. We cannot say that the Atlantic Charter rules out the kind of territorial readjustments, with transfer of populations, which is proposed here. I am afraid that I cannot accept all the arguments which the Prime Minister gave in support of his proposals as to Poland. I need not emphasize the differences except to say that the fact that Russia has liberated any part of Poland is not any reason why she should have any part of it. Nor is the fact that in Tsarist times Russia possessed Finland any reason for giving her all she wants now. We must base our decision as to the Eastern boundary of Poland on the justice which we tried to do after the last war but which we were not strong enough to do. I do not feel happy about the suggestion that Poland should be encouraged to extend Westwards into territories which are now German and which presumably will still be occupied by Germans. It is not necessary for the purpose of giving the Poles a proper homeland. The Prime Minister committed himself—I do not know whether he meant to commit the House—to certain changes in Upper Silesia. They are not in the White Paper. The Crimea Conference decided only that these things would be settled at the peace conference. I hope that they will be left to the peace conference and that there the dominant consideration will be that of making a lasting peace.

On the Government of Poland, I can speak more shortly than I would otherwise have done because, on the whole, I agree with the hon. Member for Lanark (Lord Dunglass) that it is essential for us to see that the Polish Government is one chosen to please the Poles, and not one chosen to please either Soviet Russia or ourselves. We all wish that it had not been necessary to make any settlement about the Polish Government now, but if it has to be made now, it has to be made especially for a military reason: that operations are still proceeding across Poland, and Soviet Russia must have a friendly Government in Poland which she is crossing to get to Germany. If that is the reason, it makes it all the more important to be certain that the Government which suceeeds is not necessarily a continuation of the Provisional Government.

We must take great care to make certain that those who, on our behalf, are concerned with the formation or advising as to the formation of the new Provisional Government have every opportunity for their work; that they are able to discover facts not only in Moscow but in Poland, that they are able to make certain that before the election takes place, all Poles, wherever they may be, have got back to Poland; that they should make certain that all Poles, whether pro-Russian or not can become candidates; and finally, that the election is held fairly and under international observation, which means elections held after the withdrawal of any Soviet Armies and any Soviet police. All of us must be there on equal terms as international observers. That is essential. Our honor is pledged, if we support this Vote of Confidence, to see that Poland gets an independent Government, chosen to please the Poles and no one else. We cannot accept anything that does not allow us to fulfill that obligation. If we are assured of that, we can go to our Polish friends and ask them to think not of 1772 but of 1945 and the future. We can ask them that they should become not British nationals but remain Polish nationals and should help to build up a worthy Poland. . . .

SIR EDWARD CAMPBELL (C.): I do not intend to say much about Poland, because I believe that the decision taken by the Big Three at the Crimea Conference was the best solution, in the very difficult circumstances. . . .

MR. PRITT (Lab.): I suppose it is inevitable in a Debate of this kind, that relatively small matters should occupy most of the discussion, and that what is vitally important should take very little time because it is really common ground. From a general view, the achievements of the Crimea Conference are perhaps among the most hopeful things that have happened in the world in the last 25 years or more. We ought to congratulate ourselves on having a Government with a public opinion behind them that can carry them through and support them.

The future of Poland is very important, as is the future of every country, but it would be most unfortunate if we spent half of this Debate discussing Poland. Those who are sincerely anxious about the future of Poland are entitled to voice their anxiety, but there are a good many people in this country, or a certain number in this country, and in this House, who are not really anxious about anything except nursing their own anxieties, enmities and fears about the Soviet Union, and if they were not professing anxiety about Poland, they would be about something else. The best thing we can do is to remind them that enmity and suspicion of the Soviet Union have done more in the last 25 years to bring about wars than anything else except Fascism—which is an important exception, I agree. The second thing of which we should remind them is that, when any opportunity to test them has been provided, it has been discovered that those suspicions were unfounded and the fears had no basis at all. It is a responsible matter to give credence to all the different stories about the Soviet Union's designs on Poland, because it gives the enemies of this country a handle. I am trying not to say this with bitterness, but if we were to take the type of speech already made in this House, and others that will still be made, and turn them from good English into bad German, they would simply be speeches by Hitler, and people should face that.

The first point I want to make on that subject is this. What about the good faith of the USSR? I might have dilated upon that, and probably hon. Members would not be surprised if I had given a number of instances of its good faith, but I do not wish to make my speech longer, but rather to keep it shorter. The Prime Minister, who can be trusted to form an objective judgment about it, has said a good many things about it in an unqualified way. The Noble Lord the Member from Lanark (Lord Dunglass) did not do any good service in challenging the good faith of the USSR and in suggesting to the House that there are two standards of honor—the good one, which we have, and the bad one, which they have. I can, at any rate, congratulate the Noble Lord upon his speech in that it was less mischievous than the one which he made in this House a few months ago on a similar topic.

I would like to put some practical observations before right hon. and hon. Members who are anxious about the future of Poland. They think, and a lot of others think, that the Soviet Union does not want a strong Poland, but that it does want a Poland which it can control—a puppet, if you like. I would only suggest that the Soviet Union, in common sense, quite apart from fair dealings and socialist principles, for one of which the Prime Minister praises her, but for both of which I praise her, cannot possibly want a weak Poland and a Poland that is a mere puppet. The reasons I give are these. With any government, the one vital thing to which most of their attention must be turned is peace in the future, and we can only get it by giving our attention today to the fact that Germany must be politically, morally and industrially disarmed. That is not an easy, simple or quick job, and the one thing we do want are strong countries around Germany. If we present Germany with a neighbor who is weak, we present her with a country which, as soon as Germany can get on her feet again—assuming that she does not go democratic, and I think she will, but we cannot gamble on that—will become as much a puppet of Germany as Poland, in the early stages after the last war, was a puppet of France, and, in the later stages, a puppet of Germany. It is common sense that the Soviet view in these matters is that there must be a strong Poland. Nobody thinks that Russia is a fool, and, if she has any sense, she wants a strong Poland.

The second question is, Does she want to absorb Poland herself or make a puppet of Poland? Puppets have been a very prominent feature of the international situation for a good many years, but the USSR have a very distinguished record, for what records are worth, for not wanting puppets around her. That was the reason behind her hastening in 1917 to give freedom to Finland, because Finland did not want to be with her, and, later, giving freedom to Estonia, Latvia and Lithuania. Russia never has sought to make puppets. I do not see for one moment why she should desire, in the very least, to make the Polish state a puppet. It would only lead to endless squabbles with Great Britain and the United States. Further, the Soviet Union has shown very clearly in recent months that she values, at least as much as we do, the vital business of the three Great Powers remaining friends.

I ought to look at the suggested possibility of Russia wanting to make Poland into a Soviet Poland which would enter the Union. I do not believe that hon. Members who take such a great interest in Poland need to be worried about that. Not only the history of the USSR but sheer common sense will tend to show that they do not want an unwilling member of the Union of Socialist Soviet Republics. If the people of Poland, when they get a chance to express their views in a free general election, really want to become a Soviet Republic and join the Union of Socialist Soviet Republics, every pledge that we have given pledges us to help them to do it. I do not think the Polish people want to do that. I think they want to go on for a long time to rule their own country for the first time for centuries, and I do not think they want to be a Soviet Republic, but, if they do, we are all pledged to accept it. If they do not want to join the Soviet Union, what fools the Soviet Union would be to try to make them. One of the amazingly remarkable things demonstrated in this war is that a multi-national State like the Soviet Union, with a great variety of races and with a hideous history of repression in Tsarist days of almost all these races by one of them, has remained completely strong and coherent, so that the ordinary observer does not know that it is a multi-national State. Remember that every nation within it has the absolute right to secede at any moment, but none has wanted to, because it is perfectly happy where it is. No Government with the slightest sense wants to add to 18 separate Republics, embracing 189 peoples, one more, strongly national, vigorous, quarrelsome, politically argumentative people which does not want to be there. It would be like putting one bad egg in a consignment of 100,000 to make the lot rotten. Of course, they would not do anything so foolish, and the one thing we can be quite sure of is that the last thing the Soviet Union would do would be to drag Poland into the Soviet Union by the scruff of the neck if it did not want to go.

The Noble Lord the Member for Lanark made three points about Poland. He said it was famous for opposition to tyranny. True, they are very famous for opposition to tyranny, famous for opposition to Tsarist tyranny. So were those territories which lie to the East of Poland. They destroyed it. Poland only escaped from it. The moment the Polish people instead of the Polish landlords have a real part in the government of their country, the fact that the Polish people are opposed to tyranny, and know what tyranny is like, is likely to become even more apparent.

The Noble Lord said we had all pledged independence to Poland. We have, and I hope I have shown and that other people have shown, and will show, that the independence of Poland is vital to all of us, to the Soviet Union at least as much as to anybody else. He spoke strongly about the right of peoples to choose their future. I think he was applying it to what is sometimes known as Eastern Poland, that is that territory East of the Curzon Line. I do not want, in a Debate of this kind, to go far either in substance or form in expressing the bitterness which a great many of the facts arouse in me, but if anybody is going to talk about the right of the Polish people East of the Curzon Line to choose freely, I must point out that on the most optimistic pro-Polish statistics of any reliability at all, the Poles east of the Curzon Line are less than 20 per cent of the population. Even in peace time, when landlords and their dependants, and civil servants had been counted out, I do not suppose the percentage was more than 8 or 9. If we wanted to get the views of the Polish people east of the Curzon Line the first trouble would be to find them. Then if we asked them what they thought about being in Poland they would say: "We do not mind being in a democratic Poland but all we see in Poland are pogroms against the Jews and beatings up of the other non-Polish populations," as I could prove from the columns of the "Manchester Guardian" and other reputable papers. The last people we need be worried about are the Poles to the east of the Curzon Line.

I want to say a few words about the speech of the hon. Member for Berwick-upon-Tweed (Sir W. Beveridge). I hope he will forgive me for saying that the view that he ought really to be a member of the Labor Party rather than of the Liberal Party is shown by his speech to have been quite wrong. That speech was unconsciously a very dangerous one. I do not wish to embark on criticism of it in general. I wish merely to take a few points in it. He said: "Do not let Poland expand Westwards into Germany. Compensation is a wrong basis on which to deal with these matters, and it is not just." I rather agree—I do not think much of compensation as such, and never did. But we must have a strong Poland, and a strong Poland is sufficiently near to the bone, so to speak, to come within the category of things to which almost anything must be sacrified in order to secure the peace of Europe. If we asked Poland to base the economy of the nation on anything like the population between the old Western frontier and the new Eastern frontier there would not really be a strong Poland, even giving her Lwow.

What are the objections to her expansion Westwards? There will be an ethnological objection. But a great deal of the population of the territory which is proposed to be taken from Germany is at any rate substantially Polish, and for my part I regard the wholesale exchange of populations, if necessary, as something infinitely less serious and grievous than the risk of Europe becoming a battlefield again. I would say: "Most certainly move the German population," though, I think, as the Prime Minister pointed out, a good deal has already moved out. East Prussia can strengthen Poland at the expense of Germany.

SIR W. BEVERIDGE: How many Poles does the hon. and

learned Member think would have to migrate from Eastern Poland, for whom room must be found?

MR. PRITT: From Eastern Poland in the sense I have used it there would be little migration, because there are very few Poles there. The Poles in East Prussia numbered probaboly 53 per cent pre-war [*Interruption.*] Something like 53 per cent of the whole population of East Prussia is of Polish origin. I do not think that the change will make the country too large for the people in it—not for long. . . .

CAPTAIN MCEWEN (C.): . . . I chiefly regret Poland. Poland, if not the reason for, was at any rate the occasion of, our declaring war in 1939, and it will be denied by nobody that our relations with Poland have ever since then been excellent, and moreover that the services rendered by the Poles to us and the Allied cause in every theatre of the European war have been beyond all praise. I was glad to hear from the Prime Minister—particularly because I happened to ask a Question on that subject the other day which received a somewhat Departmental answer from the Home Secretary—that facilities will be offered to such Poles as desire it, to adopt British nationality after the war.*

THE PRIME MINISTER: After consultation with the Dominions.

CAPTAIN MCEWEN: After consultation of course with the Dominions. At the same time, it was not a statement which lent any great weight to the Prime Minister's general argument, and into that I need not go any further. But even before the recent Conference, doubts were expressed in many quarters concerning what might be the result of that Conference when it was held. I have here a copy of the Memorandum given by the Polish Government to His Majesty's Government and the American Government on 22nd January,** which states that the Polish Government are confident that the Gov-

---

* See No. 21.
** See No. 17.

ernment of Great Britain will not agree to be a party to decisions concerning the Polish Government without the consent of that Government. In the same document the Polish Government expresses the hope that at the Conference of Allied Powers, the British Government will give expression of their resolve not to recognize the puppet Government and say that the recognition of such a Government in Poland would be tantamount to a betrayal of the inhabitants of Poland, in defense of whom the present war was begun. That shows, at least, that these doubts were held and felt in many quarters. Nor was it any secret that His Majesty's Government's Ambassador in Moscow was strongly of the opinion that the Lublin Committee ought to be recognized as the sole legitimate Government of Poland at an early date. I think there was no secret about that. [*Interruption.*]

MR. SHINWELL (Lab.): We cannot hear the interjections of the right hon. Gentleman the Prime Minister, which are much more important than the speech of the hon. and gallant Gentleman.

CAPTAIN MCEWEN: This is something evidently which is capable of widely divergent interpretation. On the one hand, my right hon. Friend averred that it was a masterly compromise, wherein nothing was given up and all is referred to the future. On the other, the view taken by the Polish Government, and shared by not a few in this country, is that it amounts to little more or less than a complete acceptance of the Russian point of view. This also, let me say, is my own view, and it is one which I can assure you, Sir, is at least widely shared in Scotland.

I am dealing this afternoon with one single point. There are other points in the agreement which invite argument, but I wish to confine myself to the sole point of recognition. Arguments have been put up already, and will be put up many more times in the course of this Debate, about the making of the Lublin Committee in the nucleus of the new Administration, the ignoring of the Polish Government here in the negotiations, and the apparent lack of safeguards in the matter of carrying into effect the promised elections in Poland. However, I want to deal in the first instance with the excuse which has been put forward—What else could we have done? I do not say that has been put forward today, but I have heard it before. Quite apart from the unworthiness of such a reason being put forward by a great Power which has been dealing, presumably, on an equal footing with other great Powers in a conference, in my view it would have been better to say frankly that we could not, in this instance, agree. I know that would have been a violation of the canon which governs at any rate the greater conferences, and which demands that at the close of them there should be issued a communique which states that in every detail agreement has been arrived at. I say that it covers the major conferences because it does not always cover the lesser ones, and I would instance in that respect Dumbarton Oaks and Chicago.

Then it is said: "If that is the line you take, then you would have left the Poles in Poland to what you consider to be a Russianized Lublin Government and done nothing for them." On the whole, and taking the admittedly pessimistic view of the future of the Poles under the arrangements which have been reached, which I do, I would answer: "Yes, I do not think they would have been much worse off." [HON MEMBERS: "Oh."] Believe me, I am not only thinking, or even mainly thinking, in this respect of Poland; I am thinking of this country. Had we refused to agree, and stuck to the Arciszewski Government, the "London Government" as the Lublin wireless never fails pointedly to refer to it—and incidentally, why should London become a derogatory terms in the mouths of anybody? I would like to know where Lublin was in 1940—had we stuck to that Government I say we would at least now have no cause to be ashamed. If it is said further that had we done so we would have found ourselves in complete diplomatic isolation, why then, I can only marvel that even now, at this late hour, we have still not learned the lesson of 1940—that it is a very little thing to stand alone if we are convinced that we are standing for the right, nor, in that cause, will we ever lack friends for long. It is no use harking back into the past, but I cannot help thinking that it is a pity we did not link up this question of the independence of Poland with the 20 years' pact of friendship with Russia when that agreement was concluded. I have already said that this is a difficult matter to deal with. It may seem very simple to certain hon. Gentlemen opposite, but, believe me, it is a very complicated one.

MR. PRITT: That is because the hon. and gallant Member cannot make out a case for it.

CAPTAIN MCEWEN: Therefore, without, I trust, causing any provocation, perhaps I may illustrate the situation as I see it by a simple simile. It is as if I saw someone, to whom I was bound by ties somewhat in excess of the ordinary ties of humanity, in the embrace of a bear. My expressions of concern are met by all sorts of reassuring and soothing words. I am told that this bear is, in fact, a tame bear; I am reminded that bears have many engaging qualities, that they love honey and that they occasionally indulge in a playfulness which is almost human; as to what is happening before my eyes, I am told that I can talk as much as I like about a bear's hug but that is nothing more or less than prejudice and, in fact, this is merely the bear's way of showing his affection. Well, that may be, but I cannot help feeling that history, natural and otherwise, is in this matter on my side. What has been done in the Crimea Conference has been done, but I for one cannot join in the chorus of approval which has greeted its doing, and both for the sake of my own conscience and in the hope of lessening the possibilities of this sort of thing repeating itself at some future stage, I feel I cannot allow it to pass without registering a definite but uncompromising protest.

MR. PRICE (Lab.): If hon. Members of this House have doubts in their minds as to how to vote on this occasion, I at least have none, for I wish to give wholehearted support to the Motion and to congratulate the Prime Minister on the results of this great historic Conference. In the last century the Crimea was the scene of a tragedy in the history of relations between this country and Russia. It is very fitting that it should now be the scene of an entirely new page in the history of our relations which, I hope, will prove lasting for the future. I am glad, too, that the Conference decided, apparently finally, that the Curzon Line is to be the basis of the Russo-Polish frontier. If ever there was an impartial inquiry made into the reasons for fixing the frontier on the basis of race and religion, the Curzon Line was an example. For some time past, however, that line has been challenged and the Atlantic Charter has been invoked for the purpose of claiming that there should be some other line. There is no question in my mind that the objection to the Curzon Line on the part of the London Polish Government hides, in actual fact, nothing less than an old Imperialist claim which the Poles have no right in this day to substantiate. There may have been some historical reason for it in the past when Russia was weakened, after the Mongol invasions, when the United Crown of Poland and Lithuania was able to extend into what was virtually a vacuum. But those days have long since gone, and now it is surely a waste of time. One is only too glad to feel that at the Crimea Conference a sound decision has been arrived at.

There may still be some adjustments of territory. For instance, Bialystok is a good case in point. There you have a strong Polish population, surrounded by non-Polish elements, and a little give and take there would be very desirable, and might do something to sugar the pill. I am also glad that in the matter of the future Government of Poland the Conference seems to have some to wise decisions. I am one of those who have held the view for some time that the Polish Government in London, as at present constituted, is becoming less and less entitled to speak on behalf of the Poles. At the same time, I have always held— and I said so on the last occasion on which I had the honor to address this House—that I did not feel that the Lublin Government were fully representative of all the democratic elements in Poland, and I am glad that the Conference has come to that decision—the decision to broaden the basis of that Government. I do not doubt in my own mind that the Lublin Government, even as they are now constituted, would gradually gain in experience and authority by the simple act of feeding and clothing the people with the aid of their great Eastern neighbor. But that is not enough. There are democratic Polish elements abroad who, at all costs, ought to be encouraged to go to Poland and join the Lublin Government in creating a really national, democratic, and progressive Poland. I hope that if this Debate does anything it will at least encourage those elements abroad to pluck up their courage and go there and co-operate. Indeed, I hope that those of us who speak in this Debate will try to encourage it.

There is one point which ought to be cleared up, and I noticed a passage from the Prime Minister's speech which seemed to be hopeful in that direction. There are to be elections for the new Polish Parliament as soon as possible. The importance of these elections for the future of Poland and of Eastern Europe cannot be exaggerated, but I think it is necessary that there should be present at them representatives of the Great Powers in Europe, to watch and supervise over them. I say that not because I want to cast any doubt on the great Power that is nearest to Poland, and clearly overshadows her, but I think it would create a good deal of confidence among those Polish democrats who are now doubtful, if something like that could be arranged.

If that is not done I see the danger of steering into spheres of influence—and that applies not only to Poland but to Greece as well—and it is very undesirable that that should take place. There has been a tendency to develop in that direction since the Teheran Conference. I wonder whether the Crimea Conference will change that, so that the idea of spheres of influence will be exorcised altogether, and there will be more direct cooperation between the three Great Powers in all these cases where delicate situations arise, such as in Poland and Greece. I should like to see Russian representatives present when the elections are held in Greece. I think that would be a reasonable compromise and desirable in every possible way.

I am glad that the Conference agreed to leave the question of the Western frontiers of Poland to be decided in detail at a later date. I think that is wise, because on that matter I am not altogether too happy. It seems as if Russia is rather anxious to induce the Poles to accept a wide extension of territory in the West. I think the Poles have the right to say those famous words, *Timeo Danaos, et dona ferentes*—"I fear the Greeks even when they bring gifts"—

MR. SILVERMAN (Lab.): Is my hon. Friend quite satisfied that this proposal for compensation really emanated from Russia?

MR. PRICE: It is quite clear from the Russian press that Russia is very much in favor of this, but if my hon. Friend knows something else perhaps he will inform the House if he is called in the Debate. In any case, it may be sowing dragons' teeth to extend the Polish frontier to Pomerania and the Mark of Brandenburg. It is about as unreal as claiming that the Polish frontier should be in what is clearly non-Polish territory in the East.

Moreover, I do not see why Poland should be compensated for something which she had no right to possess. There is no large or even small Slav population in Pomerania or the Mark of Brandenburg. I know that in the Spreewald, near Berlin, there are small colonies of people who once were called "Wends," originally Slavonic people. But the whole country is predominantly German miles beyond the Oder, until you get to the neighborhood of Posen. Therefore, I am sure we should create fresh difficulties by expelling the population in what is purely a German territory. I am glad that the Conference did not decide to fix anything definite in that direction, but, on the other hand, I agree with those who have expressed the view that East Prussia is an entirely different question. First of all, there is a large Polish minority there.

Moreover, East Prussia has been regarded by Germany as a colony from which she drew unprocessed raw material and to which she sent, in return, manufactured goods. Further, that unprocessed raw material was produced in the main, not by German labor at all, but by thousands of Polish natives who crossed the Frontier and worked on the Yunkers' estates. The finances of East Prussia were entirely dependent upon those of the Reich. The whole basis of East Prussia was thoroughly unsound economically and even more so now that half the population as it is reported has gone.

The second point was that not only was it an uneconomic colony, but it was the military bastion which was built up as a dagger to strike at the heart of Poland. While it might be thought very unwise to extend the frontiers of Poland right away into the West, into what was German territory, that objection does not apply in the case of East Prussia, and any decision taken by the Allies in this connection was a right one. If the Powers continue to work along the lines foreshadowed at the Crimea Conference, I feel that all will be well. Therefore, I do not hesitate to give my fullest support to the Motion moved by the Prime Minister.

CAPTAIN ALAN GRAHAM (C.): All the enemies of Nazi Germany must rejoice at the declaration made by the three Heads of Governments at the Conference at Yalta of their

> "inflexible determination to destroy German militarism and Nazism, and to ensure that Germany will never again destroy the peace of Europe."

Continued co-operation between the Great Powers, among whom we must, inevitably, include France, and continued resolution on the part of peoples concerned, even if it has to be spread over many years, and at the cost of many sacrifices, are the two essential conditions to such a happy consummation. Once, however, this is achieved the blood tears, toil and sweat will have been worth while. Our basic purposes for which we went to war, namely to secure our national and imperial security and, no less important and in direct contrast to the Nazi creed, to maintain our belief that the State exists for the individual, will have been triumphantly vindicated.

It is essential, because of this belief, that Nazism must be extirpated if our civilization is to continue. The system of government where the rights and development of the individual are sacred, cannot exist peacefully side by side with another system of government, where the individual simply does not count. For the one system to live, the other must die. Therefore it was, I presume, with an equally deep conviction on the part of the three Heads of State at Yalta of the vital necessity of the rights of the individual that, in their pronouncement on the Polish question, they insisted on free and unfettered elections being held in Poland as soon as possible and based on universal suffrage and a secret ballot. Of course it would not be possible to consider Poland truly liberated unless the Poles could claim and practice such an elementary form of democracy.

This announcement was happily reinforced by the references in paragraph 5 to Principle 3 of the Atlantic Charter, affirming the right of all peoples to choose the form of government under which they would live. If the three Heads of Government are sincere in attaching importance to this principle, how comes it that in discussing the future of Poland no representative of the London Polish Government was called into council? Two out of the three participating Governments have recognized its legality, and that Government has made its views quite plain in the Memorandum which it sent to the British and American Governments on 22nd June. The present legal Government of Poland was consulted neither before nor after the Conference. Nor was it even mentioned in the announcements of the decisions of the Conference. Yet, this is the sole legal constitutional and recognized Government of our Ally Poland. This is the Government to which the Polish Armed Forces, now numbering nearly 200,000, and the Polish Home Forces of the Underground Army have sworn loyalty and allegiance, as the rightful office-bearers of their nation and State. Their Prime Minister, Mr. Arciszewski, a veteran Socialist, and so representative of the Polish people that he was the head in Poland, until last autumn of the whole of the underground movement, has simply been ignored. He has not even been received by our Prime Minister, who legally recognized the truly representative quality of this Polish Government.

On Thursday last I was visited in this House by the representatives of half a million Polish workers and underground fighters from France, mostly Socialists and miners, thoroughly good democrats. They were unanimously supporters of Mr. Arciszewski and his Government, both in opposition to the unconditional surrender of the Eastern half of Poland, and to the surrender of the independent Government of Poland, into the hands of the Lublin puppets. I have here a cable from a body representing the 90,000 Poles in Argentina, which I propose to read:

> "The Crimea Conference has carried out once more the partition of Poland without the Polish people's consent or knowledge and has put in foreign hands the true attribute of a nation's sovereignty to create a Government. This, after six grim years of war against Germany is an incredibly hard blow. A tragedy for all of us. To form this new Government Mr. Molotov assisted by two Ambassadors has been appointed. Commissar Molotov is the one who, in 1939, signed with Ribbentrop the agreement to wipe off the Polish State, who can be held responsible for the deportation of one million and a half of Poles, who took away Polish citizenship from all Poles in the Soviet Union. In spite of this, in the Big Three's opinion the Polish people should trust Molotov more than President Raczkiewicz or one of the venerable Polish Archbishops, as arranged in Greece. We Poles are seeking for a manly conscience that would protest against such revolting facts. Shall we find it?"

On 15th December practically every speaker in the House affirmed the utterly unrepresentative quality of the Lublin Committee, yet it seems that the opinion of this House has been flouted by the decisions of the Yalta Conference.* The Lublin Committee is referred to in the pronouncement of the

* See No. 11.

Conference as the "Provisional Government now functioning in Poland" and this body, vaguely expanded, is to be the new Provisional Government of Poland charged with the holding of free and unfettered elections in that country. We know the importance which the three Heads of Government assembled at Yalta so rightly attached to these free and unfettered elections, but what sort of chance have they? The so-called Provisional Polish Government at this moment is so controling the country that no independent opinion, however democratic, is allowed to be published at all, all wireless receivers have been confiscated and broadcasts can only be heard at certain places controlled by the Provisional Government. The Lublin Minister of Education, M. Skrzeszewski, has informed the professors of Cracow University that the Rector of the University and the Deans of the Faculties will not be elected as formerly but appointed by the Government. Professors, writers, artists and scientists are forced to sign declarations denouncing the Polish Government in London as traitors to the Polish cause and especially attacking the President, M. Raczkiewicz, M. Arciszewski, and even our Prime Minister's favorite, M. Mikołajczyk. If they refuse to do this they are arrested and imprisoned or else just murdered.

At this moment members of the former Home or Underground Army, particularly officers, are being arrested, deported, and even shot. The private soldiers of the Underground Army are mostly being rounded up and forcibly enlisted under the command of General Zymierski, the Lublin Commander-in-Chief. He, incidentally, served five years' imprisonment in prewar Poland for having, when in the Quarter-Master-General's Department, embezzled money allotted to the purchase of gas-masks for the Army. I presume that the Big Three do not expect General Anders, and the honorable officers of the Polish Army still fighting by our side, to accept the leadership of such a Commander-in-Chief! Finally, since 1939, more than 2,000,000 Poles have been forcibly deported to Russia and Siberia. Such are the auspices under which these three unhappy gentlemen, Messrs. Molotov, Harriman and Sir Archibald Clark-Kerr, are expected to supervise the reorganization of the present Provisional Government, and enable free and unfettered elections to take place. What optimism, what heroic faith in the democratic behavior of the actual rulers of present-day Poland, the Russian secret police!

I will now pass to two questions—which I wish to put, in regard to the Yalta decision on the Curzon Line, although in the eyes of all Poles, frontier questions, important as they are, come second in importance to national independence.

MR. SILVERMAN: On a point of Order. An hon. Member found himself extremely puzzled a few moments ago because he did not know whether the hon. and gallant Gentleman was quoting, and therefore reading, some telegram that he had received, or whether he was reading his speech. I gather that he has long left the telegram, but it looks rather as if he is reading the whole of his speech.

CAPTAIN GRAHAM: I prefer to refer to my notes out of conscientiousness. The hon. Member is usually acute enough to know what is happening.

MR. MACK (Lab.): Could not the hon. and gallant Gentleman discard his notes?

CAPTAIN GRAHAM: Why, in a matter affecting the sovereignty and territorial inviolability of Poland, did the Big Three, who expressly reaffirm in paragraph 5 their determination "to build a world-order under law," not accept the offer contained in the present constitutional Polish Government Memorandum of 22nd January to

> "agree to any method provided for by international law for a just and equitable settlement of the dispute with the participation of both sides"?

The other question is: How can the Prime Minister reconcile the honor of this country with his ignoring of the explicit understanding at the time of the signing of the Anglo-Polish Treaty of Mutual Assistance that, if this country were to enter into any new undertakings with a third State, their execution should at no time prejudice either the sovereignty or territorial inviolability of Poland, and *vice versa?* If the right hon. Gentleman felt that, in spite of that explicit undertaking, he had, none the less, to make some arrangement which would violate the territorial inviolability of Poland, the least he could do was to take into consultation the other party to this Treaty, which is the legal constitutional Government of Poland sitting in London. It is, indeed, a mournful reflection that this Empire, which stood alone in 1940, except for Poland, against the might of triumphant Nazi Germany, cannot now, when she has mighty Allies by her side, stand up for juster treatment of her first and most martyred Ally of this war. But if, indeed, it be so, let us at least comport ourselves with dignity and honor. Do not let us pretend that something which is unjust is in reality right. Do not turn away from our own shores those who have given their lifeblood for the protection of our homes.

If we must consent to the fact of our Polish Allies being robbed of their homes, let us find them a new home in our Empire or elsewhere. Let us grant them the pensions that our own soldiers and wounded men receive, and, at least, the right to work here and if, after this treatment, they still care to receive it, British citizenship. To send them back to a Sovietized Poland, or to hand over Poland to the Government of the Lublin Committee, with the power that lies behind it, would be nothing less than the betrayal of innocent blood. We can only conscientiously consider the decision of the Yalta Conference in regard to Poland if the Government can ensure that contingents of Allied troops shall be present in the country to supervise, not merely the elections but the general conditions of life itself in Poland. Otherwise, we cannot avoid that most severe of all condemnations which lies upon those who betray innocent blood.

MR. DRIBERG (Ind.): . . . The second main danger-point is the continued existence of the Polish émigré Government in London. The Prime Minister told us this morning that at any rate formal recognition is still to be extended to it for some indefinite time; but that the dissolution of the two so-to-speak rival Polish Governments will not, of course, be simultaneous. Naturally it will not—because the Lublin Government is now in Poland and is actually doing the job, whether we like it or not, of administering Polish territory, distributing food, and so forth. On the other hand, I agree with hon. Members that a large number of the Polish Armed Forces, to whose heroism I join in paying tribute, still owe allegiance to the Polish Government in London. That makes the problem a little more intractable. I do not know whether the Armed Forces of Poland, who are fighting very gallantly in Western Europe, will feel that their allegiance to the Government in London is unshakable; but I am told that quite a number of them were seen in London last week, and even a few Polish officers, buying flags on the Red Army flag-day.

I am not suggesting that all the Poles in the London Government are completely devoid of wisdom or statesmanship. In one of the many Polish publications issued in this country I saw, in translation, some very interesting remarks the other day. I think the publication represented the Peasants' Party. In an article entitled "Elements of Hope," the writer was shrewd enough to say that Russia's very insistence on international recognition of the Curzon Line was itself proof that Russia had no designs on Polish territory as a whole, as has been so wantonly alleged in some of the more irresponsible anti-Soviet quarters in this country—including, I am sorry so say, the Scottish Roman Catholic hierarchy, copies of whose latest manifesto were distributed to hon. Members this morning.* The article went on to point out, wisely, that

* The letter of 5 Catholic archbishops and bishops in Scotland contained this statement: "It is our deep belief that the overthrow of the legal Polish Government, the toleration and approval of the rape of Polish territory by the Soviet Union against the will of the Polish nation, together with our apparent abandonment of our solemn obligations to this country—all this without the least legal foundation or justification—constitute a great act of injustice, not only with respect to our Polish friends and allies, but also with respect to the whole Christian world."

Referring to their letter of August 14, 1944 (see No. 1) to the

the break-up of unity among the major Allies would have been in the first instance a disaster to Poland, and it praises the statesmen of Yalta for their wisdom.

Although there are these saner influences in the Polish Government in London, I am afraid it must be said that for the most part that Government has been a cause of more mischief and harm among the Allies than has any other of the foreign Governments to whom we have shown hospitality. They have, indeed, built up a much larger and more expensive bureaucratic apparatus than any of the others. I do not think that the total figures have yet been published.

CAPTAIN ALAN GRAHAM: Is the hon. Member aware that the Polish troops in this country are more numerous than in the case of any other Ally, except the United States? What justification has he for alleging that they have a more expensive bureaucracy?

MR. DRIBERG: I am going to quote some of the figures of the money that has been advanced to the Polish Government in London by the British Treasury, at the expense of the British taxpayer, for bureaucratic and governmental purposes, quite apart from the maintenance of the Polish Armed Forces. I do not think that the total figures have been published yet, but, for the four-years 1941–44, we have advanced to the Polish Government well over £40,000,000. I understand that their demand from the British Treasury for this year is £15,000,000 further. I wonder whether it is going to be given to them, or whether it has already been given to them, and I wish the Foreign Secretary—

CAPTAIN GRAHAM:: Does that include money for the pay of the Polish Armed Forces?

MR. DRIBERG: No, Sir, it does not. It excludes sums for the Armed Forces, and is advanced for the maintenance of the bureaucracy alone.

Members of Parliament, the bishops feel that it is their solemn duty to advise and warn His Majesty's Government of what appears to be a crime against Poland as well as what is an affair of honor and prestige for the whole Empire.

MAJOR SIR JOCELYN LUCAS (C.): Can the hon. Member tell us how that amount compares with what has been received by other Governments in this country?

MR. DRIBERG: I have not the figures with me, but I can get them for the hon. and gallant Gentleman. In most cases the figure is considerably less. Comparing, for instance, the number of people among other Allies who have been granted diplomatic privileges, which is perhaps a rough basis of comparison, as showing the number of persons employed by Ministries, we find that whereas Czechoslovakia has 71 persons with diplomatic privileges, and Greece 16, Poland 124. Among those with diplomatic privileges, Belgium has two Army officers, Czechoslovakia eight, and Poland 11. In pretty well every case that one can check the Polish Government in London has a far more expensive bureaucracy than any of the other Allies in London.

MR. IVOR THOMAS (Lab.): The figures that my hon. Friend is giving are wholly fictitious.

MR. KIRKWOOD (Lab.): How does the hon. Member know?

MR. THOMAS: More than 90 per cent of the money advanced to the Polish Government goes for education and to paying the troops who are now fighting for our cause.

MR. DRIBERG: The figures are not fictitious at all. I have checked those figures, which come from an extremely reliable inside source—[HON. MEMBERS: "Name"]—very near to some of my hon. Friend's best friends. I am sorry to have gone on longer than I intended, but I have been interrupted quite a lot. There are one or two figures which I should like to quote, as illustrations, from the Budget of the Polish Ministry of Foreign Affairs, which for 1942 was £485,000, and by 1494 had gone up to £975,000—nearly £1,000,000. The Minister of Foreign Affairs has an uncontrolled privy purse, which amounted in 1944 to £32,000, in addition, of course, to his tax-free salary. It is from that sum, incidentally, that the lavish entertainments and banquets at luxury hotels, to which some hon. Members of this House have been good enough to go on occasion, are financed. This ministry, in particular, has built up the most elaborate network of diplomatic and consular representation throughout the world, while it has been in this country. Establishments have been set up in all sorts of countries which never had diplomatic or consular relations with Poland before. In 1942 a Polish *chargé d'affaires*, with consular officials and clerks and so on, suddenly turned up in Addis Ababa—and all at our expense. They set up a most elaborate organization at Chungking, too.

I have no time to quote the figures for the Polish Ministry of Information, but they are even more staggering than those for the Ministry of Foreign Affairs. In 1944 the sum was getting on for £1,000,000, and there have been large subsidies for all sorts of publications in this country. "Free Europe" got £4,800 from them. Also, an extremely interesting Polish "information" activity is the Soviet Research Center which increased—[*Interruption*]. Yes, The Soviet Research Center is maintained by the Polish Ministry of Information in London. It cost £5,000 in 1943, and £14,400 in 1944. I do not know what its purpose is, except to put out the usual kind of poisonous propaganda against Soviet Russia which is always circulated by the Polish Ministry of Information. Such a disreputable rag as the "Weekly Review" is another of the publications which have been subsidized in one way or another by the Polish Ministry of Information, in that case by the buying up for free distribution of large quantities of copies of the periodical. I apologize to the House for having taken up so much time. I would only urge that at the earliest possible moment recognition should be withdrawn from this bogus émigré Government, that it should not be allowed to become in future the focus of anti-Soviet propaganda and activities in this country, and that the members of it, now that their country has been liberated by the Red Army, should be invited to repatriate themselves.

COLONEL SIR A. LAMBERT WARD (C.): The hon. and gallant Member for Wirral (Captain A. Graham) has dealt with the position in Poland. He described the situation which had arisen during the formation of this Lublin Government, and compared its position *vis-à-vis* the Polish Government in London. It is not my intention to follow him at any great length, first because I have not any great time, and second, because I have other things to say, but in my humble opinion everybody admits that Poland and the Poles have suffered in the last five or six years terribly—"terribly" is not a sufficiently strong word to express it. All the same, to say that the adoption of the Curzon Line is tantamount to another partition of Poland is nothing less than an exaggeration. It appears to have been forgotten during the Debate today that the Polish Government themselves have done a bit of partitioning on their own. It will be well within the recollection of the House that, when the Germans invaded Czechoslovakia and occupied it, when one might have expected that the Poles would have come to the assistance of a race who were their relations, both by race and language, on the contrary they at once took the opportunity to occupy Teschen and the surrounding country. They stabbed their relations in the back.

CAPTAIN GRAHAM: The Czechs, in fact, in defiance of the Council of Ambassadors in 1919, seized Teschen in spite of the Polish majority there. Thomas Masaryk himself admitted, "We only took Teschen because we needed the coalmines of Karwina."

SIR A. LAMBERT WARD: Let us take another case. In 1919, after the Council of Ambassadors had decided and delineated the frontier between Lithuania and Poland, what did the Poles do but invade Lithuania and occupy the capital Vilna, of which they remained in possession until turned out in 1939? What right have the Poles to the line East of the Curzon Line, except the right of might, which enabled them to take it in 1920? I am not attacking the Poles in any way, but I think it is fair and necessary to say that the Poles will not come to the peace conference with absolutely clean hands. The Prime Minister spoke at some length of what one might call the makeweight, to make up to the Poles on the West the territory that they are about to lose on the East. He said that, instead of the Polish Corridor, they were to have Danzig. But is that all? Are they not going to have the deep-water harbor of Neufarvasser, which is the deep-water harbor of Danzig? Unless Danzig has been extensively dredged in the last few years, no vessel drawing more than six or seven feet could reach Danzig itself. It seems to me that the whole of East Prussia, including Koenigsberg, should be transferred to Poland. If we want future peace it would be advisable to have, one might almost say wholesale transfers of population between Poland and East Prussia. We have heard suggestions that 53 per cent of the inhabitants of East Prussia were Polish by descent. It is very difficult to define the descent of East Prussians. Certainly 90 per cent of them speak the German language. That is countered by the fact that a very large number of the better educated classes are bilingual. The position can be ascertained only by something like a plebiscite. It would be a platitude, in fact almost an impertinence, on my part to praise the wonderful speech which we listened to—

* * *

Debate on February 28, 1945.

MR. PETHERICK (C.): I beg to move, at the end of the Question to add:

> "but, remembering that Great Britain took up arms in a war of which the immediate cause was the defense of Poland against German aggression and in which the overriding motive was the prevention of the domination by a strong nation of its weaker neighbors, regrets the decision to transfer to another power the territory of any ally contrary to treaty and to Article 2 of the Atlantic Charter and furthermore regrets the failure to ensure to those nations which have been liberated from German oppression the full right to choose their own government free from the influence of any other power."

In moving the Amendment which stands in my name and to which the names of a number of my hon. Friends are also attached—and to which other hon. Members have added their names since it was put on the paper—I hope that the House will sympathize with me in the very difficult task that I have set myself today. The Amendment is the result of no idle *putsch*. Nor has it been hastily conceived. Those hon. Friends of mine who feel very deeply on this matter have had long and various consultations. We have considered every possible course of action, but we have come to the very reluctant conclusion that we must put upon the Order Paper of the House of Commons an Amendment which would express our views. I hope that the moderation of the words that I propose to use today, will be taken for what in fact, it is, an understatement, and that hon. Members will not think that, because of that moderation, my hon. Friends and I do not feel most deeply and sincerely in this matter. That may sound pompous for a back-bencher, but after all even the humblest back-bencher in these days never knows how far his words may carry, probably well outside this country, or whether some unfortunate remark may not be taken down abroad, and used against his own country.

Not only during but before the war, whenever international conferences were proposed, my heart always started to jump a beat, because I had an uncomfortable feeling that at every conference, there was to be an agreement, and that the agreement had to be reached generally through compromise, very often an unfortunate compromise. It seems to me that this aspect of foreign politics should contain one very great attribute, and that is the art of knowing when to say "No." I remember two occasions when British statesmen went abroad and came back without an agreement. One was the case of the late Lord Snowden and another was recent, the case of Lord Swinton, who allowed a conference partially at any rate to break down, rather than make a concession which he believed would damage this country.

I venture upon another point before coming to the main part of my Amendment and I hope it will not be out of Order. I believe the country is rather anxious. It sees the Prime

Minister constantly going from conference to conference and risking his life, which is of inestimable value to this country. As the right hon. Member for Wakefield (Mr. A. Greenwood) asked yesterday, I also would ask whether it is not time that we had a conference here. It may be a slight exaggeration, but I think there is a feeling in the country that there is too much going-about, with the savor of the cap in hand, to other countries. We know perfectly well the old saying that if the mountain will not go to Mahomet, Mahomet must go to the mountain, but there is no reason why Mahomet should go to a whole range of mountains.

The Amendment contains a direct criticism of the policy of the Government, and the decisions which were arrived at, as a result of the Yalta Conference. It contains, therefore, a criticism of the Prime Minister as head of His Majesty's Government. It seems to me that one of the great forces of this country lies in our Parliamentary system, which has sustained us through this war for the great reason that, even in war time, a strong, virile democracy, not fearing to criticize even the highest in the land may, even in the darkest days, get things done and errors rectified. That can never happen under dictatorship régime, because everybody is in a conspiracy of silence to shield those in high positions. The Prime Minister —and never let it be thought that I am attempting to curry favor in this matter—is a great man of war. He is a well-found, stout battle-cruiser. [AN *HON.* MEMBER: "A Dreadnought."] Let it not be thought that those who have put their names to this Amendment, are not conscious of the immense service that the Prime Minister has done for this country, but nobody is a superman. Everybody makes mistakes. If any back-bench Member of Parliament feels that he is justified in criticizing even the Prime Minister, then he should not in any way hesitate to do so. The late Lord Grey said that a politician must always be examining his motives; our motives in moving the Amendment are absolutely sincere, and we do not expect any political reward as a result.

It would be wholly out of Order to discuss the whole of

the Yalta Agreement in the course of considering this Amendment, but we are not criticizing all the decisions reached. I, personally, believe, although some of my hon. Friends may not share the view, that the decisions reached with regard to Germany are completely sound and represent a policy which we should like to see followed towards Germany after the war. On certain other parts of the Yalta Agreement I would reserve judgment. The great matter on which we disagree, and which has caused us to put down the Amendment is the case of Poland. Let it not be thought that those of us who take this view very strongly are more Polish than the Poles. We have immense sympathy for that very valorous, brave Ally, who have fought the Boche for five years inside and outside their own country, a country which has always maintained its national consciousness through four partitions.

We are looking at this matter through British eyes. We know that the Poles feel their national entity strongly and that is partly why we sympathize with them so much in this case. We feel also strong views in the matter from a British point of view. We feel that we are British, through and through and out the other side, and it is particularly for that reason that we regret anything which might be done or is done which will have the effect of casting British honor into doubt. The only difference between the cases of Estonia, Latvia, Lithuania and Poland in this matter is that Poland was the country for which Great Britain took up arms in 1939. It was a *casus belli*, as we know. There was the greater overriding motive of preventing the domination of Europe by sheer force of arms. I certainly should not wish to repeat everything that I and others said in presenting the case on 15th December, but I would say that as a result of this Yalta Agreement, if it goes through, Poland is to lose nearly half her territory, a third of her population, 85 per cent of her oil and natural gas, half her timber and peat, half her chemical industry, nearly half her grain, hemp and flax, and nearly 40 per cent of her water power, potassium mines and phosphates and the ancient Lion City of Lwów which stood up for centuries against attacks from North and South and from the East.

Poland is not all Pripet marshes. It has stood for countless generations against invader after invader, coming from different parts of Europe and the East. I have told the House what is happening; can all that be made good by a postdated cheque, by the cession of territory now belonging to Germany and containing we know not what? That is all in complete defiance of four treaties, particularly those entered into between Poland and Russia. It is contrary to the Atlantic Charter, about which I would like to have something to say before I sit down. It is also contrary to the Anglo-Polish Treaty of Mutual Assistance of 1939. I am referring to the Treaty and the secret Protocol attached to it of the 15th December.* This is what was said in sub-section (3), Article 6 of the Treaty:

> "Any new undertaking which the Contracting Parties may enter into in future shall neither limit their obligations under the present Agreement nor indirectly create new obligations between the Contracting Party not participating in these undertakings and the third State concerned."

As I understand it, that means that if Great Britain and Poland both made a new agreement with another country, that new agreement should not prejudice either partner to the Treaty.

This is what the secret Protocol says. In Clause 3, the relevant part reads:

> "The undertakings mentioned in Article 6 of the Agreement, should they be entered into by one of the Contracting Parties with a third State, would of necessity be so framed that their execution should at no time prejudice either the sovereignty or territorial inviolability of the other Contracting Party."**

I do not over-estimate the importance of that secret Protocol because it seems to me that the passages in that Treaty have a direct connection with my next question—how about the Atlantic Charter. In the Yalta Agreement, the Atlantic Char-

---

* No. 11.
** Vol. I, p. 191.

ter is, I think, rather ingenuously and certainly unctuously mentioned on more than one occasion. I have always felt and I am sure it is right that when our country is engaged in war, it is in the highest degree unwise at any time to mention war aims or peace aims of any kind whatever, no matter how innocuous they may appear to be. It is all the more dangerous, if anything specific is laid down, because it is bound to come back like a haunting ghost out of the past, rattling its chains at us.

This Atlantic Charter was brought out with all the pontifical "bally-hoo" of the Thirty-nine Articles, the Ten Commandments, President Wilson's Fourteen Points and the Beveridge Report, rolled into one. I should say perhaps the Berwick Report. Article 2 of the Atlantic Charter was the one which worried me most at the time because I feared that it applied to Germany, and I did not wish to apply Article 2 to Germany. What has happened since? About two years later, the Prime Minister was obliged to say—and I was most grateful to him—that Article 2 did not in fact apply to that country. But I did at least think that it applied to our Allies. What does it apply to now?*** It is only a guide and no longer a rule. I suppose the Atlantic Charter with that Clause in it, applies only to those countries who are so strong as to be able to protect themselves or so remote as to be out of danger.

I have heard it said that the Poles are a difficult people. Perhaps they are. So would we be, if our country were to be given away to somebody else. The Poles have no monopoly of being difficult in the world today. But the Poles have not been conquered. They are still fighting. They are fighting with us and they are fighting in the underground movement. This is not a case of *vae victis*. We know perfectly well that when a country has been defeated, she must bear the consequences. She may have to bear the most dreadful horrible consequences but that is because she lost the war. In this case Poland has not lost the war, she is our Ally, she is our continuing Ally and she is still fighting by our side.

*** No. 20.

May I now come to the terrible situation with which we are now faced as a result of Yalta. This is the fifth partition of Poland although it is only the first in which this country has taken part. In the last 200 years this is the fifth time in which Poland has been cut up by adjoining Powers. Hon. Members have said in the course of this Debate, that they look upon the second part of our Amendment, which refers to the question of a free and independent Poland, as being paramount, and that the question of territory does not matter so much. I do believe very strongly in a free and independent Poland, and I hope the hon. and gallant Gentleman who is to second the Motion will deal more particularly with this. But do not let us think that this question of territory does not matter at all. You can argue perfectly well about the ethnological lay-out on the east of the Curzon line. We have been given some figures which show that there are two-fifths Poles, two-fifths Ukrainians and one-fifth Ruthenians and Jews. That is not the point. The point at issue, it seems to me, is not a question of the rearrangement of boundaries. I think it was Pitt who said "Roll up the map of Europe." The map of Europe has be rolled and unrolled a good many times since then —but in this case this territory of Poland was guaranteed by treaty, freely entered into between Russia and Poland and three times re-affirmed by implication and by the whole tenor of succeeding treaties. So much for the question of boundaries. I believe you will get no peace in Europe, unless the sanctity of treaties which confirm boundaries as a result of discussions freely entered into, is recognized and honored. There will be no peace in Europe for 100 years unless we return once more to that principle.

I would like to say a little now about the question of Lublin Government, and the Provisional Government which is proposed as a result of Yalta. It is to be chosen, we understand, by three eminent men—a brace of Ambassadors and a Foreign Secretary. I wonder if we would like that very much and if we would show much confidence in a Government so chosen for us. Would any country in the whole wide world, accept such a Government? Surely one of the principles of the Atlantic Charter is the right of every people to choose its own form of Government. But this Government is being chosen for the Poles. There is one more point I should like to make on this. There are in part of the Yalta communiqué dealing with Poland, some sinister references to the suggestion, or the fact that only anti-Nazis will be allowed to vote and take part in these elections. What does that mean? Does it mean that anybody who is declared by the Provisional Government—or it may be by the Lublin Government for all I know, to be a Nazi is not to be allowed to vote. If this is the case, there can be no possible free elections in Poland, because it has only to be declared that a man is a Nazi—and he may be the leader of the Socialist party for all we know—and he will not be entitled to vote. I would ask the Foreign Secretary when he replies to deal with that point, and to tell us why that peculiar expression "anti-Nazi" was put in that document. I suggest it is clearly dragged in for this reason. There are no Nazis in Poland and there never have been—they have no Lavals, no Darlans, no Quislings, no collaborationists. Why then was this expression introduced into that part of the document? I am sure the House would be glad to know.

I am coming rapidly to my conclusion. I do believe most fervently not only that we should continue to work with Russia but that we can continue to work with Russia. But co-operation is not a one-way street. There must be give-and-take in all these matters. We have not heard Russia's case at all. The Prime Minister yesterday did not deal with Russia. We have been waiting for the Russian case to be stated in this Debate, but we have not yet heard of it. There must be a case, because it must be strong enough to over-ride four treaties and the Atlantic Charter, all of which the Russian Government have signed. Let us then hear from the Foreign Secretary what Russia's real case is.

The Prime Minister referred yesterday to Sir Eyre Crowe and Lord Curzon who, in considering the Curzon Line, said that it was a fair agreement at the time. Neither of them however is here to give evidence, nor so far as I know does that evidence appear in any of the documents or the telegrams of the time. What did appear was the fact, the perfectly plain and established fact, that the Curzon Line was an armistice line, on which both armies, then contending, were invited to stand and there was a specific reference back to the decision of the Allied Supreme Council, made in Paris, I think in 1919, which laid down the territory in which the Polish Government would be formed, but specifically reserved the question of the frontiers of Poland which were then classed as purely provisional.

EARL WINTERTON (C.): If I may put a perfectly friendly point to the hon. Member, I would point out that this was accepted by this House. I think this has some bearing on the subject which is being discussed at the moment, and I would emphasize the Curzon Line was accepted by this House.

MR. PETHERICK: It was accepted as an armistice line. I had hoped to have the approval of the Noble Lord in this matter in full and flowing tide, but all I can descry is a backward eddy.

I am afraid the Russian case is a sad one in this matter. If the Prime Minister had come back to the House and said, "Well, I have done my best to argue with them. I cannot admit that they are right, and all I can admit is that they are in occupation in the country. They are our strong Allies on whom we are going to depend for the future. Therefore I have done my best." If he had said that I should not now feel so critical. But what the Prime Minister did say was something different. He regarded it as a fair and just settlement. In spite of this, as I think, shocking decision, I do not believe that all that has happened in this war has been lost, and that the lives which have been given up in so many different territories and climes have been surrendered in vain. One great thing at least will come out of this war, and that is the complete and utter crushing of Germany as a military Power. Then we are asking what comes after that? Is there to be another Power acting in similar fashion growing up in the world? I refuse to believe it. I believe that if Russia can be persuaded that her interest lies in dealing with her neighbors on fair, just and honorable terms, there is real hope of peace, and lasting peace in Europe, and all the efforts of His Majesty's Government should be devoted—if I may respectfully point that out, as they seem sometimes not to be—firmly, honestly and determinedly, to show to the Russians where their own self-interest lies. [An HON. MEMBER: "They know."] I am sorry to hear that interruption from my hon. Friend. I had hoped that the Russians might think once again in this matter, because, after all, countries do things in the heat and excitement of war, and in the flush of victory, which they regret afterwards.

I believe that when some of us tried to state the case on 15th December in this House, we stated what was true. Speaker after speaker said that they believed—and we had an idea this was going to happen—that the proposed treatment of Poland was wrong. Speaker after speaker got up and, shrugging their shoulders, accepted it, as it were, as a *fait accompli.* My right hon. Friend the Foreign Secretary, and the Prime Minister, who are such very good judges of the temper of this House, must have known, in the course of that Debate, that the House was profoundly uneasy and anxious. For all the good it did, so far as the Yalta Conference which succeeded it was concerned, we might as well have done absolutely nothing and spent the day in bed, because the views of the Commons House of Parliament were completely and utterly ignored.

We did not want this Vote of Confidence. We did everything we could to avoid it being made a Vote of Confidence. We tried as hard as we could, by conversations and every other means we could reasonably think of to have it put down and discussed on an ordinary Motion which would not entail a Motion of Confidence. We felt ourselves obliged to put down this Amendment, which, broadly speaking, expresses our views. We did so with sorrow but with no misgiving at all, because this is no small moment in history. The Yalta Conference, it seems to me, is a curtain-raiser to the Peace Treaties that are to come, and on those Peace Treaties will depend the whole future of Europe and the world. Is this curtain-raiser to be a grim, grisly *Grand Guignol* piece, followed perhaps by a happier and a more joyous cavalcade, or is it to be the forerunner of another grim and hideous tragedy? We have put down this Amendment, confident in the righteousness of the motives which caused us to do so, and in the knowledge that divisions do not destroy decency, nor do Votes of Confidence over-ride justice.

COMMANDER SIR ARCHIBALD SOUTHBY (C.): I beg to second the Amendment.

My hon. Friend moved it with a charm and with a skill which I cannot hope to emulate, and I rise with very much the same feelings as those which I experienced on the day when I first had the honor to address this House. I do not mind confessing that this is, for me, the most difficult speech I have ever made, or probably shall ever make. It seems to me that so momentous are the issues involved by the Yalta Agreement, that where an hon. Member is dissatisfied or apprehensive he must, before casting a Vote or abstaining from voting tomorrow, either speak in the Debate, if that is possible, in order to justify his actions, or alternatively, put his name to some Amendment on the Order Paper, which would indicate the point of view he holds. That is why my name is on this Amendment. I do not have to remind the House that this Debate is, perhaps, the most important which has occurred in our time. We must, of course, answer to our contemporaries for what we say and what we do during these three days, but it is at the bar of history that we shall really come up for judgment, and not at any election held amidst the confusion inseparable from war conditions and the propaganda which is part of them. Surely, in a matter so far-reaching as this, Parliament should have been permitted to express its views free from the suggestion of coercion which is inherent in a three-line Whip and a Vote of Confidence. As it is, today we are, in fact, expressing our views under threat.

Outside this House people are confused by the flood of propaganda with which they are continuously assailed. They are asking, "Where is all this leading to? To what are we being committed? How will it affect our children?" But is it any wonder they are perplexed? They saw this war begin as a fight between dictatorship and democracy or, I should say, the democratic ideals of free men. They have seen it develop, in one aspect at least, into a clash between two rival forms of dictatorship, Communism and Nazism, in neither of which way of thought is there any room for democratic freedom as we know it. They find democracy in alliance with Communism in order to accomplish the overthrow of Nazism, and they fear and suspect—not without cause—the sacrifice of those democratic principles upon which alone man's freedom can be rooted and secured. I have studied the Report of the Crimea Conference with care, and it is not so much what is in the White Paper which justifies apprehension, as what remains undisclosed, even after the speech of my right hon. Friend the Prime Minister.

If I am critical, I must not be taken as criticizing this great man or that great man, and certainly not that very great man, Marshal Stalin, whose courage, vision and genius have led the Russian people through their darkest hours to victory. I respect him all the more because he never deviates for one moment from his course. His first consideration is always the advantage of his own people. Indeed, I sometimes wish the same could be said of our own Government. Criticism of the Yalta Agreement then is not an attack upon Russia; it is an expression of a British point of view. I fully recognize that Russian aims, methods and outlook may quite rightly differ from ours, but although they may be right and suitable for that great country, they are not necessarily right or desirable for us. I hold that it is absurd to suggest that there are only two courses open to us, one to accede to everything that Russia desires, and the other to oppose Russia so violently that war becomes inevitable. Surely, we can put our point of view to our Ally, Russia, as plainly and as forcibly, and I hope as courteously, as to any other nation with whom we were dealing. But if it is argued that so great is the strength of Russia in Europe that she must inevitably in the end obtain what she wants by force, then although we might not be able to influence that fact, there can be no reason why we should now deliberately underwrite any action which we believe to be morally wrong. To be pro-British is not to be anti-Russia, but even if it were, we, as the representatives of the British people, can neither evade nor ignore our plain duty or our responsibilities.

The Yalta Agreement is the basis upon which the whole post-war set-up is to be erected. If we acquiesce in all that is now proposed, it will be too late afterwards for us to make any effective protest. Most people, I think, would find themselves in accord with what the Yalta Agreement has to say in respect of Germany. If there is one universal determination above all others, it is that never again shall it be possible for German lust for world domination to engulf mankind in war. But while we are anxious to exact from the Germans reparation and compensation for the destruction they have wrought, it behooves us to proceed with caution. Is it intended, for example, that Germans shall be taken to other countries and employed on forced labor? If so, nothing is more likely to sow the seeds of further wars than the transference of unwilling populations. Further, what happened after the last war should be a warning to us to tread warily in the matter of the receipt of goods in reparations. In the words of the Agreement we all want to meet

> "the political and economic problems of liberated Europe in accordance with democratic principles."

and those great men who signed the Report declare their intention of enabling the liberated peoples of Europe

> "to create democratic institutions of their own choice."

and

> "to build in co-operation with other peace-loving nations a world

> order under law, dedicated to peace, security, freedom and the general well-being of all mankind."

But one is bound to ask, Is that the case regarding Poland? For make no mistake about it, our treatment of Poland is the touchstone by which our post-war relationships will be measured. It is a tragic fact that the only place where the voice of free Poland and the Baltic Republics can be heard today is in this House of Commons. Why is it that in the Yalta Report there is not one single word regarding the Baltic Republics? Are they not to be given the unfettered right to choose their own Government? Further, what is to be the state of Syria and the Lebanon? Will they enjoy the independence they have been promised or is the Yalta Agreement the writing on the wall for them—a writing which will be read to our disadvantage throughout the Arab world. I am bound to say that although I listened carefully to what the Prime Minister said yesterday, my anxiety regarding the future of these two countries remains. It is significant that a few days ago a Swiss newspaper said this:

> "When we tremble for the future of the small States, we tremble for the world as a whole."

and it went on to say:

> "We cannot but take note of the marked tendency of the 'Big Three' to ignore the smaller States."

I have, on past occasions, tried to plead the just cause of Poland and the Baltic States. I have no desire to go over old ground, but I cannot see, either in the contents of the White Paper, or in what the Prime Minister has said, anything which shakes my belief that no solution of the Polish problem has yet been reached to which my assent could honorably be given. Incidentally, it is significant that nowhere in those portions of the White Paper dealing with liberated Europe and Poland do the words "justice" or "honor" occur.

I want to ask the Foreign Secretary—I am sorry he is not on the Front Bench at the moment—if, when he replies, he will be good enough to answer specifically two questions which I now wish to put. Mr. Neville Chamberlain, the late Prime Minister, has been bitterly criticized because he failed to come to an agreement with Russia in 1939—the suggestion being that had he done so this war would not have taken place. Is it or is it not a fact that we could have had a treaty with Russia in 1939 had we been prepared to agree to a demand by Russia that she should have Eastern Poland up to the so-called Curzon Line, the three Baltic republics, and certain bases in Finnish territory, and that because we, to the lasting honor of the late Mr. Neville Chamberlain, refused an agreement based on such an arrangement, Russia then entered into the Ribbentrop-Molotov Agreement with Germany, by which she did in fact secure just those things?

From that arises my second question. When in 1941 we concluded our Treaty with Russia did we or did we not make it clear that we could not agree to what I suggest we had refused to agree to in 1939? Did we stipulate that the integrity of our Ally Poland and of the neutral Baltic republics should be preserved? If we did, is there any secret annex to that Treaty, observing what has now taken place and the fact that part of the 5th Article of that Treaty reads as follows:

> "and they will act in accordance with the two principles of not seeking territorial aggrandizement for themselves and of non-interference in the internal affairs of other States."

Perhaps it is as well to recall again Article 3 of our Agreement with Poland, of 1939, as follows:

> "Should a European power attempt to undermine the independence of one of the contracting parties by process of economic penetration or any other way, the contracting parties will support each other in resistance to such attempts."

It is quite obvious that in order to safeguard her lines of communication while occupying Germany, Russia must continue to occupy part of Poland. No one will deny that. But the information from Poland today makes it clear that under the Lublin Government the internal economy of Poland is now being irrevocably organized on Communist lines. In addition, officers and men of the Polish Army and underground forces are being confined in concentration camps.

MR. S. O. DAVIES (Lab.): What exactly does the hon. and gallant Member mean by his statement that the economy of Poland is being organized on Communist lines?

SIR A. SOUTHBY: A good many other hon. Members want to speak, and I do not want to take up too much time. [*Interruption.*] I mean, on the lines which would be accepted by the Communist Government of Russia: the expropriation of the owners of businesses and small farms and so on, and the destruction of the sort of economic system which we enjoy. The Foreign Secretary will not, I think, deny that in September, 1944, he was officially acquainted with the fact that since the occupation of part of Poland by Russia, from one district alone near Lublin 21,000 officers and men of the home army had been placed under arrest. It is clear that there must be safeguards much more definite than anything that appears in the White Paper, if Poland is to be able to hold really free and unfettered elections in order to choose her own Government. Apart from the fact that the legal Government of Poland is here in London, how can a Polish Provisional Government, as envisaged in the White Paper, be in fact established when the entire Press in Poland is under the control of the Moscow-sponsored Lublin Government, when people have no means of listening to free and independent broadcasts, and when no Pole in Poland is free to express a view except in one direction?

The White Paper says that only democratic and anti-Nazi parties may take part in the election, and put forward candidates. What is the exact meaning of a qualification like that when, for example General Bor and members of the Polish underground forces, whose heroic struggle against the Germans in Warsaw will live for all time, are now accused of being pro-Nazi for no other reason than that they do not share the political views of those Poles and others who constitute the Lublin Government. I appreciate the grave complexity of the Polish problem, but I suggest that, instead of setting up a Provisional Government of National Unity as envisaged in the White Paper, it would be far better that both the legitimate Government here in London and the Lublin Government in Poland should surrender all their functions and authority to an international commission which should govern Poland until and during the elections, by which the Polish people would choose a Government for themselves. This would constitute a definite guarantee that the elections would be free and unfettered.

But whether that course were followed or whether our Government insists upon the exceedingly doubtful procedure outlined in the White Paper, other Members of this House besides myself believe that the following seven requirements are essential if Poland is to receive from the Allies the just treatment which is her right. Firstly, that all deportations from the whole territory of Poland should now cease, that all Polish subjects who have either been deported from or who have left any part of Poland should be entitled to return as soon as possible, and that those who are in concentration camps should be released. Secondly, that any decree or such like which could prevent the free exercise of political rights should be rescinded, and that as a token of good faith there should be no exercise of influence by either Russian troops or civilians, and that the NKVD should be withdrawn. Thirdly, that if the elections are to mean anything, then, subject, of course, to the military censorship necessary to preserve security until Germany is defeated, freedom of speech and of the Press and the right to hold meetings and to broadcast on the wireless should be restored at once. Fourthly, that only persons of Polish nationality—that is to say, people who were Polish subjects before September, 1939, or those who would have been entitled to political rights had the war not taken place—should be entitled to be candidates or to vote. Fifthly, that it is essential that the elections should be conducted under the supervision of a neutral, or alternatively, an inter-Allied, Commission, which should be established at once, and that from the time of such establishment order should be maintained by mixed garrisons of inter-Allied troops. Sixthly, that all members of the armed forces of the Polish Republic serving outside Poland should be entitled to vote in the same way as our own British Forces will be entitled to vote in our own elections, either directly if that is possible or alternatively by postal ballot. Lastly, that foreign Press correspondents should be admitted into Poland without delay, and without the imposition of any political restrictions. Those, I believe, are the minimum requirements if the Polish elections as envisaged in the Crimea Report are not to be a mockery.

In conclusion, I want to tell the House of an incident which is not without significance. Last week, a discussion took place in a certain British officers' mess. At the end of it a young and exceedingly brilliant officer said this: "Of course, it is perfectly obvious that we have fought the war in vain; every principle for which we started the war has been sacrificed." I believe that what he said expresses the opinion of a growing number of the British people. It is an opinion which the Government would do well to heed. If the mistakes of the past are to be forgiven and undone, and if a happy and peaceful world is to arise—not just a short period of peace, followed by another yet more terrible war—we dare not depart from the principles, whatever the temptation may be and no matter whence it comes. With much of the Yalta Agreement I am in accord, but if our foreign policy is to be based upon expediency and not upon principles then it is bound to fail, and I cannot in honor express my confidence in it, no matter what the consequences of my decision may be to me personally. I hold that there is a greater loyalty than that which we owe to any one man, Government or party—the loyalty to those fundamental ideals of justice, liberty and honor to uphold which we have twice in our lifetime seen the British sword drawn.

DR. HADEN GUEST (Lab.): This Amendment seems to me to be a singularly unfortunate one, and, while I understand that the Mover and the Seconder were laboring under strong emotion, I have to regret some of the observations that fell from their lips, as being not calculated to do this country any good in the eyes of the world. The Mover of the Amendment said that statesmen going into a conference should know when to say "No." Does he mean to imply by that that the Prime Minister at the Yalta Conference should have been ready to wreck the whole proceedings, as he would have done, by saying that we could not agree to the proposals with regard to Poland? If the hon. Member does not mean that, I suggest that he does not mean anything at all. It seems to me most unfortunate to suggest, as was suggested, that the Prime Minister acted under some kind of duress. The Mover of the Amendment also talked about a sinister statement in the Report of the Crimea Conference, that pro-Nazi parties were not to be allowed to vote. It was said by the Mover and the Seconder of the Amendment that there were no Nazi parties or parties affiliated to the Nazi party in Poland. That was a bold statement. When I passed through Poland in 1936 it was certainly not my opinion; and it was not the opinion of many people in the country at the time. They thought that Poland then had a very strong Nazi tendency. It is very unfortunate that statements of that kind should be made, and I do not think that they strengthen the case that might have been made.

Both the Mover and the Seconder of the Amendment made many apologies. The Mover said that he had not criticized the Prime Minister in the past, and so on. It is on record that I have, on occasions, made severe criticisms of the Prime Minister. On this occasion, I find myself wholeheartedly and entirely behind the right hon. Gentleman. He has helped to produce a statesmanlike solution of an extremely difficult and intricate problem, and I believe it is one which will redound to the credit of this country and be of the greatest assistance to the world. It is quite clear that both the speakers to whom I have referred are, if not full of prejudice against the Soviet Union, at least very much afraid of it. I am very sorry that it should be so, because they really have no reason to be afraid. The last speaker asked whether we could have had a treaty in 1939 with the Soviet Union. The answer to that question is not my affair and was addressed to the Secretary of State for Foreign Affairs, but I will tell the hon. Gentleman and the House that we could have had a treaty for the purpose of setting up a world organization on the lines of the Crimea Conference in 1936, if our Government had been willing to approach the Soviet Government. I had that from a very high authority on whose opinion and influence with the Soviet Government I can entirely rely. That could have been done if our Government in those days had not gone so colossally and stupidly wrong in an anti-Soviet direction. I hope that the moving of this Amendment is not an indication that we are to have a revival of anti-Soviet feeling in this country, although I feel that that was the sense of the speeches of the Mover and Seconder.

This Amendment seems to be singularly unfortunate. I think it is worth while, in order that the unfortunate nature of this Amendment may be understood, to underline what is the object of the Motion, which I support. Its object is to support the recommendations of the Report of the Crimea Conference. The object of those recommendations is to approve the declaration of policy signed by the representatives of the United Kingdom, the USSR and the United States, which is not only the outline of a policy to be adopted on the defeat of Germany, but the outline of a policy to be adopted by a United Nations Conference to be called at San Francisco on 25th April of this year. This is to prepare a charter for the world organization, to establish world security and to establish an international organization to carry it out on the basis of the conclusions arrived at at Dumbarton Oaks. I regard these proposals of the Crimea Conference as a triumph of statesmanship, not of British statesmanship alone, but of world statesmanship. I regard the proposals which are embodied in the conversations which took place at Dumbarton Oaks, and which it is now proposed should be embodied in a charter of the United Nations, to be ratified by a meeting of the United Nations at San Francisco on 25th April, as a step forward in world statesmanship which generations in the future will look back upon as the beginning of a new and better era in the international relations of mankind.

To the Motion on the Paper we now have put forward an Amendment which delves into the muddle and obscurity of anti-Soviet prejudice and its foolishness and shows almost abysmal ignorance of international affairs. The hon. Member who moved the Amendment did not seem to be aware of the fact that an international organization was proposed. He very carefully guarded himself, at any rate, against any possibility of accepting that wholesale by saying that there were things in this document on which he would reserve judgment. All he did agree with was the agreement come to at Yalta with regard to the treatment of Germany. I wonder how far the hon. Member's agreement does go? Is he in favor or not of setting up a world organization? Is he in favor of the attempt to set up a world organization that will guarantee mankind against the disasters of war from which we are now suffering, or is he not? Are those who support and have put their names to this most unfortunate statement of policy in favor of, and believers in, the possibility of these things to which the greatest minds in the world have set their hands, and to which three of the greatest men in the world have set their names, in the signature of the Report of the Crimea Conference? One would like to know how they stand in relation to this. I will not examine in greater detail their speeches, and some of the very unfortunate things which I think were said in those speeches, reflecting on the Soviet Union. It is quite unnecessary, because I think that even to examine them afresh would add further damage to the cause of Anglo-Soviet unity, on which the peace of the world in future very largely depends.

There is no doubt whatsoever that the passing of this Amendment—if it is conceivable that it could be passed, which I do not believe—would undermine the confidence not only of the people in this country but of wide masses of people on the Continent of Europe and all over the world in the integrity and common sense of Great Britain. For they will think that this proposal has been put down to hamper the establishment of the Dumbarton Oaks plan, because it has necessitated a day being devoted to a Debate on a very small part of the world picture instead of being devoted to those greater and more spacious causes which we ought to have been examining. Do the hon. Members and the hon. Lady who have put their names down to this Amendment know what the purpose of the Dumbarton Oaks Conference was?

MR. DEPUTY-SPEAKER (MR. C. WILLIAMS): This is a matter not really within the scope of the Debate, and I do not think that we should go into a discussion, fully or in any detail, if at all, of the Dumbarton Oaks scheme. I am sorry to interrupt the hon. Member, but we should try to keep the discussion on this Amendment to the Polish question, even though the Amendment may seem rather wide.

DR. GUEST: I will endeavor to do that, Mr. Williams, but I think I may at least be justified in referring to proposals which the Motion approves, because the Amendment is a criticism of them, though only in that sense. I bow to your Ruling and will keep myself on the narrow and straight path so far as it is possible. I must ask the supporters of the Amendment whether they really are trying to delay the coming into existence of the proposals set forth in the Report of the Crimea Conference? Do they not consider that a very much better body to consider the matters they have brought forward would be the whole body of the United Nations which is to meet at San Francisco on the 25th April? Or do they think that all this, about which I have been speaking and which is set out in the document on Dumbarton Oaks and in the Report of the Crimea Conference, is just a cynical pretense? Do they accuse the Prime Minister of giving way to force? One hon. Gentleman very nearly did that. Do they really think that the Prime Minister, whom I have criticized more severely than the two hon. Gentlemen opposite, is a man to give way to a threat of force? I may criticize the Prime

Minister on a number of things, but I would never say that he would give way to force. I am sure he never would.

SIR A. SOUTHBY: I never said so.

DR. GUEST: I think it was suggested in one of the speeches made, and it was a most unfortunate suggestion. Do the hon. Members suggest that Poland has been unfairly treated, and is not given the right to choose its own Government? Hon. Members have said that. Are not the facts given by the Prime Minister yesterday that the utmost efforts were made to get Poland to choose some kind of Government which would really be responsible, and the fact that when M. Mikołajczyk went to Moscow, he came back with the terms of an agreement which would have enabled a compromise Government to be set up in Poland embodying people representing those inside Poland as well as those outside, and that the possibility of that agreement, which would have meant that the Lublin Committee would never have been formed, as the Prime Minister himself said—is it not the fact that the London Polish Government killed that agreement? They did not want to discuss anything with anybody else. They wanted to have it entirely and only their own way, and in this world it is not possible for any nation to have entirely its own way. It must co-operate with others if it is to get on in this world.

It is essential, in the interests of all nations, and not least in the interests of Poland itself, that a settlement should be arrived at, and I believe that the settlement set out in the Report is wise and fair and will establish a strong, free and independent Poland on a firm foundation. I see no reason whatever for this talk about Poland east of the Curzon Line, and how it depends on certain treaties, and I would remind the House of the fact that this territory was taken from the Soviet Union when Poland was attacking the USSR and it was established as Polish by military conquest, and, subsequently, owing to the weakness of the Soviet Union, was embodied in a treaty. This conquest is thought to be sacrosanct, and that nothing that comes afterwards can be regarded as having any justification. I do think that this is a rather nonsensical position for the supporters of the Amendment to take up, because what they propose is that we should go back on this agreement arrived at in the Crimea, and should move that reference back to a further meeting of the Big Three. Do they really think that, in the sixth year of the war, we can endure that delay and set up another conference which would then bring forward its conclusions, which, no doubt would be equally unacceptable to the hon. Members and those who put their names to this Amendment. It seems to me that no more dangerous mistake could be made. I do not think it is realized sufficiently that we cannot afford to delay the setting up of this world organization. I was never more glad of any statement on public policy than I was of the statement made that the Conference of the United Nations is to be called on 25th April at San Francisco. We need that. This Amendment, if carried, would postpone that, disrupt it and put a spoke in the wheel. It would throw sand into the machinery. It would put despair into the hearts of agonized Europe.

I have just come back from a visit to Europe. I visited France, Belgium, a portion of Holland and a little bit of Germany. I saw the agony which people are suffering there and the urgency of the actual economic and social problems waiting to be solved. I saw the intensity of economic struggle and the extreme difficulties of organization under present circumstances. Now when a new proposal comes forward for straightening out the general outline of world organization, which involves straightening out the general outline of European organization, and getting Europe and the world to work again, it is regrettable that there should be this niggling and miserable amendment designed to bring forward anti-Soviet prejudice of the worst possible kind, and brought forward as the contribution of hon. Members of the party opposite. They will come to regret the day they ever put their names to this Amendment, which can only be regarded as a spoke in the wheels of international organization. It does not seem that it could by any possibility help on the rehabilitation of Europe or help Poland itself.

Poland needs help. Poland needed help after the last war. I was one of those who went into Poland—and I know something of the country—to help to give that relief and I saw the disorganization then. I daresay that disorganization is now as bad, but the first need of Poland certainly is to get these major problems settled in such a way that they are settled, finally and once and for all as in the proposals of the Crimea Conference, and then to get on with the work of rebuilding and rehabilitation. Anyone who knows Poland—and I wish to say nothing against Poland—knows that that certainly is her chiefest need. I believe that the Agreement which the Members who have moved and seconded this Amendment are so anxious to discredit and who would be, I daresay, delighted if it could be sent back for revision is a document of first-class importance. It incorporates the great traditions of 1,000 years of the British Empire, the traditions of Soviet civilization and the traditions of the United States, that great free republic of America. I believe that on the basis of this settlement which some hon. Members wish to undervalue, minimize and decry, there can be built a great and lasting structure of world organization which will help Poland as much as any other country in the world. It is a great and outstanding achievement of world statesmanship. We should salute it. Mankind now can lift its head above the fog and miasma of the present conflict, into the purer air of world politics, planning, through a world assembly of nations the ways of future peace, progress and prosperity.

MR. W. J. BROWN (Ind.): We have listened this morning to the speech of the Mover of this Amendment which, he will allow me to say, is a most noble and moving utterance, and we have listened to the equally sincere speech of the Seconder, to which I pay the same tribute. But I want to say at once that I am going to oppose them. I propose to do it on grounds manifestly different from those which have been advanced by the hon. Member for North Islington (Dr. Guest). If there were any truth at all in his charge of anti-Soviet propaganda or feeling behind the speeches which have been delivered from the benches opposite, I could only say that those hon. Members would be justified in retorting that there was nothing but pro-Soviet propaganda in the speech which the hon. Member has just delivered. The problem of Poland is not merely a political problem, but a problem of conscience for this country. And so far from regretting that this Amendment appears on the Order Paper, I welcome its presence. Whenever any serious body of opinion in Britain is sincerely moved in its conscience by a given issue, that issue ought to come here and be threshed out. Therefore, as I say, I do not regret that this Amendment is on the Paper or that we are having this Debate.

I would ask the Mover and the Seconder of the Amendment to believe that, if I oppose them, as I now want to do, I do not do it because I am either a Communist or a disciple of Stalin. I regard the economic case of Communism as not yet proven, and as regards the political aspect of Communism, I hate totalitarianism whether of the Left or the Right. I deplore the tendency to totalitarianism that I sometimes see on the opposite side, and I equally deplore the tendency to totalitarianism that I sometimes see on this side of the House. And I shall continue to rebuke both sides, with magnificent impartiality, as long as I see those tendencies. Roughly, my view may be put in a sentence. When I consider every vile report of wrong and outrage wherewith the earth is filled, my general conclusion is that civilization ends at the cliffs of Dover! I am not animated either by anti-Soviet emotions or by pro-Soviet emotions, but I am looking at the problem as I think we must do. The main criticism I would make of the speeches of the Mover and Seconder of the Amendment is that they were complaining of two things. First, that history does not stand still. And secondly, that you cannot make international agreements in a political vacuum!

I speak as a trade-union official, who in the course of his somewhat disturbed life has made some hundreds of agreements. The test that I would apply to the making of an agreement by myself, must be the test that I ought to apply to the making of an agreement by the Prime Minister. What is the test? It is this. If any particular agreement extracts from a given political situation the maximum advantage that that situation can be made to yield, then, whether the yield be large or small, that agreement is a good one. Conversely, if an agreement fails to extract from a given situation the maximum that that situation will yield then, even if the yield appears to be substantial, that agreement is a bad agreement. That is the test that I would apply to any agreement that I made in a trade-union capacity and that is the one I must apply to this particular agreement. We must have regard to the Prime Minister's position at Yalta. He had, I was going to say, two alternatives, but I do not think they were really open to him. But there were two or three alternative theoretical possibilities. One was not to have tried to reach an agreement. That was theoretically a possible approach. The second was to defer an agreement. And the third was to make an agreement. I cannot see any other possibility than those three.

Was the Prime Minister right in trying to make any agreement? I cannot but answer that question in the affirmative. I do not believe that either the concluding stages of this war, or the problems of the setting up of a world organization to safeguard peace in the future, or the problems arising out of resettlement in Europe, could have been effectively handled by agreement between this country, America and Russia, if the Prime Minister had sought to dodge the Polish problem. I hold that he was right. He would have been wrong in trying not to reach some kind of settlement. Would he have been justified in delaying a settlement until a further international conference? In my opinion, No. The Russians have a point of view on this which is entitled to respect. There is, unhappily a long record of bad relations between this country and Russia which, unless its psychological effects can be removed, will poison relations for an indefinite period of years. I believe that every suspicion between Russia and this country would have been intensified if we had sought further delay on this question. I conclude, therefore, that the Prime Minister was right in trying to reach an agreement at this conference.

Then the only question which remains is, Does he bring back to us, in that Agreement, the maximum that the situation could be expected to yield? That is the acid test. I want to be quite blunt about this. The Prime Minister has brought back in that Document a great deal more than I expected him to bring—a great deal more. We do not make agreements in a political vacuum. And looking at either the military or the political set-up in which the Yalta Conference had to take place, can one fail to realize that most of the cards were in Stalin's hands, and not in the hands of our Prime Minister? It was not the British Army that liberated Warsaw. It was not the American Army that liberated Poland. It was the Russian Army. Suppose that the Prime Minister, because he feared that Stalin had too many cards, had come away with no agreement at all I wonder what the effect would have been in Poland? I imagine that the effect of no agreement there would have been infinitely worse than the worst that could happen under this document, and the two hon. Members who moved and seconded the Amendment today would before long have been making this House ring with what was happening in Poland, because there was no agreement of any kind.

MR. IVOR THOMAS (Lab.): The hon. Member has made an analogy of trade-union agreements, but where do the Poles come in this? Is any agreement regulating the conditions of the Civil Service made between the Ministry of Labor and the workers' association without consulting the latter association?

MR. BROWN: I should regard that as being plasphemy of the worst order. I should do my best to denounce it and undo it. But I submit that there is no analogy between the two cases. If it is agreed, first, that something had to be done about Poland, secondly, that it should be done by agreement between the Powers, and thirdly, that there had to be some sort of Polish Government to work out the further stages of this document, I cannot see any escape whatever from what the Prime Minister did at Yalta. We have had a complaint today that the London Government were not consulted, which we are told is the only legal Government of the Poles. But I would point out that history has unpleasant habits. One of its unpleasant habits is that it does not stop short at constitutional legal points. It is a dynamic process, and not a static one. Is not the real difficulty about consulting the London Poles that whereas they regard themselves as representatives of the Polish people, very large sections of the Polish people do not? If the Lublin Committee regard themselves as representative, there are many Poles who do not.

In those circumstances, what better practical line of approach could have been advanced than that of trying somehow to bring those two elements together, and to get some sort of Government of national unity? I am not a passionate advocate of Coalitions. I regard Coalitions, generally speaking, as possessing the vices of both parties—with knobs on. But Poland has to have a Government and a representative one. With the seven things that the seconder of this Amendment wants done—the ending of deportations, the return of deportees, the removal of restrictions on the exercise of political rights, the freedom of the Press, the elimination of the veto on holding meetings, and so on, I agree. But I do not know of a word in the White Paper which makes any one of them impossible. Hon. Members are entitled to say that the White Paper does not aver positively that they shall do this, but I am entitled to say that there is not a single word in the White Paper which prevents any one of those issues being raised by the Polish Government. Supposing one wanted to argue those issues now, who is to argue? Is it the Lublin Government, or the Government in London? Either or both? If it is either, one would not get a settlement; if it is both one would get chaos. But there is nothing whatever to prevent the proposed provisional Government raising every one of those seven points and possibly getting some satisfaction on them.

The Prime Minister is entitled to have from me the same judgment as I would pass on myself. I give this judgment, an honest judgment, the best that I can give. It is that the Yalta document, having regard to the historical, political and military realities of the situation, represents the maximum that could be expected. That being so, I must, as an honest man support the Prime Minister on that particular issue.

The last thing I want to say is this. I would beg the House to recognize that Poland is not the only issue that was involved at Yalta. There seemed to be a disposition in the speeches of the Mover and the Seconder of the Amendment to suppose that our Prime Minister should have gone to Yalta with an open mind, a blank check, a pen and an unspoiled piece of paper, and have written on it exactly what he liked. If that were so, then, believe me, I should not be accepting this document, nor would the House. The House would be ranged entirely behind the Mover and the Seconder of the Amendment. We have to look at the concrete situation at Yalta, and, above all, at issues other than Poland. I shall not pursue this, Mr. Deputy-Speaker, because under your earlier ruling it would be out of Order for me to do so, but you will, I feel pretty sure, regard as not out of Order what I am now about to say. I do not know what hope there is for the establishment of permanent peace in the world, but I do know that unless those three Powers can be kept together, there is no hope at all.

Even supposing the Prime Minister had given way more than he should have done, which I do not agree, in my opinion his supreme purpose at that Conference had to be to keep the Allies together, to prepare the way for the establishment of the world order, to ensure that there was not a break up of the alliance at the time when its responsibilities reach their maximum. There were other issues besides Poland, and even more important ones, and though I have not been without my share of criticism of the Government I must say, as an honest man, that I thought the way in which the overriding issues have been combined with other important but lesser issues was masterly. I thought that the line of solution proposed was a practical one, and whatever criticisms I have of other aspects of the Prime Minister or his policy, I must say that I think this document enormously increases the debt which this country and the world owes to him—enormously increases what was already a very vast debt indeed. In those circumstances, much as I respect the sincerity of the Mover and the Seconder of the Amendment I must take my responsibilities on my shoulders. And I wish to say that if there is a Division on this matter, I shall go into the Government lobby. I will do that because we here cannot dodge our responsibilities either.

What would be the consequences of passing this Amendment? One would be the defeat of the Government. I shall not waste tears about that—it is time I superseded it—but I doubt whether this is the right time to do it, on the eve of the final battles of the Western Front. I doubt if this is the time to change horses—if we want to change horses. Secondly, we have to consider that the passing of such an Amendment as we have here today would enormously increase the political difficulty of the President of the United States in handling his problem there——

CAPTAIN ALAN GRAHAM (C.): With 6,000,000 American Poles?

MR. BROWN: The mover and the Seconder of the Amendment today did not put their case on a numerical basis but on the moral basis. As I say, its second effect would be to increase enormously the difficulty of the President in handling his political problems. Thirdly, and most important of all, if this Amendment were carried every bit of suspicion and distrust between Russia and this country—which the Prime Minister's superb political handling of Russia has had some effect, I hope great effect, in allaying and dispelling—would be revived and intensified one hundred-fold, and any hope of an agreed approach between the three Great Powers, without whom there can be no peace, would be effectively and probably permanently destroyed. In all those circumstances, I propose to go into the Government Lobby today if this matter is forced to a Division.

MAJOR LLOYD (C.): I am among those who have the honor, of which I am proud, to put my name to this Amendment. I believe that those of us who have signed that Amendment and have the opportunity of speaking on it today, represent an enormous number of ordinary folk in this country who are deeply disquieted at the particular references in the Yalta Agreement to Poland. In spite of a spate of propaganda, which I suppose has never been exceeded in our history, and in spite of our diplomatic correspondents and special correspondents, who seem to have been able to get very much the same handout from the Public Relations Officers of the Department concerned, they cannot concur with that portion of the Agreement which refers to Poland. I look upon the intentions of the Yalta Agreement as downright annexation of a large portion of Poland's territory without the consent of her Government and, in fact, without the consent of her people. I believe myself that it is a very definite breach of the Anglo-Russian Treaty, the wording of which has been referred to already in this Debate. I believe that it is a very definite moral breach of the Anglo-Polish Treaty, and I am quite certain that we have once and for all departed, with our eyes wide open, from even the guidance of the Atlantic Charter, which has now been whittled down to a mere meaningless symbol. I believe that, whatever our contemporaries may say, and whatever the result of this vote is today or tomorrow, history and our descendants will say that those of us who speak for, and have signed this Amendment, were in fact right. It is on that basis, because I believe that history will say that we are right, that I am so glad to have the opportunity of saying what I am saying today.

I see no reason whatever why the subject of boundaries of Eastern Poland could not have been left over until the peace treaty. I would like to be allowed the privilege of reading to the House a statement I discovered the other day which was issued by the Ministry of Information on 17th September, 1939, the day after the Russian armies took that portion of Poland which is now on the east side of the Curzon Line. That is what the British Government, through its Prime Minister, unanimously authorized the Ministry of Information to issue to the world:

> "The British Government have considered the situation created by the attack upon Poland. . . . This attack made upon Great Britain's ally at a moment when she is prostrate in face of overwhelming forces brought against her by Germany cannot in the view of His Majesty's Government be justified . . . the full implication of these events is not yet apparent"—

and I would ask the House to listen to this solemn statement issued by His Majesty's Government to the world—

> "but His Majesty's Government take the opportunity of stating that nothing that has occurred can make any difference to the determination of His Majesty's Government with the full support of the country, to fulfill their obligations to Poland and to prosecute the war with all energy until their objectives have been achieved."*

There is a solemn pledge to the nation and to the world which is today being deliberately broken and ignored. There is not any shadow of doubt about the truth of that.

Now I want to come to the question of the supersession for it is supersession—of the legal Government of Poland which we have recognized all these long years, by a prefabricated Government to be hand-picked by three estimable gentlemen. It is in future to be recognized by all the three Great Powers concerned, and will supersede the legitimate Government of Poland which commands the Armed Forces of the Polish Republic. They have done splendidly throughout the war, and I firmly believe, still retain the overwhelming loyalty of the majority of the Polish people. The prefrabricated, Lublinized Government is to be the future Government

* Vol. I, p. 270.

of Poland. I leave it at that. It is adding insult to injury not only to break our pledges to Poland but to compel the Polish people to accept a prefabricated Government of this type.

I come to the all-important question of free elections. I agree with everything that has been said. Although I feel strongly on the boundary question, although I think it is unjustified and unwarrantable, something of which we should in fact be ashamed, something that is contrary to all our obligations and treaties, I still realize that it is of no importance really compared with the fundamental issue of whether Poland is to be truly free, truly democratic, and truly independent. So this matter of free elections is vital. Are they to be held, as one presumes they will be, with the Red Army in occupation? What is far more important, are they to be held when the whole of every village and town in Poland is completely under the control and in the iron grip of the secret police? If they are, they can never be free.

After all, who are the people who are to be classified, apparently, as "Anti-Nazis" and ruled out? The Lublin Government, and those who think with them, appear to be willing and anxious to do their best to extirpate them. The House may not have heard of a radio appeal—if I can call it that—put out by the Prime Minister of the Government of Lublin the other day in which he said that it was necessary to extirpate the traitors, bandits, incorrigible malefactors and brawlers of that home Army, and also all the followers of the London Government. No doubt those who so heroically defended Warsaw, and the followers of the London Government—and they number hundreds of thousands, including more than 90 per cent of the Polish Armed Forces—will be called malefactors and brawlers, and treated accordingly. Unfortunately, there is all too good reason to believe that many of these unfortunate people have already suffered greatly and gravely, and that some, indeed, have lost their lives.

The whole question resolves itself into whether it is the obvious intention to impose upon Poland a policy that can be checked by this new prefabricated Government. If it was possible for me to believe that this artificially appointed Government would overrule the intense desire of the secret police to communize Poland, and the intense desire of the Lublin Government to communize Poland, I would not feel so strongly as I do today. But one must be skeptical. I would like to read to the House a statement made on the subject of Communism by an important British statesman, which I came across the other day. One must to some extent weigh up for oneself whether one can have confidence in the goodwill and good intentions of a Government which is to be formed in Poland in the way it is. This great British statesman wrote:

> "Communism is not only a creed; it is a plan of campaign: A Communist is not only the holder of certain opinions, he is the pledged adept of a well-thought out means of enforcing them. The anatomy of discontent and revolution has been studied in every phase and aspect, and a veritable drill book prepared in a scientific spirit for subverting all existing institutions. The method of enforcement is as much a part of the Communist faith as the doctrine itself. At first, the time-honored principles of Liberalism and Democracy are invoked to shelter the infant organism. Free speech, the right of public meeting, every form of local political agitation and constitutional right are paraded and asserted. Alliance is sought with every popular movement towards the left. The creation of a mild Liberal or Socialist régime in some period of convulsion is the first milestone. But no sooner has this been created than it is to be overthrown. Woes and scarcity resulting from confusion must be exploited. Collisions, if possible attended with bloodshed, are to be arranged between the agents of the new Government and the working people. Martyrs are to be manufactured. An apologetic attitude in the rulers should be turned to profit. Pacific Propaganda may be made the mask of hatreds never before manifested among men. No faith need be, indeed may be, kept with non-Communists. Every act of good will, of tolerance, of consolation, of mercy, of magnanimity on the part of Governments or statesmen is to be utilized for their ruin. Then, when the time is ripe and the movement opportune, every form of lethal violence, from mob revolt to private assassination, must be used without stint or compunction. The citadel will be stormed under the banners of Liberty and Democracy; and once the apparatus of power is in the hands of the Brotherhood, all opposition, all contrary opinions, must be extinguished by death. Democracy is but a tool to be

> used and afterwards broken; Liberty but a sentimental folly unworthy of the magicians. The absolute rule of a self-chosen priesthood according to the dogmas it has learned by rote is to be imposed upon mankind without mitigation progressively forever. All this, set out in text books, written also in blood in the history of several powerful nations, is the Communist's faith and purpose. To be forewarned should be to be forearmed."

I did not say that: it was written by the present Prime Minister of this country. We have no need to prolong indefinitely the arguments that could be brought forward in favor of this Amendment. One of the reasons that influences me is this: I believe that we are the trustees of Poland, of this weak country which has done so much to help us in this war. We are her trustees, and we dare not let her down. We are about to let her down, and that is an act of which I shall always be ashamed and in which I will not participate today. We are asked to underwrite something which I for one look upon as shameful. No underwriter at Lloyd's would take such a risk, and no member of the Lloyd family, certainly not this one, will take part in it.

CAPTAIN THORNEYCROFT (C.): I rise to support the Government in resisting this Amendment, and I hope the arguments I put forward will not be too embarrassing to the Government. I believe that the decisions which were arrived at at the Crimea Conference and, in particular, the decision relating to Poland, were wise decisions which were taken in circumstances of very considerable difficulty. As my hon. Friend the Member for Penryn and Falmouth (Mr. Petherick) has said—and, if I may say so, I think few of us have ever heard him make a better speech—although the Amendment refers to Poland this is not a Polish issue. The fact is that at the Crimea Conference three men, each of them the head of a great State, were laying down the future road we were to follow in our foreign affairs——

MR. PICKTHORN (C.): The Prime Minister is not head of our State.

CAPTAIN THORNEYCROFT: I do not want to enter into constitutional niceties with my hon. Friend, but, as I have said, each of these heads of States was laying down the future path we were likely to follow in our foreign affairs, and on the choice of that road hangs the issue as to whether in another 20 years, we shall have another war or peace. We have had to face these kind of issues before. They are horribly familiar.

Twenty-five years ago, towards the end of another war, we were also discussing the rights of small Powers, and the future organization of peace, and I have no doubt that on that occasion we made many mistakes. At any rate, it is certain that in the unhappy years which followed we made mistakes, and none of us wants to reiterate the sad story of the path which led a Germany not totally disarmed to the reoccupation of the Rhineland, through Munich and Berchtesgaden, and eventually to war. It seems to me, looking at that past history, that the mistakes we made were not so much on detailed decisions of British statesmen trying to stave off disaster, as in the failure to face the real issues in foreign policy at an early enough date.

Let me say at once to those Members who support this Amendment that although I disagree with them in their conclusions, I respect them because their motives are entirely honorable and proper—and in saying that I do not want to appear to be pompous. They are not actuated, as the hon. Member for North Islington (Dr. Guest) suggested, by some hatred of Russia, or anything of that kind. Their desire is that these issues of foreign policy should be faced, and faced now. In that they represent a very widespread feeling in this country, and I share their view. If we are to enter into another period in which the facts of a certain situation in foreign affairs are to be tortured to fit into some international document to which we have affixed our signature we shall enter upon a course which must eventually lead us to another war, a war in which we shall have very few friends, and a process which will be detrimental to British honor.

As I have said, I differ from my hon. Friends in their conclusions. I do not believe that this Crimea Conference is the first milestone in the downward path. I do not believe that this Polish settlement is a betrayal of Poland or of British honor. Polish and British interests are to a large extent the same. We each have an interest to see that no one Power should dominate the whole of Europe. But the first British intrest that we have is to finish this war at the earliest possible date. It is common ground that the German people have, or had, until recently, only one hope, and that was that the Allies would fall out among themselves. If the decisions taken at the Crimea Conference are supported by this House then that hope will be finally dispelled, and I am sure my hon. Friends who have put their names to this Amendment would think carefully before any action of theirs could be interpreted as restoring that hope to the German people.

There is one other aspect of the war side I want to refer to, and this is a matter which could not be mentioned from the Front Bench but which can be mentioned from the back benches. It is that the German war is not the only war in which we are engaged. We are faced with a long, arduous and probably costly campaign against the Japanese. We cannot compel the Russians to share the burden of that campaign, but if co-operation means anything the greatest act of co-operation we could ask for would be for Russian co-operation in that war. It would save thousands of British lives and misery in thousands of homes, and we ought to watch that no words of ours will discourage the Russians in that matter. If our first interest is to conclude this war, the second is to see that another war does not happen, and to make sure that the territorial agreements we come to are honored in future.

I do not want to elaborate on the international organization, because I think that that would be out of Order now, but I think that when it is said that Poland can rely upon an international organization to see that this settlement is kept she is entitled to ask what that international organization will amount to. If there is one lesson we have learned from the history of the last quarter of a century it is that an international organization, unless backed up by military power, is both valueless and dangerous. Under the Yalta Agreement, we are committed to the provision of an occupation Army on German soil. We are committed to a number of agreements which, if not worldwide, will be very wide indeed. I presume that the Government have gone into the logistics of this matter. I presume that they have estimated what Forces will be required in order to carry out these commitments. The next step which is required is not so much a decision on voting rights at San Francisco as a forthright statement from this Government, a National Government, to the British people as to what sacrifices will be involved. What is required is a statement as to the Forces we shall have to raise in order to carry out what we shall have to do, and a clear statement as to whether compulsory military service will be necessary, as I think it will be.

Sympathy with Poland extends far beyond those who happen to call themselves friends of Poland, or even members of the Scottish Catholic Hierarchy. Sympathy with that country is based on the recognition of one gallant people for another. We have both made sacrifices in this war; we have common interests. I believe the settlement we have reached with regard to Poland is the best settlement we could have got. It is worthwhile remembering that in statesmanship and politics what counts is not the art of getting what is best, but the art of getting what is possible. I concede at once—and this may be embarrassing for the Government—that I do not regard the Polish settlement as an act of justice. It may be right or wrong, it may be wise or foolish, but at any rate it is not justice as I understand the term. It is not the sort of situation in which you get two parties to a dispute putting their case forward in front of a disinterested body and in which the strength and power of one of the parties is never allowed to weigh in the balance. The sooner we recognize that we are a long way from that sort of thing happening the better.

The Government had two choices only. They could have

postponed this issue. The hon. and gallant Member for Berwick and Haddington (Captain McEwen) suggested that that was the course that they ought to take. They could have said, "No, we want this submitted to arbitration. We cannot do anything without the consent of the London Polish Government." No one knows what would happen in those circumstances, but one can safely say that it is unlikely that there would in any circumstances be a free, independent and democratic Poland. The Red Army is in occupation of that country and the Lublin Committee is in control. The policy which was advocated by the hon. and gallant Member for Berwick and Haddington and others today is a policy of inactivity and no more. The Poles could get nothing from it. For these reasons, I believe the Government were right in rejecting that course.

The second course that they could adopt was to make the best settlement they could and impose it deliberately on the Poles. They have done that. They have bargained the Eastern frontier for the chance of a free Government of Poland within the new frontier. I could not quite follow my hon. Friend the Member for Penryn and Falmouth when he criticized the appointment of a provisional Government by the Council of the three Ambassadors. It seems to me that some provisional Government is essential. Europe is not in a situation where it can hold free democratic elections. Europe is on the brink of revolution. You will have to have some provisional Government in order to attain the very points outlined by my hon. and gallant Friend the Member for Epsom (Sir A. Southby). It seems to me that our policy in the past was mistaken. Up to date what we have done is this. We have encouraged the London Polish Government to negotiate, and have criticized them because they did not negotiate very well. We have told them they must make concessions, and then we have blamed them because they did not make concessions. I do not regard that as a sensible or an honorable course. I do not believe you can ask a Pole to decide to hand over a half of his country. I do not think it is a fair thing to ask any

Pole to do. If they agree to do that, they would divide Poland for a generation, perhaps for all time, into those who thought they were patriots and those who thought they were traitors. That is to perpetuate civil war. Nor could you ask the Poles as an act of policy to take a large slice of their powerful neighboring State. It is a big decision to take from Germany the whole of East Prussia or the land up to the Oder. It is like taking Wales from England. That is a decision which must be taken by more powerful States. I do not believe that you save your honor in this matter by imposing on others the obligation of making a decision which you ought to make yourself.

I believe the real difficulty in which my hon. Friends find themselves is not so much Poland at all. I believe it is in the apparent conflict between documents like the Atlantic Charter, and the facts of the European situation. We talk to two different people in two different languages. In the East we are talking to the Russians. The Russians are nothing if not realists. I believe Marshal Stalin's motives are entirely honorable. I believe that the Russian Foreign Office is perhaps more in tune with the advice which would be given to the Tsars than to the potentates of the twentieth century. In such circumstances we talk in language not far removed from power politics. In the West we are faced by the Americans. They are nothing if not idealists. To them we talk in the polite language of the Atlantic Charter. Somehow or other we have to mary those two schools of thought. If I could persuade the Americans, particularly in the Middle West, to have something of the Russian realism in international relations, and persuade the Russians to have the idealism that exists on the East coast of America, we might get somewhere but let us face the fact that the process will be a long and painful one. You do not move suddenly from a world in which there are international rivalries, into a world where there is international co-operation. It is the world that we are in that the Prime Minister has to deal with. We could not come back from Yalta with a blue-print for a new Utopia. The fundamental error into which my hon. Friends have fallen is this. The rights of small nations are not safeguarded by signing documents like the Atlantic Charter, and quarrelling with anyone who does not agree with your interpretation of them. The rights of small nations are safeguarded by a mixture of diplomacy and military power and, in using those things, you are liable to come into conflict with your friends.

In the last two months we have had two cases. In the case of Greece one body in the country was seeking, with arms in its hands, to take power. Our Government took action in that matter which, as I believe, safeguarded it and gave Greece the opportunity for a free and democratic existence. On that occasion, the Government were criticized by a small number of Members of the party opposite. [An HON. MEMBER: "Not a small number."] A small number voted and the rest could not make up their minds. Today it is Poland. The Government are trying to obtain a free, independent and democratic Poland, when the country is occupied by a foreign, though a friendly army belonging to a country which has not quite the same interpretation of what is free, independent and democratic as ourselves. In those circumstances—and they are difficult circumstances—the Government are attacked by a small group of Members of my own party. There is nothing in common between members who attack the Government today and those who attacked it over Greece.

But throughout this process the Government have pursued a consistent course. They have sought by every means in their power to obtain from the wreck of Europe two independent and free States. To the Poles I would say that I believe this settlement gives them an opportunity of playing a part in the future of their country which they can never do from London. They should take that opportunity. To the Russians I would say that this is regarded as a test case. The proof of this pudding is in the eating. Russia has many friends in this country. On the decision and action that she takes in the coming weeks with regard to Poland will depend not only whether she keeps those friends but the whole future of co-operation between our two countries. As regards ourselves, I would say that this document provides what may be the basis of future peace. It will only be that, if we are prepared to face up to the sacrifice and the efforts which it involves and to recognize that those sacrifices and efforts are, indeed, worth while.

SIR PERCY HARRIS (L.) : We have just listened to a very eloquent and convincing speech. On the whole, I prefer the doctrine of the young Tory, to the more ancient brand. But I should like to congratulate the Mover of the Amendment on a well-reasoned and fair statement of his case. I have no fault to find with the form and character of his speech. He made a great point that there was a Motion before the House, and suggested that he would have preferred the Debate to take place on an Adjournment Motion. I do not agree with him. It is far more satisfactory that the House of Commons should have an opportunity to express its view of the important Agreement put forward by the Government. As a matter of fact, in this case we are largely making history. There is only one precedent for a Motion of this kind, and it goes back to the palmy days of the Goverment of Earl Lloyd George in 1922, when a Motion of this character was moved endorsing the Genoa Conference. I hope that this precedent will be followed. I did press for the submission of the Atlantic Charter to the approval of this House. Now this precedent has been established, it will straighten the claims of Parliament to control the Government in the commitments they make. I think it is right that Parliament should keep control of foreign affairs and that we should have the right and the chance, to approve or to negative, important international agreements.

I have no quarrel with the hon. Member for moving his Amendment—it is right that he should move it if it expresses his sentiments—and I hope the House will have an opportunity to vote on it. In his eloquent plea for the Polish people, I am satisfied that he has the whole House behind him. I cannot forget the tragic month in September when Poland was invaded, in spite of our protests and all the efforts of our Government to prevent the war. We pledged ourselves to go to war if Poland was invaded, and Poland has been subject to untold suffering. The Prime Minister referred to the massacre of 3,500,000 Jews. The Polish Jews have been wiped out. There is no Jewish question in Poland: they have been simply liquidated. It was cold-blooded murder of the most appalling kind. But millions of Poles also have been persecuted, and subjected to every kind of cruelty. We know the story of the underground movement, unrivalled by any underground movement in any part of Europe. As far as I know, no Quisling has been found in the whole of that country. But let us be frank with ourselves. Poland owes its liberation to Russia. [HON. MEMBERS: "No."] Russia brought her freedom. We must be realists.

COMMANDER AGNEW (C.): It is true that Russia has done valiant feats of arms in freeing Poland and Eastern Europe, but is it not true to say that she would not have been able to do that but for the British convoys of munitions which went all the way round to Russia?

SIR P. HARRIS: I am the last person to suggest that there have not been indirect contributions from this country and the United States.

VICE-ADMIRAL TAYLOR (C.): Is not the right hon. Baronet also aware of the immensely important part played by the underground movement in Poland in defeating the Germans?

SIR P. HARRIS: I have already paid tribute to the valiant efforts of the Polish people in throwing off their chains, but their direct liberation—let us be blunt about it—is due to Russian arms. Poland would still be in the hands of the Germans if it were not for the valiant work of the Russian soldiers. Let us be quite clear that Poland has a claim for freedom and self-government, and that this country has a special obligation to see that they are ensured. The suggestion is made that the Prime Minister and the President of the United States have been outmanoeuvred, and that they were innocent lambs bullied by the Russian bear. That is a new kind of role for our Prime Minister to assume. This Amendment raises the question of the capacity not only of the Prime Minister, but also of the President, and it amounts to a censure, because, if it were carried, there would be no alternative but for the Prime Minister and the Foreign Secretary to resign. The Prime Minister divided this problem into frontiers and freedom. I think that he made his case for the frontiers and that it does not need to be further argued. The Curzon Line was not only approved by the Government of the day, but it was adequately discussed for two days in this House. It was the subject of the closest examination at the time when there were very few friends of Russia in this country. Lord Curzon could not be suspected of being pro-Russian. Apart from the difficult problem of race, the fact that this line was arrived at by an impartial tribunal gives it great moral authority.

On the question of giving complete self-government and freedom to Poland, I submit that all that the Crimea Agreement does is to set up machinery. It lays down two principles with which we can all agree—first, that a strong, free, independent and democratic Poland should be set up; and, second, that the new Polish Provisional Government of National Unity should command recognition from the three Powers. The commission, I understand, is to be composed of M. Molotov, the Russian Foreign Secretary; Mr. Harriman, the American representative; and Sir A. Clark Kerr, the British representative. I think it is reasonable to assume that they will see that Poland gets reasonable treatment and that the Polish Government in this country will be allowed to state its case. If, in due course, this House is not satisfied that the results of the work of the commission are fair, we shall be justified in examining the results again. Obviously, the Government which will be set up will only be provisional. The same kind of thing is happening in Greece. The British Government are pledged to have free elections on the basis of universal suffrage and a secret ballot. That is not the simple thing it sounds. When we were discussing the same provisions for Greece, I pointed out what a complex thing it was to provide electoral machinery. It has been known that Ministers of the Interior have made elections.

There is a strong case for some form of international control to see that the Polish people have a fair deal. There is also an overwhelming case for allowing the deportees to return to Poland. I have heard of vast numbers of Poles being deported to Siberia. We do not know the exact facts and figures, and perhaps they are exaggerated. The commission should demand as proof of the genuineness of the general election that the deportees should be allowed to return before the election, and should be enabled to take an active part in it. There is, too, a strong case for the Servicemen. We have spent many days discussing the right of our Servicemen to vote. Would it be unreasonable for the Government to demand that the quarter of a million men, who have fought so magnificently in the war on our side and proved themselves such splendid fighters, should have the same opportunity to vote in the election which is to take place in Poland as our Servicemen are to have in our election? I recognize that Poland has not the same political traditions as we have in this country, but that is not an unreasonable thing to try and achieve. I suggest, therefore, that when the commission is set up and arrangements are made for the election, which we are assured is to be a genuine one, not only are deportees allowed to return but Servicemen shall have some say in the future form of Government to which they are to be subjected. I attach great importance to that.

Right through the Yalta Agreement there is much use of the word "democracy." "Democracy" is often used to cover a great multitude of sins, and it is interpreted in very different ways. The American conception of democracy is very different from ours, and the Russian conception of democracy is also very different from ours. The average Russian would claim to be quite as good a democrat as the British democrat, if not better, but the Russian idea of democracy is entirely different. We think of it as Government of the people, by the people, for the people, and with that ideal goes all the paraphernalia of propaganda, speechmaking, a free Press and controversy. The Russians attach more importance to economic equality and the absence of privilege and class. It may be that we will be able to educate them to our view, and I am sure that my hon. Friend the Member for West Fife (Mr. Gallacher) and his associates will do their best to educate us to the Russian conception of democracy.

MR. STOURTON (C.): Is it not about time we stopped talking about democracy in Russia? Is not the right hon. Gentleman aware that there is only one party in Russia and that it represents only 2 per cent of the people?

SIR P. HARRIS: I have been saying that their conception of democracy is very different from ours. Let us make it clear that we demand for Poland the kind of democracy that we have in this country, and that there shall be genuine free elections, freedom of the Press and freedom of propaganda. If we get that we can have a feeling that we have given Poland a fair deal. The White Paper which contains the agreement not only mentions democracy a good deal, but there is constant reiteration of the phrase "joint action." Joint action, as I understand it, means that unilateral intervention in the liberated countries should cease. I regretted that Greece was subject to that unilateral action. I would have liked to see Russia and America associated with the liberation of that country. We have a right to claim that not only in Poland, but in all the liberated countries, neither ourselves nor the United States nor Russia should have the sole responsibility, but that there should be a real joint association and joint policy of all three Powers. I hope the Foreign Secretary will say that we are not merely paying lip service to joint action, but that there will be genuine association in the formation of the new Government in Poland, at any rate, of the three great Powers. I do not claim that for Great Britain alone, but I particularly ask the United States to be intimately associated with both the organization of the election and the selection of the new Government.

I do not take the question of Poland as an isolated matter. We ought to look at the Yalta Agreement as a whole, and the Polish policy must be judged as part and parcel of the proposed new international organization. The machinery of Dumbarton Oaks is to be completed at San Francisco. Is it unreasonable to ask that the final fate of Poland, not only its Government, but also the drawing up of its frontiers, should be entrusted to this new international organization which is to see the light of day in a few months and which is to be responsible for the future peace of the world?

MAJOR LORD WILLOUGHBY DE ERESBY (C.): It is with some diffidence that I intervene in this Debate as I am only too conscious of the fact that I cannot claim to speak with any very great knowledge or authority on foreign affairs. I have, however, during the past five years, been associated with men who fought, suffered and, alas, died for their country, and whose views, for that reason alone, although not better informed than my own, are entitled to a hearing here today.

When I saw the report of the Yalta Conference I did have a feeling of having been let down. I can only speak for myself personally, of course, but I cannot help feeling many who were with me in the Army might have the same feeling. Perhaps I may attempt to give my reasons. On instructions from the War Office it was our habit, as many hon. Members know, to hold once a week what became known as A.B.C.A. discussions. One of the most popular, and indeed, the most frequent of those discussions was the question of what we are fighting for. I was known to be connected with what was —possibly rather impolitely—called "the political ramp," and it often fell to my lot to reply to those discussions and explain to the men the full implications of the Atlantic Charter and how it was hoped that the somewhat elaborate international machinery envisaged at Dumbarton Oaks could be worked in the chaotic conditions of Europe that we saw all around us. I had also to explain the meaning of "freedom" and "democracy." The fault may be mine, but although I did my best to follow the instructions in the colorful A.B.C.A. handbook and tried not to impress, too forcibly, my own views, I was afraid that the result, at the end of many of those discussions, was that those who attended were a bit shaky as to what constituted democracy and democratic Government. They were a bit uncertain what measure of individual freedom had to be enjoyed by the people of any country, to claim that it was a free country. Some thought it meant that you could get a glass of beer whenever you liked, and then one had to explain that ours was a free country although we could get a glass of beer only at the times the Government thought was good for us, and that America was the land of the free, although at one period of her history people could not get a glass of beer there at all. That example may show some of the difficulties that we encountered. We were rather divided on whether some of the principles of democracy and the machinery envisaged at Dumbarton Oaks, could hope to work in the chaotic conditions of post-war Europe.

We very soon realized that when you told the men they were fighting for freedom and democracy, it meant something rather different to each one of them. I am afraid I have to admit that, to the more cynical and less political-minded amongst us, it meant precisely nothing at all. But there was one thing about which we were all quite clear and all agreed which was that we were fighting for Poland. When I say "Poland," I do not mean, and we did not mean, Poland as decreed by Soviet Russia or underwritten today by the British Government, or Poland as imagined by the late Lord Curzon, but a Poland with similar frontiers to those we guaranteed, and over which we went to war at such very great cost in life and suffering—frontiers extended possibly at the expense of a defeated Germany. I cannot help regretting that I shall be asked soon to approve of an agreement whereby the boundaries of Poland are to be radically altered from those which we pledged ourselves to preserve, an agreement embodying a settlement which we know is distasteful to those many heroic and gallant fellows who have fought for us on land, on sea and in the air during the past five years.

I must admit that I was very much relieved to hear the Prime Minister say that he was ready to see whether it was possible to have those Poles who fought for us, admitted into the British Empire. I would ask whoever is to reply to the Debate to give us a more definite assurance. We should make a gesture at this moment, and without any question of duty, offer safe asylum, either within our shores or within the British Empire, to those Poles who do not wish to go back to a dismembered and, to my mind, sovietized Poland. I am reminded of a remark made by a Canadian soldier in France. During an engagement, one of the first tanks to go forward was hit by an 88mm. gun, and then the next was hit. Eventually, the officer came along and asked this fellow what he was doing and why he was hanging back. The Canadian replied: "There doesn't seem to be much future in it to me." I cannot help feeling that if many of these Poles who declared themselves, quite openly, in my presence, and that of many other people, as being more anti-Russia than anti-German, might have a better future within the British Empire than within this new Free State that we are now setting up.

I frankly admit that I am violently prejudiced on this question. I happen to have lived and trained during the past five years with the Polish Army. I have had Polish officers attached to my regiment, and I have often fought alongside the Polish Armored Division. I can assure the House that a more friendly, charming and cooperative body of men one could not find anywhere, or a more determined and courageous body among whom to fight. I have seen and heard only one side of the case. I realize as well as anyone the immense difficulties and the vital considerations which have had to be taken into account by the Prime Minister when arriving at the Agreement, and I am prepared to bow to the superior wisdom of my elders and betters. But I do find it hard, indeed impossible, to wed this Agreement with the Atlantic Charter. Painstakingly, though possibly erroneously, I have tried to explain the matter to the men who were under my command. I tried to show earlier in my speech that the words "freedom" and "democracy" mean something slightly different to almost everyone. We know that the Prime Minister said in his speech yesterday that diversity of view between this side and that side of the House on this question existed, as applied to economic or political science, but I doubt whether any two Members in this House would give exactly the same definition of those words. I am afraid it is obvious that those two words have a very different meaning in Eastern Europe to what they have in Western Europe. The word "democracy" either as adjective or as noun appears more frequently than any other word in this part of the Conference Report, in so far as it deals with liberated Europe and Poland. It talks of:

> "democratic principles . . . democratic means . . . democratic elements . . . broader democratic basis . . . free and unfettered elections."

and so on. It would be disappointing, and to my mind disastrous, after the long journeys which the Prime Minister undertook to get to the Crimea and all the hard work that was done, if we found that he, the President of the United States and Marshal Stalin were not all speaking exactly the same language. In fact, a slightly different definition was given to this word by all three of them. I am sure many of us would be grateful if the Foreign Secretary, in his reply, would give us his definition, and an assurance that it was not only understood but accepted by the President and Marshal Stalin.

I do not want to detain the House any longer. I realize as well as anyone that the future peace and prosperity, not only of our own country, but of Europe and the world, depend upon the cooperation between what are known as the "Big Three." But to my mind we cannot hope for true and lasting cooperation unless it is based on a real understanding and not on a sham, and to my mind to attempt to marry up this solution of the Polish problem, as my hon. and gallant Friend the Member for Stafford (Captain Thorneycroft) tried to do, and much else that has happened in Eastern Europe, and is still happening today in Eastern Europe, with the Atlantic Charter, is really nothing more than a sham. As such, I do not think it is likely to prove a lasting settlement for peace, or contribute a sound and lasting basis for that true cooperation between the three Great Powers on which so much depends. Several hon. Members whom I have heard speak in opposition to this Amendment struck me as being possibly with us in spirit, but not prepared to come out openly on our side. It seemed that they felt that, although we might have made a point, bigger issues were involved. Dumbarton Oaks was mentioned, and the conference which is to take place at San Francisco.

I seem to find today, after an absence of some five or six years, that the roles are rather reversed in this House. Before I left, on many occasions both my right hon. Friend the Prime Minister and the Foreign Secretary—in the latter case he saw fit to resign—spoke up in this House, when they thought questions of British honor were involved, and that the signatories of various treaties were being treated in rather an off-hand manner. In view of that I am certain that however much we may hope for out of the conference at San Francisco, however much faith we place in the machinery envisaged at Dumbarton Oaks, none of these will be any good unless there is a certain sanctity in treaties, and unless people honor their word. I hope that I am wrong in my interpretation of events, but I am certain the House will not think any the worse of those of us who feel that way for expressing our views, and I am quite certain my right hon. Friend the Prime Minister will understand the motives for which we have spoken here today.

MR. GALLACHER (Com.): I am quite certain that there were those in this House and in the country who hoped that when the Crimea Conference took place there would be a breakdown. It was a breakdown on which Hitler, Himmler and Goebbels placed their hopes. Their desire was to see what this Amendment proposes—disagreement between the representatives of the three Great Powers. The Members who have put forward this Amendment fail to understand the significance of the unity expressed at that Crimea meeting—a unity that presents a great hope, not only for the people of this country, but for the people of Europe and the world. We have not only the closer unity expressed in the Crimea Agreement; we have tasks set before us in the White Paper that are completely ignored by the supporters of the Amendment. We have the tremendous task set before us of building up a world organization to maintain peace and—of the greatest significance—"to remove the political, economic and social causes of war." Never from any international conference in the history of the world has there come such a document, with the expression of such sentiments and such tasks. I regret all the more, therefore, that the Deputy Leader of the Labour Party did not utilize this opportunity to give an inspiring call to the people of this country for the carrying out of these tasks.

MR. PICKTHORN: Let the Hon. Member try.

MR. GALLACHER: In the first place, I will deal with the promoters of the Amendment. I agree with much of what was said by the hon. and gallant Member for Stafford (Captain Thorneycroft), but I did not agree with him when he accepted the sincerity of the promoters of the Amendment. There never was such a hollow sham.

MAJOR PETO (C.): Why, may I ask?

MR. GALLACHER: I am going to tell the hon. and gallant Member. I have never listened to so many references to "the fundamental principles of honor, freedom and independence" as were made by the Mover and Seconder of the Amendment. Arising out of the Crimea Conference and the White Paper, and the tasks that are set before us, the test for this country is not the relations between Soviet Russia and Poland. The test for this country, and for those who speak here, and who used such grandiloquent language, is the relations between this country and India, and when I hear anyone of these Members, in a Debate on India, talk about the fundamental principles of honor, freedom and independence—

MAJOR PETO: On a point of Order. Is it in Order to debate the question of India on this occasion?

MR. DEPUTY-SPEAKER (MAJOR MILNER): I understood the hon. Member to be giving an illustration, but the subject should not be developed.

MR. GALLACHER: I am giving an illustration to make my point that there is nothing genuine in all these protestations about freedom and independence.

I will give another instance. I am not a new convert to the demand for independence and freedom for Poland. Thirty-five years ago I was speaking in this country, at great mass demonstrations, in support of the demand for freedom and independence for Poland.

Where were the hon. Members then? [*Interruption.*] It may be that I am going too far back. All right. Ten years ago I was speaking at mass meetings, supporting the demand for free elections in Poland. Was any of those hon. Members supporting it? Had one of these new converts to the idea of a free and independent Poland a word to say about democratic elections or freedom in Poland, or the right of every party to take part in elections and use the radio before the war? I would not hesitate to join with what has been said in tribute to the Polish soldiers and to the Polish people—a great people, a people with a history of terrible hardship and suffering, who have endured it all, and who deserve, if ever any people deserved, to have freedom and independence. But while I pay that tribute to the Polish soldiers and the Polish people, neither I nor anyone else can pay tribute to the wisdom of the Polish gentry; and it is the Polish gentry who are represented by the other side. What determines the attitude of these Members? Not love for Poland, but hatred for the Soviet Union. These Members have never at any time before been apostles of democracy or freedom. Where were they when the Spanish war was waged?

General Anders issued a statement that "This is the hour of Polish tragedy." He is wrong; it is the hour of Polish rebirth. Out of the fury and fires of devastating war a New Poland is being born. If there is a tragedy it is a personal tragedy for General Anders, not a Polish tragedy—although "tragedy" is too dignified a word to use for General Anders. Everyone understands that the actual operating force for the liberation of Poland was, and could only be, the Red Army. Not that Russia did the job by herself; the British and American Armies, fighting on the various fronts, contributed to this great task. But the actual operation of fighting on the Eastern Front and liberating Poland could be done by no other power than the Red Army. General Anders left Russia, with a great Polish Army, because of his hatred of the Soviet Union. He refused to march with the Red Army for the liberation of his own country. Is that not the truth? Did he not withdraw his army from Russia?

CAPTAIN ALAN GRAHAM: The withdrawal of the Polish Army was concerted between Marshal Stalin and General Sikorski. It was agreed to by the Russian Government, because it was agreed that the Poles could fight better elsewhere, as the Russian Government could not clothe and equip them.

MR. GALLACHER: The Russian Government did clothe and equip them. It was because General Anders would not fight with the Red Army.

MR. IVOR THOMAS (Lab.): Will my hon. Friend allow me—

MR. GALLACHER: No. I can understand Members on the other side of the House associating themselves with the Polish gentry against the Polish people, but I do not appreciate it on this side. General Anders took the Polish Army out of Russia. If General Anders, instead of being a reactionary obscurantist had been a man of vision, he would have marched at the head of the Polish Army into liberated Warsaw. He was incapable of that heroic task. That is what is behind this Amendment! That is what is behind all the trouble—hatred of the Soviet Union.

It is said that this country went to war to guarantee the frontiers of Poland. Nobody would ever suggest that we should retain the frontiers of Poland. I have said that here before, and I have asked Members opposite to deal with the point. Keep the frontiers of Poland where they are, and it is impossible for Poland to be free and independent. Before she can be free and independent, she must have a free outlet to the sea; otherwise, she is hemmed in and encircled. The Polish Corridor was no solution. Would any supporter of the Amendment suggest that the frontiers should be retained as they were? The most sensible solution to the question of Polish freedom and independence was made by the Soviet Union. They would do away with the partition in the Ukraine and White Russia. If the Eire Army had come to the assistance of this country, and in the process had wiped out partition in Northern Ireland, would hon. Members suggest that they would have to go back behind the partition line again, before this country would have anything to do with them? The partition from the Ukraine and White Russia has been wiped out, and we do not want them restored, we don't want any more partition. The Soviet Army has wiped out the partition, and the Soviet Government have put forward the proposal that Poland to be free and independent must have an open seaboard and an open outlet to other countries. That is the position we have to face.

We have to face not only the question of Poland, but that of the bigger task that was accomplished at the Crimea Conference and that is presented in this document. If we are to have not only a free and independent Poland, but free and independent countries throughout the world, it is essential that the Yalta Agreement, as presented here in the White Paper, be accepted, understood and applied. There must be world organization "to remove the political, economic and social causes of war." Often references have been made to the phrase used by Litvinov, that "peace is indivisible." Just as peace is indivisible, so war cannot be isolated. I say to Members of this House, those who are supporting the Government and those who are supporting the Amendment, that this must be understood. The causes responsible for the class war are the causes responsible for general war. As peace is indivisible, so war cannot be isolated. If we are to end war, it must be completely ended. It can be ended completely only "by removing the political, economic, and social causes" that produce it. For that there is needed a great inspiring call to the people of this country. The nation must be united behind these decisions and the implementing of these decisions. It is a great responsibility, but a great opportunity to the Labor movement in this country, to gather together all the great progressive forces, to ensure that Yalta and the Agreement arising out of Yalta open up a new road to peace and progress for the people of this country and the people of the world.

MR. MANNINGHAM-BULLER (C.): This is the first occasion on which I have intervened in a Debate on foreign affairs, and I do so with some degree of nervousness. One of the reasons is that it was my misfortune not to have been able to be present yesterday, but I have remedied that to the best of my ability, by reading through the whole of yesterday's HANSARD. I have also been influenced by the fact that my views on this matter differ from those of many of my hon. Friends, whose sincerity I would be the last to question, and whose judgment I completely respect. I confidently believe that, although our views may differ, our objects are entirely the same. I am with them in their admiration of the Polish forces, of the way they have fought for the last five years. I am with them in their sympathy with the Polish people through all they have suffered during that time, and like them I wish to see "a free and independent" Poland, a Poland in which "all men of all lands may live in freedom from fear,' in which the "rights of all people to choose the form of government under which they wish to live," are respected. Wherein lies the difference between me and my hon. Friends who moved the Amendment? Having listened to them I think it lies in this: that they regard the Yalta Agreement as putting an end to those hopes for that sort of Poland. I take the contrary view. I believe that the Yalta Agreement is a real step forward towards the attainment of that end. The future will prove which of us is right, and I would not express these views without having thought them over as carefully as I can.

When one looked through HANSARD of yesterday one found no criticism at all of the Declaration in the White Paper on Liberated Europe. That Declaration was agreed to by the three signatories. I do not propose to take up the time of the House reading out, in full, paragraph 5 but it begins:

> "To foster conditions under which the liberated peoples may exercise their rights."

Those signatories are bound to those obligations. The part about Poland must, in my view, be read in the light of that Declaration; the whole document must be construed together. I do, however, regret as a lawyer—because as a lawyer I do not like anything that is unconstitutional—that the Polish Government in London were not a party to the Agreement. Who could doubt the width of the gulf between that Government and the Government of Russia? Is that position to be allowed to go on? What hope of a new Poland is there if it goes on, with Russia and a puppet Government exercising authority over a Poland behind the Russian lines, and the Polish Government in London only exercising authority over those outside Poland? What hope is there in that? What hope is there that at the Peace Conference you will be able to secure something better for Poland than has been obtained now? I, personally, doubt if that hope is very great. I do not think it is worth while taking a chance of getting more in the Peace Treaty than has been obtained now, bearing in mind that, during the intervening period liberated Poland would be governed by the Lublin Committee. It is now but if the Yalta Agreement is carried out the Lublin Committee will merge into the background.

What about this new Provisional Government? Hard words have been said about it. It has been referred to as a prefabricated government, and terms of that sort have been applied to it. What is clear from this document, if any importance is to be attached to it at all, is that the Provisional Government is to include democratic leaders from the Poles abroad. We know who these Poles abroad are. If the Provisional Government is to satisfy the terms of the White Paper, it follows that it must contain a number of people whom we know to be democratic leaders of Poland. If that Agreement is to be implemented, that, it seems to me that must follow. This Government will contain these leaders; it is to act as a Government pledged to free and unfettered elections. If any bar is put in the way of free and unfettered elections, surely the democratic leaders among the Poles now abroad will let us know. Why should we assume the contrary, that there will be no free and unfettered elections? One criticism of the Provisional Government is that it is based upon the Lublin Committee. I, personally, do not like the Lublin Committee at all, but it seems to me that there is something to be said in favor of having the new Government or the organization which is now seeking to exercise some sort of authority. When the full organization is set up, the Lublin Committee should disappear in the background; I hope it will.

With regard to the territorial changes I want to say one word. If we are to have a Polish Government over the Poles, and the Russians in Germany surely we must have some boundary drawn between the Poles and the Russians. If there is to be an independent Polish Government, there must be a frontier—I cannot and I do not feel that I am competent to express an opinion on where it should be—but it seems to me to follow, quite clearly, that there must be agreement on a frontier now.

If the Yalta Agreement is carried out in the letter and in the spirit, can it possibly be said that the Poles will have any real cause for complaint? On the other hand, are not my hon. Firends rather jumping to conclusions? Is not their Amendment really based upon the assumption that the Yalta Agreement will not be carried out? As I said before the answer to that question lies in the future, but I myself am not prepared to say that the signature of Marshal Stalin is not worth the paper it is written on. I see no satisfactory evidence to justify that conclusion.

One thing that does astonish me is the number of reports that we receive in this country which are accepted, apparently, without any reservations. I am surprised both by the contents of these reports, and also by the speed with which they appear in this country. I was in Moscow on 2nd February and I was told then of the news of the capture of Lodz, and of the fact that the machinery in the factories in Lodz were undamaged by the Germans when they retreated. I have seen what the Germans did at Stalino, and I know what such destruction means. I was back at this country on the 15th February, but the news had already got here, not only of the machinery being recaptured intact, but, apparently, that it was already being taken away by the Russians. It may be true; I do not know, but I am surprised at the swiftness with which this news travels. The reports are all contradictory. I agree that not much importance can be attached to any report of diplomatic or other correspondents which appears in "The Times." On 23rd February I read this in "The Times" from their Moscow correspondent:

> "I witnessed on more than one occasion the enthusiastic welcome accorded the Red Army in Eastern Poland, and this, from all accounts, was but a shadow of that received in the Western regions."

Frankly, I do not know whether that is true or false. The gentleman said he witnessed it himself, but it may be that it is as inaccurate as reports from Greece. Again, I do not know, but I do suggest that we ought to treat all these contradictory reports with a great deal of reserve. I am sorry that we have not got true information from that area of Poland, and I think that Russia has herself to blame for some of the things that have been said about her hard treatment of Poland. I should like to see observers sent to that country, admitted and allowed by the Russians to travel wherever they like, and not merely conducted tours by foreign correspondents from Moscow. Then we should know whether the fears expressed in some quarters are justified, and, if they are not justified, no harm could flow from the visits of such observers.

I hope that will be possible soon, and, indeed, once there is a Provisional Government exercising authority over that area, I do not see why they could not admit such observers to see that the elections are, in fact, free and unfettered.

To conclude, I see no reliable evidence which would justify me in treating the Agreement as of no value whatever. I see nothing to justify treating the signatures to is as valueless. There has been a long history of hostility between Russians and Poles. We must not ignore the fact that there may be some Poles in this country whose hatred of Russia is such that they are prepared to go to any steps in opposition to Russia. I would like to say this: I talked to people of all classes, university students, factory workers, factory directors, soldiers, sailors and others, and I was impressed, wherever I travelled, by the real desire for friendship for this country, by the real desire to have the good regard of this country. It is for those reasons that I believe this Agreement will be honored. I am not prepared to pass sentence in advance in respect of a crime which has not been committed and which I trust never will be committed. I am prepare, rather, to believe that those who desire our friendship and our regard, and who must realize that, if this Agreement is not implemented in the spirit and in the letter, they will forfeit not only our friendship but our respect, will carry out this Agreement in the way which we desire.

MR. HAROLD NICOLSON (N. Lab.): I agree with all that my hon. Friend has just said, and especially when he disagreed with the hon. Member for West Fife (Mr. Gallacher), who attributed false motives to the Mover and Seconder of this Amendment. I am very glad indeed that the Amendment appears on the Order Paper. It does express a very general regret, felt, I think, in every part of this House, that the circumstances of war and the tremendous alterations that have taken place in the proportions of power have rendered it absolutely impossible that Poland should be restored to the exact geographical and political position which she enjoyed in 1938. That regret is very wide and very deep. I am glad also that the Amendment has led to a Debate which has been characterized by two of the best speeches I have ever heard in this House—those by the Mover of the Amendment and by the hon. and gallant Member for Stafford (Captain Thorneycroft) who opposed it. I am glad also because it has given an opportunity for hon. Members in all parts of the House not merely to express their sympathy with and admiration for the Polish Army, but also to indicate the shock to British opinion of all classes and complexions who know of the deportations and actual ill-treatment meted out to Poles by the Russian authorities. The Mover of the Amendment raised again this question of the permanence of international agreements, and thereby made it quite clear to the Soviet Government that those concessions which my right hon. Friend made in the Crimea were not such easy concessions to make, and, in making them they were really paying a considerable price, in terms of feeling in this country, in return for showing how anxious, in every way, we were to establish and maintain close relations with the Soviet Union.

But I would not, for one minute, vote for such an Amendment. As the hon. Member for Penryn and Falmouth (Mr. Petherick) was honest enough to say, it is, in fact, a criticism of what has been done at Yalta, and I regard what has been done at Yalta as without question, the most important political agreement that we have gained in this war. Far from little having been achieved, it is amazing that so much was done. Let us consider what alternatives there were. I have heard the argument "What else could the Prime Minister have done?" That is an absurd argument: the Prime Minister is not the man to follow the line of least resistance. On the contrary, he has throughout his life sought out the pricks, and kicked them hard. The Foreign Secretary, too, is a man who, I think often disguises under his charming manner the fact that he is a "tough." He is moreover not a man who is deficient in diplomatic ingenuity. There are three main policies that might have been followed. One was to oppose the Russian conception of the Polish settlement, and to oppose it by force. That was what Lord Castlereagh and Talleyrand did in 1814, by making a secret agreement to declare war. That secret treaty was never called into operation, but imagine what, in fact, would have happened if it had been effected. We should never have had the Battle of Waterloo; Napoleon would have been re-established upon his throne, and England and Europe would have been denied the 100 years of prosperity and repose which the Congress of Vienna gave them. I do not think any sane man could say that we could have defended the Polish Treaty and position by force.

The other line which might have been adopted and one which I regret to see reflected in the Amendment before the House, is the Pontius Pilate line; to send for water to wash our hands; and then to say, "Holier than thou, I will have nothing to do with you." That would be, in truth, unworthy of a great country which in this war has increased its prestige and repute and risen to heights which were never equalled even in the Napoleonic war. To say "I do not like this but I cannot do anything about it"—and that is what is implicit in the Amendment—would be just as disgraceful as if we had said to Russia, "Do what you like to Poland. I disapprove, but I am not going to do anything about it." If that had been done I would not dare to look a Pole in the face again. That would have been contrary to all our tradition. Then there is the third line, namely, an attempt to save something by negotiation. That means giving something up, which means admitting things which, in some ways, are unjust. I agree with the hon. and gallant Member for Stafford that it is unjust. We have to give up something, but the point is did we give up too much.

I was myself a pessimist in considering the future of Poland. I realized that Russia, outraged as she was by the horrible attack made upon her by the Germans—triumphant as she was rendered by her amazing recovery and the onward march of her quite unexpected armies—dazzled as she might have been by the fact that it was she, once again, who had reached the Oder, and conquered the enemy of the world;

might be determined, as I thought she would be, that whatever came out of this war, one thing was certain was that Russia would be restored to her old Tsarist frontiers. It would have been a very natural thing for Russia to take a rapacious view. But no, they have not done so. They have agreed in a very important way to modify the Tsarist frontier. They have agreed at Yalta to make a concession to Poland. I cannot see anyone who has studied at all the continuity of Tsarist and Communist policy, who understands what it means to Russia, to remember the humiliation to which the Bolshevik system was exposed in the early years of its existence—I do not think, unless you realize how sensitive they are on that point, for them to say, "We do not care what the Western nations say, we will come out of the war with the whole map of Europe what it was in 1912, with our frontiers stretching where the Tsarist frontiers stretched." That they have not done that is a matter of immense relief. When I read the Yalta communique I thought, "How could they have brought that off? This is really splendid!"

The Prime Minister has simplified the matter and clarified our minds very much by dividing the problem into its two main compartments of frontiers and liberty. On the frontiers, I do not wish to repeat what people have said so far about the Curzon Line, or what the Prime Minister has said. I was there at the time, and can remember exactly what we were all thinking when the Curzon Line was drawn up. It was used as an Armistice line, but I do not see that that indicates anything very derogatory. It was a scientific line. The point was there came a stage in Paris when we had fixed the Western frontiers of Poland against Germany, Austria and Czechoslovakia, and when we felt we simply must know what the Eastern frontiers were to be. As has been said so often in this Debate—but it is very important—that examination was truly objective. It was a scientific medical analysis. If the slightest element of subjectivity came into it, that element would be entirely against the Russians and entirely in favor of the Poles. But actually it was a solid, scientific examination of the question put to the people who did the job. That question was: "What ought the frontier of Poland to be?" They said, after three weeks very hard study, it ought to be this:—the Curzon Line. I do not want to say one word against Poland at this moment but I must confess that when their arguments were received I felt and we all felt—and you can read it in the history of the Paris Peace Conference—that if Poland should go beyond those frontiers she would be something very foolish indeed.

CAPTAIN GRAHAM: Is the hon. Member speaking of the Curzon Line to the East, or to the West?

MR. NICOLSON: I was coming to that point. We all felt that it was unwise for Poland to go beyond that. We were enraged and indignant when, later on, Poland took Vilna; and I can remember speaking in this House in terms of severe reprobation of the Polish attitude towards Czechoslovakia, when Czechoslovakia lay bleeding on the ground. They got these areas by force; they must lose them by force. As regards the Lwów area, I agree that I would not like to see Lwów taken away from the Poles. I would like to feel that there was some hope that the Soviet Government, realizing the sentimental and cultural value that Lwów has in Polish hearts, would make a concession on that point. I am sure that if they did, everybody in this House would realize that this settlement is really a fair settlement, and that as far as it could be rendered fair it was so.

In conclusion I must say a word about the other aspect of the agreement—the aspect of freedom. What is written in the Yalta communiqué could not be more precise, definite and absolutely compulsory; no written words could better express the obligation to see that the independence, freedom and integrity of Poland of the future are preserved. What we are discussing is therefore a matter of some impertinence; namely whether you can trust Russia. That is really what we are discussing. We are discussing a perfectly imaginary contingency. But is it so imaginary? In the course of this war, Marshal Stalin has made many promises, public and private, to his Allies: and as far as my knowledge goes every one of those has been kept, not only in their letter and according to time-table and program, but in their spirit as well. I believe that the House is entitled to consider—and I beg my hon. Friends behind me to consider this—with what loyalty Marshal Stalin behaved to the Prime Minister in the Greek crisis. In that crisis of three weeks, when there were great dangers was there one word or one whisper from Moscow that would have increased our difficulties? Not one. That is what I call complete loyalty. To say, "Oh, but you cannot trust Marshal Stalin"—when he has demonstrated by his actions ever since the war that he is about the most reliable man in Europe—is to say something which I think is a little pessimistic, to use an understatement.

I say this to hon. Members who cast doubts upon the scheme for a Provisional Government: I do not see what else could have been done. You cannot hold elections without some sort of Government, you cannot hold elections under the London Government or under the Lublin Committee; the obvious thing is to get fusion. It is very painful for everybody concerned, but once you have that fusion, supervised, engineered, and helped on by the Ambassadors' Commission in Moscow, you have the beginnings of a working system whereby you can proceed to elections, and, I hope and pray, release people from internment camps and so on.

What is the test which will convince Members, which would convince myself, that things are really being carried out on the basis of the Yalta Agreement? The test will come much sooner than hon. Members think. It will be the day when I read that Mikołajczyk and Romer had been invited to Moscow. Then I shall know the thing is going through. Once a fusion is made, and the Government of national unity is created then I really think that some of the terrible sufferings and injustices which have been going on will be removed.

MISS RATHBONE (Ind.): Will it be enough if Mikołajczyk

and Romer to go to Moscow if they are not assured a reasonable proportion of the new Government for their powers? Last October they were offered one-fourth and the Communist Party were to have three-fourths.

MR. NICOLSON: I wish the hon. Lady had not referred to last summer, because if it had not been for the haggling last summer there would not have been so much unhappiness and uncertainty. If the Poles are encouraged to go on haggling, as they did last summer and to say, "We must have a few seats more" then we shall again get into a mess. In more direct reply to the hon. Lady's question, I feel that Mikołajczyk and Romer and let us say Sapieha with the help they will certainly get from M. Molotov and the Commission will exercise an immense influence, to put it mildly, on those difficult problems. I look forward to this National United Government being formed, and carrying out elections which will be as good as elections in that part of the world ever are and creating something which, though not perhaps as powerful, not perhaps as completely free to flirt once with one side and once with another (as my right hon. Friend's friend, Colonel Beck used to do), will none the less have a certain continuity of foreign policy, and will still be the center of Polish life, culture, language and history.

I trust that hon. Members will realize that if we vote for this Amendment in any large numbers, or if we abstain in any large numbers, the effect abroad will not be good. I trust also, whatever the voting may be on this Amendment, that tomorrow, when we have a chance of expressing our gratitude—for gratitude is the word—and tremendous admiration for the work accomplished by the Prime Minister and the Foreign Secretary at Yalta, we shall do so by an overwhelming vote.

MR. SHINWELL (Lab.): This has been a day of remarkable speeches from both sides of the House, and all that I can do is to add some observations which explain the general position taken by hon. Members on these benches. Before I do so, however, may I be permitted to express my admiration of the highly commendable speech delivered by the Prime Minister yesterday? There was, in my view, only one blemish—his reference to Greece. It seemed to me that he was chuckling over the discomfiture of his opponents on that issue. Well the Prime Minister is entitled in all the circumstances to some relaxation, both here and when addressing the populace of Athens, but I would remind him, without any special knowledge of the classics, that many public orators addressed public gatherings in the squares of Athens who came to a bad end; they were subsequently liquidated or, in the more elegant language of my right hon. Friend, extirpated. Let that be a warning to him.

Let me make the position of the party on these benches unmistakably clear. We seek as much as any hon. Member on the other side a free and independent Poland, a Poland not at variance with its neighbors but a Poland that has reached an understanding with them within the policy that was adumbrated at the Yalta Conference, and that implies the early restoration of Europe. Moreover, and this is highly important as I see it, it implies the maintenance of unity among the three great Powers. What is more important from the standpoint of the Polish people? Is there to be a dispute, temporary or permanent on the subject of frontiers, or as to whether this or that Government should prevail in Poland, or reaching an understanding with her great and powerful neighbor which, in the long run, can provide that security, military and otherwise, without which a free and independent Poland is impossible.

I want to say to hon. Members opposite who have sponsored this Amendment, that if they seek to maintain this agitation, to pretend to the Poles that by continuing these controversies they can in the long run extract from Soviet Russia greater advantage, they are doing an ill-service to the Poles. I do not want in this Debate to exacerbate feelings, but am bound to say that when I looked at the Order Paper, and studied the names of Members who are sponsoring the Amendment, it was reminiscent of the Chamberlain era, of the Anglo-German Fellowship era, and the Friends of France era, and many other questionable episodes that have occurred in the past. However, I do not want to impute motives to those who are sponsoring the Amendment; I am willing to accept their professions of sincerity; I am willing to believe that they really believe in their cause; but I must say that having regard to their public record—there is nothing secret about it—it appears to me that they are much more concerned about hostility towards Soviet Russia than they are about promoting the best interests of Poland.

There has been a great deal of talk in this Debate about free elections, democratically conducted, in Poland. First of all, I would observe that the date of those elections is very remote; we may be a long way from them. Even if the war ends in the next few months, even if a provisional Government, satisfactory to all concerned, is established in Poland, there is no reason to assume that immediately afterwards there will be free and democratic elections. It depends on the situation. After all, that provisional Government, when it is created, must consider economic and industrial restoration, and that is a formidable task. But let us assume that free elections take place in Poland, and also assume—and this is an assumption which is not ill-founded—that the people of Poland democratically decide to set up a Government of the Left or, if you like, a Communist Government. Are we to understand that the Members who are sponsoring this Amendment are quite willing to support that Government, and lend it their support?

COMMANDER BOWER (C.): Certainly, always provided that elections take place under secret conditions.

MR. SHINWELL: I am much obliged to the hon. and gallant Gentleman for what he has said. Let it be emphasized, and put on record, that provided there is a democratic election in Poland, and it produces a Government of the Left, ready to distribute the land of Poland among the peasants, ready to nationalize industry and finance and the like, hon. Members opposite will accept it, and render every service.

COMMANDER BOWER: Certainly.

MR. SHINWELL: I am delighted to hear the hon. and gallant Gentleman say so, but why was it that in Spain, when a free and democratic election produced a democratic Government, hon. Members opposite were not so willing to give it their support?

MR. PETHERICK (C.): I can give the hon. Gentleman an immediate answer. We were all for non-intervention in Spain, and we are also for non-intervention in Poland. It is right that the people should choose their own Government, without influence from outside.

MR. SHINWELL: I entirely agree with the hon. Gentleman, but it seems to me that while he and others who have spoken in support of the Amendment paid lip service to the right of the Poles to choose their own Government they themselves would prefer to choose that Government.

MR. PETHERICK: Nobody said that.

MR. SHINWELL: They would like to have safeguards.

MR. PETHERICK: Look in HANSARD tomorrow.

MR. SHINWELL: If the hon. Member is in favor of non-intervention, it seems to me that the speech he made today was a contradiction of that principle. He certainly had a great deal to say as to how the affairs of the Polish people ought to be conducted. I am all for non-intervention, but it must be non-intervention on both sides, and certainly non-intervention by the people who have not rendered any service to those concerned. What is the situation as regards Poland and her relations with Russia? Let me ask hon. Members opposite this question: Suppose there had been a victorious Germany and Poland had been crushed—indeed, she was crushed for a time —defeated overwhelmingly and overrun, and her people put on the rack and tortured—[HON. MEMBERS: "Russia was also overrun."] Let us deal with one thing at a time; let us not be in too much of a hurry. Suppose Germany had defeated Poland, and was triumphant, and there had been a Conference at Yalta or elsewhere to determine the fate of Poland, what would have been the situation of that unhappy country and people?

CAPTAIN A. GRAHAM: The Ribbentrop-Molotov partition.

MR. SHINWELL: The less the hon. and gallant Member for Wirral (Captain A. Graham) says about his friend Ribbentrop the better.

CAPTAIN GRAHAM: Will the hon. Gentleman be good enough to explain what he means by that obviously false insinuation? Ribbentrop has never been a friend of mine, and I have never been a member of the Anglo-German Fellowship or anything of that sort.

MR. SHINWELL: If—[HON. MEMBERS: "Withdraw."] If the hon. and gallant Gentleman says that he has never been a friend of Ribbentrop, and has never been associated with the Anglo-German Fellowship, or with the Friends of Franco movement—

CAPTAIN GRAHAM: That is different.

MR. SHINWELL: I will withdraw, Mr. Deputy-Speaker, with the sole exception of "Friends of Franco"—

CAPTAIN GRAHAM: I am grateful for that withdrawal.

MR. SHINWELL: —because that is certainly a big enough stick with which to belabor the hon. and gallant Gentleman. What is the argument that is advanced by hon. Members opposite in support of Poland? What positive alternatives have they presented? There has not been one. If hon. Members come to the House and criticize the Government—as I sometimes do myself—the responsibility lies heavily on their shoulders to put forward constructive proposals, but today there has not been one—

SIR A. SOUTHBY: I do not think the hon. Member was here when I made my speech, or he would have observed the constructive points—at any rate, I hope they were—which I put forward, and which I said I hoped would help to make the elections a reality.

MR. SHINWELL: I will tell the House what the constructive proposals were, because I took note of them. Let me take the hon. and gallant Gentleman the Member for Berwick and Hadington (Captain McEwen), who is the chairman of the Conservative Committee and speaks with authority. This was his constructive proposal, that we should have rejected the Soviet proposals out of hand. Is that a constructive proposal? What would have been its effect? Would it have changed by a single inch the territorial adjustments? Of course not. Would it have led to free elections? Would it have promoted unity among the Allies? No. Would it have represented an advance in the direction of a durable peace? The advice of the noble Lord the Member for Lanark (Lord Dunglass) was that we should set up a new Government, neither Lublin nor London. How do you set up a new Government, and who is to set it up? There was a suggestion from the hon. and gallant Gentleman the Member for Epsom (Sir A. Southby) that there should be an international commission which should appoint the Government. That is intervention with a vengeance.

SIR A. SOUTHBY: The hon. Member misinterprets me. I did not say anything of the sort. I said there should be an international Commission to govern Poland until and during the free elections.

MR. SHINWELL: That is not government at all and, if an international commission is set up what is to happen in the meantime to the London Government? Are they to be disbanded? Are they no longer to rely on the monetary assistance that they receive from His Majesty's Government, or are they to go out of action? If they receive no Government assistance they will go out of action unless hon. Members opposite come to their assistance. We shall wait and see. What about the Lublin Government? Does anyone suggest that it will go out of action simply because an international commission is set up?

MR. KEELING (C.): The hon. Member said he was going to deal with constructive suggestions that have been made. Will he carry out his promise? First of all he has referred to statements which nobody claims were constructive and then he misquoted the constructive suggestions.

MR. SHINWELL: I listened with great care to the suggestions of the hon. and gallant Gentleman the Member for Epsom. There was nothing constructive about them—nothing that could be carried out in a practical fashion. Now I come to the matters raised by the Noble Lord the Member for Lanark, who was supported by many others. What arguments did he adduce? Away with expediency. You must settle these matters on the basis of principle and justice. Is that customary? Was there any question of principle or justice in the Spanish affair? Indeed, is there even any justice in international affairs? We have to be realists and accept practical proposals which are related to the situation that exists at the time. We cannot expect more than that. Therefore, when we speak about principles and justice I beg hon. Members not to be talking *in vacuo*. If they are seeking to render a service to their Polish friends let them apply themselves in a practical fashion to a solution of the problem.

I want to deal also with the question of the Lublin Government. The hon. and gallant Gentleman said it was no Government at all. Anyway it was a Government that was unsatisfactory, and he made all sorts of allegations about it. One thing can be said about the Lublin Committee. It has made a real attempt to distribute the land within its supervision among the peasants. I can understand Tory landlords objecting to that. It is very natural.

MAJOR LLOYD: Other things can be said about the Lublin Government. It deported thousands and shot many.

MR. SHINWELL: I am not here to defend the Provisional

Government any more than I want to condemn the policy of the Government in London. That is not part of our purpose. We seek a solution of the problem—a very vexatious one—and no solution can be brought about by condemning Lublin or London. Surely the proper course is to try to bring both parties together to form this truly Provisional Government, under which to fashion a free election, and a democratic and economic Poland, which offers some hope to the people of that country, instead of adopting this mischievous and misguided device of trying to pretend to the Polish Government in London that by keeping up this agitation there is some hope of better terms being achieved.

There is a further and final point, which seems to me crucial. Hon. Members question the good faith of Russia. We on the Benches, while favorably disposed towards Russia and sympathetic to Soviet ideals, are not wedded to the political dispensations of that country. We never have been. We believe in the British method of approach. We believe in the democratic method, and we do not require to accept the political dispensations of Soviet Russia. Therefore I am not defending Soviet Russia. But, if we question the good faith of the Soviet Government, there is no hope of unity in Europe. What is the good of talking about an alliance with Soviet Russia, and then questioning the good faith of Marshal Stalin, Molotov or the Soviet rulers? There is no hope in that direction. Surely, it is much more important from the standpoint of the people concerned, the Poles, and indeed from our standpoint, because our future in Europe is closely bound up with the future of Soviet Russia and indeed with the economic policy of Soviet Russia, that we should accept the good faith of Marshal Stalin. Test his word, try it out and then, if we discover on some future occasion that we have been let down, let us complain of it, but do not let us complain in advance. Surely that would be a very great blunder, and it would render no service to the people who have now come under the wing of hon. Members who have sponsored this Amendment.

I think this has been a useful Debate. I am glad the

Amendment was put down, but I shall be equally glad to see it overwhelmingly defeated. It is of the highest importance that it should be, because unless it is overwhelmingly defeated what sort of message do we convey to the Conference that is to take place at San Francisco? What is the good of going into that Conference unless we are prepared to take something along with us—the good word of Marshal Stalin, the assurance of President Roosevelt and the assurance of His Majesty's Government to protect as far as practicable the people of Poland, to render what assistance we can? Unless we are ready to project into San Francisco those assurances of good faith, what is the use of going on with it? It would be better to abandon the Conference and all hope of international cooperation.

There is one last word I want to say, and I hope it will be a word of realism. There is a great deal of talk about international cooperation. We on this side are all for international cooperation; it has been our ideal for many long years. I am bound to say, however, that there is very little hope of promoting international cooperation, as we understand it, unless we can get unity among the three great Allies. That is the prerequisite of international cooperation. If there is a cleavage, any kind of fissure or generation of suspicion among the three great Allies, what is the use of pretending to the small nations that we can offer them protection and safeguards in the future? I have frequently opposed the Government, and may do so again, but I want to say that the declarations of Yalta are a magnificent advance on anything that has gone before. I believe they have taken the first definite step towards an enduring peace. We ought not, at this early stage, to shatter the hopes of the peoples of the world. We should endeavor to make the best of this Agreement with the necessary safeguards and, in due course, seek to mold it nearer to our heart's desire. I hope that we shall support the Government on this occasion, and defeat the Amendment.

MR. RAIKES (C.): Unlike some hon. Members I propose to impute no dishonest motives to anybody, but I would remind the hon. Member that those who impute dishonest motives to their political opponents seldom have clean hands. It is not easy to make the final speech in support of the Amendment, and if I am anxious about it, it is not because I am alarmed that the Prime Minister or the Foreign Secretary will dispose of this case; I am nervous lest I do not do full justice to something in which I deeply believe. Having said that, I must return to the first thing which has emerged from this Debate. The Prime Minister, when he called for a Vote of Confidence, made it abundantly plain that he wanted the Vote to show to the world that this House was behind him not simply in what he had done, but in the justice of what he had done. Since then several speeches have been made. The most eloquent speech made on the Government side today was made by the hon. and gallant Member for Stafford (Captain Thorneycroft.) He did not base it on justice; with great honesty he said he thought it was an unjust settlement. The hon. Member for West Leicester (Mr. Nicolson), in rather gentler language, agreed with him. One thing is certain—however great the Vote may be today, it will not be able to go out that all who voted for the Motion voted for it because they believe that the Motion was just. Well may the Prime Minister say, like Canning, "Save, oh save me, from my candid friends."

The real issue on this Amendment is far wider than Poland. It is the issue of the good name of Britain among the nations of the world. Are we, in the attitude we are adopting at the present time, encouraging, as the result of the Yalta Agreement, the nations of Europe to say, as they have often said in the past, that Britain is the friend and hope of the weak? That is the touchstone and test, and on that touchstone I propose to speak. The territorial issue of Poland and the independence of Poland are both matters which are interwoven with British honor. Much has been said upon the territorial boundaries, and I do not propose to deal with the question at any length. The Prime Minister, with a great flourish, assured the House yesterday that, after all, Poland would have been utterly destroyed if it had not been for Russia. I think his tone has been rather that of a man who regards Poland as a defeated country which has to get the best it can after defeat. Did the Prime Minister and the Foreign Secretary, after a Polish guarantee had been given and when in August, 1939, the Ribbentrop-Molotov Agreement had been made, turn to Poland and say "We are sorry, but in view of the fact that Germany and Russia have come together, total destruction is all you can hope for if you stand up to Germany, whatever the democracies may do"? We know quite well that that was not the line and that that was not in their hearts at the time. It was in the heard and mind of every ordinary citizen in 1939–40 that, though Poland might fall, Poland would rise again, and we believed it long before Russia ever came into the picture. It is a rather unjust argument to hurl at Poland now, after the days of 1939, that she would have been completely destroyed by the Germans and that, therefore, she ought to be grateful for what she can get today.

I come to the next point where I am rather shaken over Yalta. Whatever may have been the advantage or disadvantage of the territorial settlement, it seems astounding that, having as we had a legitimate Polish Government, in London, precisely recognized by the Foreign Secretary in a speech in December last year, that Government should not have had even one word of consultation, whether its advice were taken or not. I think I am right in saying that after the fall of Mr. Mikołajczyk, whose fall was deplored by the Prime Minister —he made that very plain in December—neither Mr. Arciszewski, the Prime Minister, nor the Foreign Secretary of the new Government have been permitted one word with either the Prime Minister or the Foreign Secretary of England. It seems to me that their treatment was a little ungenerous. It is a little hard that the legitimate Government should, as it were, have been put in cold storage while Yalta settled the fate of the Poles. I do not want to labor that point, but I thought it ought to be made.

So far as frontiers are concerned, say what you will, the Atlantic Charter was finally repudiated at Yalta. It started as a principle; it afterwards became a guide; tomorrow it will leave off becoming a guide and will become what Mr. Ramsay MacDonald would have called a "gesture." We shall want something more than a gesture if a new Europe and a new world are to be built on the basis of civilization and justice. The Prime Minister said that the Curzon Line was a just line. The hon. Member for West Leicester said it was a just line. Apparently, however, they were dealing with two different lines. The line at Yalta was a line West of Lwów, and the line which the hon. Member for West Leicester was referring to was, apparently, a line which included Lwów. When the Prime Minister said that it was the old Curzon Line over again, as he did yesterday, I think he might at any rate have reminded the House that Eastern Galicia now goes to Russia, a province that has never been Russian at any time and was never contemplated in 1919, 1920 or 1921 as likely to become Russian.

The greatest danger in this new territorial settlement is —not that the old basis was of necessity a perfect settlement, as I think the Polish line did go too far to the East—that the line should have been settled in flat contradiction to treaties which have been made. The Treaty of Riga, in 1921, was reaffirmed in 1932 and I think in 1934, and of course was again reaffirmed in the Sikorski-Stalin agreement, after Russia had come into the war. I hope the Prime Minister will forgive me if I try to deal with the points in his speech seriatim. I am going to be bold enough, as I have a right to do, to deal with the speech point by point. He said that after 30 years during which British, Russians, Americans and French had struggled against Germany, all the three great Allies had agreed what Poland should receive. If that is to mean throughout the world that any treaty made in Europe between 1914 and 1944 can come to an end because there has been a war in between, I tremble for the future of Europe and the world.

I do not want to go on farther, in regard to the Curzon Line, except to put one point to the Prime Minister which I have longed to put to him for some time. In speech after speech since Teheran, the Prime Minister has said that he regarded the Curzon Line as necessary for Russian security. He has said it with firmness and vigor, and I am sure that he believes it. What did he say yesterday? He said that the new Poland moving further West would have no great fear of danger from Germany, because drastic steps would be taken to prevent any offensive action by Germany for many years to come. If that is so, what have 180,000,000 Russians to fear from 80,000,000 broken and disunited Germans. As regards Poland, it is therefore quite unnecessary for the Russians, except by friendly negotiation, to extend their land and to seek for "Naboth's vineyard" at the expense of a smaller neighbor.

I now turn to the question of independence. I agree that it is of more importance even than boundaries, unless the boundaries are so shrunk that they hamper independence. I think every one realizes that the most significant thing proposed in regard to the future provisional Government of Poland is that they are to have what appears to be an extension of the present Government of Poland, with no reference to the London Government at all. If that means anything, it surely means that the new Government of Poland will be based upon Lublin. That is the view of Lublin. I venture to quote from the Lublin radio of 15th February. After the Yalta proposals had come through, they welcomed them and said that the fact that the provisional Polish Government of national unity was to be based upon the present provisional Polish Government showed confidence in its present authority in Poland, since the London emigré Government had not even been mentioned. That was the reaction of Lublin. What was the reaction of Moscow? The European service of "Red Star"—and, as we know, what any paper says in Moscow is the view of the Moscow Government more than what any paper says in London is the view of our own Government—said, on 16th February, through its commentator:

"Roosevelt's personal representative stressed the democratic Government of Warsaw as the only Government of Poland, and on its basis the Provisional Polish Government of national unity will be formed, which will be recognized immediately by the Allied Powers."

We may be told by the Foreign Secretary, as I hope we shall be, that he does not propose to base the new Government upon Lublin, but I venture to suggest that there must have been misunderstanding at Yalta, if the Lublin Press and the Soviet Press have come to an erroneous conclusion that the basis of the New Government of Poland is to be Lublin. The Prime Minister went further. He made one astounding statement. He said that the Poles in London should have been wise and taken the advice of the British Government a year ago, in which case there would have been no Lublin. What does that mean? It means, the Prime Minister knows and we all know, that Lublin is a fake and nothing more. Yet that fake, so far as we can read from Yalta—although there may be some safeguards—is supposed by both Lublin and Moscow to be the foundation of the new Government.

Let us consider for a few moments one or two further things in regard to the independence of the Poles. First, what sort of Poland will be able, even under the Ambassadors' Conference, to take part in the new Government? We have not been told, of course, what proportion the Lublin or any other Poles will have. The Foreign Secretary denied, in reply to the hon. Lady the Member for the English Universities (Miss Rathbone), that at Moscow the suggestion was 75 per cent to Lublin and 25 per cent to Mikołajczyk. I wonder whether we can, at last, hear today what proportion was offered either by Lublin or Moscow to Mikołajczyk, and why we have never been told. One thing we know is that the terms offered now will not be better than the terms which were offered at Moscow in August.

Reference has been made to the decree which was pronounced by M. Bierut on 17th January outlawing the Polish Home Army and denouncing not only the Prime Minister of the Polish Government in London and General Bor-Komorowski as criminal adventurers, but dealing in a very rough-handed manner with M. Mikołajczyk. I should have thought that if at Yalta it was desired to get the support and the friendship of Poles both in this country and serving abroad, if there was one way in which that could have been assisted it would have been by the rescinding of that decree. Are we to hear that perhaps it will be rescinded? I am sure the Foreign Secretary wishes it to be. But why has it not been rescinded? That is not all. Not only have these criticisms been passed in the Russian Press, but even since this Conference M. Mikołajczyk himself has been held up to ridicule. I do not want to give too many quotations, but I think I ought to make one or two. There was a dispatch from Lublin on 3rd January this year —this was before Yalta—from Henry Shapiro, a war correspondent. He said that there could be no question of compromise between the two Governments, and that feeling was particularly bitter against ex-Premier Mikołajczyk, to whom the Lublin Poles were so anxious to offer the Premiership only three months ago. He was now considered to be a public enemy in the same class as General Sosnkowski. Premier Morawski said recent documents proving Mikołajczyk to have been responsible for cases of terrorism in liberated areas had been seized by the Lublin Government. Not a very pleasant sort of party to join, even with a safeguard from the British Government to see that you get there. That is not all. At the beginning of this year there was a Soviet communiqué dealing with the so-called Peasants Congress in occupied—Western—Poland. I quote only the final passage:

> "At the end of the session the Congress demanded the expulsion of the leaders of the emigré Government—Arciszewski, Mikołajczyk and others from Polish citizenship as traitors to the Polish nation."

It seems to me that they will be bold men who, until some safeguards are produced, will be prepared to go out to Poland. They will, indeed, unless certain safeguards are proposed and certain decrees are rescinded, be men who could almost be accused of wishful thinking. But this is no matter for jest.

The reason for this Amendment is that certain hon. Members of this House, of whom I am one, believe profoundly that even though Great Britain might not be able at this stage to do much for Poland, we could do something more than underwrite a charter for Poland which, without proper safeguards, must be the end of Poland. The Prime Minister said in his speech that of course all parties will have free elections, except pro-Nazi and anti-democratic parties. I challenge him now: Can he name one pro-Nazi party in Poland? If there is one country which, under suffering and misery, has kept its soul, it is Poland. We know so well that the Russian, and indeed the Lublin, definitions of "democracy" and "pro-Nazi" are rather different from ours. Everybody with whom you disagree in Russia is a pro-Nazi or an anti-democrat. In view of the fact that the new Polish Government, however it is created, will be formed after consultations between two ambassadors and Mr. Molotov at Moscow, and will be formed with the background of this continued abuse of every known Polish leader and every great political party, whether it be the National Party or the Socialist Party, it seems rather unlikely that the old parties, and the supporters of these old parties, who have supported the underground movement, will be recognized as being either anti-Nazi or democratic. We have even had General Bor himself, the hero or Warsaw, described as a capitulating traitor in the pay of Berlin.

I do not think that the Prime Minister, whose greatness I appreciate as much as any man in this House, or any of the other members of the Government, can feel surprised if, under these circumstances, we are inclined to say, "Would it not have been better not to have come to any agreement upon the final Eastern frontiers until the war was over, and the thing could have been settled at the Peace Conference? Would it not have been better, instead of forming a Government which is bound to be formed, as Press cuttings alone show, in an atmosphere of fear and terrorism, to have had some inter-Allied Commission to carry on until the war was over, and the parties themselves could be properly supervised, and given an opportunity of free elections, under Inter-Allied control, on the basis of the Saar plebiscite. The only really fair international plebiscite we have seen for many years?"

That is our case. The last time I opposed the Government on what was made a Vote of Confidence, I followed the Prime Minister himself into the Lobby—in 1935. I did it because I believed he was right. Because I differ from him today I do it, not because I am anti- the Prime Minister—I have stood by him in days when he was far less popular than he is today—but because I believe that for all his greatness, today, insignificant as I am, I speak with the voice of my country.

THE SECRETARY OF STATE FOR FOREIGN AFFAIRS (MR. EDEN): I think those of us who have listened to this discussion have been conscious that we are discussing an issue on which the House feels deeply. Hon. Members, whatever their point of view on the issue, have fully expressed themselves and that is as it should be, for after all there are very few institutions anywhere in the world which could conduct such a discussion as has been conducted here during the last two days.

I am sure that not one of our critics will deny that we have a right, as a Government, to come to the House and ask for their judgment on the work that we did in the Crimea. Let me correct one thing that my hon. Friend said, at the beginning of his speech. He referred to my right hon. Friend's speech, and to the position of the Prime Minister in this matter. I must make it absolutely clear to the House that at every stage of this anxious Polish business, lasting as it has now done over almost the whole of the war period—and indeed starting from long before that—at any rate, so long as this Government have handled it—all the decisions have been taken by the War Cabinet; and the responsibility is the responsibility of the War Cabinet. We have worked together in all we have done, and my right hon. Friends in the War Cabinet want me to say that we have worked, in the Crimea and other occasions, as a united War Cabinet, and, be our treatment of this subject right or wrong, it is the treatment of a united Government, who took all their decisions with a knowledge of the facts put before them.

My hon. Friend also spoke of our relations with the Polish Government, and asked, was it true that I have not had direct contacts with the Polish Prime Minister or members of his Government? It is true that we have not had personal contacts with them, but it is also true that I have frequently seen the Ambassador who represents that Government. I have seen him, naturally, since I returned from the Crimea. Perhaps I ought to add, as a matter of historical accuracy, that I had arranged an interview with the Polish Prime Minister and his Foreign Secretary just before we went to the Crimea, but an incident occurred, which will be fresh in the mind of the House—that we had a sudden and unexpected Greek Debate; and I, therefore, asked my Permanent Under-Secretary, Sir Alexander Cadogan, to see them instead. I think the House will accept it that there has not been any discourtesy on the part of His Majesty's Government. I cannot, however, pretend that we have the same cordial relations with the present Polish Government as we had with the Government which preceded them, and which included, as, unhappily, this Government do not, all the main Polish parties represented in London.

I want to deal with this question, taking two mains issues—first, and the more briefly of the two, the question of the frontiers, and, second, the question of whether under the arrangement which we have devised in the Crimea there can be and will be a free and independent Poland. A word about the frontier itself. My hon. and gallant Friend the Member for Epsom (Sir A. Southby) and others, including the mover of the Amendment, who raised this issue, always begin at the Treaty of Riga; but it is really completely unrealistic to begin this discussion at the Treaty of Riga. I admit that it is true—there is no question of it—that the Soviet Government accepted the Treaty of Riga, but nobody with a knowledge of the history of those parts is going to contend that Russia was content with that solution, or, indeed, that we were content with that solution.* As the House knows, and as I have stated before, we more than once urged the Polish Government at the time not to extend their frontiers East beyond the Curzon Line, and for two years after the Treaty of Riga withheld our recognition of that arrangement. In 1923, when the Conference of Ambassadors did eventually recognize the Treaty, that Conference made it plain, on our initiative, that the responsibility for the Line rested with the two Governments concerned, and not with us.

More than that, the Conference made it clear that in their recognition of the Riga frontier, two years after the Treaty had been signed, there was called for—put it this way—the setting-up of an autonomous regime in Eastern Galicia for ethnographical reasons. In point of fact, that autonomous regime was never set up. What happened was that, after fighting between the Poles and Ukrainians, the Polish armies were victorious and obtained control of the country. I hope the House is not going to assume that, on account of that, what happened at that time was accepted by the population as a whole. It was not. Although the area was placed under the Minority Treaty, because of the disputes and the anxieties about it, the provisions of that Minority Treaty were never fully carried out, and disturbances, as the House will see if they look up the records, were unhappily frequent. What happened was this. It is not in any way surprising or a criticism of anybody. As the Eastern Galicia area—which is the one, I think, in most dispute—was an area of mixed population, with Poles in the minority, the Poles sought to increase their own population in that area by bringing other Poles in, with

* After signing in Riga the peace treaty with Poland on March 18, 1921, the chairman of the Soviet delegation, Adolph Joffe, stated: "We have concluded a peace treaty giving full satisfaction to the vital, legitimate and necessary interests of the Polish nation. . . . The peace negotiations lasted several months and encountered considerable difficulties, especially in the settlement of economic and financial problems . . . " (Quoted from Grabski S. "The Polish-Soviet Frontier", p. 35).

The author of this book participated as the Polish military expert to the Riga Conference and was a member of the frontier commision. He can state that the Polish-Soviet frontier commission worked very well and that the Soviet delegation never raised any objection to the Polish-Soviet frontiers stipulated as in the treaty.

the result that that, in its turn, led to friction. Further, there was the issue which, the House must bear in mind, underlies the whole of this frontier problem: the religious issue between the Roman Catholic elements and the Orthodox Church. The religious difference in that area is far older than the national issue, and it is religion which lies at the root of much of the feeling on this issue.

I have explained before, and I am not going over it again, the basis on which the Curzon Line was delimited, but this at least can be accepted by everybody, whatever else we dispute—that east of the Curzon Line there are no areas where the Poles are in the majority except the two cities of Vilna and Lwów, which, in their turn, are surrounded by large and non-Polish areas. On that particular aspect of the question there is no dispute between us at all. I, therefore, say that when the Soviet Government say that they will accept the Curzon Line, with certain adjustments, minor adjustments, but all in favor of Poland—the importance of which I must emphasize, for the Curzon Line, it is true, is not a frontier but a line drawn on the map, and it is of importance to the Polish Government that all adjustments, and there must be many, shall favor them—I cannot stand at this Box and say that I regard that as a gross injustice to Poland. It is the position which successive Governments in this country have consistently taken. I would put this to my hon. Friends. Are they absolutely convinced that the structure of the Polish State is strengthened by the inclusion of large, or considerable, non-Polish elements in it? I wonder.

MR. A. BEVAN (Lab.): On the west West, too?

MR. EDEN: The assumption in regard to the West is that the populations shall be removed. That is the whole basis. In most cases, I can tell the hon. Gentleman, they have gone already. But let me deal with this matter—I am sorry the hon. Gentleman has put me off my stroke—about the minorities in the Polish State. I should have said that there were two weaknesses in the Polish State, as it existed before the war.

One was these very considerable minority elements, who came frequently and made their complaints before the International Tribunal at Geneva, and the other was the Corridor. I am amazed that in the speeches which the Mover and Seconder of the Amendment made neither of them—I listened carefully—made even the slightest reference to the significance to Poland of the fact that this Corridor problem would cease to exist. If my hon. Friend's concern is solely for Poland, surely they must take some account of that?

May I ask them this? Which Poland would be stronger—the Poland with Vilna and with the Corridor as it was, or a Poland without Vilna and without the Corridor? I have not the slightest doubt, nor, I believe, has any student of international affairs the slightest doubt, which Poland would be the stronger. I am going to say a word or two about this Corridor business. I made one reference to it before, but, if the House will allow me, I am going into it a little deeper, because I had to handle this myself year after year at Geneva, when the unfortunate British representative on the Council was *Rapporteur* for Danzig. I promise the House that I never chose the job; I inherited it, and it was the most thankless task that ever fell to the lot of man, because, at every single meeting, we were faced with these issues, demands, charges and counter-charges between Poles and Germans. I think the only other person who had this experience to the same extent is the present Lord Chancellor. We were never able to obtain a solution of real value, because no solution was possible as long as the Corridor existed.

I remember one occasion—it will probably be fresh in the minds of many hon. Members—when the German representative had behaved in a particularly insulting manner to the Council. After he had withdrawn, I thought it my duty to say to the Council, in private, of course, the Press having withdrawn, that, in view of his behavior, we ought to know whether the Polish Government would take action in the event of a German infraction by violence of the Free City, for which we were responsible. I put that question, and the Polish answer was "Yes." I mention that only to show that it would be a cardinal sin on our part to perpetuate that state of affairs. I have been engaged in these last years in this Polish-Russian dispute, and, for what my own judgment is worth, I have come to the decision that there are two alternatives. Either you must deprive Poland of all outlet to the sea, or East Prussia must cease to be German and the Corridor must go. Of these two alteratives, I unhesitatingly command the second to the House; but do not let anybody say that that is not something of importance for the Poland of the future, and do not let people merely say "You are taking half Poland away" without putting into the balance what this means.

I turn to another aspect. It is not only the question of what the elimination of the Corridor means. The House must also put into the balance the position of Oppeln Silesia, which we are all agreed should go to Poland, and which is a territory of great value industrially. Poland tried hard to get it after the last peace settlement, but her claim was rejected. That must be put into the balance, too. I believe that, when a settlement is finally reached—and here let me say again that what we have expressed is our view of what a settlement should be with our Ally, a settlement which we would wish to discuss with the new Polish Government when it is created—I believe it may still be found—and I say this with respect to some of my hon. Friends—that the new Poland when so constituted, will be as strong as, or stronger than, the Poland that existed in 1939. That depends, of course, on how the agreement is carried out.

Therefore, I turn to that, and to the setting up of the new Government. I was asked by my Noble Friend the Member for Lanark (Lord Dunglas) yesterday, and I have been asked today by both the mover and the seconder of the Amendment, why it was that, when we approached this problem in the Crimea, we did not make an end of the Lublin Government, as it were, "de-recognize" the Lublin Government and "de-recognize" the Government here, and start entirely afresh. Of course, that is an attractive suggestion, and it was, in fact, the point from which we started our examination of the matter, but this is the difficulty with which we were faced. The Russians said to us, and it is inescapable, that they must have some authority on their lines of communication through Poland. Whether we like or dislike the Lublin Committee—and personally I say I dislike it—for the moment it is the authority which is functioning there in fulfilling the requirements of the Russian military authorities. What they said to us was "We do not know how long it will take to form a new Polish Government; it may take weeks, it may take months." I do not know, either; it takes quite a long time to form a British Government. Nobody can say. During that time there could not be a vacuum in Poland, and so it is that we agreed eventually, that pending the creation of the new Government—and I beg the House to note that phrase "new Government" occurs twice in the Declaration—the Soviet Government will continue to recognize the Lublin Government and we and the United States will continue to recognize the Government here. I hope I have been able to remove the doubts expressed by hon. Friends today.

The right hon. Member for Wakefield (Mr. Greenwood) yesterday complained that we had taken our decision, or come to our agreement behind the back, I think his phrase was, of the Polish Government. As I understand his argument, it was that we ought to have summoned the Polish Government to our councils in Yalta when we reached a certain point in our discussions and talked matters over with them. Of course, we thought of it. Let me therefore ask the right hon. Gentleman which Polish Government were we to summon? Were we to summon the Lublin Government, for both we and the United States Government hold that that Government is not fully representative of the Polish people? Or were we to summon the government here in London, which the Soviet Government hold is not representative of the Polish people? Or were we to summon both Governments? Apart from certain physical difficulties, this last arrangement would not have been satisfactory. Moreover in my belief, probably, those Polish statesmen who have most following in Poland—and all this is a matter of one's own conjecture—are Poles in Poland and Poles in London, who are members neither of the Lublin Government nor of the London Government. What did we do? We could not bring them all to Yalta; if we had done, no doubt we should still be there. It was impossible to do that, and so we decided to appoint this Commission to carry through the task for us.

My right hon. Friend said something about this Commission of the Soviet Foreign Secretary and two Ambassadors, and one of the speakers seemed to indicate that he thought that there was a weakness in our position; but let me assure the House that our Ambassador will act under instructions of His Majesty's Government and will not deviate from those instructions. The hon. and gallant Member for Berwick and Haddington (Captain McEwen), said that our Ambassador had said that the Lublin Government should be recognized. I do not know when he said that. He never said anything of that kind to me, to my right hon. Friend the Prime Minister, or to anyone of our colleagues, and, certainly, he knows well enough what is the attitude of His Majesty's Government in that respect.

Let me now try to answer some of the questions that have been put. My hon. and gallant Friend the Member for Berwick and Haddington, and indeed, the hon. Gentleman who has just spoken, really put what was the only alternative course. They said that better than what we have done, would have been to have left it alone. I cannot accept that view. That really is an absolute policy of despair. What would that have meant? It would have meant that the Lublin Government would have continued to operate with the support of the Soviet Government. We do not know what the conditions are there at the present time, and I am not by any means sure all the information that hon. Friends get about the state of opinion in Poland is accurate. I am not even sure that the politicians who have been five years out of the country know exactly what their country feels. There have been revolutions in thought as well as in spirit in Poland in these last years. There was an account the other day—one has to be very careful from which newspapers one quotes—in the "Manchester Guardian"—whose foreign correspondents I have always found very reliable, so far—which gave an account of some American officers who came out from Poland. They said they saw the first Russian forces drive on, the Poles, delirious with delight, cheering both the Russians and their Western Allies. I do not know whether it is true or whether it is not. I should think that very likely it was so. Maybe it was only so at the beginning and it may be so now, but one cannot tell, as one cannot be sure. But I beg of hon. Members not to accept every report that comes and is suddenly thrust upon us in the House of Commons by our friends.

MR. PETHERICK: Would not a perfectly simple solution be for the Russian Government to accept British war correspondents and British correspondents to look after the interests of civil affairs in Poland?

MR. EDEN: That is going a little ahead of what I was going to say. I would like first to answer two questions asked by my Noble Friend yesterday about our desires in connection with this Polish situation. He asked for two specific answers to his questions. First, Is it our desire that Poland should be really and truly free? Yes, certainly, most certainly it is. In examining that Government, if and when it is brought together, it will be for us and our Allies to decide whether that Government is really and truly, as far as we can judge, representative of the Polish people. Our recognition must depend upon that. We would not recognize a Government which we did not think representative. The addition of one or two Ministers would not meet our views. It must be, or as far as it can be made, representative of the Polish parties as they are known, and include representative national Polish figures. That is what we mean. There is only one consideration—I do not think we could call it more than that—that we would ask of the new Polish Government; that is that they would enter into a treaty of friendship and alliance with Russia. I do not think that anybody would think that unreasonable because at the same time that Government would have treaties of friendship and alliance with us and the French Government.

The second question was, Do we favor the establishment of machinery for Allied supervision of elections? That was a question which was also discussed. The Greek Government have asked for such supervision and we have invited, or shall invite when the time comes, our Russian and American Allies to join in it. It may be, if and when this new Polish Government is formed, they will also ask for international supervision. I hope so. If they do then we shall certainly be prepared to join in it. We could not agree to any inter-Allied supervision to which we were not parties in view of our treaty relations with Poland. I think the House will agree that the final decision on that cannot be taken until the moment comes, if and when this new Polish Government is formed, because that new Government must have a say as to their supervision and, if they desire it, as to its nature and the conditions. But I will make plain our own position, as it is made plain to our Allies, that, if there should be such supervision, we shall be glad to take part in it ourselves. There is one more question which my Noble Friend asked. He said that, in the arrangement for Yugoslavia, we included a provision that the acts of the Yugoslav Committee should be ratified by the new Parliament, and he asked why we did not include a similar provision in the Polish Agreement. But to be honest with my hon. Friend, we did not think of it. We did not think we had got to a stage far enough for that to be operative but I see no reason whatever why that proposal should not be made. In view of the fact that it was once accepted by our Allies in relation to Yugoslavia, I have no reason to think that it will not be accepted in relation to Poland, and I think it is a good thing that that proposal should be put forward. It would be an additional safeguard.

Let me turn to the question of information from inside

Poland. We should certainly like people from this country to have an opportunity of seeing for themselves conditions inside Poland. There have been newspaper correspondents, but apart from them, we would like other opportunities, and I have every reason to believe that our Russian Allies would certainly not object to it. Indeed I am inclined to think from something I have had today that they would probably welcome it, but I would rather not go further at the moment than to say that we are in correspondence with our Russian Allies about making arrangements so that people from this country can go to Poland to see what is going on. We shall do all we can to bring these arrangements to early fruition. I feel that nothing would give more reassurance to this House than a sense that there would be an opportunity to see what was going on in Poland.

I come on to the other questions. My hon. and gallant Friend the Member for Berwick and Haddington* said, "Why when you are signing the Anglo-Soviet Treaty do not you consider this Polish matter and did not you put special provisions into your agreement about it?" There was a similar question asked in another form by my hon. and gallant Friend the Member for Epsom (Sir A. Southby). The answer is that at the time the Anglo-Soviet Treaty was made fortunately Soviet Russia and the Polish Government here were in relations. It was one of the few comparatively calm and encouraging periods of Soviet-Polish relations, and they were in relation very largely as the outcome of the efforts of His Majesty's Government to bring about the agreement of 1941. Of course, the Soviet Government are aware of our engagement towards Poland on which I propose to say a word. I must repeat and make plain—I am not sure that it is plain to some hon. Members—exactly the position about recognition. I hold the House out no pledge. No one can be certain how it is going to work out but we hope that the discussions in Moscow will be attended by representative Poles from inside Poland and from outside Poland and that as a result of

* Captain McEwen.

those conversations a thoroughly representative Polish Government will come into being. If it does and if it is in the words of the communique, "properly constituted" then we and our Allies will recognize that government as the provisional government of Poland—provisional until the elections take place. If it does not come into being then we remain as we are today, we and the United States recognizing the Government in London and the Soviet Government recognizing I presume the Government in Lublin. That, may I add, would not be a very happy state of affairs either for Poland or for unity between our Allies.

Now may I say a word or two about the Amendment which we are now discussing? The Amendment suggests that the recommendations which the three Great Powers have made for the solution of the Polish problem are contrary to treaty. That is not so. We have at no time guaranteed Poland's pre-war frontier. Nor, let me add, can I accept that to agree to recommend the line which was worked out at the time as giving as near as might be an ethnographical boundary is to run directly counter to the terms of the Atlantic Charter. As to the last part of my hon. Friend's Amendment, I must say that I am frankly puzzled as to how that can be regarded as a criticism of the policy which we are now advocating. If my hon. Friends will read the wording, it seems to me to be a precise description of what we are seeking to do in Poland. We are seeking to ensure to Poland the full right to choose her own government free from the influence of any other power, or any other powers let me add. So that in that respect I do not understand where we are open to criticism. As I have said, whether we shall succeed or not I cannot pronounce upon now, but I have not the least doubt, and I hope the House has not the least doubt, that it is not only our right but our duty to make this attempt.

I come to a criticism made by my hon. Friend the Member for Penryn and Falmouth (Mr. Petherick) who maintained that in the course which we have jointly agreed, we have in some way violated the Anglo-Polish Agreement of

1939, and he referred to a secret Protocol in this connection. I can assure my hon. Friend that his fears are entirely unfounded. There is nothing in the Anglo-Polish Treaty, or in any other document, which guarantees the frontiers of Poland. The Government of 1939 gave the House, of course, full information about the Treaty but, quite rightly, they went further than this and made clear the effect of the secret Protocol from which my hon. Friend quoted. I must read to the House the reply given by my right hon. Friend the present Minister of Education who was then Under-Secretary for Foreign Affairs.

MR. BELLENGER (Lab.) : Has the Protocol been published?

MR. EDEN: No, Sir.

MR. BELLENGER: Will the right hon. Gentleman do that?

MR. EDEN: I will now have to consider that.* Naturally I had it in my mind as my hon. Friend has raised the question—I do not make any complaint about that. I am now going to read the answer which was given to Parliament at the time. I was not a Member of the Government myself. This is what he said in reply to a Parliamentary Question on the 19th October, 1939, asking whether the references to aggression by a European Power in the Anglo-Polish Agreement were intended to cover the case of aggression by Powers other than Germany including Russia, and my right hon. Friend replied:

> "No, Sir. During the negotiations which led up to the signature of the agreement, it was understood between the Polish Government and His Majesty's Government that the agreement should only cover the case of aggression by Germany, and the Polish Government confirm that this is so."—[OFFICIAL REPORT, 19th October, 1945, Vol. 352, c. 1082.]**

That is the exact position of the Agreement. There was no question whatever of any engagement having been made about the Eastern frontiers at that time or at any other time.

* The secret protocol was published April 5, 1945.
** Vol. I, p. 349.

MR. PETHERICK: May I interrupt the right hon. Gentleman? He is referring only to the main Treaty of mutual assistance. I asked about a Protocol of which I read out an extract and it was perfectly plain. I will do it again if he likes. Clause 3 of the secret Protocol says:

> "The undertakings mentioned in Article 6 of the agreement, should they be entered into by one of the contracting parties with a third State"—

shall we say Russia or some other State?—

> "would of necessity be so framed that their execution should at no time prejudice either the sovereignty or territorial inviolability of the other contracting parties."

MR. EDEN: I do not know that my hon. Friend has got the complete document. In fact I do not know what he has got. I must frankly say, if he has got the complete document, he will see that that refers to an earlier Article, and the earlier Article makes it quite plain——[An HON. MEMBER: "What are these?"] My hon. Friend did not tell me he was going to read out from a secret document but, naturally, as he did so, I have looked it up, and I have seen exactly what the position is. I can assure my hon. Friend, and my right hon. Friend the Minister of Education will confirm it, that the answer I have just given was precisely intended to cover that secret Protocol. I can assure him there is no catch about the matter at all and that what that Clause refers to, if he will look back, is to Article 3 of the agreement which refers to certain undertakings that might in the future be made——

MR. PETHERICK: I am extremely sorry but Clause 3 says "undertakings mentioned in Article 6." Nothing could be more specific.

MR. EDEN: I beg the hon. Gentleman's pardon but I have taken the trouble to look up this matter since he raised it. I was not even a member of the Government then, but I consulted those who were and I think my right hon. Friend will bear me out that they spared no pains to tell the House exactly what the postion was, and it would have been wrong if the Government had not done so. What they made absolutely plain was that these measures only applied to aggression by Germany, and it does not in the least surprise me, if I may say so. I am now going to look into these documents and lay them on the Table. I do not ask my hon. Friend how he obtained this secret Protocol.

MR. A. BEVAN (Lab.) : Is it not rather disquieting, during this period when there was so very much interest in foreign affairs, that His Majesty's Government should be making secret commitments with other Powers?

MR. EDEN: I really do not think so. We must not let a wrong impression to go out. I have consulted my legal advisers and in their judgment, and in the judgment of those concerned at the time, the effect of this secret Protocol was to limit—precisely to limit—the obligations put before the House, not to increase them.

MR. SILVERMAN (Lab.) : On a point of Order. Now that both the right hon. Gentleman and the hon. Member who moved the Amendment have referred to a document, and quoted from it, is not the House entitled to see it?

MR. EDEN: I have told the hon. Gentleman I will go into that, but I cannot lay these documents without consulting others—I do not mean other persons in this country but other Governments. There is no mystery about it. I hope the House will not think that. There is no mystery. I have convinced myself in looking into these matters that the Government of the day behaved with absolute correctness in the information they gave the House, and the House was in no way deceived at all.

MR. BEVAN: Further to the point of Order. Surely it is not sufficient to accept the assurance of the Government, which is deeply concerned in this matter, about what is the significance of the document; once the document has been referred to, there is an obligation to lay the documents on the Table so that we may ourselves form our judgment.

MR. EDEN: The hon. Gentleman, if I may say so, is wrong. There is no obligation to lay documents because they are referred to.

MR. SILVERMAN: On a point of Order——

MR. EDEN: If the hon. Gentleman would let me answer——

MR. SILVERMAN: Mr. Deputy-Speaker, I have raised this matter as a point of Order and I submit that I am entitled to a Ruling from the Chair on whether my point of Order is right or wrong.

MR. DEPUTY-SPEAKER (MAJOR MILNER): It is a rule that such documents should be laid, but not if it is against public interest, or if they are in the nature of private or secret documents.

MR. EDEN: Really we need not get heated about this because the position is quite clear. There is no obligation to lay a document unless you quote from it. I have not quoted from it, I have referred to it. We propose to lay these documents but I must consult others. I am quite confident, or at least I am advised, by those who dealt with the matter at the time, and by my legal advisers, that the effect was to limit the engagement as it was announced to the House in 1939.

MR. MACK (Lab.) *rose*——

HON. MEMBERS: Order!

MR. MACK: I am not going to be restrained by hon. Members on the other side. Can the Foreign Secretary tell me what right the hon. Member for Penryn and Falmouth (Mr. Petherick) has to have access to a document which is denied to other Members of the House, and what right he has to quote from it?

MR. EDEN: That is certainly not a matter for me. Let me now come back to some of the points which have been raised, because I want to carry the House with me in the remaining arguments I have to make. My hon. and gallant Friend the Member for Epsom* asked what were the reasons why we failed to conclude a treaty with Russia in 1939. Here, again, I am dealing with matters which I did not handle, but I think the correct answer is something like this: Russia said at that time that if she was to conclude a treaty, she must have the right to move her troops across Poland, or across the Baltic States, in the event of war with Germany. The Polish Government at that time was consulted on this point and would not agree to the Russian demand. Although I do not pretend to be a historian, I think that that was, approximately, the main cause of the breakdown of those negotiations.

SIR A. SOUTHBY: Do I understand my right hon. Friend to mean that our failure to come to agreement in 1939 was due to Russia's demand for those portions of territory which I mentioned in the question I asked him in my speech?

MR. EDEN: Perhaps my hon. and gallant Friend will put down a Question about it on the Order Paper; it is a little difficult for me to give a detailed answer at short notice. But I have consulted those who were concerned, and I think the answer I gave was the main cause of the breakdown.

Now I come to the main issue. Some of my hon. Friends have said, with warmth, that the decisions we arrived at at Yalta have become a matter of world anxiety. I really cannot accept that that is true. So far as I know, the deepest anxiety of all was caused to Goebbels. If the House will read some of the stuff put out by Goebbels, after the Yalta Agreement, they would see in that the measure of the success of that Agreement. But not only that. If the House would look at reviews of the American Press and, still more so, of the Swedish Press—Sweden has had a long traditional friendship with Poland—and of the Turkish Press, they would find in them a general and wide endorsement of what we set out to achieve at Yalta. It really is a wild exaggeration to say that

* Commander Sir Archibald Southby.

the work we did there was a cause of anxiety. I cannot tell how these matters will work out in their later stages. I know how infinitely difficult the problems will be. It may be that we shall not succeed, but I think some of my hon. Friends would have been wiser had they reserved judgment until a later stage. There is no such thing as a perfect solution of this problem, but surely it is a step forward that the three Great Powers have agreed upon a method of handling it.

Since the Polish-Soviet Agreement of 1941 was unhappily broken by an incident which is fresh in the minds of the House I have been faced with two main anxieties in dealing with the problem. First, what would be the effect of failing to restore relations of Poland with Russia and, second, what would be the effect on the three great countries joined together in the prosecution of the war? Those are the problems we have to confront. If we are to restore Poland as a true, independent State she will need the help of each one of the three Great Powers to restore her devastated frontier. She cannot do that unless there is agreement between them. Some of my hon. Friends have said that a policy of continuing to recognize the Government here while the Lublin Government is recognized by Russia is of no assistance to Poland, although it may give us a great moral position. I am surprised at my hon. Friends using that argument. My hon. Friend the Member for South-East Essex (Mr. Raikes), who has just spoken, chided me once, I remember, for being an idealist. I am not so sure that he would do that today, because he himself once said:

> "As has been so often proved, those who are prepared for the sake of ideals to disregard the realistic facts of the present situation, may indeed, as has been the case in the past, cause more unnecessary suffering than perhaps any other people."

MR. RAIKES: Perhaps I have gained a little idealism while my right hon. Friend has lot a bit of it.

MR. EDEN: It seems then that we must be near agreement at last. Let me put the issue broadly. I share the feeling which my right hon. Friend expressed yesterday. It is difficult at times not to be oppressed by the weight of problems which lie upon Europe. They are infinitely greater than they were after the last war. There have been six years of war on an unparalleled scale; there has been the devastation of air bombardment, which there was not last time, and the dislocation caused by the movement of millions of workers to slavery in Germany. If any life is to be restored to Europe, if it is to be saved from anarchy and chaos, it can only be done by the three Powers working together. The right hon. Gentleman opposite spoke yesterday of the difficulties of maintaining unity in peace. Of course, he is right, but after what we have endured there is no duty more encumbent upon statesmanship than to try and strengthen that unity, and to try to find together in good faith a full solution of the problems which confront us all.

In conclusion, I would like to say a word or two to some of my hon. Friends. As I listened to their speeches I felt the sincerity of the feeling which underlay them. Some of them expressed the view that my right hon. Friend the Prime Minister and I did not stand up with sufficient authority for the point of view of His Majesty's Government. I repudiate that, and I would ask my hon. Friends to question themselves a little, if they would. The foreign policy of this country has been based for centuries on the determination that no one country should dominate Europe. We believe in Europe, we are part of Europe and I myself am convinced that no one country is ever going to dominate Europe. It is too big for any one nation to succeed in doing that. It is because of that instinct of our own that we have a special position in Europe, and that a special measure of confidence is extended to us. It is for that reason that there were the wars with Philip II of Spain, with Louis XIV, with Wilhelm II, and now with Hitler and the Third Reich.

As I listened to some of the speeches I could not help feeling that some of my hon. Friends, in talking about Poland, had not only Poland in mind, but the fear that Russia, flushed with the magnificent triumphs of her Armies, was also dreaming dream of European domination. This, of course, is the constant theme of German propaganda. It is poured out day by day and night after night and comes to us in all sorts of unexpected forms and guises. It was their theme before the war. It was then the Bolshevik bogy, and how well Hitler used it. How often visitors to Nuremberg were told by the Germans they met, of the fear of Russia. I have had plenty of it chucked at me at interviews with Hitler myself. Can anyone doubt that that theme, before the war, was an element in making it difficult for us to establish an understanding with Soviet Russia? Can anyone doubt that, if we had had in 1939, the unity between Russia, this country and the United States that we cemented at Yalta, there would not have been the present war? I go further. Can anyone doubt that, so long as we hold that unity, there will not be another war? We do not say that we can establish conditions in which there will never be war again, but I believe if we can hold this unity we can establish peace for 25 years or 50 years or—who can say? But unless we can hold it there will be no peace for anything like that period of time.

Finally may I say this word, again to my hon. Friends? Make no mistake. The moment this fighting ceases, Germany will be out on the old theme of propaganda again. She will again try to play us off against Russia, and Russia against America and ourselves. She will play on all their pity, which she knows so well how to do. The whole orchestra of German self-pity will work up again to fortissimo. Let us be very careful that we do not fall victims to that.

What is my conclusion? I say that, while we must be watchful, active and vigorous and do all in our power to secure the real freedom and independence of our Polish Allies while that is our right and our duty, do not let us at the same time fall victims too easily to suspicion of another Ally. I think we have to be on our guard. I assure the House that the Government will do all that lies in their power to see that the objectives the Prime Minister and I described are carried out. We are in the midst of this business. We are not through it. We have many difficult stages to fulfill. Neither my right hon.

Friend nor I can give any undertaking what our measure of success may be, but unless hon. Members feel that we should not try—and I cannot believe that they do—I would ask them to give us the encouragement to go forward. I would ask them to give it with a really strong and definite voice, otherwise we are going to confuse the mind of the world and the minds of our Polish friends for, after all, this cannot be solved at all unless the elements which represent Poland can be brought together. I would ask the House to consider again and give us full support for the work we are doing and, in the light of the assurances that I have given to the House, to say that in what we have done we have their confidence, and in what we are going to do we shall have their confidence, provided we fulfill the engagements that we have given. I in turn will tell them that we will report ourselves faithfully to this House.

Question put, "That those words be there added."

The House divided: Ayes, 25; Noes, 396.

AYES.

Bower, Commdr. R. T. (Cleveland)
Donner, Squadron-Leader P. W.
Graham, Capt. A. C. (Wirral)
Greene, W. P. C. (Worcester)
Hopkinson, A.
Little, Sir E. Graham- (London Univ.)
Lloyd, Major E. G. R. (Renfrew, E.)
McGovern, J.
Mellor, Sir J. S. P.
Morris, J. P. (Salford, N.)
Nunn, W.
Peto, Major B. A. J.
Raikes, H. V. A. M.
Savory, Professor D. L.
Shute, Col. Sir J. J.
Southby, Comdr. Sir A. R. J.
Stephen, C.
Stokes, R. R.
Stourton, Hon. J. J.
Taylor, Vice-Adm. E. A. (P'd'ton, S)
Teeling, Flight-Lieut. W.
Thornton-Kemsley, Colonel C. N.

Wayland, Sir. W. A.
Williams ,Sir H. G. (Croydon, S)
Willoughby de Eresby, Major Lord

TELLERS FOR THE AYES:—
Mr. Petherick and Mr. Keeling.

NOES.

Acland, Sir R. T. D.
Acland-Troyte, Lt.-Col. Sir G. J.
Adams, Major S. V. T. (Leeds, W.)
Adamson, Mrs. Jennie L. (Dartford)
Adamson, W. M. (Cannock)
Alexander, Rt. Hon. A. V. (H'lsbr'h)
Allen, Lt.-Col. Sir W. J. (Armagh)
Amery, Rt. Hon. L. C. M. S.
Anderson, F. (Whitehaven)
Anderson, Rt. Hon. Sir J. (Sc'h Univ.)
Assheton, Rt. Hon. R.
Astor, Lt.-Col. Hon. J. J. (Dover)
Astor, Hon. W. W. (Fulham, E.)
Attlee, Rt. Hon. C. R.
Barnes, A. J.
Barstow, P. G.
Bartlett, C. V. O.
Baxter, A. Beverley
Beamish, Rear-Admiral T. P.
Beattie, F. (Catheart)
Beauchamp, Sir B. C.
Beaumont, Hubert (Batley)
Beaumont, Maj. Hn. R. E. B. (P'tsm'th)
Beech ,Major F. W.
Beechman, N. A.
Beit, Sir A. L.
Bellenger, F. J.
Bennett, Sir P .F. B. (Edgbaston)
Benson, G.
Berry, Hon. G. L. (Buckingham)
Bevan, A. (Ebbw Vale)
Bevin, Rt. Hon. E. (Wandsworth, C.)
Bird, Sir R. E.
Blair, Sir R.
Boles, Lt.-Col. D. C.
Bossom, A. C.

Bower, Norman (Harrow)
Bowles, F. G.
Boyce, Sir H. Leslie
Brabner, Comdr. R. A.
Bracken, Rt. Hon. B.
Braithwaite, Major A. N. (Buckrose)
Brass, Capt. Sir W.
Briscoe, Capt. R. G.
Broadbridge, Sir G. T.
Brocklebank, Sir C. E. R.
Brooke, H. (Lewisham)
Brooks, T. J. (Rothwell)
Brown, Rt. Hon. E. (Leith)
Brown, T. J. (Ince)
Brown, W. J. (Rugby)
Bull, B. B.
Bullock, Capt. M.
Burden, T. W.
Burke, W. A.
Burton, Col. H. W.
Butcher, H. W.
Butler, Rt. Hon. R. A.
Beveridge, Sir W. H.
Cadogan, Major Sir E.
Campbell, Sir E. T. (Bromley)
Cape, T.
Carver, Colonel W. H.
Cary, R. A.
Castlereagh, Viscount
Channon, H.
Chapman, A. (Rutherglen)
Charleton, H. C.
Chorlton, A. E. L.
Christie, J. A.
Churchill, Rt. Hon. Winston S. (Ep'ing)
Clarke, Colonel R. S.
Cluse, W. S.
Cobb, Captain E. C.
Cocks, F. S.
Colegate, W. A.
Colindridge, F.
Colman, N. C. D.
Conant, Major R. J. E.
Cook, Lt-Col. Sir T. R. A. M. (N'f'k, N)

Cooke, J. D. (Hammersmith, S.)
Cove, W. G.
Cox, Captain H. B. Traver
Craven-Ellis, W.
Cripps, Rt. Hon. Sir Stafford
Critchley, A.
Crookshank, Capt. Rt. Hon. H. F. C.
Culverwell, C. T.
Cundiff, Major F. W.
Daggar, G.
Dalton, Rt. Hon. H.
Davies, Clement (Montgomery)
Davies, Major Sir G. F. (Yeovil)
Davies, S. D. (Merthyr)
Davison, Sir W. H.
De la Bére, R.
Danville, Alfred
Dobbie, W.
Doland, G. F.
Douglas, F. C. R.
Dower, Lt.-Col. A. V. G.
Drewe, C.
Driberg, T. E. N.
Duckworth, Arthur (Shrewsbury)
Duckworth, W. R. (Moss Side)
Dugdale, John (W. Bromwich)
Duncan, Rt. Hon. Sir A. R. (C. Ldn.)
Duncan, Capt. J. A. L. (Ken'gton, N)
Dunglass, Lord
Eccles, D. M.
Ede, Rt. Hon. J. C.
Eden, Rt. Hon. A.
Edmondson, Major Sir J.
Edwards, Rt. Hon. Sir C. (Bedwellty)
Edwards, N. (Caerphilly)
Edwards, Walter J. (Whitechapel)
Ellis, Sir G.
Elliston, Captain Sir G. S.
Emrys-Evans, P. V.
Entwistle, Sir C. F.
Erskine-Hill, A. G.
Evans, Col. Sir A. (Cardiff, S.)
Evans, D. O. (Cardigan)
Everard, Sir W. Lindsay

Fermoy, Lord
Fildes, Sir H.
Findlay, Sir E.
Fleming, Squadron-Leader E. L.
Foster, W.
Fox, Squadron-Leader Sir G. W. G.
Frankel, D.
Fraser, Lt.-Col. Sir Ian (Lonsdale)
Furness, S. N.
Fyfe, Major Sir D. P. M.
Galbraith, Comdr. T. D.
Gallacher, W.
Gammans, Capt. L. D.
Garro Jones, G. M.
Gates, Maj. E. E.
George, Maj. Rt. Hon. G. Lloyd (P'b'ke)
Gibbons, Lt.-Col. W. E.
Gibson, Sir C. G.
Glanville, J. E.
Gledhill, G.
Gluckstein, Col. L. H.
Glyn, Sir R. G. C.
Goldie, N. B.
Cower, Sir R. V.
Grant-Ferris, Wing-Commander R.
Granville, E. L.
Green, W. H. (Deptford)
Greenwell, Colonel T. G.
Greenwood, Rt. Hon. A.
Gridley, Sir A. B.
Griffiths, J. (Llanelly)
Grigg, Rt. Hon. Sir P. J. (Cardiff, E.)
Grimston, Hon. J. (St. Albans)
Grimston, R. V. (Westbury)
Groves, T. E.
Guest, Lt.-Col. H. (Drake)
Guest, Dr. L. Haden (Islington, N.)
Gunston, Major Sir D. W.
Guy, W. H.
Hacking, Rt. Hon. Sir D. H.
Hall, Rt. Hon. G. H. (Aberdare)
Hambro, Capt. A. V.
Hammersley, S. S.
Hannon, Sir P. J. H.

Harris, Rt. Hon. Sir P. A.
Helmore, Air Commodore W.
Henderson, A. (Kingswinford)
Henderson, J. (Ardwick)
Henderson, J. J. Craik (Leeds, N.E.)
Heneage, Lt.-Col. Sir A. P.
Hepburn, Major P. G. T. Buchan-
Hepworth, J.
Herbert, Petty Officer A. P. (Oxford U.)
Hewlett, T. H.
Hicks, E. G.
Higgs, W. F.
Hill, Prof. A. V.
Hinchingbrooke, Viscount
Hogg, Hon. Q. McG.
Holdsworth, Sir H.
Hollins, J. H. (Silvertown)
Horabin, T. L.
Hore-Belisha, Rt. Hon. L.
Horsbrugh, Rt. Hon. Florence
Hubbard, T .F.
Hudson, Sir A. (Hackney, N)
Hughes, R. Moelwyn
Hulbert, Wing-Commander N. J.
Hume, Sir G. H.
Hunter, Sir T.
Hurd, Sir P. A.
Hutchinson, G. C. (Ilford)
Hutchison, Lt.-Com. G. I. C. (E'burgh)
Hynd, J. B.
Isaacs, G. A.
James, Wing-Com. A. (Well'borough)
James, Admiral Sir W. (Ports'th, N.)
Jarvis, Sir J. J.
Jeffreys, General Sir G. D.
Jenkins, A. (Pontypool)
Jennings, R.
Jewson, P. W.
John, W.
Johnstone, Rt. Hon. H. (Mids'bro, W.)
Jones, A. C. (Shipley)
Jones, Sir L. (Swansea, W.)
Jowitt, Rt. Hon. Sir W. A.
Joynson-Hicks, Lt.-Cmdr, Hon. L. W.

Keir, Mrs. Cazalet
Kendall, W. D.
Kerr, H. W. (Oldham)
Kimball, Major L.
Kirby, B. V.
Lakin, C. H. A.
Lamb, Sir J. Q.
Lambert, Rt. Hon. G.
Lancaster, Lieut.-Col. C. G.
Law, Rt. Hon. R. K.
Lawson, H. W. (Skipton)
Lawson, J. J. (Chester-le-Street)
Leighton, Major B. E. P.
Levy, T.
Lewis, O.
Liddall, W. S.
Linstead, H. N.
Lipson, D. L.
Llewellin, Col. Rt. Hon. J. J.
Lloyd, C. E. (Dudley)
Lloyd, Rt. Hon. G. W. (Ladywood)
Lucas, Major Sir J. M.
Lyle, Sir C. E. Leonard
Lyons, Colonel A. M.
Lyttelton, Rt. Hon. Oliver
Mabane, Rt. Hon. W.
McCallum, Major D.
McCorquodale, Malcolm S.
MacDonald, Captain Peter (I. of W.)
McEntee, V. la T.
McGhee, H. G.
Mack, J. D.
McKinlay, A. S.
Maclay, Hon. J. P. (Paisley)
Magnay, T.
Maitland, Sir A.
Makins, Brig.-Gen. Sir E.
Mander, Sir G. le M.
Manning, C. A. G.
Manningham-Butler, R. E.
Markham, Major S. F.
Marlowe, Lt.-Col. A.
Martin, J. H.
Mathers, G.

Mayhew, Lt.-Col. J.
Messer, F.
Mills, Major J. D. (New Forest)
Mitchell, Colonel H. P.
Molson, A. H. E.
Montague, F.
Morgan, Dr. H. B. W. (Rochdale)
Morgan, R. H. (Stourbridge)
Morrison, Rt. Hon. H. (Hackney, S.)
Morrison, Major J. G. (Salisbury)
Morrison, H. C. (Tottenham, N.)
Morrison, Rt. Hon. W. S. (Cirencester)
Mort, D. L.
Mott-Radclyffe, Major C. E.
Muff, G.
Murray, J. D. (Spennymoor)
Naylor, T. E.
Neven-Spence, Major B. H. H.
Nicolson, Hon. H. G. (Leicester, W.)
Oldfield, W. H.
Oliver, G. H.
O'Neill, Rt. Hon. Sir H.
Owen, Major Sir G.
Palling, Rt. Hon. W.
Peake, Rt. Hon. G.
Pearson, A.
Peat, C. U.
Perkins, W. R. D.
Peters, Dr. S. J.
Pethick-Lawrence, Rt. Hon. F. W.
Plugge, Capt. L. F.
Poole, Captain C. C.
Power, Sir J. C.
Prescott, Capt. W. R. S.
Price, M. P.
Prior, Comdr. R. M.
Pritt, D. N.
Proctor, Major H. A.
Pym, L. R.
Quibell, D. J. K.
Rankin, Sir R.
Reakes, G. L. (Wellesey)
Reed, A. C. (Exeter)
Reed, Sir H. S. (Aylesbury)

Reid, Rt. Hon. J. S. C. (Hillhead)
Reid, W. Allan (Derby)
Riley, B.
Robertson, D. (Streatham)
Robertson, Rt. Hon. Sir M. A. (M'ham)
Robinson, Wing-Com. J. R. (Blackp'l)
Robinson, W. A. (St. Helens)
Ross Taylor, W.
Rothschild, J. A. de
Rowlands, G.
Royds, Admiral Sir P. M. R.
Russell, Sir A. (Tynemouth)
Salt, E. W.
Salter, Rt. Hon. Sir J. A. (Oxford U.)
Sanderson, Sir F. B.
Sandys, Rt. Hon. E. D.
Schuster, Sir G. E.
Scott, Donald (Wansbeck)
Selley, Sir H. R.
Shaw, Capt. W. T. (Forfar)
Shephard, S.
Shepperson, Sir E. W.
Shinwell, E.
Silverman, S. S.
Simmonds, Sir O. E.
Sinclair, Rt. Hon. Sir A.
Sloan, A.
Smiles, Lt.-Col. Sir W. D.
Smith, Sir Bracewell, (Dulwich)
Smith, E. (Stoke)
Smith, E. P. (Ashford)
Smith, T. (Normanton)
Smithers, Sir W.
Snadden, W. McN.
Somerset, Sir T.
Somervell, Rt. Hon. Sir D. B.
Spearman, A. C. M.
Spears, Maj.-Gen. Sir E. L.
Stanley, Col. Rt. Hon. Oliver
Stewart, J. Henderson (Fife, E)
Stewart, W. Joseph (H'gton-le-Spring)
Storey, S.
Strauss, G. R. (Lambeth, N.)
Strickland, Capt. W. F.

Studholme, Major H. G.
Sueter, Rear-Admiral Sir M. F.
Suirdale, Colonel Viscount
Summers, G. S.
Sutcliffe, H.
Sykes, Maj.-Gen. Rt. Hon. Sir F. H.
Tasker, Sir R. I.
Taylor, Major C. S. (Eastbourne)
Taylor, H. B. (Mansfield)
Thomas, J. P. L. (Hereford)
Thorneycroft, Maj. G. E. P., (Stff'd)
Thorneycroft, H. (Clayton)
Thurtle, E.
Tinker, J. J.
Tomlinson, G.
Tufnell, Lieut-Comdr. R. L.
Turton, R. H.
Viant, S. P.
Wakefield, Sir W. W.
Walkden, A. G. (Bristol, S.)
Walker-Smith, Sir J.
Ward, Col. Sir A. L. (Hull)
Ward, Irene M. B. (Wallsend)
Wardlaw-Milne, Sir J. S.
Waterhouse, Captain Rt. Hon. C.
Watkins, F. C.
Watson, W. McL.
Watt, Brig. G. S. Harvie (Richmond
Webbe, Sir W. Harold
Wells, Sir S. Richard
Weston, W. Garfield
Westwood, Rt. Hon. J.
White, C. F. (Derbyshire, W.)
White, Sir Dymoke (Fareham)
White, H. Graham (Birkenhead, E.)
Wickham, Lt.-Col. E. T. R.
Wilkinson, Rt. Hon. Ellen
Williams, Rt. Hon. T. (Don Valley)
Willink, Rt. Hon. H. U.
Wilmot, John.
Windsor, W.
Windsor-Clive, Lt.-Col. G.
Winterton, Rt. Hon. Earl
Womersley, Rt. Hon. Sir W.

Woodburn, A.
Woolley, Major W. E.
Wootton-Davies, J. H.
Wright, Group Capt. J. (Erdington)
York, Major C.
Young, Major A. S. L. (Partick)
Young, Sir R. (Newton)

TELLERS FOR THE NOES:—
Mr. James Stuart and Mr. Whiteley.

* * *

Main Question again proposed.

SEVERAL HON. MEMBERS *rose*—

It being Six o'Clock, the Debate stood adjourned.

Debate to be resumed Tomorrow.

Debate on March 1, 1945.

MR. SILVERMAN (Lab.): When the right hon. Gentleman the Member for Wakefield (Mr. Greenwood) spoke on the first day of this Debate, he promised support for the Motion on the Order Paper on the understanding that it should not be used in evidence against anybody and permitted a number of reservations. I find myself in the happy, if not altogether usual, position of being exactly the same mind. I see nothing in this Motion which need arouse any very acute controversy. I was surprised that anyone should have thought it necessary to devote quite so much of our three day Debate as was yesterday devoted to one question. Nobody would wish to reopen that issue now, but I would like to say that my reservations with regard to this Motion, the Yalta Conference and to the White Paper have no reference whatsoever to the position of Poland. As far as I can see, that decision was eminently right and just and ought to be defended not as the best compromise obtainable but as very much the best thing that could happen in circumstances that were admittedly difficult. Neither do the reservations necessitate responding to the invitation by the hon. Member who opened today's Debate. He seemed, after making a very realistic and valuable contribution to this Debate, rather to challenge people who are critical to defend or to withdraw their past criticisms. That would be a very useless waste of our time in this Debate . . .

MR. JEWSON (L. Nat.): . . . Almost every word that could be said about the Polish question was said yesterday, and I do not want to detain the House for more than a minute or two on the subject. I have to admit that one unhappy man I did meet among the representatives of other nations was a Polish Minister, but it seemed from our conversation that his difficulties and troubles arose more from the internal dissension of his own people than from any feeling against what we had done or not done. The more I have considered this Polish question—and I do not claim to have any special knowledge—the more clear it seems to me that the Curzon Line is the correct basis for Poland's Eastern boundary. However, that is all I want to say about the frontier question. I agree that the question of freedom is very much the more important of the two, but I want to say, for the comfort of my hon. Friends who had some doubts on the matter, that I, at any rate, do not feel any doubt as to the *bona fides* of our Russian friends and their intentions in this matter. It is often very difficult for us to discover what a Russian is really thinking. It may be difficult at times to obtain from the Russians a decision about a matter—I do not know—but I am confident that not only are they extremely friends towards us, but that when they have given a decision they will stand by it through thick and thin. I think we may take that for our comfort. It is true, of course, that in dealing with people who speak another language, and have another viewpoint, you must be careful to see that the words you use have the same meaning to them as they have to you, but I am quite sure that my right hon. Friend the Foreign Secretary needs no advice from me on so elementary a point as that . . .

MR. MCGOVERN (I.L.P.): . . . There is the further question of Poland, which was debated yesterday. One Member said that we are not going to return to it today, but I will say a few words about it. We are told that we must not, on any occasion, doubt the word of Marshal Stalin, or the word of the Prime Minister, or the word of the President of the United States. This is not, however, a mutual admiration society; we are not collected here to pass compliments to one another. Members of the House can talk as glibly as they like on the Floor or in the Press, but the great bulk of opinion in this country does not believe that the Polish plan will be carried out in a decent and democratic manner. I would be enthusiastic if there were a coming-together of Russia, Poland, Germany and France and if they were prepared to work with one another in a decent atmosphere, but, with the deportation of millions of Poles, and the putting to death of a large number of Polish politicians and trade union leaders, and of every individual who does not subscribe to the totalitarian ideas of Marshal Stalin, I have grave doubts about the carrying out of this democratic plebiscite. I have seen these democratic plebiscites carried out before. I have also seen attempts made from time to time to involve people in a decision which is made to appear as if unity prevails. A plan is decided upon before you get to the meeting, and everybody has to be blackballed into submission or dubbed as traitors or dishonest.

I am a person who does not mind the attacks that will come on me, because I always remember this and take consolation from it. At one time the right hon. Gentleman the Deputy Prime Minister and the Leaders of the Labor Party were on the show-grounds of Moscow and other Russian cities, and the people threw balls at them as the social Fascists of Great Britain.

THE DEPUTY PRIME MINISTER (MR. ATTLEE): Does the hon. Member suggest that I was there?

MR. MCGOVERN: Not in person. The right hon. Gentleman was there, but he did not know it. He was an effigy. That was at the time when the Communist Party wandered into the Labor Party and tried to catch them. At that time they had these figures in the show-grounds in Moscow, and the children were taught to make dollies of the British Labor and trade union leaders, who were regarded as the social Fascists of Great Britain and Hitler's pals. I see these changes taking place. Now they want to woo you. It is a change of tactics, just as Stalin's approach to the Polish issue is a change of tactics. The Prime Minister and the President of the United States would not admit that they were compelled to accept the decision because their pride would not let them do otherwise. The fact is, however, that they found an accomplished fact in Poland. Marshal Stalin had created the Lublin Committee, and he backs it every inch of the way, because it is his Committee and his Government. He created it and he is determined that it will operate. There will be further deportations and murders until he carries his way in the plebiscite. I wish it were otherwise, but I cannot see it as anything other than that. Members talk of the great foundation that has been laid in the great unity of the three Allies which is to operate for 25 years. They are not realists in talking in that way. They are only "kidding" themselves, but they are not "kidding" thinking men and women, who know that the great Powers are all preparing to get the mastery of each other economically and militarily for the time when it arrives.

This Yalta Agreement is more important for the things it does not say, than for the things it does say. It presents, like the Atlantic Charter and the Teheran decisions, a jumble of words with no meaning or reality to any individual who is politically honest. If Members think otherwise, although they are quite honest about it, they are badly deluded. The Yalta Conference did not face the position. As a Socialist, I maintain that war is brought about by the rival antagonisms, both financial and industrial, of the ruling classes of each country. You will have shed the blood of millions of people, you will have destroyed millions of homes and broken hundred of thousands of hearts in every country, but unless you lay low that ecenomic and financial power which causes war, then a further outbreak will take place as the next rival rises up, too powerful for the present combination. I condemn the Yalta Agreement as being only a hypocritical declaration that has no real foundation of any kind.

MAJOR-GENERAL SIR EDWARD SPEARS (C.): Like other speakers today, I would like to say a few words about the Polish question because I imagine that my case is that of many other speakers yesterday. The question that I put to myself is this: Was the Agreement arrived at Yalta in conformity with the principles upon which this war is being fought? That is the question I imagine many other Members put to themselves. Having heard the Prime Minister, I came to the conclusion that he, at any rate, was convinced that that was so. I was prepared to accept that, and to support him; if I had not felt that, not even a six-line Whip would have made me vote for the Government.

I regret one thing in the Yalta Conference very much, and that is that so much has been laid upon the Ambassadors' Conference. I have the highest opinion of our Ambassador in Moscow. I think he is one of the finest men in the service—

MR. MACLAREN (I.L.P.): Does the hon. and gallant Gentleman mean the French Ambassador?

SIR E. SPEARS: I mean the British Ambassador.

MR. MACLAREN: I was not quite sure.

SIR E. SPEARS: I have a hideous memory of a similar conference that took place in Berlin after Munich where we were represented by an Ambassador, and I think the teaching of history ought not to be so lightly disregarded. I have been reading a book which I think that all Members would do well to study. It is Mr. Sumner Welles' book, "The Time for Decision." This book shows clearly that all the evil effects which flowed from the last Peace Conference were due to the abandonment of the high principles which had inspired millions of people to bear the burdens of a terrible war. Expediency took the place of principles, the masses lost faith in the peace settlement, and another war became inevitable. For this reason I was frankly horrified by what was said by the hon. Member for Seaham (Mr. Shinwell) yesterday. He put forward the view that foreign affairs must, inevitably, be governed by expediency alone, and he appeared to accept that fact. If that is the view of the Labor Opposition, they are doomed, and rightly doomed. It is not only incredibly sordid, but terribly disappointing.

MR. SORENSEN (Lab.): Would the hon. and gallant Gentleman allege that the Yalta Agreement has been primarily reached through morality rather than expediency?

SIR E. SPEARS: I have just attempted to explain that, all things considered, and taking the facts as they were, the moral basis upon which this war has been fought is the basis of the Yalta Agreement. To say that expediency alone governs foreign affairs is to accept Hitler's principles and the principles of "Mein Kampf." I was horrified to hear those principles put forward here yesterday . . .

THE DEPUTY PRIME MINISTER (MR. ATTLEE): . . . I am glad that today we are getting on the main question, which has been diverted by the Polish question. It is natural that we should have devoted a great deal of attention to the Polish question. That is a subject that arouses very much sympathy, very much pity. I do not want to add much to what has been said but I would like to say a word because I have very many close friends among the Poles.

I have visited the Polish troops, both in their training camps and in the line in Italy; and I have personal friends in various parties, and indeed among members, who think as I do on most subjects of the London Polish Government. I am not unacquainted with the history of Poland, and I have a great admiration for the qualities of the Polish people, but I cannot say that political wisdom is an outstanding quality among them. I have pleaded very often with my friends on these matters, and I have, to my sorrow, seen chance after chance lost. I have seen the position getting worse and worse. I have begged my friends to remember their place in the world as neighbors of the Russians; and we have to take into account our neighbors in this world. Some I have seen take a realist view; others, I think, take an ultra-romantic view.

I recall very well receiving a card this Christmas from one of my Polish friends. It was rather characteristic. It consisted of a map of Poland in the 17th century. It is this tragic harking back by so many peoples of Central and South-Eastern Europe into the past, instead of looking to the future, that makes the establishment of a permanent peace so difficult. I noticed in the Debate yesterday, and indeed in all Debates on frontiers, that Members tend to be too historical, and everyone has his particular year from which he likes to start the argument. I want to see this Polish question in the general picture of Yalta, because we have to think of what the statesmen gathered there had to do. They had two preoccupations; one with the present, the winning of the war, and the second with the future, the winning of the peace. Those two things are much more important than the past.

CAPTAIN COBB (C.): But my right hon. Friend will agree that they also had a very great concern with the maintenance of British honor.

MR. ATTLEE: I quite agree—the maintenance of British honor in the past, the present and the future. But it is not useful to encourage claims on the past. My hon. Friends so often beg the question, because they assume exactly what the point of honor is, which they often base on the principle of regarding as sacrosanct some particular arrangement at some particular point of time that happens to suit their particular point of view. I suggest that that is not really useful.

VICE-ADMIRAL TAYLOR (C.): Could my right hon. Friend explain what right the Lublin Committee had to decide anything as regards Poland?

MR. ATTLEE: The Lublin Committee does not enter into it at all. We have not recognized the Lublin Committee. I was not dealing with the Lublin Committee: I was dealing with certain points of the past. We have to look at these things from the point of view of the future of the peoples of Europe. Over all these countries the storms of the past have gone. You have to try to unravel a tangle that has grown up through the 18th century. We ought to appreciate the magnitude of the storm that has now passed over Europe, killing millions of people, wrecking the lives of people; with 5,500,000 Jews or more done to death; Poles killed; many people, workers of various States, carried off from their homes; homes wrecked by war; Germans deported by their own Government from some places; Germans driven out by Russian armies. There have been unprecedented movements of population. The same thing has occurred in other places in Europe. You have an immense area of disturbance. You have to try to see how that is going to settle down in the future. I suggest that we should not always be thinking that it must necessarily settle down into the position of the past. One thing is quite certain. If you ask who is responsible for these movements, this terrible thing that has smitten Europe, there is no doubt at all that it is the Nazi rulers of Germany, and the people of Germany who actively supported them, and, in a lesser degree, those who have acquiesced, and who have been quite satisfied as long as things went well. I do not suggest that you can draw an indictment against a whole people, but neither can you relieve of responsibility a whole people?

MR. SILVERMAN: Who can be relieved of responsibility for that? Did not all Europe acquiesce for six years?

MR. ATTLEE: I really do not think so. I recognize the generosity of the hon. Member: I realize how he feels on this subject; but I do not think it is reasonable or right to suggest that the responsibility here is at all equal. I think it lies quite definitely on the Nazi leaders. Nor do I believe that the Nazi leaders are just the tools of some wonderful form of secret capitalist organization. I believe that the German capitalists were in it; whether they were the tools of Hitler, or Hitler the tool of them—which befooling which—I do not know. You have to recognize fairly and squarely that this terrible thing which has come upon Europe is the responsibility of the German leaders and of the German people—and I am afraid that there are a great many who accepted those ideals. They have broken down the old barriers, and therefore I say that they cannot appeal to the old Europe. If they have to yield, to make restitution, they are not entitled to appeal on the basis of the moral laws that they have disregarded or the pity and mercy that they have never extended to any others. I do not believe in treating them as they have treated other people, but I cannot admit that they have a claim to appeal to rights and moral principles which they have utterly disregarded.

Therefore, if it is necessary to take some German soil, to make it up to the entirely innocent Dutch people who have seen their land destroyed, I shall not complain; if it is found necessary to take certain areas in order to enable the Polish people to lead a free, full life, I shall not complain—and I do not think that the Germans have a right to complain. I shall judge all these changes, not by whether they fit into past history or whether they are performing an act of revenge, but entirely as to whether they will make for a peaceful Europe in future. The shifting of population at the present time may be very, very painful, but it may be far better than a long drawn out sore of populations under peoples whom they hate. It may be that a single adjustment will be better. It is therefore precisely here that, I think, we can see the importance of the conclusions of the Crimea Conference.

If we look at Europe, looking backwards to the past, we see a whole congeries of armed States competing with each other, anxiously looking to see whether they are going to be attacked, or looking possibly for opportunities for attack. We ought to try to look forward to a Europe which, free from the fear of war and secure, will consist of citizen States living peacefully together, developing the arts of peace, and not perpetually trying to make war against each other. Therefore,

I say that these difficulties of adjustment are far less when you look at them in the light of a world organization. I hope that the San Francisco Conference will result in the establishment of a system of security, under which the nations of Europe may at long last settle down and live together. It is necessary to get the section dealing with Poland into its right perspective in the White Paper. It is one of the many problems which we must deal with if we are to have an established peace.

I say the same on the question of settling on an interim Polish Government. Some people seem to think it is very easy to get interim Governments, fully representative of all people, although those countries have been swept by war and occupation. Believe me, it is extremely difficult. Even the technical constitutionality of the existing Government does not always carry you through. Governments in exile change their membership. They become more or less representative as time goes on. I claim that it can be shown, in the dealings of this Government, that in every influence we have been able to bring to bear we have steadily striven to get the Governments with whom we are in contact, the Governments in exile, more and more broadly based. It is not so very esay. The Government which came out of Greece was not a democratic Government; it gradually grew, and we took the utmost pains to get it as fully representative as possible, by getting people from the resistance movements into it . . .

MR. RHYS DAVIES (Lab.) : As the House is aware, I represent a minority view here, and it is just as well that it should be put in the very short time at my disposal. I hope my right hon. Friend the Deputy Prime Minister, will forgive my saying that I agree with a great deal of what he said, and the only comment I make to him is that, if our Labor Party had never joined the Coalition, he might well be delivering the very speech that I am now about to deliver. I have listened to the whole of this Debate, and I had better say how it has affected me. I do not want to dwell unduly on Poland, but hon. Members have dealt with only the Eastern side of Poland;

I want to say something about the Western side. As it happens, I have been in Danzig, the Corridor, Silesia and Poland and know just a little about that part of the world.

The first thing I want to say about the Polish question is this. I was really amazed yesterday at what came from the Foreign Secretary about the Polish situation. The right hon. Gentleman said—if hon. Members will be quiet, they will hear me better—that Poland was, in effect, a ramshackle State in 1939. How on earth came it about, therefore, that the British Government could give a promise to defend the independence of a ramshackle State like that? The second thing that astonished me was—and I am sure the people of this country have been deceived in regard to Poland—that the only guarantee we gave for its independence was in the event of an attack on Poland by Germany. It did not matter if Russia, or any other Power, apparently, attacked her. It was, in effect, and I hope I am not being biased, an invitation to Poland to stand up to Germany in order that we might make war on Germany. The right hon. Gentleman the Foreign Secretary made another statement that, generally, the avowed policy of this country for centuries was that no great Power should be allowed to rise in Europe to challenge the liberty of the peoples of this continent. If that is our policy, let me say that the next generation in this country will have to be prepared for a war on Russia, because it will be the next State to be involved in that policy of balance of power.

That is an awful state of affairs, and I do not like the situation at all. If my right hon. Friend—and I hope he does not mind my reminding him—looks up his own speeches delivered before the outbreak of this war and before our party joined the Coalition, he will find that they do not tally with some of the statements he has made today. That is one thing about Coalition Governments, and I am not blaming him personally. One of the results of a Coalition, to be quite blunt, is that members of all parties soil their political shirts, and their collars and ties as well by joining it.

Let me now turn to the Western side of Poland; this is

the one thing that puzzles me in the Crimea Declaration. If it is the policy of the Allied Powers to hand over Danzig and East Prussia and other patches of Germany to Poland, to establish a new State by giving patches of Poland to Russia on the other side, do they imagine for a moment that they are likely to establish a durable peace in Europe? If they think that they cannot really be called three big men, we might as well christen them three blind mice instead. Does my right hon. Friend, and his colleagues, imagine for one moment that millions of Germans will live in peace under the control of the Poles? My right hon. Friend shakes his head. I know his answer, it is that the Germans have left those territories already; have evacuated them. Supposing the people of Wales and Scotland were compulsorily evacuated to England and left their schools, institutions and the graves of their people behind them, does my right hon. Friend imagine that they would be satisfied and would not desire to return to their native country? That is human nature.

MR. ATTLEE: I do not think that my hon. Friend is quite right there. There is a little piece of Flintshire which is detached and I do not think that there would be serious trouble if we moved those people from Wales.

MR. DAVIES: My right hon. Friend had better try it on and see what would happen. I think that all Members of this House, whatever their views upon the war may be, are looking forward to something more hopeful for mankind emerging from the San Francisco Conference. . . .

MR. PICKTHORN (C.): . . . I have only one other piece of hastily fetched foreign information, about which I would like to ask my right hon. Friend the Foreign Secretary a question. I take no responsibility for this, but as a statement I think it has enough evidence to make it fair to ask the question, which is this: Is it true that Madame Arciszewski, the wife of the Prime Minister of the Polish Government, recognized by his Britannic Majesty's Government, has been arrested? I think it is of some importance that we should know. I should be the last to start such a rumor, or even to help it into circulation, if it was not already quite clear that it was in circulation, but so soon as it is clearly in circulation, I think it ought to be answered.

I want to say one other thing about the Polish side of the case which is, I think, a little different from what taking them together, I may recall the incomparable eloquence of four or five of my hon. Friends in the last few days. I do not think I can say better what they said, but I think I am trying to say something slightly different. Incidentally, if my right hon. Friends the Prime Minister and the Foreign Secretary can remember the far off times when they were on these back benches, I want to tell them that I am just as anxious as ever they were to draw myself to the favorable attention of the leaders of the Tory Party. What I want to say is this: It really is not any good their telling us that it would be improper, impolite or impolitic to question the word of Marshal Stalin and M. Molotov. I should not think of questioning their word, but if I did, and wanted to annoy them, which is the last thing in the world I wish to do—[*Laughter*]. Yes, it is the last thing in the world I wish to do, and I do not think that what I am going to say will annoy them, or cause them to be critical if they do me the honor of reading my remarks. As I was saying, if anybody did wish to annoy them I think it is very dubious which of their utterances they would have found it most insulting to have questioned. I have taken a good deal of pains to read Marshal Stalin's books and M. Molotov's speeches. I do not think it is I who throw doubt on the intentions and engagements they hold.

Suppose I wished to lend £1,000 to my hon. Friend the Member for Peckham (Mr. Silkin), because I liked his face, and I was sure that he was wholly trustworthy. Suppose I wanted to lend him £1,000—if I had £1,000—there would be no reason in the world why I should not do it, as the seductive advertisements say, "On note of hand alone." But if, on note of hand alone, I lent him £1,000 which were not mine, but which were deposited with me, and in relation to which I was in a fiduciary capacity, then no amount of politeness would excuse me for that. I should need not only assurances but securities .

The essential thing about this Yalta Agreement on Poland seems to be not whether it is the best arrangement which could possibly be made at that time. That still begs the question. For instance, we were told yesterday that this and that had happened because of the existence of the Lublin Committee. But His Majesty's Government were not wholly without influence in the days before that Committee came into existence. There are all sorts of things which we do not know about what relations were between His Majesty's Government and the Soviet Government. The main point is this: This thing is presented to us as the first step towards a great new world organization. I will be frank with the House. I am not very easily taken with love for great new world organizations. Perhaps I am too skeptical about them. But I make this small boast. By an accident of the date of my by-election I was, I think, the first Member of this House to say that now that all parties have agreed to enter upon the path of sanctions, no party could have any duty which conflicted with the duty of re-armament. Therefore, I was a League of Nations man in that sense, which is more than can be said of all League of Nations men.

I am, perhaps, over suspicious about great world organizations, but a feel sure that such an organization can be built up only by taking up all that there was in the modern world of international law and international comity, and building as from that. It seems to me that however much this may be much the best arrangement, and however much it may be said that the Poles may be idiots for wanting to keep their old provinces or for not wanting to have chunks of Germany, what sticks in my gizzard, what I find it impossible to give positive approval to, is that so far as I know it is the first time in history that one country has had both its *régime* and its boundaries altered in the course of a war by three other nations—all in alliance with it, or at least, two of them are in alliance in every sense of the word, and the third is in alliance in one sense or another—without that country being present. It may be that that was necessary. It may be that at the point we reached in January, 1945, which, judging by the Prime Minister's speech in October, was a point very different from that which we reached three months sooner, this was the best and only thing to do. But to say that it should be done with candles, bells, flags, ribbons, rejoicings, and jigs, because this is the way to start building a new world organization, to say that is too much with which to face every Member as has been done by the demanding and the advocacy of this Vote of Confidence. Therefore, with the utmost reluctance, I find myself unable to give that Vote. And I would ask my right hon. Friend, Is it really wise to go out of your way to make this three days' Debate, on what my right hon. Friend the Foreign Secretary will admit to be a debatable act of foreign policy, a test between the Government and every individual Member of this House, however faithful any particular individual may be?

The Prime Minister was twitted two or three years ago, I think it was, for what I thought was an unimpeachable utterance of his, when he said that he hoped that when the long day was done the Tory Party would prove to have been the main rock upon which victory had been built. That was a perfectly fair thing for any party leader to say. [*Laughter.*] Yes, it was a perfectly fair thing for any party leader to say, or for any patriot or any Englishman to say. I do not know what else any Englishman could say in time of war for his party. I never understood the questioning of it which came from certain quarters. I would not endeavor to cut this House up into parties, still less would I endeavor to cut up my own party. I have never belonged to any organized clique in it which has tried to be a party inside a party. I have always thought such things wrong. There are, however, recognizable strains in a party, as in any other biological collection of people, but those of us most troubled about this question can fairly boast that not before in the course of this war have any of us been the ones who have been tiresome in moments of crisis. We have not been the ones who, if our war machinery has been proved to be a death-trap, if our ships have been sunk, or the battle has swayed the wrong way, or a great Ally has thought that a second front ought to be opened at a point of time when to do such a thing would have been a certain way of losing the war, have asked awkward questions and have gone into the wrong lobbies on those occasions.

I ask the Government, before they repeal this experiment: what happens if this goes wrong? I am all for it going as right as it stands, but supposing it goes wrong? Suppose it becomes plain within the next six weeks or six months that there was never any real chance of getting any real expression of opinion or independence of provisional Government in Poland. It is certainly going to be difficult. Anyone who listens to the Lublin wireless will know that you are not allowed to have a typewriter, or listen to any wireless except at a communal listening point. All parties and papers are strictly controlled. We have been trying for 18 months to settle on a way to have a general election in this country and we have not yet brought it off and, when it does come, we know that it will be a sweepstake.

MR. MOELWYN HUGHES (Lab.): A sweep.

MR. PICKTHORN: That remains to be seen. The hon. and learned Gentleman may yet find himself winning a moral victory. Very confident politicians have done it in the past. But we know how immensely difficult it is. From Lublin information alone we know that it is almost inconceivably difficult to arrange anything like a real election there.

If this goes wrong, what is to happen to the next Vote of Confidence? Are we still unanimously to express confidence or to have the whole of our policy in relation to our great Ally suddenly very much altered? Are we suddenly to go right off the foot on which we have been for the last two or three years? I am by no means persuaded that the policy and the way it has been presented to us is not that most likely to arouse difficulties. I admired my right hon. Friend the Foreign Secretary's speech yesterday very much. It was a very persuasive speech, exactly calculated for its audience, and I thought it was extremely successful and on the whole fair, though I thought he slipped into what was unfair towards the end in the stuff about Goebbels. But, again, "my withers are unwrung." When I was a small boy in 1900 my father told me that the South African war was the beginning of the attempt by the German Empire to conquer the world through the British Empire. I believed it then and I have believed it ever since. I have never had the least pro-Germanism or tenderness for Hitler. But let all that be as it may—this surely is true of the Goebbels propaganda: it has all been based upon the argument that, if you knock out the German military machine, the Russian military machine will be irresistible. I have never believed it and I do not believe it now. I do not think there is any necessity to be frightened of Russia. I have never been frightened of Russia. Those who supported the Government yesterday are those who took that line. They continually got up and said, "What else could you have done? It was the best bargain that could be made in a very tight corner." It is a little hard that that particular reproach about Goebbels' reaction should be levelled at those of us who, with the bitterest regret, are critical of the Government at this historic moment.

MR. MACK (Lab.): Whatever one may think of the political opinions of the hon. Member the Senior Burgess for Cambridge University (Mr. Pickthorn), at least he is entertaining, and he was none the less so on this occasion because he purported to be serious. But, behind all the arguments advanced and the *jeux d'esprit* which he introduces into his speeches, the first thing that will be apparent is the fact that he himself, together with a number of others whose identity we know very well, are strongly opposed to the Soviet Union. Despite the fact that yesterday we had a long discussion on the particular case of Poland, I think it is right and proper to say a word or two about the type of people who in large part constitute the Polish Government in this country and to compare them, as far as we can, with those elements of the Poles inside Poland. The Polish Provisional Government which is in Poland at present is not composed of Communists alone or people who have ideological relationship with Russia. They are highly representative of various political parties, including the Polish Democratic Party, which is, I understand, similar to our Liberal Party in outlook, the Socialist Party, which is analogous to our Labor Party, the Workers' Party, which may roughly be regarded as a Communist Party, and the Peasants' Party, which is agrarian and contains Conservative elements. It might be of interest to know how much the Polish Government in Britain is costing the taxpayers. Something like £45,000,000 is being expended annually, out of which £21,000,000 is going to officials of various kinds, and I am advised that medium officials are receiving something like £40 to £60 per month, whereas Ministers are receiving £120 per month, all free of Income Tax. They have conducted a continuous spate of anti-Soviet propaganda.

In this House, I am sorry to say, in spite of the commendable efforts made by the Prime Minister and the Foreign Secretary to reach a solution on the basis of equity, because they regard the solution as just in all the circumstances, these two Ministers are being arraigned, mostly by Members of their own political party. If the gloves are to come off in this fight I have no objection at all. Someone has said we are not afraid of Russia. There is no need to be afraid of Russia's military might, because she would never use it to do injustice to any small nation in order to seize some small advantage.

It follows the Shakespearean maxim:

> "It is excellent to have a giant's strength; but it is tyrannous to use it like a giant."

I was not surprised, though I did raise an eyebrow, to read two days ago in an editorial of the "Daily Express," a paper with 3,000,000 circulation:

> "Russia, in her dealings with the outside world, has shown full integrity and honesty. She has dealt with her conquered foes

> with the most remarkable fairness and restraint. Stalin gave Finland a peace which astonished the world by its moderation. Speak as you find is a good maxim. For the people of Britain it means TRUST RUSSIA."

I shudder to think what would have happened if another Power had conquered Finland in the then circumstances. Would it have given her the opportunity to rebuild the country, resuscitate herself and live a free and independent life, as Russia did? I would remind hon. Members opposite in particular, when they talk of frontiers being destroyed and about Poland not being consulted in the matter, of the immediate pre-war record of that country, which endeavored to seize a part of Czechoslovakia and tried to make territorial depredations in the direction of Vilna. Its policy was definitely aggressive for years before the war. But in pre-war years hon. Members seldom rose to speak about Poland, because the country was relatively little known. It is only now, when there is a possibility of driving a wedge in the relationship between Russia and ourselves, to say nothing of America, that they wax indignant. May I be permitted a slight reference to one of the most detestable speeches ever made in this country by an hon. and gallant Gentleman, the Member for Cleveland (Commander Bower) recently at a Northern seaside resort when he impugned and bitterly attacked the good motives of Marshal Stalin? If he is right, all I can say is that the Prime Minister and the Foreign Secretary, who have met and deliberated with Marshal Stalin, are guilty of a crime of the first magnitude if they deliberately deceived us as to the intentions of the leader of the USSR. I do not believe that they would do that for a moment. I was satisfied that they spoke with a feeling of honesty when they said they had implicit trust in Russia's word. To talk about 47 per cent of Polish territory being given over to Russia——

MR. DEPUTY-SPEAKER (MAJOR MILNER): I am sorry to interrupt the hon. Member, but I must point out that we have devoted a day and a half to the question of Poland and Russia and had a Division, and I should regard it as approaching a misuse of the time of the House if further extensive reference, or the whole of the hon. Member's speech were devoted to that subject alone.

MR. MACK: I think I shall be in Order in referring to the general position of Russia as distinct from the Polish situation and the relationship between that great country and ourselves. I will bear your suggestion in mind, Sir. If it were true that it was the intention of the USSR to tear up every democratic country in Europe, they could have adopted the policy of saying: *"J'y suis, j'y reste"* and no one could have shifted them. People will say that is *force majeure.* They will say: "We have no desire to interfere with a country of that size and importance."

COLONEL VISCOUNT SUIRDALE (C.): Is not that what they have done in Estonia, Lithuania and Latvia?

MR. MACK: No, most certainly not. I think it is generally conceded that in war a country that has to cross the frontiers of smaller countries which are in geographical contiguity to it must, of necessity, establish some form of influence and control of those countries during the operations of war. I do not concede that they have used that influence in the aggressive sense that my hon. and gallant Friend suggests.

CAPTAIN SIDNEY (C.): According to my recollection, the Soviet Republic went into the Baltic Republics before they were engaged in any war in Europe.

MR. MACK: The hon. and gallant Member is quite right, but there was a free vote and these small countries decided themselves to become an integral part of the USSR. This to me is an important factor. The purpose of this Debate surely is to give support to the Government in their most difficult task in bringing about the Yalta Agreement. One of the important things achieved at Yalta was to succeed in convincing American opinion, or alternative for America to convince British opinion, that the intentions of Russia, as far as these countries are concerned, have at least been honest.

MR. GALLACHER (Com.): Would the hon. Gentleman agree to give India the same opportunity of a plebiscite as was given to the Baltic Republics?

MR. MACK: My hon. Friend knows and endorses my views in that respect. All I am saying is that my views are antithetical to those of hon. Members opposite. There are some Members in this House whom I would regard as plasticine politicians; they can be shaped any way. At one moment they vote for the Government and the next day they vote against the Government. They speak with sincerity and loyalty to the Prime Minister and go up and down the country using every argument they can against certain people, suggesting that they are not behind the war, yet today and yesterday we have seen the greatest disloyalty on their part, and something worse, whether they realize it or not; they are making it extremely difficult for the Government to carry out these protracted and difficult negotiations.

On 25th April the Allies are going to meet in San Francisco, a very nice place for a meeting. They are going to meet for the purpose of arranging the new world. I regard it as essential, if we are to go into the future with a sense of reality, that we should have good faith and believe with all our hearts in the honest intentions of other people. There is an old and trite saying that the proof of the pudding is in the eating. The blood that has been spilled by Russia and other countries, but particularly by Russia, is a practical and physical proof of the sincerity of their efforts. There is nothing more contemptible and despicable than sneering, slanting references against the integrity of the USSR. It is a reflection of the minds of those who make them. As far as this is concerned, there should be a showdown. I often wonder why the leaders of the Conservative Party do not deal very drastically with those Members who have done all they can by their speeches and conduct to render more difficult the work of the Government.

There are two points which I should like my right hon. Friend to deal with in his reply. At Birkenhead a number of

Polish seamen who are alleged to hold certain political opinions are not allowed to enter vessels of the Polish Shipping Federation. I would like to know whether the Polish Shipping Federation are to be allowed to do that in this country after the Yalta Conference, and whether the accredited representative in this country of the Lublin Committee is to be given any facilities to make his case and to meet the Government. I should like to ask, also, whether Lady Sinclair's Fund to help Warsaw will be handed over to the Provisional Government once that is brought into being upon a broad democratic basis. I should like to ask, too, if we are to have foreign broadcasts by the London Poles which cast aspersions on the good faith of at least one of our Allies. These are things which are very pertinent and are exacerbating good opinion.

This Debate has had one good effect. It has proved itself to be a clearing house of opinion and it has shown hon. Members in their true colors. This period of the war is not the least important. In the penultimate state of a war unity is essential between one country and another, and in this fight for democracy and freedom we should be bound together by sincere motives. There are, however, people who are allowing their prejudices—their religious prejudices in some cases—to operate to the disadvantage of the relationships between Britain and Russia. If that is to be allowed to obtain I am sorry for the future policy of this country. I believe that the combination of the three Powers, plus China, France, Czechoslovakia, Yugoslavia and the smaller Powers, can, with good will, lead to lasting peace. I believe that the prestige of Britain stands higher in Russia today than it has for a long time. I was one of those who in the past bitterly opposed the Prime Minister for some of his utterances. I now applaud him for having the magnanimity, decency and honesty to admit that what he said in years gone by does not affect his attitude at the present time, in the light of the new facts. We ought to support the Government, and I shall support them in the good work they have been doing and give them a chance at San Francisco to build on democratic lines a world which will mean a great deal for the millions of suffering people in all the countries of Europe.

SIR GEOFFREY MANDER (L.): . . . I have no intention of going over the ground of the Polish Debate, but I would like to make one point. I hope that the Poles, whether in the Polish Government in this country, whether outside the Government or in Poland, however bitter and disappointed they may be feeling, will take the opportunity that now presents itself to try to get something done. I urge them not to reject it out of hand by a precipitate refusal to play any part in the negotiations. It is their duty in the interests of their country to make the best of the situation which presents itself and try to obtain a reasonably representative Polish Government in Poland. We ought not to allow emotional sympathy for ideal solutions of particular problems to blind us to the overriding consideration that the three Great Powers are the people on whom we must rely for peace in the world for a considerable time to come. I believe that these three, so different in their history, constitutions and methods, are at one in sincerely desiring peace and the onward and upward march of mankind. . . .

LIEUT.-COLONEL SIR THOMAS MOORE (C.): . . . Your predecessor, Mr. Deputy-Speaker, said that the question of Poland should not be dealt with at great length today, and I quite agree. Members have expressed their views, and the Government are well aware of them on both sides. I am a friend and ally of suffering, desolate, courageous Poland, but I am also a friend and ally of outraged, heroic and conquering Russia. All that I ask is that the generous treatment which was indicated by the Prime Minister on Tuesday shall be fully accorded. Frontiers are not of the same importance today as they were long ago. V. 1's and V. 2's take no notice of frontiers: the weapons of the future will take still less; and, although it may be necessary for Marshal Stalin to seize that territory behind which his Armies will have room to deploy for immediate defence and ultimate victory, now that victory is in his hands, now that he can afford to be, as he is, generous, let him err on the side of generosity. That is all I have to say about Poland. I would be happy to know that our foreign policy and Russia's foreign policy march hand in hand. I do not know what Stalin's foreign policy is; but I want to be sure that they are marching together. . . .

SIR HERBERT WILLIAMS (C.): I intervene for only a few moments to raise a matter of very great importance. I quite understand why the Foreign Secretary is not in his place at the moment, but I would be grateful if his right hon. colleagues will convey what I have to say to him. Many of us have been informed that the wife of the Polish Prime Minister in London, together with a number of other ladies working for the Red Cross in Poland, has been arrested. This seems to me, in the light of this Debate and of the Crimea Conference, a very grave issue indeed, and, before this Debate ends, we ought to learn from the Foreign Secretary whether it is true or not, and if it is true, we ought to know what steps His Majesty's Government are taking to safeguard the rights and liberties of these people against the actions of the Lublin Committee.*

MR. PETHICK-LAWRENCE (Lab.) . . . Now I come to the question of boundaries, which has proved in the past to be a fatal germ of war. Before we meet here in this House every day, we pray that our deliberations may be guided from above, and that the highest wisdom may be given to us in coming to our decisions. That prayer must be doubly necessary in the case of those who take part in determining the frontiers of the world at the Peace Conference. I am sure my hon. Friend the Member for West Leicester (Mr. Harold Nicolson), who, I think, took part in some of those Conferences, would bear out what I say. It is essential to settle at the Peace Conference not merely what seems just at the present time but what will appear just 20 years hence, and this applies in particular to the frontiers of Germany herself. For that reason I was very

---

* See No. 31.

glad to read in the Yalta Agreement, and to hear the remarks of the Prime Minister, about the Eastern frontier of Germany towards the mouth of the Oder. I think it would have been disastrous if the Eastern frontier of Germany had been fixed along the Oder all the way to the sea in advance of the peace settlement. I do not think that could have promoted the peace of the world and, as I understand it, it is not desired by the Poles. The inclusion of great tracts of Pomerania in the Polish Republic would be fraught with grave danger to the security of Poland and to the peace of Europe and the world, and I do not think that the British people in 10 or 20 years' time would go to war in order to enforce that settlement. . . .

. . . But important as are these material matters, frontiers, the economy and the standard of life, behind them all lies the restoration of the confidence of nations in the pledged word of treaties. The nervous system of the international body politic is perhaps the hardest thing of all to repair. In this connection, I should like to make one observation with regard to the question of Poland, which was the principal subject of yesterday's Debate. I appreciate the chagrin of my Polish friends at having a decision about the future of their country taken in their absence. I appreciate their feeling of intense regret that their Eastern frontier, in particular, has been decided against their wishes; I appreciate their anxiety with regard to the future. But I would beg them not to carry their lament over these "might have beens" to the extent of failing to grasp the opportunities which are still in front of them. If I have learned one thing in life I have learned this: that when a thing has happened, and has happened irrevocably, then so far as possible it must be put on one side, and one must turn one's mind to the future. Whatever may have been the theoretical case before the Division took place yesterday, it must be perfectly clear that Yalta is now settled policy and that its decisions cannot be undone. I would appeal to those who sponsored the cause of Poland yesterday to face that fact. They may regret—we all regret—that Poland has not been able to reach by consent a settlement with Russia in which both sides would feel they have a satisfactory solution. We may regret the proposed frontier, we may regret all kinds of things, but what is absolutely essential is that such advantages as Poland does get out of the Yalta settlement shall be implemented and seized to the full.

I said I thought that the Debate yesterday was on a very high level, and that the case for Poland was put with cogency and sincerity. But I do think this: that if a good deal more time had been spent, not in criticism of the Government, but in trying to discover exactly what opportunities now remain, it is possible that the fruits of that Debate might have been even more valuable than they are. We have had the promise of the three Great Powers that there shall be a free and independent Poland, that there shall be a fair transitional Government, and that there shall be, in future, elections of a free kind. To that the three Powers have put their hands and, in particular, the Prime Minister of this country has put his hand. The prestige and honor of this country are, therefore, bound up in that decision, and it is my advice to my Polish friends, and to those who so valiantly advocated their cause yesterday, that we should seek to develop that promise, and make sure that it is carried out in the spirit as well as in the letter. I recognize that this may be hard advice, but I believe that it is in the true interests of friends to give advice which is founded upon judgment, and not merely upon emotion. Therefore, I venture to give that advice, believing it to be in the best interests of the Polish nation, and those who have the interest of Poland at heart.

I have done, and I will say only this, in conclusion: In my opinion Yalta marks a great step forward. It may have its limitations, it may have its blemishes, but I never knew of a settlement, agreed to by three parties, that was without them. Nevertheless, taken as a whole, it does represent not merely a tremendous effort but a tremendous achievement in obtaining unity between three Great Powers that are fighting this war. Not only is it a great step forward, but it is a sincere step towards world unity, and on behalf of my party I can assure the Government that if it comes to a Division tonight we shall go into the Division Lobby in support of the Yalta decisions.

THE SECRETARY OF STATE FOR FOREIGN AFFAIRS (MR. EDEN): . . . The hon. Gentleman the Member for Newcastle-under-Lyme (Mr. Mack) asked a question which I should like to answer because it helps once again to clarify a point about which there seems to be some doubt. He asked whether facilities are now to be given to the representatives of the Lublin Government to have contact with Polish seamen here, just as the representatives of the London Government have contact with them. The answer is, "No." We have in no sense recognized the Lublin Committee, and may I add, we have no intention of recognizing the Lublin Committee. We do not regard it as representative of Poland at all. When my right hon. Friend and I met the representatives of this Committee in Moscow, I must say that they did not make a favorable impression upon us. There is no question, and the House need not be anxious that there is any question of our affording recognition to them—not at all. I hoped that I had made that clear yesterday, but from some of the comments in the Debate, I am not sure that I did. It does not surprise me to hear, for instance, as I was told in this Debate, that the Lublin Radio is pouring out streams of contentious stuff. I have no doubt what the Committee want. Their purpose is to maintain the position that they already hold; but that is not what we want, nor is it what the Yalta Conference decided upon. The Foreign Secretary of Soviet Russia and the Ambassadors are now beginning discussions in Moscow, and we shall see whether a broadly representative Polish Government can be created. If it can be created, and if we are satisfied that it is representative, then and only then will we and the United States Government recognize it. If it cannot be created, we shall stay as we are. If it can be, then that is a satisfactory solution. I hope that on this point there is now no further misunderstanding.

MR. MACK: Is it the intention of my right hon. Friend, if he is not satisfied that the Lublin Committee is representative of Poland, to continue to recognize the present Government in London?

MR. EDEN: We have recognized this Government in London, which has gone through many changes. We will continue to recognize it until a new Government is created—if it is created—as a result of the conversations in Moscow, and provided it can be regarded as broadly representative of the Polish people. I received a message a short while ago, to which I understand the hon. Member for South Croydon (Sir H. Williams) referred, of the reported arrest of the wife of the present Polish Prime Minister in London and a certain number of people working with her in the Red Cross. [*Interruption.*] She is reported to have been arrested in Poland. I have had no report about that except a message just before I came to the House, from the Polish Ambassador in London. Of course, we shall take that matter up, not with the Lublin Committee, which we do not recognize, but with the Soviet Government, at the same time informing our American friends of the message we have received. I will then, in due course, when we have made our inquiries, report to the House the outcome of those inquiries, and of those representations.

My hon. Friend the Member for Cambridge University* and others who have been a little critical again today—and I must reply to them—really have not told us what alternative course we ought to pursue. What they have said is, "We do not think you ought to have got into this position." Let me assure the House that we did not want to get into this position. It was because we did not wish to arrive at this position that, a long time ago, my right hon. Friend and I began our efforts—the moment when Polish-Russian relations were broken off—to try to restore them. I repeat what the Prime Minister said, that if little more than a year ago the Polish Government had felt able to come to a decision about

* Mr. Pickthorn.

the frontier position in the East, I am quite certain it would have been possible for us to make arrangements with our Allies whereby that Government would now be in Warsaw with Mr. Mikołajczyk as its Prime Minister. It is just because we feared this present situation was going to arise that we made those efforts. Faced with that situation, neither my hon. Friend, nor anyone else in this Debate, has told us of any course we could pursue, except to sit still and take no action at all. I think it was the hon. Member for Cambridge University who referred to some reference I made to Goebbels in the House yesterday. All I said—I do not think there was very much harm in it, and it seems to be literally true—was:

> "Some of my hon. Friends have said with warmth, that the decision we arrived at at Yalta has become a matter of world anxiety, I really cannot accept that that is true. So far as I know the deepest anxiety of all was caused to Goebbels. If the House will read some of the stuff put out by Goebbels, after the Yalta Agreement, they will see in that the measure of the success of that Agreement."—OFFICIAL REPORT, 28th February, 1945; Vol. 408, c 1512.

I was not passing any reflection on any hon. Member of this House. I was only expressing, I hope, not unnatural satisfaction that Goebbels found himself anxious.

Finally, I want to deal with the question which has been brought into this Debate as to whether or not the Government were right or wise to ask the House to express its opinion on the work we have done in the Crimea. This raises, I fully understand, a very important issue, and we did not lightly take our decision. We gave a three days' Debate, so that all Members of the House, as far as possible, should have a chance to express their views. But after that, after there has been this wide range of opinion, I think it is not only reasonable, but absolutely essential, that the Government should ask the House for an expression of its opinion. Surely, that is how our Parliamentary institutions are carried on. I beg my hon. Friends to believe that it is not a question of trying to test anybody's loyalty. After a work of this kind, whether they agree with it all or not, everyone will agree it is a work of great magnitude and of immense significance for the future—the Government endorse the work our own Prime Minister did, and surely it is not only right, but necessary, that we should ask the House to express its views. If we did not do so, let the House think for a moment what the consequences would be. Each foreign country would assess the opinion of this House in a different way. Everybody who knows the House can judge, or thinks he can judge, though he may not always do this rightly, how the trends of opinion are moving, but foreigners cannot judge that; foreign Governments cannot judge that. They will read the speeches, and it is very natural that in almost any of these Debates it is the critics who are most anxious to speak. That is as it should be. If you are well content there is not much point in getting up and purring once or twice. If you do not feel that way, it is a more agreeable exercise to get up and scratch once or twice. That is always the effect Debates have. If we do not ask the House to take a decision, I do not know how foreign opinion would assess the view of the House on the work we have done.

What are we asking? We are not asking for a detailed approval of every line and comma of this document, though much trouble was taken over those lines and commas. What we ask for is, in the terms of the Motion, for approval of our work and for authority to go on with it. It is an endorsement which we must have. My hon. Friend said, "What will happen if you fail in this Polish business, despite having got the support of the House?" That would be a very serious state of affairs, I do not deny it at all. All I am asking the House to say is we must try, not only in respect of Poland, but of all the other big issues, to go forward.

May I conclude with these words? My right hon. Friend on whom the heaviest burden fell, strove, and I think with success, to bring out of the Crimea a contribution to the future. Let the House remember for a moment the state of our relations as they appeared before the Crimea Conference, and let them look at them now. Let them look at the disappointment our unity has been to the enemy, and surely they must approve in general of what we have done, which is all we ask of them. If they will give us that message, we will go forward, and do our best to be worthy of their trust.

Question put:

> "That this House approves the declaration of joint policy agreed to by the three great Powers at the Crimea Conference and, in particular, welcomes their determination to maintain unity of action not only in achieving the final defeat of the common enemy but, thereafter, in peace as in war."

The House divided: Ayes, 413; Noes, 0.

House of Lords Debate on March 1, 1945.

THE SECRETARY OF STATE FOR DOMINION AFFAIRS (VISCOUNT CRANBORNE) (*Lord Cecil*): My Lords, I rise to move the Resolution which stands in my name:

> "That this House approves the declaration of joint policy agreed to by the three great Powers at the Crimea Conference and, in particular, welcomes their determination to maintain unity of action not only in achieving the final defeat of the common enemy but, thereafter, in peace as in war."

This Resolution is one of the outcomes of the most recent journey of the Prime Minister and the Foreign Secretary to foreign parts in connection with the business of the nation...

The results of the Crimea Conference have been remarkable and far-reaching, and it is right and proper, I think, that they should be approved by Parliament. Your Lordships will have read the Prime Minister's own account of the discussions that took place at Yalta and the conclusions that were reached there, and I will not weary the House by repeating what he has already said. I think that the most convenient course would be for me formally to move this Resolution and then, at the end of the debate, for me to speak again by leave of the House and answer points which have been raised by noble Lords. I understand that that arrangement is acceptable to the leaders of the other Parties, and therefore without more ado, I beg to move the Resolution standing in my name.

Moved to resolve, That this House approves the declaration of joint policy agreed to by the three Great Powers at the Crimea Conference and, in particular, welcomes their determination to maintain unity of action not only in achieving the final defeat of the common enemy but, thereafter, in peace as in war.—*(Viscount Cranborne.)*

LORD ADDISON (Lab.): . . . I would like now to say a few words on the much-discussed subject of Poland. I remember, as some others of your Lordships do, the discussions that went on in 1919, and before, as to the reports on the populations on the eastern borders of Poland, and I have a very clear recollection—and I have, in fact, reminded myself by looking at the papers—of the discussions and memoranda that related to this subject at that time. I think that it was true then, and it is true now, that the Curzon line in the main was as fair a boundary as one could reasonably draw. The Prime Minister quite rightly, I am glad to say, stated that the British support for this boundary was based upon population and other considerations, which have not altered substantially in the last twenty-five years; and that it constitutes a fair and just delimitation; that our support was not due to fear of, or bullying by, Russia or anybody else, but to a just and right appreciation of the case. I am sure that is a well-warranted statement.

Some Papers have been issued, and I expect your Lordships will have received copies, in which we are told about a further partition of Poland. Well, that is not related to reality. It is not a further partition of Poland. I do not forget, and I think it is well to remind ourselves of the fact, that some of the protagonists putting out documents about this imaginary partition of Poland are, or at all events were, in sympathy with those who when Czechoslovakia was invaded by Germany promptly grabbed a piece of the former country. We do not forget actions of that kind and they do not inspire confidence in the fair-mindedness of their promoters. I am glad that the Prime Minister, without any qualification whatever, repudiated these suggestions that it involved a partition of Poland. I believe it is as fair a boundary as could reasonably have been drawn.

It is really a great tragedy that the opportunity presented nearly a year ago through the previous Prime Minister was not allowed, by some influential Poles in London, to be taken as it ought to have been. It would, we are assured, at all events have led to an agreed form of Provisional Government in Poland. I do not see myself that there is any sufficient ground for the complaint that the three collaborators did not bring together in the Crimea representatives of the Lublin Committee, of the London Government and of others. I should have thought that that would have been better calculated to promote discord than anything one could possibly imagine. I cannot see that they had any alternative, in view of the position, than to act as they did. As the Prime Minister said, "We had to settle it." It was essential. I am glad that he went on to say:—

> "The Three Powers are agreed that acceptance by the Poles of the provisions on the Eastern frontiers and, so far as can now be ascertained, on the Western frontiers, is an essential condition of the establishment and future welfare and security of a strong, independent, homogeneous Polish State."

That is a firm statement and I think it should be welcomed.

I confess that one cannot escape the impression that some of the extreme protagonists of the extension of Polish boundaries far to the East, apart from being unacquainted with the population and ethnological facts, seem to be much more inspired by a hatred of Russia than an enthusiasm for Poland, and it is as well to say so. That frame of mind is altogether deplorable. And, after all, we have to remember—and I wish it could be more prominently born in mind by these extreme protagonists of discord—that it is the Russian Armies that have liberated Poland. If it were not for the valor and organization of the Russian Armies, Poland would still be under Germany. It is Russian arms that have given this opportunity, and I think that it is right that we should bear that governing fact in mind.

On the other side, however, I am very glad that whilst there was a feeling that a decision must be arrived at on the question of the Eastern frontiers, so far as it was humanly possible pledges were given and arrangements made to see that there was set up a Free Government in Poland and, so far as one could do so, for the establishment of the machinery for bringing it into being. I can imagine that the three Ambassadors in Moscow will have a very difficult task before them. They will need to exercise all the diplomacy that lies in them. We can only hope that their efforts will be attended with success, because whatever may be said of ourselves, it is unfortunately true from their history that many of our Polish friends are quite disposed to be a bit quarrelsome. That makes the task of conciliators rather more difficult than it otherwise would be. I am sure at all events that the Ambassadors and others deserve every support we can possibly give them. If good will and a reasonable measure of confidence in others can be promoted, it ought to be possible to get together what can be recognized by all three Powers as a sufficiently responsible and representative Provisional Government to inaugurate the establishment of popular government in Poland and to establish what is called, in the jargon of today, a democratic régime.

When I have said all this I hope it will not be thought that I am in any way lacking in sympathy with Poland. We owe a tremendous lot to the valor of the Polish airmen and the Polish troops, and never should we forget it. If we can think more of our obligations to one another and be less suspicious of others that would do a great deal to make things smoother in the future. Speaking of the suspicions of others, I was very glad that the Prime Minister quite definitely refused to be any party to challenging the good faith of our Russian Allies. We cannot hope to get a stable system started in Poland in present circumstances without their good will and help. Geography alone makes that indispensable. I do not know of any case where business men and others who have had dealings with our Russian Allies long before they were

Allies have said that they have not kept their undertakings completely. They have paid their bills for their purchases in this country promptly and honestly for many years past, which is more than can be said of everybody. The record of the Russian Government in its dealings in this country with the business world before the advent of this war is a fine example to all, and I think the Prime Minister was fully warranted in protesting against any suggestion that our Russian Allies are not going to play fair. Nothing could be more ruinous to the future of the world than that we should listen to people who seek to sow distrust between ourselves and our Allies. The whole safety of the world depends upon good will and mutual confidence between us, and we owe a great debt to the Prime Minister for his frank and definite stand in that respect . . .

VISCOUNT SAMUEL (L.): . . . Happily the question of Greece has receded from the theatre of controversy. Now its place is taken by Poland. I have no doubt that some of your Lordships may feel some anxiety as to the policy which has been pursued in regard to Poland. For my own part I support the Motion now before your Lordships' House and not least in its application to the affairs of Poland. It is to that that I shall mainly address my remarks today. The history of Poland for 600 years has been one of constant conflict with the fellow Slavs of the Poles in Russia and of continually shifting frontiers. At one time, 300 years ago, the Polish Empire was the largest in Europe and covered an area as great as that of Germany and France together. That vast Empire which she acquired raised enemies against herself in every direction and in the seventeenth- century the Poles enjoyed only fifteen years of peace as contrasted with 85 years of war. Then, after constant conflicts, wars and diplomatic struggles, Poland was the victim of the three partitions which ended in the disappearance of her name from the map of Europe. In our own day, in 1919, she was re-created and, after the last Great War, she insisted upon her Eastern frontier being extended far beyond any line that was justified by the character of the population. Once more the Polish leaders showed an unhappy lack of restraint and moderation. It was a moment when Russia was *hors de combat* and the Poles seized that moment to extend their frontiers in that manner against the earnest advice of their friends in Western Europe.

No official estimate has ever been published, made by the Poles, as to the ethnographical character of the population between the Curzon Line and the 1939 frontier, but an article by a Polish publicist published in *Free Europe* on April 21, 1944, quotes the census of 1931, which is the latest census of that area. It gives these figures to which I would very specially invite your Lordships' attention. The total population of the area in dispute was 10,768,000. The Poles in that population were 3,914,000—in round figures 4,000,000 out of a total of 11,000,000. The rest were Ukrainians and White Ruthenians 5,649,000, and others 1,200,000. Mr. Eden in the House of Commons at the end of last year—on December 15—used these words:

> "It would be fair to say that, while there are no later figures than those of 1931, the Poles have never constituted more than a third of the total population of this area."*

Nevertheless, in 1919, without any plebiscite, without any consultation with the people of that area, the Poles established their frontier along the line that was maintained until 1939. The British Government refused recognition of that frontier, so wholly did they think it unjustified, and for two years it was not agreed to. Then, at last, it was consented to as a *fait accompli,* but with that very clear pronouncement that we took no responsibility for it and that it was the work only of the Poles and the Russians who then were induced to agree to it. In 1921 the Poles by a military *coup* took Vilna, then alloted to the ancient State of Lithuania. That resulted in open hostility between Lithuania and Poland and a closed frontier which was maintained until quite recently. In 1939, after Munich, the Polish Government sent an ultimatum to

---

* See No. 11.

President Benes of Czechoslovakia, who at that moment was in no position to resist, and seized the district of Teschen.

Meanwhile, in 1920, Poland had entered into an Alliance with France against both Germany and Russia, intended to contain Germany and, at the same time, to establish what was called a *cordon sanitaire* against Bolshevist Russia. Now, viewing the whole situation historically and quite impartially, we must come to the conclusion that this policy of the Poles has been an impossible policy. The history of the last two hundred years shows that Poland cannot live in a state of hostility with both Germany and Russia. She must make friends with either one or the other. When I had the opportunity, some months ago, of having conversations with some of the Polish Ministers I most earnestly pressed that view upon them. They asserted that their great desire was to make friends with Russia, but one is forced to the conclusion that that desire has not been in any degree effectively carried out. The efforts of the Prime Minister and the Foreign Secretary have been devoted continuously to a mediation between Poland and Russia, both of them Allies of our own, and it is of great importance, from every point of view, that there should be a reconciliation. Those efforts unhappily have been unavailing.

A year ago, in the House of Commons, the Prime Minister said:**

> "I may remind the House that we, ourselves, have never, in the past, guaranteed on behalf of His Majesty's Government any particular frontier line in Poland. We did not approve of the Polish occupation of Vilna in 1920. The British view in 1919 stands expressed in the so-called Curzon Line."

The necessity for coming to terms with Russia was recognized by no less a person than the Prime Minister of the Polish Government established in London, namely, Mr. Mikołajczyk, who went to Moscow particularly with that purpose in view, and came back with proposals which he believed were reasonable

** February 22, 1944. See Vol. II, p. 341.

in themselves, and would effect that object. He was, however, immediately deposed from office by his colleagues.

One can understand the unwillingness of many Poles to consent to so great a sacrifice as to give up the four million Poles who inhabit the territories beyond the Curzon Line, and particularly the unwillingness of the landed classes belonging to that region who, with their families, have been established there often for centuries, and who are, most naturally, exceedingly reluctant to be uprooted from the districts in which they have lived for so long. There are also the interests of the Catholic Church which, as we all know, in Eastern Europe has been engaged in continuous rivalry for a thousand years or more with the Orthodox Church and with fluctuating fortunes, and which would be exceedingly reluctant to see important Catholic communities transferred not merely to a Government under the influence of the Russian Church but to a Government which, very possibly, is more or less antagonistic to all Churches. That motive, as Mr. Eden mentioned in the House of Commons yesterday, is a very important factor in the whole situation. Nevertheless, looking at the matter from the point of view of the requirements of statesmanship, neither of these considerations can be regarded as the ultimate and decisive factor, and it is futile for the present Prime Minister of Poland merely to declare—as he has declared—"We shall never surrender."

The matter must be viewed on its merits. The Polish people are a very valiant people. There is none more heroic. In this war, the Polish airmen have won great glory and the highest praise from all who know their work. Their only fault is said to be that they are too brave. Their troops and their seamen also have won great distinction. As we all know, the Poles are an attractive people, very persuasive, and eminent in many of the higher branches of civilization such as literature, music and scholarship. But this must in candor be confessed—in statesmanship they have shown little aptitude. Their history has been an ambitious history, turbulent and checkered and, on the whole, unsuccessful. We, looking at it from the outside, can see quite clearly that it is not in the interests of the Polish people to hold on to provinces in which there is a majority of two to one against them. To hold on to those provinces would be inviting the sustained animosity of Russia while, at the same time, the Poles would always have to face the danger of a revived hostility from Germany. On the other hand, the proposal of the three Powers, made in the Crimea and previously, is that while they surrender this impossible territory they should obtain certain other territories from which the Germans should be withdrawn. Let it be remembered that, at the beginning of this war, Hitler himself required the compulsory emigration from the Baltic States of the Germans who had been established there for centuries —the Balts who had been an outpost of Germanism. They were all withdrawn on Hitler's order, and settled on Polish lands. It is not an impossibility that a similar withdrawal should be made from other areas in that part of Europe, and if that were done then the Poles who wish to remove from east of the Curzon Lines would be able to establish new communities there and look forward to a different future. Furthermore, the Corridor would disappear, that Corridor which, as Mr. Eden mentioned yesterday, has been a source of incessant difficulty and a cause of continuous friction.

So, looking at the matter, as I say, from the outside, we can see a future Poland under the new arrangements, far stronger, with greater material resources and with a much improved geographical position compared with a Poland within the frontiers which they would wish to retain. Then they ask: "Is this to be the recompense for all our sufferings and for our valiant fight in the common cause, that we should submit to territory which has been ours for twenty years, since 1919, being taken away from us?" It is hard, no doubt; but if the matter is regarded as a conflict of interest between the Poles and the Russians, and not as a question to be decided on ethnographical grounds, surely the sufferings of the Russians should be taken into account as well. Have they not suffered also? No one can recount the story of their agonies. If the claim is made because Poland is a small nation and Russia is a great one, is it just to say that only the sufferings of the small nations are to be taken into account, and that the equal and even greater sufferings of the great nations are to be wholly ignored?

Again, it is said that the British people went to war to guarantee Poland, and now we are to end it by abetting an Ally in seizing half the territory of Poland; but, as has been said by the Government and repeated today, we never guaranteed the eastern territory of Poland. On the contrary, we disapproved of the eastern frontier, and it is absurd to say that we should feel that we are bound to use our efforts to secure that that line is continued. We gave no guarantee of the eastern frontier. We went to war in order to prevent Poland being annexed to or dominated by Germany. That will be accomplished. When it is said that this territory is being taken by force, let us remember that it was annexed by the Poles in direct contravention of what may be regarded as an impartial award. It is a territory in which four million people seek to control seven million.

We should all have preferred this issue to be reserved for settlement after the war by regular procedure, but the Russians insist that it is impossible for them, in view of the campaign which is now proceeding in that part of Europe, to agree to such a postponement. They must have in power in Poland a Government which is not animated by bitter hostility to themselves, and they say that they cannot consent to employ their Armies to conquer territory at immense cost, both material and human, only in order to hand it over to a Government animated by such hostility. In view of all the facts of the case, it seems to me wrong to require the British Government to make the postponement of this issue a *sine qua non*. That could only lead to a most serious rift in the alliance between ourselves and Russia, which would conduce in no way to the advantage of Poland...

LORD VANSITTART: . . . On the question of Poland I will say a few words, but so much has been already said that there is little to add. I think that the Polish Government in London would have been better advised to find some words of welcome for the agreement as a whole, seeing what benefits it confers on mankind generally, particularly, for example, the destruction of German militarism by which everybody, including the Poles, stand to gain immeasurably. We were given to understand that the agreement at Yalta was a compromise. Territorially the compromise is not apparent, but politically I do see distinct possibilities and I hope they will be followed up successfully. It remains to be seen how far we shall get, but I have hopes. We are told that the basis of the Polish Government is to be broadened. Well and good; nothing could be better. How far will that take us? I think we must wait to see the outcome of the discussions at Moscow between M. Molotov, Mr. Harriman and Sir Archibald Clark-Kerr, but I doubt whether we shall get very far unless there is a change of heart and habit on the part of the Lublin Committee. Some time ago I made a speech in your Lordships' House in which I urged that they should change their manners in one important respect, that is that they should cease their vindictive abuse of those who do not think quite the same way as they do, and above all cease the persecution of people who have born the brunt of the fighting against the Germans. I rather regret that the suggestion was not followed at the time. Since then these habits have not changed and the result has been that the Lublin Committee has made a poor impression abroad. They can still easily retrieve that reputation with a little good will and I earnestly hope this may be taken as a start for a change.

The case in this particular respect seems to me rather a simple one. Speaker after speaker, headed by the Prime Minister, has gone on record saying that the real and genuine independence of Poland is of more importance than a demarcation of frontiers. There is very great force and truth in this observation. In consequence, everybody is committed to see that this free, independent, strong democratic Poland—all the epithets that were used at Yalta—really comes into being. I have hopes that that may be the case; but what does that exactly mean? In plain English it means this. We all of us have abundant evidence going back a long way—to the 1921 Constitution, in fact; although I do not wish to go back as far as that—which shows clearly that the people represented by the Lublin Committee have always been a minority. If there is to be real justice in the settlement—and I take it that there will be—then the Lublin Committee must loyally accept its true position and proportion. And that means participation but not domination. The "Big Three," or, as Viscount Samuel, before lunch, preferred to call them, the "August Triumvirate," are all committed to that. They have taken a pledge, and it is, I think, for all of us to accept without question that they mean to live up to their obligations. There is no cause whatever for questioning that. If that is true, we shall, again, be within sight of a real compromise in this sphere. If we are going to get this free and unfettered election, based on universal suffrage and the secret ballot, the future will really be very much brighter. We have not yet been told exactly what means it is intended to adopt to ensure that result, and as we are all committed we shall all be entitled to scrutinize . . .

EARL DE LA WARR: . . . Many of your Lordships wish to speak and debate will be very difficult if we all feel it necessary to ramble over the whole field of the agreement. I wish to say that on grounds of higher policy alone we must approve the agreement. Any agreement that makes it possible for the Prime Minister to say, as he did say in another place,

> "The Crimea Conference finds the Allies more closely united than ever before, both in the military and political sphere. Let Germany recognize that it is futile to hope for division among the Allies and that nothing can avert her utter defeat"

must present itself to our minds as one to be considered good. We all of us know that the one and only hope that any German has had for the last few months is that somehow or other it might be possible to bring about division among the United Nations.

But, having said that, I think it would be a pity to imply that this agreement has to be justified or apologized for in terms of the need for unity. The agreement will stand on its own feet. Certainly, as has been said repeatedly before, in this debate and elsewhere, there is no surrender for this country in accepting as the frontier of Poland the Curzon Line. After the enforcement of the Riga Line there were two years before we agreed to it, and then our agreement was, in fact, a mere acceptance of what had happened and what at that moment did not seem capable of being altered. But it is not on the question of the frontier that the gravest concern lies. The Poles main fears were, I think, expressed by the Prime Minister himself, speaking in another place, when he asked the question in his speech "Are the Poles to be masters in their own house?" And later when he asked the question:

> "How will this declaration be carried out? How will phrases like 'Free and unfettered elections on the basis of universal suffrage and secret ballot' be interpreted?"

I might add, What is going to be the fate of Polish prisoners in Russia?

It is not so much the agreement that is concerning some of us, it is how far this agreement is going to be carried out. We all of us hesitate to express any question as to the good faith of any of our Allies. I think we all feel extremely hopeful that this matter will in fact be adjusted according to the lines laid down in this agreement. What is the machinery that is being set up for ensuring its being carried out? We are told by the Prime Minister that arrangements are now being made by the Commission of three consisting of M. Molotov, Mr. Harriman and Sir Archibald Clark-Kerr. How far will they succeed in establishing machinery that will ensure "free and unfettered elections on the basis of universal suffrage and secret ballot?" To be completely successful we are going to need the cooperation of the Poles—if I may say so, more cooperation than sometimes has always been accorded on their behalf; but, subject to the cooperation of the Poles, I would assert that on the success of the arrangements that are being made depends not only the future of Poland but British honor, which is deeply committed, and also the final possibility of our people really being able to work happily in future with the Russian people.

As your Lordships are aware, we are a queer mixture in this country, a queer mixture of realism based on a fundamental belief in certain principles which go deep down into our nature; and it is up to those who speak for us to Russia, or to any other country, to make them realize that we are a democracy. We can have our twenty-years agreements or anything else between Governments, but fundamentally there has to be understanding and confidence between peoples. We are a democracy, and if arrangements are come to that offend deeply the principles in which our democracy believes, then indeed real full cooperation between our peoples is going to be very difficult. If arrangements are come to between the Ambassadors that in fact do not bring about the free and unfettered elections that have been promised, if they merely formalize the rule of Lublin, to which the noble Lord, Lord Vansittart, referred, then I am afraid we shall have a setback in the final unity between our countries. I hope I am not speaking over-frankly, but I am convinced that in the future friendship between nations can only be obtained through complete frankness. I know there are those who say, "We must remember the great mass of Russian strength, we must remember what we owe to Russia in this war. Where would we be today in this great struggle if Russia had not now been in the war?"

THE EARL OF WARWICK: Where would Russia be?

EARL DE LA WARR: When I hear that remark made I find myself saying, as the noble Earl behind me said, "Where would Russia be without our efforts—our efforts during those first two lonely years of the war, our efforts in Africa, our efforts in the Mediterranean and on the high seas, in the air, in Italy and on the Western Front?" And I do hope that in our dealings with Russia, as a people who essentially speak straight to those with whom we are dealing, we shall make them realize that we regard cooperation with them as absolutely essential, not only to our future existence but to the future peace of this world; and that if we are prepared to give cooperation we are prepared also to ask for it. Cooperation must be real; it must not be appeasement...

VISCOUNT ELIBANK: . . . There is one arrangement about which I am not so happy and that is in regard to Poland. The Prime Minister in his great speech on Tuesday told the House of Commons that it was the most difficult problem that they had to deal with at Moscow, and of that there can be no manner of doubt. A more complicated tangled skein of tragic and adverse circumstances has never been presented to any statesman to solve than that provided by Poland today. In his speech Mr. Churchill, with his extreme skill in directly reaching the pith of any question or problem, divided the Polish issue into two parts—frontiers and freedom. Let me deal with the question of frontiers first. The Poles in this country feel that they have had a pretty raw deal with regard to their Eastern boundary. It is true that the Curzon Line now adopted by the three Powers was the armistice boundary line provisionally fixed as ethnographically correct by a Commission after the last war and supported by His Majesty's Government. But it was not agreed by the Polish people and they showed by the military action they took on the first opportunity that they did not agree with it. They succeeded in extending the line considerably further eastwards. Twenty years afterwards, without any consultation with the Polish Government in London, which His Majesty's Government still recognize, this boundary is to be arbitrarily put back by an approximation of the Curzon Line. If I were a Pole I should feel very strongly about this. A great many Poles do feel very strongly about it and I, for one, would be glad if something yet can be done to obtain a compromise boundary which would give them a larger slice of the territory of which they are being deprived or, still better, restore to them the old Polish town of Lwów which lies not very far from what is called the Curzon boundary.

But having said that, I should like to make an appeal to the Poles, as a Scotsman who has been closely associated with them in many ways. In my own county in Scotland we still have several thousands of Poles and the Polish military staff college has been functioning there for the past three years. I have also associated with Poles in London, and I have learnt to admire and respect their many good qualities and the courageous manner in which they have faced their adversities. I have made many friends among them and I feel, therefore, that I shall not be misunderstood in what I say to them today from my place in your Lordships' House.

I would suggest to them that, looking to the future, there are other and even more important points to settle than the eastern boundary if they are once more to become a strong, free, united independent nation. What are the points? They fall under the heading of freedom as described by the Prime Minister in his speech. I will enumerate them very briefly. The first is to establish new boundaries with territorial extension in the west and north; the second is to establish a Provisional Government of national unity which will have the confidence of the Polish nation; the third is to establish a strong, free and independent Poland, and the fourth is to make arrangements for free and unfettered elections which will return a Government which will consolidate all those matters I have mentioned. I should like to suggest to my Polish friends that it is worth while for the moment to ignore the eastern boundary and to give their whole-hearted cooperation in solving these other points in which their whole freedom and the whole welfare of their nation is involved.

I should like to deal with these points individually. Let me first take the question of boundaries on the west and the north. It is proposed, as we heard in the speech of the Prime Minister, that part of East Prussia, the whole of Danzig and Upper Silesia, the Corridor, shall be added to Poland and made part of Polish territory. By this they will get a very large and important territory and almost certainly a richer territory, taking all the resources included in it, than they possessed before the war. But the readjustment of that territory does not, by itself, create a strong and independent Poland. It does not necessarily confer upon the Poles the freedom which the Poles are seeking—that is to say, freedom from outside control and freedom to live their lives according to their own choice, politically, economically and socially. No change of territory can do this. It must come from another source altogether. This is a matter which I particularly urge His Majesty's Government should never lose sight of now or in the future.

Then there is the question of establishing a new Polish Provisional Government of National Unity. As was stated by the noble Lord, Lord Addison, this will be a very delicate and difficult task. It will be an almost impossible task unless the Polish Government in this country assist, so far as they can, in broadening the basis of that Government. I do not see, if my Polish friends here are not going to play—if I may use that expression—in connection with the formation of that Government, how they can expect to have proper representation in it. There again I appeal to them to take up a somewhat different attitude from the attitude they have taken up to the present to my own personal knowledge.

Next there is the question of free and unfettered elections on the basis of universal suffrage and secret ballot. We have Marshal Stalin's word that he will do all he can to support those proposals, and I do not doubt his word. I believe that so far as he can he will carry out that pledge. But I venture to suggest that some of his agents and people may not be so trustworthy as he is, and I urge His Majesty's Government not to agree to elections taking place until all Russian troops have been withdrawn from Poland, together with their secret police and agents. Until this has been done, I venture to believe that there can be no possible guarantee of free and unfettered elections. Even so, I am somewhat skeptical about really free and unfettered elections taking place in the atmosphere which has been created in Poland during the past five years of hideous war and suffering. And, probably, in the last resort—I do not know whether this is being discussed at the moment, but I have heard it suggested—it may be found that it will be necessary to have these elections under international control, on a basis somewhat similar to that which was adopted in regard to the Saar some years ago.

I wish to say to my friends the Poles that so much depends upon their cooperation today that I feel that unless they really come to the practical conclusion that it is necessary to step out and extend a measure of good will and cooperation in regard to what His Majesty's Government here are trying to achieve for them, and the efforts now being made do not succeed, then in a great measure the failure may be attributed to them in the future. I believe that our Government, headed by the Prime Minister, have done their best to obtain the most practicable settlement of this vexed Polish question. I am sorry that the Prime Minister has had to do this work without consultation with the Polish Government here. Nevertheless, having done what has been done, I suggest that there rests a very grave responsibility on the shoulders of His Majesty's Government, as well as upon the shoulders of the other two signatory powers, to see that the settlement in all its details is carried out in the letter as well as the spirit.

THE EARL OF ELGIN AND KINCARDINE: My Lords, what I had intended to say to your Lordships has already been said so eloquently by other speakers that I shall detain you only for a few moments. I would wish to add my tribute to those of others to the splendid leadership given to us by the untiring energy and devotion of the Prime Minister, and also to express acknowledgment of the call to unity among the Allies which is embodied in the Motion before us. I should wish also without any reserve to acknowledge the splendid contribution given to the cause in which we are all engaged by Soviet Russia; but having done that, I confess I feel some anxiety, as other speakers have already done in regard to the position of Poland now and in the future. The noble Viscount, Lord Samuel, in a most impressive and eloquent speech analyzed the tangled history of Poland and gave us a very graphic description of the difficulties which have confronted her through the ages, and which have been increased by her own actions. But not one of us here will deny that in a struggle in which we have been engaged for five years Poland has taken her part without reserve, and with a courage and skill which cannot be surpassed. She has taken her part in every field of action, on land, on sea and in the air, and in every field she has shown herself well qualified in the art of warfare. Latest of all we have had her participation in that epic achievement at Arnhem in which the Polish Parachute Brigade took such an influential part.

Acknowledging that, we do feel, as the noble Viscount, Lord Elibank, explained in greater detail, that there are special difficulties confronting Poland at the moment, created and emphasized by the Yalta Conference. The noble Lord, Lord Addison, in his opening speech referred to the fact that Poland was liberated by the action of Soviet Russia. That is perfectly true, but we cannot shut our eyes to the fact that the liberation, involving as it does the acceptance of the Curzon Line, means that probably between 3,000,000 and 4,000,000 Poles have to leave an old-established home and seek a new one, and the fact has been brought home to us during the debate in another place by the offer of British citizenship to such Poles as do not feel it possible to return to their homeland. It is the tragedy of that situation which, I think, must prompt us to do anything we can to help in a practical way in the present situation.

How is the establishment of a free and independent Poland to be accomplished? The noble Earl, Lord De La Warr, in his speech dealt with certain aspects of that, and stressed the importance which must be given to the liberty of the Poles to vote. He mentioned various categories of those Poles, but there is another category to which no reference has yet been made by any speaker, and that comprises those Poles who are actively taking part in the Fighting Services in Italy, on the Western Front and elsewhere. How are their votes to be recorded? They must, certainly, if justice is to be done, be given an opportunity of recording their wishes in the establishment of a free and independent Poland and in the formation of its Government.

The noble Lord, Lord Vansittart, also stressed the vital need of cooperation, and both he and the noble Viscount, Lord Elibank, referred to the fact that the present Government of Poland find it difficult to cooperate; but Lord Vansittart rightly stressed also that cooperation must be obtained from the Lublin Committee, that they must enter into the spirit of the formation and foundation of this free and independent Poland with the idea of cooperation, and not domination. Here, again, I think our influence might be brought to bear to help in the solution of this difficulty. Our efforts therefore must be to help in any way we can to establish a feeling of trust, co-operation, and friendly helpfulness in all elements of Poland itself, and of Poland in whatever part of the world it may be operating.

I had the opportunity of bringing the subject of Poland and her sufferings before your Lordships in a debate in December, 1942.* You accepted unanimously the Motion which I then presented to you, and may I quote the final words of the noble Earl who spoke then for the Government, Lord Selborne:

> "The Polish nation, led by its great Prime Minister, General Sikorski, will march to final victory. All our pledges to Poland, to which the Noble Earl referred, will be honored. Great Britain drew the sword to fulfill the first pledge that we gave to Poland; we shall not sheathe our sword until the last pledge has been fulfilled."

I do hope that every one of us will do all we can to help Poland in this time of her tragedy, and help her to build a glorious, free Poland in the time to come.

VISCOUNT TEMPLEWOOD: . . . The Government would, I

---

* Vol. II, No. 21.

believe, be the first to admit that while we have before us a great plan, not only for the immediate future but for the longer distances, that plan must be judged upon its actual results. All the great questions that were dealt with at Yalta depend on what actually is done, not only by the Great Allies but by the United Powers generally, in the months and the years to come. There is the question of Poland, a question that has loomed very largely in the discussions of today, and perhaps still more largely in the discussions in another place. I approach the Polish question not in any way as a partisan. I do not pretend to understand the extraordinarily complicated intricacies of the Polish question, still less do I approach them with any bias against our Russian Allies. I have seen enough of foreign affairs to know that we are dealing with one of the most difficult questions in Europe—one of those difficult questions in which both sides are right, always the most difficult of all questions in human experience. If every one were as reasonable as the noble Viscount, Lord Samuel, who gave such a remarkable analysis of Polish history this morning, there would be no difficulty in finding a reasonable and permanent solution of the difficulties. Unfortunately that is not the case. We are dealing with a problem fraught with historical prejudice, with bitter racial sentiments, with strong religious convictions; and not least perhaps we are dealing with a people who have suffered every kind of horror in the last six years.

Let us not judge too easily these Poles, whatever may be their particular opinions. Let us not judge too easily the Government in London. It seems to me that an emigré Government, whatever may be its views, is in a terribly difficult position. There it is, separated from its own country, its members knowing that every kind of horror is being perpetrated upon their relatives; inevitably in a state of strained nerves, inevitably almost upon the verge of hysterical emotion. That being so, let us be patient with those sections of the Polish people with whom, it may be, some of us disagree. I do not believe that the best way to obtain a workable arrangement is to abuse the Poles in London or to abuse the Poles in Lublin. I agree very much with the views expressed by the noble Viscount, Lord Elibank, and by the noble Earl, Lord Elgin. It is for us to do our utmost to be peacemakers between those two sections of Polish opinion.

For what it is worth, my advice to the Poles in London would be upon the lines given by Lord Elibank. I would advise them to accept, in the letter and in the spirit, the Yalta Agreement, and I would advise them subsequently to judge by results and to do their utmost, in cooperation with the great Allies, to ensure the safeguards that are explicitly set up in the Yalta Agreement. Having given my humble advice to the Poles in London, I would also venture to say that as far as the Soviet are concerned I am convinced that they would greatly improve the atmosphere here for obtaining a workable arrangement if they could use the influence of the Soviet Government to stop the newspaper attacks upon the Poles in London, just as I hope that the Poles in London would stop their attacks upon the Poles in Poland. Further than that, I think almost the keenest test of the sincerity of the arrangements made for the Polish compromise would be that the Poles who were members of the underground resistance movement in Poland and who subsequently were arrested and deported should now be liberated. I do not know whether noble Lords take the same view as I do upon this matter, but what has most moved me in all this terrible history in Eastern Europe in recent months has been the magnificent, forlorn-hope fight by the Poles in Warsaw. It may have been mistimed—I do not know—it may have been misguided, but there you had men laying down their lives day after day not abandoning the fight until most of them were exterminated. I do hope that when the noble Viscount comes to reply he will be able to tell us that those members of the resistance movement who were subsequently arrested and deported have already been liberated or that they are going to be liberated as a result of the Yalta Agreement . . .

THP EARL OF PERTH: My Lords, I would like, if I may, to call your Lordships' attention to the Resolution itself. That

Resolution falls into two parts. The first asks for your Lordships' approval of the declaration of joint policy agreed to by the three Great Powers at the Crimea Conference, and the second part "welcomes their determination to maintain unity of action not only in achieving the final defeat of the common enemy but, thereafter, in peace as in war." I think it will be universally agreed that unless the three Great Powers hold together and are united the future outlook for the world must be a very somber one. I feel therefore that the Government should be encouraged to do everything in their power to promote and preserve that unity between the three Great Powers. We ought to bear that aim in mind when we discuss the first part of the Resolution which asks for approval of the joint policy framed at the Crimea Conference.

That policy, as far as I am aware, has been subject to only one point of criticism—namely, on the question of Poland. That is obviously a question of deep importance since, by many people, it is considered the test case. I hope, therefore, your Lordships will allow me to present a few considerations in addition to the vast amount that has been already said and written on the subject. The case of Poland, as has been pointed out, has two quite different aspects. There is first the boundary problem and secondly the establishment of a strong, free and independent Poland. On the question of the Eastern boundary I am frankly a strong supporter of the Curzon Line. As the noble Viscount, Lord Samuel, pointed out, there is no Polish ethnographical majority east of that line. If there had been I have no doubt such a fact would have weighed heavily with those who suggested that line because, at the time, very special account was taken of population statistics and ethnographical factors. It is true, of course, that there are a very large number of Poles east of that line—more than 3,000,000—but that is due to the extreme intermingling and mixture of populations which we find in that part of Europe which has always rendered any clear-cut settlement extremely difficult.

The fact that there is this large population must be faced,

and I would urge that all Polish families and individuals east of the line who desire to leave their territory and go to what will be the new Poland, should be allowed to do so, that they should be allowed to take with them, as far as practical arrangements allow, their movable goods and to receive—again, if possible—compensation for immovable property which they would have to abandon. I do not know how far the stories are true of large numbers of Poles being sent to remote parts of Russia. I fear something of this kind may have happened, perhaps largely owing to considerations of war operations, but this being so I hope that His Majesty's Government will appeal to the sense of right and justice in the Soviet Government and urge, if necessary, that these Poles should be allowed to go back and settle among their compatriots in the new Poland.

I hope very much that the noble Viscount, the Leader of the House, will be able to give me some reassurance on this particular point. I think all of us—I in particular, realize fully the ancient historic appeal which the cities of Lwów and of Vilna make to Polish sentiment. Nevertheless, those who have studied this question, and in particular those of us who know in what conditions Vilna became Polish after the last war, cannot, however much our emotions may be moved, allow these particular facts to influence our final and unbiased judgment. I need not labor the point but I would like to add one word. If I had been asked by anyone during the last twenty years what was a fair and proper boundary between Soviet Russia and Poland I should have unhesitatingly replied: "The Curzon Line." Ever since the last war we have had continual racial troubles and disturbances in that part of the world. The Foreign Secretary referred to his experiences at Geneva during a certain number of years and the troubles he had in connection with minority questions. I think the noble Viscount, the Leader of the House, will remember his difficulties as well. But those difficulties were only difficulties which used to occur four times a year. We had to serve up the dish and they tasted it, but I had to look at the pot once a week and see that it did not boil over.

We have to accept different standards for the eastern boundary of Poland and the western. The eastern boundary is to be fixed now. I quite realize that there may be material necessities which force us to accept that view, but I think most of us agree that we should have liked, as a matter of principle, that the whole matter should have waited for final determination by the United Nations as a whole. As regards the western boundary I am not going to weary your Lordships with the reasons which I have given before why in my view East Prussia should, most certainly, be transferred to Poland. I think the reasons are unanswerable. I would, however, like to lay stress on one point. East Prussia must not be given to Poland as compensation for the territories she will lose in the east. It should go to Poland because it is right that it should go to Poland, for economic, strategic and geographical reasons, and also because—and I believe this to be the fact—the transfer of this territory to Poland will make for an enduring peace. I know that there has been some criticism of this proposal of transference on the ground that it runs contrary to Clause 2 of the Atlantic Charter—"no territorial changes that do not accord with the express wishes of the peoples concerned." But the Charter must be taken as a whole, and underlying and inspiring the whole of that magnificent instrument—for I think that it is a magnificent instrument—is, surely, the principle of an enduring peace based on justice, on free peoples, on "freedom from fear, and freedom from want." And, additionally, I hope very much that the Atlantic Charter on this particular point will be met, because I think there ought to be a large transfer of the main German population of East Prussia to Germany proper.

Now I come to my second point, the establishment of a strong, free and independent Poland. The constitution of such a Poland is a debt of honor which we, and indeed all the great Allies, owe to a very gallant and chivalrous nation upon whom a most bitter burden of suffering has fallen. That burden has been most gallantly and courageously borne. Frankly, I do not very much like the kind of argument used by the noble Lord, Lord Addison, and also, I think, in another place, by the Prime Minister to the effect that without the magnificent achievements of the Russian forces Poland would never have been liberated from German domination. Of course, it is true but let us go a little further back in time. Suppose that Poland—and this is unthinkable, I am glad to say—had joined Germany against Russia: where would Russia have been then? I am not going to pursue the argument. I leave it at that point.

It seems to me to be essential for the future that we should secure a really representative Government of Poland, a Government representing and based on the freely expressed will of the Polish people. It is quite clear that the London Government today, and still less the Lublin Committee, do not represent the freely expressed will of the Polish people. Poles who have been removed from their homes must be allowed to go back—unless, of course, they are collaborators. But there are very few, if any, Polish collaborators. It is a most remarkable thing: here is a country that could not find one Quisling. I think this calls for a great tribute to the Poles. I hope that there will be some outside supervision to see that there is real liberty at the election and that no coercion is used. That is a matter that is worrying all the people of Poland and our Polish friends here, and indeed all of us. I am not going to detain your Lordships any longer. There is no doubt that the declaration and the principles laid down at the Yalta Conference are excellent. The principles and intentions are admirable. But, to my mind, the touchstone will lie in their execution. His Majesty's Government have undertaken a very grave responsibility, a very great responsibility. Many of us will judge the Yalta Conference in the light of how that responsibility is effectively fulfilled. Today, surely, we cannot do more than fully approve of the declarations, which have been made, and warmly congratulate the Government on them.

THE SECRETARY OF STATE FOR DOMINION AFFAIRS (VIS-

COUNT CRANBORNE): . . . I think I have now dealt broadly with the more general questions which were discussed in the Crimea. They are far-reaching and comprehensive and the decisions which have been reached should go far to lay the foundation stones of the new world. But opportunity was also taken, as your Lordships know, to tackle another problem, more limited in scope but equally important for the preservation of peace, and that is the problem of Poland, to which so much of today's debate has been devoted. As the noble Viscount, Lord Templewood, with all his long experience of these questions, said in his speech this afternoon, this is in many ways the thorniest question of the day, and he added —and I cordially agree— that this is not a time for abuse, it is a time for clear, cool thinking by ourselves and the Poles. On the last occasion when I addressed your Lordships on this subject, the House will perhaps remember that I said that a complete deadlock appeared to have been reached and that the only hope seemed to be that some solution would be found at the forthcoming meeting of the Big Three. Now the Big Three have met, and they have produced a plan which covers every aspect of this thorny problem.

The details of the plan are already well known to your Lordships. They have been described in full in the Crimea Declaration, and they have formed the subject of powerful speeches by the Prime Minister and by my right hon. friend the Foreign Secretary. As the Prime Minister said in his speech, any plan which seeks to solve the problem of Poland must deal with two main questions: the question of the Polish boundaries and the question of Polish independence. It is the first of these, the boundary question, which, rather curiously I think, has throughout the whole of this long controversy occupied the main attention of the public in this country. Perhaps that is only natural because, after all, the loss of territory is always painful, and it is particularly painful when the country which is to lose the territory is not one of the vanquished but one of the victors in the war, and when it is a country, too, which has earned the admiration of the world for its unconquerable spirit in the face of cruelty and oppression.

On the other hand, while I think it would be quite wrong to suggest—and I certainly do not propose to suggest—that the transfer of these lands east of the Curzon Line from Poland to Russia will not constitute a very painful sacrifice for the Polish people—because it clearly does—it would be equally wrong to assume that the new proposals, taken a a whole, will not prove of benefit to Poland in the long run. It would be extremely difficult, as has been said today, for us to maintain that Poland has an inalienable right to these territories, when our own experts took the view, after the last war, that they were not ethnologically part of Poland and when we had already advised, with what turns out now to be extremely wise forethought, that they would be a constant bone of contention between her and her great neighbor, were she to retain them. As Lord Addison said in his speech, we advised and indeed protested against the occupation by Poland of those particular territories. The fact, which was mentioned by Lord Elibank this afternoon, that the Polish Government did not agree with us and took these territories, where they were in a minority, by force, cannot be held to bind us.

Lord Addison said that this cannot be called a further partition of Poland, and of course it cannot. What she is going to lose is, at best, debatable ground, and she is going to gain infinitely richer territory, with a wide seaboard. The need for the Polish Corridor, which has been the source of so much strife in the last twenty years, is now abolished, and vast proportion of East Prussia and the rich industrial regions of Southern Silesia will come within her boundaries. That is not a bad exchange, if one looks at it in a cool and objective manner. It may very well be that had this settlement, instead of the earlier settlement, been reached at the end of the last war, Poland would have been very much better off than she was in the inter-war years. I believe profoundly that this new delimitation of Polish boundaries is a far sounder one, both politically and economically, than the one reached at the end of the last war, and that future experience will justify it. Perhaps it would have been better, as Lord Perth remarked, in an ideal world, that all these territorial decisions should have been left over until the end of the war. Unfortunately, as your Lordships know, events did not permit of that.

At the same time, as Lord De La Warr said in his speech, no territorial settlement, however satisfactory that territorial settlement may be, will be of any value unless Poland is truly independent and not a mere vassal of Russia. To the people of this country, who have gone to war on this very issue of Polish independence, that must be a vital consideration, and I think it is perfectly right and proper that Parliament should submit this portion of the Crimea proposals to the very closest scrutiny. I would like, if your Lordships will allow me, once more to examine these proposals, which have not been discussed together this afternoon. Reference has been made to one or other of them but not to the proposals as a whole. Your Lordships will have noted that the Crimea Declaration, of which I would remind your Lordships Russia is a signatory, reaffirms unequivocally—I quote the words—"our common desire to see established a strong, free and independent Poland." The Declaration then proceeds to define how this end is to be attained. First of all, the present Provisional Government, which is now functioning inside Poland—what we have called the Lublin Committee—is to be reorganized by the inclusion of democratic leaders from both inside and outside Poland. It is to be made a new Government, fully representative of all the democratic and Anti-Nazi Parties. To ensure that all the three Powers are satisfied that this is in fact being done, a Commission is being set up in Moscow, composed of the Soviet Commissar for Foreign Affairs and the British and United States Ambassadors, to consult with representative Poles with a view to the reorganization of the Government on the lines approved at Yalta. I can assure the House, most sincerely, that it is the firm intention of His Majesty's Government that these consultations shall in fact be free and unfettered, and that these representative Poles, who come from both inside and outside Poland, shall be given a full opportunity of making their views known.

When the new Provisional Government has been formed, it is to be pledged at the earliest moment possible to hold, as has been said this afternoon, free elections on the basis of universal suffrage and the secret ballot,and at these elections all democratic and anti-Nazi Parties are to have the right to put forward their candidates. It will be seen that these provisions—your Lordships will forgive me for having gone through them again—which are designed to ensure that the new Provisional Government will be as representative and as democratic as possible, are extremely comprehensive. I do not think they could be more comprehensive than they are. Certainly much care and trouble was taken by the Prime Minister and the other representatives at Yalta to ensure this. Moreover, there is one further safeguard which is provided. There are to be Ambassadors appointed by the three Powers to the new Provisional Government, who will be able to report to their Government that it is not abusing its authority, either at the time of the elections or at any other time. The point was made in one of the speeches, how was it to be ensured that we should be able to keep an eye on the election? That will be one of the duties of the Ambassadors who will be appointed.

Finally, until it is certain that the new Provisional Government is properly formed on a basis more representative than either the Polish Government in London or the Lublin Committee, His Majesty's Government will continue to recognize the London Government and will not recognize the Lublin Committee. Unless we are going to take the view that the Soviet Government is utterly unreliable, these safeguards should surely be effective. If we take that black view about Russia, of course there is no hope for the future at all, not merely in regard to the Polish Agreement but in regard to every other agreement. The World Organization itself, which is to be negotiated at San Francisco, will be so much waste paper. That seems to me to be a counsel of despair and I do not think any of us will take that view.

I have now gone very fully into the proposals of the Crimea Conference with regard to Poland.

THE EARL OF PERTH: Will you allow me for one moment? There was a point which I raised—the position of the Poles east of the Curzon Line.

VISCOUNT CRANBORNE: I am going to deal with that. I have still several points with regard to Poland to deal with. It may I repeat possibly be considered that I have gone into the proposals too fully. But the issues are so important that it seems to me essential that there should be no misunderstanding. It would be very easy to suggest modifications or amendments to these proposals, and some of them have been suggested today. Lord Templewood asked me a question as to whether any undertaking had been given for the release of Polish patriots who have been arrested or deported by the Russian Armies. There is no provision made in the actual Declaration. But I can say to your Lordships that this is a matter to which His Majesty's Government attach the highest importance, and this aspect of the matter will, I understand, be raised in Moscow in connection with the Commission. Then there was a similar question from the noble Earl, Lord Perth, the one to which he has just referred. He asked His Majesty's Government, as I understand him, to do what they can with the Soviet Government to ensure that the Poles east of the Curzon Line will be allowed to settle with their goods as far as practicable in the new Poland. The answer to his question is this. His Majesty's Government would certainly be in favor of all Poles east of the Curzon Line, who opt to move into the new Poland, being allowed to do so freely. The Lublin Poles—that is to say the Polish authorities on the spot—are understood to have already concluded an agreement with the Ukrainian, the White Russian and Lithuanian Soviet Republics providing for the exchange of populations and it is understood such an exchange is already beginning. I think that is the answer for which the noble Earl was asking.

Then the noble Earl, Lord Elgin, asked two questions. The first was, will members of the Polish Forces fighting at present under the British Command be eligible for British citizenship? That question was in fact answered by the Prime Minister in his speech in the House of Commons. What he said was that he hoped that as a result of the new proposals the Polish soldiers in question would be able and willing to return to Poland; but, if not, he hoped it would be possible to arrange for them to receive British citizenship. But he added, what I am sure the noble Earl will understand, that this is of course not a matter merely for us but for the Dominions also. Lord Elgin also asked whether there would be voting rights for Poles in the Fighting Services now under the British Command. In answer to this question, I think I had best refer the noble Earl again to another passage in the Prime Minister's speech, in which he said that "His Majesty's Government are resolved that as many as possible of the Polish troops should be enabled in due course to return to Poland of their own free will and, under every safeguard, to play their part in the future life of their country." I understand it is the view of His Majesty's Government that, if this can be achieved, Polish troops now serving under British Command in the British Isles and in Italy would be enabled to take part in the elections. My Lords, I do not say that if we alone had been given the task of solving the Polish problem, we should have produced a scheme absolutely identical with the Crimea proposals. No doubt, that is equally true of the Soviet Union. This is a joint scheme which had to be acceptable to all the Powers gathered at Yalta. It is, as Lord Vansittart has said, in the nature of a compromise. But, if it is carried out in its entirety, it should, I believe, satisfy the essential requirements both of ourselves and of the Polish people. I recognize that preoccupations on this subject still exist. Some of them were expressed this afternoon by Lord De La Warr and others by the noble Viscount, Lord Templewood.

Lord Templewood asked, I gathered, in connection with the Polish problem, whether I could define the United Nations attitude to the Atlantic Charter. That, I thought, was a rather strange request. For it is clearly impossible for the spokesman of one Government unilaterally to define the attitude of all the United Nations. But I think the best answer I can give him is one that has already been given in this House this afternoon. I think he gave it himself, when he quoted the words which were used by the Prime Minister in another place on the 21st February, to the effect that the Atlantic Charter was to be regarded as a guide and not as a rule. Still less, in my view, is it to be regarded as a strait jacket. It would be contrary to all British tradition to be entirely hide-bound by any written constitution of that kind. The noble Viscount, Lord Templewood, has himself been Foreign Secretary and he knows very well, as we all know, the fate of policies which have no chance of acceptance by the main countries concerned. We must take account of realities in framing our policy. But subject to that brief comment, I would assure Lord Templewood that it is the aim of His Majesty's Government to frame their policy in accordance with the principles of the Atlantic Charter.

And now, to return to the policy recommended at Yalta with regard to Poland: What alternative is there to that policy? I have felt all along that there are only two possible policies regarding Poland. One is to find a settlement acceptable to Russia, and that to my mind is as essential to Poland as to us. The other is to stand aside and wash our hands of the whole thing. The second policy would have been an extremely easy one to adopt. It would have been far easier than the one which we in fact did adopt. But how would it have helped the Poles? What would be their position now if we had adopted that policy? The whole country of Poland would have been handed over to the Lublin Committee, undiluted by the elements who are now to be brought in, and the situation for the Poles would have been infinitely worse than it is. Moreover, a position would have continued in which Russia recognized one Government and we and the United States recognized another. I cannot imagine any situation more dangerous for world harmony than that. I believe that the policy of washing our hands would have been universally condemned by the British people, and that it would have been regarded as a contemptible abandonment of our heroic Ally in her extremity. Today, we can at any rate say that we have done our best for our Polish Allies. It is for the critics, if there are any, to produce a better alternative. Personally I have not seen it yet...

* * *

Motion agreed to nemine dissentiente.

27. AIR CONNECTION WITH POLAND*

SIR ARCHIBALD SINCLAIR (L.): . . . The other activity of Bomber Command to which I referred . . . is one of which little public mention has yet been made. When the peoples of Europe awoke from the nightmare of 1940, they found themselves powerless against the mechanized might of Nazi Germany. To the Royal Air Force fell the task of supplying arms to the resurgent peoples of Europe. A plan to arm the patriots of Europe was drawn up between the Services. A small force of aircraft was allotted to the task. . . . In difficult country the navigation risks were almost as formidable as the risks from the enemy. Frequently pilots had to land their aircraft in occupied territory to bring out leading members of the Underground movement.

For example, it became necessary last Spring to bring out of South East Poland some staff officers of the Polish Underground Forces. Two days before the operation was due to take place, the suspicion of the Germans in the district was aroused. The local peasants and farmers, all members of the under-

* House of Commons. Vol. 408, Mar. 6, 1945, p. 1859–1860.

ground organization, were mobilized. Their rifles, pistols, and hand grenades were taken out of the hiding-places where they were kept between the battles which the Polish Secret Army had been fighting for four years and were put into action. For 48 hours the brave Poles fought. They lost 42 men killed and many wounded, but they kept the landing ground—a field of stubble—clear. A Dakota aircraft, flown by a British crew with a Polish navigator flew in, landed safely, and five minutes later took off with its important passegers.[1]

28. EAST PRUSSIA — KOENIGSBERG*

PROFESSOR SAVORY (C.) asked the Secretary of State for Foreign Affairs on what ethnological or historical grounds His Majesty's Government have agreed to the City of Koenigsberg being ceded to Russia.

THE SECRETARY OF STATE FOR FOREIGN AFFAIRS (MR. EDEN): As has been frequently stated it is the view of His Majesty's Government that East Prussia should be detached from Germany and the German population removed from it. In such conditions it would seem that the Soviet claim to Koenigsberg has justification. So far as I am aware, there is no considerable Polish element in the city.

PROFESSOR SAVORY: Have we abandoned Clause 5 of the Anglo-Soviet Treaty under which we mutually renounced all territorial aggrandizement in this war?[2]

MR. EDEN: My hon. Friend had better re-read Clause 5 and the second part of the Anglo-Soviet Treaty, which refers to the post-war period. The Prime Minister made it quite clear, in respect of the Atlantic Charter, that we did not consider that it applied to enemy territory.

---

[1] No confirmation could be found in the Archives of the Polish Home Army of the information given here by Sir Archibald Sinclair.
* House of Commons. Vol. 408, Mar. 6, 1945, p. 1997–1998.
[2] Vol. II, no. 15.

MR. GALLACHER (Com.): Is the right hon. Gentleman aware that the hon. Member is afraid that this might be used as a precedent for ceding Belfast to Ireland?

29. TARNOPOL, VILNO, LWOW*

ON SEPT. *9, 1944 the Lublin Committee reached an understanding with the Ukrainian and White-Russian Governments with respect to the transfer of populations. Following is the communique issued on Sept. 14 on this subject:*[1]

Negotiations have taken place between the Polish Committee of National Liberation and the Government of the Ukrainian Soviet Socialist Republic and the Byelorussian Soviet Socialist Republic and an agreement has been signed concerning the evacuation of Polish citizens from the Ukraine and Byelorussia to Poland, provided the citizens were Polish subjects before Sept. 17, 1939, and the evacuation of the Ukrainian and Byelorussian population from Polish territory to the Ukraine and Byelorussia.

The agreement provides that the evacuation will be voluntary and its conditions made known to the population by special representatives of the Polish Liberation Committee and the Councils of People's Commissars of the Ukraine and Byelorussia who will supervise the evacuation.

The settling and provision of employment for the evacuees will be provided for by respective Governments. Persons evacuated from Poland to Ukrainian and Byelorussia territory will be either fixed up in collective farms or alloted plots of land for the cultivation of individual peasant homesteads. Persons evacuated from the Ukraine and Byelorussia to Polish territory will also receive land on a scale in accordance with law governing agrarian reforms in Poland.

Evacuated peasants who held no land will also receive land on the general basis.

The agreement provides for various privileges for the evacuees. All their arrears of deliveries in kind, arrears in taxes and payments for insurance are to be written off. All evacuated homesteads in the three territories are freed from all State taxes and insurance payments for two years. The evacuees will be granted

* House of Commons. Vol. 408, Mar. 6, 1945, p. 1998–1999.
1 Stosunki polsko-sowieckie, 1943–46, p. 236.

assistance in each the sum of 5,000 zloty (or rubles) per homestead to buy agricultural equipment, etc. This sum is to be paid off in five years.

The evacuees will also be permitted to take with them various household and agricultural articles to the total weight of two tons per family and the cattle and fowl they own. When an evacuee has to leave his harvest behind the State will provide full compensation, a harvest of equal quantity, for him at the place to which he is being evacuated. All evacuees who have sown winter crops on their present holdings, will receive an equal amount of winter crops at their destination.

The cost of movable and immovable property left behind after the evacuation is to be paid to the evacuees according to the laws existing in Poland, the Ukrainian SSR and the Byelorussian SSR.

The agreement was signed on behalf of the Government of the Ukrainian SSR by Comrade Khrushchev, on behalf of the Polish Liberation Committee by Osóbka-Morawski, and on behalf of the Byelorussian SSR by Comrade Pomarenko.

PROFESSOR SAVORY (C.) asked the Secretary of State for Foreign Affairs if he is aware that persons of Polish nationality form, according to the census of 1931, a majority of the inhabitants of the city of Tarnopol; and what steps the Allies are proposing to take in order to safeguard the rights of the Polish majority in this city as well as those in the cities of Wilno and Lwów.

THE SECRETARY OF STATE FOR FOREIGN AFFAIRS (MR. EDEN): The Polish census of 1931 did not give separate population figures for the city of Tarnopol. The figures for the whole province of Tarnopol showed that neither by language nor by religion were the Poles in an absolute majority, though they did form a majority in the urban areas as a whole. The Poles in this area have under the agreement concluded in September, 1944, between the Lublin Committee and the Government of the Ukrainian Republic of the USSR the same right as those in other parts of Eastern Galicia to transfer to the West of the Curzon Line.

PROFESSOR SAVORY: If the right hon. Gentleman will look up the figures again, he will find that in the city of Tarnopol the Poles have an absolute majority of 77 per cent and a similar majority in the administrative district of Tarnopol. Further, will he put in a word for the thousands of Poles, Ukrainians, and White Ruthenians who have been arrested and deported to unknown destinations?

MR. EDEN: I am dealing with the last part of the question in another answer. One of the reasons why we were so anxious that these conversations in Moscow should proceed and reach a conclusion was in order that this situation, and reports of various kinds, may be finally checked and, I trust, the situation disposed of. I believe I have given accurate figures but I will check them again.

MR. PRICE (Lab.): Do not those figures include Jews and Greek Catholics as well as Polish Roman Catholics?

MR. EDEN: I do not know. I did not quote the figures.

PROFESSOR SAVORY: No.

30. RELIEF FOR POLAND*

MISS RATHBONE (Ind.) asked the Secretary of State for Foreign Affairs whether any reply has now been received from the Government of the USSR giving permission for a delegation or supplies from UNRRA to reach Poland or any districts in Russia where Polish or other deported persons are in need of assistance; and whether similar permission has been given for missions or supplies to be sent by any bodies other than UNRRA.

THE SECRETARY OF STATE FOR FOREIGN AFFAIRS (MR. EDEN): I am informed that the Russian authorities have promised UNRRA facilities for the transit of supplies to Poland. Arrangements for the transit of a delegation are not yet concluded, but the dispatch of supplies is not being delayed on

* House of Commons. Vol. 408, Mar. 6, 1945, p. 1999. See also no. 24.

that account. As regards the last part of the Question, I have no information.

MISS RATHBONE: Considering that the USSR was one of the three Great Powers which initiated UNRRA, is not this very long delay, lasting over two months, in giving permission for a personal delegation very unsatisfactory? Why should Russia be afraid of impartial observers?

MR. EDEN: I am neither responsible for the Soviet Government nor for UNRRA. All I can do is to give the House information. I also regret the delay and I am glad that at last shipments have apparently begun.

31. MADAME ARCISZEWSKA*

MME. ARCISZEWSKA, *wife of the Polish Prime Minister in London, was arrested in Poland along with several members of the Polish Red Cross.*

Debate on March 6, 1945.

CAPT. ALAN GRAHAM (C.) asked the Secretary of State for Foreign Affairs if he can yet inform the House as to the result of his inquiries from the Soviet Government in regard to the arrest of the wife of the Polish Prime Minister and other Red Cross workers recently in Warsaw.[1]

MR. STOURTON (C.) asked the Secretary of State for Foreign Affairs if he has any statement to make concerning the arrest in Poland of Mme. Arciszewska, wife of the Polish Prime Minister in London.

SIR HERBERT WILLIAMS (C.) asked the Secretary of State for Foreign Affairs if he has now received any report with regard to the arrest in Poland of the wife of the Prime Minister of Poland.

---

* House of Commons. Vol. 408, Mar. 6, 1945, p. 1999–2000; Vol. 409, Apr. 11, 1945, p. 1798–1799.

[1] No. 26.

THE SECRETARY OF STATE FOR FOREIGN AFFAIRS (MR. EDEN): The Soviet Government have informed His Majesty's Ambassador at Moscow, in reply to the inquiries which he made upon my instructions, that to meet the wishes of His Majesty's Government they are taking steps at once to set Mme. Arciszewska free.

MR. EDMUND HARVEY (Ind.): Has the right hon. Gentleman any information as to why this lady was arrested?

MR. EDEN: I have been given some but I thought, in the light of the conclusions of my representations, the House would think it wiser to leave it there.

Debate on April 11, 1945.

CAPTAIN ALAN GRAHAM (C.) asked the Secretary of State for Foreign Affairs whether the release from arrest by the Soviet authorities of Mme. Arciszewska, the wife of the Polish Prime Minister, has yet been confirmed by His Majesty's Ambassador in Moscow?

MR. EDEN: As I informed my hon. and gallant Friend in reply to his Question on March 6, His Majesty's Ambassador received an assurance that the Soviet Government were taking steps to set Mme. Arciszewska free. I understand that the Polish Government shortly afterwards received confirmation of her release.

MR. AUSTIN HOPKINSON (Ind.): Can the right hon. Gentleman say whether the wives of any other Prime Ministers are in danger in Russia?

MISS RATHBONE (Ind.): Could my right hon. Friend say whether the people belonging to the Polish Red Cross, who were arrested simultaneously with Mme. Arciszewska, have been released.

MR. EDEN: I am afraid that I could not. I cannot recall whether I made representations for them at the time; I do not think that I did.

PROFESSOR SAVORY (C.): Is the right hon. Gentleman aware that the wife of the Polish Prime Minister is still obliged to report every day to the police, and can he protest against this continued indignity?

MR. EDEN: I have had information about that and I would like to consider it. I made representations to secure the freedom of this lady, and I would like to consider whether I ought to make any further representations.

32. POLISH HOME ARMY — DISSOLUTION SUMMARY OF ACTIVITIES OF THE POLISH ARMED FORCES*

WHEN THE WARSAW UPRISING *ended without success and units of the Home Army were taken prisoner by the Germans, Gen. Bor-Komorowski named General of the Brigade Leopold Okulicki as his successor in command of the Home Army on Polish soil. On Dec. 21, 1944, Pres. Raczkiewicz in London confirmed the nomination and Gen. Okulicki became commander of all armed forces in Poland.*[1]

The fall of Warsaw shook the delicate secret network of the Home Army down to its very foundations, which led to a loosening of organization and authority. A lot of time was needed to tighten up the organization and re-establish authority. Gen. Okulicki planned mainly: 1) to break off the general armed activity in Poland and to limit it only to the cases to act against German punitive expeditions and the diversion against Germans, and, 2) to stop Home Army members from revealing themselves to the Red Army, instructing them to stay underground.

Since the beginning of 1944 the Polish Goverent in London had been trying to get the British and U.S. Governments

* House of Commons. Vol. 408, Mar. 6, 1945, p. 2000–2001.

[1] Polskie Siły Zbrojne, vol. 3, p. 905.

to send an allied mission to Poland to become acquainted with the actual state of affairs in the underground organization there—the same as the British Government had done with Yugoslavia and Tito. Britain and the U.S. had always replied in the negative. Not until late in December of 1944 was a British mission of 5 officers under Col. Hudson sent into Poland by air.[2] *This mission landed near Radom and was immediately taken under protection of the Home Army. On Jan. 1, 1945 they were attacked by the Germans and the Home Army fought a delaying action until the mission could withdraw into the neighboring woods. On Jan. 4 the mission met with Gen. Okulicki. When this area was occupied by the Soviets this mission came out from hiding, was disarmed by the Russians, arrested and taken to Moscow, from which city they were returned to England.*

The January offensive of the Soviets quickly forced the Germans to leave Poland. As far as the Polish underground was concerned, the German occupation was only succeeded by a Soviet occupation. But, under existing political conditions, there could be no battle against the Soviets. Therefore, implementing a decision of the Polish Government in London, Gen. Okuclicki issued his last order of the day on Jan. 19, 1945, dissolving the Home Army.

Thus began the long and complicated task of dissolving an underground army of 350,000.[3] *About 50,000 of these lay down their arms and presented themselves to the Red Army.*[4] *These were taken to Russia. Part of the Home Army returned to their normal occupations; others did not lay down their arms, but, forming a new organization for independence, began to fight the Soviets.*

On Feb. 8 Polish Pres. Raczkiewicz broadcast over the radio this speech to the soldiers of the Home Army:[5]

---

[2] Ibid, p. 922.

[3] This is the number of the highest level of the Polish Home Army in the middle of 1944 (Polskie Siły Zbrojne, p. 124).

[4] Ibid, p. 926.

[5] Ditto.

"Soldiers of the Home Army!

When the German invaders were thrown out of Poland by the Red Army, fighting ceased on Polish soil and the Home Army was dissolved.

You soldiers of the Home Army performed your duties honorably, carrying out the firm desire of the people to fight the German invaders. You were an armed force of the Polish Underground and of the Republic of Poland. To the last minute you struck blows against the ruthless enemy, you protected the people from German barbarity, you liberated the Polish prisoners and evacuated people, sent by Germans to perdition, you saved cities and farms from destruction.

For more than 5 years, under the most difficult conditions and with superhuman self-denial and great sacrifice, you heroically fought an unequal struggle, presenting history and the world with proof that the Polish nation has a right to independence, at the same time showing absolute faithfulness to the accepted responsibilities of our allies.

Battles at Volhynia, Vilno, and Lublin district and the unparalleled bravery and dedication of the Warsaw uprising all have heaped, for all the world to see, immortal glory on the Polish flag. In the name of the Republic of Poland I thank all the soldiers of the Home Army for their great courage, their sacrifices without limit, and I thank their commanders for their splendid leadership.

To the fallen I pay tribute.

Although we are forced to dissolve the armed forces of the Republic of Poland on Polish soil, we all have a responsibility to continue to have the faith of our convictions and to so conduct ourselves that our cause will find a sympathetic response in the conscience of the world, and a just solution in the post-war settlement.

Polish Armed Forces on foreign soil are continuing to fight unflinchingly and are striving to be worthy of you—soldiers of the Home Army. Long live a free and independent Poland!"

On Jan. 17, 1945 the Lublin Committee issued a decree aimed against the soldiers of the Home Army, calling them "traitors, bandits, incorrigible malefactors and brawlers" and declaring that the government would not hesitate to take most severe measures to stamp them out. About Gen. Bor-Komorowski's heroic command during the Warsaw uprising the de-

cree stated that "his provocative rising and later surrender of arms considerably helped the Germans"

In a dispatch of Feb. 3, 1945, Premier Arciszewski notified Pres. Roosevelt of this Lublin Committee decree maligning the Polish underground.[6]

SUMMARY OF ACTIVITIES OF THE POLISH ARMED FORCES AGAINST GERMANY DURING THE SECOND WORLD WAR[7]

1. The Campaign in Poland (Sept. 1-middle of Oct. 1939) where the whole Polish Army (about 800,000 soldiers) took part.

2. Polish Highland Brigade fought in Narvik (Norwegian Campaign) in Apr. and May 1940.

3. Polish Army in France fought in the battle of France (June 1940).

4. The Polish Air Forces, organized in England, took part in the war starting from the Battle of England until the end of the war in Fighter, Bomber and Coastal Commands. In the Battle of Britain alone (summer and autumn 1940) Polish pilots destroyed 219 and probably destroyed 39 German planes, i.e. 15% of enemy losses in this battle.

The Polish Air Forces took part in the air offensive over France and Belgium, the defense of Malta, the attack on Tunis, in the invasion of the Continent and in all campaigns of 1944–45. They defended London against flying bombs, and raided Germany and military targets in other countries.

5. The Polish Navy which escaped from Polish ports to Great Britain took part together with the Royal Navy in many naval battles in the Channel, the North Sea, the Atlantic, the Mediterranean, at Narvik, Dunkirk, Lofoten, convoys to Murmansk, to Malta, on the beaches of Normandy.

---

6 See No. 17.

7 It Speaks for Itself, p. VIII-XI. Also Polish Facts and Figures, No. 7.

6. The Carpathian Brigade, formed in Syria, took part in the North African campaign (1941) in Tobruk, El Gazala and Bardia.

7. Some of the First Polish Army Corps in Britain took part in the invasion of France (June 1944), in the battle of Falaise and farther in France, Belgium, Holland and Germany. The Independent Polish Parachute Brigade fought at Arnhem.

8. The Second Polish Army Corps formed in the Middle East from Polish soldiers evacuated from Russia fought in 1943–44 in Italy and distinguished itself in the battles of Monte Cassino, Ancona, Bologna.

Altogether about 200,000 Polish soldiers fought abroad.

9. In Poland during the whole war the Polish Home Army of about 350,000 soldiers fought against the Germans. The rising of Warsaw (August-September 1944) where about 48,000 soldiers of Polish Home Army took part was the most important action of this army.

10. Finally, together with the Soviet Forces a Polish Army organized by the Soviet Government fought against the Germans. This Polish Army totaled:

10 infantry divisions, one armored corps, one armored brigade, one cavalry brigade[8] *(from October 1943 till the end of the war).*

MR. STOURTON (C.) asked the Secretary of State for Foreign Affairs whether an approach has been made to the Soviet Government with a view to securing cancellation of the decree of the Lublin Committee outlawing the Polish Underground Army.

THE SECRETARY OF STATE FOR FOREIGN AFFAIRS (MR. EDEN): I have no evidence that any decree has been issued by the Lublin administration outlawing the Polish Home Army as a whole. The Home Army has been formally dissolved by

[8] Jaklicz, J. The Pattern of Life in Poland. X. The Armed Forces, p. 9, 12.

the Polish Government in London. Many of its members, however, are alleged to have resisted the Lublin administration's measures of registration, conscription, etc., and to have refused to submit to its authority. This administration have announced their intention of taking severe measures against these allegedly irreconcilable elements of the Home Army, and against supporters of the Polish Government in London, and special courts have been set up to hold Polish treason trials. In the view of His Majesty's Government, if the necessary atmosphere of confidence is to be created, which alone can ensure the success of the present consultations in Moscow, it is imperative both that the Lublin administration should take no measures against Poles merely because they do not recognize their authority and that such Poles should cease active resistance to the local authorities, which endangers the lines of communication of the advancing Soviet armies. His Majesty's Government will continue to use their influence to this end.

MR. STOURTON: Will my right hon. Friend bear in mind that the proper treatment of the Polish Underground Army is a vital preliminary step to obtaining lasting accord between Russia and Poland?

MR. EDEN: My hon. Friend will see that I have dealt with that point, not exactly in his terms, but in a rather similar way.

MR. MOLSON (C.): Is the right hon. Gentleman satisfied that the British Ambassador at Moscow has access to full information about what is going on in East Poland?

MR. EDEN: I should be obliged if my hon. Friend will put that down. The question of information in Poland is one of those at present under discussion in Moscow.

33. BALTIC COUNTRIES*

SIR H. WILLIAMS (C.) asked the Secretary of State for Foreign Affairs the countries which are outside of the second part of Article 5 of the Anglo-Russian Treaty of May 26, 1942.[1]

THE SECRETARY OF STATE FOR FOREIGN AFFAIRS (MR. EDEN): As is made plain in the Treaty, the Article in question will apply to the post-war period, and all countries will come within its scope except Germany and perhaps certain of her associates in Europe.

SIR H. WILLIAMS: I take it that Latvia, Lithuania and Estonia come within the scope?

MR. EDEN: It applies to the post-war period, that is to say, the period after the peace. If my hon. Friend wishes to know the Soviet Government's attitude to Latvia, Lithuania and Estonia, that is another question.

SIR H. WILLIAMS: When the treaty was signed, were not these countries nominally independent although occupied by Germany?

MR. EDEN: They were not so regarded by the Soviet Government, and that has many times been made plain.

34. DANZIG**

MR. STOKES (Lab.) asked the Secretary of State for Foreign Affairs whether he can state the number of Germans living in the Free City of Danzig prior to the war; and what population they bore to the whole population.

---

* House of Commons. Vol. 408, Mar. 6, 1945, p. 2002.
1 See Vol. II, no. 15.
** House of Commons. Vol. 409, Mar. 14, 1945, p. 203.

THE SECRETARY OF STATE FOR FOREIGN AFFAIRS (MR. EDEN): The last official census was in 1929, when the total population of the Free City was 408,000. At that time, the number of Polish-speaking persons was estimated at about 10,000.

35. BRITISH NATIONALITY FOR POLISH CITIZENS*

Debate on March 14, 1945.

CAPTAIN ALAN GRAHAM (C.) asked the Prime Minister whether the question of British citizenship for members of the Polish Fighting Forces will be on the agenda of the forthcoming meeting of the British Empire delegates to the San Francisco Conference or by what other means he proposes to bring it to the official cognizance of the various Dominion Governments.

THE PRIME MINISTER (MR. CHURCHILL): Consultation with the Dominion Governments on this matter is already proceeding through the customary channels.

CAPTAIN GRAHAM: Is my right hon. Friend aware that that news will give the greatest satisfaction to our gallant Allies as, at the present time, the fulfillment of this suggestions of his constitutes in their eyes their only war aim and their only peace hope?

THE PRIME MINISTER: No, Sir, I had in mind—I am glad this point has been raised—in saying this that I know from personal inquiries that there are a certain number of Poles who will be very unhappy and will not adapt themselves to the new conditions which may be established. In that event, this must be regarded as their final security. If everything else fails, here are open the portals of the British Empire.

* House of Commons. Vol. 409, Mar. 14, 1945, p. 224–225; Mar. 21, 1945, p. 803–804; Vol. 410, May 3, 1945, p. 1587; May 17, 1945, p. 2625; Vol. 411, June 13, 1945, p. 1670.

Debate on March 21, 1945.

MR. LIPSON (Ind. C.) asked the Prime Minister if he will extend the discussions with the Dominions concerning the possibility of Polish citizens being granted British nationality to include the request of many other nationalities and of some Stateless persons, who are fighting in the British Forces, to be allowed to become British citizens.

THE DEPUTY PRIME MINISTER (MR. ATTLEE): The existing law contains provisions to the naturalization of persons who have been in the service of the Crown, and as far as concerns aliens who are serving in the British Forces it seems unlikely that any sufficient reasons will arise for an amendment of the law. The position of members of the Polish Forces is different, and it is because of the special considerations which affect their position that the Dominions are being consulted on the question of an amendment of the British Nationality Act.

MR. LIPSON: Is the right hon. Gentleman aware that many of these men who are fighting in the Forces of the Crown are very concerned about their future, and are very anxious to have British nationality? Could not the Government be a little more generous in this matter?

MR. ATTLEE: This supplementary question seems to relate to administration. I have been answering my hon. Friend on a question of what the law is.

MISS RATHBONE (Ind.): Is my right hon. Friend not aware that in this matter we have behaved far more meanly than the United States or any of our Dominions? In view of the smallness of our numbers compared with many of the larger States, both Allied and enemy, may I ask whether we can afford to reject gallant men who have been thought good enough to fight for us, but apparently are not thought good enough to bear the responsibility of becoming citizens?

MR. ATTLEE: I do not think the hon. Lady could have heard my reply. I said that the law already provides for those who are serving in our Forces. The question of what is done under the law is not a matter for me. I do not administer the Nationalization Acts and the question should not be put to me at all. The specific point put to me was about persons who are serving in the British Forces.

COMMANDER LOCKER-LAMPSON (C.): Will the Deputy Prime Minister not forget the Jews, who are Stateless and ought perhas to come first?

MR. ATTLEE: No, I do not forget them.

MR. SILVERMAN (Lab.): The right hon. Gentleman says that there are already laws, but that he does not administer them; will he bear in mind that the Home Secretary has declared more than once that the question of naturalization will have to be postponed until the end of the war? Does he think it is necessary to postpone a question of this urgency?

MR. ATTLEE: If my hon. Friend wants an answer to the question he must put it to the Home Secretary.

* * *

Debate on May 3, 1945.

COMMANDER LOCKER-LAMPSON (C.) asked the Secretary of State for the Home Department how many Poles have taken advantage of the British offer of British nationality; and how many Jews are among them.

THE SECRETARY OF STATE FOR THE HOME DEPARTMENT (MR. H. MORRISON): No statement has yet been made as to the method of implementing the offer of British nationality to members of the Polish Forces who fought with us and may be unable or unwilling to return to Poland. It is possible that legislation may be required to give effect to the offer, but any forecast of the precise method to be adopted would be premature at the present stage. The steps to be taken can only be settled when more is known as to the size and nature of the problem which may arise in future circumstances.

COLONEL SIR ARTHUR EVANS (C.): Have His Majesty's Government also considered the just claims of people of foreign nationality who have served, generally with distinction, in the ranks of the Armed Forces of the Crown?

MR. MORRISON: I answered a question on that subject some time ago.* The statement which was made by the Prime Minister on the matter arose specifically in relation to Polish Forces, and resulted from the proceedings at the Crimea Conference.

MR. SILVERMAN (Lab.): With reference to the latter part of the Question on the Paper, can the right hon. Friend say that in considering any such application there will be no kind of racial or religious discrimination?

MR. MORRISON: My hon. Friend may be quite sure of that.

* * *

Debate on May 17, 1945.

MISS WARD (C.) asked the Prime Minister whether his assurance that under certain circumstances British nationality will be available for personnel of the Polish Forces applies to women members of the Polish Forces as well as men.

THE SECRETARY OF STATE FOR FOREIGN AFFAIRS (MR. EDEN): If the conditions are similar, sex will not be a bar.

MISS WARD: Will women of the Polish Underground Army be eligible?

MR. EDEN: I doubt whether that is a matter for my jurisdiction.

MR. SEABORNE DAVIES (Lab.): Can the right hon. Gentleman tell us whether any replies have been received from the Dominion Governments on this matter of according British nationality to these people?

MR. EDEN: Perhaps my hon. Friend will put that question down.

* * *

---

* See No. 21.

Debate on June 13, 1945.

FLIGHT-LIEUTENANT TEELING (C.) asked the Secretary of State for the Home Department whether he has any statement to make as to how far his negotiations with the Dominions Governments have gone concerning the granting of British nationality to Polish subjects who have fought with the Allies; and whether such a granting of British nationality can be extended to officers and men of the Royal Yugoslav Forces.

THE ATTORNEY GENERAL (SIR D. SOMERVELL): Preliminary consultations with the Dominions are proceeding satisfactorily. The extension of the offer to other nationalities is not contemplated.

36. POLISH RED CROSS—ARRESTS*

MR. GLENVIL HALL (Lab.) asked the Secretary of State for Foreign Affairs whether he will make representations to the Soviet Government to secure the release of M. Madejski, member of the Board of the Polish Red Cross, and those of his staff arrested with him on Feb. 20 in Piotrkow.

THE SECRETARY OF STATE FOR FOREIGN AFFAIRS (MR. EDEN): I have no detailed knowledge of this case. If my hon. Friend has information, perhaps he will give it to me.

37. SAN FRANCISCO CONFERENCE— POLISH REPRESENTATION**

THE POLISH GOVERNMENT *in London was not one of the 39 governments invited to participate in the San Francisco Conference. Because of this the Polish Government sent the*

* House of Commons. Vol. 409, Mar. 14, 1945, p. 244.
** House of Commons. Vol. 409, Mar. 21, 1945, p. 835.

following protest to the British, U. S. and Chinese Governments on Mar. 12, 1945:[1]

"On Mar. 5, the Polish Government learned from radio broadcasts and the Press that the Government of the United States had sent on their own behalf and on that of Great Britain, China and the Soviet Union, an invitation to 39 States to take part in a United Nations Conference to be held on Apr. 25, 1945, at San Francisco, to prepare a Charter for a general International Organization for the maintenance of international peace and security.

The Polish Government notes that they have not received an invitation to take part in this Conference.

2. Considering that the Polish nation took up arms in the defense of freedom, security and right on Sept. 1, 1939, and was the first nation to make a stand against German aggression; and that from that time on, relentlessly and regardless of sacrifice, it has been fighting at home and abroad, on land, on sea and in the air;

Considering also that the Polish nation having fought longest in the defense of these ideals it has sustained in relation to its potentialities heavier losses in human life and property than any other nation in the world;

Furthermore considering that the war, begun in the defense of Poland, has created a spirit of unity among the free nations of the world which led to the promulgation and realization of the ideals of the United Nations;

And, finally, considering that at the San Francisco Conference the United Nations are to create a permanent World Peace Organization for the prevention of future aggression which is to be based on respect of law and the sovereign equality of all peace-loving nations;

The Polish Government, as the sole legal and independent representative of the Polish State emphatically insist on their indisputable right to take part in the World Security Conference and solemnly protest against their omission from the invitation to the San Francisco Conference.

3. The Polish Government wish to state that the noninvitation to the San Francisco Conference of Poland whose constitutional President and Government are generally recognized by all the United Nations, with the exception of only one of the Powers, and also by the neutral States, is the first disquieting case of

[1] Stosunki polsko-sowieckie, 1943–46, p. 503.

the application of the right of veto of Great Powers which has been made even before the United Nations have approved or accepted the proposals concerning an International Security Organization.

4. The Polish Government have already submitted certain preliminary suggestions on the Dumbarton Oaks proposals and intended participating to the fullest in the work of setting up an International Security Organization.

In these circumstances the Polish Government declare that they have been deprived of the possibility of presenting to the Conference their considered comments on the Dumbarton Oaks proposals as also on the suggestions regarding the voting procedure in the Security Council worked out at the Crimea Conference."

On Mar. 31 the Soviet Government issued a communique asserting that the Provisional Polish Government in Warsaw should be invited to participate in the San Francisco Conference. The communique reads as follows:[2]

"In connection with the Conference opening on Apr. 25 this year in San Francisco for establishing an international organization for the maintenance of peace and security, the Provisional Polish Government as already reported in the Press, on Mar. 22 addressed the Government of the Soviet Union, the United States of America, Great Britain and China with a Statement, point out that to hold the San Francisco Conference without the participation of Poland would be unfair and an absolutely unjustified insult to the Polish nation.

In this Statement the Provisional Polish Government also expressed the hope that representatives of the Polish people in the person of the Provisional Polish Government would take part in the Conference, and that democratic Poland would occupy a proper place in the family of the United Nations.

According to information received from authoritative sources, the Soviet Government, even before the Provisional Polish Government made this Statement, had informed the Governments of the United States of America and Great Britain that if reorganization of the Provisional Polish Government was not effected or completed in the near future, representatives of the Provisional Polish Government in Warsaw should be invited to the San Francisco Conference, as this Government exercises power throughout

[2] Stosunki polsko-sowieckie, 1943–46, p. 510.

the territory of Poland and enjoys the support of the Polish people.

In this Statement the Soviet Government pointed out that the absence of representatives of Poland at the broad international Conference in San Francisco could not be explained by such reasons as the absence of diplomatic relations between the Governments of Great Britain and the United States on the one hand, and the Provisional Polish Government on the other, since the Soviet Government similary has no diplomatic relations with such countries as India or Haiti, Liberia or Paraguay: however, it met the desires of Great Britain and the United States, and agreed to the participation of these countries in the San Francisco Conference. The Soviet Government suggested that the Allied Governments discuss this question and pass a corresponding decision.

The Soviet Government has informed the Government ot the Unted States that it expects an early reply to the proposal made by it concerning the invitation of Poland to the Conference in San Francisco.

The Soviet Government has also informed the Governments of Great Britain and China that it fully supports the Statement of the Provisional Polish Government, and expects that Poland will be given the possibility of taking part in the San Francisco Conference."

As it happened, Poland had no representative at the San Francisco Conference. The flag of Poland did not appear among the flags of the allied nations on display at Opera House where the meetings took place.

A couple of days after the opening of the conference this same Opera House was the setting for a concert by Arthur Rubinstein. The great pianist, after playing the American national anthem, as was the custom during the war, stood up and announced to the audience that though he did not see the flag of his native country, Poland, displayed among the many others, he would like to play the Polish national anthem "Poland is not yet dead, for we still live" ("Jeszcze Polska nie zginęła.") The loud and long applause that followed was a spontaneous manifestation of the great regard held for Poland.

On Apr. 27 the Assembly of the United Nations, on the motion of Belgian Minister for Foreign Affairs Paul Henri Spaak, admitted into the record the following resolution:

"The Governments of the United Nations extend to the people of Poland their sympathy and admiration. They hope the construction of the Polish Government recognized as such by the sponsoring nations will enable them to come and take part as soon as possible in the work of the Conference."

COLONEL THORNTON-KEMSLEY (C.) asked the Secretary of State for Foreign Affairs if he will give an assurance that Poland will be invited to participate in the San Francisco Conference, and that in default of the formation of a new Provisional Government of National Unity in Poland in time for its representatives to attend the Conference, the President of the Polish Republic will be invited to nominate delegates.

THE UNDER-SECRETARY OF STATE FOR FOREIGN AFFAIRS (MR. GEORGE HALL): Invitations to the San Francisco Conference are issued by the Government of the United States of America on behalf of itself and of His Majesty's Government in the United Kingdom, the Soviet Government and the Chinese Government. It is thus essential that all four Governments should agree before any invitation can be issued. The Soviet Government do not recognize the Polish Government in London, and the other Allied Governments concerned do not recognize the Provisional Government established in Warsaw. In these circumstances Poland can only be invited to the Conference if a Polish Provisional Government of National Unity, which will be recognized by all four Powers, can be formed in Poland in accordance with the recommendation of the Crimea Conference.

His Majesty's Government in the United Kingdom, like their Allies, attach the highest importance to Poland being represented at the Conference, and they therefore earnestly hope that a united Polish Provisional Government may be formed in time.

38. POLAND—ARRESTS*

CAPTAIN ALAN GRAHAM (C.) asked the Secretary of State for Foreign Affairs whether he will make representations to the Soviet Government to obtain the immediate release of those members of the Polish Christian Labor Party and National Democratic Party, whose names have been sent to him, and who were arrested by the N. K. V. D. on March 8 in Brwinow, near Warsaw, as well as the Red Cross delegate M. Lewandowski, arrested at Milanowek, near Warsaw, at about the same time; and whether he will inform the Soviet Government of the prejudicial effect upon Anglo-Russian relations of their policy of arrests and deportations of the friendly citizens of our ally, Poland.

PARLIAMENTARY UNDER-SECRETARY TO THE FOREIGN OFFICE (MR. LAW): His Majesty's Ambassador at Moscow has been instructed to bring these reports to the notice of the Soviet Government and to ask them whether the facts are as stated.

39. CREATION OF POLISH PROVISIONAL GOVERNMENT IN MOSCOW**

IT WAS THE INTENT *of the Yalta Conference decisions to create a new Polish Provisional Government of National Unity through the reorganization of the existing Polish Government in Warsaw. This task was to be done by a committee in Moscow composed of Molotov and ambassadors A. Harriman and A. Clark Kerr.*[1]

But discussions of this committee dragged on for a long

---

* House of Commons. Vol. 409, Mar. 21, 1945, p. 835–836.

** House of Commons. Vol. 409, Mar. 21, 1945, p. 785–786; Apr. 11, 1945, p. 1796–1800; Vol. 411, June 13, 1945, p. 1622–1623; June 14, 1945, p. 1786–1787.

[1] See No. 26.

time in Moscow and produced no results. It was Molotov's opinion that each Polish candidate had to have the prior approval of Warsaw—this prevented any decisive action. In the meantime the Government in Warsaw took over completely in Poland, arresting Home Army soldiers and all others who were politically opposed to them. This was done quietly, profiting from the fact that even representatives of the western press were not allowed into Poland.[2]

This situation caused alarm in the British Government. Minister Eden in a talk with Ambassador Raczyński on Mar. 15, 1945 admitted that he had been deluded.[3] *He felt that Moscow's behavior was incomprehensible and downright illogical, since it would seem that a just solution of the Polish-Soviet dispute would be of great benefit to Russia. Prime Minister Churchill was also alarmed with the apparent impossibility of carrying out with Molotov the Yalta resolutions. On Mar. 10 he telegraphed to Pres. Roosevelt:*[4]

> "The Lublin Poles may well answer that their Government can alone ensure 'the maximum amount of political tranquility inside', that they already represent the great mass of the 'democratic forces in Poland', and that they cannot join hands with émigré traitors to Poland or Fascist collaborationists and landlords, and so on, according to the usual technique.
> Meanwhile we shall not be allowed inside the country or have any means of informing ourselves upon the position. It suits the Soviets very well to have a long period of delay, so that the process of liquidation of elements unfavorable to them or their puppets may run its full course. This would be furthered by our opening out now into proposals of a very undefined character for a political truce between these Polish parties (whose hatreds would eat into live steel) in the spirit and intent of the Crimea decision, and might well imply the abandonment of all clear-cut requests, such as those suggested in my last telegram to you. Therefore, I should find it very difficult to join in this project of a political truce . . ."

Churchill suggested sending a categorical dispatch to Stalin demanding more effective action by the committee in

[2] Churchill, W. Triumph and Tragedy, p. 423.
[3] Stosunki polsko-sowieckie, 1943–46, p. 505.
[4] Churchill, W. Op. Cit. p. 423.

Moscow. Roosevelt would not agree to such a strong move and suggested waiting for results from the talks in Moscow. But, on urgent demands from Churchill, Roosevelt sent a dispatch to Stalin on Mar. 29 stating:[5]

". . . The part of our agreement at Yalta . . . has aroused the greatest popular interest and is the most urgent relates to the Polish question. You are aware of course that the Commission which we set up has made no progress. I feel this is due to the interpretation which your Government is placing upon the Crimea decisions. In order that there shall be no misunderstanding I set forth below my interpretation of the points of the agreement which are pertinent to the difficulties encountered by the Commission in Moscow.

In the discussions that have taken place so far your Government appears to take the position that the new Polish Provisional Government of National Unity which we agreed should be formed should be little more than a continuation of the present Warsaw Government. I cannot reconcile this either with our agreement or our discussions. While it is true that the Lublin Government is to be reorganized and its members play a prominent rôle, it is to be done in such a fashion as to bring into being a new Government. This point is clearly brought out in several places in the text of the agreement. I must make it quite plain to you that any such solution which would result in a thinly disguised continuance of the present Warsaw régime would be unacceptable and would cause the people of the United States to regard the Yalta agreement as having failed. It is equally apparent that for the same reason the Warsaw Government cannot under the agreement claim the right to select or reject what Poles are to be brought to Moscow by the Commission for consultation. Can we not agree that is it up to the Commission to select invitations to be sent out accordingly? If this could be done I see no great objection to having the Lublin group come first in order that they may be fully acquainted with the agreed interpretation of the Yalta decisions on this point. In order to facilitate the agreement the Commission might first of all select a small but representative group of Polish leaders who could suggest other names for the consideration of the Commission. We have not and would not bar or veto any candidate for consultation whom Mr. Molotov might propose, being confident that he would not suggest any Poles who would be inimical to the intent of the Crimea decision. I feel that it is not too much to ask that my

[5] Churchill, W. Op. Cit., p. 744.

Ambassador be accorded the same confidence. It is obvious to me that if the right of the Commission to select these Poles is limited or shared with the Warsaw Government the very foundation on which our agreement rests would be destroyed.

While the foregoing are the immediate obstacles which in my opinion have prevented the Commission from making any progress in this vital matter, there are two other suggestions which were not in the agreement but nevertheless have a very important bearing on the result we all seek. Neither of these suggestions has been as yet accepted by your Government. I refer to:

(1) That there should be the maximum of political tranquility in Poland and that dissident groups should cease any measures and counter-measures against each other. That we should respectively use our influence to that end seems to me so eminently reasonable.

(2) It would also seem entirely natural, in view of the responsibilities placed upon them by the agreement, that representatives of the American and British members of the Commission should be permitted to visit Poland . . ."

Churchill also sent a dispatch to Stalin on Apr. 1 completely supporting Roosevelt.[6] *At the end of his dispatch Churchill wrote*:

". . . If our efforts to reach an agreement about Poland are to be doomed to failure I shall be bound to confess the fact to Parliament when they return from the Easter recess. No one has pleaded the cause of Russia with more fervor and conviction than I have tried to do. I was the first to raise my voice on June 22, 1941.[7] It is more than a year since I proclaimed to a startled world the

[6] Churchill, W. Triumph and tragedy, p. 437.

[7] Churchill's broadcast on June 22, 1941: ". . . Now I have to declare the decision of His Majesty's Government, and I feel sure it is a decision in which the great Dominions will in due course concur . . . We have but one aim and one single irrevocable purpose. We are resolved to destroy Hitler and every vestige of the Nazi regime. From this nothing will turn us—nothing . . . We shall give whatever help we can to Russia and to the Russian people . . . We have offered to the Government of Soviet Russia any technical or economic assistance which is in our power and which is likely to be of service to them. We shall bomb Germany by day as well as by night in ever-increasing measure, casting upon them month by month a heavier discharge of bombs and making the German people taste and gulp each month the sharper dose of the miseries they have showered upon mankind . . . The Russian danger is . . . our danger, and the danger of the U. S., just as the cause of any Russian fighting for his hearth and home is the cause of free men and free peoples in every quarter of the globe." (The Times, London, June 23, 1941).

justice of the Curzon Line for Russia's western frontier, and this frontier has now been accepted by both the British Parliament and the President of the U. S. It is as a sincere friend of Russia that I make my personal appeal to you and to your colleagues to come to a good understanding about Poland with the Western democracies, and not to smite down the hands of comradeship in the future guidance of the world which we now extend."

In his answer of Apr. 7 Stalin blamed the failure of the commission in Moscow to reach any decision on lack of co-operation from the British and American ambassadors. He stated that in his opinion it would be necessary to accept the following principles to retrieve the Polish affair from a blind alley:[8]

The Lublin Government must be reconstructed, not liquidated, by replacing some of its existing Ministers by new ones from outside it; only eight Poles should be invited for consultation, five from Poland and three from London, and all must accept the Yalta decisions and be friendly to the Soviet Government; the Lublin Government must first be consulted because of its "enormous" influence in Poland and because any other course might insult the Polish people and make them think we were trying to impose a Government upon them without consulting public opinion. "I think," he concluded, "that if the above observations were taken into account an agreed decision on the Polish question could be arrived at in a short time."

On Apr. 7 Stalin also sent to Churchill a personal message:

"The British and American Ambassadors, who are members of the Moscow Commission, are unwilling to take account of the Provisional Polish Government, and insist on inviting Polish personalities for consultation without regard to their attitude to the decisions of the Crimea Conference on Poland and to the Soviet Union. They absolutely insist on summoning to Moscow for consultation, for instance, Mikołajczyk, and this they do in the form of an ultimatum. In this they take no account of the fact that Mikołajczyk has come out openly against the decisions of the Crimea Conference on Poland. However, if you think it necessary, I should be ready to use my influence with the Provisional Polish Government to make them withdraw their objection to inviting Mikołajczyk, if the latter would make a public statement accepting the decisions of the Crimea Conference on

8 Churchill, W. Op. Cit., p. 438.

the Polish question and declaring that he stands for the establishment of friendly relations between Poland and the Soviet Union. . ."

During all this time the plight in Poland of political underground leaders was becoming increasingly more difficult. So, when the Soviet military authorities tried to make a contact with Polish underground authorities, the Poles decided to cooperate. On Mar. 27 the assembly of the Polish underground, consisting of Vice Premier S. Jankowski, Speaker of the Council of National Unity K. Puzak, and Gen. Okulicki, last commander of the underground military forces in Poland, met with representatives of the Red Army, and immediately they disappeared; the next day 13 leaders of Polish political organizations met with the same fate. Only on May 4 in San Francisco did it come to light that all of these were arrested by the Soviets and forcibly transported to Moscow.[9]

Pres. Roosevelt died on Apr. 12, 1945. Pres. Truman therefore conferred with Mr. Eden who was at that time in Washington to discuss the problem of a new government for Poland.

On Apr. 15 Churchill and Truman sent a joint dispatch to Stalin suggesting that the following persons be invited to Moscow for consultation, without delay:[10] *"Bierut, Osóbka-Morawski, Rola-Żymierski, Bishop Sapieha, one representative Polish political party leader not connected with the present Warsaw Government (if any of the following were agreeable to you, he would be agreeable to us: Witos, Żuławski, Chaciński, Jasiukowicz), and from London: Mikołajczyk, Grabski and Stańczyk." These persons could then suggest others in Poland and in exile so that all major Polish groups would be represented in the discussions.*

In the same dispatch Churchill and Truman pinpointed the differences between their statements and Stalin's on the subject of the creation of the Provisional Polish Government: "Actually, the point at issue between us is this: does the War-

---

[9] See No. 43.
[10] Correspondence vol. 1 no. 430, p. 326.

saw government have, or does it not have, the right to veto individual candidates participating in the consultation. We do not feel that this is the interpretation reached during the Crimean decisions. It seems to us, that you are reverting to the original stand of the Soviet delegation at Crimea, a stand which was subsequently revised in the final resolution. It is uppermost in our minds that we are presently speaking only of a group of Poles who are to be invited to Moscow for consultation."

At the end Churchill and Truman emphasized that they could not agree to an arbitrarily set principle for the formation of a new Polish government until such a time as Polish leaders had been consulted, and under no circumstances could they approve a Yugoslav precedent for Poland.[11]

While this was going on Churchill had a talk with Mikołajczyk at Chequers at which time he prevailed on Mikołajczyk to issue a statement in accordance with a demand made by Stalin in a dispatch of Apr. 7. Accordingly, Mikołajczyk gave out this statement on April 15:[12]

> "I belive that a close and lasting friendship with Russia should form the cornerstone of future Polish policy and should be included within the framework of a broader amity with the United Nations.
> To remove all doubts as to my stand, I wish to state that I accept the Crimea decisions with regard to the future of Poland, her sovereign and independent position, as well as the formation of a representative Provisional Government of National Unity. I support the decisions made at Crimea with respect to the convocation of leading figures with a view to forming a Government of National Unity, which might represent the Polish nation as broadly and as truly as possible and which might be recognized by the Big Three."

But this did not satisfy Stalin, and on Apr. 17 he telegraphed Churchill:[13]

---

[11] On Nov. 1, 1944 an agreement was reached between Premier Subasic and Tito which approved the creation in Yugoslavia of a Council of Regents and United Yugoslav Government composed of representatives from the National Committee for Freedom and the Royal Government.

[12] Mikołajczyk, S. Op. Cit. p. 114.

[13] Churchill, W. Op. Cit., p. 489.

"Mikołajczyk's statement represents of course a great step forward, but it is not clear whether Mikołajczyk also accepts that part of the decisions of the Crimea Conference which deals with the eastern frontiers of Poland. I should be glad, first, to receive a full text of Mikołajczyk's statement, and, secondly, to receive from Mikołajczyk an explanation as to whether he also accepts that part of the decisions of the Crimea Conference on Poland which deals with the eastern frontiers of Poland."

Churchill answered on Apr. 22 by sending this statement by Mikołajczyk in which Mikołajczyk dispelled all doubts:[14]

"On the demand of Russia the three Great Powers have declared themselves in favor of establishing Poland's eastern frontier on the Curzon Line with the possibility of small rectifications. My own point of view was that at least Lwów and the oil district should be left to Poland. Considering however first that in this respect there is an absolute demand on the Soviet side and secondly that the existence side by side of our two nations is dependent on the fulfilment of this condition, we Poles are obliged to ask ourselves whether in the name of the so-called integrity of our republic we are to reject it and thereby jeopardize the whole body of our country's interests. The answer to this question must be "No'."

This declaration pleased Stalin, and in his dispatch of April 24[15] *he told Churchill that he would recommend that the Provisional Polish Government take this declaration under consideration and withdraw its objections regarding inviting Mikołajczyk for consultation on the problem of a Polish government.*

Stalin also emphasized that the stand taken by Churchill and Truman in not considering the Provisional Polish Government as the nucleus of a future Polish Government of National Unity, but only as one of many groups of Poles, did not correspond to the Yalta decisions.[16]

All this while the Warsaw Government in Poland and the Soviet Government were busy developing a situation in Poland which would strengthen the hand of the Warsaw Government in the Moscow talks for establishing a new Polish

14 Ditto.
15 Perepiska, vol. I, no. 439, p. 335–336.
16 Churchill, W. Triumph and Tragedy, p. 492.

Government. One thing they did was to conclude, on Apr. 21, 1945, a treaty of friendship, mutual assistance and post-war cooperation between the Soviet Union and Poland. Here is the text:[17]

ARTICLE I. The High Contracting Parties will continue jointly with all the United Nations the struggle against Germany until final victory. The High Contracting Parties undertake to render each other military and other assistance in this struggle by every means at their disposal.

ARTICLE II. The High Contracting Parties, convinced that the interest of the security and prosperity of the Soviet and Polish peoples call for the preservation and strengthening of a stable and permanent friendship in time of war and after the war, will strengthen the friendly collaboration between the two countries in conformity with the principles of mutual respect for their independence and sovereignty as well as non-intervention in the internal affairs of the other State.

ARTICLE III. The High Contracting Parties undertake also after the termination of the present war with Germany to take jointly all measures at their disposal in order to eliminate every threat of a repetition of aggression on the part of Germany or any other State which would unite with Germany directly or in any other form. To achieve this aim the High Contracting Parties will participate, in a spirit of most sincere collaboration, in all international actions aimed at ensuring the peace and security of the nations, and will contribute their full share to the cause of the materialization of these lofty aims. The application of the present Treaty by the High Contracting Parties will conform to international principles in the adoption of which both Contracting Parties have participated.

ARTICLE IV. In the event of one of the High Contracting Parties in the post-war period finding itself involved in hostilities with Germany, the latter having resumed her aggressive policy, or with some other State united with Germany directly or in any other form in such a war, the other High Contracting Party will immediately render to the Contracting Party involved in hostilities military or other assistance and support by every means at its disposal.

ARTICLE V. The High Contracting Parties undertake not to conclude without mutual consent an armistice or peace treaty

---

[17] Soviet-Polish Relations, p. 16.

either with the Hitler Government or with any other authority in Germany which encroaches or would encroach on the independence, territorial integrity or security of either of the High Contracting Parties.

ARTICLE VI. Each High Contracting Party undertakes not to conclude any alliance and not to take part in any coalition directed against the other High Contracting Party.

ARTICLE VII. The High Contracting Parties will also after the termination of the present war collaborate in a spirit of friendship with a view to further development and consolidation of economic and cultural ties between the two countries, and assist each other in the economic rehabilitation of both countries.

ARTICLE VIII. The present Treaty comes into force from the moment of its signing, and is subject to ratification within the shortest possible time. The exchange of Ratification Instruments shall be effected in Warsaw as soon as possible. The present Treaty shall remain in force for 20 years from the moment of its signing. If at the end of this 20-year period either of the High Contracting Parties does not declare, twelve months prior to the expiration of the term, its desire to renounce the Treaty, it shall remain in force for the next five years and thus each time until either of the High Contracting Parties, twelve months prior to the expiration of the current five-year term, gives notice in writing about its intention to renounce the Treaty.

Further talks on the Polish problem were held by Molotov, Eden and Stettinius in San Francisco, but they produced no results. At this time Churchill and Stalin exchanged strongly-worded dispatches as to the interpretation of the Yalta resolutions on forming a new Polish Government, but this also produced no results. And, when, on May 4 in San Francisco, Molotov announced that 16 leaders of the Polish underground had been arrested by Russian authorities,[18] *Eden and Stettinius said that in view of this new serious development, the talks could not continue.*

On May 7, 1945 the Germans surrendered. So, another meeting of the Big Three was planned for July in Potsdam, to discuss post-war European problems. However, many important problems, among them the Polish-Soviet dispute, had not yet been settled. Thus, at the end of May, Pres. Truman

[18] See No. 43.

sent Harry L. Hopkins to Moscow, to talk over these problems with Stalin.[19]

During his many talks with Stalin between May 26 and June 6 Hopkins tried to explain the allied stand on the Polish problem:

"He (Hopkins) said the question of Poland per se was not so important as the fact that it had become a symbol of our ability to work out problems with the Soviet Union. He said that we had no special interests in Poland and no special desire to see any particular kind of government. That we would accept any government in Poland which was desired by the Polish people and was at the same time friendly to the Soviet Government. He said that the people and Government of the U. S. felt that this was a problem which should be worked out jointly between the U. S., the Soviet Union and Great Britain and that we felt that the Polish people should be given the right to free elections to choose their own government and their own system and that Poland should genuinely be independent. The Government and people of the U. S. were disturbed because the preliminary steps towards the re-establishment of Poland appeared to have been taken unilaterally by the Soviet Union together with the present Warsaw Government and that in fact the U. S. was completely excluded."

Stalin mentioned that during the course of 25 years Poland had twice been attacked by the Germans, something which neither England nor the U.S. had experienced.

"He (Stalin) said that Germany had been able to do this because Poland had been regarded as a part of the cordon sanitaire around the Soviet Union and that previous European policy had been that the Polish Government must be hostile to Russia. In these circumstances either Poland had been too weak to oppose Germany or had let the Germans come through. This Poland had served as a corridor for the German attacks on Russia. He said Poland's weakness and hostility had been a great source of weakness to the Soviet Union and had permitted the Germans to do what they wished in the East and also in the West since the two were mixed together. It is therefore in Russia's vital interest that Poland should be both strong and friendly. He said there was no intention on the part of the Soviet Union to interfere in Poland's internal affairs, that Poland would live under the par-

---

[19] Sherwood, R. Roosevelt and Hopkins, p. 890–907 (this quotation and those following).

liamentary system which is like Czechoslovakia, Belgium and Holland and that any talk of an intention to Sovietize Poland was stupid. He said even the Polish leaders, some of whom were communists, were against the Soviet system since the Polish people did not desire collective farms or other aspects of the Soviet system. In this the Polish leaders were right since the Soviet system was not exportable—it must develop from within on the basis of a set of conditions which were not present in Poland. He said all the Soviet Union wanted was that Poland should not be in a position to open the gates to Germany and in order to prevent this Poland must be strong and democratic."

"In fact the United States had more reason to be a world power than any other state. For this reason he fully recognized the right of the United States as a world power to participate in the Polish question and that the Soviet interest in Poland does not in any way exclude those of England and the United States. Mr. Hopkins had spoken of Russian unilateral action in Poland and United States public opinion concerning it. It was true that Russia had taken such unilateral action but they had been compelled to. He said the Soviet Government had recognized the Warsaw Government and concluded a treaty with it at a time when their Allies did not recognize this government. These were admittedly unilateral acts which would have been much better left undone but the fact was they had not met with any understanding on the part of their Allies. The need for these actions had arisen out of the presence of Soviet troops in Poland; it would have been impossible to have waited until such time as the Allies had come to an agreement on Poland. The logic of the war against Germany demanded that the Soviet rear be assured and the Lublin Committee had been of great assistance to the Red Army at all times and it was for this reason that these actions had been taken by the Soviet Government. He said it was contrary to the Soviet policy to set up Soviet administration on foreign soil since this would look like occupation and be resented by the local inhabitants. It was for this reason that some Polish administration had to be established in Poland and this could be done only with those who had helped the Red Army. He said he wished to emphasize that these steps had not been taken with any desire to eliminate or exclude Russia's Allies.

He felt that we should examine the composition of the future Government of National Unity. He said there were eighteen or twenty ministries in the present Polish Government and that four or five of these portfolios could be given representatives of other Polish groups taken from the list submitted by Great Britain and the U. S. (Molotov whispered to Stalin who then said he meant four and not five posts in the government). He said he thought the Warsaw Poles would not accept more than four ministers from other democratic groups. He added that if this appears a suitable basis we could then proceed to consider what persons should be selected for these posts."

"Mr. Hopkins said that as far as the U. S. Government was concerned we had no interest in seeing anyone connected with the present Polish Government in London involved in the new Provisional Government of Poland and he did not personally believe that the British had any such idea."

On May 31 several candidates were named for the new Polish Government. Hopkins thus felt some progress had been made. But, Stalin did not yield from the stand that the new government must be formed around the existing Warsaw Government, with the addition of some new members from London and Poland.

After Hopkins' departure, the ambassadors continued their talks and on June 12 they issued this statement (published June 13):[20]

"The people's Commissar of Foreign Affairs of the USSR, Mr. V. M. Molotov, the British Ambassador, Sir A. Clark Kerr, and the Ambassador of the U. S., Mr. W. A. Harriman, authorized by the Three Allied Powers to consult with members of the Provisional Polish Government and other democratic leaders in Poland and abroad about reorganization of the Provisional Polish Government on a broad democratic basis, with inclusion of democratic leaders from Poland itself and from Poles abroad, and about the formation of a Provisional Polish Government of National Unity, have agreed that for the above-mentioned consultations provided for in the Crimea Agreement on Poland the following persons shall be invited:

1. REPRESENTATIVES OF PROVISIONAL POLISH GOVERNMENT: According to information received from Warsaw the following have been appointed representatives of the Provisional Polish Government: Bolesław Bierut, Edward Osóbka-Morawski, Władysław Kowalski, Władysław Gomułka.

2. DEMOCRATIC LEADERS FROM POLAND: Wincenty Witos, Zygmunt Żuławski Stanisław Kutrzeba, Adam Krzyżanowski Henryk Kołodziejski.

---

[20] Stosunki polsko-sowieckie, 1943–46, p. 559.

3. DEMOCRATIC LEADERS FROM ABROAD: Stanisław Mikołajczyk, Jan Stanczyk, Julian Żakowski.

All the above-mentioned have been invited to arrive in Moscow for June 15th."

Upon receipt of this statement the Polish Government in London on June 15 issued a communique.[21] The communique enumerated the arrest of the Polish underground leaders, the reign of terror existent in Poland, the lack of freedom of speech, press, and assemblage, and the presence on Polish soil of the Red Army. The statement then continued:

". . . In the face of these tragic realities the creation of a legal and independent government of national unity, based on the freely expressed will of the people is a practical impossibility so long as the Polish Republic is occupied by the Soviet army and the Soviet political police (NKVD), and so long as Poland is cut off from her Western Allies and the whole civilized world.

The presence of the Soviet army on the territory of the Polish Republic after the termination of hostilities against the Germans in Europe is not justified by any considerations of war, and is moreover contrary to Point VI of the Joint Declaration by the Four Powers on Oct. 30, 1943, which lays down that: ". . . After the termination of hostilities they (the Four Powers) will not employ their military forces within the territories of other states . . ."

Any action on the part of the great Western Democracies with a view to normalizing conditions in Poland should be preceded by:

(a) The immediate withdrawal from Poland of the Soviet Army and political police;

(b) The liberation of all Polish citizens arrested and deported since 1939;

(c) Desistance from imposing upon Poland a political system which is extraneous to her."

Debate on March 21, 1945.

MAJOR-GENERAL SIR ALFRED KNOX (C.) asked the Secretary of State for Foreign Affairs whether the negotiations in Moscow with the object of forming a new Government of Poland have made any progress.

---

21 Stosunki polsko-sowieckie, 1943–46, p. 561.

CAPTAIN GAMMANS (C.) asked the Secretary of State for Foreign Affairs how many meetings have been held in Moscow of the Ambassadors of Great Britain, the U.S.A. and the U.S.S.R. with a view to the organization of a Polish Provisional Government of National Unity as agreed at the Yalta Conference; and whether any invitation has yet been sent to the Polish Government in London to send representatives to Moscow for discussion.

MR. MARTIN (Lab.) asked the Secretary of State for Foreign Affairs whether he can make any statement on the progress of the Allied Commission in Moscow in the formation of a new Polish Government.

THE PARLIAMENTARY UNDER-SECRETARY TO THE FOREIGN OFFICE (MR. LAW): His Majesty's Government fully understand the importance which the House attaches to these most important negotiations. The Prime Minister or my right hon. Friend the Foreign Secretary will make a statement at the earliest opportune moment.

SIR A. KNOX: Has no progress been made so far? Have any members of the Polish Government been invited yet to go to Moscow?

MR. LAW: I ask my hon. and gallant Friend to await the statement that will be made. The Foreign Secretary assured the House that he would report on the matter, and he will keep that assurance.

CAPTAIN DUNCAN: Have His Majesty's Government taken, or are they taking, the same action as the American Government in reinforcing their Ambassador in Moscow with officials from the Foreign Office?

MR. LAW: I cannot answer that question off-hand, but I can assure my hon. and gallant Friend that we are at one with the United States Government in this matter.

MR. PURBRICK (C.): When does my right hon. Friend expect a statement to be made?

MR. LAW: I cannot tell the hon. Member now. A statement will be made at the soonest opportune moment; we must leave that to the Prime Minister or the Foreign Secretary.

MR. MANNINGHAM-BULLER (C.): Will the statement be made before the Recess?

MR. LAW: I cannot say when the statement will be made, but I can assure my hon. and gallant Friend that either the Foreign Secretary or the Prime Minister will inform the House of developments at the earliest moment that is opportune.

* * *

Debate on April 11, 1945.

SIR A. KNOX (C.) asked the Secretary of State for Foreign Affairs what progress has been made in the negotiations in Moscow with the object of forming a new Government of Poland.

SQUADRON-LEADER DONNER (C.) asked the Secretary of State for Foreign Affairs whether any progress has been made at Moscow in constituting a new Polish Government.

VICE-ADMIRAL TAYLOR (C.) asked the Secretary of State for Foreign Affairs whether the final composition of the Polish Provisional Government has yet been completed.

MAJOR PETO (C.) asked the Secretary of State for Foreign Affairs whether he has received any further reports of arrests or deportations of Poles from the territories both east and west of the provisional demarcation line fixed at Yalta since the conference held at that place; how many persons are involved; and whether they have since been returned to their homes.

MR. RALPH ETHERTON (C.) asked the Secretary of State for Foreign Affairs what arrangements have now been come to in relation to the holding of free elections in Poland.

MR. GRAHAM WHITE (L.) asked the Secretary of State for Foreign Affairs if he is in a position to make a statement on the progress of the negotiations for the formation of a Polish Provisional Government.

MR. SORENSEN (Lab.) asked the Secretary of State for Foreign Affairs if he will make any statement respecting progress towards the establishment of a provisional government for Poland that will correspond to conditions acceptable to Great Britain, the U.S.S.R. and the U.S.A. and whose representatives will be recognized at the forthcoming San Francisco Conference.

CAPTAIN ALAN GRAHAM (C.) asked the Secretary of State for Foreign Affairs whether he has yet obtained from the Soviet Government any explanation of their policy of arrests and deportations of prominent Polish citizens, Red Cross workers, democratic party leaders and other patriotic loyal Allies of Great Britain and the U.S.A.

THE SECRETARY OF STATE FOR FOREIGN AFFAIRS (MR. EDEN): As at present advised my right hon. Friend the Prime Minister proposes to make a statement next week, probably on Thursday, on the work of the Commission of Three in Moscow and on certain other aspects of Russo-Polish relations. I would therefore ask my hon. Friends and the House to be good enough to await that statement. My right hon. Friend the Prime Minister may also take this opportunity on Thursday of next week to say something about the war situation in general.

MR. RHYS DAVIES (Lab.): Does it follow from what the right hon. Gentleman has said, that the statement of the Prime Minister will be debatable?

MR. EDEN: My right hon. Friend will make his statement, and if there is a general desire for a Debate, certainly a Debate will follow. We had that in mind.

MR. PICKTHORN (C.): Are we to have the Debate, which

I think was promised, on San Francisco, before or after this potential Debate on the Prime Minister's statement?

MR. EDEN: That is a matter of Business, which I will deal with later; it does not arise out of these Questions. . . .

CAPTAIN ALAN GRAHAM (C.) asked the Secretary of State for Foreign Affairs which political parties in Poland are defined by His Majesty's Government as democratic and non-democratic, respectively; whether these parties are similarly so defined by our Soviet Ally; and whether His Majesty's Ambassador in Moscow is satisfied that all democratic parties in Poland have at the present time freedom to express and to work for their political opinions.

THE SECRETARY OF STATE FOR FOREIGN AFFAIRS (MR. EDEN): His Majesty's Government, the United States Government and the Soviet Government are at present concerned with the first step proposed at the Crimea Conference, the setting up in Poland of a broadly representative new Provisional Government of National Unity such as would command recognition by the Great Powers. When this has been done and His Majesty's Government are represented in Poland, they will be in a better position to form a final opinion as to what parties should be entitled to take part in elections, which clearly could not take place for some considerable time after the formation of the new Government. The scanty information at present available to His Majesty's Government about conditions in Poland indicates, as one would expect, that, as a result of the long German occupation and the recent operations in Poland, Party political warfare is not yet working in a normal manner. It may also clearly be that before elections were held new parties might emerge.

CAPTAIN GRAHAM: Is my right hon. Friend aware that the British Government sought, on January 27, the names of Polish politicians in Poland who might enable the Committee of Ambassadors to form a Provisional Government? Were they then in a position to secure the lives and liberties of those politicians, and are they now in that position?

MR EDEN: What we are at present trying to do is to secure agreement about Polish democratic leaders. The question of parties comes afterwards. Certainly, it would be part of any arrangement, so far as we are concerned, that if any Polish leaders were invited they should have full security and full right to go where they wished.

VICE-ADMIRAL TAYLOR (C.): Is the intention that all the members of the National Polish Provisional Government shall be Polish citizens?

MR. EDEN: I should have thought that the answer was, "Yes."

MR. GALLACHER (Com.): The right hon. Gentleman says that he is awaiting a new Provisional Polish Government. There is nothing about that in the Yalta Agreement.

MR. EDEN: If the hon. Gentleman will read it he will find there the word "new," because I was anxious that it should be there.

* * *

Debate on June 13, 1945.

MR. MARTIN (Lab.) asked the Secretary of State for Foreign Affairs whether he has any further information about the setting up in Poland of a Government representative of the various parties in Polish life.

MR. PRICE (Lab.) asked the Secretary of State for Foreign Affairs whether, with a view to implementing the decision of the Yalta Conference, he will invite the Government of the U.S.S.R. to put forward names of persons living both inside and outside Poland who, in their opinion, might be suitable candidates for membership of an enlarged Polish Government.

THE PARLIAMENTARY UNDER-SECRETARY TO THE FOREIGN OFFICE (MR. LAW): Hon. Members will no doubt have seen the announcement issued this morning. Following upon the recent conversations between Marshal Stalin and Mr. Hopkins the Moscow Commission on Poland established by the Crimea Conference has resumed its work and has issued invitations to an agreed list of Polish leaders from within Poland and from abroad to consult under the auspices of the Commission on the composition of a Polish Provisional Government of National Unity in accordance with the Crimea decisions. These consultations will only be the first step towards the fulfillment of those decisions but it is the hope of His Majesty's Government that they may lead to the formation of a Government acceptable to all parties in Poland such as will command the recognition of all the Great Powers.

MR. PRICE: Should these conversations prove successful, as we all hope, will the Foreign Secretary reconsider the whole status of the Polish Government in London?

MR. LAW: Up till now we have been governed in this matter by the declaration on Poland of the Crimea Conference. Perhaps I ought to read to the House the relevant part:

> "When a Polish Provisional Government of National Unity has been properly formed in conformity with the above"—

that is, the Agreement—

> "the Government of the Union of Soviet Socialist Republics, which now maintains diplomatic relations with the present Provisional Government of Poland, and the Government of the United Kingdom and the Government of the United States will establish diplomatic relations with the new Polish Provisional Government of National Unity and will exchange ambassadors, by whose reports the respective Governments will be kept informed about the situation in Poland."

That still governs our attitude.

MR. GLENVIL HALL (Lab.): Is the Polish Government in London a party to these new moves and in agreement with them?

MR. LAW: I think the hon. Member will have seen in the Press today the list of representatives who are going, and they do seem to us to be as fully representative of Polish feeling as we can hope to have at the present time. I do not think there are members of the London Polish Government.

MAJOR-GENERAL SIR ALFRED KNOX (C.): Will my right hon. Friend state whether these delegates will have their safety guaranteed by the British Government?

MR. LAW: I have no reason to suppose that their safety is in any jeopardy.

MR. DRIBERG (Ind.): Pending the conversations, in order to improve relations, will some of the Polish agencies in London be invited to refrain from publishing anti-Soviet propaganda at our expense?

PROFESSOR SAVORY (C.): Can my right hon. Friend say whether the President of Poland has been consulted as being the only persons entitled to appoint a Polish Government?

* * *

Debate on June 14, 1945.

THE PRIME MINISTER (MR. CHURCHILL): Our relations with Russia have undergone a marked improvement in the last week or so, because one difficult matter connected with Poland has already been settled. Invitations have been sent to Mr. Mikołajczyk and other Poles in this country and to Mr. Sapieha and Mr. Witos and others in Poland who were nominated by the British or United States Governments. Invitations have been sent to them to proceed at once to Moscow, where the Conferences between the two Ambassadors and Mr. Molotov will be reinforced by Conferences in a larger circle in which the present Warsaw Polish Government will be assisted by representatives of the Poles from outside the country and others outside the scope of that government. . . . In respect of the people who were invited to Russia . . . it must be remembered that they are only going to take part in a consultation, the object of which is to see whether the Warsaw Government can be extended or not, and we had rather hoped that that would have been settled three months ago.

40. PRESS CORRESPONDENTS IN POLAND*

CAPTAIN GAMMANS (C.) asked the Secretary of State for Foreign Affairs if members of His Majesty's Embassy in Moscow and Press correspondents are now able to visit that part of Poland which has been liberated by the Russian Army.

MAJOR LORD WILLOUGHBY DE ERESBY (C.) asked the Secretary of State for Foreign Affairs the number of British and American reporters now in Poland.

THE SECRETARY OF STATE FOR FOREIGN AFFAIRS (MR. EDEN): Since His Majesty's Government do not recognize the Polish Provisional Government in Warsaw, no member of His Majesty's Embassy at Moscow has yet entered liberated Poland. A number of Press correspondents have been able to visit Poland since the New Year, but no British correspondents are now there.

CAPTAIN GAMMANS: Is my right hon. Friend aware that the good faith of the Yalta Agreement, to which His Majesty's Government are committed, is very largely dependent upon whether or not facilities of this sort are going to be permitted?

MR. EDEN: My hon. and gallant Friend asked whether a representative of His Majesty's Embassy in Moscow has gone and I explained to him that, as we do not recognize the Provisional Government, that cannot be. As regards Press representatives, we should very much welcome the very widest circulation of Press representatives.

---

* House of Commons. Vol. 409, Apr. 11, 1945, p. 1795–1796.

41. PERSONAL MESSAGES TO POLAND*

Debate on April 11, 1945.

MR. HENRY BROOKE (C.) asked the Secretary of State for Foreign Affairs whether any facilities yet exist for persons in this country to make inquiries about friends or relatives in Poland, or to send personal messages to them.

THE SECRETARY OF STATE FOR FOREIGN AFFAIRS (MR. EDEN): I understand that the British Red Cross accept inquiries about persons in Poland, although they cannot undertake that such inquiries will reach their destination or that replies will be received. Inquirers are informed accordingly. There are yet no facilities for transmitting personal messages.

MR. SILVERMAN (Lab.): Is the right hon. Gentleman aware that, for some time past, the radio in Lublin has been publishing lists of survivors with relatives outside Poland; and would he make those lists available to interested persons in this country?

MR. EDEN: If there is any means by which I can do that, and it is desired, I will certainly consider it.

* * *

Debate on April 18, 1945.

LADY APSLEY (C.) asked the Secretary of State for Foreign Affairs if His Majesty's Government is aware of the concern felt by officers and other ranks of the Polish Forces serving with the British Navy, Army and Air Force who, unable to obtain definite news of their relatives in Poland, are a prey to rumors of deportations and arrests among their families; and what steps are being taken to obtain information from

---

* House of Commons. Vol. 409, Apr. 11, 1945, p. 1797–1798; Vol. 410, Apr. 18, 1945, p. 228–229.

the Soviet Government for our Polish Allies as to the safety and whereabouts of their parents, wives and children.

THE PARLIAMENTARY UNDER-SECRETARY TO THE FOREIGN OFFICE (MR. LAW): His Majesty's Government are indeed aware of the concern felt by those who are serving so gallantly in the Polish Armed Forces under British command about the safety of their relatives in Poland from whom they have for so long been separated. It will be understood, however, that His Majesty's Government are not in a position to make inquiries of this sort of the Soviet Government on a large scale, although they have done so in certain special cases. They have been given to understand by the Soviet Government, however, that the pressure of business upon the Soviet Administration makes it difficult for them to carry out the necessary investigations in cases of this nature, and that they can only undertake to do so in so far as means are available for doing so.

42. CONCENTRATION CAMPS IN POLAND*

MR. PETHERICK (C.) asked the Secretary of State for Foreign Affairs whether, in view of the Yalta Agreement, he can give the House any information about the concentration camps in the province of Lublin, Poland, for officers of the Polish Home Army and others.

THE PARLIAMENTARY UNDER-SECRETARY TO THE FOREIGN OFFICE (MR. LAW): No, Sir. Since His Majesty's Government do not recognize the present Provisional Government in Warsaw there are no official British representatives on the spot to confirm the existence of such camps.

MR. PETHERICK: Will my right hon. Friend make arrangements with the Russian Government for British journalists to go to Poland to inquire whether there is any truth in any of the allegations that are now being made?

* House of Commons. Vol. 410, Apr. 18, 1945, p. 185–186.

MR. LAW: The Prime Minister said yesterday, I think with the general assent of the House, that this was not an opportune time to discuss these matters, and I think it would be inadvisable to pursue the discussion now.[1]

PROFESSOR SAVORY (C.): Can my right hon. Friend give us any information with regard to M. Witos, the venerable leader of the Peasant Party and former Prime Minister, who was carried away from his home near Cracow on March 31st?

MR. LAW: I really do not think I can add anything to the reply that I have given, especially since my hon. Friend has raised quite a different question.

MR. MCGOVERN (I. L. P.): If the Government have not recognized the Lublin Committee, can the right hon. Gentleman state why Members of Parliament are today receiving documents concerning the Lublin Government from an office in London?

MR. LAW: I have no information about that. I can assure the hon. Member that I am not responsible for it.

MAJOR-GENERAL SIR ALFRED KNOX (C.): Surely the Prime Minister did not express a wish that these atrocities should continue and that we should make no protest?

MR. GALLACHER (Com.): On a point of Order. Is it right to make allegations about atrocities where there is no proof of any kind?

MR. SPEAKER: I cannot stop Members saying what they like as long as it is in Order.

---

[1] House of Commons, April 17, 1945. THE PRIME MINISTER (Mr. CHURCHILL): . . . I do not think it would be a good opportunity for a Debate on Poland or on the general war situation. I think it might lie akwardly with the general movement of events. Serious changes in the world position have taken place since this order of Business was planned and now the Foreign Secretaries of Russia, Britain, and the United States will have an opportunity of meeting, which has been greatly needed since we left Yalta. I should not like to plunge into discussions which might in any way impair the prospects of a definite improvement in regard to the various subjects which were discussed at Yalta and have not yet reached their full fruition . . ."

MR. PETHERICK: As we have been asked to await the Prime Minister's statement, would my right hon. Friend say when that statement is likely to be made?

MR. LAW: I cannot possibly say that. It is a matter that concerns the general Business of the House. I have no doubt that a statement will be made at the earliest possible moment.

MR. STOKES (Lab.): Is the right hon. Gentleman aware that this matter will be raised tomorrow in connection with the Business of the House?

43. THE CASE OF THE SIXTEEN*

DURING ALL OF THE WARSAW UPRISING *in 1944 members of the Polish underground government, including Deputy Premier J. S. Jankowski and leaders of the Council of National Unity (Polish underground Parliament) with Speaker Kazimierz Puzak at the head, stayed in Warsaw in constant contact with the Home Army. After the uprising they left bombed Warsaw and continued their underground activity in various Polish cities still under German occupation. They had radio contact with the Polish Government in London. After Warsaw was occupied by the Russians the underground government gradually returned the base of its operations to the capital.*

Before the Yalta Conference, on Jan. 27, 1945, Under-Secretary of State for Foreign Affairs Sir Orme Sargent, in a talk with Ambassador Raczyński, said that Minister Eden felt it would be important and useful if he could have the names of Polish underground leaders. Such information might help him, he felt, to guarantee the security of these individuals against reprisals by the Soviet authorities or the Lublin Government.[1]

---

* House of Commons. Vol. 409, Apr. 11, 1945, p. 1798; vol. 410, Apr. 18, 1945, p. 227–228; Apr. 25, 1945, p. 807; May 2, 1945, p. 1382–1384; May 9, 1945, p. 1882–1884; vol. 411, May 30, 1945, p. 190, June 6, 1945, p. 892; June 13, 1945, p. 1623–1624.

[1] Stosunki polsko-sowieckie, 1943–46, p. 450.

Discussions with Deputy Premier Jankowski of the Polish Government in Poland lasted some time. Finally, on Mar. 9, a note was sent by the Polish Government to Minister Eden giving the names of the following ministers in Poland, who were actually members of the Polish Government in London:[2] *Jan Stanislaw Jankowski (Independent), Antoni Pajdak (Socialist), Stanisław Jasiukowicz (National Democratic Party), and Adam Bień (Peasant Party). Ambassador Clark Kerr gave these names to the Soviet Government with the statement that if any harm came to these persons the British Government would consider it a serious violation of the Yalta Agreements.*[3]

At this same time, Deputy Premier Jankowski wired the Polish Government in London that since Feb. 27 he had been in indirect contact with Soviet Col. Pimienov who was stationed in the city of Pruszków near Warsaw and was acting as an intermediary for the 1st Byelorussian Front Command. On Mar. 6, Deputy Premier Jankowski said, both he and Gen. Okulicki received letters from Col. Pimienov[4] *suggesting that they come to a conference with Col.-Gen. Ivanov, the representative of the High Command of the 1st Byelorussian Front within the next few days. Both letters ended with this statement:*

> ". . . I myself, as an officer of the Red Army to whom it fell to carry out a mission of such importance, am giving you a full guarantee and pledge of my officer's word that after your arrival here, when your fate will depend on me, you will enjoy full security."

On Mar. 17 and successive days, Col. Pimienov had separate talks with Deputy Premier Jankowski, and members of the Polish Peasant Party, National Democratic Party, and Christian Labor Party. On Mar. 19 Deputy Premier Jankowski said that in answer to his questions Col. Pimienov gave him to understand that:[5]

---

[2] Ibid. p. 503.
[3] Ibid. p. 504.
[4] Stosunki polsko-sowieckie, 1943–46, p. 496.
[5] Ibid. p. 409 (Jankowski's telegram of Mar. 19, 1945).

"1. Gen. Ivanov would come by air in the very near future to hold conversation with us.

2. Gen. Ivanov was acting on the authority of the High Command of the Red Army to which he was appointed with the approval of Stalin.

3. He was anxious that the matters under discussion should be settled speedily.

4. Gen. Ivanov had decided to put an airplane at my (Jankowski's) disposal so that a delegation could be sent to London.

I came to the conclusion that the Soviet authorities attached great importance to the conversations and considered them as urgent. If they grant facilities for a delegation to travel to London it will be a real proof of good will."

The Polish Government informed the British Government of these happenings.

On Apr. 1, 1945 the Polish Government in London received news from Poland that on Mar. 27 Deputy Premier Jankowski, Gen. Okulicki, and Speaker of the Council of National Unity K. Pużak had gone to Pruszków for conversations with Col.-Gen Ivanov, and had failed to return to attend the meeting of the Council of National Unity scheduled for the afternoon of the same day.

On Mar. 28 the 3 remaining ministers (A. Bień, S. Jasiukowicz, and A. Pajdak) and delegates of four political parties went to Pruszków for conversations with Gen. Ivanov. The party delegates were: Kazimierz Bagiński, Józef Chaciński, Eugeniusz Czarnowski, Kazimierz Kobylański, Stanisław Michałowski, Stanisław Mierzwa, Józef Stemler-Dąbski, Zbigniew Stypułkowski and Franciszek Urbański. All failed to return. Earlier, on Mar. 8, Aleksander Zwierzyński, Chairman of the National Democratic Party, had been arrested.

The British Government, informed of this, on Apr. 2 instructed Ambassador Clark Kerr in Moscow to intervene in this affair. He received no answer.

To understand how the Polish underground could fall so easily into a trap set by the NKVD it is necessary to realize the plight of the existent underground organization in Poland. Contact with the Government in London was very weak, inasmuch as after the fall of Mikołajczyk's Government the British authorities had made radio communication between the London Government and its ministers in Poland extremely difficult.[6] *In addition, when Poland was already occupied by the Red Army, underground soldiers more and more wanted to come out into the open and take into their own hands the administration of the country and to oppose the Polish communists who were also aiming at the same goal. The conspiracy started to disappear because the Polish communists who during the war worked in the underground knew it very well. Besides the underground government knew that names of its leaders had been given to the Soviet authorities by the British and trusted that the western allies would not let the Soviet do any harm to them. The growing tendency to establish contact with the Soviets in Poland was given an added push by Mikołajczyk's dispatch, received by the Council of National Unity on Mar. 25*[7] *in which he advised just such action.*

This was the situation when Col. Pimienov appeared with the suggestion for discussions—discussions which ended with the arrest of 15 Polish underground leaders.

On Apr. 6 the Polish Government issued this communique:[8]

> At the end of February this year the Deputy Prime Minister and Delegate of the Polish Government in London, and the last commander of the now disbanded Home Army, received an indirect invitation from Col. Pimienov, of the Soviet Political Police, to take part in a conference with the representatve of the High Command of the 1st White Ruthenian front, Gen. Ivanov. Soon afterwards, on Mar. 10, they received a written invitation signed by Col. Pimienov, on behalf of Gen. Ivanov, asking them to come to a meeting and laying stress on the necessity and exceptional importance of the meeting.
>
> The note added that Col. Pimienov, as an officer of the Red Army, guaranteed the safety of the invited persons. Later it was explained by the Soviet authorities that the political aim of this invitation was to discuss the coming into the open of the Polish

[6] See No. 11.

[7] Baginski, K. "Sprawa szesnastu!" (IN: Nowy Świat, New York, Mar. 30, 1955).

[8] Stosunki polsko-sowieckie, 1943–46, p. 520.

political parties which have so far not revealed themselves, "in order to include them in the general current of democratic powers in independent Poland."

Col. Pimienov also at the same time approached the Polish political parties with a similar request.

On Mar. 20, in reply to requests from the Polish side, Col. Pimienov announced that the Soviet authorities agreed to allow 12 Polish political leaders fly to London in order to confer with the Polish Government and political leaders here. On Mar. 27, the Deputy Prime Minister, the Chairman of the Council of National Unity, and the last commander of the Home Army presented themselves to Gen. Ivanov in accordance with his invitation. They have not so far returned from their visit, and have sent no messages to their families or to anybody else.

On Mar. 28, three Polish Cabinet Members then in Poland, eight members of the Polish political parties and an interpreter presented themselves to Gen. Ivanov in accordance with his invitation. They also have not returned from this visit. There has been no further news of the whereabouts of any of these 15 persons.

When, after a period of 4 weeks, no news had been received of the date of the disappeared, Polish Minister for Foreign Affairs A. Tarnowski sent a telegram to Eden and Stettinius in San Francisco asking them to do all they could to find out what had happened to these individuals.

The Polish American Congress, on May 3, also sent a dispatch to Secretary of State Stettinius asking him "to obtain from Mr. Molotov, before his departure from San Francisco, a clear and definitive reply to the question: What has become of the fourteen[9] kidnapped Polish Underground leaders?"[10]

On May 4 Molotov informed Eden and Stettinius that these men were being held in Russia, and on May 5 TASS News Agency issued this Soviet Government communique:[11]

"Several British newspapers have of late disseminated all sorts of rumors regarding a number of Polish political leaders who are alleged to have disappeared from Poland.

[9] This figure is not correct—it should be: 16. (Together with Mr. Zwierzynski).

[10] National Committee of Americans of Polish Descent. Biuletyn Organizacyjny, No. 31, p. 8.

[11] Stosunki polsko-sowieckie, 1943–46, p. 540.

On May 2 questions about these Poles were asked in the House of Commons, and 15 names were mentioned. The name of the former Polish Prime Minister, Mr. Witos, who is alleged to have been arrested, was also mentioned.

At the same session of the Commons, the question was raised regarding rumors about the killing and shooting of Poles in Siedlce.

According to available information received from fully authoritative sources TASS is able to state that these reports are mendacious. The facts are as follows:

The groups of Poles mentioned in the British Press and referred to in the House of Commons is composed of 16 and not of 15 people. It is headed by the well-known Polish General, Okulicki, about the disappearence of whom the British reports intentionally keep silent in view of the special odiousness of this general.

Gen. Okulicki's group as especially he himself are accused of preparing diversionary acts in the rear of the Red Army, as a result of which more than 100 officers and men of the Red Army lost their lives.

This group of 16 persons did not disappear but were arrested by the military authorities of the Soviet Command and are now in Moscow pending the investigation of the case.

The group is also accused of the installation and maintenance in the rear of Soviet troops of illegal radio transmitters, which constitutes an act punishable by law. All these persons, or some of them, as the investigations may warrant, will be commited for trial.

As regards British reports of murder and shooting of Poles at Siedlce, which matter was raised in the House of Commons, such reports are false from beginning to end and were probably insinuated to the members of Parliament who raised the question by Arciszewski agents. The report of the arrest of Witos is equally false."

The same day a following statement was issued on behalf of the British and U. S. Governments:

"The British and United States Governments have been making persistent enquiries of the Soviet Government about the group of prominent Polish democratic leaders who were reported to have met the Soviet military authorities in Poland for discussions at the end of March. They have now been officially informed by Mr. Molotov, on behalf on this Government, that these leaders have been arrested on the charge of 'diversionary activities against the Red Army'.

Mr. Eden and Mr. Stettinius immediately expressed their grave concern to Mr. Molotov at receiving this most disquieting information after so long a delay, and asked him to obtain a full explanation concerning the arrest of these Polish leaders, a complete list of their names and news of their present whereabouts.

The Foreign Secretary has reported this most serious developement to His Majesty's Government, and has informed Mr. Molotov that, meanwhile, he cannot continue discussions on the Polish issue."

On May 6 the Polish Government sent to Stettinius, as chairman of the San Francisco Conference, an appeal[12] *stating that "the Polish Government urgently appeals to the Governments of all the United Nations to do all that is in their power to induce the Soviet Government to set free immediately the leaders of the Polish Underground Movement and to guarantee personal safety to them and to their families."*

On May 10 Minister Eden, at a press coference in San Francisco on the Polish problem, said that it would now be for Britain, the U. S. and the Soviet Government "to take stock of the situation and determine what the next step should be." About the arrested Polish leaders Mr. Eden said: "Our information about events in Poland is incomplete today, but I must emphasize that the list of 16 Poles reported as having disappeared and about whom we inquired of the Soviet Government more than a month ago included nearly all the leading figures of the Polish underground movement. These men maintained an excellent record of resistance against the Germans throughout the war. . . . Most of these men were just the type who should, in our view, have been consulted about the new National Government in Poland."[13]

On May 11 Moscow correspondent of the London Times, R. Parker, sent a letter to Stalin asking for a statement on this subject in order to enlighten public opinion which had shown interest in this matter.

---

[12] Stosunki polsko-sowieckie, 1943–46, p. 542.
[13] Ibid, p. 549.

Stalin sent this reply to Mr. Parker on May 18:[14]

"1. The arrest of the 16 Poles in Poland, headed by the notorious diversionist, Gen. Okulicki, is in no way connected with the question of the reconstruction of the Polish Provisional Government. These gentlemen were arrested by virtue of a law dealing with the safeguarding of the rear of the Red Army from diversionists, analogous to the British law of the Defense of the Realm. The arrest was made by the Soviet military authorities in conformity with an agreement made between the Polish Provisional Government and the Soviet military command.

2. It is not true that the arrested Poles had been invited for the purpose of negotiations with the Soviet authorities. The Soviet authorities do not and will not conduct negotiations with breakers of the law relating to the safety of the rear of the Red Army.

3. As regards the question of the reconstruction of the Polish Provisional Government, this can only be settled on the basis of the Crimea resolutions. There can be no deviation from these resolutions.

4. I am of opinion that the Polish question can be solved by agreement among the allies subject to the fulfilment of the following conditions:

a) That when the Polish Provisional Government is reconstructed the latter is recognized as the kernel of the future Polish Government, by analogy with Yugoslavia, where the national council of liberation was recognized as the nucleus of the united Yugoslav Government.

b) That as a result of reconstruction, such a Government in Poland is formed as will carry out a policy of friendship with the Soviet Union and not a policy of a cordon sanitaire directed against the Soviet Union.

c) That the question of the reconstruction of the Polish Provisional Government is decided with Poles who have ties at the present time with the Polish people and not without their participation."

Fallacies in Stalin's statement were pointed out in a communique of the Polish Government on May 22 which once again gave a factual account of the events leading up to the arrest of the 16 Polish leaders.

Towards the end of May Harry Hopkins was in Moscow for talks with Stalin.[15] *Among instructions received from*

---

[14] Ibid, p. 550.
[15] See No. 39.

Pres. Truman, Hopkins was to bring up the arrest of these 16 Polish leaders. On May 31 he brought up the subject emphasizing how important it was for American opinion to resolve this problem of the arrested men. Here is what Hopkins has to say about this discussion:[16]

> "Stalin then said that he was unwilling to order those Poles released who were charged only with use of illegal radio sets. He stated that he had information in regard to these prisoners which was not available to us and inferred that all of them were engaged in what he called diversionist activities. He stated that he believed that Churchill had misled the United States in regard to the facts and had made the American Government believe that the statement of the Polish London Government was accurate. Just the opposite was the case.
>
> Marshal Stalin stated that he did not intend to have the British manage the affairs of Poland and that is exactly what they want to do. Nevertheless, he stated that he believed me when I told him it was having an unfavorable effect on public opinion in America and he assumed the same was true in Great Britain, and therefore he was inclined to do everything he could to make it easy for Churchill to get out of a bad situation because if and when all the evidence is published it would look very bad for the British and he does not want to make the situation worse than it is. He stated that the men must be tried but that they would be treated leniently and he clearly inferred that he was going to consider at once what could be done in regard to these prisoners that I was concerned with to clear the matter up."

Just before the court trial was to begin in Moscow, Pres. Raczkiewicz sent an appeal to Pres. Truman asking him "to use every means at your disposal to prevent such a grievous injustice which can only intensify the Polish Nation's sense of wrongful treatment and evoke profound indignation throughout the whole civilized world, and that you do all in your power to obtain the release of the arrested persons and a guarantee of personal security for them and their families."[17]

The court trial, in the Military Collegium of the Supreme Court of the USSR in Moscow, took place on June 18–21, that is, at the same time as the ambassadors' commission and Po-

---

16 Sherwood, R. Op. Cit., p. 909.
17 Stosunki polsko-sowieckie, 1943–46, p. 563.

lish representatives were meeting in Moscow, for the purpose of establishing a new Provisional Polish Government.[18]

The 16 were accused[19] *of conspiratorial activity in the rear of the Red Army, of sabotage and espionage, of possessing, despite Soviet orders, radios, printing presses, arms and ammunition; and of using these for criminal purposes. Gen Okulicki was accused of wanting to cooperate with the Germans against the USSR, citing as proof his directive to a subordinate in which he wrote:*[20]

> ". . . Until Japan is defeated we cannot expect any improvement in our political situation. The Western world will try to obtain Russia's help in the struggle in the Far East, and will be inclined to make further concessions for this. Later they will see how much Soviet greed and power will become a menace to an extremely terrified Europe. The Anglo-Saxons will have to mobilize all their forces in Europe to enable them to halt the Soviets. We shall then come to the front in the defense line, and we shall probably even see some Germans there who will be under Anglo-Saxon command."

The trial was a public one, attended by foreign press correspondents. The acused were allowed to speak freely—thus they acknowledged some of the accusations—such as ownership of radios and arms—and Gen. Okulicki and underground leaders acknowledged activity in an underground organization.

The sentences delivered on June 21, 1945 were, as compared to usual Soviet sentences, unusually lenient—this can be attributed to Hopkins' intervention with Stalin. The sentences were: Gen. Okulicki—10 years in prison, Deputy Premier Jankowski—8 years; Ministers Bień, Jasiukowicz and Pajdak (sentenced separately because of ill health)—5 years; Puzak—18 months; Bagiński—12 months; Zwierzyński—8 months; Czarnowski—6 months; Mierzwa, Stypułowski, Chaciński, and Urbański—4 months each. Michałowski, Kobylański and Stemler-Dąbski were set free.

---

[18] See No. 53.
[19] Trial of the organizers, leaders and members of the Polish diversionist organizations in the rear of the Red Army. Verbatim report.
[20] Stypułkowski, Z. Invitation to Moscow, p. 317.

Immediately after the trial Premier Arciszewski sent a dispatch to Churchill[21] *with an appeal to him "as to one who can give testimony and whose voice will carry conviction and weight with the conscience of the world. I am also appealing to you to demand of the Soviet Government the immediate release of the sentenced men and permission for them to live wherever they themselves may choose. To voice the truth about the Moscow trial is essential not only in the defense of Poland, in the defense of all the oppressed nations, and also in the defense of these high ideals in the name of which Great Britain entered the war."*

After ten years, on Apr. 21, 1955 the U. S. Government intervened in the matter of these leaders with this note:[22]

> The Embassy refers to representations which were made in 1945 by a United States official with Premier Stalin at Moscow and by the then Secretary of State with Foreign Minister Molotov at the San Francisco Conference on the United Nations Charter with respect to the arrest of 16 leaders of the Polish Underground by Soviet authorities on Mar. 28, 1945.
>
> It is recalled that the Underground had waged a bitter struggle on the side of the Allies and in the defense of Poland against foreign aggression and occupation in the Second World War. The arrest of these men, members of various Polish political parties and groups, aroused great concern throughout the world. It may also be noted that the 16 Polish leaders were arrested at a time when the Western Allies were making an effort in accordance with international discussions, to have a new Polish Government formed on a democratic basis by the inclusion of Polish leaders from abroad and from the Underground in Poland. In virtue of this interest the U. S. made its inquiries to the Soviet Government in 1945 with a view to obtaining information regarding the arrested men. The U. S. Government now wishes to raise this matter again.
>
> Certain developments subsequent to this arrest are well-known. The men were transported from Poland to the Soviet Union and were tried by a Soviet court in June 1945. Most of them were imprisoned in the Soviet Union. Some were re-arrested in Poland and sentenced to imprisonment in Polish jails. The

---

21 Stosunki polsko-sowieckie, 1943–46, p. 572.
22 U. S. Dept. of State Bulletin, May 2, 1955, p. 737.

longest Soviet sentence was that of ten years, imposed on Major Gen. Okulicki.

The U.S. Government notes that if Gen. Okulicki's sentence began on the date of his arrest he has now presumably completed his term of imprisonment. Since all of the other Soviet sentences were of lesser length it is assumed that none of the sixteen men originally arrested are now held in Soviet jails.

The U. S. Government also wishes to point out that despite continued interest in the fate of these Polish leaders, nothing is known of the whereabouts of several of them and there is even some doubt as to how many are still alive.

So far as the U. S. Government is aware the following three members of the group, in addition to Gen. Okulicki, have not yet returned to Poland: Jan St. Jankowski, St. Jasiukowicz and Antoni Pajdak. Dating from the time of their original arrest, Jankowski's sentence would have ended Mar. 28, 1953, and that of Jasiukowicz, and possibly of Pajdak, on Mar. 28, 1950.

Under these circumstances the U. S. Government wishes to request that the Soviet Government provide information as to which of these sixteen men are still in the Soviet Union, and under what circumstances. Information is also requested regarding any of the men who may have died in the USSR.

A similar note was sent to the Polish Government in Warsaw, with this addition:

"It is also understood that Stanisław Michałowski and Kazimierz Kobylański were re-arrested following their return to Poland from the Soviet Union. Their ultimate fate, as well as that of Adam Bień, Aleksander Zwierzyński and Józef Stemler-Dąbski is unknown."

Both governments, Soviet and Polish, refused to accept the notes from the U. S.

Much later, only on Oct. 19, 1955, Gen Okulicki's wife in London received, through the English Red Cross from the Soviet Red Cross, the news that Gen Okulicki had died "of natural causes" on Dec. 24, 1946—that is, 10 years earlier.[23]

According to the Warsaw radio "Kraj" of Aug. 31, 1956, the fate of other members of the Polish Government jailed in Russia, was as follows:[24]

---

[23] "Nowy Świat", New York, Oct. 21, 1955.

[24] "News from Poland" (Free Europe Press) no. 36/139, Sept. 4, 1956, and "Nowy Świat" (New York) Sept. 22, 1956.

Kazimierz Bagiński—on his return to Poland he was arrested, spent several years in a Polish prison, after which he was able to escape, and he is now in the USA. Adam Bień—after his return to Poland, he was sentenced to 5 years in prison, after which he was released. The following died in Poland: Józef Chaciński in 1954, Eugeniusz Czarnowski in 1952, Franciszek Urbański in 1955. Stanisław Jasiukowicz, according to information from the Warsaw Government, returned to Poland in 1945 and died there several years later. Actually, it is believed that he never returned to Poland and that he died in Russia.

Vice-Premier Jan S. Jankowski died in a Soviet prison probably on March 13, 1953. Kazimierz Kobylański, Stanisław Michałowski and Stanisław Mierzwa returned to Poland where they were arrested. Antoni Pajdak returned to Poland in 1955, Kazimierz Pużak returned to Poland in 1945 whereupon he was arrested by Polish authorities and he died in prison in 1950. Józef Stemler-Dąbski returned to Poland. Zbigniew Stypułkowski returned to Poland, from which he later escaped and he is now in the U. S.

Aleksander Zwierzyński died in Poland in 1958.

Debate on April 11, 1945.

MISS WARD (C.) asked the Secretary of State for Foreign Affairs whether he has any information regarding the whereabouts of the Polish representatives who left for the Soviet Union to discuss the formation of the New Provisional Government of Poland.

THE SECRETARY OF STATE FOR FOREIGN AFFAIRS (MR. EDEN) : While I have no confirmation of the reports that these Polish representatives have gone to the Soviet Union to discuss the formation of the new Provisional Government, I have instructed His Majesty's Ambassador at Moscow to make inquiries concerning their whereabouts. When I learn the result of these inquiries, I will report further to the House.

MISS WARD: Can the right hon. Gentleman say when that telegram was dispatched and how long it is likely to take?

MR. EDEN: I think it was either yesterday or the day before; I am not sure.

* * *

Debate on April 18, 1945.

COMMANDER BOWER (C.) asked the Secretary of State for Foreign Affairs if, in the course of the discussions culminating in the Yalta Agreement, a procedure was contemplated such as that now being followed in the negotiations initiated on March 15, 1945, between the Vice-Premier of the Polish Government in London, the Polish Underground Leaders, and representatives of the Government of the USSR.

THE PARLIAMENTARY UNDER-SECRETARY TO THE FOREIGN OFFICE (MR. LAW): No, Sir. But the main aim of the Crimea Declaration on Poland was the establishment of a new Polish Provisional Government of National Unity by the reorganization of the present Provisional Government on a broader democratic basis with the inclusion of democratic leaders from Poland itself and from Poles abroad. Although the Crimea Declaration did not contemplate discussions of the character described by my hon. and gallant Friend, there is no reason why they should be ruled out if they contributed to achieving the main aim of the Crimea Declaration.

COMMANDER BOWER asked the Secretary of State for Foreign Affairs if he is aware that on March 28, 1945, after several preliminary meetings with a high officer of the NKVD, the Vice-Premier of the Polish Government in London, who is resident in Poland, together with three other Ministers and eight representatives of four political parties, visited the headquarters of the Russian General Ivanov, at his invitation in order to discuss means for sending 12 delegates from Polish political parties and the Underground Movement in London; and when the arrival in London of these delegates may be expected.

MR. LAW: The reports which my right hon. Friend has received of such meetings as are referred to in the question do not suggest that their purpose was to discuss means of sending Polish political leaders to London, and I have no information as to their possible arrival here.

* * *

Debate on April 25, 1945.

PROFESSOR SAVORY (C.) asked the Secretary of State for Foreign Affairs (1) whether he has now received any information as to the whereabouts of M. Jankowski, Vice-Premier of Poland and delegate at Warsaw of the Polish Government, who, with 14 other Polish representatives, was taken away by the Soviet authorities on March 28; (2) whether he has now received information with regard to M. Witos, the former Polish Prime Minister, who was taken away from his home near Cracow on March 31.

MR. LAW: His Majesty's Government still await a reply to the inquiries which they have made of the Soviet Government on these matters.

PROFESSOR SAVORY: Does my right hon. Friend realize that three out of the 14, in addition to the Vice-Premier, are members of the Polish Government, and that their colleagues await news of them with the most intense anxiety?

MR. LAW: This is a matter which, as the House knows, is occupying the earnest attention of His Majesty's Government, and in particular of the Foreign Secretary, at this moment. I do not think that the work of the Foreign Secretary would be helped by discussion of these matters now, and I have really nothing to add to what I have said.

MR. STOKES (Lab.): May I ask——

MR. SPEAKER rose——

MR. STOKES: On a point of Order. I beg to give notice that I shall return to this matter at the earliest possible moment.

* * *

Debate on May 2, 1945.

PROFESSOR SAVORY (C.) asked the Secretary of State for Foreign Affairs (1) whether he has now received any answer to the inquiries addressed by him to the Soviet Government with regard to M. Witos, the former Polish Prime Minister, who was taken away from his home near Cracow on March 31; (2) whether he has now received a reply to the inquiries which he has made of the Soviet Government as to the whereabouts of M. Jankowski, the Vice-Premier of Poland, three Cabinet Ministers and 11 other representatives who were carried away by the Soviet authorities on March 28.

COMMANDER BOWER (C.) asked the Secretary of State for Foreign Affairs whether he has yet any information concerning the whereabouts and condition of the Vice-Premier of the Polish Government in London, the three other Ministers and eight representatives of four Polish political parties who visited the headquarters of the Russian General Ivanov at his invitation on March 28, 1945.

MAJOR LLOYD (C.) asked the Secretary of State for Foreign Affairs whether he has yet received from the Russian Government information with regard to the fate of the 15 Polish political leaders who have disappeared, and about whose disappearance the gravest concern is felt by the Polish Government in London.

CAPTAIN MCEWEN (C.) asked the Secretary of State for Foreign Affairs whether the inquiries which he has made of the Soviet Government regarding the whereabouts of a number of Polish representatives, including Messieurs Witos and Jankowski, have, as yet, placed him in a position to give any information on the subject.

MR. LAW: His Majesty's Government have not ceased to press the Soviet Government as to the whereabouts of the prominent Poles referred to. No information has, however, been received by His Majesty's Embassy at Moscow in reply to their repeated inquiries. I regret that I can give the House no assurance as to the safety of the persons mentioned in the Questions.

PROFESSOR SAVORY: Does not the right hon. Gentleman realize that a month has now elapsed since these gentlemen were carried off and that the anguish of their Polish colleagues in the Ministry is intense? Were they not offered a safe conduct by General Ivanov?

MR. LAW: I certainly fully understand the point which my hon. Friend has made. As I said, we have made repeated inquiries of the Soviet Embassy and in Moscow, and so far have had no reply whatever. That is a matter which His Majesty's Government regret.

COMMANDER BOWER: Does my right hon. Friend realize that not only the Polish authorities are suffering from great anxiety, but public opinion in this country is violently aroused about this?

CAPTAIN MCEWEN: In view of this situation in which between Allies we apparently are unable to get a civil reply to a civil question, will not my right hon. Friend take some extra steps to ensure obtaining a reply?

VISCOUNTESS ASTOR (C.): Will my right hon. Friend have this brought up at San Francisco?

COMMANDER AGNEW (C.): Will my right hon. Friend telegraph at once to the Foreign Secretary to ask him to talk to Mr. Molotov about this and ask Mr. Molotov to give personal attention to it?

MR. LAW: I can assure my hon. and gallant Friend that the Foreign Secretary has done, and is still doing, all he can to obtain information on this point.

MR. GALLACHER (Com.): Is the Minister aware that hundreds of people have been taken from their homes in Ulster and their relatives are suffering great anxiety, and will he take that matter up?

EARL WINTERTON (C.): On a point of Order, Mr. Speaker. Is it open to an hon. Member to raise an entirely different question which has got nothing to do with the Question on the Paper, and if so, can we have a debate on it?

MR. SPEAKER: A supplementary Question must always be relevant to the Question on the Paper.

COMMANDER BOWER (C.): asked the Secretary of State for Foreign Affairs if he is aware that a public meeting was held, on Apr. 14, in Siedlce, Poland, at which representatives of the Lublin Government announced forthcoming elections on a one-party basis; that 24 Poles who opposed the speakers were publicly executed in the marketplace by Lublin special police in the presence of senior officers of the Russian police; that on 15th April five other Poles were shot, two of them were American citizens of Polish descent; that on 16th April a further six Polish farmers were publicly hanged without trial; and if, in view of the Yalta Agreements, he will make representations to secure the avoidance of such incidents in future.

MR. LAW: His Majesty's Government have received one report which appears to bear upon two of the incidents described by my hon. and gallant Friend, but does not altogether correspond with the details he has given. They are, however, unable to confirm the truth of this report or to acquire information regarding events in Poland, since they do not recognize the present Provisional Government in Warsaw and, therefore, are not officially represented in Poland; nor have the Soviet authorities granted facilities for British observers to proceed to areas which are on the lines of communication of the Red Army. Inquiries have been made, however, of the Soviet Government regarding the reports referred to by my hon. and gallant Friend.

COMMANDER BOWER: If we are to collaborate with our Ally successfully in the time before us, is it not very necessary that there should be a great deal more frankness in the communications which we receive from the Soviet Government on this and allied matters?

* * *

Debate on May 9, 1945.

PROFESSOR SAVORY (C.) asked the Secretary of State for Foreign Affairs whether he is now in a position to inform the House of the result of his inquiries addressed to the Soviet Government with regard to M. Witos, the former Polish Prime Minister, who was taken away from his home near Cracow on March 31.

MR. LAW: His Majesty's Charge d'Affaires in Moscow has been instructed to ask the Soviet Government for confirmation of the report that M. Witos is now at liberty. He has also been instructed to ask for information regarding the reports which have been brought to the notice of His Majesty's Government that other member of the Peasant Party have recently been arrested.

PROFESSOR SAVORY asked the Secretary of State for Foreign Affairs whether he has now received any information concerning the whereabouts of M. Jankowski, Vice-Premier of Poland, three Cabinet Ministers and other Polish representatives who were taken away by the Soviet authorities on March 28.

MAJOR LLOYD asked the Secretary of State for Foreign Affairs whether he has yet received from the Russian Government information with regard to the fate of the 15 Polish political leaders who have disappeared, and about whose disappearance concern is felt by the Polish Government in London.

MR. EMMOTT (C.) asked the Secretary of State for Foreign Affairs whether His Majesty's Government have now received from the Government of the U.S.S.R. an answer to the repeated inquiries they have made about certain Polish personages.

CAPTAIN GAMMANS (C.) asked the Secretary of State for Foreign Affairs if he will make a statement about the breakdown of negotiations at San Francisco concerning the formation of a national Government in Poland.

MR. KEELING (C.) asked the Secretary of State for Foreign Affairs whether he can make a statement about the Polish democratic leaders who were arrested by the Soviet military authorities after accepting their invitation to enter into discussions.

MR. LAW: I have at present nothing to add to the statement issued jointly by my right hon. Friend the Foreign Secretary and by Mr. Stettinius on this grave matter.

PROFESSOR SAVORY: Does the right hon. Gentleman realize that these gentlemen were invited to a conference and were promised absolute immunity for their personal safety?

MR. LAW: I can assure my hon. Friend that His Majesty's Government realize the full significance of the facts, in so far as they know them.

MR. EMMOTT: Will my right hon. Friend confirm or deny the statement made by the Tass Agency on Saturday that these Polish personages constitute a group which is led by General Okulicki, since the introduction of the name of this officer appears to constitute quite a different element?

MR. LAW: I have, of course, seen the report to which my hon. Friend refers, that of the Tass Agency. In reply to his question I can only say that the information at the disposal of His Majesty's Government certainly does not confirm what is contained in that report.

CAPTAIN GAMMANS: In view of the fact that most of the missing gentlemen were members either of the Polish trade union movement or of the Socialist movement in Poland, has the right hon. Gentleman had any protest from members of the parties of the Left in this country, at their detention?

MR. LAW: I am not absolutely certain about the premises

stated by my hon. Friend, but certainly when these matters have been discussed here, I have not been conscious of any such protest.

MAJOR LLOYD: Can my right hon. Friend inform the House whether there is, in fact, any sound reason for believing that any of these gentlemen are still alive?

MR. LAW: I regret very much that we have no further information than that with which the House is already familiar.

MR. SHINWELL (Lab.): If the Government are disposed to interfere in matters of this sort—[Hon Members: "Oh."] —will the right hon. Gentleman take note of the fact that General Franco caused a colonel of the French resistance forces to be shot last week?

CAPTAIN MCEWEN (C.): Can my right hon. Friend indicate how soon the Foreign Secretary will be able to make a statement in this country?

MR. GEORGE GRIFFITHS (Lab.): Not before he comes home.

MR. LAW: I do not think I can better the answer which has just been given by the hon. Member from the other side of the House. As to when the Foreign Secretary will be back, I am afriad I cannot give the House any information at the present time.

* * *

Debate on May 30, 1945.

MAJOR LLOYD (C.) asked the Secretary of State for Foreign Affairs whether he has yet received from the Russian Government information with regard to the 16 Polish democratic leaders who have been arrested by the Russians, about whose fate concern is felt by the Polish Government.

MR. IVOR THOMAS (Lab.) asked the Secretary of State for Foreign Affairs whether he has any further report to make on the 16 arrested Poles.

THE SECRETARY OF STATE FOR FOREIGN AFFAIRS (MR. EDEN): I have received no further information additional to what has been published.

MR. THOMAS: Is it the case that the only offense with which the Poles are charged is the possession of wireless sets?

MR. EDEN: I do not think it would be true to say that that is the only offense, though it is one of the offenses. I asked M. Molotov when I saw him at San Francisco to let us have a full explanation and list of the names. I hope we shall receive them.

MR. MCGOVERN (I.L.P.): Can the right hon. Gentleman say where these men are housed?

MR. EDEN: No, Sir. The hon. Member knows that we have no access of any kind.

* * *

Debate on June 6, 1945.

MR. MACK (Lab.) asked the Secretary of State for Foreign Affairs, in view of Marshal Stalin's statement that the 16 arrested Poles were not invited to Russia for negotiations, what steps he proposes taking, in the interests of our alliance with Soviet Russia, to correct the public impression that these Poles had been lured to the U.S.S.R. for subsequent arrest.

THE PARLIAMENTARY UNDER-SECRETARY TO THE FOREIGN OFFICE (MR. LAW): As my right hon. Friend stated in reply to Questions on May 30, he has not yet received the full explanation of this episode for which he asked M. Molotov at San Francisco. In the absence of full information His Majesty's Government are scarcely in a position to correct any misapprehensions that may exist in the public mind.

* * *

Debate on June 13, 1945.

MR. MARTIN (Lab.) asked the Secretary of State for Foreign Affairs whether any further information has been received from the Soviet Government on the Polish leaders under arrest in Russia.

MR. PRICE (Lab.) asked the Secretary of State for Foreign Affairs whether in view of the increasing suspicion over the intention of the U.S.S.R. in Poland and Eastern Europe arising in part from the arrest of the 16 Poles, he will invite the Government of the U.S.S.R. to state in greater detail than hitherto whether all the 16 persons are charged with offenses; and if not, who are so charged and the nature of the indictments against them.

MR. LAW: The Soviet Government are well aware of the desire of His Majesty's Government for full information on this subject. The early release of these men would, I am sure, contribute to the success of the important consultations which will shortly begin in Moscow.

MR. MARTIN: In view of the satisfaction which we all feel at the answer to the previous Question, could the right hon. Gentleman represent to the Soviet Government the great importance to Anglo-Soviet relations and the future organization of world security of releasing these people?

MR. LAW: I am sure the Soviet Government are fully aware of our anxiety in this matter, but I will certainly see that what the hon. Member has said is brought to their attention.

MR. SILVERMAN (Lab.): Can the right hon. Gentleman assure us that the Polish Government in London will themselves refrain from abusing the special powers that we have conferred upon them in relation to their Army by arresting political opponents?

MR. SPEAKER: That is another question.

44. ELECTIONS IN LIBERATED COUNTRIES*

THE EARL OF MANSFIELD had the following Notice on the Paper: To ask His Majesty's Government whether they are aware that when the first General Elections are held in the liberated countries of Europe, there is grave danger that, in certain cases, political groups may be able, by violence and and intimidation, to produce electoral results in no way representative of the real wishes of the populations concerned; whether they are therefore considering, in consultation with our Allies, the advisability of arranging that such elections, in all countries of Central and Eastern Europe, shall be supervised by an Allied Commission, in which as many as possible of the United Nations shall be represented, in order to ensure in the suffrage the free expression of popular opinion; whether this question is to be discussed at the San Francisco Conference; and to move for Papers.

The noble Earl said: . . . Each country must be responsible for its own destiny, but it is my firm belief that the United Nations, having freed these countries from the German yoke, have still incumbent upon them the obligation to ensure that the first Government to be set up in each country by popular election shall, so far as is humanly possible, conform to the wishes of the great majority of the population of each country concerned. Unfortunately, as I have said, there is only too much reason to fear that in several countries, unless some control is exercised from outside, the result of a so-called popular election will be decidedly unpopular, the resulting Government will be one based upon force rather than consent, so that the countries concerned will have an unstable regime, subject to overthrow by force again in a few years' or indeed a few months' time, and the condition of the peoples of those countries will be likely to be very un-

* House of Lords, Vol. 136, Apr. 25, 1945, p. 28–34, 38–42, 48–49.

satisfactory from the economic, as well as from the political, point of view.

This is particularly the case in regard to that most unfortunate of all our Allies and of all the victims of German aggression, Poland. His Majesty's Government have very rightly made it abundantly clear that they do not consider the Lublin Committee, at present calling itself the Provisional Government of Poland, a body which is truly representative of Polish opinion. Not only does the personal record of many of the members of that Government induce little confidence in their impartiality, but they are also all, without exception, members of extremist organizations whose voting power in the Poland of before the war was negligible and whose influence is by no means likely to have increased to such an extent as would justify them in assuming that they genuinely represent the great majority of the population.

In view of the all-too-well authenticated stories which are now coming out of Poland, I suggest that it is urgently necessary that the first election to take place in that country, above all others, should be supervised by an Inter-Allied Commission, not a Commission appointed by a single one of the Great Powers. It would be desirable that as many of the Allied Nations as possible should take part in such a Commission. Obviously the most important of the Allies—Great Britain, the United States of America and Russia—will contribute each a large proportion of the officials concerned, and I hope that fair representation would also be given to France, who can justly complain of somewhat cavalier treatment having been meted out to her for a considerable time past. It would be highly desirable that all of our smaller Allies should also be represented, and, indeed, I would include in the invitation the Governments of countries like Sweden and Switzerland who have a Parliamentary system. The more nations taking part in such a Commission, the less would there be the chance of any nation being able to exert undue influence and thereby bring about results not in accordance with the will of the electors . . .

LORD STRABOLGI (L.): The noble Earl talks quite glibly of this election in Poland being supervised by the Swedes and the Swiss, the Americans, the Russians and as many others of the Allies who can be brought in, but when does he think that is to take place? Poland is a devastated country. I do not imagine there is anything in the nature of an electoral roll from one end of Poland to the other. Everyone knows that the records have had to be destroyed to keep them out of the hands of the Gestapo during the German occupation. Then there are vast numbers of Poles who have not yet returned. There are the Poles who have been and are fighting with us, and the displaced persons. Presumably they will have to go back before there can be an election. Many thousands of Poles are fighting most gallantly in our Armies in Holland and Italy and presumably these soldiers must return before there can be elections. When does the noble Earl think these elections can take place in Poland and how does he think we shall be able to spare the Forces and organizers and administrators for a very long time to supervise the elections? The suggestion of a vast international supervision of the elections in Poland is fantastic...

THE EARL OF PERTH: My Lords, the problems raised by the noble Earl in the Motion which he has brought before your Lordships and developed in his speech are of great difficulty, and they are certainly worthy of the serious consideration of your Lordships' House. I do not intend to follow him and the noble Lord who has just spoken, in making a tour of the various countries of Central and South-eastern Europe. I think, myself, that discussion of the nature of the Governments now existing and the personalities which compose them could only have rather unfortunate results at the present time. There are just two points which I should like to take up. The first refers to Greece, to which the noble Lord devoted a very considerable portion of his speech. I should like to say that, contrary to his view, I believe that the policy adopted by His Majesty's Government has been highly successful, and if the policy which he suggested had been the policy carried out I believe that civil war would still be going on in Greece. The other point relates to Poland. I regret that the noble Earl spoke about Poland in the way in which he did. Some little time ago, we had a debate about the Crimea decisions, a very full and lengthy debate, and it was quite clear from the answer given by the noble Viscount the Leader of the House that His Majesty's Government fully recognized that they had undertaken very grave responsibilities with regard to the future of Poland. I, for one, would like to give them adequate time to allow them to do their utmost—as I am sure they are doing—to discharge those responsibilities, and to fulfill the pledges which they have given.

There are one or two general considerations which I should like to put before your Lordships apart from matters relating to these countries which have been specially mentioned. The Motion which the noble Earl has moved can well be defined as dealing with the methods to be adopted to secure fulfillment of point 3 of the Atlantic Charter—namely, the right of peoples to choose the form of government under which they desire to live, and that the rights of self-government shall be fully restored to those who have been deprived of them. Most of us have wondered whether this can possibly be effected. I think that our minds—probably owing to our happy historic past—turn rather naturally to General Elections, and to the forms of Parliamentary government which result from those elections. We believe that such a system is best fitted to democratic government, that is a Government chosen in accordance with the freely-expressed wishes of the majority of the people of a particular country. But I do not think that as regards other countries we ought to be too dogmatic. Our Parliamentary methods of government may not be immediately practicable for them, and indeed they may not be those which the inhabitants, the people generally, of a particular State, may desire. If that is so, then surely we ought not to try to impose our methods upon them.

It seems to me that what is essential, in the first place, is a Government which commands the support and approval of the majority of the people concerned. In the second place, I believe it to be essential—indeed I think it is the hall mark of democracy—that the people should be able, by constitutional means, to change the Government when it has lost their confidence. The Motion of the noble Earl refers to General Elections. Of course, it would be very gratifying to us to think that in the liberated countries the people have decided to, or wish to, adopt either the British Parliamentary system or the American system. But I rather doubt—indeed I feel quite convinced of the contrary—whether any suggestion of that kind would, today, be a practicable proposition. What, in my view, the existing circumstances require is a Government which will represent, broadly, the feelings of the population as a whole, so far as they can be ascertained. It is obvious that such a Government must be composed of people of varying political ideas, in fact, probably, of utterly opposed political theories, because the principal task of such a Government, as pointed out by the noble Earl, must be to maintain order and to repair, as far as practicable, the immediate ravages of war and restore the economic and social life of the people.

Such a Government, in my view, ought not to remain in office longer than is absolutely necessary, and in many cases it will have to pave the way for a Constituent Assembly. The duty of that Constituent Assembly would be to formulate the methods and the form of Government which the people would wish to obtain in the country for the future. For instance, the Constituent Assembly would be the right body to decide whether the monarchial or the republican principle should prevail. It is clear that the formation of the kind of Government to which I have alluded is not to be an easy task, and it is clear, I think, that the principal Allies and the United Nations should be prepared to give help and advice, and, indeed, if necessary, to take the initiative. I, myself, doubt whether this problem is a subject which can be discussed at the San Francisco Conference proper. I do not think that it would fall within the purview of such a Conference. These problems do require an exchange of views between the principal Powers; the negotiations are likely to be extremely delicate and their success might, indeed, be impaired by any undue or premature publicity. I think, however, that San Francisco may quite well afford a good meeting place for the intimate exchange of views which I have indicated.

I feel very strongly that we must be prepared to be patient on these questions. Some three months ago I was talking to a French friend on whose political judgment I place very great reliance, and I asked him what was the general trend of political opinion in France. He said that the people as a whole were not greatly concerned with politics; their minds were concentrated on a sufficiency of food for themselves and their families, on heating, on clothing, on health, and on other material necessities of life. It was indeed, in his view, doubtful whether men and women who had undergone so many years of suffering and misery were yet sufficiently recovered to resume normal political activities. Naturally there are exceptions to that, but that expression of opinion seemed to me at the time to be very sound. There is also another factor—namely, the return of the numerous prisoners of war and of the large numbers of workers who were deported. It will be necessary to await their return before anything in the nature of a true expression of popular opinion can be taken.

If that is true as regards such a highly-developed political entity as France, it is surely even more applicable to the countries of Eastern and Southern Europe, to which the noble Earl alludes. Assuming that the national territory has been liberated, or that a sufficient amount of national territory has been liberated, from enemy occupation—though even in those cases there may be very complex questions as to the need for safeguarding Army communications—I think, to sum up, that the right procedure to follow would seem to be first of all the establishment of a Government representing the general national trend of opinion. The chief duty of that Government would be to keep order and to provide as far as may be food and work for the people and to prepare, as I have said, for a possible Constituent Assembly. I think that such a Government ought to have the approval and support, both material and moral, of the Allied Nations.

The election of a Constituent Assembly would be the second step, and here I think it would be well, if it were practicable, that some measure of inter-Allied supervision should obtain. The noble Earl was rather scornful about the possibility of international supervision, and spoke somewhat slightingly, I thought of the plebiscites which have taken place. I would remind him of one which took place in the Saar which was a great success, and which did not require an enormous amount of preparation or very many troops to enforce it. There was a certain number of observers, but it was not by any means an army of occupation. At any rate, if that does not prove feasible, and if there cannot be Allied observers, it is essential that the Press should have full liberty of access and full liberty to report. That would be most helpful. The last stage of all would be a General Election for a Parliamentary system or such other system as may be determined by the Constituent Assembly. I obviously exclude Fascism or Nazism, for those are utterly outside our purview and outside the Atlantic Charter. I am therefore convinced that it would be a cardinal error to try to proceed too quickly on these really vital matters. To do so would in my view merely weaken the cause of democratic government, which we believe to be best fitted for the future peace of Europe and of the world.

* * *

THE MINISTER OF ECONOMIC WARFARE (THE EARL OF SELBORNE): . . . The Foreign Secretary, speaking in another place on December 20 said:

> "If our help is needed it will be available, and if our Allies will come and help, that help will be valuable. We ask nothing of the Greeks. It is our wish to bring our troops away as soon as is practically possible."

The attitude of His Majesty's Government in that respect is

unchanged, and provided that the Government and people of any liberated country clearly ask for it, we should be willing to help that country on the path to freedom and Parliamentary government.

I should like to make clear, beyond the possibility of misunderstanding, what we mean by those terms. I do not think I can do better than quote from the Prime Minister's farewell letter to Italy after his recent visit. He wrote:

> "The question arises 'What is freedom?' There are one or two quite simple practical tests by which it can be known in the modern world in peace conditions—Is there a right to free expression of opinion and of opposition and criticisms of the Government of the day; have the people the right to turn out a Government of which they disapprove, and are constitutional means provided by which they can make their will apparent? Are there Courts of Justice free from interference by the Executive, free from all threats of mob violence and all association with any particular political Party? Will these Courts administer old and well-established laws which are associated in the human mind with the broad principles of decency and justice? Will there be fair play for the poor as well as the rich, the private person as well as the Government official? Will the right of the individual, subject to his duties to the State, be maintained and asserted and exalted? Is the ordinary peasant or workman earning decent living by his daily toil and striving to bring up his family free from the fear that some great police organization under control of a single Party, like the Gestapo started by the Nazi and Fascist Party, will tap him on the shoulder and take him off without fair or open trial to bondage or ill treatment? These are some of the title deeds on which a new Italy could be founded."

Or as the Foreign Secretary more pithily put it:

> "Government by ballot instead of by bullet."

As I have said, the state of Europe immediately after the conclusion of hostilities will be such that we cannot hope to arrive at this condition equally quickly in all countries. The road will not be an easy one nor a quick one to traverse, and we must beware of drawing analogies from our own country with countries whose history and whose temperament are very different. In Britain our Parliamentary institutions are built on a thousand years of constitutional evolution and are in conformity with the will and genius of the British people. It is therefore no use ignoring the immense difficulties that lie before us, but the goal of freedom of the subject and Parliamentary government, as I have defined it, is our aim and we must pursue it with resolution and patience.

45. POLISH PRISONERS OF WAR*

Debate on May 1, 1945.

COMMANDER BOWER (C.) asked the Prime Minister if he is aware that owing to the delay in forming a democratic Government in Poland, many thousands of liberated Polish prisoners, both civil and military, cannot return to Poland without fear of reprisal; and whether he will take steps, in conjunction with the U.S.A. authorities in Germany, to ensure that no liberated Polish prisoners are repatriated against their will.

THE PRIME MINISTER (MR. CHURCHILL): The large numbers of Polish prisoners liberated by the advance of the Allied Armies are being given shelter and maintenance under the authority of the Supreme Commander-in-Chief at various centers set up for their reception. They will continue to be cared for in this way so long as conditions make it impracticable or undesirable for them to be repatriated or otherwise provided for. The matter is one for inter-Allied discussion, but I cannot conceive that Poles in danger of reprisals would be sent back to Poland against their will. I trust however that the conditions which will be created in Poland as the result of the inevitable further discussion on this subject between the Great Allies will be such that the numbers failing to return to their native land may be very few.

---

* House of Commons. Vol. 410. May 1, 1945. p. 1224; May 8. 1945, p. 1836; May 17, 1945, p. 2621–2622; Vol. 411, May 29, 1945, p. 56–57; June 5, 1945, p. 705–706; June 14, 1945, p. 1816–1817; House of Lords, Vol. 136, June 14, 1945, p. 639.

MR. GALLACHER (Com.): Would it not be desirable that all those who have influence in this country should use it towards the end of getting conditions in Poland and a Government in Poland which would allow most of these people to return?

THE PRIME MINISTER: It is a question of interpretation.

* * *

Debate on May 8, 1945.

MAJOR LORD WILLOUGHBY DE ERESBY (C.) asked the Secretary of State for War why prisoners of war from the Polish Army who fought in Poland in 1939 and from the Polish Underground Movement, who fought in Warsaw were recognized as combatants by the British and Allied Governments, receive different treatment from British and other Allied prisoners of war.

THE SECRETARY OF STATE FOR WAR (SIR J. GRIGG): I should be grateful if my Noble and gallant Friend would give me particulars of what he has in mind. Meanwhile I would refer him to the reply given by the Prime Minister to my hon. and gallant Friend the Member for Cleveland (Commander Bower) on May 1st.

* * *

Debate on May 17, 1945.

MRS. CAZALET KEIR (C.) asked the Prime Minister whether, before taking the decision to employ German prisoners of war in helping with our rebuilding program, any invitation had been conveyed by the Government to liberated Polish citizens, who are, at present, unable to return to their own country, to volunteer to come here and do similar work.

THE SECRETARY OF STATE FOR FOREIGN AFFAIRS (MR. EDEN): I have been asked to reply. The answer is "No, Sir."

MRS. KEIR: Does not my right hon. Friend think that by allowing a certain number of these liberated Poles to come over and work here, it will be both doing ourselves a good service and helping some of our brave Allies?

MR. EDEN: This is a separate issue from that of the employment of prisoners of war. Certain arrangements are being made to find useful opportunities of service for our Polish Allies, but it is important not to confuse them with the issue of the employment of prisoners of war.

* * *

Debate on May 29, 1945.

MISS WARD (C.) asked the Secretary of State for War whether he is aware that among the women soldiers of the Polish Home Army at present in prisoner-of-war camps in Holland and Western Germany are nurses, teachers, lawyers, engineers, doctors, etc., whose services would be of the greatest value to the Allies; and when these women can be brought to this country for recuperation.

THE ATTORNEY GENERAL (SIR D. SOMERVELL): I have been asked to reply. My right hon. Friend the Prime Minister has already informed the House on May 1 that Polish prisoners liberated by the advance of the Allied Armies are being given shelter and maintenance under the authority of the Supreme Commander-in-Chief at various centers set up for their reception and that for the present they will continue to be cared for in this way.

MR. G. WHITE (L.) asked the Secretary of State for War whether members of the Polish Forces, prisoners from 1939 onwards, who have been liberated from various camps in Germany are being classed as displaced persons or as prisoners of war.

THE SECRETARY OF STATE FOR WAR (SIR J. GRIGG): All Poles held as prisoners of war by the Germans and who have been uncovered in prisoner-of-war camps by the Allied Expeditionary Forces are dealt with as recovered United Nations prisoners of war; those found outside such camps are initially dealt with as United Nations displaced persons until identified as prisoners of war.

* * *

Debate on June 5, 1945.

SIR R. GLYN (C.) asked the Secretary of State for Foreign Affairs how many Poles are now being cared for by British and Allied Forces in Germany and other occupied areas: whether these persons are to be returned to Poland even against their wishes; if not, what immediate action it is proposed to take to relieve the strain now falling on the relief organization; and whether the Soviet Government has now given leave for British representatives to visit Poland and ascertain the position of the relatives of those Poles now in our hands.

LORD DUNGLASS (C.): I am informed that the number of Poles accounted for in assembly centers and camps in Supreme Headquarters Allied Expeditionary Force's zone up to May 27 was at least 700,000. The Prime Minister has already made it clear to the House that the Poles are at present being sheltered and maintained by S.H.A.E.F. and that they will continue to be cared for in this way for as long as conditions make it impracticable or undesirable for them to be repatriated or otherwise provided for. As regards the last part of the Question, it has not yet proved possible to arrange for British official representatives to enter Poland, since His Majesty's Government do not recognize the Polish Provisional Government now functioning there.

* * *

Debate on June 14, 1945.

MISS WARD asked the Secretary of State for the Home Department whether he is aware that there is an outbreak of suicide among Polish women members of the Polish Home

Army, due to continued retention under prisoner-of-war conditions; and will he, in view of the Polish organization available in Scotland, reconsider the proposal to allow them to come to this country to recuperate under free conditions.

SIR D. SOMERVELL: I regret that I cannot add anything to the reply which I gave to a similar Question by my hon. Friend on May 29.

* * *

House of Lords. Debate on June 14, 1945.

THE EARL OF MANSFIELD asked His Majesty's Government whether they are aware that there are 1,700 Polish women and girls held in prisoner-of-war camps within the British Zone in Germany, as well as 600 within the United States Army Zone; and that conditions in these camps are by no means satisfactory; and whether they will state if steps are to be taken at an early date to bring these women to this country, where many have husbands or fathers in the Polish Army, and where use could be made of them in the Polish Women's Services.

THE PARLIAMENTARY UNDER-SECRETARY OF STATE FOR THE HOME DEPARTMENT (THE EARL OF MUNSTER): Polish prisoners liberated by the Allied Forces are being given shelter and maintenance under the authority of the Supreme Commander-in-Chief at various centers set up for their reception, and for the present they will continue to be cared for in this way.

46. TRIBUTE TO THE POLISH ARMY IN ITALY*

THE PRIME MINISTER (MR. CHURCHILL): If we look over the whole list of those men who have fought, we find, taking first our own contribution, which was the largest, the British, and a British Indian division of the highest quality. In addition to the British divisions, we had the Poles, who

* House of Commons. Vol. 410, May 2, 1945, p. 1509.

have always fought with the greatest loyalty, the New Zealanders, who have marched all the way from the beginning right up to the very spearpoint of the advance, the South African armored division, which was very forward in the fray, the great Forces of the United States, second in numbers only to our own . . .

47. GERMAN SURRENDER*

THE INSTRUMENT OF UNCONDITIONAL *surrender of Germany was signed at Reims by Gen. Bedell Smith and Gen. Jodl on May 7, 1945. Hostilities ceased at midnight on May 8; ratification took place in Berlin on May 9.*

In answer to a congratulatory telegram on the occasion of the German surrender, King George VI sent Polish President Raczkiewicz this telegram on May 8:[1]

> "It is with deep emotion, Mr. President, that I send you this message of greeting on the day of final triumph over Germany.
>
> It will ever be to Poland's honor that she resisted, alone, the overwhelming forces of the German aggressor. For over five tragic years the British and Polish nations have fought together against our brutal foe, years of terrible suffering for the people of Poland borne with a courage and endurance which has won my heartfelt admiration and sympathy. The gallant Polish soldiers, sailors and airmen have fought beside my forces in many parts of the world and everywhere have won their high regard. In particular, we in this country remember with gratitude the part played by Polish airmen in the Battle of Britain, which all the world recognizes as a decisive moment in the war.
>
> It is my earnest hope that Poland may, in the tasks of peace and international cooperation which now confront the Allied Nations, achieve the reward of all her courage and sacrifice."

In his broadcast to the British people on May 13 Prime Minister Churchill recounted the five years of struggle for

---

* House of Commons. Vol. 410, May 8, 1945, p. 1868.
1 Stosunki polsko-sowieckie, 1943–46, p. 545.

victory, but emphasized also that the real aims of the war were yet to be attained:[2]

> "On the continent of Europe we have yet to make sure that the simple and honorable purposes for which we entered the war are not brushed aside or overlooked in the months following our success, and that the words freedom, democracy, and liberation are not distorted from their true meaning as we have understood them. There would be little use in punishing the Hitlerites for their crimes if law and justice did not rule, and if totalitarian or police governments were to take the place of the German invaders. We seek nothing for ourselves, but we must make sure that those causes which we fought for find recognition at the peace table in facts as well as words, and above all we must labor that the world organization which the United Nations are creating at San Francisco does not become an idle name; does not become a shield for the strong and a mockery for the weak."

THE PRIME MINISTER (MR. CHURCHILL): . . . The German war, Mr. Speaker, is therefore at an end. After years of intense preparation Germany hurled herself on Poland at the beginning of September, 1939, and in pursuance of our guarantee to Poland, and in common action with the French Republic, Great Britain and the British Empire and Commonwealth of Nations declared war against this foul aggression. After gallant France had been struck down we from this Island and from our united Empire maintained the struggle single handed for a whole year until we were joined by the military might of Soviet Russia and later by the overwhelming power and resources of the United States of America. Finally almost the whole world was combined against the evil-doers, who are now prostrate before us. Sir, our gratitude to our splendid Allies goes forth from all our hearts. We may allow ourselves a brief period of rejoicing, but let us not forget for a moment the toils and efforts that lie ahead. Japan, with all her treachery and greed, remains unsubdued. The injuries she has inflicted upon Great Britain, the United States and other countries and her detestable cruelties call forth justice and retribution. We must now devote all our

---

[2] Stronski, S. What Poles want. p. 3.

strength and resources to the completion of our tasks both at home and abroad. Advance Britannia! Long Live the Cause of Freedom! God Save the King!

48. POLISH ARMY IN ITALY—ANTI-SOVIET PROPAGANDA*

MR. PRITT (Lab.) asked the Secretary of State for War whether he is aware that Polish officers in Italy are distributing broadcast to officers and men of the British Forces anti-Soviet and to some extent anti-British propaganda in the English language printed in this country, in Italy, and in Palestine; and whether he will take steps to put a stop to this activity and to provide facilities for the dissemination of true information as to the British policy of preserving the friendship of the United Nations.

THE SECRETARY OF STATE FOR WAR (SIR J. GRIGG): I am finding out the facts about this. I will then consider whether any action is necessary.

49. TEHERAN AND YALTA DECISIONS**

Debate on June 5, 1945.

MR. STOKES (Lab.) asked the Prime Minister whether he will publish as a White Paper the full decisions arrived at both at Teheran and Yalta with regard to the readjustment of territory in Europe, the treatment of enemy peoples, the reparations to be made by enemy countries and the zones of influence allocated to each of the Great Powers, as also any decisions with regard to the use of slave labor for reparations purposes.

* House of Commons. Vol. 411, May 29, 1945, p. 17.

** House of Commons. Vol. 411, June 5, 1945, p. 687; June 7, 1945, p. 1064–1065.

THE PRIME MINISTER (MR. CHURCHILL): No, Sir.

MR. STOKES: Does the Prime Minister recollect the categorical statement made in this House by the Foreign Secretary that no secret engagements of any kind have been entered into; and if that is so, will he tell the House what is the objection to publishing the information now?

THE PRIME MINISTER: I do not think it would be a good thing.

MR. KIRKWOOD (Lab.): The right hon. Gentleman is not giving very much away.

Debate on June 7, 1945.

MR. STOKES asked the Prime Minister what agreements were arrived at at Teheran or Yalta with regard to relations with other European Powers not so far disclosed to the British public.

THE PRIME MINISTER (MR. CHURCHILL): I have nothing to add to the official statements which have already been made on the results of these Conferences.

MR. STOKES: Will the Prime Minister repeat the assurance given by the Foreign Secretary that no secret engagements of any kind whatever were entered into either at Yalta or Teheran?

THE PRIME MINISTER: I cannot give a guarantee that the newspaper reporters were there all the time.

MR. PRICE (Lab.): If it is a fact that there are no undisclosed conditions to the Yalta decisions, why is it that the Russian Government have acted in the matter of the broadening of the Polish Government in a way totally in conflict with the declared decisions of the Yalta Conference?

THE PRIME MINISTER: Certainly there were no secret engagements entered into there at all, except that we kept secret the addition of two members to Russia, Byelo-Russia and the Ukraine. Those were kept secret at the desire of the United States so that the President could get home and make the necessary arrangements on the spot. Otherwise, there were no secret engagements, but the conversations, of course, proceeded in a very intimate manner, and I am not prepared to say that everything discussed at Yalta could be made the subject of a verbatim report.

MR. STOKES: With great respect to the Prime Minister, his answer was quite irrelevant. I was not talking about newspapers. Will he repeat the assurance given to the House by the Foreign Secretary that no secret engagements were entered into at either of those conferences?

THE PRIME MINISTER: Yes, Sir, I have, but I do not accept the view that it is absolutely necessary that there should never be on any occasion a secret clause in some arrangement, provided that is reported to a wide Cabinet. It may very often be necessary to do so. It would hamper very much the whole proceedings if no understandings could be made which had not to be immediately published. I should not approve of that myself, although I know that a lot of claptrap is talked about it.

50. DISTURBANCES AT POLISH CAMP IN SCOTLAND*

THE POLISH CAMP AT *Findo-Gask, Pertshire, in May 1945 was the scene of disturbances created by soldiers who wanted to be discharged (about 20 soldiers). Military authorities soon restored order. This situation was used for propaganda purposes by local representatives of the Warsaw Government, as well as by the League for the Defense of Personal Rights at Glasgow. They spread false reports that two soldiers had hung themselves at the camp and that one had been shot to death by a Polish guard.*

This was utterly false—it was proved that there had

* House of Commons. Vol. 411, June 5, 1945, p. 708–709.

been only one case of suicide—that of a private who had become very neurotic over worry about the fate of his family in Poland.[1]

Incorrect accounts of happenings at the camp had been forwarded from Glasgow to several Members of Parliament.

MR. DRIBERG (Ind.) asked the Secretary of State for War if he can now make a statement about recent events at a Polish camp at Findo-Gask, near Perth, where there have been disturbances resulting in deaths by hanging or shooting, and where Polish soldiers who have served in fighting units of the German Army and as guards in Nazi concentration camps are terrorizing other Polish soldiers for refusing to participate in military training avowedly designed to fit them for war against the Soviet Union.

THE SECRETARY OF STATE FOR WAR (SIR J. GRIGG): I am informed that some Poles at this Polish camp wished to be discharged from their forces on medical grounds and made trouble when they were not. But I understand that there have been no cases of shooting or hanging. Polish ex-prisoners who have served as guards in Nazi concentration camps are rejected as unsuitable for the Polish Army.

51. GENERAL BOR-KOMOROWSKI*

MAJOR-GENERAL SIR ALFRED KNOX (C.) asked the Secretary of State for Foreign Affairs if his attention has been drawn to an article in the "Soviet News" of May 25, issued by the Russian Embassy, which characterizes General Bor, the defender of Warsaw, in most insulting terms; and whether he will protest against the circulation in Britain of attacks of this nature on a representative of another Ally.

THE PARLIAMENTARY UNDER-SECRETARY TO THE FOREIGN OFFICE (MR. LAW): I have seen the article to which my hon.

---

[1] Sikorski Historical Institute, London, Archives.
* House of Commons. Vol. 411, June 6, 1945, p. 860–861.

and gallant Friend refers, and I share his regret that statements of the sort contained in it about one of our Allies should appear in an official publication of another.

SIR A. KNOX: Will the right hon. Gentleman do anything to stop attacks of this kind? Does he realize that this article called the heroic General Bor "an agent provocateur" and "a dirty adventurer?" Is it seemly that the Press department of an Embassy in London should publish this sort of thing?

MR. LAW: I think that the view of His Majesty's Government on this matter is already known. If it was not known before, it should be known now, from the terms of the reply I have just given.

MR. GALLACHER (Com.): Is the right hon. Gentleman not aware that, for years, so-called official publications in London from the Polish Government have been uttering the most atrocious slanders about the leaders of the great Ally, the Soviet Union, and we have had no protests from the Foreign Office? Will he protest about those slanders now?

MR. LAW: I have heard protests in this House on the point the hon. Member has made.

MR. A. BEVAN (Lab.): Is it going to be the policy of the Government to interfere with the expression of opinion by another Power? Is it not a fact that, on several occasions, protests have been heard from this side of the House about the anti-Soviet propaganda of the Polish Government in London?

MR. GALLACHER: Why does not the right hon. Gentleman deplore that?

MR. LAW: I do not think it is a question so much of policy as of what is seemly, and, as I say, we do regret that statements of this kind about any Ally should appear in the publications of another Ally.

52. RELIEF FOR POLAND*

MR. STOURTON (C.) asked the Secretary of State for Foreign Affairs if he will take up with the Soviet Government the question of admitting representatives of the International Red Cross into Poland by the Government responsible, in order that medical aid and supplies for countering an outbreak of bubonic plague, typhus and typhoid, may be brought to Warsaw.

THE PARLIAMENTARY UNDER-SECRETARY TO THE FOREIGN OFFICE (MR. LAW): His Majesty's Government are always ready to consider any suggestion as to how they might be of service in such matters. But they have not in the present case received any request from the International Red Cross Committee for assistance of the nature indicated by my hon. Friend.

MR. STOURTON: Will my right hon. Friend bear in mind that there is an almost complete dearth of medical supplies in Warsaw and throughout Poland?

MR. LAW: I will certainly bear in mind the point that my hon. Friend makes, but he must remember that we have at present no first hand opportunities of informing ourselves of conditions in Poland at all.

MR. SHINWELL (Lab.): In view of the absence of accurate information on the subject, could the right hon. Gentleman do anything to suppress these Tory attacks on Soviet Russia?

MR. LAW: I cannot see that there is any attack on Soviet Russia.

---

* House of Commons. Vol. 411, June 13, 1945, p. 1624–1625.

53. NEW PROVISIONAL GOVERNMENT IN WARSAW. WITHDRAWAL OF RECOGNITION FROM POLISH GOVERNMENT IN LONDON.

THIS CONCLUDES THE DEBATES *on Poland in the British Parliament during World War II.*

This also marks the end of the war-time (and 37th) Parliament which lasted 10 years (from 1935). It was dissolved on June 15, 1945, and new elections brought into being on July 26 a new (38th) Parliament with the Labor Party in power rather than the Conservative Party.

Thus ended Prime Minister Churchill's war-time leadership in British politics and on July 26 he handed in his resignation to the King.

World War II ended in Europe on May 7 and in the Far East on Aug. 14.

This point marks the end of one era in Polish politics and the beginning of another era. The meeting of ambassadors in Moscow with Warsaw agents resulted in the creation of a new Polish Provisional Government of National Unity in Warsaw, recognized by the Soviet Union, Great Britain, and the U.S. on July 5, 1945. The same day the western allies withdrew recognition from the Polish Government in London.

This study of Poland in the British Parliament comes to an end with the cessation of hostilities in Europe. There remain to be appended, however, several documents of importance before closing the pages of this era of Polish history.

On June 24 representatives of the Polish Provisional Government met with democratic leaders from Poland and abroad and "came to an understanding on the method of reorganizing the Polish Provisional Government" resolving to include in the new Government several persons from Poland and from abroad.[1]

---

[1] Stosunki polsko-sowieckie, 1943–46, p. 574.

The Polish Government in London issued a declaration on June 25 in which it explained Poland's role as a faithful ally in the war against the Germans and then continued:[2]

"The Polish Government as the sole authorized and independent Government legally appointed by the President of the Republic, and universally recognized declares that the so-called "Polish Provisional Government of National Unity" is illegal, and cannot be volutarily recognized by the Polish Nation. It has been created on the basis of an unprecedented procedure while the whole of Polish territory is occupied by the Soviet army and at a time when the Poles are deprived of the elementary rights of man and citizen.

The Polish Government declares that it will hand over its authority solely to a government which has been formed on free Polish soil, consonant with the laws in force in Poland, and one which reflects the freely expressed will of the people."

At the same time the Polish Government in London sent an appeal to the Polish nation on June 26 in which were explained its activities during the war, and stating:[3]

". . . The present Polish Government has been often called in sarcasm—government of stubborn resistance. This appellation is accepted by it with pride. Indeed it is a government of resistance, of resistance against all attempts to destroy the independence of Poland.

The Polish Government could not agree to annexation of half of the territory of the Polish Nation including the towns so dear to the whole Polish Nation, such as Lwów and Wilno.

The Polish Government could not agree to the imposition on Poland of a social regime alien to her fundamental concepts of freedom, lawful order and moral traditions.

The Polish Government could not agree to grant any rights to the self-appointed committee composed of members of a numerically weak communist party and subordinated to foreign power.

The Polish Government could not agree to the destruction of legal order on which the existence of the Polish State was based.

The Polish Government could not agree to severing of thousand years old links between Poland and the world of western culture and civilization.

---

2 Stosunki polsko-sowieckie, 1943–46, p. 577.
3 Ibid, p. 578.

These decisions were taken by the Polish Government fully conscious of the responsibility it bore. It could not have acted differently if it had known at the time when it took these decisions the present course of events. The Polish Government was not appointed by the President of the Polish Republic to take hand in the liquidation of the independence of Poland.

Poland was first to fight with the arms in hand the German bid for world domination. She always desired friendly coexistence with Russia and rejected all German suggestions of a joint attack upon the Soviet Union. She fought at a time when other powers were still practicing with Hitler. She never had any misgivings in her faithfulness to her Allies and in the crucial days of 1940 she stood by the side of Great Britain in her lonely fight. In the great air Battle of Britain which decided the issue of the war Polish airmen contributed their bit to the Allied Victory. The Poles have not abused the friendly hospitality and friendship which was shown to them by the people of Britain. During the long and arduous years of war the Polish Nation endured, fought and believed.

Today, over the charred remains of the Polish Republic an entirely new body is to be constituted, without the frontiers which are due to Poland, without legal and constitutional continuity, deprived of the traditions in which Poland lived and thrived for a thousand years.

The lawful authorities of the Polish Republic cannot recognize such an imposed solution. The President and the Government of the Polish Republic are mandatories of the national will up to the moment when free and honest elections are held in Poland. It seems that the leading statesmen of the west are basing their hopes on the Yalta promise of the holding in Poland of "free and unfettered elections". It is clear, however, that no such elections are possible as long as there is no freedom of political life, of the press, of meeting and association and as long as the iron screen separating Poland from the world is not lifted.

Even when the recognition will be withdrawn from it, the Polish Government will not cease to be the lawful Government of Poland. It is the lawful Government not because it is recognized by other Powers, but because it expressess the will of the Polish people and because it has been constituted in accordance with the laws of the Polish Republic . . .

We are fully aware that our words are reaching men and women who have suffered heavily and are greatly exhausted. The future fate of the Poles will not be alike everywhere. While most will suffer in Poland the cruel realities of a police regime, others will remain in the free world to be spokesmen of those who must remain mute.

Our future path is a hard one, but at journey's end we shall see the Poland for which we are all striving from the bottom of our hearts: a Poland free and independent, a Poland of liberty and justice, a Poland in which love of God and man shall prevail."

On June 28 a radio communique from Warsaw announced the members of the Polish Provisional Government of National Unity, named to office by Bolesław Bierut, President of the National Council in Poland. E. Osóbka-Morawski was to continue as premier; first vice-premier was W. Gomołka, second vice-premier and minister of agriculture was Stanisław Mikołajczyk, minister of national defense was Gen. Rola Żymierski, and minister of foreign affairs was W. Rzymowski.

Of the 21 ministers named 16 were former members of the Lublin Committee and 5 were newcomers.

Successive events came quick and fast. A flood of protests from Poland, the Polish Government in London, the Polish Army, and Polish organizations from all over the world, including the Polish American Congress and the National Committee of Americans of Polish Descent, failed to deter the course of inevitable official moves by Great Britain and the U.S. On July 5 the governments of both these countries announced the recognition of the Polish Provisional Government of National Unity in Warsaw. Here is Great Britain's statement:[4]

"His Majesty's Government in the United Kingdom have received from the Prime Minister of recently formed Polish Provisional Government of National Unity in Warsaw a formal notification to the effect that the Government was established on June 28, and that it has recognized in their entirety the decisions of the Crimea Conference on the Polish question. The message requested the establishment of diplomatic relations with His Majesty's Government and the exchange of representatives with the rank of ambassador.

His Majesty's Government welcome the establishment of the Polish Provisional Government of National Unity as an important

[4] Ibid, p. 585.

step towards the fulfilment of the decisions regarding Poland embodied in the declaration on Poland issued by the Crimea conference. In full agreement with the United States Government they have conveyed to M. Osóbka-Morawski their recognition of the Polish Provisional Government of National Unity and have informed him of their readiness to establish diplomatic relations with it. In doing so they have recalled that the Crimea decisions on Provisional Government of National Unity shall be pledged to the holding of free and unfettered elections as soon as possible on the basis of universal suffrage and secret ballot, in which all democratic and anti-Nazi parties shall have the right to take part and put forward candidates.

The appointment of a British Ambassador to Warsaw will, it is expected, be announced shortly. Pending his appointment, it is proposed to send to Warsaw as soon as possible the Hon. Robert A. Hankey as Chargé d'Affaires ad interim."

On the same day Pres. Truman announced in Washington:[5]

"It is with great satisfaction that I announce that effective today as of 7:00 P.M. Eastern War Time the Government of the U. S. has established diplomatic relations with the newly-formed Polish Provisional Government of National Unity now established in Warsaw. The establishment of this Government is an important and positive step in fulfilling the decisions regarding Poland reached at Yalta and signed on Feb. 11, 1945.

The new Polish Provisional Government of National Unity has informed me in a written communication that it has recognized in their entirety the decisions of the Crimea Conference on the Polish question. The new government has thereby confirmed its intention to carry out the provisions of the Crimea decision with respect to the holding of elections.

Mr. Arthur Bliss Lane, whom I have chosen as U. S. Ambassador to Poland, will proceed to Warsaw as soon as possible, accompanied by his staff."

At the same time diplomatic relations were discontinued with the Polish Government in London.

To supervise the orderly liquidation of the machinery in Great Britain of the London Polish Government, a committee entitled the Interim Treasury Committee for Polish Questions was formed by the British Government.

---

5 Ciechanowski, J. Op. Cit., p. 387.

Immediately upon receipt of these announcements Polish Ambassador in London, Edward Raczyński, and Polish Ambassador in Washington, Jan Ciechanowski, delivered practically identical notes, in the name of the Polish Government in London, to the respective governments to which they had been accredited.

Here is Ambassador's Ciechanowski's note of July 5, 1945:[6]

"The Ambassador of Poland presents his compliments to the Secretary of State and has the honor to acknowledge receipt of the note of the Secretary of State of July 5, 1945, quoting the text of a public statement which the President is to make at 7.00 P.M. Eastern War Time, today, and the text of the communication which the American Chargé d'Affaires ad interim near the Polish Government in London has been instructed to deliver to the Polish Foreign Minister.

In reply to this note informing him that the Government of the United States has recognized effective at 7.00 P.M. Eastern War Time, July 5, the new Polish Provisional Government of National Unity, as the Government of the Republic of Poland, and that it has withdrawn the Mission of the American Embassy near the Polish Government in Exile in London as of that time, the Ambassador, acting on instructions of his Government has the honor to state the following:

1) I was appointed to my present functions as Ambassador of Poland to the United States by the legitimate Polish Government which has not recalled me nor instructed me to relegate my functions to any other person. The Polish Government has not ceased to exist for the Polish Nation whose sole constitutional and independent representative it continues to remain. Being an official of the Republic of Poland I am pledged to remain loyal and obedient to that Government and without instructions from it I have no right to relegate my functions and powers to anyone appointed by the so-called Polish Government headed by Messrs. Bierut and Osóbka-Morawski.

2) The authority of the Polish Government to which I owe my allegiance is based on the Constitution of Apr. 23, 1935, which the Polish Nation has not changed and which it is not in a position to change freely and according to its own will in the conditions of pressure and under which it finds itself today.

---

[6] Ibid, p. 389.

On the basis of the aforesaid Constitution the Polish authorities have maintained diplomatic relations with the Government of the United States and on the same basis they concluded agreements with that Government. When Poland entered into the present war against Germany, the Constitution of 1935 was in force. It is also in accordance with this Constitution that the President of Poland, before leaving his country in September, 1939, relegated his powers to the present President of Poland, by appointing him as his successor. The powers of the latter have until now not been questioned by any Power with the exception of the Soviet Union.

Throughout the war the Polish Nation made enormous sacrifices for the cause of Freedom. The Resistance Movement in the Homeland as well as the Polish Armed Forces on all fronts—on land, on sea, and in the air—fought the enemy unceasingly. The occupied Homeland and the leaders of the Resistance in Poland never ceased to recognize the authority of the Polish President and of the Government appointed by him.

Consecutive Polish Governments formed on the basis of this Constitution concluded the principal agreements concerning Poland with other States. Among these, which include in their number also all the bilateral undertakings entered into during the war and concerning military, naval, aviation, financial, economic, and shipping matters, I wish in particular to mention:

a) The Agreement between Poland and the United Kingdom signed at London on Aug. 25, 1939, concerning Mutual Assistance.

b) The Polish-French Protocol, signed at Paris on Sept. 4, 1939, concerning the execution of the Polish-French Alliance.

c) The Agreement between Poland and the USSR, signed at London on July 30, 1941.

d) The Agreement concluded at Washington between the Polish Government and the Government of the United States on July 1, 1942, concerning Lease and Lend, known as 'Mutual Aid Agreement'.

Furthermore, multilateral agreements to which the Polish Government is a party include:

1) Declaration of the United Nations, signed at Washington on Jan. 1, 1942, embodying the Atlantic Charter and known as the 'Declaration of the United Nations'.

2) Inter-Allied Declaration against acts of dispossesion committed in territories under enemy occupation or control, signed at London on Jan. 5, 1943.

3) The final Act of the United Nations Food and Agricultural Conference, signed at Hot Springs on June 3, 1943.

4) Agreement to set up a United Nations Relief and Rehabilitation Administration, signed at Washington on Nov. 9, 1943.

5) Final Act of the Monetary and Financial Conference of the United Nations, signed at Bretton Woods on July 22, 1944.

6) Agreement of Principles having Reference to the Continuance of Co-ordinate Control of Merchant Shipping, signed at London on Aug. 5, 1944.

7) International Sanitary Convention, signed at Washington on Jan. 5, 1945.

8) The International Agreement and the Final Act of the International Civil Aviation Conference, signed at Chicago on Dec. 7, 1944.

When all the said Agreements were being concluded not one State questioned the validity of the Constitution of 1935 or of the powers of the Polish President and of the Government of his appointment. Neither was any doubt ever raised by such States as to the right of the Polish President and Government to lead the Polish Nation in the struggle against the German aggressor and to exercise supreme command over the Polish Armed Forces fighting at the side of the Allied Nations.

3) Poland, still now remaining as it does under a foreign occupation and under the ruthless control of foreign military and police forces, is not in a position to change its Constitution by legal means and to choose freely a parliament and executive authority; nor is in position to carry out these changes, if it so desired, by revolutionary means. Any changes, therefore, which have occured in Poland are not the result of the will of the Polish people, expressed legally or by revolution. The war which started in Poland in defense of her independence ended in depriving her of that independence and in placing our country under the direct control of a neighboring Power.

In these circumstances neither my Government nor I, as its Representative, are in position to recognize such changes.

4) The first attribution of the independence of a State is its freedom to choose its Government. In the present circumstances, the source of the authority of the government headed by Messrs. Bierut and Osóbka-Morawski is a decision made not by the Polish Nation but by three foreign Powers, one of which controls de facto the whole administration of Poland through its army and police forces. The legal basis of the authority of that government cannot be regarded as better founded than that of the so-

called governments set up in occupied countries during the war by Germany. In both cases they are based on the will of a foreign Power.

The persecution which thousands of Poles are enduring in Poland today, and which affects in the first place those who have given active evidence of their desire for an independent State by opposing with arms the German invader, is a further proof that the government of Messrs. Bierut and Osóbka-Morawski in no way represents the will of the Nation but constitutes a puppet government imposed on Poland by force from without.

5) In hese circumstances, acting upon instructions from my constitutional Government, I protest most solemnly against the recognition of Messrs. Bierut and Osóbka-Morawski by the Government of the United States, for this amounts to recognition of the suppression of Poland's independence and of the foreign rule in Poland which is already being exercised there in actual fact. For the second time in history the Polish Nation is being deprived of its independence, though this time not as a result of events which took place in Eastern Europe alone, but as result of war which the United Nations waged in the name of law and justice. Notwithstanding the recognition of this state of things by other States, the Polish Nation will never give up its right to an independent State, and for this right it will struggle unwaveringly."

Between July 17 and Aug. 2 there was a meeting in Potsdam of the heads of the governments of the U.S., Great Britain, and the USSR: Pres. Truman, Prime Minister Churchill (after his dismissal, replaced by Prime Minister Attlee), and Marshal Stalin. They arrived at several important decisions during the course of this conference. The decision on Poland is as follows:[7]

The Conference considered questions relating to the Polish Provisional Government of National Unity and the western boundary of Poland.

On the Polish Provisional Government of National Unity they defined their attitude in the following statement:

A. We have taken note with pleasure of the agreement reached among representative Poles from Poland and abroad which has made possible the formation, in accordance with the decisions

---

[7] Soviet-Polish relations, a collection of official documents, 1944–1946, p. 35.

reached at the Crimea Conference, of a Polish Provisional Government of National Unity recognized by the Three Powers. The establishment by the British and United States Governments of diplomatic relations with the Polish Provisional Government has resulted in the withdrawal of their recognitions from the former Polish Government in London, which no longer exists.

The British and United States Governments have taken measures to protect the interest of the Polish Provisional Government of National Unity as the recognized Government of the Polish State in the property belonging to the Polish State located in their territories and under their control, whatever the form of this property may be.

They have further taken measures to prevent alienation to third parties of such property. All proper facilities will be given to the Polish Provisional Government of National Unity for the exercise of the ordinary legal remedies for the recovery of any property belonging to the Polish State which may have been wrongfully alienated.

The Three Powers are anxious to assist the Polish Provisional Government of National Unity in facilitating the return to Poland as soon as practicable of all Poles abroad who wish to return to Poland, including members of the Polish Armed Forces and the Merchant Marine. They expect that those Poles who return home shall be accorded personal and property rights on the same basis as all Polish citizens.

The Three Powers note that the Polish Provisional Government of National Unity in accordance with the decisions of the Crimea Conference, has agreed to the holding of free and unfettered elections as soon as possible on the basis of universal suffrage and secret ballot in which all democratic and anti-Nazi parties shall have the right to take part and to put forward candidates, and that representatives of the Allied Press shall enjoy full freedom to report to the world upon developments in Poland before and during the elections.

B. The following agreement was reached on the western frontier of Poland:

In conformity with the agreement on Poland reached at the Crimea Conference the three Heads of Government have sought the opinion of the Polish Provisional Government of National Unity in regard to the accession of territory in the north and west, which Poland should receive.

The President of the National Council of Poland and members of the Polish Provisional Government of National Unity have been received at the Conference and have fully presented their views. The three Heads of Government reaffirm their opinion that the final delimitation of the western frontier of Poland should await the peace conference.

The three Heads of Government agree that pending the final determination of Poland's western frontier, the former German territories east of a line running from the Baltic Sea immediately west of Swinemunde, and thence along the Oder River to the confluence of the Western Niesse River and along the western Niesse to the Czechoslovak frontier, including that portion of East Prussia not placed under the administration of the Union of Soviet Socialist Republics in accordance with the understanding reached at this conference and including the area of the former free city of Danzig, shall be under the administration of the Polish State and for such purposes should not be considered as part of the Soviet zone of occupation in Germany.

* * *

The Conference reached the following agreement on the removal of Germans from Poland, Czechoslovakia and Hungary.

The Three Governments, having considered the question in all its aspects, recognize that the transfer to Germany of German populations, or elements thereof, remaining in Poland, Czechoslovakia and Hungary, will have to be undertaken. They agree that any transfers that take place should be effected in an orderly and humane manner.

Since the influx of a large number of Germans into Germany would increase the burden already resting on the occupying authorities, they consider that the Allied Control Council in Germany should in the first instance examine the problem with special regard to the question of the equitable distribution of these Germans among the several zones of occupation.

They are accordingly instructing their respective representatives on the Control Council to report to their Governments as soon as possible the extent to which such persons have already entered Germany from Poland, Czechoslovakia and Hungary, and to submit an estimate of the time and rate at which further transfers could be carried out, having regard to the present situation in Germany.

The Czechoslovak Government, the Polish Provisional Government and the Allied Control Council in Hungary are at the same time being informed of the above, and are being requested meanwhile to suspend further expulsions of the German populations pending the examination by the Governments concerned of the report from their representatives of the Control Council.

The elections in Poland as ordered by the Yalta and Potsdam resolutions did not take place as Stalin had promised, one month after the creation of the Polish Provisional Government, but a full one and one half years later—on Jan. 19, 1947. These elections, according to observations by ambassadors accredited to Warsaw and foreign correspondents, violated all the principles of free and democratic elections, and were a distinct breach of the obligations of the Polish Provisional Government accepted at Potsdam. Only the Soviet Government declared these elections to be fair. Here is the U.S. position on the conduct of these elections:[8]

"On January 19, 1947 a general election was held in Poland, the results of which are expected to be announced shortly. The United States Government has followed closely the developments leading up to this event in accordance with the commitments it accepted at the Yalta and Potsdam Conferences. On numerous occasions it has expressed its concern over the course of events in Poland, which increasingly indicated that the election would not be conducted in such manner as to allow a free expression of the will of the Polish people. On August 19 and November 22, 1946, formal notes were addressed to the Polish Provisional Government on this subject. On January 5 this Government brought the situation in Poland to the attention of the British and Soviet Governments and expressed the hope that those Governments would associate themselves with the Government of the United States in an approach to the Polish Provisional Government of National Unity. This proposal was rejected by the Soviet Government. On January 9 this Government delivered a further note to the Polish Provisional Government which stated among other things that if the repressive activities on the part of the Provisional Government did not cease immediately there was little likelihood that elections could be held in accordance with the terms of the Potsdam agreement. The British Government has also protested to the Polish Provisional Government the violation of its election pledges.

The reports received from the United States Embassy in Poland in the period immediately prior to the elections as well as its subsequent reports based upon the observations of American officials who visited a number of Polish voting centers confirmed the fears which this Government had expressed that the

---

[8] U. S. Dept. of State Bulletin, vol. 16, no. 397, p. 251.

election would not be free. These reports were corraborated by the general tenor of the dispatches from foreign correspondents in Poland. It is clear that the Provisional Government did not confine itself to the suppression of the so-called "underground" but employed wide-spread measures of coercion and intimidation against democratic elements which were loyal to Poland although not partisans of the Government "bloc". In these circumstances the United States Government cannot consider that the provisions of the Yalta and Potsdam agreements have been fulfilled . . . The United States Government considers that the Polish Provisional Government has failed to carry out its solemn pledges."

On Feb. 4, 1947, when receiving the Letters of Credens from the new Polish Ambassador, Joseph Winiewicz, Pres. Truman, among other things, said:[9]

". . . The Government of the United States gave expression to this interest in the Polish people when it joined with the British and Soviet Governments in the important decisions concernng Poland that were taken at the Yalta and Potsdam Conferences. One of these decisions provided for the holding at a free election and the Polish Provisional Government of National Unity pledged itself to carry out this decision. It is a cause of deep concern to me and to the American people that the Polish Provisional Government has failed to fulfil that pledge . . ."

On Feb. 3, 1947, the problems concerning the elections in Poland were taken up in the British Parliament. When the government was questioned regarding this matter, Mr. Mayhew, the Under-Secretary of State for Foreign Affairs, said:[10]

"Our information regarding the conduct of the Polish elections, unfortunately, confirms reports from reliable British Press correspondents, which have already been published. The powers of the Polish Provisional Government were extensively used to reduce to a minimum the vote of those opposed to the Government bloc. Opposition lists of candidates in areas covering 22 per cent. of the electorate were completely suppressed. Candidates and voters' names were removed from the lists; candidates were arrested; Government officials, members of the Armed Forces and many others were made to vote openly, and other forms of intimidation and pressure were used. The count was conducted

[9] U. S. Department of State Bulletin, Vol. XVI, No. 398, p. 299.
[10] Hansard, Vol. 432, p. 1376.

in conditions entirely controlled by the Government bloc. His Majesty's Government cannot regard these elections as fulfilling the solemn contract which the Polish Provisional Government entered into with them and with the United States Government and Soviet Government that free and unfettered elections would be held. They cannot, therefore, regard the results as a true expression of the will of the Polish people.

On 9th of January, the United States Government addressed His Majesty's Government and the Soviet Government suggesting joint representations to the Polish Provisional Government, and on 11th January His Majesty's Ambassador in Moscow had a conversation with Monsieur Molotov in which he expressed the deep concern of His Majesty's Government. The Soviet Government replied both to His Majesty's Government and the United States Government that they did not agree that there was discrimination, that the arrests were necessary to prevent disorder and terrorism and that the Soviet Government did not consider there was any cause for intervention. My right hon. Friend did not agree with this view, but it was clearly useless to pursue the matter further in Moscow. My right hon. Friend, however informed the Polish Provisional Government once more of his very grave concern at the situation. Every possible effort was thus made, but without success, to secure the execution of the Yalta and Potsdam agreements. Naturally, our sympathy is with the Polish people who have thus been deprived of their democratic rights which we thought had been secured for them by allied agreement, which we honestly believed would be kept."

SELECT BIBLIOGRAPHY

Akademiia Nauk SSSR. Institut Slavianovedeniia. Istoria Polshi. Vol. 1–3. Moscow, 1958.

Alleged incorporation of the Polish eastern provinces in the Soviet Union; conditions and circumstances. London, 1943.

Anders, Władysław. An Army in exile; the story of the Second Polish Corps. London, 1949.

Anders, Władysław. Bez ostatniego rozdziału; wspomnienia z lat 1939–1946. London, 1949.

Annexation of eastern Poland by the USSR. London, 1941.

Apenszlak, Jakób. Armed resistance of the Jews in Poland. N. Y., 1944.

Apenszlak, Jakób. Black book of Polish Jewry, an account of the martyrdom of Polish Jewry under the Nazi occupation. N. Y., 1943.

Atholl, K. M. The tragedy of Warsaw and its documentation. London, 1945.

Barrell, L. L. Poland and Eastern European Union, 1939–1945. (IN: Polish Review, vol. 3, no. 1–2, 1958, p. 87–127).

Bartoszewski, Władysław, Prawda o Von dem Bachu. Poznań, 1961.

Bathe, Rolf. Der Feldzug der 18 Tage; Chronik des polnischen Dramas. Berlin, 1939.

Beck, Józef. Dernier rapport; politique polonaise, 1926–1939. Neuchâtel, 1951.

Beck, Józef. Final report. N. Y., 1957.

Bellona; kwartalnik wojskowo-historyczny. London, 1941– .

Benes, Edvard. Memoirs; from Munich to new war and new *victory.* London, 1954.

Berbecki, Leon. Pamiętniki. Katowice, 1959.

Biegański, Stanisław. Na drodze do Teheranu. (IN: Niepodległość, London, vol. 2, 1950, p. 90–153).

Bilmanis, Alfreds. Baltic essays. Washington, 1945.

Black book of Poland. N. Y., 1942.

Blumenthal, N., ed. Obozy; dokumenty i materiały. Łódz, 1946.

Bolshaia sovietskaia entsyklopedia. 2d ed. 1949–58.

Bonnet, G. E. Défense de la paix. Vol. 1: De Washington au quai d'Orsay. Geneva, 1946.

Boratyński, Stefan. Dyplomacja okresu II wojny światowej; konferencje międzynarodowe, 1941–1945. Warsaw, 1957.

Borkiewicz, Adam. Powstanie warszawskie, 1944; zarys działań natury wojskowej. Warsaw, 1957.

Boswell, A. S. The eastern boundaries of Poland. Birkenhead, 1943.

Bregman Aleksander. Dzieje pustego fotela; konferencja w San Francisco i sprawa polska. London, 1948.

Bregman, Aleksander. Faked elections in Poland as reported by foreign observers. London, 1947.

Bregman, Aleksander. Najlepszy sojusznik Hitlera. London, 1958.

Byrnes, James. Speaking frankly. N. Y., 1947.

Churchill, Winston. Onwards to victory; war speeches. Boston, 1944.

Churchill, Winston. The Second World War. 6 vols. Boston, 1948–53.

Ciano, Galeazzo. The Ciano diaries, 1939–43. Garden City, N. Y., 1946.

Ciechanowski, Jan. Defeat in victory. N. Y., 1947.

Comité pour l'assistance à la population juive frappée par la guerre. L'extermination des juifs en Pologne. Dépositions du témoins oculaires. 3. série. Les camps d'extermination. Geneva, 1944.

Comité pour l'assistance à la population juive frappée par la guerre. L'extermination des juifs polonais. IV. Le martyr du ghetto de Varsovie. Geneva, 1944.

Council of Polish Political Parties. Poland accuses, an indictment of the major German war criminals. London, 1946.

Czapski, Józef. The inhuman land. N. Y., 1952.

Czapski, Józef. Wspomnienia starobielskie. Italy, 1944.

Dallin, D. J. Soviet Russia's foreign policy, 1939–1942. 1943.

Degras, J. Soviet documents on foreign policy. Vol. 3: 1933–1941. London, 1953.

Documents on American foreign relations. Vol. 2–7. Boston, 1940–47.

Documents on international affairs. Vol. 1–2. London, 1939–46.

Epstein, Julius. The mysteries of the Van Vliet report, a case history. Chicago, 1951.

Estreicher, Karol. Straty kultury polskiej. 2 vols. Glasgow, 1945.

Facts and documents concerning Polish prisoners of war captured by the USSR during the 1939 campaign. London, 1946.

Feis, Herbert. Between war and peace; the Potsdam Conference. Princeton, N. J., 1960.

Feis, Herbert. Churchill, Roosevelt, Stalin; the war they waged and the peace they sought. Princeton, N. J., 1957.

Finland. Ministeriet för Utrikesärendena. The Finnish blue book; the development of Finnish-Soviet relations during the autumn of 1939, including the official documents and the Peace Treaty of Mar. 12, 1940. Philadelphia, 1940.

Fisher, Louis. Soviets in world affairs, Princeton, N. J., 1952.

For freedom and independence of Poland; documents, June-Nov. 1945. London, 1946.

France. Ministère des affaires étrangères. Documents diplomatiques, 1938–1939. Paris, 1939.

Free Europe; fortnightly review of international affairs. London, 1943–44.

Friedman, Filip. Zagłada Żydów polskich w okresie okupacji niemieckiej, 1939–1945. Munich, 1947.

Gafencu, Grigore. Derniers jours de l'Europe; un voyage diplomatique en 1939. Paris, 1946.

Gamelin, M. G. Servir. 3 vols. Paris, 1946–47.

Gąsiorowski, Z. J. Polish-Czechoslovak relations, 1918–1922. (Reprinted from: Slavonic and East European Review, vol. 35, no. 84, 1956).

Gąsiorowski, Z. J. Polish- Czechoslovak relations, 1922–1926. (Reprinted from: Slavonic and East European Review, vol. 35, no. 85, 1957).

Germany. Auswärtiges Amt. Amtliches Material zum Massenmord von Katyn. Berlin, 1943.

Germany. Auswärtiges Amt. Documents and materials relating to the eve of the Second World War. 2 vols. Moscow, 1948.

Germany. Auswärtiges Amt. Documents on Germany foreign policy, 1918–45. Series D. Vol. 5: Poland; the Balkans; Latin America; the smaller powers (June 1937-Mar. 1939). Vol. 6: The last months of peace Mar.-Aug. 1939. Vol. 7: The last days of peace Aug. 9-Sep. 3, 1939. Vol. 8: The war years, Sep. 4, 1939-Mar. 18, 1940. Vol. 9: The war years, Mar. 18-June 22, 1940. Vol. 10: The war years June 23-Aug. 31, 1940. Vol. 11: The war years, Sept. 1, 1940-Jan. 31, 1941.

Germany. Auswärtiges Amt. Documents on the events preceding the outbreak of the war. N. Y., 1940.

Germany. Auswärtiges Amt. The German white paper; full text of the Polish documents issued by the Berlin Foreign Office. N. Y., 1940.

Germany. Auswärtiges Amt. Nazi-Soviet relations, 1939–1941; documents. (Dept. of State Publication 3023). Washington, 1948.

Germany. Auswärtiges Amt. Polish documents relative to the origin of the war; first series. Berlin, 1940.

Germany. Wehrmacht. Oberkommando. Der Sieg in Polen. Berlin, 1940.

Goebbels diaries, 1942–43. N. Y., 1948.

Grabski, Stanisław. The Polish-Soviet frontier. N. Y., 1943.

Great Britain. Foreign Office. The British War Blue Book. N. Y., 1939.

Great Britain. Parliament. House of Commons. Parliamentary Debates. Vols. 344–412. London, 1939–45.

Great Britain. Parliament. House of Lords. Parliamentary Debates. Vols. 112–136. London, 1939–45.

Halecki, Oskar. Poland. N. Y., 1957.

Henderson, H. W. An outline of Polish-Soviet relations. Glasgow, 1944.

Henderson, Nevile. Failure of a mission; Berlin, 1937–39. N.Y., 1940.

Hull, Cordell. Memoirs. 2 vols. N. Y., 1948.

Institute of Jewish Affairs of the American Jewish Congress, World Jewish Congress. Hitler's ten-year war of the Jews. N. Y., 1943.

International Military Tribunal. Sprawy polskie w procesie norymberskim. Poznań, 1956.

International Military Tribunal. Trial of the major war criminals, Nuremberg, 14 Nov. 1945-1 Oct. 1946. 42 vols. Nuremberg, 1947–49.

Jaklicz, J. Kampanja wrześniowa 1939 r. w Polsce. (IN: 11. XI. 1941. Grenoble, 1941).

Jaklicz, J. The pattern of life in Poland. X: The Armed Forces. Paris, 1952.

Jakobson, Max. The diplomacy of the winter war; an account of the Russo-Finnish War, 1939–40. Cambridge, Mass., 1961.

Jędrzejewicz, Wacław. Polonia amerykańska w polityce polskiej; historia Komitetu Narodowego Amerykanów Polskiego Pochodzenia. N. Y., 1954.

Jordan, Z. Oder-Neisse line; a study of the political, economic and European significance of Poland's western frontier. London, 1952.

Kamiński, A. Mobilizacja polska we Francji. (IN: 11. XI. 1941. Grenoble, 1941).

Karski, Jan. Story of a secret state. 1944.

Kertesz, S. D., ed. East Central Europe and the world; developments in the post-Stalin era. Notre Dame, Ind., 1962.

Kiedrzyńska, Wanda. Ravensbrück, kobiecy obóz koncentracyjny. Warsaw, 1961.

Kirchmayer, Jerzy. Kampania wrześniowa. Warsaw, 1946.

Kirchmayer, Jerzy. Na marginesach "Polskich Sił Zbrojnych." (IN: Wojskowy Przegląd Historyczny, Warsaw, rok 2, no. 3, 1957, p. 287–330).

Kirchmayer, Jerzy. Powstanie warszawskie. Warsaw, 1959.

Kirchmayer, Jerzy. 1939 i 1944; kilka zagadnień polskich. Warsaw, 1958.

Kirchmayer, Jerzy. Uwagi i polemiki na marginesie londyńskiego wydania "Polskie Siły Zbrojne w II wojnie światowej." Warsaw, 1958.

Kirkien, Leszek. Russia, Poland and the Curzon Line. Duns., Scot., 1944.

Klimaszewski, Tadeusz. Verbrennungskommando Warschau. Warsaw, 1959.

Kliza, Jan. Cieszyn Silesia; bond of union between Poland and Czechoslovakia. London, 1944.

Klukowski, Zygmunt. Dziennik z lat okupacji Zamojszczyzny (1939–1944). Warsaw, 1958.

Komarnicki, Titus. Rebirth of the Polish Republic; a study of the diplomatic history of Europe 1914–1922. London, 1957.

Komorowski, Tadeusz. Armia podziemna. London, 1951.

Komorowski, Tadeusz. The secret army. London, 1950. (Also, N. Y., 1951).

Konovalov, Serge. Russo-Polish relations, an historical survey. Princeton, 1945.

Kopański, Stanisław. Wspomnienia wojenne, 1939–46. London, 1961.

Korboński, Stefan. W imieniu Rzeczypospolitej. Paris, 1954.

Korboński, Stefan. Warsaw in chains. N. Y., 1959.

Kostarbowski, T. I. Sprawa mordu w Katyniu. 1946.

Kot, Stanisław. Listy z Rosji do Gen. Sikorskiego. London, 1956.

Krasuski, Jerzy. Stosunki polsko-niemieckie, 1919–1925. Poznań, 1962.

Kuśnierz, Bronisław. Stalin and the Poles, an indictment of the Soviet leaders. London, 1949.

Kwapiński, Jan. 1939–1945 (kartki z pamiętnika). London, 1947.

Landau, Ludwik. Kronika lat wojny i okupacji. Tom 1: wrzesień 1939 — listopad 1940. Warsaw, 1962.

Lane, A. B. I saw Poland betrayed; an American ambassador reports to the American people. Indianapolis, 1948.

Leahy, W. D. I was there; the personal story of the Chief of Staff to Presidents Roosevelt and Truman. N. Y., 1950.

Leitgeber, Witold. It speaks for itself; what British war leaders said about the Polish Armed Forces, 1939–1946. London, 1946.

Lukacs, J. A. The great powers and eastern Europe. N. Y., 1953.

Łukasiewicz, Juliusz. Pamiętniki. (Unpublished manuscript in the Józef Piłsudski Institute of America, New York, N. Y.)

Łukasiewicz, Juliusz. Sprawa czechosłowacka w 1938 r. na tle stosunków polsko-francuskich. (IN: Sprawy Międzynarodowe, London, no. 6–7, 1948, p. 27–56).

Lwów and south-eastern Poland. London, 1944.

McInnis, Edgar. The war. 6 vols. London, 1940–45.

Mackiewicz, Josef. The Katyn Wood murders. London, 1951.

McNeill, W. H. Britain and Russia; their cooperation and conflict. London. 1943.

Majdalany, Fred. The Battle of Cassino. N. Y., 1957.

Mańkowski, Zygmunt, i Naumiak, Jan., eds. Ruch oporu na Lubelszczyźnie. Gwardia Ludowa i Armia Ludowa na Lubelszczyźnie (1942–44). Lublin, 1961.

Markiewicz, Jerzy. Odpowiedzialność zbiorowa ludności polskiej powiatu biłgorajskiego podczas okupacji hitlerowskiej. Warsaw, 1958.

Mass murder of Polish prisoners of war in Katyn. London, 1946.

Matuszewski, Ignacy. Great Britain's obligations towards Poland and some facts about the Curzon Line. N. Y., 1945.

Matuszewski, Ignacy. Wybór pism. N. Y., 1952.

Mendelsohn, Shlama. The battle of the Warsaw ghetto. N. Y., 1944.

Mikołajczyk, Stanisław. The rape of Poland; pattern of Soviet aggression. N. Y., 1948.

Montanus, B. Polish-Soviet relations in the light of international law. N. Y., 1944.

Moscow trial of the 16 Polish leaders. London, 1945.

Moszyński, Adam. Lista katyńska; jeńcy obozów Kozielsk, Ostaszków, Starobielsk, zaginieni w Rosji sowieckiej. London, 1949.

Namier, L. B. Diplomatic prelude, 1938–1939. London, 1948.

Namier, L. B. Europe in decay; a study of disintegration, 1936–1940. London, 1950.

Namier, L. B. In the Nazi era. London, 1952.

National Committee of Americans of Polish Descent. Biuletyn informacyjny. N. Y., 1942–48.

National Committee of Americans of Polish Descent. Od apelu do Kongresu, zbiór dokumentów Komitetu Narodowego Amerykanów Polskiego Pochodzenia. N. Y., 1944.

Neumann, W. L. Making the peace, 1941–45. Washington, 1950.

Niepodległość; czasopismo poświęcone najnowszym dziejom Polski. London, 1948–

Noel, Leon. L'aggression allemande contre la Pologne. Paris, 1946.

Norwid-Neugebauer, Mieczysław. The defence of Poland (September 1939) London, 1942.

Norwid-Neugebauer, Mieczysław. Kampania wrześniowa 1939 w Polsce. London, 1941.

Olszewicz, Bolesław. Lista strat kultury polskiej, 1939–1945. Warsaw, 1947.

Piątkowski, Henryk. Bitwa o Monte Cassino. Rome, 1945.

Pierwsza dywizja pancerna w walce; praca zbiorowa. Brussels, 1947.

Pobóg-Malinowski, Władysław. Najnowsza historia polityczna Polski, 1864–1945. Vol. 1, Paris, 1953. Vol. 2–3, London, 1956–60.

Pobóg-Malinowski, Władysław. Wojskowy i konspiracyjny wysiłek Polski we Francji, 1939–45. Paris, 1946.

Poland. Ambasada. U. S. Polish-Soviet relations, 1918–1943; official documents. Washington, 1943.

Poland. Główna Komisja Badania Zbrodni Hitlerowskich w Polsce. German crimes in Poland. 2 vols. Warsaw, 1946–47.

Poland. Główna Komisja Badania Zbrodni Hitlerowskich w Polsce. Obóz koncentracyjny Oswięcim-Brzezinka (Auschwitz-Birkenau). Warsaw, 1956.

Poland. Główna Komisja Badania Zbrodni Hitlerowskich w Polsce. Zburzenie Warszawy. Zeznania generałów niemieckich przed polskim prokuratorem przy Międzynarodowym Trybunale Wojennym w Norymberdze. Katowice, 1946.

Poland. Ministerstwo Informacji. The Black book of Poland. N. Y., 1942.

Poland. Ministerstwo Informacji. Concise statistical year-book of Poland, Sept. 1939-June 1941. London, 1941.

Poland. Ministerstwo Spraw Zagranicznych. Documents on the hostile policy of the U. S. Government towards People's Poland. Warsaw, 1953.

Poland. Ministerstwo Spraw Zagranicznych. The mass extermination of Jews in German occupied Poland; note addressed to the governments of the United Nations on Dec. 10, 1942, and other documents, N. Y., 1943.

Poland. Ministerstwo Spraw Zagranicznych. L'occupation allemande et sovietique de la Pologne; note addressée le 3 mai 1941 aux Puissances Alliées et neutres. London, 1941.

Poland. Ministerstwo Spraw Zagranicznych. Official documents concerning Polish-German and Polish-Soviet relations, 1933–1939. London, 1940. (Polish White Book).

Poland. Ministerstwo Spraw Zagranicznych. Polska i zagranica. 1944.

Poland. Ministerstwo Spraw Zagranicznych. Stosunki polsko-sowieckie od kwietnia 1943 r. do września 1946; zbiór dokumentów. London, 1946.

Poland. Naczelna Dyrekcja Archiwów Państwowych. Straty bibliotek i archiwów warszawskich w zakresie rękopiśmiennych żródeł historycznych. Piotr Bańkowski, ed. vol. 3. 1955.

Poland. Polskie Siły Zbrojne. Komisja Historyczna. Polskie Siły Zbrojne w drugiej Wojnie Światowej. Vol. 1, pt. 1–3; vol. 2, pt. 1, vol. 3, London, 1940–59.

Poland and Great Britain before and after the Crimea Conference; documents. London, 1945.

Polish American Congress. Selected documents, showing various phases of Polish American Congress activities, 1944–48. Chicago, 1948.

Polish facts and figures. Nos. 1–17. N. Y., 1944–45.

Polish Government Information Center. Jews in post-war Poland; a digest of documents. N. Y.

Polish Jewish observer (weekly). London, 1943–44.

Polish-Soviet relations, 1917–1945; facts and documents. Glasgow, 1945.

Pologne, 1919–1939. Neuchâtel, 1946–47. 3 vols. Vol. 1: Vie politique et sociale.—vol. 2: Vie économique.—vol. 3: Vie intellectuelle et artistique.

Polska Akademia Nauk. Instytut Historii. Najnowsze dzieje Polski. Materiały i studia z okresu II Wojny Swiatowej. Vol. 1–4. Warsaw, 1957– .

Polska Akademia Nauk. Wydział Nauk Społecznych. Sesja naukowa poświęcona wojnie wyzwoleńczej narodu polskiego 1939–45. Materiały. Warsaw, 1961.

Polska i Rosja w stosunkach wzajemnych. London, 1943.

Polska Wojskowa Misja Likwidacyjna we Francji. Wojskowy i konspiracyjny wysiłek Polski we Francji, 1939–1945. Paris, 1946.

Pomian, Andrzej. The Warsaw rising, a selection of documents. London, 1945.

Porwit, Marian. Obrona Warszawy, wrzesień 1939; wspomnienia i fakty. Warsaw, 1959.

Pragier, Adam. Polish peace aims. London, 1944.

Principal allied powers in the first World War and the eastern boundaries of Poland.

Protokół spisany z okazji zbadania masowych grobów oficerów polskich w Katyńskim lesie koło Smoleńska, przeprowadzonego przez Komisje wybitnych przedstawicieli medycyny sądowej i kryminalistyki europejskich wysokich szkół oraz innych znanych profesorów medycyny na wysokich szkołach. Smoleńsk, 30 kwietnia 1943.

Pusta, K. R. The Soviet Union and the Baltic states. N. Y., 1943.

Raczyński, Edward. Polska polityka zagraniczna w czasie drugiej Wojny Światowej. London, 1953.

Raczyński, Edward. W sojuszniczym Londynie; dziennik ambasadora Edwarda Raczyńskiego, 1939–45. London, 1960.

Report on the massacre of Polish officers in Katyn Wood; facts and documents. London, 1946.

Retinger, J. H. All about Poland: facts, figures, documents. London, 1941.

Ripka, Hubert. Eastern Europe in the post-war world. London, 1961.

Roberts, H. L. Foreign affairs bibliography, 1942–1952. N. Y., 1955.

Rómmel, Juliusz. Za honor i ojczyznę. Warsaw, 1959.

Rozek, E. J. Allied wartime diplomacy, a pattern in Poland. N. Y., 1958.

Russia. Ministerstvo Inostrannykh Del. Correspondence between the Chairman of the Council of Ministers of the USSR and the Presidents of the USA and the Prime Ministers of Great Britain during the Great Patriotic War of 1941–1945. 2 vols. Moscow, 1957.

Russia. Ministerstvo Inostrannykh Del. Perepiska Predsedatelia Soveta Ministrov SSR s prezidentami SSA i priemier-ministrami Velikobritanii vo vremia Velikoi Otechestvennoi Voiny, 1941–1945 gg. 2 vols. Moscow, 1957.

Rzepecki, Jan. Wspomnienia i przyczynki historyczne. Warsaw, 1956.

Shapiro, Leonard. Soviet treaty series; a collection of bilateral treaties, agreements and conventions, etc. concluded between the Soviet Union and foreign powers. Vol. 2: 1929–1939. Washington, 1955.

Sherwood, R. E. Roosevelt and Hopkins, an intimate story. N. Y., 1948.

Shotwell, J. T. Poland and Russia, 1919–1945. N. Y., 1945.

Sikorski Historical Institute, London. Documents on Polish-Soviet relations, 1939–1945. Vol. 1: 1939–1943. London, 1961.

Skarzyński, K. Katyń i Polski Czerwony Krzyż. (IN: Kultura, no. 91, 1955, p. 127–141).

Smogorzewski, K. M. About the Curzon line and other lines. London, 1944.

Smogorzewski, K. M. Lwów and Wilno. London, 1944.

Sosabowski, Stanisław. Najkrótszą drogą. London, 1957.

Soviet-Polish relations; a collection of official documents and press extracts, 1944–1946. London, 1946.

Soviet war documents; addresses, notes, orders of the day, statements, July 1941-Nov. 1943. Washington, 1943.

Soviet war of aggression and the annexation of Polish territories in 1939 (political background and aspect of military operation). London, 1943.

Sprawy międzynarodowe. (quarterly). London, 1947–49.

Stettinius, E. R. Roosevelt and the Russians; the Yalta Conference. N. Y., 1949.

Stroński, Stanisław. What Poles want. London, 1945.

Stypułkowski, Zbigniew. Invitation to Moscow. London, 1951.

Suchodolski, B. The development of Polish science, 1945–1955. Warsaw, 1956.

Sumiński, Tadeusz, ed. Pamiętniki żołnierzy baonu "Zośka." Powstanie warszawskie. Warsaw, 1959.

Super, M. L. The case for Poland. Ann Arbor, Mich., 1945.

Super, M. L. Poland and Russia, the last quarter century. N. Y., 1944.

Supplementary report on facts and documents concerning the Katyn massacre. London, 1946.

Survey of international affairs, 1939–1946. London.

Sworakowski, W. An error regarding eastern Galicia in Curzon's note to the Soviet government. 1944.

Szembek, Jan. Journal, 1933–1939. Paris, 1952.

Taborsky, E. Benes and Stalin, Moscow 1943 and 1945. (IN: Journal of Central European Affairs, vol. 13, 1953, p. 162).

Taborsky, E. A Polish-Czechoslovak Confederation. (IN: Journal of Central European Affairs, 1950, p. 392).

Timasheff, N. S. The great retreat. N. Y., 1946.

Trial of the organizers, leaders, and members of the Polish diversionist organization in the rear of the Red Army on the territory of Poland, Lithuania and the western regions of Byelorussia and Ukraine, heard before the Military Collegium of the Supreme Court of the USSR, June 18–21, 1945. Moscow, 1945.

Truman, H. S. Memoirs. Vol. 1: Years of decision, N. Y., 1955.

Turlejska, Maria. O wojnie i podziemiu; dyskusje i polemiki. Warsaw, 1959.

Turlejska, Maria. Rok przed klęską, wrzesień 1938-wrzesień 1939. Warsaw, 1960.

Turlejska, Maria. Rozkazy i odezwy dowództwa głównego Guardii Ludowej (1942–1944). Warsaw, 1956.

Umiastowski, Roman. Poland, Russia and Great Britain, 1941–1945; a study of evidence. London, 1946.

Umiastowski, Roman. Russia and the Polish Republic, 1918–1941. London, 1945.

United Nations Review; a monthly summary of documents on the allied fight for freedom. N. Y., 1943–45.

U. S. Congress. House. Select Committee on Communist Aggression. Hearings and interim reports. Washington, 1954.

U. S. Congress. House. Select Committee on Communist Aggression. Special report. (House report no. 2684). Washington, 1954–55. 16 parts.

U. S. Congress. House. Select Committee on the Katyn Forest Massacre. Interim report of the Select Committee to Conduct an Investigation and Study of the Facts, Evidence, and Circumstances of the Katyn Forest Massacre. Washington, 1952.

U. S. Congress. House. Select Committee on the Katyn Forest Massacre. The Katyn Forest Massacre; hearings. Washington, 1952. 7 parts. (Contains numerous documents, among them the text of the Soviet Special Commission for Investigating the Katyn Forest Massacre (p. 225–309) and Polish "White Book" (p. 1623–1823).

U. S. Congress. Senate. Committee on Foreign Relations. A decade of American foreign policy; basic documents, 1941–49. (Senate document no. 123). Washington, 1950.

U. S. Dept. of State. Bulletin. Washington, 1939–45.

U. S. Dept. of State. Foreign relations of the U. S. Diplomatic papers. 1938, vol. 1. Washington, 1955. 1941, vol. 1. Washington, 1958. The conferences at Malta and Yalta, 1945. Washington, 1952–55 (later called: Yalta papers). The Soviet Union, 1933–1939. Washington, 1952. The Conferences at Cairo and Teheran. Washington, 1961. Vol. 3, Europe. Washington, 1961.

U. S. Dept. of State. Official record of the Yalta Conference. N. Y., 1955.

U. S. Library of Congress. Legislative Reference Service. Events leading up to the World War II; chronological history. Washington, 1944.

Vilno and north-eastern Poland. London, 1944.

Vołacic, M. The Curzon line and territorial changes in eastern Europe. (IN: Belorussian Review, publ. by Institute for the Study of the USSR, Munich, no. 2, 1956, p. 37–72).

Wandycz, D. S. Polish Americans and the Curzon line. President Roosevelt's statement at Yalta. N. Y., 1954.

Wandycz, D. S. Zapomniany list Piłsudskiego do Masaryka. London 1953.

Wandycz, P. S. Czechoslovak-Polish Confederation. Bloomington, Ind., 1956.

Wandycz, P. S. France and her eastern allies, 1919–1925. French-Czechoslovak-Polish relations from the Paris Peace Conference to Locarno. Minneapolis, 1962.

Wojan, Ryszard. Bydgoszcz, niedziela 3 września 1939. Poznań, 1959.

Wójcik, A. J. The Teheran Conference and the Odra-Nisa boundary. N. Y., 1959.

Wojskowy przegląd historyczny, kwartalnik. Warsaw, 1958–

Woodward, Llewellyn. British foreign policy in the Second World War. London, 1962.

Zabielska, Janina. Bibliography of books in Polish or relating to Poland, published outside Poland since Sept. 1, 1939. London, 1953–59. Vol. 1: 1939–1951; Vol. 2: 1952–1957, and supplements to 1939–1951.

Zachodnia Agencja Prasowa. War losses in Poland. Poznań, 1960.

Zagórski, Wacław (Lech Grzybowski). Wicher wolności; dziennik powstańca. London, 1957.

Zaremba, Zygmunt. Powstanie sierpniowe. London, 1946.

Zbrodnia katyńska w świetle dokumentów. London, 1948.

Zeszyty historyczne. Zeszyt pierwszy. Paris, 1962.

Związek bojowników o wolność i demokracje. Palmiry, 1940–41. Warsaw, 1960.

INDEX

ERRATA

VOLUME I

Page x. 19th line from top: Sir Halford Mackinder.
8th line from bottom: Sir Halford Mackinder.
Delete 1st line of footnote. Asterisk should precede next line: *Quoted from 1942 edition . . .

Page xi. 7th line from top: Sir Halford Mackinder.
22nd line from top: Sir Halford Mackinder.

Page 2. Last line: . . . "That.

Page 18. Last line: Read February 21, 1921 for February 19, 1921.

Page 105. 2nd line from bottom should read: . . . munitions or war material on . . .

Page 261. 6th line from top: . . . Luftstreitkraefte . . .

Page 334. 6th line from bottom: to Germans, too . . .

Page 471. 11th line from bottom: from the British Government . . .

VOLUME II

Page 13. Last line: . . . particular importance to the attitude.

Page 71. 10th line from top: . . . military service . . .

Page 99. 16th line from bottom: . . . Minister of Economic Warfare.

Page 101. 17th line from top: amount . . .

Page 106. 14th line from top: . . . reverend Prelate . . .

Page 113. 14th line from top: THE MINISTER OF ECONOMIC WARFARE . . .
Page 126. 10th line from bottom. . . . in the village . . .
Page 138. 17th and 19th lines from top: correct twice 1491 to 1941.
Page 141. 7th line from top: in the eastern part of Poland . . .
Page 150. 13th line from top: . . . Soviet note of Jan. 5, 1942.
Page 173. Paragraph third must be read: During all this time the Soviets had maintained that all the Polish officers had been freed. They never once mentioned that such a large number of officers had been abandoned to the Germans during the Russian retreat from Smolensk.
Page 186. 9th line from top: correct respects to prospects.
Page 227. Last line: read Forces for Fordes.
Page 246. 16th line from top: relations between Poland and the USSR . . .
Page 265. 3rd line from top: read article for aricle.
Page 329. 2nd line from top: view of the Soviet Union.
Page 334. 17th line from top: . . . east of Wilno . . .
Footnote, 3rd line from top: I agree that the Polish Government . . .
Page 375. 9th line from top: . . . extraordinarily dangerous . . .
Page 467. 17th line from bottom: . . . no body of soldiers.
Page 485. 5th line from top: . . . Polish Minister of Defense . . .
Page 501. 1st footnote: Komorowski, T. . . .

VOLUME III

Page 416. 6th line from bottom: . . . 1944
Page 433. 14th line from top: . . . 1942 . . .
Page 694. 11th line from top: . . . these . . .